The Velvet Glove

The Velvet Glove

Paternalism and Conflict in Gender, Class, and Race Relations

Mary R. Jackman

UNIVERSITY OF CALIFORNIA PRESS
Berkeley   Los Angeles   London

University of California Press
Berkeley and Los Angeles, California

University of California Press
London, England

Copyright © 1994 by The Regents of the University of California

Library of Congress Cataloging-in-Publication Data

Jackman, Mary R.
    The velvet glove: paternalism and conflict in gender, class,
and race relations / Mary R. Jackman.
        p.   cm.
    Includes bibliographical references and index.
    ISBN 0-520-08113-7 (cloth : alk. paper)
    1. Equality. 2. Social conflict. 3. Paternalism. 4. Intergroup
relations. 5. Ideology. I. Title.
HM146.J33   1994
305—dc20   93-6064
                                                     CIP

Printed in the United States of America

1 2 3 4 5 6 7 8 9

The paper used in this publication meets the minimum requirements of American
National Standard for Information Sciences—Permanence of Paper for Printed Library
Materials, ANSI Z39.48-1984 ∞

To my parents,
Ed and Lil Peretz

Iron hand in a velvet glove

—ATTRIBUTED TO CHARLES V (1500–1558)
FROM THOMAS CARLYLE,
LATTER-DAY PAMPHLETS, II

CONTENTS

ACKNOWLEDGMENTS   xiii

PROLOGUE   1

The Expropriative Basis of Social Inequality   2

The Pursuit of Resources   3

Long-term Relations of Social Inequality   5

The Ideological Pressures of Long-term Inequalities   7

The Sweetest Persuasion: Paternalism   9

Paternalism versus Benevolence   11

Mastering the Illusion of Benevolence   14

The Wages of Love   15

Outline of the Book   16

PART I • THE WIND AND THE SUN

1 THE SEARCH FOR CONFLICT   23

Class and Class Conflict   24
     The Debate about Marx   25
     Attempts to Salvage the Class Concept   29
     Exploitation and Conflict   32
     Empirical Questions and Measures   33

Racial Prejudice as Irrational Antagonism   33
   The Concept of Prejudice   34
   Realistic Group Conflict Theory   38
   Reassertions and Modifications of the Prejudice Concept   40
   Empirical Questions and Measures   42

Political Tolerance as Hostility Defused   43
   Tolerance and Democracy   44
   The Resolution of Conflict through Consensual Rules of the Game   45
   Rising above Hostility   46
   Empirical Questions and Measures   46

Gender Relations as Hostility Revealed   47
   The Racial Analogy   49
   Gender Violence   50
   Women's Resistance—Or Lack Thereof   51
   Conservative Theoretical Pressures   51
   Empirical Questions and Measures   53

Summary   55

2   IDEOLOGY AND SOCIAL CONTROL   59

The Limits of Force   61

Implicit Power and Ideology   64
   Expropriation Embedded   64
   Ideology as Communication   67
   Amorphous and Flexible Ideology   69
   The Sensitive Shroud   71

Coercive Love and Reasoned Persuasion   71
   The Inclusive Reach of Dominant Ideology   72
   Communication under Constraints   73
   Intimate versus Distal Relations   74
   Intimacy and Coercive Love   78
   Distal Relations and Reasoned Persuasion   86

Summary   91

PART II • THREE CASES OF INEQUALITY

3   EXPRESSIONS OF INEQUALITY: CLASS, RACE, GENDER   97

The Three Cases: Definitional Parameters   97
   Distributive Basis for the Inequality   98
   Ascription to Groups   102
   Race, Gender, Class: Defining Parameters   108
   Empirical Definition of Group Memberships   109

A Comparative Case-Study Analysis   111
   A Comparative Analysis of Intergroup Attitudes   112
   Intergroup Attitudes as Relational Communications   114
   Intergroup Attitudes as the Property of Groups   115
   A Comparative Case-Study Analysis: Analytic Issues   120

Summary   124

4 THE STRUCTURE OF INTERGROUP CONTACT   127

Role Segregation and Spatial Segregation   127
   Role Segregation   128
   Spatial Segregation   131
   Differentiation and Communication   138

Data: Intergroup Contact in the Three Cases   138
   Physical Insulation of Groups   139
   The Terms of Intergroup Contact: Role Segregation   146
   Affiliative Behavior   152

Summary   161

PART III • DIALOGUES OF DOMINANCE AND
SUBORDINATION

5 INTERGROUP FEELINGS AND THE DEFINITION OF GROUP
   INTERESTS   167

The Issues   168
   Prejudice   169
   Tolerance   171
   Group Consciousness   172
   Measurement Issues   177
   Dispensable Hostility   180

Data: Intergroup Feelings   182
   Measures   183
   Results   185

Data: The Definition of Group Interests   197
   Measures   198
   Results   199

Conclusions   205

6 THE ARTICULATION OF POLICY GOALS   208

The Issues   209
   Prejudice   210
   Tolerance   211

Gender Attitudes 211
Class Consciousness 212
Overview 213
Measurement Issues 214
The Constrained Pursuit of Resources 219

Data: Abstract Policy Principles 228
Measures 228
Results 231

Data: Specific Policy Goals 238
Measures 238
Results: Prescriptive and Existential Beliefs 241
Results: Affirmative Change, Conservatism, and Reaction 251

Conclusions 256

7 THE IDEOLOGICAL MOLDS OF PATERNALISM AND
CONFLICT 261

The Issues 263
Attitudinal Consistency and Ideological Constraint 263
Inconsistent Attitudes in Ideology 269

Data 273
The Relationship between Intergroup Feelings and Policy Goals 273
Alternative Attitudinal Compounds 279

Conclusions 291

8 THE COGNITIVE EMBROIDERY OF INTERGROUP
RELATIONS 296

The Issues 298
Stereotypes 301
Folk Wisdom about Group Distinctions 307
Attributions as Embroidery 309

Data: Trait Attribution to Groups 321
Measures 322
Results 325

Data: Popular Explanations of Group Differences 338
Measures 338
Results 339

Conclusions 343

PART IV • THREADS OF PATERNALISM AND CONFLICT

9 IDEOLOGY AND COERCION   353

   The Politics of Intergroup Ideology   358

   Strategy of Inquiry   366

   The Pattern of Evidence   371
      The Three Cases   371
      The Dynamics of Intergroup Ideology   376

   Love and Enmity   382

   REFERENCES   385

   SUBJECT INDEX   409

   AUTHOR INDEX   419

ACKNOWLEDGMENTS

During its long gestation, this book has benefited from the support, proddings, arguments, and diversions of a large number of people.

First, I am grateful to several sources for the funding that made this book possible. Grants from the National Institute for Mental Health (MH–16433) and the National Science Foundation (SOC 75–00405 and SOC 78–16857) provided for the data collection and the analysis of the data. A Research Scientist Development Award from the National Institute for Mental Health (MH–00252) provided me with fellowship support, enabling me to devote more time to the development of the central ideas that drive this manuscript. A year at the Center for Advanced Study in the Behavioral Sciences in 1986–1987 was absolutely invaluable in rescuing me from all my normal professional responsibilities and granting me the solitude I needed to read and to begin writing this book. Finally, since coming to the University of California at Davis in 1989, I have received generous support from the University's Research Committee, the dean's office, and the Institute for Governmental Affairs.

The data for this book come from a sample survey of the United States, conducted by the Survey Research Center of the University of Michigan. I thank the staff of the Survey Research Center for their excellent fieldwork and coding of the data. In particular, Jeanne Castro expertly managed the fieldwork and made sure that deadlines were met as the data were collected. Jeanne and other members of the field office (including people from the interviewing staff) and the coding section also provided invaluable advice and resourcefulness during the pretesting of a questionnaire that contained more than its fair share of novel items and sensitive material.

A number of wonderful research assistants have contributed to this project over the years since its inception—with their dedicated work, enthusiasm, and perceptive criticisms and commentary. Their cumulative contributions are countless, and their intellectual vitality and sense of fun have added immeasurably to this project. Mary Scheuer Senter threw herself into the project with her boundless energy, intellectual sensitivity, and exacting standards. It is hard to find someone quite as compulsive as me, but Mary kept me on my toes with long hours and endless iterations until items were made right, the data could be declared fit for analysis, and analyses were sufficiently thorough. Several other research assistants have built on Mary Senter's initial contributions over the years: Marie Crane, Michael Muha, Anne Adams, Emily Kane, Paula Rust, Arlene Sanderson, Maria Kousis, Suzanne Purcell, and Margalit Tal at the University of Michigan, and Myrna Goodman, Ellen Scott, Ron Ruggiero, Eric Cain, and Ross Miller at the University of California, Davis. Their contributions have been both tangible and intangible. They and other students in my seminars on Ideology at the University of Michigan and UC-Davis have continued to prod me to refine my ideas about the nature of coercion and compliance and the use of ideology in lieu of violence as a primary mechanism of social control in longstanding relations of inequality.

I have also been fortunate in receiving support and encouragement from a number of other people. Joyce Lazar (at the National Institute for Mental Health), Donald Ploch (at the National Science Foundation), Sheldon Stryker, and William J. Wilson gave the project a vote of confidence when it was at a fledgling stage, and they offered indispensable advice. Gerald Gurin and Patricia Gurin welcomed me to the Institute for Social Research at the University of Michigan when I was a very junior scholar and offered me intellectual companionship and moral support: their support and encouragement were critical in the early days of this project. During my year at the Center for Advanced Study in Stanford, Bob Scott and the other members of the staff provided all kinds of superb services and good friendship that still take on a golden hue as I look back on that wonderful year. In particular, Frances Duignan found us housing in a very difficult housing market and provided innumerable other kind services during the year. Margaret Amara and Roseanne Torre promptly retrieved many books for me from the libraries of the Bay Area. In addition, Margaret brightened the days with her warm companionship and luscious advice about the scenic delights of the area. Stanley Holwitz at the University of California Press has shown extraordinary patience and offered unfailing support as I have tried to prepare and finish this book. And the production staff at the Press have also been most helpful and collegial. I am especially grateful to Rebecca

Frazier for her thoughtful attention to the book's production and to Diana Feinberg for suggesting the title.

I have drawn copiously on the social resources of friends and family as I faced the marathon of finishing this book. Ken and Sandy Waltzer have generously given their caring friendship and steadfast support. Larry Cohen has upheld my sense of the absurd with his trenchant wit, and he has offered endless debates and unflagging support. Bruce and Arlene Bueno de Mesquita have sustained me with their warmth and comradeship; they also have given us the use of their house as a second home, and much of this manuscript was typed up on the computer in their kitchen. Marie Crane and Bill Kelly have maintained a sensitive interest in the progress of the manuscript, and they have kept me going with their kind thoughts and sweet company. Our neighbors Jim and Kathy West have given us many wonderful meals on days when I was too busy or too exhausted to cook, as well as their continual friendship, encouragement, and support. Aram Yengoyan has kept up a steady flow of entertainment, warm concern, and critical intellectual commentary. Randy Siverson has enhanced our table with the bountiful produce of his garden, and he has offered constant support for my scholarly endeavors.

I would like to thank my family for doing their best to keep me human during this project. I have tried to learn from the wise counsel of my parents, which comes from their varied encounters with life, and I am deeply appreciative of their love and support. Paul Peretz, my brother, never fails to advise me that I am working too hard, as I advise him—and I am pleased to say that we have mutually ignored the other's advice but much enjoyed the giving and receiving of it. Robert Jackman has been my steadfast colleague and friend, helping in countless ways with the completion of this project, and he has bravely endeavored to distract the kids from their mother long enough to let me finish this book. Finally, Saul and Rachael have shown great patience in the past few months, helping and showing consideration for their often preoccupied mother in ways that seem beyond their years. I thank them for letting me get in some quality time with my manuscript and for enhancing my life with a continual feast of enchantments and distractions.

It is perhaps a truism that this project would not have been possible without the accumulated knowledge that others have generously shared with me. Over the years, several people have read various portions of this manuscript and given me incisive and thoughtful comments. I especially thank Sheldon Stryker, Barbara Reskin, Lowell Hargens, Jim Cramer, Larry Cohen, and Robert Jackman. Nancy Denton and an anonymous reviewer for the University of California Press gave an earlier version of this manuscript a most thorough and thoughtful reading: their comments were uncommonly helpful in tightening up my argument and clarifying the presentation. The book has also been enriched by discussions and debates with colleagues from Michigan and California. I have benefited especially from the commentary and advice of Barbara Reskin, Ken Waltzer, Bruce Bueno de Mesquita, Larry Bobo, Don Kinder, James Jackson, Aram Yengoyan, Clarence Walker, Larry Cohen, and Robert Jackman. They have directed my reading and stimulated my thinking about the nature of ideology and coercion. Beyond those personal discussions, I have also profited immeasurably from the written work of others, most of whom I have never met. Paradoxically, the works that are the subject of closest critique in my book are often the ones from which I learned the most. Whether this reflects a perversity in my character or the intrinsic nature of scholarly learning I know not. In any event, I thank all those scholars whose work has provided intellectual guidance and provocation. The errors and lapses that remain in the book must regrettably be attributed to me alone.

Davis, California
September, 1993

Prologue

The Wind and the Sun
A dispute once arose between the wind and the sun over which was the stronger
of the two. There seemed to be no way of settling the issue. But suddenly they
saw a traveller coming down the road.
"This is our chance," said the sun, "to prove who is right. Whichever of us
can make that man take off his coat shall be the stronger. And just to show you
how sure I am, I'll let you have the first chance."
So the sun hid behind a cloud, and the wind blew an icy blast. But the harder
he blew the more closely did the traveller wrap his coat around him. At last the
wind had to give up in disgust. The sun came out from behind the cloud and
began to shine down upon the traveller with all his power. The traveller felt the
sun's genial warmth, and as he grew warmer and warmer he began to loosen
his coat. Finally, he was forced to take it off altogether and to sit down in the
shade of a tree and fan himself. So the sun was right, after all!

Application: Persuasion is better than force.
AESOP'S FABLES, 1947

This book is an analysis of the coercive gleam of persuasion in relations of inequality. Through a comparative analysis of three different intergroup relationships in the United States—race, gender, and social class—I hope to define the varying forms of ideological persuasion that dominant groups espouse as they seek to maintain control of different kinds of relationships as well as the ideological responses that find expression among their potential protagonists. I explore the attitudes that are exchanged between unequal groups as they respond to the structural exigencies of their mutual relationship and to the pressures and symbols created by their contenders in the delicate game of dominance and subordination.

My approach departs from the primary thrust of research on the ideology of inequality. Our intellectual agenda has been shaped by the enduring debate over "conflict versus consensus." Those who endorse the moral view that social inequality is contrary to human freedom have been drawn to the conflict perspective that anticipates friction, discontent, and concerted rebellion. Those who regard inequality as necessary for human productivity and fulfillment have argued that inequality is

1

a constant feature of social life which enjoys spontaneous consensual endorsement. This forced-choice paradigm has implicitly treated conflict as the exclusive symptom of exploitative relations and consensus as the indelible sign of functional integration. What has been overlooked by both sides is that the exploitation of one group by another may be buttressed more effectively by sweet persuasion than by hostile force. Once this is recognized, we can abandon the overriding significance that we have attached to conflict in intergroup relations. It becomes clear, instead, that consensus is only as spontaneous as the removal of one's coat in hot weather.

My purpose is to make the case that neither dominants nor subordinates actively seek open conflict and that hostility is rarely the active ingredient of exploitative relations. The ideological pressures created by dominant groups are more likely to be subtle and insidious than blatant or hostile. Thus, we need to abandon our preoccupation with conflict. We should redirect our attention to the many ways that dominant groups subvert conflict by befriending or at least emotionally disarming those whom they subordinate.

THE EXPROPRIATIVE BASIS OF SOCIAL INEQUALITY

I begin with the premise that inequality between social groups in the distribution of finite resources intrinsically entails a relationship in which one group expropriates resources from another.[1] I mean this in the most rudimentary sense: the advantage that one group enjoys depends inextricably on the disadvantage that another suffers. Although some have argued that social inequality can be portrayed in benign or neutral terms, my premise is that if one group enjoys a larger portion of a finite resource, the only place from which it can have come is the other group or groups who reside in the same social system. This holds whether the distributive asset be material, social, or political.

The material wealth of one group depends on the availability of relatively cheap labor from others. If the gap between rich and poor is to be narrowed, the price must be paid by the wealthier members of society, who will no longer be able to afford all the services and accouterments of the standard of living to which they have become accustomed. Similarly, it is logically impossible for one group to possess more status, pres-

---

1. I use the term "expropriation" in preference to the commonly used term "exploitation." The latter term has carried various meanings and as a result it is burdened with ambiguities. The term "expropriation" is adapted from Cohen and Machalek (1988), who divide people into "producers" and "expropriators" to identify those who illegally steal the goods produced by others. I am generalizing the concept of expropriation: my point is that most forms of expropriation take place within the bounds of the law.

tige, or social privileges without assigning less to other members of society. If there are to be gains for a subordinated group, these can only be accomplished by cutting into, and thus diminishing, the prestige and privileges enjoyed by a dominant group. Indeed, terms such as "prestige" and "privilege" intrinsically connote a relational inequality: their value is measured in terms of the exclusiveness of their attribution to some members of society. Finally, in the case of political inequality, it is perhaps intuitively clearest that the advantage of one group can stem only from the disadvantage of another. Moves toward political equality can only be achieved by subtracting from the advantaged group's control over decision making. In relationships between social groups, the gains of one group and the losses of another are thus inextricably bound together.[2]

THE PURSUIT OF RESOURCES

My approach is also premised on the assumption that groups are comprised of individuals who strive to maximize their control over resources. Thus, I assume humans are self-interested.[3] In the endeavor to preserve and possibly to enhance their control over material, social, and political resources, people are driven into social relations with others. As Weber points out, the self-interested person can ill afford to disregard other actors:

> . . . the stability of action in terms of self-interest rests on the fact that the person who does not orient his action to the interests of others, does not "take account" of them, arouses their antagonism or may end up in a situation different from that which he had foreseen or wished to bring about. He thus runs the risk of damaging his own interests. (Weber [1947] 1964, 123)

2. For purposes of simplicity, this discussion has been restricted to a dichotomous allocation system. If there are more than two groups, the same principle holds, although inequalities may involve more complex interactions among the participating groups. Within the general condition of inequality, any one group may experience relative gains or losses without necessarily affecting the outcomes of all other groups. However, the achievement of complete equality in distribution among all groups would require each group to forfeit or gain in proportion to the relative size of its current holdings.

3. The term "self-interested" has been one of the most confused, misused, and misunderstood terms in recent social science (see, for example, the multiple uses of the term in the articles assembled in Mansbridge's volume, *Beyond Self-Interest*, 1990; see also R. Jackman, 1993, for a discussion of the various ways in which the concept has been misunderstood by social scientists). My truncated discussion here cannot do justice to the topic, and I request the reader's patience in my use of this term. My approach has been most influenced by Downs's conception of the motivational basis of political behavior in his classic book, *An Economic Theory of Democracy* (1957). I ask that my conception of self-interest be taken on its own merits, as a working assumption.

For this reason, "self-interested" should not be confused with "selfish." As individuals negotiate their social world in the endeavor to make out as well as they can, they enter into both collaborative and expropriative relations with others. In either case, the self-interested actor is bound to communicate and interact with other parties.

In that process, self-interest has motivational primacy, although it need not be the only factor working on people's responses. For example, self-interest does not preclude a capacity to feel compassion or sympathy for others or even to act on behalf of others. However, I do not expect people to manifest such behaviors when they believe it puts their own interests at risk. Thus, instead of asking, "If people are self-interested, why do they give to charity?", it is more appropriate to ask, "If people are *not* self-interested, why do they give such a miniscule portion of their incomes to charity, and why do charitable contributions go up when they are tax-deductible and go down during recessions?" It is taken for granted that people donate to charity after they have met their own financial needs. No one is expected to demonstrate his sympathy for the starving people of Somalia by selling his home and giving his earnings over to the relief effort. Similarly, the fact that many religious organizations resort to the practice of tithing suggests that they recognize the importance of self-interest, even among the pious. Thus, I am assuming that self-interest has primacy, but not a monopoly, in determining human behavior.

People generally utilize whatever assets they initially possess to enhance their control over material, status, and political resources. They are also sensitive to whatever deficits they initially possess that make their control over resources vulnerable to incursions by others. Thus, as people attempt to make the most of their lives, they are inclined both to take advantage of opportunities and to be sensitive to risks.

When individuals share similar attributes that position them in the same way in the pursuit of resources, the evolving patterns of social life are molded by those similarities, and social groups are formed. Those with an initial advantage in their possession of vital assets collaborate with one another to establish expropriative relations with weaker members of the community. In this way, advantaged groups consolidate and promote their control over resources. Those with an initial disadvantage in their possession of vital assets must yield to the stronger contenders. For weaker parties, the struggle becomes one of preventing further incursions on their resources and trying, as best they can, to better their conditions.

Because humans are efficient problem solvers, they do not expend a great deal of conscious thought on every issue that is a part of their lives. People are not inclined to give careful deliberation to each and every aspect of their lives, and they develop habitual responses to those aspects that appear to be stable fixtures (Downs 1957). For the same reason, people do not have to test each potential behavioral strategy firsthand. Instead, they tend to gravitate to solutions and strategies that do not seem to put them at risk, and they rely on information from others as well as their own past and present experience to make such assessments. Sometimes they make mistakes, either because of poor information, misinterpreting information, or miscalculating outcomes, but people generally learn from their mistakes as well as from the mistakes made by others.

In the process of information gathering, people also develop habits according to a source's accessibility and its time-proven credibility as either a positive or negative reference (Downs 1957). On these principles, people draw information with differential confidence from their mothers, fathers, brothers, sisters, friends, schoolmates, teachers, co-workers, employers, sons, daughters, extended family members, neighbors, newspapers, television, radio, books, and any other sources that come their way.

People grope through the welter of experiences and information with which they are daily bombarded, as they contend with the day-to-day exigencies of their lives and shrink from the sea of uncertainties that lies beyond. Mistakes can be costly. In this ongoing struggle, their surest strategy is to succumb to the pressures that bear down on them—in other words, to follow the path of least resistance.

LONG-TERM RELATIONS OF SOCIAL INEQUALITY

When resources are expropriated from one group to another iteratively over a period of time, a long-term relationship of inequality is delineated between the participating groups. Even if there are alterations in the specifics of the resource allocation, we may consider a relationship between groups to be one of long-term inequality when the overall imbalance in the distribution of resources between the groups remains in place. It is such long-term, unequal intergroup relations that are the focus of this book. The relations that exist today in American society between men and women, whites and blacks, and among social classes have evidenced considerable change in the specific allocation of resources and in the manner in which the inequalities are practiced. But all three cases involve long-term relations of social inequality: all three have been a significant part of organized social life in this country throughout its history.

I presume that the ideological dynamics of long-term relations of inequality are distinct from other kinds of intergroup relations. First, they should be distinguished from relations involving either greater instability in the share of resources going to each group or only a narrow advantage

allocated to one group. Many relations between ethnic or religious
groups (for example, between Indians and ethnic Fijians in Fiji, or between Christians and Moslems in Lebanon) involve closer contests between groups and significant uncertainty about which group is to dominate the distribution of assets. As it becomes less clear which group is
dominant, the ideological dynamics shift progressively away from the
model that I explore in this book and travel instead toward more explicit
assertions of group interests and more open hostility and conflict.

Long-term relations of social inequality are also distinct from those
relations involving geographic proximity between culturally incompatible groups with little or no functional interconnection. Many states incorporate groups that are mutually distinctive in terms of culture, religion,
or language. The primary, and sometimes the only, connection between
the affected groups is that they happen, by historical accident, to be
residing in the same political unit. In such instances, there is not an
expropriative relationship between the groups—neither group offers
the other group the prospect of enhancing its control over resources
through an expropriative arrangement. The members of each group
would like to have complete control over their state's resources, and the
continued presence of the other group or groups only presents an obstacle to that end. Examples of such cases are the French and English Cana-
dians in Canada, the contact between Europeans and Native Americans
in America, Moslems and Hindus in colonial India, Europeans and Ab-
origines in colonial Australia, and relations between many ethnic groups
in the African states (such as between Christians and Moslems in Sudan,
and among Ibos, Hausa, and Yoruba in Nigeria).[4] Under these circumstances too, open hostilities are likely to develop between the groups.
When the groups are evenly balanced in the distribution of assets, a
struggle ensues. When one group clearly has the advantage in its control
over resources, it may initiate hostile actions toward the other group or
groups—it may dictate restrictive terms by which the other group or
groups can continue to reside in the state, or it may resort to expulsion
or genocide in order to eliminate the threat posed by the target group(s)
to its own dominance.[5]

4. Competitive interethnic relations have been a hallmark of politics in many African
states—a legacy of the carving up of African territory by the European colonial powers
with no regard for the geographic distribution of the preexisting ethnic nations of Africa
(see van den Berghe 1983 for an interesting discussion of ethnic divisions in Africa).

5. The treatment of middleman minorities comprises a special case of this general type,
since their functional relationship to other groups in society is circumscribed by restrictive
conditions that are subject to rescission. Middleman minorities have the following attributes: (1) they are immigrant groups who are culturally distinct from the "host" population,
(2) they have been granted residence in a nation on specific terms that restrict their eco-

Past research has tended to treat all intergroup relations as subject to the same competitive pressures, as is manifested, for example, in the frequent citation of Sherif's famous boys' camp experiment (1965) in which competing (or warring) social groups were created and their hostile interactions analyzed. Although many researchers have regarded Sherif's study as holding fundamental, universal truths for the dynamics of intergroup relations, I treat the situation of outright competition between groups as the limiting case rather than the prototype. The political pressures generated in such cases are much different from those that exist in long-standing relations of inequality. The puzzles that have intrigued scholars about relations between social classes, men and women, and whites and blacks in American society cannot be solved without considering the distinctive pressures that are generated in longstanding, expropriative relations of inequality.

Long-term relations of social inequality are marked fatefully by one pivotal factor: one group has a vested interest in maintaining the existing relationship, with the distribution of resources that it brings. The members of the dominant group have vested their interest in the ongoing institutional arrangements that deliver their benefits. This has important consequences for the strategies pursued by the members of the dominant group and for the responses of subordinates to their predicament.

THE IDEOLOGICAL PRESSURES OF LONG-TERM INEQUALITIES

Most fundamentally, the existence of ongoing institutional arrangements that bear the primary burden of distributing resources means that the individual members of the participating groups need not be explicitly cognizant of the relationship that exists between them. Lack of awareness

---

nomic role to specialized occupations that are unattractive to the indigenous population for economic or cultural reasons, and (3) they thereby occupy a buffer role between the main contending groups in that society. Middleman minorities have historically occupied a very vulnerable position. They retain an "outsider" status, and their continued presence is tolerated only insofar as they perform tasks that are distasteful to the indigenous population and they function to deflect the hostilities of indigenous subordinate groups away from the dominant group. Whereas the members of the dominant group maintain a long-term interest in expropriating resources from indigenous subordinates, their interest in the middleman group is only conditional and is thus highly volatile. Depending on the state of the economy and their success in expropriating resources from subordinates, the dominant group's main intentions toward the middleman group may be, variously, to encourage its specialized economic activity, to incite open hostilities against its members by subordinates, to expel them, or to exterminate them. The Jews have historically experienced all those fates. (For more detailed treatments of the special case of middleman minorities, see Blalock 1967; Bonacich 1973; van den Berghe 1981.)

among subordinate groups has been the frequent subject of commentary
and analysis, but what is often overlooked is that the collective and institutionalized character of the expropriation renders it particularly invisible
to its beneficiaries. When a relationship is regularized and institutionalized, it is simply a case of "c'est la vie." Personal acts of aggression are
not required to claim one's due as a member of the advantaged group:
benefits simply fall into one's lap. There is thus no need for deep, personal insight into how things work, nor is there any feeling of personal
accountability or guilt for the expropriated benefits one enjoys. Indeed,
it is remarkably easy to view one's benefits as the natural outcome of
individual endeavor and to overlook the dreary fact that those benefits
have been delivered at someone else's expense.

Yet the dominant group does strive for a subjectively plausible understanding of its collective experience, and there is an abiding need to
protect current arrangements from the omnipresent possibility of challenge. From these pressures there develops an ideology that gains popular acceptance within its ranks. Far from identifying the bleak reality of
the expropriation, this ideology provides an interpretation of social life
that is less offensive to the sensibilities of its beneficiaries and more diver-
sionary from the incipient complaints of subordinates.

Because individuals in the dominant group do not feel personally
accountable for the expropriated benefits of their existence, there is no
impetus for them to contrive knowingly to manufacture such an ideology. Instead, out of the pressures created by their collective relationship
with subordinates, there evolves naturally an interpretation of social reality that is consistent with the dominant group's experience. That ideology
is a collective property. It permeates the main institutions and communications networks of organized social life and is propagated with an easy
vehemence that can come only from uncontrived sincerity. The individuals who comprise the dominant group are caught in the prevailing current; without any exercise of personal guile, they learn to defend their
interests with aplomb. Lasswell has given an animated description of the
process:

> A well-established ideology perpetuates itself with little planned propa-
> ganda by those whom it benefits most. When thought is taken about ways
> and means of sowing conviction, conviction has already languished, the
> basic outlook of society has decayed, or a new, triumphant outlook has not
> yet gripped the automatic loyalties of old and young. Happy indeed is that
> nation that has no thought of itself; or happy at least are the few who
> procure the principal benefits of universal acquiescence. Systems of life
> which confer special benefits on the other fellow need no plots or conspira-
> cies when the masses are moved by faith and the elites are inspired by self-
> confidence. (Lasswell 1936, 29–30)

This implies, of course, that the effectiveness of a particular ideology cannot be gauged simply by assessing the sincerity and easy following that it engenders within the ranks of the dominant group. Minimally, the dominant ideology provides an interpretation of current social arrangements that seems coherent and reasonable to its beneficiaries. Beyond this, the vital question is the extent to which the dominant group can induce subordinates to fall in with its way of thinking. A perspective that develops effortlessly from one side of experience might by the same token seem quite inappropriate from the other side. The degree to which the dominant group can persuade subordinates to accept its proffered interpretation of the meaning of their social relationship is a measure of the dominant group's success in controlling that relationship.

Thus, the beneficiaries of a relationship of inequality must not only make sense out of their experience in a way that is personally reasonable and satisfying. They need also to engage subordinates in the same way of thinking. Both of these needs form a constant source of pressure on the ideology that dominant groups espouse.

The shape of dominant ideology varies according to the structure of the relationship with subordinates and the exigencies created by that structure. But whatever the specific circumstances that the dominant group faces, the overriding propellant of its ideology is the unmeditated pursuit of a persuasive message that obscures the bare bones of expropriation and thus prevents or at least mitigates resistance. The costs of overt conflict are painfully high for dominant groups, and thus the enduring proclivity of such groups is to try to prevent conflict by obscuring the basis on which it might coalesce. As with the sun in Aesop's fable, the dominant group seeks to obviate the possibility of defeat by structuring the terms of the encounter to its advantage. And as in the fable, the dominant group understands implicitly that the use of force only structures the game in combative terms, making resistance the readiest response, whereas persuasion radiates with disarming warmth at the same time as it is relentless and pervasive in its effects.

THE SWEETEST PERSUASION: PATERNALISM

Dominant groups resort to alternative modes of persuasion as circumstances change, but the enduring beacon to which they are drawn and from which they depart only reluctantly and by degrees is an ideology of paternalism. Webster's definition of paternalism is "the principle or system of governing or controlling a country, group of employees, etc. in a manner suggesting a father's relationship with his children" (Webster 1975). An earlier edition of Webster's (1965) defined paternalism in more detail:

Paternalism: the care or control of subordinates (as by a government or
employer) in a fatherly manner; *esp*.: the principles or practices of a government that undertakes to supply needs or regulate conduct of the governed
in matters affecting them as individuals as well as in their relations to the
state and to each other. (Webster's 1965)

The traditional father-child relationship on which the term is based was
one in which the father authoritatively dictated all the behaviors and
significant life-decisions of his children within a moral framework that
credited the father with an unassailable understanding of the needs and
best interests of his children. They, in turn, accepted implicitly and absolutely the authority of their father—occasional bouts of independence
were not unexpected, but never tolerated. Good children learned to comply with and defer to the wishes of their fathers.

No arrangement could be more desirable for a group that dominates
another. Yet fathers love their children, and thus the traditional father-
child relationship might seem an inappropriate analogy for the ideology
that accompanies and bolsters a relationship of inequality between social
groups. Because of our ensnarement in the "conflict versus consensus"
debate, we have implicitly regarded discrimination as the inalienable
expression of hostility: within that framework, affection and exploitation
are incompatible. In this book, however, I separate hostility from discrimination. I argue that it is only in the limiting case that they become
linked. Affection, far from being alien to exploitative relations, is precisely the emotion that dominant groups wish to feel toward those whom
they exploit. The everyday practice of discrimination does not require
feelings of hostility, and, indeed, it is not at all difficult to have fond
regard for those whom we subordinate, especially when the subject of
our domination accedes to the relationship compliantly. To denote this
phenomenon of discrimination without the expression of hostility, I use
the term paternalism.

Paternalism is a time-worn term that has had indefinite meaning in
common usage. Among analysts of intergroup relations, it has occupied
an uncertain and marginal role because of the overriding concern with
conflict and hostility. In one of the few explicit analyses of paternalistic
relations, van den Berghe (1967) relegated it to preindustrial societies
in which a numerically small minority dominates over more numerous
subordinates. Myrdal (1944), in his classic treatment of black-white relations in the United States, regarded paternalism as a cultural anachronism, out of place in an industrial, democratic society. Paternalism found
its most penetrating exposition in Genovese's work on master-slave relations in the antebellum American South (1974), and more recently, some
scholars have applied the concept to an analysis of management-labor
relations in anachronistic pockets of the developing industrial enterprise

(Lockwood 1966; Newby 1977*a*, 1977*b*; Burawoy 1984; Staples 1987). More commonly, paternalism indefinitely connotes the colonial days and the "white man's burden" of the nineteenth century. The prevailing effect has been to associate paternalism with a bygone era. Most research on contemporary intergroup relations has brushed the phenomenon aside, like a relic, to be regarded occasionally with quiet dismay.

My argument, however, is that paternalism has a significance that is both general and contemporary. It is a powerful ideological mold that offers the most efficient and gratifying means for the social control of relationships between unequal groups. The attitude structure that it comprises—the combination of positive feelings for a group with discriminatory intentions toward the group—has been underestimated by students of intergroup relations and unheeded in research on intergroup attitudes. And yet the ideology of dominant groups departs from the comforting mold of paternalism only reluctantly and under duress. The abiding quest is to preserve an amicable relationship with subordinates and thus to preempt or subvert conflict. The expression of hostility invites the exercise of force, and that remains the option of last resort.

PATERNALISM VERSUS BENEVOLENCE

An awkward ambiguity has pervaded both popular and scholarly uses of the term "paternalism" over the extent to which paternalism connotes benevolence. Fathers, after all, were presumed to have benevolent intentions toward their children, even as they exercised absolute authority over them. And in the analysis of intergroup relations, the tendency to link malevolence with hostility has been so habitual that analysts have inferred that the development of bonds of affection between the members of dominant groups and their subordinates must erode the ability of dominant-group members to control their relations with subordinates.

Thus, the observation of affection toward subordinates in paternalistic systems has promoted the inference that paternalism involves at least some degree of benevolence. For example, in a discussion of "Paternalism in Industry," Blumer wrote:

> [A] sense of responsibility and of obligation for the welfare of the worker
> is the most outstanding mark of paternalism. It is a tempering influence
> on the mere proprietary and control relationship and imparts to that rela-
> tionship a personal and benevolent character. (Blumer 1951, 26)

A similar confounding of affection and benevolence is found in a more recent treatment of paternalism by Weiner (1985/1986). In assessing the effect of slave-owners' wives on the institution of slavery, Weiner comments:

Allston was not the only plantation mistress who found pleasure in plantation life or developed strong bonds of affection for slaves. The teachings
of the ideology of domesticity and southern paternalism together defined
caring for slaves as central to southern womanhood. . . . While men created
paternalism as a mechanism of social control, women inadvertently assumed a significant portion of the responsibility for putting it into practice
on a daily basis. . . . In their efforts to ameliorate the physical and emotional hardships experienced by slaves, women quite unwittingly became
the agents of paternalism. . . . Ironically then, one result . . . was to enable
slavery to continue to exist by making life more tolerable for slaves and
thus helping to defuse discontent. (Weiner 1985/1986, 382).

Even the most critical exponents of paternalism have seen it as an
ideological system fraught with contradictions, stemming from a tensive
intermixture of domination with benevolence (see, for example, Genovese 1974; Newby 1977*b*). Dominant-group members are seen as being
trapped by their affectionate inclinations and by paternalism's moral
shroud of mutual obligation into giving more than they might otherwise
to subordinates.

The appearance of benevolence in paternalistic intergroup relations
is indeed pervasive, but it is important to recognize that it is nothing more
than an appearance. It is helpful here to consider a neutral definition of
paternalism that portrays the phenomenon as benevolently motivated.
In VanDeVeer's exhaustive and probing book, *Paternalistic Intervention:
The Moral Bounds of Benevolence*, paternalistic acts are defined as those
"in which one person, A, interferes with another person, S, in order
to promote S's own good" (1986, 12). VanDeVeer specifically rules out
callousness or maliciousness as a motive for paternalistic acts. He cites
many diverse examples of paternalistic acts: his long list includes legal
requirements that motorcyclists wear helmets, compulsory education of
the young, legal prohibitions on voluntary euthanasia, required courses
at universities, required waiting periods for divorce, distribution of welfare in kind (e.g., food stamps) rather than in cash, involuntary steriliza-
tion, and compulsory participation in systems providing for adequate
income on retirement (e.g., Social Security) (VanDeVeer 1986, 13–15).
What all these acts have in common is the intervening party's presumptive claim to a superior understanding of the subject's best interests than
the subject may possess him- or herself. In essence, then, VanDeVeer's
paternalistic actor is distinguished by the coupling of two characteristics:
an un-self-interested, benevolent intent, and a presumption of greater
moral competence than the subject of his or her intervention (VanDe-
Veer 1986).

We now return to the inferred benevolence of the father's authority
over his children. The father's benevolent exercise of authority is, of

course, based on the notion that children are not the maturational or moral equals of their parents. An argument can be made that the exercise of authority over those who lack the maturity or moral competence to make the "wisest" decisions for themselves may be construed as being in the best interests of those who are thus treated, as "taking care" of them. Individuals who are encompassed by this criterion might (arguably) include children, students, the seriously retarded, the mentally ill, and people who are physically unconscious.

However, even here, legitimate disputes can arise about both the definition of the morally incompetent population (at what point does someone cease to be a child or a student? is someone who is depressed and wishes to commit suicide to be considered mentally ill?), and about the extent of intervention that is justified (should parental consent be required for teenagers to have abortions? should involuntary hospitalization be required for the mentally ill?). These moral ambiguities hover over even the most neutral examples of paternalism (VanDeVeer 1986), and they are compounded by yet another tier of difficulties.

When an actor presumes to have superior moral competence, he or she becomes the final arbiter of what is considered to be the best interests of the subject of the intervention. What protection does such a system offer for a truly disinterested assessment of the subject's best interests? Indeed, is the paternalist capable of assessing the best interests of others, separate from his or her own interests and free from the limitations of his or her own moral perspective? Bear in mind that when fathers exercised paternalistic authority over their children, they did not selflessly evaluate the best interests of their children. Children owed an allegiance to their families: their personal interests were defined, at best, as inseparable from those of their families, and in the event of a conflict, personal interests were subjugated to the financial, status, or political interests of the family. To what extent do similar constraints operate when faculty decide what is "in the best interests" of students, or when civil authorities decide what is "in the best interests" of the mentally ill or the seriously retarded? Do faculty consider what knowledge students should learn without consideration to what would be easiest for the faculty to teach and uninfluenced by their own prior investment in a particular body of knowledge? Do social institutions consider what is best for social dependents without concern for the costs to the rest of society of alternative options?

And, finally, how is the observer to distinguish acts that are altruistically or benevolently motivated from malevolent acts that merely purport to be benevolent? VanDeVeer acknowledges the existence of "illegitimate constraints placed on persons 'for their own good'—with the invitation to comfortable self-righteousness implicit in such an expression." He adds: "Given our strong desire to believe that we are 'reasonable persons of good will' we . . . are less likely to avoid the self-deceptions associated with acts which are seemingly innocent instances of 'doing good' " (Van-DeVeer 1986, 426).

These layers of doubts and ambiguities plague even a generous interpretation of paternalism, as when an agent intervenes with good will on behalf of a subject who is maturationally younger or morally incompetent. But these issues are heightened dramatically when an agent presumes superior moral competence over a subject who is the equal of the agent either maturationally or in the physical ability to think and reason. Indeed, VanDeVeer argues that even acts of benevolently motivated paternalism are unjustified in such cases: when we "view and treat other competents as our moral inferiors," we indulge our own moral sensibilities at the expense of others' liberties (VanDeVeer 1986, 423–424).

These issues are heightened still further when a social group presumes moral superiority over another group from whom it is expropriating valued societal resources. To begin, the lack of reciprocity implicit in such a presumption of moral superiority (that is, the dominant group does not grant that subordinates may at times have a superior understanding of the interests of dominant-group members) carries with it a tacit status-ranking of the two groups. Insidiously, that status-ranking coincides with the expropriative pattern in the intergroup relationship. The preexisting relationship between the two groups hardly positions dominant group members for disinterested, benevolent intervention on behalf of subordinates. In such circumstances, it is implausible that the members of the dominant group might dissociate their own best interests from those of the group that is providing their privileges. The presumption of moral superiority over a group with whom one has an expropriative relationship is thus flatly incompatible with the spirit of altruistic benevolence, no matter how much affection and breast-beating accompanies it. In the analysis of unequal relations between social groups, paternalism must be distinguished from benevolence.

MASTERING THE ILLUSION OF BENEVOLENCE

But the agenda for dominant groups is to create an ideological cocoon whereby they can define their discriminatory actions as benevolent. In this way, the beneficiaries of the inequality assuage their own sensibilities at the same time as they avoid the awkwardness of having to withhold something from the demanding grasp of subordinates. Subordinates do not demand something unless they define it as a need. Dominant groups thus mimic the traditional father-child relationship by claiming superior moral competence and attempting to define the needs of subordinates.

They can then provide—with pleasant sentimentality and with a satisfying *feeling* of benevolence—for the fulfillment of those needs.

To that end, their unequal relationship is swathed in a morality that identifies subordinates' worth and value within the terms of that relationship. Such an orientation must rest on persuasion rather than on force and can only be really effective in the circumstance of mutual affection between the groups. With affection comes the ability of those in command to shape the needs and aspirations of subordinates and to portray discriminatory arrangements as being in the best interests of all concerned. Conflict is obviated because those who must initiate it—the have-not's—are bound emotionally and cognitively in a framework that is of the dominant group's definition. Far from undermining their domination over subordinates, the expression of affection for subordinates thus strengthens the dominant group's control.

THE WAGES OF LOVE

A great deal has been written, spoken, and, above all, sung, about the virtues of love. Love in all its forms is extolled. Whether it is in reference to the relations between parents and children, sexual partners, siblings, friends, social groups, or nations, we are daily exhorted to strive for love. Before its radiant power, problems melt. We all know that "love is blind," that to love is to give of oneself, to embrace the other to oneself, to lay oneself open, and to dissolve barriers. We revere love as the highest human emotion.

But something is missing. Many husbands who profess to love their wives beat them, and after humble contrition and apologies, they beat them again. Many fathers who profess love for their children beat them or sexually abuse them. Slave-owners in the Old South who professed affection for their slaves subjected their slaves to harsh physical punishments. I submit that love is overrated. It seems to offer little protection in human relations.

Is love given freely, or is it offered on terms? Does love instill feelings of protectiveness, or feelings of possession? Is love blind, or carefully circumscribed? Does love make people do anything for someone, or does it give them a license to do anything *to* someone? Do we give more to those whom we love, or do we demand more from our loved ones? Is love a feeling of dependence ("I can't live without her"), or a feeling of being indispensible ("He needs me")? The problem is that almost anything can be done, and has been done, in the name of love. Idealized love and the practice of love appear to have little connection.

The single achievement of love is to entangle the affected parties with an intricate and complex emotional bond. That bond does not dissolve other elements present in the relationship. It neither alters the personalities of the participants nor changes the way resources are distributed between them. If one participant has more resources, love does not move him to give those advantages up. The distinction between the pleasures afforded by love and by privilege is brought out sharply in the words of an upper-middle-class white Virginian, interviewed in the 1940s:

> As a boy I played with colored children. I loved my Negro mammy and kissed her as I would my white mother. The social side has nothing to do with the human side. I wouldn't have gone to school with the colored boys, but I was in sports with them, camped out with them, ate and slept with them. I remember one old friend, Jim, who had been a body guard to an old general. I saw him in back of the house when I was home last—he almost opened his arms to me. I shook his hand, just as familiarly. That's the human side of your old type Negro. If he came to my house he'd go around to the back door; he wouldn't think of going to the front. (Quoted in Johnson 1943, 210; for similar reports showing the acute distinction between affection and status differentiation in whites' relations with African Americans in the South in the early twentieth century, see Powdermaker [1939] 1968, 31–32)

What love does accomplish is to infuse the inequalities in a relationship with an intricate bond that lubricates the contact points between the participants. By these sweet means, the actor with more resources is granted an ease of access to the other party of which he might otherwise only dream.

Longstanding relationships of social inequality are not driven by feelings of hostility; nor do such feelings provide a sound bolster for the inequality. In such relations, the intent to discriminate springs directly from the privileged interests of the dominant group, and the emotional accompaniment of choice is not hostility, but affection. Groups who dominate social relationships strive to keep hostility out of those relationships, not in order to foster equality, but rather to deepen and secure the inequality. They have learned that persuasion is better than force.

OUTLINE OF THE BOOK

These ideas about conflict and its avoidance in intergroup relations are elaborated in part I. I begin, in chapter 1, by discussing the prevailing concerns and assumptions of the literature on class relations, racial prejudice, political tolerance, and gender attitudes, and I identify the ways in which each of these disparate bodies of research has been shaped by the pivotal significance attached to conflict and hostility. In chapter 2, I elaborate an alternative view of the relational process of dominance and subordination. My argument is that the preoccupation with conflict and

hostility has seriously misdirected our efforts to understand and interpret the dynamics of social inequality. I assess the limits of explicit power
relations and force as a means of social control and the role of ideology
in channeling social control into more implicit and less combative avenues. This leads to a consideration of the different forms of ideological
persuasion that are nurtured by varying structural conditions. I appraise
the coercive properties of love as an instrument of social control and
the congeniality of conditional love in the control of relations that are
structured with high physical intimacy between the groups. I then suggest an alternative form of ideological persuasion into which dominant
groups drift when their relations with subordinates are structured more
distally and the threat of conflict is heightened. When love is impractical,
dominant groups turn to reason as they grope to restrain hostility and
maintain control without the exercise of force.

In part II, I address issues that bear on the comparative, empirical
analysis of the ideologies that accompany different cases of intergroup
relations. In chapter 3, the factors that define the distinctive physical
profiles of my three empirical cases—race, gender, and social class in
the contemporary United States—are assessed, followed by a discussion
of the rationale that underlies my comparative case-study analysis. In
chapter 4, I consider the ways in which intergroup contact is structured in
race, gender, and class relations in the United States. The distinguishing
elements of role segregation and spatial segregation as modes of differentiation are assessed, as well as the implications of each mode for the
character of communication channels between groups. I then examine
empirical data from my 1975 survey of the American public to evaluate
the degree to which these two forms of segregation have shaped the
pattern of contact between groups in race, gender, and class relations
in the United States.

In part III, I dissect and compare empirically the intergroup attitudes
that are exchanged between groups in the three cases. The attitudes of
a representative sample of the adult population of the United States in
the mid-1970s give us a revealing camera shot of the intergroup attitudes
that pervade alternative forms of inequality. Those data allow us to explore the ideological intricacies of dominance and subordination as each
group responds to the structural exigencies of the relationship and to
the messages received from its unequal cohabitants. I focus piece by
piece on evidence for different kinds of ideological tendencies and the
presence of conflict or the quieter ideologies of paternalism or reasoned
persuasion from one intergroup relationship to another.

This begins, in chapter 5, with an assessment of the emotional and
cognitive wellsprings of intergroup attitudes. To what extent do the
members of contending groups manifest hostility or warmth in their

basic affective dispositions toward one another and a sense of mutual disparity or universally shared interests in their cognitive understandings of the relationship between them? Those questions have lain at the foundation of theories on prejudice, tolerance, and group consciousness. I suggest that the data do not lie in patterns that conform to the expectations of past theories. The emotional and perceptual framing of intergroup attitudes is frequently softened by warm or neutral emotional expressions and by perceptions of shared group interests. The introduction of hostility and disparity varies across different groups and intergroup relations, but it appears to be tentative rather than strident.

In chapter 6, the focus shifts to the policy goals of contending groups, to assess their construction and substance and the degree to which they suggest competing or merged political agendas. To address the shape of grassroots political alignments, I consider the distinctions between abstract and specific policy goals, egalitarianism and individualism, and existential and prescriptive beliefs. The differing existential views that frame people's policy prescriptions help us to distinguish those who advocate affirmative policy change from the conservatives who want no change and, at the other extreme, those who urge reactionary change. The varying shape of political discourse between dominant and subordinate groups can then be traced for race, gender, and class relations.

In chapter 7, I turn to the key issue of how people's intergroup emotional dispositions are linked with their policy goals on behalf of groups: to what extent are negative emotional dispositions the catalyst for competitive policy goals? Despite the scholarly preoccupation with consistent attitudes, what are the alternative ways that intergroup feelings and policy goals are compounded by people in dominant and subordinate groups? And how do the attitudinal configurations on each side of an intergroup relationship dovetail with one another as the participating groups respond to the constraints presented by their mutual relations?

In chapter 8, the cognitive embroidery of intergroup relations is examined. What kinds of beliefs prevail in each intergroup relationship about the salient characteristics of the contending groups, and what is the folk wisdom about the causes of group differences? I argue that the scholarly emphasis on stereotypical beliefs that are categorical, sharply differentiating, irrational, rigid, and derogatory has been misplaced. I examine intergroup attributions as political, elastic stories introduced by the dominant group to address the various stress-points that exist in their relations with subordinates. I assess the varying substance and style of intergroup attributions in unequal relations that are marked by different constraints and the varying success of dominant groups in persuading subordinates to see things their way.

Finally, in part IV, the broad issues that have motivated this book are assessed. In chapter 9, I begin by outlining the central precepts of my theoretical and methodological approach to the ideology of inequality, identifying the key ways in which my approach diverges from other models. The data from race, gender, and class relations are then reviewed. What features distinguish the structure of each intergroup relationship and the accompanying exchange of ideologies between groups? I appraise the extent to which the attitudes of individual participants are bound by aggregate pressures stemming from the general structure of contact between groups and the messages received from contending groups in the ongoing affair of dominance and subordination. What does the evidence from gender, class, and race relations in the United States suggest for the roles of hostility and persuasion in the ideological pursuit of group interests?

PART I

The Wind and the Sun

CHAPTER ONE

The Search for Conflict

In his well-known essay on "The Subjection of Women," John Stuart Mill (1869) made the following argument about what he regarded as the special character of the unequal relationship between men and women:

> They [women] are so far in a position different from all other subject classes, that their masters require something more from them than actual service. Men do not want solely the obedience of women, they want their sentiments. All men, except the most brutish, desire to have, in the women most nearly connected with them, not a forced slave but a willing one, not a slave merely, but a favory. They have therefore put everything in practice to enslave their minds. The masters of all other slaves rely, for maintaining obedience, on fear—either fear of themselves, or religious fears. The masters of women wanted more than simple obedience, and they turned the whole force of education to effect their purpose. ([1869] 1970, 141)

Mill's argument is important, both for what it says and for what it does not say. First, Mill identified the clear advantages to a dominant group of obtaining the unthinking compliance of subordinates and the significance of ideology ("the whole force of education") as a weapon to achieve that effect. But, second, Mill assumes that relationships of inequality in general are not governed by such considerations. He argues that male-female relations are an exception (and, as I shall show later, only a partial exception at that) to the general rule of overt hostility between unequal groups and the forced compliance of subordinates. The first point is an important insight into the ideological dynamics of dominance and subordination. The second point is an equally important oversight that undermines the potentially broad significance of Mill's analysis.

Mill's oversight has been endemic to the disparate literature on the

ideology of inequality. The attitudes that are espoused by groups who
are engaged in a relationship of inequality have been analyzed and dis-
sected by students of class relations, racial prejudice, political tolerance,
and gender relations. Each of these bodies of literature has operated
independently, each caught up in its own specialized language and research agenda. But what each corpus of research does share is the pivotal,
implicit assumption that conflict and hostility are the exclusive hallmark
of problematic social relations. I turn now to an overview of the motivating concerns of each of these bodies of literature on the ideology of
inequality. Such an overview reveals both the discrete concerns of each
corpus of research and the common thread—expressed in various
ways—of the assumption that there is an indefatigable link between
problematic social relations and conflict.

CLASS AND CLASS CONFLICT

Karl Marx's analysis of class relations put conflict squarely at the center
stage of debate about the existence and meaning of social class. The
abiding role that Marx assigned to conflict in the expression and resolution of exploitative social relations is made clear in Engels' succinct summary of Marx's approach in his introduction to "The Manifesto of the
Communist Party":

> The fundamental proposition . . . is that in every historical epoch the pre-
> vailing mode of economic production and exchange and the social organi-
> zation necessarily following from it form the basis upon which is built up,
> and from which alone can be explained, the political and intellectual history
> of that epoch; that consequently the whole history of mankind (since the
> dissolution of primitive tribal society, holding land in common ownership)
> has been a history of class struggles, contests between exploiting and ex-
> ploited, ruling and oppressed classes; that the history of these class strug-
> gles forms a series of evolutions in which, nowadays, a stage has been
> reached where the exploited and oppressed class—the proletariat—can-
> not attain its emancipation from the sway of the exploiting and ruling
> class—the bourgeoisie—without, at the same time, and once and for all,
> emancipating society at large from all exploitation, oppression, class dis-
> tinctions, and class struggles. (Marx and Engels [1888] 1959, 4)

Capitalism would bring to a climax the evolutionary history of exploitation and conflict, and it would therefore intensify the strains that had
been the catalyst for change throughout history. The language of conflict
and struggle abound in Marx's analysis of capitalism:

> The modern bourgeois society that has sprouted from the ruins of feu-
> dal society has not done away with class antagonisms. It has but established
> new classes, new conditions of oppression, new forms of struggle in place
> of the old ones.

Our epoch, the epoch of the bourgeoisie, possesses, however, this distinctive feature: it has simplified the class antagonisms. Society as a whole is more and more splitting up into two great hostile camps, into two great classes directly facing each other: bourgeoisie and proletariat. (Marx and Engels [1888] 1959, 8)

The Debate about Marx

Marx's thesis drew the first powerful lines of the framework that was to lock in the debate about social class. Those who wished to promote the view of class as exploitative felt compelled to show evidence of its injurious effects on social harmony. Those who sought to portray inequality as benign pointed to the lack of strife along class lines as vital evidence. Indeed, in the ensuing "conflict versus consensus" debate, the concept of class itself became tied-to the inseparable pair, exploitation and conflict. To claim no evidence of class conflict was tantamount to denying the existence of class at all as an organizing factor in social life.

The powerful impact of Marx's analysis on the concept of social class reflects not only the radical nature of the theory itself, but the particular quality of the criticisms it engendered. Although some analysts disputed the exact basis of class organization (for example, authority relations at work or type of work rather than relationship to the means of production), the most threatening criticisms that defined the other extremities of the framework for debate did not challenge the internal logic of Marx's theory or the logic of its empirical deductions. Attempts to discount Marx's analysis primarily took the form of working backwards from the ultimate empirical prediction, class conflict: using the absence of class conflict as their logical starting point, critics sought to establish that the notion of class exploitation on which conflict was predicated was therefore wrong.

Criticisms of Marx came in a series of waves. Indeed, until the relatively recent advent of neo-Marxist thought, Marx's influence on the literature on class inequality seemed to be primarily indirect, through the counterarguments that it spawned. The first enduring criticisms came from Max Weber. A second line of dispute came from Emile Durkheim and the subsequent development of the functionalist school of thought. Further criticisms were developed by scholars from the pluralist and postindustrial/postmaterialist schools of thought. Without giving a full account of each of these waves of criticism, I would like to draw attention to those aspects that reinforced the equation of exploitation with conflict and hostility.

Weber.   Max Weber took issue with Marx on both methodological and theoretical grounds. In his advocacy of the "ideal type" methodology, he held that theory construction was a misleading tool for the analysis of social life. He did not want to argue that Marx's theory was wrong in the sense that an alternative theory would be better. He argued that any theory of social life would be limited both by the elusively changeable nature of social phenomena themselves and by the baggage of personal values that the social scientist brings to the world in which he is both a participant and an observer (Weber 1949). The analytic goal of Weber's "ideal type" methodology was to construct an abstraction of some social phenomenon and then to use that abstraction, not as a lens through which to observe and interpret social reality, but as a reference against which reality could be compared. In this way, he hoped to identify the regularities of social life as well as to highlight the idiosyncracies. Weber's purpose, therefore, in criticizing Marx was not to advocate an alternative theory but to treat Marx's theory as though it were an "ideal type" and to elucidate those aspects of social life that did not square with Marx's model of it. Because of this methodological slant, Weber's legacy was more a series of questions about various pieces of Marx's theory than the development of an alternative conception of the dynamics of social inequality.

Weber raised numerous questions about Marx's theory, but the statement that had the most profound effect on the shape of the literature on social inequality was his fragmentary essay, "Class, Status, Party" (Weber 1946a). In that paper, he argued that classes may be nothing more than bare, economic categories devoid of the sense of community or shared purpose that come out of status distinctions. Pointing to social distinctions that have no direct basis in economic inequality (and especially racial and ethnic distinctions), Weber argued that they "interfered with the sheer market principle" by providing alternative, more socially salient magnets for social exclusiveness and intergroup antagonism.

In the subsequent desire to move away from a class analysis of society, social scientists seized upon this idea of Weber's. Specifically, they attempted to demote the analytic importance of class by arguing that other culturally based distinctions (especially race and ethnicity) evidenced more conflict and hostility than did class. In this way, Weber's legacy was to heighten even further the significance attached to social conflict in the analysis of social inequality.

Durkheim.   Durkheim's ideas about social inequality reinforced the linkage of conflict with problematic social relations more directly. Durkheim viewed social differentiation, not as the product of exploitative relationships, but as a benign and functionally integrative feature of organized social life (Durkheim [1897] 1951, [1893] 1965). At the same time, he denied the normality of conflict—he acknowledged its contemporaneous existence but portrayed it as an aberration from normal social intercourse brought about only by minor maladjustments in a complex but overwhelmingly balanced, integrative social system. Social inequality was functionally integrative, and under "normal" circumstances this would be tacitly demonstrated in its consensual endorsement (Durkheim [1895] 1964). Thus, whereas Marx depicted conflict as intrinsic to the course of human history, Durkheim regarded conflict as abnormal. For Durkheim, consensus and harmony typically govern social intercourse, and this was taken as a manifestation of the functional integration of the underlying structure of society. Outbreaks of conflict were taken as a signal that things had slipped temporarily out of kilter, indicating that the system required repair to nudge it back to its normal state of integrated balance. Thus, Durkheim preserved the logic of a link between pervasive social struggle and exploitative social inequality. Even sporadic outbreaks of conflict were taken as evidence of a social problem, albeit a lapse capable of repair rather than an endemic structural flaw. In Durkheim's view, absence of conflict was the normal condition of human society and it demonstrated the absence of exploitation and even the absence of any divisive social problem.

Davis and Moore. In their functional theory of stratification (1945), Davis and Moore promoted Durkheim's line of reasoning, and, in so doing, they sealed the course of the debate about the meaning of social inequality into a choice between conflict (symptomatic of exploitative relations) and consensus (indicative of functional differentiation). Davis and Moore argued that socioeconomic inequality, far from being a weapon that frustrates human creativity and freedom, is the necessary instrument by which the potential of both society and its individual constituent members is realized. An unequal distribution of rewards does not indicate that one group is taking something from another but rather an implicit social contract in which all participants mutually understand their respective contributions to the common good. Tasks that contribute more are awarded higher benefits, especially if their fulfillment requires a greater personal investment.

Such an argument rests implicitly on the idea of consensual social relations: if one argues that social inequalities are freely and spontaneously entered into, it is inconvenient to find those with fewer rewards restive and complaining that something has been taken from them. The conception of society as a collective whole further encouraged an emphasis on consensual social behavior, rather than on discord with its implication of disparate social groups. Indeed, the holistic view of the functionalists made the very concept of discrete classes inappropriate and encouraged instead the perception of an unbroken continuum of inequality: the constituent functions and rewards of society provided no basis for the coalescence of distinct socioeconomic groups. The debate

over the meaning of social inequality was now shaped into well-demar-
cated positions that hinged critically on the constancy or infrequency of
group conflict.

Pluralism. The inevitability of the connection between entrenched
relations of exploitation and sustained group conflict was also taken as
a given by scholars in the pluralist school of thought. Asserting that
American society was characterized by an absence of repeated conflict
along class lines, pluralists argued that the critical ingredient of sustained
class exploitation was missing (for example, Coser 1956; Polsby 1980).
Rather than seeing the political system as reflecting a reiterative bias in
favor of one segment of society at the expense of another, pluralists
conceived of the political system as fragmented and fluid (for example,
Dahl 1961; Rose 1967). Issues on the political agenda were seen as constantly shifting and as relatively specialized in their import. Allegiances
that might coalesce around one issue would disband for the next and
possibly be transformed on opposing sides of a later issue. No group
was seen as the systematic loser. Instead, the system would deal with each
issue, one at a time, responding to the investment of effort of contending
parties without any accumulation of bias from the resolution of previous
issues. Such a system prevented the buildup of a sustained social cleavage
along class (or other) lines. Individuals belonged to multiple groups with
shifting and sometimes conflicting interests (for example, Coser 1956;
Hodge and Treiman 1968; Polsby 1980). The allegiances of individuals
were too transitory and fragmented to provide any basis for the development of sustained conflict between groups.

Embourgeoisement, Postindustrialism, Postmaterialism.   In a variant on the
pluralist theme, some analysts have argued that the idea of riveting class
conflict has been rendered obsolete by the increased level of affluence
and altered occupational structure in advanced industrial societies. In
an era of postindustrialism, the embourgeoisement of the working class,
the expansion of the middle class, and the growth of the service sector
of the economy were held to move society away from traditional class
distinctions into more individualistic orientations toward personal better-
ment and into increasing concern with "postmaterialist" issues bearing on
noneconomic aspects of the quality of life (see, for example, Dahrendorf
1964; Wilensky 1970; Bell 1973; Inglehart 1977, 1990; Lipset 1981).
This line of thought, too, has assumed that if an exploitative relationship
between the economic have's and have-not's were the principal organizing factor of social life, that relationship must find expression in passionate, conflict-laden ideologies. If the latter have wilted, the cause must lie

in changed economic relationships that have muted exploitation and thrown open multiple, competing foci for political energy.

Attempts to Salvage the Class Concept

On the other side of the debate about class are scholars in the "neo-Marxist" and "interest-group" schools of thought who wish to promote the concept of socioeconomic exploitation, either in the form of Marx's class categories or in some other class framework. These scholars have not strayed from the original conception of class as a source of conflict. This has confronted them with some awkward choices as they go about interpreting empirical data on class ideology which have repeatedly shown an embarrassing lack of outright conflict. Indeed, the lack of blatant conflict in contemporary class relations has been the most pressing theoretical challenge facing analysts of class ideology. Various resolutions of the problem have been pursued.

Accentuating Class Conflict.   The simplest strategy has been to interpret data in a way that highlights the disparity of ideological positions between socioeconomic groups rather than dwelling on the extent to which the views of the groups converge (for example, Centers 1949; Huber and Form 1973). Meanwhile, analysts who are less sympathetic to the concept of class have interpreted similarly modest differences between groups as clear evidence of the nonexistence or demise of exploitative class relations (for example, Dahrendorf 1964; Nisbet 1970; Wilensky 1970; Polsby 1980; Lipset 1981). These disagreements tend to lock empirical debate into a dispute over "half-empty versus half-full," as one side bravely emphasizes the evidence of dissension between classes while the other side draws attention to the evidence of consensus.

Hidden Resistance.   A second attempt to salvage conflict from the jaws of consensus has been to claim that oppositional orientations lie simmering beneath the surface among subordinate classes (for example, Scott 1985, 1990). Known usually as "hidden resistance," this argument has been very appealing to students of class. It postulates that the governed, although they appear to have acceded to their position, nevertheless are cognizant of their exploitation; and that although they refrain from engaging the dominant class in major, organized confrontations, subordinates routinely engage in small, personal acts of resistance that are hidden in the everyday practice of life. This argument rightfully calls attention to more subtle forms of behavior and reminds us that, as with all things social, we should not rely on outward appearances alone to decipher the levels and nuances of human interaction.

Unfortunately, however, the search for hidden, private forms of resistance involves the application of an awkwardly weighted accounting procedure. Any action that might be interpreted as less than fully compliant, no matter how small, private, or inconsequential, is given disproportionate weight in making inferences about the state of consciousness of subordinates—meanwhile, unambiguous and socially significant acts of compliance are discounted as instrumentally contrived. This weighting procedure involves an awkward presumption about which actions are true reflections of someone's state of mind and which are either "false" or instrumentally contrived.

The hidden resistance argument also uses ambiguous rules of evidence, making it impossible to draw a clear empirical line between resistant and accommodative acts. Indeed, in Genovese's sensitive interpretation of day-to-day resistance among African-American slaves in the antebellum South (1974, 597–621), he discusses the ambiguity inherent in such behaviors as lying, stealing, dissembling, and shirking, and he refers to them as "simultaneous accommodation and resistance" (1974, 597). Although such behaviors may buffer subordinates from the worst exactitudes of their status, they also pander to the prejudices and foibles of the dominant class, thereby helping to perpetuate the inequality between the classes by feeding the dominant class's preexisting conceptions of the limitations of their subordinates. For these reasons, Genovese argues that hidden resistance qualifies "at best as prepolitical and at worst as apolitical" (1974, 598).

"False Consciousness" and Cultural Hegemony. There has been a third general attempt to grapple with the lack of class conflict within a conflict model, and that has been to attribute the passivity and conservatism of the working class to an artificially induced state of "false consciousness." There are slightly different variants of the false-consciousness argument, but their common feature is to credit the dominant ideology with a pervasive power that pummels the thinking of subordinates. The idea originates with Marx and Engels' famous dictum, laid out in *The German Ideology* in 1846:

> The ideas of the ruling class are in every epoch the ruling ideas, i.e., the class which is the ruling *material* force of society, is at the same time its ruling *intellectual* force. The class which has the means of material production at its disposal, has control at the same time over the means of mental production, so that thereby, generally speaking, the ideas of those who lack the means of mental production are subject to it. (Marx and Engels [1846] 1970, 64)

As Abercrombie and Turner (1982) point out, this postulate flatly contradicts Marx's primary prediction that people's consciousness will be

THE SEARCH FOR CONFLICT

shaped directly by their experiences, that is, that people rationally perceive and interpret their experiences and that from this ability stems the
inevitability of eventual class conflict. According to the dictum of false
consciousness, the working class, which is designated by Marxist theory
as the key agent of change in the capitalist dialectic, fails to perceive its
true interests and hence lapses into a deceived acceptance of its own
oppression.

Analysts have explored this idea in slightly different ways. Mann
(1970) argued that, because subordinate classes display stronger support
for the tenets of dominant-class ideology when they are asked about
relatively abstract principles than when they are asked about specific
applications of those principles, this constitutes evidence that the conservatism of subordinate classes is "false." Mann's logic is that specifics
are more likely to be perceived in their context and are thus perceived
with the clearer vision that comes from direct experience, whereas abstractions are imposed by dominant ideology and represent an incomplete socialization attempt. Similar arguments about the disjuncture between the abstract and the applied perspectives of the working class have
been made by Parkin (1971) and Huber and Form (1973), but without
the terminology of "false consciousness."

Perhaps the most sophisticated treatment of false consciousness is to
be found in the concept of "cultural hegemony" developed by the Italian
communist, Antonio Gramsci (Gramsci 1971). Because it offers an interpretation of the absence of class conflict within a conflict perspective,
the concept of cultural hegemony has proved alluring to an increasing
number of scholars. And the complexity of Gramsci's ideas and the lack
of precision with which he expressed them has left room for a variety
of interpretations of the concept (see, for example, G. Williams 1960;
Marcuse 1964; Femia 1975; Anderson 1976–1977; R. Williams 1980;
Lears 1985; Bocock 1986). The essential argument is that all the major
institutions of society are infiltrated by the dominant ideology, blunting
the working class's perceptions and molding its values so that the class
is rendered impotent as an agent of change. The cultural hegemony of
the dominant class prevents the working class from realizing its true
interests or, indeed, from developing a value system that would provide
the ideological infrastrcture for revolutionary change. From Gramsci's
point of view, as a political activist, this meant that changing working-class
values was to be an important priority in the political agenda; without a
concerted effort to alienate working-class values from those of the cultural hegemony, a true revolution (that would abandon capitalist values)
could not be realized.

The concept of cultural hegemony, like that of hidden resistance,
offers important insights into the dynamics of ideological control. But,

like the concept of hidden resistance; cultural hegemony is hamstrung by its confinement within a conflict model of class relations. Although various interpretations of cultural hegemony have tackled the concept slightly differently, none of them has been able to resolve the intrinsic difficulties. First, the depiction of working-class consciousness as "false" involves an a priori decision about what the true interests of the working class are (is this a form of analytic paternalism for scholars to pronounce what the working class's interests are, irrespective of what people in the working class themselves believe?), and it leads to inconclusive debates about how to assess the "true" interests of a group (see, for example, Connolly 1972). A related problem (Mann's efforts notwithstanding, 1970), is that the concept of false consciousness is not empirically falsifiable—the falseness of a particular ideological postion can only be determined on a priori grounds. A second and more fundamental problem is the intrinsic contradiction noted above between the ideas of material determinism and cultural ascendancy. If the dominant class prevents subordinates from perceiving their true interests by the imposition of a cultural hegemony, this implies a persistent lack of rationality among subordinates—but the primary prediction of class conflict rests pivotally on the assumption that humans process and act on their experiences rationally. Thus, in an attempt to salvage the prediction of class conflict, some analysts have undermined the rationality assumption on which the prediction of conflict rests.

Exploitation and Conflict

Serious interpretive ambiguities or conceptual contradictions plague all three attempts to preserve the concept of class conflict in the face of class quiescence. It is more than a little awkward to deal with the empirical absence of open conflict within a theoretical approach that is driven by the expectation of conflict as the rational expression of exploitative social relations.

Within the confines of the established debate about class, the cleanest interpretation for an observed lack of conflict remains a lack of exploitation. And, indeed, an analyst's interpretation of the extent of class conflict in a society is generally an accurate barometer of his claims about the significance of class organizationally. Thus, for Nisbet, class conflict is absent and therefore class does not exist (Nisbet 1970). For Lipset, class exists in muted form as one of many weak divisions in the industrial democracies, and thus the "democratic class struggle" presents a picture of muted class conflict crosscut by a variety of other political issues (Lipset 1981). For Centers, classes are enduring, socioeconomic interest groups, and this is manifested in significant ideological conflict between socioeconomic groups (Centers 1949). For Wright, classes are carved out by the relations between different positions in the means of production, and herein lies the fuel that energizes class conflict (Wright 1979, 1985).

Empirical Questions and Measures

The lines of debate about class and class conflict have molded the kinds of questions that have been central to empirical analyses. A large literature developed around the assessment of subjective class identification (for example, Centers 1949; Hodge and Treiman 1968; Jackman and Jackman 1973, 1983; Kleugel, Singleton, and Starnes 1977), as analysts sought to determine whether and in what form class exists in the public consciousness. Note that there has been no comparable empirical effort to measure baseline identification with race or gender groups. For class, however, the underlying issue has been that if people do not identify subjectively with social classes, then classes do not exist. Considerable empirical effort has also been devoted to the assessment of people's perceptions of the economic system and their economic policy dispositions, to determine whether people seem to define and pursue conflicting class interests (for example, Centers 1949; Landecker 1963; Wilensky 1970; Mann 1970; Huber and Form 1973; Jackman and Jackman 1983).

In short, the very existence and definition of class has come to be linked critically to the notion of class conflict. Marx's conception of politics and culture as epiphenomena reflecting underlying economic relationships has been commonly accepted in its most literal, direct sense. If classes have conflicting economic interests, it is assumed that they must eventually find expression in ideological conflict.

RACIAL PREJUDICE AS IRRATIONAL ANTAGONISM

The analysis of racial prejudice in the United States drew strength from two main sources, one pragmatic and the other theoretical. On the pragmatic side, the analysis of racial prejudice was propelled by the clear, in fact pressing, existence of a racial cleavage in American society between whites and blacks. As Pettigrew brings out in his excellent history of American scholarship on race relations (Pettigrew 1980), from the early years of this century the starkness of the racial problem has spurred a social-reformist approach among analysts of prejudice. The overriding concern of these scholars has been to find an answer to the policy question: how can whites' hostility to blacks be reduced, possibly even eliminated?

The analysis of racial prejudice gathered theoretical legitimacy primarily from Max Weber's argument that status differentiation should be separated from the issue of economic differentiation and that the former is a highly salient independent factor in the formation of social cleavages (Weber 1946a). The way was thus opened for the analysis of racial prejudice as an important field of inquiry in its own right, not merely as a subsidiary of the structural problem of class relations. As I argued above, Weber's legacy was even to encourage the conception of racial prejudice as an *alternative* problem to class relations, rather than something that interfaced with it.

The result was that the analysis of racial prejudice generally became divorced from the analysis of class—each corpus of research has operated under its own assumptions about the primacy of its subject matter and the critical dynamics of intergroup ideology. There have, of course, been some important studies in race relations that have examined the intersection of class and race stratification (for example, Dollard's classic book, *Caste and Class in a Southern Town*, 1937; Bonacich's work on split labor markets in the United States, 1972, 1975, 1976; more recently, William J. Wilson's influential books, *The Declining Significance of Race*, 1980, and *The Truly Disadvantaged*, 1987; and the subsequent flourishing line of research on the dual effects of economic pressures and racial discrimination on the quality of life for urban, poor blacks, such as Jencks and Peterson 1991; Massey 1990; Massey and Eggers 1990; and Massey and Denton 1993). Scholars have also occasionally argued that much of race prejudice may be due to class prejudice (for example, Bayton, McAlister, and Hamer 1956; Blalock 1967; Smedley and Bayton 1978). However, these studies have had little impact on the main thrust of theory and research about racial prejudice. The conception of racial prejudice as a product of independent cultural forces has been preserved.

If racial and ethnic cleavages did not have their origins in the class structure of society but in exogenous cultural factors, the human mind could be credited with an inventive capacity that Marx had not acknowledged. While the debate about class relations pertained to the *structure* of society, students of racial prejudice departed on their own path and came to define their problem in *social psychological* terms.

The Concept of Prejudice
The two propellants, pragmatic and theoretical, determined the definition of the problem and the approach to its analysis. Racial prejudice reflected an error of the human mind, a cultural anachronism that was out of keeping with democratic and scientific thinking. Gunnar Myrdal encapsulated this thinking when he posed the problem as "An American Dilemma"—the parochial anachronism of racial prejudice and discrimination embedded within a society that was governed by democratic, egalitarian ideals (Myrdal 1944). Analysts assumed that all racial and ethnic groups share the same, universal human values and that racial and ethnic

hostility must be driven by misperceptions and misunderstandings that grew out of ignorance and parochialism. Allport, in his seminal work *The Nature of Prejudice* ([1954] 1979, 265), emphasized this reasoning with a parable:

> See that man over there?
> Yes.
> Well, I hate him.
> But you don't know him.
> That's why I hate him.

From ignorance came misunderstanding, and from misunderstanding came hatred. This framework led Allport to conclude optimistically that "knowledge and acquaintance are likely to engender sounder beliefs concerning minority groups, and for this reason contribute to the reduction of prejudice" (Allport [1954] 1979, 268).

The task of progressive social reform was to eradicate parochialism and thereby to break down the walls of hostility that are a barrier to human understanding and social harmony. These themes were forcefully expressed by Marshall Field in his foreword to Deutsch and Collins' landmark study, *Interracial Housing: A Psychological Evaluation of a Social Experiment*:

> There are barricades in the United States restricting and confining Negroes, Mexicans, Orientals, and other segments of our population to ghettos which are as real as the walls that surrounded the Jews in Warsaw. They are intangible; *they exist in the customs of society and in the minds of men.* . . . The *walls of custom and belief* which keep Negroes segregated from whites are not only a *blot on our own national, democratic ideals* but they are also a serious blow to our reputation among the nations. . . . This study. . . may be of great value to those who would *replace superstition with science* in making up their minds about interracial housing. (Deutsch and Collins 1951, v, vi, emphasis added)

The issues that motivated the literature on racial prejudice are captured in Allport's classic definition of prejudice:

> Ethnic prejudice is an antipathy based upon a faulty and inflexible generalization. It may be felt or expressed. It may be directed toward a group as a whole, or toward an individual because he is a member of that group. ([1954] 1979, 9)

Allport emphasized two ingredients that identify prejudice: first, definite hostility and rejection, and second, rejection based on categorical (and therefore erroneous) criteria (Allport [1954] 1979, 5). Many other definitions of prejudice have been offered in the literature, but almost all share Allport's emphasis on irrationally founded antipathy as the core of the problem (see, for example, Newcomb, Turner, and Converse 1965,

430–431; Harding et al. 1969, 3–6; Ashmore 1970; Simpson and Yinger 1972, 24; Berry and Tischler 1978, 235; Kinder and Sears 1981; Pettigrew 1982, 1–5; Dovidio and Gaertner 1986, 2–3; Marger 1994, 74–75).

Prejudice as Hostility.   The concept of prejudice puts racial hostility in center stage. Whereas the significance of conflict for analysts of class relations was as a reflexive indicator of underlying structural disunity, students of racial prejudice focused on hostility as the definitional core of the problem itself. This was the form in which race relations manifested itself as an ugly social problem, and the social problem was what motivated the analysis of race relations. If there were no intergroup hostility, there would be no problem that required analysis. That spirit is illustrated in an early bulletin published by the Social Science Research Council on *The Reduction of Intergroup Tensions* (Williams, Jr. 1947), which was "Prepared under the direction of the Committee on Techniques for Reducing Group Hostility." The mandate of that prestigious committee has continued to dominate the agenda of research on racial attitudes (see, for example, Stephan's chapter on "Intergroup Relations" in the third edition of *The Handbook of Social Psychology*, 1985).

Prejudice as Blatant and Unitary.   By the same token, prejudice was assumed to have a unitary character. Because prejudice was a purely expressive phenomenon (rather than a politically motivated articulation), the irrationally founded hatred on which it was based might manifest itself in a variety of modes—beliefs, feelings, social avoidance, discrimination. In the prejudiced individual, hostility would dominate all his dispositions toward the group in question or toward individuals from that group. Measurement might rely on any of these indicators, and assessment of the general extent of the problem in society could draw on any measure that reflected intergroup negativism. And because they were a product of parochialism, the personal feelings of antipathy that drove prejudice were also expected to find blatant and unsubtle expression. Prejudice was conceived as an uncontained expression of parochial negativism.

Prejudice as an Individual Phenomenon.   Finally, because prejudice was divorced from the question of the economic structure of society, it was conceived as a phenomenon that resided in people's heads and therefore as a property of individuals. The way to understand the problem was to analyze the variance across individuals in expressed racial hostility and to match this with individual differences in personality (for example, the theory of the "authoritarian personality") or cultural experience (for example, the theory of "working class authoritarianism" and the "contact theory"). As others have observed, this conception of the problem in individually based psychological terms also carried over into the analysis of ethnic relations more generally because of the prominent position occupied by the concept of prejudice in the literature on race and ethnic relations (Schermerhorn 1970, 6–8; Wilson 1973, 3–5; Wellman 1977, 20–22; Pettigrew 1980, xxxi-xxxii; Giles and Evans 1986).

Dominant Hostility and Subordinate Passivity. The hostility manifested in prejudiced attitudes has been regarded as an undesirable outcome by those who study it. This is, of course, implicit in what I have said in the preceding pages, but it deserves explicit note, because it contrasts sharply with the literature on class consciousness. Students of socioeconomic inequality have been divided as to whether they regard that phenomenon as functionally integrative or exploitative. Only the latter group have seen conflict as an integral part of the phenomenon, and they have viewed class hostility as a desirable outcome, the fuse that would tear apart the current structure of society and forge positive social change. Students of prejudice, however, have been unified in their perception of the existence of racial hostility. And because they have viewed the hostility as lodged in people's heads (rather than being driven by structurally induced differences in interests), it is viewed as an undesirable property that has damaging effects on everything that it touches, from the moral certitude of society as a whole to the reduced opportunities and self-esteem of the unfortunate target group.

Those who regarded socioeconomic inequality as the product of exploitative relations assumed hostile attitudes on the part of those above toward those below, and they eagerly sought evidence of a reciprocated hostility from those below. Marx's description of capitalist society as divided into "two great hostile camps" exudes an excitement that has never been shed in the search for hostility among the victims of exploitation in the class relationship. The development of the prejudice literature, however, reflects an overwhelming concern about the degree of hostility in the racial attitudes of the dominant group, whites. The victims, blacks, were generally regarded in passive terms. Whites constituted the most probable agents of change, in part because the locus of the problem was in the minds of whites and in part because blacks had been rendered relatively powerless by the discriminatory practices that white prejudice had installed.

Students of socioeconomic inequality viewed the lower echelons in more active terms and focused primarily on their attitudes, as indicative of either spontaneous approval of inequality or assertive decrying of the system. By contrast, students of prejudice viewed the essential energy as coming from the dominant group, whites. To the extent that blacks'

attitudes were investigated, it was primarily in passive terms, to assess
the damage wrought by whites on the black psyche (see, for example,
Clark and Clark's classic study of ethnic self-devaluation among black
schoolchildren, [1947] 1958; and Brand, Ruiz, and Padilla 1974). Studies
by Johnson (1943) and Williams, Jr. (1964) were important early exceptions that examined the racial attitudes of both whites and blacks. For
most scholars, it was not until the black urban riots of the late 1960s that
there was a shift in emphasis, and that shift has been only partial and
gradual. Interest in blacks' racial attitudes was initially propelled by questions about the new social problem of mass black violence (for example,
G. Marx 1967; Campbell and Schuman 1968), but increasingly black
identity and black consciousness emerged as a legitimate field of inquiry
in its own right (see, for example, Schuman and Hatchett 1974; Gurin
and Epps 1975). The realization has crept into the field that a full investigation of racial attitudes requires the inclusion of blacks' as well as whites'
perceptions and attitudes (Schuman, Steeh, and Bobo 1985; Sigelman
and Welch 1991). At the same time, however, inclusion of blacks in analyses has not led to any fundamental recasting of the dynamics of racial
attitudes in more politically interactive terms. The concept of prejudice
has not been dislodged and the powerful core of the problem is still seen
as residing with whites. Assessments of racial prejudice among whites
have continued to flourish as a discrete line of inquiry (for example,
Selznick and Steinberg 1969; Campbell 1971; Katz 1976; Fairchild and
Gurin 1978; Pettigrew 1979; Sears, Hensler, and Speer 1979; Kinder
and Sears 1981; Apostle et al. 1983; Dovidio and Gaertner 1986;
Sniderman et al. 1991).

Realistic Group Conflict Theory

A divergent strand in the prejudice literature, usually identified as realistic group conflict theory, has been attracting growing interest in recent
years. This loose school of thought warrants separate discussion because
it represents a different attack on the problem of racial attitudes which
abandons many of the central tenets of the prejudice literature; at the
same time, it does not abandon the primary concern with conflict as the
core factor in intergroup attitudes. The exact arguments made by scholars using the realistic group conflict perspective vary somewhat, but the
perspective may be described as roughly analogous to the interest-group
approach in the class literature: racial groups are seen at least in part as
having distinctive interests that engender conflict. LeVine and Campbell
(1972, 29) provide a clear summary of this approach:

> This theory assumes that group conflicts are rational in the sense that
> groups do have incompatible goals and are in competition for scarce re-

sources. Such "realistic" sources of group conflict are contrasted with the psychological theories that consider intergroup conflicts as displacements or projective expressions of problems that are essentially intragroup or intraindividual in origin. . . . Not all of them eschew psychological explanations. . . . But for all, realistic sources of group conflict are a primary emphasis.

Blumer's essay on "Race Prejudice as a Sense of Group Position" (1958) provides the roots (albeit rather tenuously) for this school of thought. Blumer made the case that prejudice should not be seen as a property of individuals, but of groups seeking to protect their position against possible incursions by subordinates. He introduced the idea of prejudice as motivated by feelings of threat, but he held back from locating those feelings in tangible advantages enjoyed by the dominant group. Blumer's "sense of group position" was a subjectively shared, group-level "sense" rather than a response to tangible, group-level interests (see also his discussion of the impact of industrialization on race relations, 1965). The small school of thought that has grown from Blumer's argument has generally assigned a clearer role to tangible group interests (see, for example, Wellman 1977; Giles and Evans 1986), although an irresolution about the extent to which prejudice derives from irreconcilable, mutually opposed group interests or merely subjectively felt feelings of threat characterizes some of the work in this approach (see, for example, Bobo 1983). The prevailing social-reformist goals of the prejudice literature have pervaded even this school of thought to some degree, constraining espousal of an interest-group approach with its attendant enthusiasm for conflict as a positive rather than as a negative outcome. Doubtless an influential factor here has been that, although realistic group conflict theory implicitly views subordinates in more active terms as part of a power relationship, empirical analysts in this framework have shared with most other analysts of prejudice a primary concern with the attitudes of the dominant racial group, whites (see, for example, Wellman 1977; Smith 1981; Bobo 1983; Giles and Evans 1986). When viewing the attitudes of the more powerful group, expressions of hostility have connotations that analysts find harder to endorse.

Thus, this small but growing school of thought has moved away from the traditional conception of prejudice as an entirely irrational phenomenon lodged in individuals' heads and has instead stressed the need to be attentive to group-level pressures and interests. However, scholars in this school have continued to be attentive primarily to the attitudes of the dominant racial group, whites. Perhaps for this reason, their view that conflict follows inevitably from opposed group interests is accompanied by less enthusiasm than it is among interest-group theorists of class, who focus more on the attitudes of subordinates.

Reassertions and Modifications of the Prejudice Concept
The traditional concept of prejudice has remained essentially intact over the years, and some of its elements have even been reaffirmed. However, there has been a growing sense among students of prejudice that the concept needs some modification and refinement to address the complexities of contemporary racial prejudice.

The Cognitive School.   The conceptual proclivities of the traditional prejudice literature have been reasserted in the recent explosion of research on intergroup attitudes conducted within what is broadly termed the cognitive school. Experimental research on the "minimal group paradigm" has promoted the idea that the creation of even a "minimal group" (on the basis of an arbitrary criterion or even random assignment, with no personal interaction among fellow "group" members) generates own-group bias and out-group discrimination, in terms of both evaluations and allocation of rewards (see, for example, Tajfel 1969, 1978; Billig 1976; Brewer 1979).

A related, rapidly growing body of research has focused on stereotyping and discrimination as an outgrowth of normal social categorization and social comparison processes (see, for example, Tajfel 1969; Hamilton 1979, 1981; Pettigrew 1979; Stephan 1985). The assumptions and predelictions of that literature are captured in an empirical question posed by Taylor (1981, 98): "Given that stereotyping appears to be rooted in basic categorical processes, what are the individual differences that would influence the propensity to categorize or the ability to make within-category discriminations?"

Although some of this research has been attentive to the influence of power or status differentials on the shaping of individuals' perceptions (see, for example, Tajfel and Turner 1979; Tajfel 1982), the governing premise has been psychologically reductionist: that intergroup hostility is rooted in cognitive and motivational mechanisms that are intrinsic to individual behavior. Like Allport before them, these scholars have conceived of the problem in terms of affectively constrained cognitions, and they have directed their energies toward specifying the mechanisms that convert basic cognitive processes into prejudice and discrimination.

"Modern Prejudice."   At the same time, there has been an increasing appreciation over the years that the traditional conception of prejudice is inadequate to reflect the complexities of contemporary racism. Particularly troubling to investigators has been the repeated observation of a sharp discrepancy between, on the one hand, whites' apparent progress toward racial liberalism on traditional measures of prejudice, and, on the other, their continued resistance to specific policies of affirmative

racial change (see, for example, Jackman 1978, 1981*a*; McConahay, Hardee, and Batts 1981; Schuman, Steeh, and Bobo 1985; Schuman and Bobo 1988). The ensuing debate about whether white racial prejudice has "really" declined quickly devolved into disagreements about what the critical elements of interracial attitudes are.

I have suggested elsewhere that the concept of prejudice be abandoned in favor of a conception of interracial attitudes that views them as politically motivated communications to defend group interests rather than as expressions of parochial negativism. In the context of political challenge from blacks, many of the symbolic messages in whites' racial attitudes have become more moderate and subtle, but whites continue to defend their privileged position by opposing specific policies for affirmative racial change (Jackman and Muha 1984). This approach puts primary emphasis on whites' support for specific affirmative racial policies as a gauge of their dispositions toward blacks (Jackman 1978, 1981*a*, 1981*b*; Jackman and Muha 1984). As whites seek to maintain their privileged position in the face of challenge, they have moved away from inflammatory racial epithets and learned to rely instead on the seemingly more neutral principle of individualism.

Some other scholars have shared my position that whites' racial attitudes have become more subtle and nuanced, rather than clearly more positive, but they have retained the basic conception of prejudice as an irrationally founded antipathy. The theories of "symbolic racism" (McConahay and Hough 1976; Kinder and Sears 1981; Kinder 1986) and "modern racism" (McConahay, Hardee, and Batts 1981; McConahay 1986) have maintained that prejudice lives on in the white American psyche but that it has found a more subtle expression that is more in keeping with contemporary cultural norms. The expression of prejudice becomes manifest in specific policies that bear on race relations: these policies are thought to symbolize whites' longstanding repugnance for people who are seen as violating the old-fashioned American values of individualism and self-reliance.

Both these arguments place considerable emphasis on the norm of individualism in the shaping of whites' racial attitudes, although the precise way that individualism and racial attitudes are thought to intersect is different. Individualism is represented either as a politically driven rationale for opposition to affirmative policy interventions (Jackman and Muha 1984) or as an intrinsic part of the prejudice syndrome (e.g., Kinder and Sears 1981). Still other scholars have rejected both these interpretations and have maintained that individualism is an independently held American value that unfortunately confounds policy interventions on behalf of blacks even as whites have become genuinely less prejudiced (for example, Sniderman and Hagen 1985).

Indeed, several scholars have voiced considerable irritation with the new conceptions of racial attitudes. For example, Sniderman and Tetlock conclude their critique of "symbolic racism" with an ardent allusion to "genuine prejudice—a deep-seated, irrational insistence on the inferiority of blacks, and contempt and hostility toward them" (1986, 186). Nonetheless, whatever their predilections, scholars have begun to distinguish in their terminology between "traditional prejudice" and "modern prejudice" (or "new racism"), the former being more blatant and unitary and the latter more subtle and nuanced (see, for example, Firebaugh and Davis 1988; Bobo and Kluegel 1991; Sniderman et al. 1991). And the role of individualism in the formation of racial attitudes remains prominent but uncertain in its meaning.

Empirical Questions and Measures
The questions and measures that have occupied a central position in empirical research on prejudice reflect the themes I have discussed. Analysts have probed into what aspects of individuals' backgrounds and experiences might account for variance in their racial prejudice. The emphasis on prejudice as an expression of parochialism has led to a continuing interest in the effects of formal education in reducing prejudice (see, for example, Lipset 1960; Selznick and Steinberg 1969; Jackman and Muha 1984; Bobo and Licari 1989). The individual, psychological cast of the prejudice concept led some researchers to investigate prejudice as an aspect of personality (most notably, Adorno et al.'s theory of the authoritarian personality, 1950). The casting of prejudice as a symptom of authoritarianism has continued to hold an allure for empirical scholars, especially among those who have seen education as a positive influence (for example, Lipset 1960; Selznick and Steinberg 1969; Bobo and Licari 1989). The question continues to hang over research on prejudice about the extent to which it is a product of individual personality or individual experience (for example, Pettigrew 1958; Allport 1962; Selznick and Steinberg 1969; Kinder and Sears 1981; Yinger 1983). The social-reformist spirit of prejudice research has flowered in the longstanding prominence of the contact theory of prejudice, which postulates that increased intergroup contact, under the right conditions, reduces prejudice (for example, Deutsch and Collins 1951; Wilner, Walkley, and Cook 1955; Miller and Brewer 1984; Jackman and Crane 1986; Kinder and Mendelberg 1991). Social-reformist concerns have also produced a long tradition of studies devoted to monitoring the trends in whites' racial attitudes over time (for example, Hyman and Sheatsley 1956, 1964; Greeley and Sheatsley 1971, 1974; Schuman, Steeh, and Bobo 1985; Firebaugh and Davis 1988).

The most common measures that have been used in analyses of prejudice are those reflecting stereotypical beliefs, feelings of social distance, and support for racial integration and other affirmative racial policies. Stereotypes were conceived as irrational, negative, categorical beliefs about a group. Because of their propinquity to the essence of prejudice itself, stereotypes assumed a preeminent importance, and a vast literature developed that was devoted to their conceptual and empirical analysis (see, for example, Lippmann 1922; Katz and Braly 1947; Vinacke 1957; Karlins, Coffman, and Walters 1969; Brigham 1971; Mackie 1973). Interest in stereotypes has continued to thrive, promoted by social psychologists in the cognitive school (for example, Tajfel 1969; Hamilton 1979, 1981; Hamilton and Trolier 1986) and pursued by other students of prejudice as well (for example, Selznick and Steinberg 1969; Dovidio and Gaertner 1986: Bobo and Kluegel 1991). There has also been a growing interest in assessing people's explanations of the causes of racial differences: do people think racial differences are physically inherent, cultural, or caused by societal discrimination and bias? (See, for example, Pettigrew 1979; Apostle et al. 1983; Kluegel and Smith 1986.)

The concept of social distance was devised by Bogardus (1925). In a historical era when racial inequality was marked by physical segregation, the notion of personal acceptance was readily adopted as a vital signal of the breakdown of negative attitudes (see, for example, Deutsch and Collins 1951; Greeley and Sheatsley 1974).

For the same reason, rejection of racial segregration became widely interpreted as laden with significance for the breakdown of negative racial attitudes (see, for example, Hyman and Sheatsley 1956, 1964; Campbell 1971; Greeley and Sheatsley 1971; Taylor, Sheatsley, and Greeley 1978). And in recent years, analysts have become increasingly interested in probing whites' support for various affirmative racial policies, as they have tried to grapple with the discrepancy between the linear decline in whites' subscription to traditionally racist ideas and their continued resistance to affirmative policies of racial change (for example, Jackman 1978; Schuman, Steeh, and Bobo 1985). That discrepancy has engendered an increasing debate about how best to measure prejudice in order to capture the nuances of its contemporary expression (for example, Jackman 1977, 1978, 1981b; Crosby, Bromley, and Saxe 1980; McConahay, Hardee, and Batts 1981; Pettigrew 1985; Kinder 1986; McConahay 1986; Schuman and Bobo 1988).

POLITICAL TOLERANCE AS HOSTILITY DEFUSED

The literature on political tolerance developed independently of the two currents of research that we have just considered on class conflict and racial prejudice. Some familiar strands reappear in research on tolerance, but they are fused uniquely to produce an alternative approach to the issue of intergroup conflict.

Like some analysts of class, students of tolerance accepted as a given that society was comprised of groups with contending interests. However, students of tolerance did not concern themselves with the root causes of those competing interests, whether they reflected deep rifts in the organizational structure of society or mere differences in beliefs, lifestyle, or skin color. Like analysts of prejudice, they did not view the unbridled expression of intergroup hostility as a progressive outcome, and they were especially concerned about the attitudes of more powerful groups toward political, religious, and ethnic minorities. But unlike students of prejudice, those who studied tolerance were not concerned with how to eliminate hostility—they concentrated, instead, on how to defuse it. Tolerance does not imply positive feelings toward a group—it means the equal treatment of those whom we dislike. In the words commonly attributed to Voltaire, "I disapprove of what you say, but I will defend to the death your right to say it" (Bartlett 1968).

Tolerance and Democracy

The analysis of tolerance evolved within the literature on empirical democratic theory. In that setting, democratic society was viewed as an unwieldy amalgam of contending groups: the stability of democratic institutions depended on a delicate balance between the dual principles of majority rule and minority rights. The first principle provided for the peaceful rule of the declared winner in political competition; the second principle provided for the preservation of political competition by granting full civil liberties to the losing side (Dahl 1956). Within this context, tolerance of those with whom we disagree (whatever the basis of the disagreement) is vital to democratic stability.

The initial concern was with the issue of maintaining freedom of speech so that majority rule would not deteriorate into the tyranny of the majority. The empirical literature on tolerance was launched in the aftermath of the McCarthy era with Stouffer's book, *Communism, Conformity, and Civil Liberties* (1955). The title to the book reflects the concern that many liberals felt at that time over the threat that McCarthy's anticommunist witch-hunt posed for the democratic principle of freedom of speech. Stouffer focused on the extent to which political leaders and members of the mass public were inclined to restrict the civil liberties of political and religious nonconformists—communists, socialists, and atheists. Most of his questions centered on freedom of expression directly, but he also addressed the broader civil libertarian issues implied in hiring and firing decisions. In a historical era when the extension of full civil rights to blacks became a prominent public issue, the broader significance of tolerance was highlighted, and some analysts applied the concept to the arena of black civil rights (for example, Prothro and Grigg 1960; Jackman 1977, 1978). The primary concern of the literature has remained with attitudes that bear specifically on the openness of political life (see, for example, Sullivan, Piereson, and Marcus 1982; McClosky and Brill 1983), but tolerance has assumed a more general application to the broad democratic principle of "equality of opportunity, regardless of race, color, or creed."

The ability to disconnect one's behavioral dispositions from one's personal feelings toward a group was regarded as a uniquely democratic quality. Thus, students of tolerance, like their counterparts who studied prejudice, implicitly regarded the primary institutions in democratic society as a progressive force that offered the promise of a more enlightened existence. The more people were exposed to democratic institutions, either through formal education (for example, Stouffer 1955; Lispet 1960; Prothro and Grigg 1960) or through active political participation (for example, Stouffer 1955; McClosky 1964; McClosky and Brill 1983), the more eroded would become the raw tendency to take action against groups who are the object of dislike. Democratic institutions were seen as mechanisms that socialize people into the benefits of diversity and teach them the reciprocal advantages of removing positive personal feelings as a requirement for positive treatment.

The Resolution of Conflict through Consensual Rules of the Game

Although analysts of tolerance have not explicitly concerned themselves with the issue of what underlies the divisions between social groups or the nature of the relationship between unequal groups, implicit assumptions about these questions do provide the contextual logic for the concept of tolerance. It is important to remember that the issue of tolerance was raised within the framework of empirical democratic theory. That body of theory specifies that democratic stability requires a fundamental working consensus among the populace on rules of the game; such a consensus is not considered viable in a society marked by deep cleavages (e.g, Dahl 1956; Almond and Verba 1963). Thus, although analysts of tolerance deviate from those who study prejudice in their acceptance of group conflict as a normal part of life, this deviation is not as great as it might seem, because the basis for the conflict must be sufficiently shallow to prevent intense feelings from being aroused.

But if the inequality between groups is in fact expropriative, where one group's gain is the other's loss, there might be too much at stake for tolerance to be practiced with ease. Add to this the awkward point that the most salient rifts in society do not involve relationships among equals who are buffeted about in a political game of give and take, trading places from time to time as winners and losers. In the most serious cleavages that American society faces—those based on race, class, and gender—it is not too difficult to identify which groups are repeatedly winners and losers.

The concept of tolerance implicitly neutralizes the issue of social inequality. By directing attention to the defusing of conflict without regard to its underlying causes, it places more weight on societal stability than on the substantive resolution of group differences. What takes precedence is the procedural issue of *how* the game will be played, rather than the substantive issue of what the game is about. The libertarian concern with freedom of speech and equality of opportunity more generally does not address the problem of the unequal positions from which different groups may avail themselves of those opportunities (Schaar 1967; Parkin 1971; Jackman and Muha 1984). Instead, the concept of tolerance lends itself more easily to the pluralist view of a society unmarked by deep rifts between have's and have-not's. And, indeed, some of the most prominent contributors to our empirical understanding of tolerance have promoted such a view (for example, Stouffer 1955; Lipset 1960; McClosky 1964).

Rising above Hostility

Like students of prejudice, those who study tolerance are interested in getting society beyond conflict. Students of prejudice implicitly assume that there are no hard substantive grounds for racial conflict, but that intense interracial dislike can be generated by malleable cultural forces. Thus, the critical problem for them is to undermine the negative intergroup feelings that drive discrimination. Students of tolerance implicitly assume that intergroup hostility is not intense, because the gap in interests between contending groups is neither profound nor irreconcilable. If there are no grounds for intense emotional rift, one need not worry about feelings per se. Instead, one should concentrate on the issue of dislodging behavioral predispositions from their affective base. The task is not to eliminate intergroup hostility (as would students of prejudice) or to debate the substantive grounds for its existence (as would students of class relations). The normality of some intergroup disparity is accepted without question—the problem is how to defuse it so that it does not escalate and disturb the peaceful practice of democratic life.

Empirical Questions and Measures

The central empirical questions driving analyses of tolerance have been the assessment of its prevalence among the democratic citizens of the United States (for example, Stouffer 1955; Sullivan, Piereson, and Marcus 1979; Abramson 1980), the measurement of change in levels of tolerance over time (for example, Sullivan, Piereson, and Marcus 1979;

Abramson 1980), and examination of what factors (personality, democratic socialization, education, or demographic characteristics) produce political tolerance (for example, Stouffer 1955; McClosky 1964; R. Jackman 1972; Sullivan, Pierson, and Marcus 1982; McClosky and Brill 1983). Empirical analyses of tolerance have thus been governed by very similar kinds of questions to those found in research on racial prejudice. And, to the extent that analyses of prejudice have been pervaded by Myrdal's portrayal of prejudice as an anachronism that jars against the American commitment to democratic values and ideals (Myrdal 1944), much of the tone of analyses of tolerance also resembles prejudice research.

Empirical measures of tolerance, however, have developed along very different lines than measures of prejudice. Analysts of tolerance have usually relied exclusively on indicators of people's policy or behavioral dispositions, with positive responses being interpreted as evidence of tolerance (for example, Stouffer 1955; McClosky and Brill 1983). Students of prejudice, with their more holistic approach to attitudes, might interpret the same response as reflecting an overall favorable attitude toward the group—the elimination of prejudice. This disjuncture between the concept of tolerance and its empirical measurement has been noted by Jackman (1977, 1978) and Sullivan, Pierson, and Marcus (1979, 1982). Sullivan and his colleagues found that when one takes explicit account of people's feelings toward specific groups, the granting of full civil rights to groups that are disliked is a rare phenomenon—considerably less common than what is ostensibly required for the democratic functioning of society.

GENDER RELATIONS AS HOSTILITY REVEALED

Relations between men and women were largely neglected by scholars until relatively recently, perhaps because the manifest docility of gender relations did little to excite observers' attention (and the fact that scholarly observers tended to be male doubtless exacerbated the invisibility of anything problematic in relations between men and women). Gender relations were the subject of passing commentary from time to time, but a sustained literature on gender relations is a comparatively recent development, emerging in the shadow of already well-established bodies of research on class and race relations. If the relationship between men and women had failed to draw attention to itself by offering any blatant prospects of societal disruption, the task of those who sought to establish its significance as a field of inquiry was to reveal its dynamics in terms that analysts of class and race would clearly recognize—friction, violence, emotional disparity.

At the beginning of this chapter I quoted a passage from John Stuart Mill in which he astutely noted that gender relations are distinguished by a lack of reliance on force. Despite that insight, even Mill sought to engage the skeptic by highlighting elements of hostility and conflict in those relations. Indeed, the latter theme is the prevalent one in his essay on "The Subjection of Women":

> In struggles for political emancipation, everybody knows how often its champions are bought off by bribes, or daunted by terrors. In the case of women, each individual of the subject-class is in a chronic state of bribery and intimidation combined. . . . If ever any system of privilege and enforced subjection had its yoke tightly riveted on the neck of those who are kept down by it, this has. . . . But, it will be said, the rule of men over women . . . is accepted voluntarily; women make no complaint, and are consenting parties to it. In the first place, a great number of women do not accept it. Ever since there have been women able to make their sentiments known by their writings (the only mode of publicity which society permits to them), an increasing number of them have recorded protests against their present social condition: and recently many thousands of them have petitioned Parliament. . . . The claim of women . . . is urged with growing intensity, while the demand for their admission into professions and occupations hitherto closed against them, becomes every year more urgent. . . . How many more women there are who silently cherish similar aspirations, no one can possibly know. . . . There is never any want of women who complain of ill usage by their husbands. There would be infinitely more, if complaint were not the greatest of all provocatives to a repetition and increase of the ill usage. (J. S. Mill [1869] 1970, 136–137, 139–140)

I have quoted from Mill at length because the language of his essay demonstrates so clearly the implicit assumption that if there were no conflict between the groups, there would be no problem worthy of analysis. In his effort to draw attention to the relationship between men and women, Mill portrayed it as ridden with violence and intimidation on the part of the oppressors and protest and simmering resentment on the part of the oppressed. He conceded, by implication, that if women were found to be "consenting parties," his case would be weaker, and he set about revealing the intensity and urgency of women's discontent. Later in the essay, Mill acknowledged the affection that many men feel for their wives, and he regarded this as something that mitigates the tyranny of men over women (Mill 1970, 161–162). The affection that women may feel for their husbands, he dismissed, however, as lodged in fear: "It is part of the irony of life, that the strongest feelings of devoted gratitude . . . are called forth in human beings towards those who, having the power entirely to crush their earthly existence, voluntarily refrain from using that power" (Mill 1970, 162–163). Mill went on to appeal to the reader that it is unreasonable to judge any system of oppression by "its best instances":

> Who doubts that there may be great goodness, and great happiness, and great affection, under the absolute government of a good man? Meanwhile, laws and institutions need to be adapted, not to good men, but to bad. . . . The tie of affection and obligation to a wife and children is very strong with those whose general social feelings are strong, and with many who are little sensible to any other social ties; but there are all degrees of sensibility and insensibility to it, as there are all grades of goodness and wickedness in men. . . . The vilest malefactor has some wretched women tied to him, against whom he can commit any atrocity except killing her. . . . When we consider how vast is the number of men, in any great country, who are little higher than brutes, and that this never prevents them from being able, through the law of marriage, to obtain a victim, the breadth and depth of human misery caused in this shape alone. . . swells to something appalling. (Mill 1970, 163–164)

The hapless reader might have drawn comfort from the apparent lack of friction in gender relations. Mill's strategy was not to question the logic of that derivation, but to undermine the validity of the empirical observation on which it is based. He endeavored to reveal in gender relations the same hallmark symptoms as those emphasized in more commonly recognized systems of oppression—violence and fear, hostility and resentment.

The Racial Analogy

In his essay, Mill drew several explicit analogies between gender relations and racial oppression. The same device was used, much later, by such varied advocates of the analysis of gender relations as Gunnar Myrdal (1944), Helen Hacker (1951), and Simone de Beauvoir (1953). In appendix 5 to his epic analysis of race relations in the United States, *An American Dilemma* (1944), Myrdal presented "A Parallel to the Negro Problem," in which he argued that women and blacks alike are oppressed by the lagged presence of a paternalism that was once nourished by a preindustrial economy but which is now but an atavistic element destined to be discarded in the contemporary, industrial world. Hacker, in her classic article, "Women as a Minority Group" (1951), rested her case on an enumeration of the parallels between the condition of women and blacks (highlighted by a chart entitled "Castelike Status of Women and Negroes" with parallel columns for the two groups). Where Hacker found an exact parallel between the condition of the two groups, she drew evidence for the case that women constitute a "minority group"; where she found the condition of women to deviate from that of blacks, Hacker inferred that the minority status of women is mitigated somewhat. And de Beauvoir, too, drew on parallelism to establish her case:

> Whether it is a race, a caste, a class, or a sex that is reduced to a position of inferiority, the methods of justification are the same. "The eternal feminine" corresponds to "the black soul.". . . There are deep similarities between the situation of the woman and that of the Negro. (de Beauvoir [1953] 1973, 683)

The analysis of the ideology of gender relations was thus established in a framework based on parallelism with race. The same concepts that dominated the analysis of racial attitudes were applied to gender attitudes: hostility, stereotyping, prejudice, and low self-esteem among subordinates. Simone de Beauvoir stated the case boldly:

> It is easy to see that the duality of the sexes, like any duality, gives rise to conflict. . . . All oppression creates a state of war. And this is no exception. (de Beauvoir [1953] 1973, 681, 690)

She portrayed the relationship between the sexes as one of chronic animosity, punctuated by stereotyping of women and aggressive assertions of feminine inferiority on the one side and festering resentment and frustration on the other.

A similar argument is made by Rubin in her analysis of working-class family life, *Worlds of Pain* (1976). She portrays that life as infested with pain, not only in its economic constraints, but also in its cultural dictate of disparate worlds for husbands and wives. Those two worlds are intersected only by the uncaring negligence of men and the angry resentment of their wives. She concludes thus:

> Are there good times? Yes, a birthday remembered with joy, a happy Christmas, a loving and tender moment between wife and husband. But they stand out in memory as unique and treasured events, monumentally important because they happen so seldom, because they are so little a part of daily experience. . . . As people talk about their lives, such small events become insubstantial, slipping away before a more compelling reality. (1976, 215)

Gender Violence

The theme of dreariness and disparity in gender relations has been carried a step further by some radical feminist scholars, who portray gender relations as ridden with blatant hostility and violence. The criminal act of rape is identified as epitomizing the general quality of the relationship between men and women—a relationship in which men are depicted as subjugating women to their will through sexual terrorism, backed up by physical and institutional force (see, for example, Millett 1970; Griffin 1980; Cronan 1984). Millett states:

Patriarchal force also relies on a form of violence particularly sexual in character and realized most completely in the act of rape. . . . In rape, the emotions of aggression, hatred, contempt, and the desire to break or violate personality, take a form consummately appropriate to sexual politics. . . . Patriarchal societies typically link feelings of cruelty with sexuality, the latter often equated both with evil and with power. (1970, 44)

Heterosexuality is depicted as intrinsically misogynist, an instrument purely to subjugate women (see also Rich 1980). In another gender-race comparison, Millett compares the crimes of rape and lynching, and she argues that "unconsciously, both crimes may serve the larger group [whites or men] as a ritual act, cathartic in effect" (Millett 1970, 45). Prostitution and marriage are described in like terms as sexual and political slavery for women (see also Goldman [1910] 1969; Barry 1979; Cronan 1984). Millett sums up the relationship between men and women thus:

The history of patriarchy presents a variety of cruelties and barbarities. . . . The rationale which accompanies that imposition of male authority euphemistically referred to as "the battle of the sexes" bears a certain resemblance to the formulas of nations at war, where any heinousness is justified on the grounds that the enemy is either an inferior species or really not human at all. (1970, 46)

Women's Resistance—Or Lack Thereof

The lack of concerted resistance among women has left scholars who depict gender relations as conflictive with an empirical shortfall. As in some accounts of class and race consciousness (Genovese 1974; Scott 1985), some scholars of gender relations have attempted to reconcile the discrepancy by emphasizing the many ways in which women engage in personal behaviors that constitute hidden or private forms of protest (Cloward and Piven 1979; Anyon 1984). The same interpretive difficulties plague this argument in its application to gender relations as I noted in the earlier section on class ideology. As with the debate about class consciousness, the theoretical significance attached to the presence or absence of conflict is so great that some scholars have felt pressed to scour the minutiae of the relationship to uncover behaviors among women that might be construed as showing evidence of alienation and resistance.

Conservative Theoretical Pressures

The search for conflict in gender relations reflects not only the habits learned from the analysis of class and race relations. It has also been spurred, perhaps even more urgently than in the class literature, by the presence of powerful conservative arguments that gender differentiation reflects a "natural order" that is manifested in its consensual endorsement by both men and women. Parsons and Bales (1955) argued that gender differentiation is socially functional, serving to integrate the family unit with the larger society while providing for the nurturance and socialization of society's youngest members. The specific "expressive" role of women and "instrumental" role of men were explained as the natural outcome of differences between the sexes in their biological contributions to procreation.

There has also been a large body of literature that promotes the ideas of biological determinism in gender relations. Numerous analysts have argued that there are natural differences in male and female personality types stemming from physically complementary functions in procreation: for example, that genital penetration of the female by the male requires that the male be assertive and the female submissive, that the length of the pregnancy requires nurturant feelings and emotional commitment from the mother whereas the father's physical contribution is fleeting, and so on (see, for example, Storr 1968; Tiger and Fox 1971; Wilson 1978; Bettelheim 1984).

Perhaps because of the readily identifiable physical difference between men and women, combined with the pervasiveness of gender differentiation at the heart of everyday life, conservative arguments based on functionalism and biological determinism have had a deeper impact on the shape of the literature on gender relations than they have on race relations or even class relations. There has been no serious scholarly attempt in the past few decades to explain racial differentiation as functional. In the early years of this century, biological determinism had a central position in American scholarly debate about race (see, for example, the debate published in the *American Journal of Sociology* in 1908 between Stone and Willcox et al., as well as Pettigrew's history of American scholarship on race relations, 1980). But the scholarly impact of biological determinism on research about race has waned over this century. A few analysts have persisted with the question of whether there are genetic differences between whites and blacks in intelligence (Jensen 1969; Shockley 1971, 1972a, 1972b; Herrnstein 1990), but such arguments have had little impact on the main thrust of research on either racial inequality or racial prejudice (see, for example, the comprehensive report on the status of race relations in the United States sponsored by the National Academy of Sciences, Jaynes and Williams, Jr. 1989). Indeed, scholars of race relations have tended to dismiss arguments about immutable racial differences as Victorian or fascist. In the explanation of socioeconomic inequality, functionalism had a major impact, although still perhaps not quite to the extent that it has in the gender literature. And more blatant biological determinism, in the form of social Darwin-ism (Spencer [1862] 1958; Sumner 1883), made only a brief visitation to the literature on class. Yet biological determinism continues to be a major influence on the debate about gender differentiation (see, for example, Maccoby and Jacklin 1974; Rossi 1977a; Gross et al. 1979). A "natural order" is expected to manifest itself in spontaneous consensual endorsement: those who would depict gender inequality as other than "natural" or functional have thus taken the reflexive counterposition that gender relations are fraught with tension and conflict.

Empirical Questions and Measures

The empirical analysis of gender attitudes has been shaped by the theoretical currents outlined above, although not always explicitly. Feminist theorists with a more critical perspective have often expressed philosophical objections to systematic, public-opinion research in the "positivist" tradition (see, for example, Stacey and Thorne 1985), and survey researchers interested in gender attitudes have generally returned the compliment by ignoring theoretical work that depicts gender relations in political terms. Indeed, public-opinion studies of gender attitudes have usually had an empirically driven agenda, proceeding to the empirical business with little or no discussion of theoretical issues. However, the kinds of empirical questions that have been asked primarily reflect the influence of the liberal tradition, exemplified by John Stuart Mill and Gunnar Myrdal, juxtaposed with the functionalists and biological determinists. In more recent years, there has been an increasing tendency for empirical analysts to draw on theories that depict gender relations as expropriative (for example, Gurin 1985; Kane 1989). The resulting blend of empirical questions in research on gender attitudes shares some features with the literature on class consciousness, and some with the literature on prejudice.

Students of social class invested particularly in the attitudes of the working class. Both Marxist and functionalist theories put a heavy onus on the have-not's either to challenge or to endorse socioeconomic inequality, and this is reflected in the empirical literature on class consciousness (for example, Lane 1962; Leggett 1968; Goldthorpe et al. 1969; Hamilton 1972; Huber and Form 1973; Newby 1977b; Jackman and Jackman 1983). So too have the gender attitudes of women been the object of particular empirical scrutiny. There are numerous studies of women's gender attitudes taken alone (for example, Goldberg 1968; Horner 1972; Parelius 1975; Mason, Czajka, and Arber 1976; Thornton and Freedman 1979; Gurin 1985), along with an increasing number that compare men's and women's attitudes (for example, Sherriffs and McKee 1957; Broverman et al. 1972; Cherlin and Walters 1981; Simon and Landis 1989; Kane 1989).

Most of these studies have focused on attitudes about "sex-roles," rather than on attitudes about power relations between the sexes, suggesting an almost exclusive influence of functionalist ideas. The net result was that gender-attitudes research shared the emphasis of class-ideology research on the attitudes of subordinates, but without the attendant conception of gender relations as exploitative. Recently, however, there has been a growing awareness of this deficiency in gender-attitudes research, and an increasing number of studies are incorporating measures that show sensitivity to the power dynamics of gender relations (see, for example, Gurin 1985; Kane 1989; Simon and Landis 1989; Kane and Sanchez 1992).

There has been little tendency to follow the lead of the prejudice literature by focusing exclusively on the attitudes of the dominant group (Goode's essay on "Why Men Resist" [1982] is a rare example of a discrete discussion of men's gender attitudes.) At the same time, the liberal, social-reformist sentiment of the prejudice literature is shared by many students of gender attitudes, and that tradition too has shaped the kinds of questions that have been asked about gender attitudes—and especially women's gender attitudes.

These dual influences from research on class consciousness and racial prejudice have resulted in two broad themes of empirical inquiry about gender ideology. The first of these is a focus on prejudice against women and on women's self-esteem. A repeated question has been whether women suffer from low self-esteem and poor achievement orientation. There have been numerous studies of gender stereotyping, devaluation of women, and low achievement orientations among women. The language of these studies parallels that of the literature on racial prejudice. For example, Sherriffs and McKee state that "both men and women esteem men significantly more highly than women" (1957, 451); Broverman et al. conclude that "stereotypically masculine traits are more often perceived to be desirable than are stereotypically feminine characteristics" (1972, 75); Goldberg answers "yes" to the question "Are women prejudiced against women?" (1968); and Horner declares that women have a "fear of success" because their self-conceptions are tied to low status (1972).

A second major line of empirical inquiry has been the extent to which people, and especially women, endorse the traditional division of labor between the sexes and, more recently, the division of power and economic opportunities between the sexes (for example, Mason, Czajka, and Arber 1976; Thornton and Freedman 1979; Spitze and Huber 1980; Cherlin and Walters 1981; Helmreich, Spence, and Gibson 1982; Thornton, Alwin, and Camburn 1983; Gurin 1985; Mason and Lu 1986; Simon and Landis 1989; Kane 1989). Analysts have been interested both in

monitoring the overall level of support for "nontraditional" gender arrangements and in assessing what individual factors (personality, socialization, personal experience, or demographic characteristics) affect gender attitudes. And as in the prejudice literature, there has been a special
interest in monitoring change in gender attitudes over time, as an indicator of the wave of liberal progress. But unlike students of racial attitudes,
who have been largely unplagued by notions of a "natural" or functional
order of racial differentiation, students of gender attitudes have not been
free to lay the onus of progress unequivocally on to the dominant group.
Many analysts of "sex-role attitudes" appear to base their inferences
about the pace of change on the attitudes of women alone, implying that
women's attitudes are the prime source of energy in determining the
form of their relationship with men. Other analysts draw on concepts
about class consciousness to view women's gender attitudes within the
political context of an expropriative intergroup relationship in which
men are the more powerful group.

Thus, the empirical analysis of gender attitudes reflects a blending of
concerns from the theoretical and empirical traditions of class consciousness and racial prejudice. The resulting depictions of women are pervaded by two conflicting undercurrents: the female as victim (like the
black), beaten by prejudice into abject submission, and the female as a
conjectured collaborator (like some images of the poor and working
class), contentedly endorsing her assigned position in life or moving assertively to alter it. In this context, women are held to have some complicity in their own fate in a way that blacks are not. It is implied that the
onus is on women to indicate whether their station in life has become a
painful anachronism or continues to be the fulfillment of their biological
proclivities.

SUMMARY

I have analyzed the prevailing concerns and assumptions that have governed the study of class, race, and gender attitudes. My purpose has not
been to elucidate the full variety of ideas that are to be found in each
corpus of research—such a purpose would require volumes in itself. My
purpose, rather, has been to identify major themes that have shaped the
development of each literature.

I have attempted to draw out two important points. First, from a
common family of ideas, research on class conflict, racial prejudice, political tolerance, and gender ideology broke apart in disparate networks of
development. Second, the abiding focal point for each network has been
conflict and hostility. The result has been that, as each body of literature
followed its own course, it developed a distinctive welding of ideas to

address a common and enduring concern with conflict versus consensus in the assessment of unequal social relations.

In the analysis of social class, the legacy of Karl Marx was to weld conflict to the very conception of class as the basis for expropriative social relations. According to Marx's model, the working class signals its realization of the exploitative basis of its relationship with capitalists by becoming ideologically alienated from the capitalist system and organizing to overthrow it. Those who debated with Marx or his ghost did nothing to dislodge the theoretical expectation that exploitation would lead to conflict, and, indeed, they reinforced that expectation as they argued backwards from the lack of empirically observed class conflict to claim that class was either not exploitative or that it did not exist at all. In the face of the empirical shortfall in class conflict, some scholars have attempted to salvage the central elements of Marx's class analysis by accentuating evidence of dissension among classes, by arguing that subordinate classes engage in "hidden resistance," or by depicting subordinates' consciousness as "false." I have argued that all these attempts contain important insights, but they are weakened by their ensnarement in the conflict model. That ensnarement causes analysts to stretch their arguments out onto a thin ledge where rules of evidence lose their clarity or contradictory assumptions undermine their theoretical consistency. Empirical analyses of class ideology continue to revolve around issues pertaining to the existence and importance of class as a basis for exploitative and conflictive relations, with particular attention to the political consciousness of subordinates.

The analysis of racial prejudice has been driven by the spirit of social reform. Students of prejudice have sought to eradicate racial discrimination by developing models that approach the phenomenon in terms of individual psychological dispositions. Analysts have focused on the psychological construct of prejudice—an irrational, parochial antipathy based on faulty, categorical perceptions of the target group. The intergroup beliefs, feelings, and behavioral dispositions of prejudiced individuals in the dominant group are thought to be locked together in a negative position. Some analysts have diverged on a theoretical strand that posits that prejudice is motivated by a sense of group position (rather than by irrational parochialism), and some analysts have argued that prejudice is being expressed in more subtle and nuanced ways than the traditional prejudice concept stipulates. But all conceptions of prejudice have retained the central emphasis on intergroup hostility as the core of the problem. With relatively little attention to the dispositions of subordinates, students of prejudice have focused on trying to monitor and explain the racial animosity of the dominant group, whites.

The concept of political tolerance grew out of democratic theory. It was held that democratic systems require citizens to have consensus on rules of the game in order to resolve conflicts peacefully. According to this perspective, hostility and conflict are unavoidable aspects of social life, but democratic citizens must learn to respect the civil rights and civil liberties of all other citizens, even when they personally disagree with them or harbor animosity toward them. The problem for analysts of tolerance has been to assess how successfully democratic citizens have disconnected their behavioral dispositions from their personal feelings toward a group. Interest has focused primarily on the tolerance of dominant-group members toward political and racial minorities.

The relatively recent growth of research on gender relations has fed from themes that were developed in the analysis of class and race relations. In the attempt to draw attention to gender as a significant and problematic social relationship, analysts have depicted gender relations as ridden with the commonly recognized symptoms of oppressive systems—force, violence, and hostility on the one hand, and fear, resentment, and low self-esteem on the other. Even more than in the class literature, the analysis of gender relations has been wedged in by a theoretical debate that includes staunchly conservative arguments depicting gender differentiation as a "natural order" that is endorsed consensually by men and women. In this context, the manifest passivity of women has created serious theoretical difficulties for scholars who wish to depict gender relations as expropriative. And as in the literature on prejudice, many analysts of gender attitudes have been motivated by the liberal spirit of social reform, but their primary focus on the gender attitudes of women has implied that it is the subordinate group (as in class relations) that must bring about change, rather than the dominant group (as in race relations). This merging of somewhat incompatible themes has often left empirical analyses of gender ideology in something of a theoretical void, as analysts have proceeded with an empirically driven agenda to monitor and explain popular endorsement or rejection of traditional gender arrangements.

All these lines of research tend to depict intergroup attitudes as primarily the property of individuals and as being purely expressive, rather than as political communications. That is to say, the common working assumption is that attitudes are raw acts of individual expression, articulating the inner thoughts, feelings, and reactions that individuals generate as they march through life.

At the same time, different assumptions have been made about whether humans express themselves in ways that suggest rationality or irrationality. Analysts of prejudice have been explicit on the point that prejudice is an irrational phenomenon that bears no relation to a rational processing of valid information about the target group. In the literature on class conflict, however, it has been taken as a given that people do rationally process information and personal experiences. In the Marxist perspective, individuals are presumed to perceive and act rationally on their own behalf. Rationality in that model refers specifically to the ability to perceive one's economic interests and to act in concerted ways to further those interests, either by defending current economic arrangements (among those who benefit from them) or by rejecting those arrangements and working to alter them (among those who are hurt by them). Research on political tolerance is less clear on the issue of rationality, but it seems to assume that people rationally perceive competing interests in society: the task for democratic citizens is to learn to disregard the feelings of antipathy that arise from those perceptions as they formulate their policy dispositions toward competing groups. Research on gender ideology has embroiled competing strains of thought from theories of class conflict and prejudice, and thus no clear set of expectations about human rationality can be deduced from this line of research.

In the next chapter, I begin to raise questions about these various facets of ideology. Are attitudes raw acts of individual expression or politically motivated communications? Do intergroup attitudes originate with the individual or with the group to which he or she belongs? Are intergroup attitudes rational or irrational? How are these attitudes formed? I start by proposing a specific conception of rationality and considering some of the constraints that are present in intergroup relationships of inequality. Those considerations lead me to suggest that the preoccupation with conflict and hostility in the analysis of class, race, and gender relations is misplaced. My purpose is not to argue that such factors are devoid of significance for unequal social relations, only that their importance has been seriously overestimated. As we consider the role of ideology in social control, we will see many pressures that work against conflict and the expression of hostility. By using hostility as the flag for the inequality, students of class, race, and gender alike have misread the character of their material.

CHAPTER TWO

Ideology and Social Control

The best point at which to manage conflict is before it starts.
E. E. SCHATTSCHNEIDER (1960, 15)

Because of the abiding concern with conflict among students of inter-group relations, questions have tended to hinge on the issue of whether one group is using force to subjugate another, with all the attendant ideological trappings of hostility and derogation. But dominant groups may be playing a different game. If their energies are geared toward the prevention or containment of conflict, social control may rarely be reduced to the use or even the explicit threat of force. The question of whether subordinates' position in the relationship reflects their own volition or forced compliance is a false question, unless we are sure that force and the threat of force are the primary weapons in social control.

There are several reasons to believe that these weapons play only a minor part in the day-to-day practice of subjugation. The threat of force always hovers in the background; under extreme duress, the threat is moved to a more conspicuous position, and, if necessary, actualized. But groups who enjoy the fruits of domination prefer to obviate this necessity by managing conflict "before it starts," or failing that, to contain its incipient development. In this endeavor, they work to engage subordinates in a common view of the world that rationalizes the current order. The surest method of social control is to induce subordinates to regulate themselves. To that end, the unmediated weapon of choice is ideology.

I assume that groups gravitate to ideologies that are rationally consistent with their interests. However, my conception of rationality does not lead me to expect confrontational ideologies. A rational actor does not naively pursue goals on the basis of their desirability alone, but is sensitive to constraints. Occasional mistakes and miscalculations are to be expected, but groups do learn from their mistakes. Most of the time, the attitudes of unequal groups reflect responses that strive to maximize their control over resources, not in an ideal world, but *within the actual conditions they confront*. This assumption does not lead me to expect much confrontation or hostility from either side of an intergroup relationship. Myrdal expressed the impact of these pressures well, when he discussed the lack of protest behavior among African Americans in the 1940s:

> The accommodation motive has predominant importance in the daily life of American Negroes. . . . the influence of the protest motive is limited mainly to the propagation of certain ideas about how things *should* be. Everyone, however, has to get on with his own life from day to day, *now and here*. Even when the individual plans for future employment, for business, or for schooling, he has to reckon with the world as it is. He has to accommodate. (Myrdal 1944, 768)

For as much as people on each side of an unequal relationship might wish to increase their control over resources, they are also aware, if only implicitly, that their present holdings are not invulnerable. In that sense, even subordinates have some stake in the present system, insofar as they have not been stripped of all their resources. And members of the dominant group have a major investment that they wish to preserve. As people grope through the uncertainties of life, they have a tendency to tread carefully: rash moves carry too many risks.[1]

When societal resources are distributed to groups according to the terms of an unequal relationship, the members of those groups have no choice but to communicate with each other about those terms. The relational basis of the exchange necessitates communication across group lines, and the members of each group also compare notes with others from their own group, to whom they have ready access. The quality of all those communications will be affected by the pressures to which the members of each group are subject.

Those pressures derive initially from the structure of the intergroup relationship, which sets outer limits on the kinds of communications that are safe and potentially effective in the ongoing political exchange. As the members of each group stake out a position, that enters into the political picture by shaping the moral climate within which the members of the other group interpret their situation and make their next move. Viewed in this way, intergroup attitudes are communicative and political rather than naively expressive. This means that participants on both

---

1. Interestingly, the members of the community who are typically the most likely to make bold moves are young adults. At the initiation of adulthood, people have a smaller personal investment in the current order, and therefore they have less to lose. Young adults also have a weaker sense of history than those who have been around longer: they are less aware of the past experience of the group, and they thus have an inflated idea of what they can achieve.

sides of unequal relationships have their antenna habitually cocked to the messages coming from the other side. As they follow the path of least resistance through the day-to-day exigencies that they encounter, their perspectives on the unequal relationship that binds them are molded by the pressures that reside therein.

To explore these ideas, I begin with the constraints that face dominant groups as they seek to maintain their advantaged position. This leads me to consider the limitations of force as an instrument of social control. I then pursue the implications this has for the function and character of intergroup ideology. With those general considerations in hand, I turn, in the second part of the chapter, to the specific forms of ideology that are nourished under different structural conditions.

THE LIMITS OF FORCE

In their discussion of the politics of inequality, Bachrach and Baratz (1970) offer an insightful analysis of power and force in the dynamics of social control. They argue that in a relationship founded on explicit power, one party gains the compliance of the other through the threat of sanctions. They stress that before one can assert definitively that power has been exercised one must be sure that a threat has been made and that it is this threat (and not something else) that motivates the compliance of the other party. Thus, in an explicit power relationship, compliance is based on fear.

Such a hard-line approach to social control carries an uncomfortable dilemma. When faced with noncompliance, only two options are available. On the one hand, if threats are not carried out, they lose their credibility and hence their potency. The basis for power is undermined and further noncompliance is thus encouraged. On the other hand, if threats are carried out, the application of force is an open acknowledgment that control through threats has failed. Bachrach and Baratz conclude that in this instance as well the power relationship is undermined.

In addition, they argue that the application of threatened sanctions introduces further risks. Subordinates may find the sanctions less exacting than they had anticipated, a discovery that invites further noncompliance. Sanctions that are harsh, however, weaken the opponent sufficiently to preclude the possibility of compliance while those sanctions are in effect. Punishment by death constitutes the most complete (and irrevocable) example of compliance foregone. Short of death, sanctions must be severe enough to be punishing but not so severe that they incapacitate the opponent—a difficult assignment.

Bachrach and Baratz's argument throws a different light on force than is implied in the literature I discussed in chapter 1. Instead of seeing force as the expression of power, Bachrach and Baratz describe it as a failure of power. A similar evaluation was made by Merriam in 1934, in his analysis of political power: "Power is not strongest when it uses violence, but weakest. . . . Rape is not an evidence of irresistible power in politics or in sex" (1934, 180). In essence, any application of sanctions is an open admission that one failed to obtain the other's compliance through the use of threats, that is, one failed to exercise power—hardly a salutary observation for the party who seeks to control another.

These considerations have three important implications. First, reliance on explicit power (that is, the threat of sanctions) to gain the compliance of subordinate groups is intrinsically hazardous. Incidents of noncompliance threaten the basis of social control, whether or not force is applied.

Second, because of its conspicuous nature, the explicit exercise of power sharpens the subjective rift between groups. The subordinate group is made aware of its concessions, and under such conditions the services extracted are likely to be carefully circumscribed. This limits the dominant group's effective access to the resources of the subordinate group. In addition, the subordinate group's awareness of its concessions is more likely to heighten than to diminish its sense of grievance. In this way, the instrument of social control itself incites the motivation for noncompliance, which in turn increases the probability that force will have to be applied. Anger and bitterness might build up sufficiently among subordinates to provide them with motivation to withstand even severe privations, rather than comply with the evil oppressor. In such a situation, the use of force by dominant groups may even backfire by confirming subordinates' negative interpretation of the relationship and thus inflaming their resistance further. The latter phenomenon was evidenced in the resistance movements of Gandhi and Martin Luther King, Jr. Thus, in the best case, explicit power relations produce delimited compliance, and in the worst case, an escalation of noncompliance.

Third, the only payoff from the use of force for the dominant group is in the provision of a demonstration or deterrence effect. Dominant groups may be prepared to forfeit temporarily the compliance of some subordinates in order to instill sufficient fear in them to induce their subsequent compliance, or to cow the rest of the group sufficiently to elicit their submission. But prolonged or repeated reliance on force indicates that the demonstration effect failed.

Edmund Burke eloquently summarized many of the drawbacks of force as an instrument of control in his speech to the British Parliament "On Conciliation with the Colonies" in 1775:

> First, Sir, permit me to observe that the use of force alone is but *temporary*. It may subdue for a moment, but it does not remove the necessity of

subduing again; and a nation is not governed, which is perpetually to be conquered.

My next objection is its *uncertainty*. Terror is not always the effect of force, and an armament is not a victory. If you do not succeed, you are without resource; for, conciliation failing, force remains, but, force failing, no further hope of reconciliation is left. Power and authority are sometimes bought by kindness, but they can never be begged as alms by an impoverished and defeated violence.

A further objection to force is, that you *impair the object* by your very endeavors to preserve it. The thing you fought for is not the thing which you recover, but depreciated, sunk, wasted, and consumed in the contest. (Burke [1775] 1954, 89–90)

From this perspective, the degree of open conflict and friction in a relationship of inequality tells us how well (or rather, how badly) the dominant group has things in hand. If we rely on such features to indicate how much expropriation is involved, or the degree to which the relationship is a "problem," we may bypass the very relationships where the expropriation is the most pronounced, where the dominant group's control is the most pervasive.

Thus, although Bourdieu (1977, 192–197) and Scott (1985, 307–309) have argued that overt, physical coercion is the preferred method of domination that reflects the most complete form of control, I am led to the opposite conclusion. Whereas Bourdieu and Scott see covert forms of coercion as relatively costly, both economically and socially, my position is that those costs are trivial compared to the costs of overt coercion. An explicit power relationship, with force as its clumsy adjutant, represents the end of the line for the dominant group, leaving it with uncomfortably reduced degrees of freedom as it must cope with a hardened opposition.

Consider, for example, the increasing incidence of overt conflict in South Africa in the past decade or so. This does not signify an increase in racial exploitation, but rather a decline in the white minority's effective control of that expropriative relationship. Indeed, the South African government's suppression of news coverage about their racial conflict in the 1980s reflected an acknowledgment of its damaging implications for apartheid's legitimacy and an attempt to contain that damage. And, despite the prolonged use of violence and legal sanctions by the white apartheid government against South Africa's blacks, black protest has persisted to the point where the government has eventually confronted a choice between the long road of concessions and reform or the short road to failed governance. The South African government might well endorse Burke's proviso that "a nation is not governed, which is perpetually to be conquered."

The factors that give a relationship a high profile for researchers also give it a high profile for the participants, hardly a desirable outcome for those who benefit from the relationship. As Barrington Moore has noted, "In any society the dominant groups are the ones with the most to hide about the way society works" (1966, 523). For these reasons, groups on the top side of an unequal relationship may be expected to gravitate toward other methods of social control, methods more subtle in their technique, more flexible in their application, and more insidious in their impact.

IMPLICIT POWER AND IDEOLOGY

As a minimal step, dominant groups set up institutions to carry out the ongoing task of expropriating resources from subordinates. Those institutions become a communal property, transmitting expropriative patterns from one generation to the next. That the expropriation from subordinates is practiced via institutions, rather than by each dominant-group member singlehandedly, has profound implications for the way it is experienced and interpreted by all the participants. The ideology that evolves around expropriative arrangements is shaped by the pressures that inhere in those institutions.

Expropriation Embedded

The institutionalization of expropriative arrangements yields multiple advantages to the dominant group. Most fundamentally, the institutions stabilize and routinize the supply of benefits from one group to another. They stack the deck so that the path of least resistance for individuals on either side is to accept the fait accompli. For example, institutionalized arrangements between employer and employee preempt any risk of constant negotiations about who should get the profits from the enterprise or who should set the length of the workday. Similarly, the institution of marriage regulates behavior between men and women and removes the possibility of reiterated negotiations about how sexual access should be decided or how the products of sexual union should be nurtured.

For subordinates, institutions limit the opportunities for, and raise the costs of, noncompliance. As the individual subordinate's social and material survival is conditioned by her ability to accommodate herself to the daily demands of social institutions, adaptive behaviors become molded into everyday habits, dimming each person's vision of social alternatives and hedging in her choices. And any failure to comply with institutional directives would be a provocation to the edifice of organized life, not merely a simple act between two individuals—this means that subordinates are less likely to engage in noncompliance lightly, as the personal investment that would be required grows heavier.

This is advantageous for the dominant group in itself, but it yields the further advantage of shifting the locus of control away from the individuals in the dominant group to the institutions they have historically erected. This means that benefits are delivered to individual members of the dominant group routinely, without any need for individually initiated acts of assertion. The institutions operate as an experiential buffer, blurring the direct, expropriative basis of the inequalities between groups both from those who receive the benefits and from those who supply them.

These factors have profound consequences for the kind of ideology that the dominant group espouses and for the reception that it gets from subordinates. The institutionalization of inequality releases the individual members of the dominant group from any sense of personal complicity. As they seek to interpret the happy situation in which they find themselves, they have no reason to feel personally defensive—after all, they have personally taken no steps to extract from others the benefits that regularly come their way. Instead, the ideas that prevail are the product of pressures coming out of the institutional arrangements. Individuals pick up those ideas piecemeal without any effort. Unfettered by any need to construct their own personal motivation scheme for discrimination, the individual members of the dominant group instead succumb to the relentless institutional pressures as they grope to interpret the world in which they live. Because the members of the dominant group are released by institutions from the rude necessity of having to exact subordinates' compliance singlehandedly, they are able to espouse and promulgate ideas that are institutionally convenient with uncontrived sincerity.

Ideologies that are promoted with sincerity are more compelling. This in itself gives the dominant group an advantage in persuading subordinates that all is right with the world, but subordinates are rendered more vulnerable to such appeals because their perceptions too are constrained by the existing institutional arrangements. The dominant group thus avoids the wearying and hazardous journey into the explicit assertion of power by making the inequalities into a societal habit, ingrained into the way of life. Weber has described the process well:

> An order which is adhered to from motives of pure expediency is generally much less stable than one upheld on a purely customary basis through the fact that the corresponding behavior has become habitual. The latter is much the most common type of subjective attitude. But even this type of order is in turn much less stable than an order which enjoys the prestige of being considered binding, or, as it may be expressed, of "legitimacy." (Weber [1947] 1964, 125)

Bachrach and Baratz maintain that authority is not simply power institutionalized, that compliance in response to authority is based on an
entirely different consideration—a shared set of values. They argue, for
example, that most people obey the laws of a society not because they
fear the sanctions that are threatened but because they adhere to a set
of values that places a high stock on the necessity of a legal system to
preserve an orderly and peaceful society. Bachrach and Baratz overstate
the case—the ability of the legal system to command compliance would
be severely tested were it stripped of its ability to inflict sanctions and
compelled to rely entirely on shared values to generate compliance. But
their argument contains an important insight into the ideological dynamics of intergroup inequality.

Institutions can legitimize and stabilize inequality by removing compliance from the self-conscious realm. The authority of an institution rests
implicitly on its ability to use force, that is, to inflict punishment on those
who resist it. However, the advantage of authority over the explicit assertion of power is that the threat remains implicit, submerged beneath an
elaborate ideological edifice. Instead of being engaged provocatively in
the direct use of threats, the power differential between groups is de-
ployed more effectively in molding the institutions and accompanying
values that constitute a way of life. Compliance is more readily given if
subordinates have been induced to adopt the same values as the dominant group. Lukes has put it well:

> To put the matter sharply, A may exercise power over B by getting him
> to do what he does not want to do, but he also exercises power over him
> by influencing, shaping or determining his very wants. . . . Is it not the
> supreme and most insidious exercise of power to prevent people, to what-
> ever degree, from having grievances by shaping their perceptions, cogni-
> tions and preferences in such a way that they accept their role in the exist-
> ing order of things, either because they can see or imagine no alternative
> to it, or because they see it as natural and unchangeable, or because they
> value it as divinely ordained and beneficial? (Lukes 1974, 23–24)

In this context, even the use of force, should the dominant group be
pressed to it, assumes a safer meaning than it does in explicit power
relations. The application of sanctions against the occasional straggler
can be interpreted self-righteously by both dominant and subordinate
groups as a just punishment for transgression of the social order, not as
the cold assertion of one group's will over another. Instead of placing
the dominant group's position at risk, such a use of sanctions thus reinforces the morality of the entire social order. The benefits that the dominant group derives from that social order are pleasantly obscured beneath a value system that has been made a consensual property.

Several observers have pointed to the subtlety with which power works to constrain the institutional and moral framework within which political judgments are made. Schattschneider (1960) talked of the use of institutions to generate a "mobilization of bias"; Bachrach and Baratz (1970) discuss the process of "nondecision-making" and "decision-shaping"; Lindblom (1977) uses the concept of "constrained volitions." Although the specific emphases of those arguments vary, for our purposes they all identify a common phenomenon—the implicit use of power to prevent or contain conflict rather than the explicit exercise of power to subdue it. Rather than engaging in battle with subordinates who challenge the status quo, dominant groups prefer to constrain the vision of subordinates sufficiently to preclude the emergence of a serious challenge. The surest strategy for social control is to confine the agenda within which a challenge might take place.

Empiricists may complain that the process thus entailed is not empirically observable. Merelman (1968), for example, objected that Bachrach and Baratz's "nondecision" is by definition a nonevent that has no grounding in the empirically observed exchanges of everyday political life. But it is precisely because of its invisibility in the day-to-day arena that the institutionalization of bias is so profound. By defining the bounds of reasonable discourse, institutionalized power limits the kinds of political exchanges that may take place without sullying the awareness of any of the participants. By contrast, it is the very conspicuousness of the explicit exercise of power that reduces it to such a clumsy basis for durable social control.

Ideology as Communication

The members of the dominant group evolve a compendium of symbolic messages to interpret the expropriative institutions from which they benefit. Those messages are directed both to the other members of their own group and to the other parties in the relationship, as the continued support of established institutions is necessarily sought from both parties: the stability of expropriative institutions requires both the continued cooperation of dominant-group members and the continued compliance of subordinates. Thus, in order to have credibility, ideological messages must seem compelling to those on both sides of the relationship. Under these pressures, dominant-group members are moved to interpret arrangements in a way that is personally gratifying and that also appeals to the sensibilities of subordinates.

The symbolic messages that thus evolve are the natural accompaniment to the institutionalized expropriation from subordinates, protecting that expropriation through camouflage. The institutional arrangements within which inequalities are practiced and the symbolic interpretations of those arrangements have complementary goals—to define, respectively, the practical and the moral imperatives of social life.

In a penetrating essay on ideology and class relations, Abercrombie and Turner (1982) argue that the practical imperatives of institutionalized power alone are sufficient to coerce subordinates into compliance. They claim that moral imperatives are both ineffectual and unnecessary in the management of subordinates. Pointing to several examples of specific moral strictures that commanded stronger adherence in the dominant classes than in subordinate classes, they reason that ideology functions not as an instrument of social control, but simply as an expressive device for the dominant classes. By providing them with a moral justification of the status quo, the dominant ideology serves as a symbolic banner around which the dominant class can rally.

According to this view, the dominant ideology is a pure epiphenomenon, thrust up by the structure of inequality and serving only as the symbolic embodiment of it. This view presupposes, however, a state of open hostilities between have's and have-not's. In such a state, each side closes ranks and directs its moral energies entirely toward its own constituents. In these circumstances, subduing the other side has become a lost cause, and the adversaries on each side must instead work on motivating their own ranks to invest in the high costs of outright conflict. In this all-too-familiar scenario, people on each side then assert their group's cause by claiming a distinctive moral code and derogating their opponents.

But open conflict is precisely what dominant groups are driven to avoid. As they aim for stability rather than disruption, these groups must direct their moral exertions more inclusively toward all participants in the relationship. They are not free to indulge in moral expressions that provide psychological gratification only to those who share their side of experience. The practical coercion provided by institutionalized power relations is not sufficient to secure the stable compliance of subordinates. Habits are established and reinforced so much better when there is a compelling moral basis for them. If the institutional arrangements were left unadorned, or worse, emblazoned in a moral code that failed to embrace the sensibilities of subordinates, the dominant group would face a battle to obtain even recalcitrant compliance from subordinates. The potency of institutionalized power lies not only in its ability to constrain people's options but also in its ability to buffer the direct relationship between have's and have-not's. To complete the obfuscation, institutions must be enshrouded in a moral code that makes an inclusive, rather than an exclusive, appeal. The legitimacy of those institutions hinges critically on making them morally palatable to those whose compliance sustains them.

Amorphous and Flexible Ideology

The ideology of the dominant group provides a broad moral framework that touches every aspect of life. The amorphous quality of popular ideology has made it an elusive concept for scholars to define or measure precisely, and one finds the term used in multitudinous ways by scholars focusing on different aspects of social and political life (for example, compare the various discussions of ideology in Apter 1964; also Gramsci 1971; Thompson 1990). Researchers have experienced similar problems with the general concept of power (see, e.g., Dahl 1968). The empirical products of both power and popular ideology are so subtly shaded into every aspect of life that they elude bounded definition and observation. But from this stems their enduring significance. They work together to permeate the social structure and to mold the terms in which that structure is experienced and perceived by all the participants. Because implicit power relations necessarily have an inclusive reach, so too must the accompanying ideology.

None of these considerations imply that the dominant ideology should be applied with a uniform stamp to lock reactions into a tight consistency or to force a universal code of behavior on all participants. Indeed, the strength of an ideology lies in its loose-jointed, flexible application. An ideology is a political instrument, not an exercise in personal logic: consistency is rigidity, the only pragmatic effect of which is to box oneself in. A slight change in circumstances or a compelling challenge to one part of the ideology would render the whole ideological edifice vulnerable. Although it is advantageous to have subordinates' options hedged in, the members of dominant groups are not drawn to patterns of thinking that would limit their own maneuverability.

Another factor working against ideological consistency is that ideologies are not hatched up in a single, contrived action. They are not static but fluid, and they evolve piecemeal rather than being fabricated in toto. They develop historically, shifting and changing constantly as the specific exigencies are altered. There is not a clean sweep of the entire ideological framework with each minor change in exigencies: instead, some ideas are dropped swiftly while others linger or are slowly reshaped. In addition, the unself-conscious way in which individuals absorb the various ideas that float past them causes two forms of inconsistency. First, any individual amalgam of ideas is likely to contain idiosyncratic combinations of elements, depending on the particular currents of information to which he or she has been exposed. Second, there will be gaps or logical inconsistencies in many individuals' renditions of popular ideas, insofar as they drift into ways of thinking that are convenient rather than sign on to a clearly labeled package of ideas.

Thus, the perennial search of scholars for sharp intellectual consistency in expressions of ideology (see, for example, McClosky, Hoffmann, and O'Hara 1960; Converse 1964; Achen 1975; Nie, Verba, and Petrocik 1976; Sullivan et al. 1978; Converse and Markus 1979; Smith 1989) is misleading. In the political needs of the group, in the way in which ideologies evolve and are propagated, and in the ideological proclivities of individual group members, there is little pressure for the articulation of a tightly consistent ideology. This is especially true of ideologies that are broadly consistent with existing institutional arrangements. People who challenge the modus vivendi are more self-conscious and are forced more on their own motivational resources, both of which generate slightly greater pressure toward consistency. But this is a difference of degree only: challenging ideologies also develop in a trial-and-error historical process, and here too, tight consistency remains a political liability.

By the same token, it is misleading to take as the measure of an ideology's reach its success in implanting identical mores into the minutiae of everyday life of all participants in the relationship (as do Abercrombie and Turner 1982). If the conduct of the relationship does not require identical behaviors of all participants (and more typically it requires just the reverse), there is no advantage in imposing the same moral minutiae on subordinates as on one's own group. The insidious reach of a dominant ideology inheres in its elevation of a few abstract principles for general consumption and the subsequent application of those principles judiciously and adaptively to the various exigencies that it confronts. Broad moral principles contain enough flexibility and ambiguity that they lend themselves admirably to multiple ad hoc applications as the need arises. One marvels, for example, at the highly various deeds and practices that have been justified in the name of Christian religious principles. The unequal relationship from which the dominant group benefits creates disparate conditions of life. An ideological system that does not address itself to those conditions by developing diffuse applications will fail to be inclusively compelling.

Thus, in feudal society, the central moral precepts of loyalty, honor, and obedience were necessarily applied with sensitive discrimination to the specific daily behaviors of the peasantry and the nobility. Given this, what Abercrombie and Turner (1982) interpret as a failure to reach subordinates is instead a mark of the success of feudal ideology in adapting to the disparate conditions of life that the feudal organization of labor had created. Similarly, the moral code associated with the system of slavery in the antebellum South included a core set of tenets to which all participants were answerable (especially the moral strictures of Christianity), as well as distinct codes of ethics for slave-owners on the one hand (for example, to be protective, to advise and adjudicate over "weaker" mortals) and their slaves on the other (for example, to be loyal, hardworking, and respectful). The specific ethical codes for each group were of course compatible with its position of dominance or subordination in the expropriative business of slavery. And again, in contemporary gender relations, there is an overarching, abstract moral code that encompasses both groups, but at the same time, each group is exhorted to follow a specialized moral code that is adapted to its position in the intergroup relationship. Indeed, many conservatives in gender relations have been moved to exclaim anxiously, "Vive la difference!"

The Sensitive Shroud

In the amorphous ideological framework of the dominant group, the segment that is especially sensitive is the attempt to explain and interpret the relationship with subordinates that is at the core of social life. This topic must be broached by the dominant group, but with some delicacy. The intergroup attitudes of the dominant group are its most direct communication with those whose compliance it requires. The portrayal of the subordinate group and affective and behavioral dispositions toward subordinates are all articulated with intuitive care, constrained by the need for inclusiveness. The dominant group cannot afford to indulge in unbridled messages that gratify only the sensibilities of its own membership. As the members of the dominant group seek to preserve their privileges, they express views that swathe arrangements in a soft, protective shroud. To that end, they are drawn to ideas that are likely to soothe subordinates rather than pound them. The alternative forms that these efforts may take are the subject of the next section.

COERCIVE LOVE AND REASONED PERSUASION

Slavery identifies the interests of rich and poor, master and slave, and begets domestic affection on the one side, and loyalty and respect on the other. . . . We abhor the doctrine of the "Types of Mankind"; first, because it is at war with scripture, which teaches us that the whole human race is descended from a common parentage; and, secondly, because it encourages and incites brutal masters to treat negroes, not as weak, ignorant and dependent brethren, but as wicked beasts, without the pale of humanity. The Southerner is the negro's friend, his only friend. Let no intermeddling abolitionist, no refined philosophy, dissolve this friendship.

FITZHUGH, SOCIOLOGY FOR THE SOUTH, OR THE FAILURE OF FREE SOCIETY

(1854, 43, 95)

With friends like that, who needs enemies? But no one need doubt the sincerity of Mr. Fitzhugh's passionate defense of Southern slavery. It is instructive to read proslavery tracts such as Fitzhugh's and those collected by Elliott (1860). Absurd as it may seem through the cynical lens of temporal detachment, those essayists defended the flagrantly expropriative institution of slavery on the grounds, not of hatred, but of love and humanitarianism. Interestingly, those learned gentlemen were not oblivious to the benefits that accrued to Southern whites from slavery (see, e.g., Fitzhugh 1854, 27, 93, 163). But what is conveniently missing from their discernment is any realization that those benefits were being extracted at the direct expense of the other group in the system, blacks.

The same sticky syrup still coated the affirmations of some of the Southern whites interviewed by Johnson in the 1940s (Johnson 1943):

> "They make perfectly delightful servants. I wouldn't have any other kind." (Charleston housewife to Johnson 1943, 195)

> "The Negro in his place is really an assistant in the South. He's what the Lord Almighty intended him to be, a servant of the people. We couldn't get along without them." (Official of the Arkansas industrial welfare commission to Johnson 1943, 195)

> "The Negroes around here are not capable of doing the more skilled work. They are often helpers. The men prefer them to white helpers: they are more humble, obedient and strong. They know their place and keep it." (Union official in Georgia to Johnson 1943, 205)

The cordial, self-righteous pleasures that are sometimes offered by domination do indeed seem almost boundless. What are the conditions that nurture such warm and satisfied feelings of privilege?

The Inclusive Reach of Dominant Ideology

It has been observed before that dominant groups gravitate effortlessly toward interpretations of inequality that portray its benefits as diffuse and general rather than as specialized and lopsided. Marx regarded the neutralization of the relational basis of inequality as the primary ideological task of ascendant classes:

> For each new class which puts itself in the place of one ruling before it, is compelled, merely in order to carry through its aim, to represent its interest as the common interest of all the members of society, that is, expressed in ideal form: it has to give its ideas the form of universality, and represent them as the only rational, universally valid ones. (Marx and Engels [1846] 1970, 65–66)

In a similar vein, Dahrendorf (1959, 284) argues that "the dominant groups of society express their comparative gratification with existing conditions *inter alia* by visualizing and describing these conditions as ordered and reasonable."

What has been overlooked, however, is that such an ideological endeavor is incompatible with the expression of hostility toward subordinates. Because they seek the "loyalty and respect" of subordinates rather than their fear, dominant groups eschew hostility. Only when they are driven to abandon the quest for loyalty and respect by the existence of potent threats to their position will dominant groups let hostility slide into their ideological communications. But to the extent that dominant groups are successful in embracing subordinates ideologically, the probability that they will have to face such threats is sharply reduced.

Marx's excited prediction that capitalist society would devolve progressively into "two great hostile camps" is inconsistent with his recognition that dominant classes always strive to embrace their would-be adversaries with an inclusive ideology. The only way to reconcile these two assertions of ideological inclusiveness on the one hand and conflict on the other is by relegating ideology to a strictly expressive role, with no communicative or politically instrumental function. But the notion of an inclusive ideology itself suggests that dominant-group members are not simply venting an expressive need geared solely to their own gratification—their ideology is a means of communication to assist them in the ongoing business of social control.

The ideological outcome that Marx foresaw for capitalist class relations—class conflict—is rendered improbable precisely because of the profound workings of ideological universalism. Ideology does not work alone, but as the natural accompaniment to institutionalized, implicit power relations. Together, they obfuscate the bare reality of expropriation and constrain the moral latitude of any challenge that might surface. Like Marx, subsequent scholars of inequality have been riveted by the potential for conflict and have thus given scant attention to the conservative pressures that more typically prevail in long-term, unequal relationships—pressures that foster harmony or that spare dominant groups from more than a modicum of acrimony.

The intergroup attitudes that are exchanged between groups locked in an unequal relationship cannot be treated as naive, unconstrained acts of personal expression. Because the groups are bound together in a relationship, they have no recourse but to communicate with each other. The intergroup attitudes expressed on either side of the relationship are the symbolic representations that each side makes to the other in a continuing dialogue. Those attitudes are constrained by the structural and moral framework of the relationship within which they are formulated.

Communication under Constraints

The dominant group clearly has the primary advantage, but even so, its interpretation of the relationship with subordinates is confined by the way the relationship is structured, by the preexisting moral framework, and by the kind of attitudes that are presented by subordinates. Subordinates, in turn, are hemmed in even more tightly. Even when the structure of the relationship permits some insulation from the intergroup messages of the dominant group, subordinates are still bound by the existence of a *relationship* with the dominant group to engage in a dialogue rather than a monologue. Thus, the intergroup attitudes of subordinates are always reactive rather than independent: they are framed by the broad moral code that shades the institutional structure of the relationship and by the specific appeals that are made by the dominant group.

Within these constraints, the dominant group relies more on love or reasoning as instruments of coercion than on hostility and force. These efforts do not fall into a void, but set the moral parameters of the dialogue with subordinates. If the structure of the relationship is conducive, subordinates may be trapped by the serenade into generous compliance. If the structure of the relationship restricts the opportunity for the dominant group to infiltrate the emotions of subordinates, the general moral code that envelops the relationship shifts to a different gear, but it still operates to limit the nature and scope of subordinate complaint. Before discussing the characteristic features of the different ideological forms that find voice, I trace the structural conditions that foster each.

Intimate versus Distal Relations

It is to the advantage of the dominant group when the structure of the relationship with subordinates dictates intimate contact between them. The more the daily lives of the respective groups are intertwined, the greater and more varied are the opportunities for the dominant group to invade the emotional and cognitive vulnerabilities of their unequals. If one supposes that it might just as easily work the other way around, one must bear in mind that the intimacy between groups does not take place in a neutral setting but within the institutional structure of their organized inequality, a context that gives the dominant group the natural advantage in any encounters.

But expropriative relationships are not always structured in a way that facilitates intimate personal contact between groups. The most important limiting factor lies in the functional requirements of the productive process that is the core of the redistribution between groups. This is perhaps clearest in the case of class relations. Advances in the technology of communal production that we associate with increases in productivity and efficiency have also dictated a reorganization of work relations, creating larger and more mechanized production units and altering the functional relationship between those with unequal control over the means of production. Marx's comparison of the social organization of peasant agriculture with that of industrial production is well known (Marx 1964, 184–189). Feudal agriculture placed scattered communities of peasants within the social and economic grasp of individual landlords on a life-long, multigenerational basis. Although the amount of contact between a landlord and his peasants was still not as frequent as within-class contacts, the ties between classes were individualized, and their permanency broadened their reach beyond the utilitarian basis of the class relationship to cover all aspects of social life. By contrast, the industrial mode of production dictates a less personalized pattern of contact between different functional groups. The specialization of tasks and the accompanying aggregation of labor push the work-related communications between groups toward more utilitarian, contractual negotiations between aggregates. Enduring ties to specific individuals in other groups are no longer a normal feature of the exchange process in production.[2]

The structure of the relationship between whites and blacks in the United States was also influenced by these economic pressures, insofar as the expropriation of African American labor in economic life has always been an important component of that relationship. The pattern of contact between whites and African Americans in the antebellum South was marked by similar constraints to those that existed between landlord and peasant in feudal Europe. With the dissolution of slavery, those patterns were partially maintained through the system of share-cropping in the rural South. However, as industrial growth in the North drew blacks away from the rural South and as the South itself industrialized, blacks were gradually funneled into the aggregate of laboring masses, and their personal contact with their white masters consequently diminished.

The inequality between men and women is founded in control of sexual access and sexual reproduction. The technology of procreation has dictated one-to-one contact between sexual partners: in order to control procreation, men require intimate access to individual women, and the long maturation period for their offspring lends itself naturally to individualized, long-term relationships between members of the two

2. There have been sporadic attempts in the history of industrialism to structure industrial relations with enduring, personal ties across group lines. The most prominent examples are company towns (see Newby 1977b; Burawoy 1984), and the model of labor management followed by some Japanese firms (see Genovese 1974, 661–665). As several analysts have commented, however, the vagaries of capitalist markets make the strict application of long-term commitments to particular individuals impractical. Thus, even when industrial firms attempt to institute more personal ties to workers, they lack the certain durability of interpersonal relations across class lines that existed in the feudal organization of labor.

groups.[3] In addition, sexual access, treated as an asset in its own right, intrinsically involves physical intimacy. The enduring and individualized quality of contact between men and women permeates the relationship not only between coupling partners but also between parents and children.

The functional requirements of the productive process that establishes the inequality set outer limits on the pattern and quality of contact between the groups. Within those limits, dominant-group members have a continuing need to differentiate themselves from subordinates, and this prompts behaviors that reaffirm their status prerogatives. These, too, have a direct impact on the frequency and quality of interaction with subordinates.

When the division of labor between groups is deeply embedded in social institutions, the routinized role prescriptions alone constitute sufficient affirmation of the status prerogatives of the dominant group. In this context, close physical proximity to subordinates is "safe" because embedded rules govern interactions between members of the two groups, unambiguously defining the social meaning of any interactions and by the same token removing the possibility of challenge from the social agenda (Goffman 1956; van den Berghe 1967, 27; Reskin and Roos 1987). Personal interactions between status unequals are marked by numerous behavioral asymmetries that reaffirm the distinctions between them. These include the familiarity or formality used in terms of address (servants and patients are addressed by their first names, masters and doctors are addressed more formally), invasions of personal space and touching behavior (for example, in interactions between women and men, students and teachers, and employees and employers, the lower-status participant is more likely to be touched physically), initiating and interrupting in conversation (males interrupt females more than vice versa, work supervisors initiate conversation more than subordinates), expressions of anger (it is more acceptable for status superiors, such as work supervisors or men, to express anger than for inferiors, such as subordinates at work or women, to do so), and tone of voice (loud or soft, authoritative or diffident) (Henley 1977; Henley and Freeman 1979; West and Zimmerman 1983; Ellyson and Dovidio 1985). When these behavioral asymmetries become habitual and ingrained, repeated

3. The technological innovation of artificial insemination now makes it possible for procreation to take place without physical contact between sexual partners, but this does not alter the requirement for men to maintain intimate contact with their sexual partners if they wish to ensure ready access to their offspring. Since it is women, rather than men, who bear babies, it is women who would have presumptive parenthood if men did not link themselves unambiguously to their sexual partners (this point is, of course, a central tenet of Engels' well-known thesis [1972] about sexual inequality).

personal contact with subordinates provides a risk-devoid opportunity for members of the dominant group to reaffirm their status prerogatives.

When the practice of the expropriation does not afford the opportunity to seal status distinctions into the daily code of conduct, dominant-group members are pressed into a more defensive position. In order both to safeguard their status prerogatives and to insulate themselves from the uncomfortable possibility of personal challenge, the members of the dominant group retreat to the practice of spatial exclusiveness. Litwack (1979) provides an interesting example of how status anxiety in the dominant group affects the symbolic meaning of physical proximity between unequal groups. He reports that in the antebellum South, where it was complacently assumed that blacks were in the service and control of their white masters, blacks had relatively free access to a variety of physical settings. In the wake of slavery's dissolution, however, Southern whites quickly became more sensitive to the physical proximity of blacks: the presence of blacks in designated white areas came to symbolize a violation of racial status barriers, because the terms of blacks' physical presence were less clear-cut. The continuing symbolic significance of spatial segregation in American race relations may be interpreted as an attempt by whites to insulate themselves against the threat of encroachments on their racial status prerogatives.

In class relations, where material distinctions themselves visibly assert the differentiation between classes, dominant classes still promote status prerogatives as a way of symbolizing their gains and consolidating those gains for their offspring against encroachments by would-be competitors from outside their ranks. Snobbery associated with such nonmaterial factors as spoken accent, type of dress, and mode of personal expression help to secure the boundaries between insiders and outsiders, thus limiting the competitive field where immutable physical rules for group membership do not exist. Spatial exclusiveness encourages cultural divergences that are convenient handles for status distinctions, and it also serves directly to insulate dominant classes from too many incursions by assertive subordinates.

The contingencies that encumber physical proximity between unequal groups are seen especially clearly in the context of gender relations. Here, the functional locus of the inequality requires high physical proximity between individual men and women, the definition of group membership is immutable, and the status prerogatives of group membership have been relatively secure. Yet even here, some residual status anxiety drives the dominant group to maintain selected domains of spatial exclusiveness. In those domains that offer no clearly defined, distinctively "female" functions, the physical presence of women threatens the status boundaries between groups and is therefore unacceptable. Hence, spatial proximity to women in the workplace is threatening to many men if the women are assigned to the same occupations as themselves, but it is quite untroubling if women are there to serve men's needs (spatial proximity to secretaries and typists is desirable whereas contact with a female co-executive may be avoided). Similarly, all-male social clubs exclude women as members but may welcome women as servants or sexual playthings (waitresses, dancing girls, or prostitutes).

In short, the degree of physical proximity between unequal groups is limited by the functional constraints of their relationship and by the desire of dominant-group members to maintain status boundaries between themselves and subordinates. In domains where the functional basis of the expropriation does not dictate physical intimacy between groups, physical proximity to subordinates threatens to undermine the social boundaries between them. Such proximity is only acceptable in domains where there are clearly prescribed status-bounded tasks for each group; otherwise ambiguity hangs over subordinates' presence and threatens a violation of status boundaries. The fewer "safe" domains there are within the functional confines of an unequal relationship, the more the dominant group resorts to a policy of spatial exclusiveness to protect its position.

The organization of intergroup relations along intimate or distal principles carries indelible implications for the practice of ideology. Distinctive opportunities and constraints are thus introduced. I turn now to the varying ideological forms that are thus given life.

Intimacy and Coercive Love

In intergroup relationships characterized by a high degree of personal contact between groups, dominant-group members offer love, affection, and friendship to subordinates—on strict terms. Instead of threatening punishment if compliance is not given (an ugly scene), dominant-group members are in the happier position of offering rewards if compliance *is* given. The implied sanction is no less potent than when an explicit threat of punishment is made, but the symbolism that is invoked is warm and friendly instead of cold and threatening. After all, most parents know that it is more satisfactory to promise their child a chocolate for good behavior than to threaten a spanking for bad behavior.

The Entangling Net of Conditional Love.   Specific traits compatible with the subordinate role are idealized and subordinates are exhorted to strive for the ideal. The more successful a subordinate is in achieving the idealized traits that have been assigned to her group, the more lovable and sought-after she becomes. Within the institutionalized structure of the intergroup relationship, a subordinate's best chance of success in life is to excel in manifesting the traits and behaviors that have been designated for her group.

In this context, stereotypes about the subordinate group are in part meant as existential declarations and in part as ideals that subordinates should strive to attain. Thus, popular conceptions of the attributes of subordinates are a fusion of existential beliefs and moral strictures. The specific traits that are attached to subordinates are compatible with the tasks that are required of them in the expropriative exchange and with their subservient position in that exchange. The concept of "feminine" delineates a bundle of attributes that includes warmth, emotional and physical weakness and vulnerability, submissiveness, deference, dependence, and loyalty (Bell and Newby 1976; Rubin 1983; Cancian 1985, 1987). The inculcation of these traits in women is useful in itself, but it also makes women more vulnerable to a system of control based on conditional love. As Cancian has argued, women are rendered more dependent on male affection and protection by defining such traits as intrinsically feminine (Cancian 1985, 1987). In the antebellum South, slaves too were described and idealized as weak, dependent, deferential, loyal, and loving.

Subordinates who manifest the specified traits of their group are rewarded with love, affection, and praise. But subordinates who deviate from the stereotype are branded as "unfeminine" or as troublemakers, for which they may be punished, rebuked, ostracized, or ridiculed. The connection of these rules to the legitimation of the inequality between groups is brought out well by Bledsoe, in his *Essay on Liberty and Slavery* (1856):

> There is no form of human excellence before which we bow with profounder deference than that which appears in a delicate woman, . . . and there is no deformity of human character from which we turn with deeper loathing than from a woman forgetful of her nature, and clamourous for the vocation and rights of men. (Bledsoe 1856, 224, quoted in Myrdal 1944, 1074)

By specifying and idealizing the traits of subordinates, members of the dominant group put themselves in the enviable position of being able to define what subordinates' needs are. This permits them to cast their own role as one of magnanimously providing for subordinates' needs. Dominant-group members are thus spared the unpleasantness of withholding something from subordinates that they themselves value—after all, subordinates have different needs than they do. This then clears the way for them to define their relationship with subordinates as one of charming complementarity and mutual obligation:

> Slavery is the duty and obligation of the slave to labor for the mutual benefit of both master and slave, under a warrant to the slave of protection,

and a comfortable subsistence, under all circumstances. The person of the slave is not property, no matter what the fictions of the law may say; but the right to his labor is property and may be transferred like any other property, or as the right to the services of a minor or an apprentice may be transferred. Nor is the labor of the slave solely for the benefit of the master, but for the benefit of all concerned; for himself, to repay the advances made for his support in childhood, for present subsistence, and for guardianship and protection, and to accumulate a fund for sickness, disability, and old age. The master, as the head of the system, has a right to the obedience and labor of the slave, but the slave has also his mutual rights in the master; the right of protection, the right of counsel and guidance, the right of subsistence, the right of care and attention in sickness and old age. He also has a right in his master as the sole arbiter in all his wrongs and difficulties, and as a merciful judge and dispenser of law to award the penalty of his misdeeds. Such is American slavery, or as Mr. Henry Hughes happily terms it, "Warranteeism." (Elliott 1860, vii; see Genovese 1974 for numerous other examples of slaveholders' reconception of their expropriation of black labor as "a duty and a burden")

The relational basis of the inequality is thus cast in happier terms as a mutual interdependence between groups rather than as an expropriation of resources from one group to another.

Subordinates are unable to buffer themselves from the conditional love that is thus proffered by their betters. As long as the conditions are not violated, individual subordinates may engage in the reciprocal warmth of affectionate relationships with individuals from the dominant group. But if an individual subordinate should violate the terms of the affection, he or she cuts off that source of love or affection without having any other organized source of interpersonal gratification available. Because the daily practice of the relationship is individualized and intimate, subordinates either return the love offered them by members of the dominant group, within the terms specified, or face probable exclusion from organized social life.

The more completely the dominant group can penetrate the day-to-day lives of subordinates, the more tightly it constrains the calculable options of subordinates as well as the visibility and subjective plausibility of alternative options. An implicit understanding based on conditional love is much more satisfactory to the dominant group than an explicit contract. The implicit arrangement raises the costs of noncompliance for subordinates. At the same time, it removes the specter of noncompliance from the explicit day-to-day communications between groups.

Intimacy and Social Control.   The singularly coercive power of conditional love in relationships marked by high intimacy between groups has escaped the attention of analysts preoccupied with hostility and conflict.

Several analysts of gender attitudes have commented on the importance of individual-level intimacy in male-female relations in undermining the development of an assertive group consciousness among women (Mill 1970; Hacker 1951; de Beauvoir 1953; Rossi 1977b). But these analysts have focused primarily on the structural obstacles that this poses for women as an organizational unit. For example, de Beauvoir wrote:

> Women lack concrete means for organizing themselves into a unit which can stand face to face with the correlative unit. They have no past, no history, no religion of their own; and they have no such solidarity of work and interest as that of the proletariat. They are not even promiscuously herded together in the way that creates community feeling among the American Negroes, the ghetto Jews, the workers of Saint-Denis, or the factory hands of Renault. They live dispersed among the males, attached through residence, housework, economic condition, and social standing to certain men—fathers or husbands—more firmly than they are to other women. (de Beauvoir [1953] 1973, 678–679)

That analysis is reminiscent of Marx's famous portrayal of the small-holding peasantry in nineteenth-century France as so many "potatoes in a sack" (Marx [1869] 1959, 338). In a similar argument, John Stuart Mill saw the individualized organization of gender relations as providing men with a unique opportunity to keep women under their thumb:

> Every one of the subjects lives under the every eye, and almost, it may be said, in the hands, of one of the masters—in closer intimacy with him than with anyone of her fellow-subjects; with no means of combining against him, no power of even locally over-mastering him, and, on the other hand, with the strongest motives for seeking his favour and avoiding to give him offence. (Mill [1869] 1970, 136)

The structural dispersal of the members of a subordinate group is surely important in hindering the ease of communication amongst them that might have fostered the growth of a common sense of community. And their simultaneous individualized link to members of the dominant group does indeed allow for their close observation by dominant-group members. However, what these analysts have overlooked is that the meaning of such factors is significantly altered by more fundamental pressures that are put in place by the institutionalization of intimate ties across group lines. The primary significance of intimacy is that it permits dominant-group members to define their relationship with subordinates in a way that preempts explicit power considerations. This opportunity is pivotal, for it molds the way coercion is wielded and the way it is experienced by subordinates.

By making love the very instrument of coercion, dominant-group members swathe the unequal exchange with subordinates in the warmth of personal affection even as they hem in subordinates' options with a taut thread. Through the medium of longstanding personal relationships, men can dictate women's behaviors, condition women's perceptions of their experience, and capture their emotions. Individual subordinates are rewarded with love and praise for their fulfillment of specified, subordinate traits and compliant behaviors. There is no need to engage in explicit power negotiations with subordinates if one has an embedded, ingrained understanding that the continued exchange of affection is contingent upon the fulfillment of specific obligations. With such an institutionalized understanding in place, it is taken as a given by all the participants as they formulate their responses to one another. Their responses are thus tightly constrained even as their cognizance of the pressures is so ingrained that they have no need to deliberate about them consciously. As students of child development have long recognized, behaviors are instilled more indelibly if they are internalized as norms than if they are imposed externally through explicit threat of punishment.

Only among some radical feminists does one find discussion of the obfuscating and coercive properties of love, but the interpretation that they place on love is more as a deliberate and conscious manipulative device employed by men (see, e.g., Millett 1970, 36–37; Rich 1980). Some radical feminists even portray the role of love as one whereby men subjugate women by feeding off their love without offering it in return (Firestone 1970; Atkinson 1984). My argument, however, is that in conditions of high personal intimacy, relations between groups become infused with personal love and affection in an uncalculated gravitation. These bonds of mutual affection provide the members of the dominant group with an insidiously potent and self-gratifying vehicle for tightening their grasp around an unequal arrangement. They offer their love to individual subordinates, not freely, but within the rigid confines of an idealized and sanctified declaration of the distinctions between groups.

Love and Violence.　　Although physical coercion has little direct bearing on the day-to-day practice of social control in unequal relations that are organized around intimate one-to-one contacts, the use of violence by members of the dominant group is not precluded. Indeed, the intimate, one-to-one practice of the relationship ironically permits dominant-group members to engage in the freer locution of personal violence against subordinates than is possible in more distally structured relations. Such relations provide more opportunities for incidents of personal violence against subordinates and such incidents are less likely to damage the expropriative arrangements between the groups than would be the case in more distally structured relations. There are two ways that intimately structured relations facilitate the commission of violence against subordinates.

First, the risk of violence faced by individual subordinates from strangers from the dominant group (for example, rape of women by unknown men, or the brutal treatment of runaway slaves by slave patrols in the antebellum South) drives subordinates to find protection. The uneven distribution of resources between groups and the individualized, personal structure of the intergroup relationship leaves the individual subordinate with no option but to seek a personal tie with someone from the dominant group who can function as her protector. By attaching herself to an individual man, a woman secures protection from other men. Her awareness of her vulnerability to physical violence from unknown men thus leads her to value her attachment to an individual man more highly and deepens her emotional tie to her chosen partner. And in the antebellum South, the individual slave had little recourse but to rely on the mercies of his owner: in a world populated by slave patrols off the plantation and possibly by harsh overseers within the plantation, the slave might well regard his owner as the person who was best positioned to protect his well-being, and, by virtue of his economic investment, also the person with the biggest vested interest in his well-being.[4] Given these miserable constraints, the slave's security was best served by seeking to establish an emotional bond with his owner. Thus, the known risk of violence from members of the dominant group drives subordinates to seek the protection of a personal relationship with someone from that group. And it simultaneously encourages them to dissociate the violence committed by other members of the dominant group from their personal relation with a specific individual from that same group. The one-to-one relations that are the mainstay of the intergroup relationship are thereby reinforced by the existence of violence outside such one-to-one relations.

Second, the emotional bond that exists between the individuals in each one-to-one relationship swathes their personal interactions and makes it more acceptable for the individual from the dominant group to express anger and to indulge in physical violence within the confines of that personal relationship. Ironically, a woman often excuses physical violence against herself if it is perpetrated by the man she loves (and who she believes to love her), whereas she would not excuse the same act if it were committed by a stranger. Explosions of anger and violence are considered acceptable for a man within the context of an intimate, love relationship with a woman. If he is duly contrite after the incident,

4. The pecuniary interest of the slave-owner in the welfare of his slave property was explicitly recognized in the legal code of slavery (Elkins 1968, 58–59).

professes his love, and asks forgiveness, many women are unable to resist the appeal. In essence, the love relationship between them gives him a license to commit violence that would be unacceptable between strangers. (And the inequality that is nested in the love relationship is evident in the asymmetrical norm that such exhibitions of anger or violence would be unacceptable coming from the subordinate.) The wife's confusion is shared and reinforced by society at large. The interpretation of specific physical acts is so conditioned by the context within which they are committed that forced sexual intercourse between spouses is not usually recognized legally or morally as rape (Russell 1982). The institution of marriage seals off the intimate relationship between a man and a woman, making the interactions between them "private" and beyond the purview of other societal or governmental institutions. A man's home is indeed his castle.

Slavery in the antebellum South permitted a similar protection of violent behaviors by slave-owners, although the situation was not exactly parallel to that of contemporary gender relations. From its rather abrupt initiation, and throughout its relatively short duration, the institution of slavery relied more overtly on physical coercion than does gender relations. Slave-owners' relations with their slaves were less intimate and individuated than are men's relations with women, and physical violence was routinely and openly practiced by slave-owners or their agents as punishment administered for noncompliance among slaves. Such use of physical violence against slaves was sanctioned by the legal system and was openly acknowledged as a part of the system of social control. At the same time, the legal system and the dominant moral code did not condone wanton physical cruelty in the treatment of slaves or the sexual abuse of slaves. These niceties in the fine print did little to protect slaves who were abused, however. Slaves could not testify against their masters, and whatever happened within the confines of the plantation was a private matter.

This protection of the slave-owner's privacy in his relations with his slaves was based on a conception of the master-slave relationship as an extension of family relations (see, for example, Fitzhugh 1854; Myrdal 1944, 1073–1074).[5] Thus, although the institution of slavery did not lend itself perfectly to the intimate practice of coercive love, slave-owners nonetheless learned to adopt many of its features in order to enhance their control of slaves. Master-slave relations on small plantations or within the household often permitted sufficient intimacy to generate

5. With unintended irony, Fitzhugh defended slavery with the following analogy: "Look closely into slavery, and you will find nothing so hideous in it; or if you do, you will find plenty of it at home in its most hideous form" (Fitzhugh 1854, 89).

emotional ties between individuals from the two groups. The conditional affection that slave-owners offered their slaves under those circumstances had a coercive strength that should not be underestimated.

The practice of violence in slavery was thus nestled in the symbolism of familial affection, and this conditioned the way it was experienced and interpreted. As in contemporary gender relations, the encompassing moral framework of paternalistic love and affection facilitated the practice of violence against subordinates without contaminating the ongoing expropriative relationship. Apologists for slavery sincerely depicted the institution of slavery in the language of paternalistic nurturance rather than hostile force. That "nurturance" included the "obligation" of the slave-owner to mete out punishment for transgressions by his slaves (see the quote from Elliott above), as well as the paternal right to unleash feelings of anger freely on his hapless slaves.

This encompassing moral framework did not fail to affect the responses of slaves to their predicament. Litwack provides some revealing illustrations of the torn emotions that at least some, and perhaps many, slaves experienced as they watched their white masters suffer through the Civil War—the same war that African Americans hoped would bring their emancipation from slavery. For example, Litwack writes:

> Few slaves were immune to the human tragedies that befell the families to whom they belonged. They had known them too well, too intimately not to be affected in some way. "Us wus boys togedder, me an Marse Hampton, en wus jist er bout de same size," Abram Harris recalled. "Hit sho did hurt me when Marse Hampton got kilt kase I lubed dat white man." The tragedies that befell the Lipscomb family in South Carolina provoked one of their slaves, Lorenza Ezell, beyond mere compassion to outright anger and a desire for revenge. . . : " . . . I so mad, I could have kilt all de Yankees. I say I be happy iffen I could kill me jes' one Yankee. I hated dem 'cause dey hurt my white people." . . . As a young slave on a Virginia plantation, Booker T. Washington listened to the fervent prayers for freedom and shared the excitement with which his people awaited the arrival of the Union Army. Yet the news that "Mars' Billy" had been killed in the war had profoundly affected these same slaves. "It was no sham sorrow," Washington would later write, "but real. Some of the slaves had nursed 'Mars' Billy'; others had played with him when he was a child. 'Mars' Billy' had begged for mercy in the case of others when the overseer or master was thrashing them. The sorrow in the slave quarter was only second to that in the 'big house.' " . . . To Washington, there was nothing strange or contradictory about such behavior; the slaves had simply demonstrated their "kindly and generous nature" and refused to betray a trust. (Litwack 1979, 7, 9)

References such as these to love, to "*my* white people," and to "refusing to betray a trust" are only meaningful within the context of a paternalistic relationship, where love and coercion are insidiously intertwined.

Distal Relations and Reasoned Persuasion

When unequal groups become spatially separated, the dominant group encounters a reduced set of opportunities to exercise social control over subordinates. The essential difficulty is that the dominant group cannot afford to insulate itself completely from those whose continued compliance it requires. Physical separation of the unequal groups runs counter to the relational basis of the inequality. The dominant group must contain subordinates within a common social system, but this becomes problematic as relations between the groups are structured more distally. Stated simply, the dominant group cannot insulate itself without at the same time providing the same opportunity to subordinates. The natural rift that is thus introduced in their relationship is felt in two ways.

First, and less important, it limits the direct access that members of the dominant group have to the services of subordinates. Of course, where the core of the inequality has shifted to a more aggregated mode of expropriation, this lack of ready access to the personal services of subordinates is not critical to the maintenance of the relationship. It does, however, remove or restrict one gratifying and useful benefit of a dominant position—the ability to summon individual subordinates at will.

Second, and more critically, the physical separation of groups restricts communication channels between them and thus threatens to undermine the systemic integration of the groups within a common relationship. Indeed, were it not for the development of mass communication media and mass institutions (especially educational institutions) as an integral part of the technological advances that have worked to aggregate the mode of expropriation in class and race relations, dominant groups in those relationships might find the task of social control insurmountable.

The practice of social control through the medium of individual relationships softens the symbolic context of the expropriation and presents its rigid, group-based rules via individual, personal ties. Without the individualized mediation, the expropriative basis of the relationship is revealed in ruder, hardened terms. This makes it both more visible and less palatable to subordinates. By the same token, the replacement of personalized communications between individuals from different groups with distal communications between aggregates greatly reduces the dominant group's hold over subordinates, both perceptually and emotionally. There are fewer compelling opportunities to condition subordinates' perceptions and interpretations of their relationship. And the opportunity to exercise coercion through conditional love is foregone, as subordinates are thrown more on the emotional and cognitive resources of those who share their own side of experience.

Faced with more independent subordinates who are less generously compliant, if not downright recalcitrant, dominant groups relinquish the ideological props of conditional love reluctantly, bit by bit. A moral framework of long standing is hard to abandon: based in a long history of its past effectiveness, the patterns of thought have become habitual and ingrained. Thus, there is a natural lag between the morality that infuses people's orientations and the changed structural circumstances that make such a moral outlook anachronistic. A broad moral framework cannot be shed knee-jerk style with changed structural conditions; instead, its ineffectuality must be learned. At the same time, we might expect some cultural diffusion from one intergroup relationship to another within the same society. Moral precepts that govern one relationship may infiltrate other relationships on a trial-and-error basis. The morality of conditional love—paternalism—has an especially strong pull. The high returns yielded by its venerable practice make it difficult for dominant groups to abandon paternalism, even when changed structural circumstances render it obsolete. Added to this is the personally gratifying nature of coercion through love: it offers the members of the dominant group an unrivaled opportunity to exercise discrimination without any shadow of personal culpability or malevolence.

As dominant groups are confronted with the failure of paternalism, they do not rush headlong into the practice of explicit power relations with its attendant hazards of hostility and force. Indeed, the use of violence becomes more hazardous than in paternalistic relations, where its individualized application particularizes its interpretation and thus spares the main frame of the relationship from contamination with hostility. When violence is practiced against aggregates (as in police action against strikers or civil rights demonstrators), the group basis for the action is readily apparent: the violence is administered impersonally against groups of people, and it takes place in the public domain, where it also has high visibility. Thus, as dominant groups learn the impracticality of conditional love as the means of social control, they grope for an ideological alternative that will keep the hazards of explicit power relations at bay. Conditional love is supplanted by reasoned persuasion.

Individualism and Social Control. Whereas the practice of discrimination through personal relationships particularizes its experiential impact, the practice of discrimination against aggregates necessitates an ameliorating ideology that diverts from the hardened experience of group-based inequality. Paternalism is based on the affirmation and idealization of group differences, but dominant groups in more distal relationships become experienced in denying the group basis of social life. Instead of upholding the idealized group characteristics of subordinates as the rigid contingency for personal love and acceptance, dominant groups attempt to deny that group membership is relevant for the allocation of life's benefits. When subordinates develop resilience to the pressures of conditional love, dominant groups attempt to coax them into compliance by affirming and idealizing individualism as the guiding principle in social life. The affirmation of individualism as an existential principle is an attempt to portray social life in a way that denies the validity of group-based complaints. The concurrent normative elevation of the rights of individuals to a lofty plane is an attempt to confine the moral horizons of subordinates by denying the legitimacy of group-articulated complaints and thus to channel disaffection into less threatening, individualistic goals.

The distinction between individual rights and group rights is a subtle one, which makes it particularly well suited to an ideological defense of privilege. At a superficial level, it seems obvious that if all individual rights were respected, the problem of group rights would be obviated. Indeed, democratic values have emphasized individual rights as a way of protecting the principle of political equality, and in so doing individualism and equality have been implicitly linked.

The problem is that when the members of one group operate from a disadvantaged position, the principle of individualism does little to promote their advancement and it often stands as an obstacle. Even within the narrowly political sphere it has often been observed that the simple application of universal suffrage (that is, that each individual is given the same formal political rights) fails to provide valid political equality because it does not correct for systematic inequalities that exist in resources, access to information, and general political knowledge, all of which predetermine the ability of different groups to participate effectively (Downs 1957; Parkin 1971; Lindblom 1977). As Parkin argues,

> Political equality presupposes sufficient social and material equality to enable contending groups to utilize formal political rights in roughly the same degree. Where sharp social and material inequalities do exist, the provision of equal political rights in effect confers a major advantage on those who command the greatest resources to mobilize in defense of their interests. (Parkin 1971, 185)

Similarly, meritocracies protect the right of the individual to a job for which he or she is qualified, but where one group's access to the necessary qualifications has historically lagged behind another's, the right of the individual comes into direct conflict with the right of the disadvantaged group to advance its collective socioeconomic position. Where the historical disadvantage from which one group operates is the direct outcome of discriminatory practices, the disjuncture between individual rights and group rights is particularly rude. But whatever the origin of the inequalities between groups, the principle of individualism fails to address them.

Yet individualism provides a general, principled, seemingly neutral basis for the rejection of aggregate group demands. The rights of the individual are endorsed vehemently, as there is a systematic aversion to any representation of social problems in group terms. Society is cautioned against responding to the aggregate demands of categories of people because that would interfere with the inviolable rights of the individual—who must have free access to the ideas that interest him, to the job for which he is qualified, to the neighborhood that he can afford, and so on. By upholding individualism as a guiding principle in the empirical and normative interpretation of social life, the rights of groups are thus rendered illegitimate and unreasonable.

Symbolic Concessions. In the same vein, dominant groups learn how to respond to subordinate-group demands with symbolic, rather than substantive, concessions (Edelman 1964; Lipsky 1968). Again, unmitigated rejection of subordinate groups is avoided because it seems so unreasonable and because it is too conflictive. However, actions such as establishing a commission to examine subordinate-group grievances seem responsive and sincere: the dominant group is satisfied that it is looking into the matter and the subordinate group is placated by the show of concern. That the subsequent commission recommendations are not acted upon or are translated into legislation that is not enforced is too lengthy and obtuse a process to be noticed by most of the participants. The net result is the peaceful preservation of the status quo in the face of challenge, along with little or no injury to the sensibilities of either dominant or subordinate groups.

Channeling Egalitarianism into Equality of Opportunity. The conservative effects of individualism and symbolic concessions are felt in the pervasive reshaping of egalitarianism into the goal of equality of opportunity. Inequality in distributive outcomes is morally sanctioned so long as access to *opportunities* is not unequal (Schaar 1967; Parkin 1971). The normative shift from outcomes to opportunities offers several advantages to the dominant group. To begin, it relocates the focus of the public agenda from group conditions to circumstances affecting individuals. It also diverts attention away from the most threatening issue, redistribution of outcomes. Indeed, it legitimizes, de facto, the concept of having an unequal distribution of outcomes by implying that it is only the procedures for distribution that warrant scrutiny. Correction of the procedures removes any basis for complaint about the specific outcomes. Finally, the "success" of policies aimed at correcting procedural processes is considerably more slippery to assess than are policies aimed at tangible, distributive outcomes (Dorn 1979). When procedures replace outcomes as the policy focus, the proof is no longer in the pudding, but in the less readily observed method by which it is cooked.

The Muted Terms of Debate.   By these means, the central redistributive issues that divide the interests of dominant and subordinate groups are obfuscated and the grievances of subordinates are diverted into less threatening and less clear-cut channels. This rechanneling of subordinates' demands is a modified form of the strategy pursued by dominant groups in more intimate relationships of defining subordinates' needs completely. In distally structured relations, dominant-group members forfeit the opportunity to exercise sufficient cognitive and emotional control of subordinates to preclude their formulation of group-level grievances. In this situation, the dominant group retreats to the next-best strategy of diverting those grievances into less threatening channels.

This general goal frames the terms of the dialogue between unequal groups. The dominant group is not free to lash out at subordinates, much as it may resent their threatened incursions into the modus vivendi. Pockets of outright negativism may exist within the dominant ranks, but the prevailing current of dominant ideology runs to intergroup attitudes that try to appease rather than inflame subordinates. At the leading edge of this current are the better-educated members of the dominant group, whose worldly knowledge and cognitive sophistication give them a natural proclivity for the more complex and subtle world view that best meets the defensive needs of a dominant group under challenge (Jackman and Muha 1984).

In the web of this world view, the intergroup attitudes of the dominant group are pulled away from the rigid affirmation of group differences and group prerogatives that were de rigueur when the relationship was bolstered and cushioned by paternalistic mores. As hostility is introduced into the relationship by discontented subordinates, those who belong to the dominant group try to subdue and contain that hostility by softening and complicating their intergroup messages in a shifting line of defense.

Subordinates are not immune to these pressures. Their better insulation from the dominant group is what makes it possible for them to formulate grievances and to articulate a challenge. But the obfuscatory response of the dominant group insidiously infuses and constrains the dialogue between them. Although dominant-group members can less effectively exclude complaints from the agenda, they can still set parameters that restrict the kinds of complaints that have moral credibility. This sticky web entangles subordinates, whose energies become diverted and exhausted with skirmishes that are on the perimeter of their collective distributive deficit. The core redistributive issues are relegated to a position outside the bounds of accepted, legitimate discourse, where they slip quietly out of reach.

SUMMARY

I have argued that the role of hostility in intergroup attitudes has been widely misconstrued. Hostility, far from being the natural companion of subjugation, is instead its natural enemy. Intuitively aware of the hazards of hostility, dominant groups work to penetrate the social structure with a world view that either excludes or restrains hostility.

I began by assuming that the members of contending groups are drawn to ideologies that are rationally consistent with their interests. This does not lead people on either side of an unequal relationship to take a confrontational stance. On each side, people are sensitive to the opportunities and risks that are presented by the structure of their social relationship and its enveloping moral framework as they attempt to maximize their control over resources without putting their current holdings at risk. On each side, people have no recourse but to heed the messages from their protagonists as they formulate their own position.

With these considerations in mind, I explored the limitations of force for dominant groups seeking to secure the compliance of subordinates in their expropriative relations. Explicit power negotiations, with the threat and possible exercise of force hovering over them, make an uncomfortable and unstable basis for obtaining compliance. For these reasons, dominant groups work to institutionalize their expropriation from subordinates and to encase such institutions in a moral code that sanctifies them. Both the institutions and their accompanying ideology constrain the options of subordinates. Habitual and ingrained responses develop to institutions that are fixed quantities in their lives, and subordinates' pleas are limited to those that do not incur the wrath of their more powerful opponents and that have credibility within the established moral framework.

The process that is thus involved is one of continual trial-and-error learning over a long period of time. Individuals do not rely solely on their own resources in gathering and evaluating information. They accumulate knowledge from the historical and contemporary experience of others who share their social circumstances. They develop habitual responses to institutions that have been shown to be stable fixtures, and they concentrate their energies on those features of life that seem potentially pliable. These responses develop unself-consciously as individuals negotiate themselves around the rocks and unknown snares that await them in their day-to-day lives. The ideologies to which groups thus gravitate have accumulated piecemeal and the ideas that are welded together do not manifest tight, logical consistency. Intergroup ideologies are political communications that evolve and change in response to pressures in the relationship, not unencumbered acts of raw expression.

The ideological framework to which the members of dominant groups are drawn is constrained by their interest in pacifying rather than inflaming subordinates. And the institutional stability of the expropriation buffers dominant-group members from any feeling of personal complicity, making it easy for them to perceive the arrangements in a positive light. The specific form of sugar-coating that they adopt is constrained by the structure of their relationship with subordinates. The day-to-day business of expropriation may dictate either intimate, one-to-one relations across group lines or impersonal, aggregated patterns of interaction between groups.

In relations that are structured intimately, dominant-group members gravitate to a paternalistic ideology that permits them to practice coercive love. Subordinates' attributes and needs are defined by the dominant group in ways that are consistent with their ascribed role in the unequal relationship, and subordinates are offered love and affection if they comply with the terms of that relationship. This moral framework constrains subordinates' options tightly at the same time as it swathes the expropriation with the warm and binding ties of mutual affection.

When the expropriative basis of the intergroup relationship ruptures one-to-one contacts across group lines and necessitates more aggregated communications between groups, members of the subordinate group become less vulnerable to emotional control by the dominant group. As subordinates become more insulated from the dominant group, they are thrown more on the cognitive and emotional resources of their own group. In addition, the aggregated basis of expropriative arrangements reveals those arrangements in a harsher and less personal light. In these circumstances, the configuration of costs and opportunities shifts somewhat for subordinates, and they begin to inject more vocal notes of dissension into the relationship.

Faced with less compliant subordinates, the members of the dominant group gradually learn to cast off the venerable paternalistic mold and to adopt an alternative ideology that settles for second-best. If you cannot preempt conflict, then you try to contain it; if you cannot entrap subordinates in love, then you try to reason with them. As the group basis of social life becomes a point of contention, dominant-group members gradually learn to adopt a view that denies the existential or moral credibility of group-based demands. The dominant view shifts to a moral framework governed by the principle of individualism: the rights of individuals are given precedence over the rights of groups. Within that framework, the dominant group steers the course of debate toward symbolic concessions and equality of opportunity in order to divert attention away from the threatening specter of equality in the distribution of resources themselves.

My argument has three important implications for the analysis of intergroup attitudes. First, the process by which individuals and groups gravitate to a way of thinking is political, gradual, piecemeal, and unselfconscious. Intergroup ideologies are not raw acts of personal expression, they are not exercises in personal logic, they are not formulated in a single sweep, and they are not the result of conscious deliberation. As people grope through their lives, their sensitivity to risks and opportunities teaches them to follow the path of least resistance. Ideas gain favor or are discarded according to their political expediency. The resulting ideology is an amalgam of ideas that are flexibly linked to some core principles. Simple consistency has no place in this process: the rigidity that is inherent in consistency would be nothing more than a political liability.

Second, the character of dominant-group attitudes cannot be reduced to a formula reflecting the blatant manifestation of intergroup hostility in the cognitive, emotional, and behavioral dispositions of the dominant group. In their ongoing attempt to preserve their advantaged position and continue collecting the benefits that come their way, members of dominant groups are drawn to ideologies that obfuscate, rather than simplify, and that seek to preempt or contain hostility, rather than to inflame it.

Third, by the same token, the attitudes of subordinates cannot be viewed in a vacuum. Subordinates are not at liberty to challenge the status quo in any way, shape, or form. They are caught in the institutional and moral framework in which they are the less powerful participants. Thus, compliance should not be confused with either complicity or "false consciousness." Subordinates do not give up resources freely or gladly; nor do they fail to perceive their interests. Subordinates take what opportunities they may to chip away at the edifice that surrounds them, but outright challenge is ruled out or muted by forces beyond their control.

PART II

Three Cases of Inequality

CHAPTER THREE

Expressions of Inequality:
Class, Race, Gender

My empirical analysis centers on three cases of inequality—social class, race, and gender relations in the United States. These constitute the most prominent intergroup relationships in American society and they provide us with telling examples, within a single society, of alternative forms of social inequality. My appraisal of the intergroup ideologies that accompany those relations is in the nature of a comparative case-study analysis. It is geared toward establishing general propositions about the ideological dynamics of unequal social relations. The approach diverges from earlier research, not only in substantive emphasis, but in basic analytic goals and strategies.

In this chapter, I begin by delineating the factors that distinguish the physical profiles of the three cases at hand. The second part of the chapter is then turned over to a discussion of the methodological principles that inform my analysis of the three cases. With this as background, I turn in chapter 4 to the factors that mold the structure of intergroup contact in race, gender, and class relations in the United States, and I delineate the empirical patterns of intergroup contact that mark each of those relations.

THE THREE CASES: DEFINITIONAL PARAMETERS

Class, race, and gender have all generated prominent, longstanding relationships of social inequality in the United States. The three cases have different histories, however, and they present distinctive structural constellations. Among them, they capture a significant range of elements from the spectra of social inequality. In order to make maximal use of these cases to draw inferences about the ideological dynamics of inequality, we need to delineate the features that distinguish the structure of each relationship. In this section, I discuss two fundamental dimensions that define the broad parameters of class, race, and gender relations, respectively: first, the distributive basis for the inequality, and second, the ascriptive rules for group membership. With that material in hand, I take stock of the general profile that is presented by each intergroup relationship, and I describe the empirical definition of group memberships that are used in this study.

Distributive Basis for the Inequality

Social analysts have disagreed about the nature and form of interrelations among economic, status, and power inequalities. The well-known Marxist position has been that economic structure determines the distribution of all kinds of valued assets: any observed inequalities are explicable in economic terms, whether we are concerned with class, race, or gender relations. The Weberian approach, which has gained a wider following, has taken a more agnostic position with respect to both the primacy of economic, status, or power inequality and the question of whether there is any necessary relationship among them.[1]

I assume that economic well-being, high social prestige, and control over decision making are all prized assets. Each has intrinsic value and value as currency to acquire other distributive advantages. For this reason, it is probable that an advantage gained in one asset will be converted into another, both for the amplification of benefits and for the reinforcement of one's dominant position. Thus, I reject the Weberian argument that an important social inequality may exist on one dimension, say status, without embroiling other dimensions of inequality. Yet the deterministic Marxist position that economic inequality has universal causal primacy is also rejected: it takes an unsatisfactorily rigid view of human values and motives.

Expropriative relationships develop between different kinds of groups on the basis of specific pertinent characteristics that the groups possess. Those characteristics may bear most directly on economic, status, or power considerations. Once the primary inequality is established, however, it is quickly reinforced with other distributional inequalities. In the historical growth of an unequal relationship between groups, the three kinds of distributive assets grow into a mutually reinforcing interlock

---

1. Weber was master of the qualified statement. In his essay, "Class, Status, Party" (1946), he at times acknowledged the empirical regularity of interconnections among those three dimensions of inequality, and yet the main thrust of his argument seems to be a cautionary agnosticism with respect to the mutual independence or interdependence of class, status, and party.

that provides the dominant group with both a wide variety of benefits and a strongly fortified position. With this in mind, I now delineate what I see as the primary locus of the inequalities that exist between class, race, and gender groups, respectively.

Class. The core of class relations lies in economic distinctions that are created by the organization of economically productive work. Individuals with an initial advantage in their possession of material assets position themselves advantageously in economic exchanges. They may do this either by expropriating labor from others who have fewer resources at their disposal or by securing more remunerative occupational positions for themselves (such as by purchasing administrative posts in a feudal economy or by purchasing the educational credentials required for entry to more highly rewarded positions in an industrial economy). The economic distinctions that result are highly visible, tangible, and compelling in themselves, but they are buttressed by status and power distinctions.

Differential economic experiences divide the population into socially cohesive groups that develop identifiable subcultures and subjectively salient identifications (Jackman and Jackman 1983). These economic and social distinctions provide fuel for status distinctions that, in turn, reinforce the symbolic boundaries that divide the socioeconomic groupings from one another. Differential access to power, as well, follows effortlessly from the unequal distribution of economic and social resources, even in systems that are organized according to "democratic" principles (see, for example, Lipsky 1968; Bachrach and Baratz 1970; Parkin 1971; Schlozman 1984; Hill and Leighley 1992). And the unequal distribution of power, in turn, is of course critical in securing the continued unequal distribution of economic resources that is the primary basis for class divisions.

Race. The racial division between blacks and whites involves the same ingredients of economic, status, and power distinctions, but they are configured differently. The cultural divide between whites and African Americans provides the material for sharp status distinctions between the two groups. Whites' ability to confer higher status on their own culture and way of life has, of course, been facilitated by their advantaged access to economic resources and to power. The economic benefits that accrue to whites are considerable in themselves, but the particular historical form that whites' expropriation of black labor has taken in the United States cannot be understood without reference to whites' desire for cultural ascendancy in an emerging society. This urgent concern placed status considerations at the core of the relationship between whites and blacks from the beginning, even as white Europeans initiated their relationship with black Africans simply to obtain cheap labor.

Starting in the seventeenth century, black Africans were brought to the North American continent from an alien culture to perform servile labor for those white settlers who had the material means to procure it. White indentured servants were imported contemporaneously from Britain to meet the labor shortage in the American colonies, but black Africans were the only people who were abducted from their homeland and forcibly removed to the American colonies. This unique treatment of black Africans (which flew in the face of established English principles of personal freedom) was made possible by longstanding English beliefs about the inferiority of black people and the convenient preexistence of a slave trade in Africa (Jordan 1968). At a more fundamental level, white Europeans took advantage of their possession of superior material assets (especially in armaments, transportation, and communication) to seize control of black Africans and to assert cultural superiority to them. They also seized upon black Africans' alien language, religion, and mode of dress, their distinctive physical features, and their less advanced level of economic development as evidence to justify their assignation of greater social prestige to white European culture.

In the latter part of the seventeenth century the importation of black Africans began in earnest and legislation was initiated in the American colonies that distinguished sharply between the legal and economic rights of white indentured servants on the one hand and black slaves on the other (Elkins 1968; Jordan 1968). That legislation symbolized and sanctified the cultural abyss between whites and blacks that had already made it morally acceptable for whites to abnegate the civil rights of black Africans exclusively in abducting and transporting them forcibly to America. But once blacks began arriving in large numbers, it was important for whites to solidify their own cultural ascendancy in the colonies by enacting legislation that placed a permanent restraint on the economic and civil rights of blacks.

By sealing the subordination of the cultural aliens in the legal code, whites assured themselves of a ready supply of servile laborers. Beyond the economic benefit (which was after all enjoyed only by whites of some means), whites secured the continued cultural dominance of their group in the major institutions of the emerging colonial way of life. The economic and political degradation of blacks inflicted further pervasive injury on their social status. It also guaranteed a distinctive experience for African Americans that deepened their cultural rift from whites, thus aggravating white concern about the need for racial exclusiveness.

The easy physical identifiability of blacks served to facilitate whites' efforts to assure their cultural dominance. Status claims and prerogatives are more readily enforced because "passing" is a near impossibility, and distinctive physical features provide a constant, visible symbol for the cultural divide between groups. Racial distinctions in physical appearance have thus taken on a heavy symbolic significance that works to reinforce vividly the status differential between groups.

With so many prompts, whites have continued to attach an inferior status to blacks long after the major legal restrictions to their civil and economic rights have been removed, despite the fact that most whites have no more than a cursory historical knowledge of those legal restrictions. Economic and power distinctions continue both to serve and to amplify the status distinctions that divide whites from blacks.

Gender. In gender relations, the core of the inequality lies in control over sexual access and sexual reproduction. Men's greater physical strength gave them an initial advantage in this contest. Men have sought to ensure and maximize their sexual access to women and to guarantee their paternity over the physical offspring of sexual union. Engels ([1884] 1972) interpreted those behaviors as economically motivated (primarily men's desire to ensure that their property was passed on to their own physical offspring). But it is unnecessary to resort to economic motives in order to account for such behaviors. Women and children constitute significant property in and of themselves, providing tangible benefits both economic and otherwise to the male who has exclusive control over them.[2]

Thus, although power is a vital ingredient of any relationship of inequality, it probably has greater primacy in the gender relationship than in class or race relations. Men's control over women and children inherently provides men with tangible benefits in both their personal and worldly lives: it assures them sexual access to women of their choosing; it provides them with human property to satisfy their social, emotional, and economic needs; it maximizes their degree of personal control over their own private lives; and it provides them with tangible assets to assist their worldly standing in exchanges with other members of society. The question of power is important here, not as a means to an end (such as protecting economic and status advantages), but primarily as the central goal in itself.

In this context, the copious status and economic disparities that exist between the sexes function primarily to serve the power differential, even though the status and economic disparities provide ample benefits

---

2. The hostility that gay men and lesbians often encounter doubtless reflects the flagrant threat that their alternative sexual behaviors present to the established rules of sexual expropriation in gender relations.

of their own to men. At the same time, the core distributive inequality between the sexes in personal power has permeated day-to-day life so successfully that it is generally less apparent to the participants than are the attendant status and economic insignia of gender-group membership.

In sum, class, race, and gender relations present distinct configurations of economic, status, and power inequalities. I have argued that the core distributive asset that divides the classes is economic, between the races it is cultural status, and between men and women it is personal power. In each case, the core distributive inequality has been so embellished with others that the benefits of holding the dominant position have not only been reinforced but generously amplified.

Ascription to Groups

In the ascriptive rules for group membership, we can draw an initial distinction between race and gender on the one hand, and class on the other. Race and gender each present a dichotomous division based on a simplified categorization of physical traits that are readily visible and virtually immutable. The boundaries between classes are less sharply drawn; many analysts have pointed to the absence of rigidly defined, objective insignia and the partial mutability of class membership. Thus, scholars have regarded ascription to race and gender groups as routine, but ascription to classes has been the subject of a wide scholarly inquiry that has kindled debate about how many classes there are and the very tangibility of classes as social groups.

Although clear differences exist in the simplicity of group ascription, these differences have been exaggerated and overinterpreted. The differences are one of degree rather than of kind. In all three cases, it is important to remember that the groups are social constructions. Indeed, this is what lends the groups their significance. We can readily distinguish redheads from blondes and brunettes, but these easy physical distinctions are bereft of social significance because they have not become a basis for social organization. The main way in which race and gender differ from class is in the extent to which the rules for group definition have been commonly reduced and simplified. As we inspect those rules, it becomes apparent that their construction is not somehow intrinsically predetermined, but is bound to pressures stemming from the specific basis for the expropriative relationship between groups. I compare the rules of group ascription for race, gender, and social class in terms of two critical elements: the clarity of group boundaries, and the mutability and heritability of group membership.

The Clarity of Group Boundaries.   By social convention, the members of race and gender groups agree on a core set of differences in physical appearance between the groups. Although not everyone may agree on every detail of the physical makeup of each race and sex, the consensually recognized set of physical insignia are so instantly identifiable that they suffice to demarcate group boundaries sharply and effortlessly. In both cases, this is achieved by the rigid application of simplified rules. Those rules virtually eliminate the possibility of ambiguous stimuli and by the same token keep the categorization dichotomous.

With gender, this is achieved by attaching overwhelming significance to one sexual characteristic at the expense of others: genitalia take precedence over everything else, including sexual preference and hormonal makeup. This simplified rule reflects the centrality to the relationship of control over sexual access and sexual reproduction. Incorporation of gradations in sexual preference and hormonal makeup would not serve the distinctions that are critical to that relationship because they are not directly pertinent to its core distributive contention. In addition, those criteria are more prone to subjective definition, and their incorporation would therefore reduce the dominant group's control over group assignment on the basis of the asset in which they are most interested. At the same time, the prime criterion for gender-group membership is socially heightened and made more readily identifiable by its embellishment with gender-specific dress codes that have quick visual recognition and that become imbued with symbolic meaning (Henley and Freeman 1979).

With race, potentially ambiguous stimuli (people of racially mixed parentage) are resolved by assigning overwhelming weight to the presence of any black physical insignia: gradations in skin color or other racially associated physical features are not formally acknowledged. The so-called "one-drop rule," which specifies that just "one-drop" of "black blood" makes a person black, emerged from the American South to become the nation's definition (Myrdal 1944, 113–136; Jordan 1968, 167–178; Williamson 1980, 1–2; Davis 1991, 4–6, 31–80). By the 1920s, it was universally accepted as the rule for assignment to the white or black "race" in the United States (Davis 1991, 31–32).

This ascriptive rule, with its flagrant disregard for standard genetic criteria, is unique to the United States (Williamson 1980, 2; Davis 1991, 32). Intriguing analyses are offered by Jordan (1968) and Davis (1991) of the historical circumstances that gave rise to the "one-drop rule" in the United States, but two factors were probably especially important. First, there was a ready availability of white women to serve as the legitimate sexual partners of white male colonists. In that context, sexual encounters between white males and black women were sub rosa, and the offspring from such encounters were an embarrassment whose existence was painful to acknowledge. The solution was to define them as full members of the subordinate racial group. Second, the continued practice of this strategy was doubtless aided by the fact that white Europeans generally enjoyed the numerical advantage in the American colonies. In the 1700s, whites outnumbered blacks everywhere except in South Carolina (Jordan 1968, 102–103, 141), and over time whites came to outnumber blacks by a hefty margin. Today, blacks comprise only about 12 percent of the population of the United States. If blacks had formed a larger proportion of the population, it might have served whites' control over them to subdivide them according to degree of "blackness." But in the absence of such a constraint, racial status distinctions are preserved with greater clarity by the application of a simple dichotomous scheme in which assignment to the higher-status group is sharply restricted. In keeping with the implicit exclusiveness of white racial status-imperatives, this simplified decision-rule makes it harder to join the higher-status group than the lower one.[3]

Oddly, the lack of formal recognition of gradations in skin color (or other racially associated physical attributes) has not prevented the tendency for whites to confer favored treatment on those blacks with more white-European physical attributes. Increasing evidence has surfaced that in the antebellum South, lighter-skinned slaves were more likely to be appointed to privileged occupations (such as house servants) and to be granted other benefits, including manumission (Myrdal 1944; Mullins and Sites 1984; Keith and Herring 1991). A lighter skin has continued to be an advantage for blacks: recent evidence suggests that skin tone is a consequential predictor of socioeconomic attainment for blacks, even after controlling for such factors as parents' socioeconomic status and other pertinent background characteristics (Keith and Herring 1991). But because racial gradations are not formally recognized, whites' tendency to moderate their discriminatory treatment of blacks in accordance with their manifestation of "white" physical traits remains a sensitive topic that the members of both racial groups are reluctant to discuss openly.

The criteria for class membership are less rigidly defined and there

3. In other nations where whites have subordinated African blacks, the latter have been socially subdivided in some way. For example, in South Africa, blacks were subdivided into sharply differentiated categories: blacks are distinguished from "colored" according to whether their ancestry is entirely black African or partially white European, and further subdivisions are emphasized within the black population on the basis of tribal membership. In Brazil, racial distinctions have taken the form of multiple, amorphous categories based on racial ancestry (various combinations of white European, black African, and indigenous Indian), with boundaries as ragged as those for social classes in the United States. For more detailed discussion and comparison of the economic, demographic, social, and political factors involved in these and other cases, see van den Berghe 1967; Klein 1967; Jordan 1968; Degler 1971; Fogel and Engerman 1974; Baker 1983; Conrad 1983; de Queiros Mattoso 1986; Fogel 1989; Tomich 1990; Davis 1991; and Marger 1994.

is an absence of simplified decision-rules by which gradations in socioeconomic standing might be routinely truncated into a social dichotomy. As even some neo-Marxist scholars have acknowledged (e.g, Wright 1979, 1985), industrial economies have not disgorged two categories of socioeconomic experiences. The technology of industrial production has produced workers of varying levels of education, managerial authority, and income. That those gradations have not been reduced by social convention to a dichotomous classification is a function of forces operating from two different directions. First, the distributive asset that forms the core of the class relationship—economic inequality—has a highly tangible quality that makes it less malleable to symbolic redefinition. Variations in access to economic rewards produce vividly observable differences in the material quality of life that would be difficult to disguise. Second, there is no motivation for those at the socioeconomic pinnacles to attempt such a symbolic redefinition. Because of their relatively small numbers, it is not in their interests to align the rest of the population in a single group against them. Indeed, from a managerial standpoint, it is advantageous to highlight the distinctions within the rest of the population, in order to encourage its fragmentation rather than its social and political solidification. And the effective expropriation of labor in industrialized, capitalist economies has no need for the rigidification of group boundaries: elasticity in the supply and application of labor is more useful in responding to changing technologies and markets, and the incitement to individual achievement is better adapted to the ambitious production goal of economic growth. Indeed, if the technological and political needs of the socioeconomically dominant were operating in solo, one might find a complete absence of classes as meaningful social groups, with socioeconomic distinctions operating as unbroken continua. However, the vividness and tangibility of economic distinctions make them a highly compelling magnet for the formation of subjectively salient social clusters among those who share similar economic experiences.

The admixture of these two different kinds of pressures has resulted in the emergence of several social classes, each one representing a cluster of people with broadly similar socioeconomic experiences, and each one depending for its definition on subjective identification. There is an absence of rigid, explicitly imposed rules for group definition because that would not assist the practice of economic inequality, and, indeed, such rules might work to undermine it. The definition of social classes arises, therefore, from the subjective potency of socioeconomic distinctions that draws people with similar configurations of socioeconomic characteristics toward one another. The boundaries of these social groupings remain relatively ragged because, unlike the racially advantaged and gender-advantaged, there is no incentive for the economically advantaged to impose rigid rules for group ascription.

Thus, in order to identify social classes, analysts must rely heavily on self-placements. There is clear empirical evidence that such self-placements correspond systematically to configurations of objective socioeconomic criteria, such as educational attainment, occupational standing, earned income, capital assets, and level of job authority (those relationships are explored in detail in Jackman and Jackman 1983). But the correspondence is not rigid because rules for group definition have not been explicitly articulated or enforced. The lack of clearly visible, physical insignia for group membership (as compared to gender and race) makes it easier to leave group boundaries ragged; this, however, is not the critical factor obstructing the sharper delineation of class boundaries. Recall that physical insignia are themselves not intrinsically free of ambiguity; they must be invested with symbolic significance and cognitively simplified in order to be useful as tags for groups. By the same token, it would be possible for class boundaries to be rigidly defined according to a clear, objective, socioeconomic referent and reinforced with dress codes or other visual aids—but they are not.

Because of the central role of subjective identifications in the development of socially defined classes, the most efficient way for the analyst to identify those classes is to rely on the class terms that find frequent articulation in popular usage: poor, working class, middle class, upper-middle class, and upper class. Those terms are the symbolic magnets around which groups of people cluster who share similar configurations of socioeconomic characteristics. Although there is no single, consistently applied rule about the exact placement of the boundary between each of these classes, the magnetic force that generated the classes is sufficiently compelling to provide the basis for the growth of meaningful and salient social communities. A detailed discussion and empirical examination of the objective and subjective elements of the social communities that cluster around those commonly used class terms is provided in Jackman and Jackman (1983).

Mutability and Heritability of Group Membership.   Apart from the clarity of group boundaries, ascription to social class has often been regarded as fundamentally different from race and gender ascription because it is relatively mutable. The subjective significance of this distinction remains to be demonstrated, although the prevalence of popular norms about equality of opportunity suggests there is some psychological vulnerability to this distinction. Again, however, the difference between class and the other two intergroup relationships in this factor may have been overdrawn.

The virtual immutability of the physical insignia for race and gender groups makes membership in those groups a lifelong affair for the overwhelming majority of people. For race, group membership also extends across generations, although more rigidly for blacks than for whites. Blacks almost invariably share their racial group membership with their social parents and, even in the case of intermarriage with whites, blacks confer their racial group membership on their children. In practice, because of the small amount of racial intermarriage, most whites also have the same racial status as their parents and children; but in the (unlikely) event of intermarriage, whites cannot pass on their priviledged racial group membership to their children. For gender, this sense of permanence only partially extends across generations: the majority of people have a social parent from each gender group and have no necessary expectation about the gender group of their children.

The imperatives of economic privilege in advanced industrial societies do not rule out the possibility of movement from one class to another; and empirically, there is some mobility from one socioeconomic standing to another. However, although not immutable, the constraints imposed by economic inequalities in practice restrict the volume of such mobility in the population and make movements over short socioeconomic distances more probable than over long distances (see, e.g., Blau and Duncan 1967). The upshot is that some people may attain a different social class in adulthood than the one in which they were raised as children, although such movement is more likely to be between adjacent classes than distant ones. At the same time, most people will share the social class of their parents and their children, either because of an absence of intergenerational mobility or because their mobility is not sufficiently consequential to cause a shift in class identifications. In this respect, the loose social definition of boundaries between adjacent classes assists the retention of consistent class identifications across generations, and, in combination with the hierarchical (rather than dichotomous) structure of the categorization scheme, it diminishes the import of any shift that does take place in identifications across adjacent classes. Viewed in this way, it becomes apparent that, in practice, there is more intergenerational permanence associated with class membership than with gender group membership.

Summary.   In sum, we can delineate a crude distinction between class, on the one hand, and race and gender, on the other, in the clarity and immutability of ascription to groups. That distinction, however, is neither qualitative nor impermeable. I have emphasized that in all three cases the ascriptive rules are not intrinsically predetermined, but are social constructions. As such, their varying nature does not reflect the popular salience of the groups concerned, but instead it reflects the specific social and political pressures that arise from the expropriative basis of each relationship of inequality.

Race, Gender, Class: Defining Parameters

Variation in the expropriative basis of the inequality and in the ascriptive rules for group membership have shaped the physical profiles of the three intergroup relationships. We now take stock of the parameters that define race, gender, and class relations, respectively.

Race.   The deep, historically reinforced rift between black and white Americans is rooted in whites' desire to maintain cultural dominance as they were forcibly importing large numbers of blacks from an alien culture for the purpose of expropriating their labor. The abolition of the slave trade coupled with the continued immigration of Europeans to the United States reduced the numerical threat posed by African Americans, but the cultural divide was hardly diminished by the discriminatory practices that had been established by whites. The social distinction between blacks and whites has been maintained as a simple dichotomy, with visible physical attributes being the criterion for group membership. Gradations in skin color or other racially associated physical features are not formally recognized (as they are in, say, Brazil), and decision-rules instead emphasize a rigid demarcation between the two racial groups in which membership in the higher-status group is treated more exclusively.

Other racial and ethnic divisions have coexisted with the division between blacks and whites (for example, "white ethnics," Asians, Latinos, and Native Americans, all of which are further subdivided into multiple groups). But the presence of these other ethnic groups has not impinged on the historically durable rift between white and black Americans. Today, the physical profile of the race relationship presents itself as a dichotomous division in which the dominant group vastly outnumbers subordinates. Further tacit distinctions among blacks are made on the basis of gradations in skin color, but formally, a person's racial group membership is set at birth in one of two categories. Subordinates always transmit their group membership to their children, but dominant-group members only give their privileged status to their children if they refrain from sexual unions with subordinates.

Gender.   The gender relationship also involves a dichotomy, but here of course the two groups are of about equal size. Coexisting with the division between the sexes are distinctions among gay men, lesbians, and heterosexuals, but again, these distinctions do not impinge on the main lines of the gender relationship. The relationship between men and women is centered on control over sexual access and sexual reproduction, and people are ascribed to one group or the other on the basis of their genitalia. Secondary sexual characteristics (for example, body shape) and dress codes make ascription to gender groups usually instantaneous. As with race, gender-group membership is set at birth (with a few rare exceptions), but both men and women have only about a fifty-fifty chance of passing on their gender-group membership to their children.

Class. Class relations are centered on control over economic resources of production and consumption. They are distinguished from race and gender relations in that the affected groups are less readily determinate. The numerical minority of people who enjoy economic dominance have had little reason to accentuate the distinction between themselves and the rest of the population, and class relations are bereft of any rigidly imposed rules for group membership. The definition of social classes stems from the salience of socioeconomic distinctions that cannot be masked: social classes reflect loose configurations of socioeconomic experiences, with ragged boundaries between them. The definition of social classes and people's class membership relies on self-identification much more heavily than does race- and gender-group membership, and that process is sensitive to distinctions in socioeconomic attainment.

Many analysts have insisted that class distinctions can be treated as a dichotomy, although they have disagreed about its basis (e.g., capitalists versus workers, blue-collar versus white-collar workers, workers with and without authority in the workplace). The class nomenclature most commonly used in popular discourse, however, suggests five social classes: poor, working class, middle class, upper-middle class, and upper class. There is a strong relationship between the class membership of parents and their children, and most people form stable class memberships over their adult lives, but some experience suffecient socioeconomic mobility to alter their class identification from that of their parents or from their own class identification in an earlier career-stage.

Empirical Definition of Group Memberships

The data in this study come from a national survey that was designed to give comparable information on race, gender, and social class in the United States. The questionnaire was administered to a national probability sample of the adult, noninstitutionalized population of the United States in the fall of 1975.[4] Interviews were conducted in respondents'

4. I designed the questionnaire; the pretesting, sampling, interviewing, and coding were administered by the Survey Research Center of the Institute for Social Research at the University of Michigan. The sample is of the adult, noninstitutionalized population,

homes, and every effort was made to match the race of the interviewer with that of the respondent. Membership in race and gender groups was determined by interviewer observation; class membership was based on respondents' self-identifications.

Race. Of the total of 1,914 respondents in the sample, the study includes 1,648 whites (86.1 percent), 195 blacks (10.2 percent), and 71 respondents (3.7 percent) from other racial or ethnic groups (primarily Asians, Latinos, and Native Americans). Analyses of data on race are restricted to respondents who are either white or black.

At the time the study was in the field, the term commonly used to refer to Americans of African descent was "black." That term was used in the questionnaire, and it is thus used predominantly in the book, especially in discussions of data from the survey. However, in the past few years, the term "African American" has gained increasing popularity among many people who formerly called themselves blacks. Survey data from Detroit for spring 1992 indicate that about 32 percent of blacks in that city prefer to be called African American, whereas 44 percent prefer to be called black, and 12 percent have no preference; preference for African American is positively related to education (Farley 1993).[5] Because Americans of African descent were obliged historically to accept whatever names their captors chose to give them, the selection of a particular appellation for the group carries high symbolic significance in contemporary race relations. The term *black* came into vogue in the late 1960s as a rejection by the black community of the term *Negro*, which was associated with slavery and the Jim Crow South. In the hopeful political atmosphere of the 1960s, adoption of the term *black* symbolized a bold break with the racial practices of the Jim Crow South: "Black is beautiful." But in the disillusioned wake of the 1970s and 1980s, a significant portion of Americans of African descent have begun to adopt the term *African American* (especially among the well-educated) because of its more positive emphasis on ethnic heritage rather than on skin color. For that reason, I will at times use the term *African American* interchangeably with the term *black*.

---

aged eighteen and over, residing in the forty-eight contiguous states. The response rate was just under 70 percent, giving a total *N* of 1,914.

5. Responses were to the question, "Which term describes what you like to be called?. . ." Another 6 percent of Detroit blacks preferred to be called Negro, 4 percent colored, and 2 percent were not ascertained; the total number of blacks in the survey was 750. Among those with less than 12 years of education, 24 percent prefer to be called African American and 44 percent prefer black: with increasing education, the percentage preferring black remains fairly constant, but preference for African American steadily increases to 47 percent of the college graduates (Farley 1993).

Gender. The study includes 802 men (41.9 percent), and 1,112 women (58.1 percent). The higher response rate among women is not unusual in public-opinion surveys and is likely related to discrepancies in men's and women's social roles. The dictates of those roles affect both the availability of each gender to survey interviewers who arrive on their doorsteps and the willingness of males and females to comply with requests for an interview.

Class. Because the definition of classes as social groups depends so heavily on subjective identification, ascription to classes in the present study draws on respondents' subjective identification with classes that are frequently termed in everyday discourse. Accordingly, respondents were asked:

> People talk about social classes such as the poor, the working class, the middle class, the upper-middle class, and the upper class. Which of these classes would you say you belong to?

The structure of the class-identification item is discussed in Jackman and Jackman (1983), along with a detailed assessment of information from numerous follow-up questions that probed the meaning of people's subjective class identifications. Those data suggest that most respondents related to the class identification item with ease and that people think of the classes in terms of a graded series of status groups that have their basis in configurations of socioeconomic characteristics.

The distribution of class identifications in the study is as follows: 19 respondents identified with the upper class (1 percent); 157 with the upper-middle class (8.2 percent); 829 with the middle class (43.3 percent); 701 with the working class (36.6 percent); and 145 with the poor (7.6 percent). The tiny remaining balance of respondents gave nonclassifiable responses (1.3 percent), denied the existence of classes (0.5 percent), said "don't know" (1.5 percent), or their responses were not ascertained (0.2 percent). Analyses of data on class are restricted to respondents who identified with the upper-middle class, middle class, working class, or poor. The upper class is too small to provide for reliable inferences about the attitudes or behavior of this group in a standard cross-sectional survey, although we may make inferences about other people's attitudes toward the upper class.

A COMPARATIVE CASE-STUDY ANALYSIS

Analysis of the intergroup attitudes associated with race, gender, and class relations has a venerable but dispersed history. My study is an attempt to capture that dispersed subject matter within a single framework.

In so doing, there is an important shift in the empirical and conceptual terrain that comes into focus.

My empirical framework entails three important departures from the prevailing analytic strategies of previous empirical research on race, gender, and class ideology. First, my interest is comparative, rather than specific to a particular intergroup context. Second, my interest is in the exchange of attitudes in an intergroup relationship taken in its entirety, rather than being restricted to the attitudes that are expressed on one side of the relationship or the other. Third, I treat intergroup attitudes primarily as the property of groups, rather than of individuals, and I examine the pattern of attitudes in the group as a whole as an expression of the group's collective experience. Taken together, these three strategies allow me to shift the focus to general questions about the attitudinal dynamics of unequal intergroup relations. The three points are interrelated, but they warrant separate discussion before taking stock of the implications and limits of my empirical framework.

A Comparative Analysis of Intergroup Attitudes

Class, race, and gender relations in the United States are of considerable intrinsic interest. My analysis of them, however, is motivated primarily by what they can contribute to our more general understanding of the ideology of inequality, treated as a recurrent feature of organized social life.

As I argued in chapter 1, the analysis of class, race, and gender ideology has generally been conducted in discrete bodies of literature, each motivated by localized theoretical and policy concerns. Students of class attitudes have been engaged by the theoretical question of the significance of class as an organizing factor in social life. Reference to other intergroup relationships has only been pertinent to the extent that it bears on the significance of class, not because of any insights that it may offer about intergroup attitudes as a general phenomenon. The separate bodies of research that developed on race and gender attitudes were motivated largely by policy concerns specific to each intergroup relationship. Those concerns consumed researchers' intellectual energies and generally closed out other intergroup attitudes from consideration. Comparative work has been largely confined to the ad hoc assertion of parallels between race and gender in order to validate the credibility of gender relations as a field of inquiry (as I discussed in chapter 1). Such assertions had little impact on the empirical research agenda of either race or gender scholars.

A number of scholars have focused on the way the various forms of inequality intersect with one another, either to create special pockets of grievance in the population (as, for example, in the case of poor African-

American women) or to dilute individuals' sense of grievance among those with inconsistent statuses (as pluralists argue). I will address this issue at greater length below, but for now, we can note that evaluation of the intersections of race, class, and gender presupposes a strong comparative understanding of the three cases. That comparative groundwork is missing.

The comparative student faces a disconnected body of knowledge about intergroup attitudes as a general phenomenon. By the same token, the student of race, class, or gender relations confronts different gaps and unasked questions in any of the intergroup relationships taken singly. The central concern with hostility and conflict found expression in multiple, idiosyncratic frameworks and terminologies that had little to say to each other. Parallel ideas were usually obscured, and potentially relevant ideas from one intergroup context were left unnoticed in another.

Two bodies of literature developed which were motivated by more general questions, public-opinion research on political tolerance and experimental research on the "minimal-group paradigm." In each case, however, the search has been for universals rather than for comparison and variance. The motivating concern of the tolerance literature has been to understand a particular attitudinal phenomenon, with reference to a variety of out-groups. This has not implied a comparative interest in different kinds of intergroup relationships, but more a disregard for intergroup characteristics as a source of explanation. The minimal-group paradigm is premised on the assumption that any group division, created on the basis of any arbitrary or even random criterion, will result in preference-behavior for one's own group. Although many experimental manipulations have been introduced to exacerbate that effect, the phenomenon is conceived as originating in basic, universal, cognitive processes. The emphasis is on how experimental manipulations feed those universal cognitive processes, rather than on how different kinds of expropriative intergroup relations cause the participants to formulate specific kinds of intergroup ideologies.

My approach is directed to the latter question. I assume that in social and political life, some group divisions assume salience whereas others are inconsequential. This occurs because some group divisions impinge on important societal assets: a relationship develops between such groups that reflects their unequal control over those assets. The specific asset that is the central contention between the groups and the way in which the distribution of that asset is organized have important implications for the way the relationship between groups is structured. My purpose is to evaluate the impact of these factors on the kinds of attitudes that are espoused on each side of a relationship. Thus, intergroup attitudes are conceived not as a function of human personality or cognitive procliv-ities, but as cultural expressions that are molded by the structure of a specific unequal distribution of valued societal assets.

To address the central issues involved in the varying ideologies of unequal intergroup relations, I draw on a single, public-opinion survey that I designed to provide comparable data for race, gender, and social class in the United States. The measures that I have employed are an attempt both to capture the conceptual parallels between one literature and another and to apply unique insights from one intergroup locus to another. The use of a systematic, comparative framework opens up new questions about each case and raises more general issues that reach be-yond the confines of any one intergroup relationship.

Each intergroup relationship becomes a data-point in a broader, com-parative context. This casts a different light on each case than is possible when it is treated in solo, thus offering the prospect of a new theoretical understanding of the attitudes associated with any one of the intergroup relationships. But my analysis is not motivated by a primary concern with the indigenous characteristics of any one intergroup relationship. Instead, each relationship is analyzed with a view to its instrumental value as an instructive case of a variant social phenomenon. It is only by a systematic comparison of the ideologies of race, class, and gender rela-tions that we may ascertain the distinctive features of each as well as the general features of ideologies of inequality. By comparing the character-istics of the three relationships, we can begin to formulate ideas about the way the structure of an unequal relationship introduces pressures that shape the attitudinal dynamics between groups.

Intergroup Attitudes as Relational Communications

The second distinctive feature of my approach is that I view the attitudes found in any one group as situated within a mutual relationship that involves an ongoing exchange of communications between groups. Much previous research has been restricted to questions about the attitudes of a single group. For example, there is a readily identifiable body of re-search on whites' prejudice toward blacks, another on women's gender attitudes, another on working-class consciousness, and so on. Intergroup attitudes have in addition usually been treated as a separate issue from group consciousness, the former of interest when examining dominant groups, the latter in subordinate groups. As a result, certain theoretical questions have repeatedly been bypassed, and we have been left with a fragmented understanding. These comments are least true of the litera-ture on class attitudes, where there are a number of empirical studies that compare the attitudes of different classes. However, even there, the primary interest is in the attitudes ("consciousness") of subordinate classes, and the attitudes of other classes are included primarily as a referent, in order to assess the degree to which subordinates deviate from status quo ideology.

In contrast, I treat each intergroup relationship as a dynamic entity and examine the attitudes of both dominant and subordinate groups within that relationship. The attitudes of the members of any single group cannot be fully understood without an appreciation of the context within which the group is operating—that is, the structure of the relationship with another group and the attitudes presented by the other group. In this approach, the ideas that have been associated with intergroup attitudes and group consciousness are fused. The attitudes of dominant and subordinate groups are seen as embedded in an ongoing exchange, in which each side continually influences and is influenced by the other.

Of course, my data are static, offering a snapshot of a dynamic process that has a history and a continuing motion forward. Thus, I rely on cross-sectional comparisons to draw inferences about what causes change over time. That inferential process is framed, however, by an emphasis on the relational interchange between unequal groups. The attitudes of each group cannot be understood in a historical or political vacuum: they must be interpreted within the ongoing exchange of which they are an inextricable part.

Intergroup Attitudes as the Property of Groups

The third distinctive feature of my empirical framework lies in the shift from the individual to the group as the primary focus of attention. Previous research on intergroup attitudes and group consciousness has overwhelmingly focused on individual-level variance in attitudes in the endeavor to answer questions about the causes of those attitudes. Thus, the enduring empirical research questions have been in the following vein: Does an increase in years of formal education make whites less prejudiced toward blacks? Does an increase in personal contact with blacks break down whites' racial prejudice? Are certain personality types (especially authoritarians) more likely to be prejudiced or intolerant? What individual life experiences account for some women having less "traditional" sex-role attitudes than others? What factors in an individual's experience in the workplace (e.g., authority relations, unionization) influence the articulation of class consciousness?

Without denying the validity of variance among individuals, I wish to explore a different avenue of explanation. In this study, I shift the primary empirical burden to the aggregate level of the intergroup relationship taken as a whole. My strategy is to identify the prevailing attitudinal properties of each intergroup relationship and to focus attention on the variance that exists among different kinds of intergroup relationships. My purpose is to uncover and explore sources of variance that cannot be identified within the empirical framework of past research.

There is a necessary relationship between a specific methodology and the substantive questions that come into focus, and the present case is no exception. My shift from the individual to the group as the primary focus of attention invokes both a different methodological strategy and a different substantive emphasis from that common to past research. Individual variance exists within groups both in the intergroup attitudes that are espoused and in pertinent experiential factors. Past research sought to exploit that variance. Such an approach, of course, assumes that the variation that exists within groups captures a broad enough range to be empirically useful. At the same time, that approach places an implicit emphasis on the individual actor as the source of intergroup attitudes. This has encouraged a relatively atomized conception of the individual actor: it is assumed that something should be experienced directly and personally to enter the salient realm of human cognizance.

That assumption is evidenced in standard analytic strategies. It is taken as a given that if a proposition is valid, it will hold true at the individual level. For example, the hypothesis that intergroup contact affects intergroup attitudes has been tested by comparing those members of a group who have had personal intergroup contact with those who have not (rather than comparing groups from different intergroup relationships where the prevailing experiences are different). Similarly, it is routinely anticipated that if authority relations affect workers' level of consciousness, this should be demonstrated empirically by an observable difference in attitudes between workers whose personal experience has been with different kinds of authority relations (rather than examining how the prevailing mode of authority relations may condition the consciousness of workers as a whole). Analysts have sought to test theories by seeing whether they have explanatory power at the individual level.

This has especially been the case in the analysis of racial prejudice, where the phenomenon itself has been conceived as an expression of individual experiential and psychological factors. Thus, when Allport asked, "Prejudice: Is it Societal or Personal?" (1962), he was not posing a choice between the group and the individual as the unit of analysis, but between the individual acting according to the dictates of his personality (for example, prejudice as a function of "authoritarianism") and the individual responding to factors that derive from his social experiences (for example, prejudice as a function of formal educational attainment). In a somewhat similar vein, Tajfel's lengthy discussion of "Individuals and Groups in Social Psychology" (1981) essentially poses the question of the extent to which individual behavior is driven by indigenous biological-perceptual proclivities or is a response to factors acting on the individual from the social environment in which he lives.

In an early commentary on the prejudice literature, Blumer argued that this emphasis on the individual level of experience was misplaced:

> The dominant group is not concerned with the subordinate group as such but it is deeply concerned with its position *vis-a-vis* the subordinate group. . . . The sense of group position is the very heart of the relation of the dominant to the subordinate group. . . . To seek . . . to understand [race prejudice] or to handle it in the arena of individual feeling and of individual experience seems to me to be clearly misdirected. (1958, 4, 7)

Blumer's comments had almost no impact on the research agenda on prejudice. That agenda continued to be dominated by theories that identified individual differences in personality or experience as the root of the problem. Interestingly, even those empirical analyses that have been most influenced by Blumer's work (analyses based on realistic group-conflict theory) have still been drawn to individual-level variance as the explanatory wedge (see, e.g., Wellman 1977; Smith 1981; Bobo 1983; Giles and Evans 1986).

Blumer's notion of "the sense of group position" was perhaps too obliquely defined to have utility as a sharp analytical tool. He stopped short of seeing dominant groups as being driven by tangible interests; his conception of prejudice emphasized the same features as did mainstream conceptions, except that they were transposed to an aggregated level. Hostility toward and derogation of subordinate groups were attributed to a collective cultural process that dealt with subordinates as a symbolic abstraction. Blumer's "sense of group position" was very much a "sense" rather than a tangible "position," which made it an aggregate-level analog of individual-level prejudice. Because it was not linked to specific aspects of the structure of the relationship between groups, the "sense of group position" did not carry a clear enough set of empirical referents to suggest a particular line of empirical inquiry. But Blumer's idea that the problem of prejudice was located in a collective group process did run directly against the prevailing social-reformist current of research on prejudice. That current mandated the identification of specific individual-level factors that might be manipulated to reduce prejudice.

Research on gender and class attitudes has also placed the overwhelming explanatory burden on individual-level variation, even though the phenomenon of interest is not seen as so exclusively within the psychological realm. The literature on class consciousness, in particular, has been shaped by theories that address the macrostructure of society. Yet individual-level motivational factors are still regarded as a critical element, and those factors are seen as primarily the product of direct individual experiences (e.g., Lockwood 1966). Indeed, the common emphasis among students of class, race, and gender attitudes on hostility as a vital ingredient of expropriative intergroup relations is consistent with the broader analytic assumption that the locus of energy is in the individual. If one casts the attitudes of the group as the simple sum of its members' individually generated attitudes, personal feelings of hostility make an intuitively plausible motivational basis for the existence of discriminatory dispositions.

The assumption that the critical energy lies at the individual level is so ingrained in our way of thinking about intergroup attitudes that it is even reflected in the basic methodology of questionnaire-item construction. As Weissberg (1976) has pointed out, a requisite characteristic of good questionnaire items is that they elicit variance in responses, and it is a cardinal rule to avoid items that do not generate reasonable variance. Although this rule is dictated by the pragmatic need for individual-level variance if that is to be the fuel for analyses, it clearly has conditioned the way we define empirical problems. Issues that arouse consensual responses from all the members of a group reveal something about the shared experience of the group. Similarly, issues that elicit consensus from all participants in a relationship tell us about the prevailing values that encase the relationship and that define the limits of the political agenda (Weissberg 1976). Such issues may be especially germane to our understanding of the central currents in an intergroup relationship, but in explanations that hinge on individual-level variance, they are dismissed as "constants" with no utility.

I do not mean to deny that individual variance exists on salient issues or that differences in individual experiences bear on the expression of intergroup attitudes. However, exclusive attention to such individual variation, especially in the context of a single group in a single relationship (for example, whites' racial attitudes or women's gender attitudes), draws the explanatory endeavor away from questions about the overall structure of the relationship. The latter may impinge deeply on the participants in the relationship, constraining the amount of variance to be observed within a single group or relationship.

Consider the question of how the degree of personal contact between groups affects intergroup attitudes. This question has been studied primarily via individual variance among whites in their personal contact with and attitudes toward blacks, and yet there is only limited variance in whites' contact with blacks. Most whites have little or no personal contact with blacks and the intimate end of the continuum is marked by a small minority of whites who can name one friend who is black (or occasionally two). Contrast this with the gender relationship, where the overwhelming norm for intergroup intimacy far exceeds the extreme end of the continuum for race and where the physical separation from subordinates that most whites experience is a rare event for men. Either relationship by itself captures only a portion of the empirical range of human experience that exists across relationships. The variance between the two relationships expands the observable range dramatically and thus offers the opportunity to measure the effects of intergroup contact over a broader spectrum.

The shift to variance between intergroup relationships as the explanatory source, whether or not it increases the observable range of experience, carries with it a consequential shift in the kinds of substantive questions that come into focus. It draws attention to the structural conditions that encase an intergroup relationship and it underscores the point that individual actors are not free agents but are caught in an aggregate relationship. Unless we assume that the individual is socially atomized, her personal experiences constitute only one source of information that is evaluated against the backdrop of her manifold observations of the aggregated experiences (both historical and contemporaneous) of the group as a whole. Even if we are willing to assume that the individual is motivated entirely by selfish concerns (which I am not willing to do), it would still be hasty to assume that her inferences about how best to serve those concerns are based solely or even primarily on her direct experiences. As I argued in the prologue, because the individual is situated within social relations, she cannot help but draw inferences about her own fate from her observations of the experiences of others, especially if she has reason to believe that her fate is linked (either positively or negatively) to those others. Individuals do not have to wait until they are personally knocked down by a hurricane to understand that hurricanes are dangerous.

This is not to say that all members of a group are expected to think the same way. The structural constraints imposed by the organization of an intergroup relationship are not felt uniformly by all members of a group. People are not impervious to their direct experiences. And information is not dispersed evenly to all members of a group. There are channels of communication that systematically influence the information to which individuals are exposed. For example, educational institutions influence people's cognitive style and the kinds of ideas and information available to them: dominant-group members with an advanced formal education are thus likely to espouse a more elaborate and sophisticated ideology to defend their group's interests (Jackman and Muha 1984). Similarly, direct personal contact with members of a subordinate group alters the information available to individual dominant-group members and has been shown to influence some aspects of their intergroup attitudes (Deutsch and Collins 1951; Wilner, Walkley and Cook

1955; Jackman and Crane 1986). Some information also trickles through the group along irregular and unpredictable paths depending on the particular constellation of personal characteristics and experiences that each individual has from childhood through his adult life. And as these individuals meet and interact with one another, some idiosyncratic networks of communication are created that could be either durable or ephemeral. Thus, it should not be surprising that analyses using individual-level data have found that no single explanatory model can account for more than a small portion of the variance among group members in their intergroup attitudes.

The intergroup attitudes that people espouse are not their personal property, devised from their own experience independently, but the property of the group to which they belong. The group's collective experience provides the informational context within which individuals interpret their personal experiences. For although individual characteristics and experiences influence personal gravitation to one kind of attitude or another from those that are arrayed in the collective culture, the array is not infinite but is instead constrained by the limits of the collective experience. As ideas appear, they gain or lose currency according to their efficacy in meeting the political needs of the moment. They may spread rapidly, fizzle out, or gradually become reshaped over time. At any single point in history, the ideological baggage of the group as a whole reflects all these currents, as new ideas are heaped on top of old ones that then become discarded (rapidly or slowly) as they lose their political utility.

As we examine the pattern of attitudes that characterizes each group, we learn about the collective condition of the group as it faces another. We can then ask whether the position of a group in a relationship (dominant or subordinate) produces any systematic tendencies in attitudinal dispositions, or whether completely different rules seem to govern the exchange between groups from one intergroup relationship to another. We can observe whether unequal groups face off in competing, internally unified camps, whether they join together in a common consensus, or whether they are engaged in muted conflict that displays internal divisions within each camp or shifts from intergroup consensus to conflict from one kind of issue to another. By examining such questions across different cases of inequality that manifest widely variant structures, we can formulate ideas about the generality of the attitudinal processes that accompany inequality and their sensitivity to alternative structural pressures.

A Comparative Case-Study Analysis: Analytic Issues

As I draw on the information contained in the three cases, I follow the design of a comparative case-study analysis. This design raises some distinctive analytic issues. My sample of cases is small, all three cases come from a single society, and each embroils all or almost all of the population. I discuss the implications of each of these issues in turn.

Small Number of Cases.   Three cases do not constitute a large enough N for normal hypothesis testing, and, in any event, the cases are not a random selection of the universe of unequal intergroup relationships. Instead, the three cases have been selected purposively, both for their shared prominence in the world's preeminent capitalist-democracy and for the diverse range of characteristics that they capture. My analysis promotes a different way of asking about the sources of intergroup attitudes and of interpreting the meaning of various attitudinal expressions.

Because I am relying on a small, purposive sample of cases, constraints are imposed on the analysis that prevent normal hypothesis testing (see Lieberson 1991 for an excellent discussion of the obstacles to making causal inferences from a small number of cases). The most fundamental problem is that the number of potential explanatory variables exceeds the number of observations. Thus, the inferential process throughout the analysis will necessarily take interpretive liberties. My purpose is to exploit the distinctive features of the three cases in order to explore new propositions about the ideological dynamics of long-term relations of inequality. The three intergroup relationships of race, gender, and social class should be conceived as comparative case studies, each selected purposively to throw a different angle of light on the ideology of inequality. To the extent that the three cases manifest clearly interpretable patterns, I can establish the empirical plausibility of my theoretical framework.

Cases Drawn from a Single Social System.   All three cases are embedded in a single social system at a single historical time-point. This imposes restrictions on the analysis that are both limiting and helpful. Three main implications for the analysis should be noted.

First, patterns observed in these cases may have restricted application to societies with different political or economic structures than the contemporary United States. Since those background factors are held constant across the three cases, the analysis will be unable to elucidate their importance.

Second, by the same token, this restriction simplifies the analytic task somewhat. By holding constant the social and historical milieu, a possible confounding influence on comparisons across cases has been removed. As we compare the three cases, we can rule out the possibility of idiosyncrasies in their social or historical contexts lurking unidentified. In view of the small number of cases, it is helpful to restrict the possible gamut of competing explanatory variables.[6] It becomes possible to focus more sharply on the structural distinctions among the three cases.

Third, we must recognize that there are opportunities for cultural diffusion from one intergroup relationship to another. Ideas that pervade one relationship may creep into another, or ideas that spring from democratic, industrial, or capitalist pressures may seep into the ideology of all intergroup relationships in the society. I return to this issue in the final chapter, but for now, we should recognize that differences among the ideologies of the three cases may be muted by their coexistence within a single social system.

Overlapping Group Memberships. Individual citizens are embroiled in different intergroup relationships, and their multiple group memberships may be crosscutting (as, for example, among middle-class black males) or reinforcing (as, for example, among poor black females or upper-middle-class white males). The impact of this factor on the intensity of group loyalties and the pattern of organized political life has generated considerable speculation and discussion, especially among scholars from the pluralist school (see, for example, Truman 1951; Simmel 1955; Tocqueville [1850] 1969; Polsby 1980). Although pluralists have emphasized the potential for the muting of cleavages by the existence of crosscutting group memberships, equally plausible is the potential for the hardening of cleavages among subcommunities of people who have reinforcing group memberships. There has been increasing interest in the latter possibility (see, for example, Anderson and Collins 1992; Baer and Jones 1992; Blea 1992).

Little direct, systematic, empirical evidence has been brought to bear on this issue, and, indeed, it is premature to map out such possibilities until we have gained an understanding of the general parameters of each intergroup relationship taken on its own terms. For example, if we found that one intergroup relationship involved a deep rift between groups whereas another was pervaded by consensual attitudes, it would clearly be inappropriate to specify a model in which both sets of groups were given equal weight as a draw on people's emotional or political energies. An understanding of the distinctive experiences that belong

6. The advantages of this strategy have been noted in several discussions of comparative social research. For example, according to Lijphart, "The principal problems facing the comparative method can be succinctly stated as: many variables, small number of cases" (1971, 685). To address this issue, he recommends a focus on "comparable" cases, which are "similar in a large number of important characteristics (variables) which one wants to treat as constants, but dissimilar as far as those variables are concerned which one wants to relate to each other" (1971, 687). Parallel arguments have been made by Przeworski and Teune (1970, chapter 2) and Smelser (1976, chapter 7).

to different intergroup relationships logically precedes any expectations about the state of mind of any subcommunities that weld specific combinations of experiences.

In this study, I am concerned with the prior question. I treat each intergroup relationship as a discrete experience shared by aggregates of people on the assumption that the primary stimuli affecting the attitudes pertaining to an intergroup relationship come from the structure and dynamics of that relationship. Recall that I assume people do not rely solely on their own direct experience for information: they also gather and integrate information from other sources, and, indeed, they interpret their own experiences in the light of that other information. People thus learn to distinguish fairly reliably among the multiple sources with which they come into contact, and they develop an appreciation of the regularities in life that create groups with similar experiences. All this suggests that people develop a sensitivity to the constraints posed by the position they hold in a specific intergroup relationship, regardless of their position in other intergroup relationships. The validity of this assumption can be appraised as we assess the degree and pattern of variation in ideology across the three intergroup relationships that are the subject of this study.

Empirically, the nondiscrete nature of race, class, and gender relations bears on the cross-composition of group memberships in the sample in three ways that should be noted. First, there is a relationship between racial group and class membership: blacks are considerably more likely than whites to identify with the poor (about 28 percent of blacks versus 5 percent of whites), somewhat more likely to identify with the working class (about 42 percent of blacks versus 36 percent of whites), and less likely to be middle class or upper-middle class (about 24 percent of blacks versus 55 percent of whites). This is reflected in the racial composition of social classes such that blacks constitute about 37 percent of the poor, 12 percent of the working class, and only about 5 percent of the middle class and 2 percent of the upper-middle class. Second, although gender has no overall relationship to class, women are slightly more likely than men to identify with the poor (about 9 percent of women versus about 5 percent of men).[7] This affects the gender composition of the poor such that it has a higher proportion of women than do the other social classes (women comprise about 70 percent of the poor compared with about 53 to 60 percent of the other social classes). Finally, women are somewhat more overrepresented among black respondents in the sample

7. Women are somewhat less likely than men to identify with the working class (34 percent of women versus 43 percent of men), slightly more likely to identify with the middle class (47 percent of women versus 42 percent of men), and have the same probability as men of identifying with the upper-middle class (about 8 percent).

than among whites (women constitute about 68 percent of blacks and about 57 percent of whites).

These compositional differences and the subgroups that are created by the nondiscrete existence of the three forms of inequality are outside the main thrust of the book. I begin with the premise that people's responses to a particular social relationship are shaped by the exigencies they face in that relationship. By comparing the way race, gender, and class relations are structured and the attitudes that accompany each intergroup relationship, the plausibility of that premise is investigated. Within that analysis, however, the possibility of subgroup variation is not dismissed: all data are checked by subgroup and any instances of subgroup memberships impinging on people's responses to an intergroup relationship will be noted.

SUMMARY

The empirical framework of this study diverges from the main thrust of earlier research on race, gender, and class ideology. My objective is to compare these three different intergroup relationships in order to establish general propositions about the ideological dynamics of long-term relations of inequality. In this chapter, I have prepared for that analysis in two ways. First, I outlined the defining parameters of the three intergroup relationships that are the subject matter of my comparative case-study inquiry. Second, I delineated my strategy for their analysis, and I assessed the methodological and substantive issues that are thus brought into focus.

Class, race, and gender relations differ in terms of the expropriative basis for each relationship and the socially established rules for ascription to the pertinent groups. The social construction of groups and the rigidity and clarity of ascriptive rules are molded by the technological and political exigencies that spring from the expropriative basis of the relationship.

Thus, class relations are bereft of any rigidly imposed rules for group membership, because the numerical minority who expropriate economic resources of production and consumption from others have little reason, either technologically or politically, to define precisely the distinction between themselves and the rest of the population. The social definition of classes arises from the compelling nature of the socioeconomic distinctions and experiences that are put into place by the day-to-day practice of economic expropriation. Inequalities in such tangible items as educational and occupational attainment, income and wealth, job authority, and material standard of living are keenly felt, and people form communities with others whose socioeconomic attributes cluster close to their own. The classes that are thus formed are identified by self-placements: they have ragged boundaries and are neither immutable nor completely heritable, although class memberships are usually stable over people's adult lives and are strongly related to parents' social class. The social classes that find common expression in popular discourse fall into a loosely arranged hierarchy: poor, working class, middle class, upper-middle class, and upper class.

The deep, historically reinforced rift between white and black Americans derives from whites' anxieties about maintaining cultural dominance over African Americans as they were bringing them here for the purpose of expropriating their labor. Whites have sought to protect and solidify their status prerogatives over blacks, and demographics have generally made it unnecessary for whites to be concerned about the lower-status group outnumbering them. Under these circumstances, the social distinction between the two groups has been maintained as a dichotomy that relies on a simplified rule for attribution to groups—the so-called "one-drop rule" by which one drop of African "blood" makes a person black. This rule makes membership in the dominant group very exclusive. It also means that group membership is immutable and generally heritable—except that those whites who form sexual unions with blacks are unable to pass their racial privilege on to their children.

Gender-group membership is also based on a simplified rule that results in the social definition of two groups on the basis of genitalia. Gender relations are based on control over sexual access and sexual reproduction, and thus the basic definition of gender groups avoids acknowledgment of the many shades of sexual preference, since that would only serve to undermine clear rules of sexual dominance. Gender-group membership is generally immutable, but it is the least heritable of the three types of groups in the study—both men and women have only fifty-fifty odds of transmitting their own gender-group membership to their children.

The data for this study come from a probability survey of the American public, conducted in 1975, that was designed to gather comparable information on class, race, and gender relations in the United States. My framework for analyzing these data departs from most past research on the ideologies associated with these intergroup relationships. First, my focus is comparative. Second, I analyze intergroup attitudes as relational communications between contending groups, making it necessary to examine the exchange of attitudes in an intergroup relationship taken in its entirety. And, third, I treat intergroup attitudes primarily as the property of groups, rather than of individuals, in order to assess the pattern of attitudes in the group as a whole as an expression of its collective experience. The resulting framework is in the nature of a comparative case-study analysis. I seek to exploit variance among these three intergroup relationships to explore how the ideological communications between unequal groups are shaped by the constraints and exigencies that each group faces.

The three intergroup relations of race, class, and gender have been selected purposively for the range of characteristics that they capture. As I proceed with their analysis, we must remember that the small sample of intergroup relationships precludes standard hypothesis testing, and their representation of a single society limits our ability to assess the influence of broader historical and social factors. My purpose, instead, is to examine the patterns manifested in these three cases to evaluate the empirical plausibility of new propositions about the ideological dynamics of long-term relations of social inequality.

In the next chapter, I proceed with the core issue of delineating the structure of intergroup contact for each case. I consider different ways that social differentiation between groups may be carried out and the different kinds of constraints that are thus imposed on intergroup communication channels. I then compare the way intergroup contact is structured in race, gender, and class relations in the United States.

CHAPTER FOUR

The Structure of Intergroup Contact

The way in which contact between unequal groups is structured is crucial, for two reasons. First, it tells us how differentiation between groups is implemented in the routine practice of social life. It is this factor that frames the day-to-day presentation of the relationship in people's lives. It constrains the awareness of all participants, even of those whose personal contact with the other group is deviant, because the prevailing pattern defines the common understanding of the relationship within which meaning is attached to specific events and experiences. Second, the organization of intergroup contact has immediate bearing on the way that members of the groups communicate with each other and thus on the kinds of messages that are likely to take hold, both within and between groups. It lays the basic communication grid within which some messages may flow with greater ease than others.

In this chapter, I begin by considering the conceptual distinctions between two major forms of intergroup differentiation—role (or social) segregation and spatial (or physical) segregation. What factors shape the prevalence of one or the other type of segregation, what are the various manifestations that each type of segregation can take, what is the experiential impact of each type of segregation for the participating groups, and what are its implications for communication patterns between groups? I then evaluate empirical data on the prevailing patterns of intergroup contact in race, gender, and class relations in the United States.

ROLE SEGREGATION AND SPATIAL SEGREGATION

Some form of social differentiation is integral to any relationship of inequality between groups: the institutions that accomplish the unequal division of resources constrain the structure of interaction between groups. The specific form of differentiation that prevails in a given relationship is conditioned by the functional mechanics of the expropriation that undergirds the relationship. At the same time, dominant groups do not play an entirely passive part in the matter. Within the bounds set by the functional mechanics of their relationship with subordinates, dominant groups practice exclusionary behavior as a way of buffering their position. The nature of that behavior varies from one relationship to another, as dominant groups follow the path of least resistance and maneuver within the course that is laid out by the organization of the inequality.

In this activity, dominant groups are restrained by one important consideration. Any form of differentiation simultaneously erects some barriers to communication and thus there is a clear disincentive for piling multiple forms of differentiation on top of one another. This would represent an overachievement with accumulating risks to the ongoing task of social control. Indeed, intergroup differentiation presents a delicate dilemma between two countervailing pressures. There is an initial need to differentiate the groups sufficiently to procure the inequality. But this is balanced against the need to integrate subordinates within a common relationship, in order to preserve the orderly flow of benefits. Too much differentiation might rupture the groups apart into disconnected social systems.

In assessing the variance across intergroup relationships in the prevailing patterns of intergroup contact, I make an initial distinction between two broad forms of social differentiation. First is the separation of groups from one another by rules or norms that specify *behavior* according to group membership. This is generally discussed as *role (or social) segregation*. Second is the separation of groups from one another into different *spatial spheres*, which is generally referred to as *spatial (or physical) segregation*. As I argued in chapter 2, all systems of inequality are permeated to some extent by both forms of differentiation, but the specific representation of each varies considerably (van den Berghe 1960). Each form can be manifested in varying guises and in varying degrees, with profound implications for the quality of social interaction within and across group boundaries. I briefly discuss each form of segregation, the pressures that generate it, its different manifestations, and its experiential impact.

Role Segregation

By role segregation, I refer to social rules and customs that specify behaviors on the basis of group membership. These behaviors define the kind of role that group members fulfil in social life—stated more simply, they constrain the way group members may interact with others in society.

In this context, the term "role" takes on a political meaning that it lacks in functionalist uses of the term, which treat roles as more voluntaristic (see, for example, Parsons and Bales 1955). Role segregation incorporates three main types of behaviors. First, groups may be allocated distinctive tasks in economic and social life (occupations and social activities). Second, socially appropriate interpersonal behaviors may be specified for each group, in order to govern both the kinds of behaviors group members may manifest in any social interactions (such as displays of anger, knowledge, affection, concern, fear, or helplessness) and rules of etiquette targeted specifically at interactions across group lines (such as manifesting assertiveness and self-assurance or submissiveness and diffidence). Third, dress codes may be established for each group to aid in the identification of group members and to heighten the social distinctions between groups. Various elements of role segregation have been addressed by different scholars, and many of the pertinent issues were discussed earlier in chapter 2. For excellent discussions of the multiple aspects of role segregation, see van den Berghe (1960) and Reskin and Roos (1987).

Any system of inequality entails at least some rudimentary role segregation, insofar as the distributive process that divides the groups generates distinctive tasks and perquisites for the respective groups. It is also the case that role segregation always carries in its trail some spatial segregation, since the specialization of tasks and perquisites alters the odds of each group's presence in various physical arenas. These observations do not take us very far, however. The specific character of role segregation and its interpenetration with physical segregation vary significantly across intergroup relationships.

Role prescriptions may be highly elaborated with great specificity or they may be only loosely formulated. They may be rigidly or casually applied. They may have a broad reach that radiates over many domains of activity or they may be narrowly restricted to but one or two domains. Three factors seem especially germane to an understanding of such variation. First, role prescriptions are most likely to be found in domains of activity in which the conduct of the inequality between groups requires sustained interaction between the groups. Second, the more critically those interactions bear on the nexus of the inequality between groups, the more sharply will the role prescriptions be drawn: those are the areas in which the dominant group has the strongest interest in avoiding any ambiguity about the activities and behaviors that are appropriate to the respective groups. Third, role segregation should play a more pervasive part in the conduct of relationships in which the core distributive process throws a large portion of the people in the affected groups into personal interactions across group lines, especially when those interactions are sustained. Such relationships provide both the greatest opportunity for and the most pressing need for role segregation to maintain group boundaries. Thus, we may generally expect to find well-elaborated and strictly applied rules for behavior in at least one or two domains of activity that constitute significant distributive contact-points in an intergroup relationship. But role prescriptions are most likely to have a pervasive reach over many domains of activity and to have a rigid intrusion into the pattern of social life when the core distributive process throws the respective groups into close physical proximity.

The joint effect of these three factors on the structure and significance of role segregation is illustrated in the three intergroup relationships of interest in this book. In industrial class relations, the allocation of people to distinctive roles in the economy may be regarded as the fundamental basis of the inequality. Rules for group-appropriate behavior are thus most clearly specified in the core distributive context of the workplace, where interaction between representatives of the affected groups establishes the framework of the relationship between groups. Workers are supposed to perform the tasks that their employers dictate; it is taken for granted by all concerned that this rule conditions their relationship. But because the distributive process of industrial production tends to clump people together according to the occupational roles they perform, there has been little development of role prescriptions for personal behaviors. Thus, there is a general understanding that social class membership is associated with the performance of different kinds of occupational tasks, but this does not carry over into elaborated specifications about appropriate personal behaviors outside the workplace. Even in the workplace, the personal behaviors that are circumscribed are limited almost entirely to the conduct of work tasks and the maintenance of authority relations.

Contemporary American race relations do not contain the elaborated codes of race-specific personal behaviors that they did in the slave economy of the antebellum South when personal contact across racial lines was the norm. As the race relationship was reshaped by industrialization, African Americans continued to be assigned economic tasks that were consistent with the lower cultural status to which whites had relegated them. And in keeping with the continuing central significance of cultural status to the race relationship, some personal behaviors that have traditionally been associated with African Americans, such as the speaking of "black English," have continued to be circumscribed by whites as inappropriate for occupational tasks involving responsibility or authority. The same delimitation applies to spoken accents associated with lower-class whites, but it is more intensely and rigidly applied in the case of black English. At the same time, however, other personal behaviors have generally slipped out of the reach of racial role prescriptions: with the decline in physical proximity between the races that was engendered by industrialization, personal behaviors became less significant to the maintenance of the inequality. Rules of racially appropriate personal behaviors were sacrosanct in the master-slave relations of the antebellum South, and they continued to have high social significance in the share-cropping relations of the rural South. But they have faded from the consciousness of whites as African Americans have been banished to more distant, remote physical enclaves.

In gender relations, the core distributive process (sexuality and sexual reproduction) necessitates sustained, personal relationships across group lines, making it imperative for the dominant group to set clear rules that condition the quality of all interactions that take place. This dictates rigid role specifications that have a broad reach over many domains of activity and that infuse even minute aspects of personal behavior and dress (see, for example, Henley and Freeman 1979; Bell and Newby 1976; West and Zimmerman 1983; Cancian 1987). The most sensitive domain of activity is the home and family, and it is in this context that rules for group-appropriate behavior find their most elaborated specification. The institution of the family is saturated with commonly understood rules about the responsibilities and perquisites of its constituent members. The specification of personal behaviors is so intrinsic to the relationship, however, that the rules radiate out to be applied to any situation in which men and women find themselves in personal contact. Rules governing personal interactions between men and women are applied as ingrained habits, even in situations where the woman may have been given the same task-actitivies as the man (for example, with male colleagues in the same occupation and authority-rank at work, women may still be expected to exhibit such female traits as deference and sexual submissiveness). More commonly, as women venture out of the designated female realm of domestically focused activities, they are steered into distinctive occupations that are a consistent extension of the same ingrained rules about appropriate "feminine" personal behaviors: much has been written on the pervasiveness of occupational sex-segregation (see, for example, Blau and Hendricks 1979; Treiman and Hartmann 1981; Reskin 1984; Bielby and Baron 1986; Jacobs 1989; Reskin and Roos 1990).

Spatial Segregation

Role segregation dovetails into spatial segregation. As dominant groups seek to differentiate themselves from subordinates, they pattern their practices within the lines set by the structure of the distributive process from which their advantaged position is derived. As I noted above, any division of tasks and perquisites accomplishes some physical separation of the groups. For example, even in gender relations, which create unusually high physical proximity between the groups, role prescriptions have reduced the physical presence of women in the workplace and have led to employed women performing functionally distinctive jobs that may locate them in different physical sites within the workplace (see, for example, Reskin and Roos 1987, 1990). By the same token, in all intergroup relationships there are at least some physical sites that lack built-in task-specifications for the respective groups. In such situations, dominant-group members may rely on other group-designated behavior-codes or dress-codes to maintain boundaries, or they may resort to spatial exclusiveness. If they exercise the latter option, subordinates' physical presence might be banned completely from the site in question, or physical restrictions may be placed on their access to the site. For example, according to orthodox Jewish practice, women cannot worship side-by-side with men, but they may attend religious services if they sit in a separate section of the synagogue. Similarly, men sometimes retreat to clubs based on mutual fellowship and loyalty, such as college fraternities: in such clubs, women's presence is tolerated only if it is within the confines of designated role prescriptions, such as maids, social assistants, or sexual playthings (see, for example, Martin and Hummer 1989). For these reasons, no intergroup relationship is likely to be completely devoid of spatial segregation, just as some form of role differentiation is a given. However, the relative importance of each in the practice of the relationship depends on the degree to which the distributive process steers the groups physically together or apart. When the groups are pushed further apart, the symbolic significance of spatial separation is heightened among the participants.

As with role segregation, spatial segregation may be practiced in a variety of ways that profoundly shapes its experiential impact. Most important is the elementary point that different forms of spatial segregation impose varying degrees of physical distance between the respective groups. Spatial segregation may involve any one or a combination of the following three practices, each of which imposes increasingly greater physical distance between the groups:

1. The allocation of groups to different parts of the same facilities (such as men and women seated in different sections of an orthodox synagogue, whites and blacks seated in different parts of Jim-Crow buses) or to use of the same facilities at different times (such as whites and blacks given different times to use recreational facilities in the Jim-Crow South).

2. Allocation of different groups to separate, sometimes adjacent, fa-

cilities (such as men's and women's bathrooms, white and black bathrooms in the Jim-Crow South).
3. Allocation of different groups to distinct residential areas (such as ghettos for Jews in the history of many European and Middle-Eastern cities, residential segregation by race and class in contemporary urban America).

Racial segregation in the Jim-Crow South involved all three practices, but it relied primarily on the first two in conjunction with considerable role segregation by race as well. I believe it is that package of practices that many Americans, even today, commonly understand to be meant by the term *segregation*. Racial segregation in the contemporary United States, however, is marked predominantly by the third type of spatial segregation—urban residential segregation.

Spatial-segregation practices that introduce the least physical distance between the groups are those that specify separate use of the same facilities. This is done either by allocating a separate part of the same facility to each group (for example, as when Southern blacks were restricted to traveling at the back of the bus), or by specifying separate times of usage (for example, as when Southern blacks were granted access to sports facilities or parks at different times than whites). This is likely to be practiced in situations where physical proximity is unavoidable but where there is no embedded task differentiation along group lines. In such situations, dominant groups preempt the possibility of subordinates approaching them on an equal-status basis by imposing physical barriers between the groups. By assigning subordinates to less desirable space or times, the practice additionally serves to make a statement about status prerogatives.

This kind of physical barrier has a contrived quality that makes it more conspicuous to all the participants than are the behavioral barriers that are incorporated in role definitions. Yet this form of spatial segregation is the least removed from role segregation in its experiential impact, and, indeed, it is most likely to be practiced in relationships that are dominated by role segregation but in which there are residual arenas of activity that throw groups onto common ground that is role-neutral. In the Jim-Crow South, African Americans and whites occupied fairly well-differentiated roles in economic, social, and political life that regulated a considerable amount of personal contact between the races, but the role segregation was not pervasive enough to radiate over all realms of activity. This primitive form of spatial segregation, along with the allocation of separate facilities when feasible, covered any potentially ambiguous terrain.

The rules that governed the separate seating of blacks and whites in buses in the pre-civil-rights South exemplify the blurred line between role segregation and primitive spatial segregation. The rules regulating racially segregated seating in Montgomery buses in the 1950s blended spatial separation of the races with behavioral prescriptions for racial deference in access to seats. The first few rows were reserved for whites' exclusive use and were off-limits to blacks even if there were no whites on the bus and all blacks' seats were filled. At the same time, if all the white seats were occupied, blacks sitting in seats closest to the reserved white rows were required to yield their seats to whites entering the bus (King, Jr. 1958, 41). In this way, only the whites' seating was exclusively bounded, and the physical line between black and white seating moved backwards in the bus to accommodate white demand without removing the physical barrier between the races. Thus, Rosa Parks was arrested in 1955, not for breaking the spatial rule, but for her violation of the deference rule when she refused to yield her designated "black" seat to a white in a crowded bus (King, Jr. 1958, 43).

With increased community resources, this form of spatial segregation may be elaborated to the provision of separate, often adjacent, facilities for the respective groups (as in the Jim-Crow South). Its main effect is to place a somewhat greater physical distance between the groups in the domains of activity that are thus segregated. This further reduces the possibility of personal contact in segregated areas, thereby obviating the need for behavior prescriptions to cover situations in which members of the unequal groups might find themselves interacting with one another in the same physical space. At the same time, it allows the dominant group to reinforce status distinctions more definitively through the spatial rules themselves—by making the parallel facilities of unequal quality. For example, in 1915, South Carolina spent almost $14.00 per capita on white schools but only $1.00 per capita on black schools, and the school year for white children lasted twice as long as for black children (Robertson and Judd 1989, 176). In essence, subordinates are expected to submit to the superior status of the dominant group by accepting the inferior facilities that have been allocated to them: the deference rule is built right into the spatial rule.

Thus, the allocation of separate facilities further heightens the symbolic value that is attached to the spatial separation of the groups, and physical closeness to subordinates begins to assume a repugnance for members of the dominant group. In cases where some domains of activity are ruled by role segregation and other domains are spatially segregated, members of the dominant group learn to distinguish between the two with ease. For example, in the Jim-Crow South, a white matron might have felt quite relaxed with her black maid in her home, since the role segregation between them was sufficient to preserve her status prerogatives in that setting. But she would probably have been repelled at the prospect of eating in the same restaurant with either her maid or other "colored folk," since physical proximity in that context would violate white status prerogatives.

The provision of separate facilities for the unequal groups retains a fairly high profile in people's day-to-day lives, but it does not have quite such a high profile as the more rudimentary version discussed above. The segregation is more conspicuous when the groups can see each other seated in different parts of the same theatre than when they are seated in different theatres. It also affords subordinates more insulation from the dominant group. Once they are within the facilities that have been allocated to them, subordinates are released from the mindful supervision of the dominant group. This accords them a measure of personal freedom that they cannot achieve in situations that are spatially segregated in the more makeshift way that was described above. However, as long as the facilities are adjacent or nearly so, there is still a tacit recognition that the expropriative basis to the relationship does not permit wide physical separation of the groups. In view of this, subordinates can only break partially free from the role prescriptions that adhere to their group.

As the mode of distribution tends to clump the members of different groups into separate physical domains, the normal day-to-day practice of the relationship leads to fewer interpersonal contacts across group lines and robs such contacts of their built-in status demarcations. Under these conditions, wide physical separation of the groups becomes the natural strategy for the dominant group as it reinforces socially the structural tendencies that already exist. This strategy is facilitated by the advent of sophisticated systems of mass communication and transportation, most notably the telephone, television and radio, the automobile, and mass transportation systems, all of which make it possible for people to communicate and travel over much greater distances than was formerly possible. These technologies allow for wide spatial separation of the groups without severing all contact between them.

Those are the circumstances that have spawned the form of spatial segregation with which we are familiar in contemporary American race relations and class relations—urban residential segregation. When the conduct of the unequal relationship hinges on use of the aggregated labor rather than the personal labor of subordinates, the development of separate residential areas follows readily. Residential segregation by class is accomplished with little concerted effort: if personal access to lower-wage workers is not required for expropriative purposes, individuals with more economic resources can separate themselves from such workers residentially simply by situating their own residences in clusters (neighborhoods) that contain no properties that are small or humble enough to be within the financial reach of those with fewer resources. With the advances in mass communication and transportation, even those workers to whom one requires personal access (such as servants or other household workers) need not reside nearby.

Some residential segregation by race follows in the wake of class segregation. Because of racial role segregation, African Americans have been disproportionately relegated to lower-wage occupations and that by itself would have resulted in some racial residential segregation, given the preexistence of class residential segregation (Massey 1990). However, the extreme form of racial segregation that holds in many American cities (referred to as hypersegregation by Massey and Denton 1989, 1993) has been brought about by the intervention of governmental policies, laws, and Supreme Court decisions that fostered and enforced residential segregation by race (Taylor 1986; Robertson and Judd 1989; Judd 1991; Massey and Denton 1993). For example, during the New-Deal and post-World-War-II years, the Federal Housing Administration and the Veterans Administration actively promoted the development of racially segregated neighborhoods as they underwrote a substantial portion of the housing construction that built the suburbs. Their financing programs for housing explicitly favored white applicants or required racially segregated housing developments. These federal policies were supported by law and amplified by local government policies and the enforced racial segregation of educational institutions and public facilities.

In small towns or villages, residential segregation does not accomplish wide physical separation of the groups because the total unit size is still small. But the industrialization process that has aggregated labor relations has by the same token created large urban areas. Urban residential segregation achieves an unprecedented physical separation of the groups—it maximizes the spatial distance between the groups and it radiates over many domains of social life as separate schools, shopping, places of employment, and recreational facilities follow effortlessly from the existence of separate neighborhoods. Spatial segregation in neighborhoods thus spills over into all walks of life, creating de facto physical separation of the groups throughout social life.

In addition, Massey (1990) has demonstrated convincingly that the combined effects of class and racial residential segregation have led to further economic losses for urban, poor blacks, contributing to the problem that is commonly known as the "urban underclass": a lower tax base, poorly equipped schools, deteriorated housing, fewer stores, fewer jobs. Because of the flight of capital from such areas of concentrated poverty, negative economic outcomes spiral disastrously for the African Americans trapped there, and residential segregation thus helps whites retain a larger share of the nation's economic resources. And the poorer material quality of segregated black neighborhoods also reinforces the status differential that whites maintain between themselves and African Americans.

Even as the physical separation of the groups acquires new heights of symbolic significance in the practice of the relationship, this system of segregation places most members of the dominant group at such a wide spatial distance from subordinates that the latter become a depersonalized abstraction for them. The typical dominant-group member thus maintains the physical separation without consciously taking any active steps in his day-to-day behavior. Although racial residential segregation was promoted by governmental policies and it continues to be supported by institutionalized practices in the real estate industry, the individual white residing in a white neighborhood is blissfully unaware of such policies and practices. And because so much subsequent spatial segregation follows de facto as the afterbirth of residential segregation, the individual white is likely to feel quite blameless in the whole affair. Whereas many forms of social segregation and the two more rudimentary forms of spatial segregation require the active participation of all members of the dominant group for their maintenance (albeit by habit), individual dominant-group members can reap the benefits of residential segregation without lifting a personal finger to bring it about. This is not to say that whites are reticent to lift a personal finger when the need arises—but most of the time, the institutionalized processes are sufficient to maintain residential segregation and its afterbirth, without active participation by individual whites, and hidden from their view.

Because of the unique way in which contemporary residential segregation has been realized, it is not enforced as rigidly or consistently as the other forms of spatial segregation. The degree of racial residential segregation varies somewhat from one city to another (Massey and Denton 1987), and whites often fail to be vigilant about minor lapses in the pattern.[1] At the same time, this form of spatial segregation achieves a

1. Although the practice of racial residential segregation clearly reflects the prevailing preferences of whites, there is no evidence that individual whites who find themselves in physical proximity to blacks in their neighborhoods, schools, or workplaces do so out of personal choice (Jackman and Crane 1986, 483–485). Situations that throw whites and blacks into proximity occur in individuals' lives as accidents over which they have little or no control: such people are simply caught in a "lapse" in the prevailing (but imperfect) pattern of spatial segregation. There is no evidence that whites with positive racial predispositions self-select into neighborhoods or places of work in which blacks are present, or that the whites who are least tolerant of exposure to blacks are those who exit such situations. People's options for residential and job mobility are constrained by many factors other than their racial predispositions. This means that blacks who find themselves in physical proximity to whites may have no specific expectations about the initial reception they will

physical separation of the groups that is unprecedented in its scope and pervasiveness. Indeed, because of this, unremitting enforcement would only have the effect of rupturing social relations between the groups entirely.

Differentiation and Communication

Role segregation and spatial segregation each present their own hazards to social control, but I have stressed that the latter subjects a relationship to more strain. Strict and pervasive spatial segregation would obliterate one-to-one contacts between groups and thereby severely reduce opportunities for the dominant group to penetrate and control the social awareness of subordinates. Spatial segregation also has the effect of lumping together people within each group, fostering communication channels within groups and thus further hampering the social containment of subordinates. Strict role differentiation is primarily subject to the risk that the attendant sharp disjuncture in social experiences may throw up an impenetrable barrier to effective communication—the world frame of each group may then become unfathomable to the other (Rubin 1983; Cancian 1987). However, in the context of sustained and intimate personal interactions, this danger is mitigated critically because the members of the dominant group are provided with ready access to the hearts and minds of subordinates while communication channels within the subordinate group are simultaneously restricted.

The structure of intergroup contact is thus a sensitive indicator of the general experiential presentation of an unequal relationship, and it also tells us about the kinds of channels that are available (personal or aggregated) for communication across group lines. I expect these factors to have a profound effect on the receptivity of subordinates to different kinds of messages and on the proclivity of dominant group members for various forms of persuasion. Whether an intergroup relationship is structured intimately or distally preconditions the participants to different kinds of ideological communications.

DATA: INTERGROUP CONTACT IN THE THREE CASES

I now compare data on the prevailing features of intergroup contact between whites and blacks, men and women, and different social classes in the United States. Certain aspects of the intergroup contact in these relationships are well known. It is widely recognized that contemporary race relations in the United States manifest a pronounced form of resi-

---

receive from the individual whites involved, but there is certainly no reason for them to anticipate an initially warm reception.

dential segregation whereas the practice of gender relations relies heavily on role segregation; class relations exhibit an admixture of less pervasive forms of residential and role segregation. As we examine data for each case, the distinctions among them will be clarified. My concern is with intergroup contact as an experiential factor in intergroup relations, and my data are thus drawn exclusively from respondents' reports of their contact with the members of other groups.

The data are divided into three spheres. First, I consider the degree to which the groups are physically insulated from one another. Second, I evaluate the significance of role segregation in governing interaction between members of unequal groups. Here, I am concerned not with the opportunities for interpersonal contact across group lines but with the presence of rules that condition the quality of such interactions. These alternative kinds of differentiation impose distinctive constraints on the volume and character of affiliative ties between groups, and this is the third manifestation of intergroup contact that I examine.

Physical Insulation of Groups

Tables 4.1, 4.2, and 4.3 present data on people's reported exposure to their own and other groups in selected social settings. These data give us a picture of the degree to which spatial separation of groups is experienced in race, gender, and class relations. Because of the known pervasiveness of spatial segregation in race relations, the questionnaire contained more questions about the racial composition of various social settings than about their gender or class composition. I asked people about the racial composition of the following social settings:

The neighborhood you now live in

All the people at work whom you come in contact with at least once a week or so

The people where you go shopping

The high school nearest you

The grade school nearest you

All the people who are in clubs or organizations that you are involved in [respondents had previously indicated involvement in clubs or organizations from a list]

Respondents were provided with the same response options for each question: "all black, mostly black, about half black and half white, mostly white, all white." I asked about the gender composition of the second and last of those social domains (workplace and clubs/organizations), with the five response options ranging from "all women" to "all men" in a parallel format to that for race. I asked about the class composition of the first and last of the social domains (neighborhood and clubs/organizations); in each case respondents were asked "are they mostly poor, work-ing class, middle class, upper-middle class, or upper class?" (all mentions were recorded). In tables 4.1, 4.2, and 4.3, "don't know" responses are also included in order to show cases where there is only a hazy awareness of the pertinent group composition.

In comparing the data on spatial segregation for race, gender, and class, two constraining factors must be recognized. First, for race and gender, the group division is a dichotomy, whereas for class the division is into five graded groups. This frames the pattern of physical segregation differently for class than for race or gender. In class relations, the mem-bers of each class experience a pattern of contact with each of multiple other classes, making more complex and differentiated channels of con-tact possible among all the groups encompassed by the relationship.

Second, the relative size of the respective groups varies from one inter-group relationship to another. In the relationship between whites and blacks, the dominant group has been in the numerical majority by far (in the 1970s blacks comprised less than 12 percent of the population). The gender relationship is between two groups of about equal size. And in class relations, the working class and the middle class each comprise about 40 percent of the population, whereas the classes at either extreme are considerably smaller: the poor and the upper-middle class are each about 8 percent of the population, and the upper class is a minuscule 1 percent. These differences are important because any lapses in spatial segregation are likely to be felt disproportionately by groups that are relatively small: where physical contacts involve the same absolute num-ber of people from each affected group, this constitutes a larger propor-tion of the smaller group. This issue is discussed by Lieberson (1980, chapter 9), as it bears on the estimation of residential segregation, and Massey and Denton (1987) apply this factor to the estimation of trends in urban residential segregation for blacks, Hispanics, and Asians from 1970 to 1980. In any imperfectly practiced system of spatial segregation, the relative size of the groups is thus consequential in terms of who bears the experiential brunt of lapses in the physical insulation of the groups. When the dominant group outnumbers the subordinate group, the prac-tice of spatial segregation at anything less than a perfect level affords the dominant group the opportunity to insulate itself from subordinates without granting the same degree of insulation to the subordinate group.

This factor applies especially to contact between whites and African Americans, since whites are in the overwhelming majority. Contacts in-volving only a small proportion of the white community can effectively invade the lives of a considerably larger proportion of the black commu-nity, and blacks are more exposed to whites on a day-to-day basis than vice versa. In class relations, the two classes that have the numerical

TABLE 4.1.   Respondents' Reported Exposure to Blacks and Whites in Selected Social Settings, by Race.

	All Own Race	Mostly Own	Half & Half	Mostly Other	All Other	D.K.	Base N[a]
			Reported Racial Composition				
Whites:							
Neighborhood	65.1%	30.4	3.1	1.0	0.1	0.3	1632
Workplace	43.4%	45.6	10.3	0.0	0.2	0.3	870
Shopping Center	14.1%	65.8	18.3	0.9	0.1	0.9	1627
High School	15.9%	50.3	12.1	3.7	0.1	17.8	1631
Grade School	24.1%	47.0	9.0	3.3	0.2	16.3	1633
Clubs/Orgs.	48.3%	46.6	4.6	0.1	0.2	0.2	901
Blacks:							
Neighborhood	28.4%	39.2	19.6	11.9	1.0	0.0	194
Workplace	8.2%	24.7	37.1	21.6	8.2	0.0	97
Shopping Center	3.1%	13.4	52.1	24.7	4.6	2.1	194
High School	9.3%	23.2	37.6	14.9	0.5	14.4	194
Grade School	8.8%	34.5	31.4	13.9	0.5	10.8	194
Clubs/Orgs.	42.0%	25.0	23.2	8.9	0.9	0.0	112

[a] Excludes respondents with missing data on the pertinent variables.

advantage are the working class and the middle class. All other things equal, people in these two classes have more opportunity to insulate themselves from other classes than do people in the poor, the upper-middle class, or the upper class.

Race.   The data in table 4.1 suggest pervasive but incomplete spatial separation of blacks from whites. Because whites outnumber blacks so heavily, the system works asymmetrically, affording more racial insulation to whites than to blacks. In addition, racial segregation attends some social settings more than others.

Whites are more likely to be insulated from blacks in their neighborhoods than in any other setting, with 65 percent describing their neighborhoods as "all white" and another 30 percent saying they are "mostly white." Whites are somewhat less insulated from blacks in their workplaces and in the clubs or organizations to which they belong, with fewer than half describing either of those settings as "all white." Whites are most likely to be exposed to blacks in their shopping districts, which are described as "all white" by only 14 percent of whites. Local schools are also less likely to be described as "all white," but note that schools are the only place where any appreciable number of respondents say they don't know the racial composition: some respondents without school-age children presumably pay little attention to their local schools. If one disregards the "don't know" responses, 19 percent of the remaining whites describe their high schools as "all white" and 29 percent describe their grade schools in this way.

Although these six settings vary considerably in the extent to which they afford racial exclusiveness to whites, it is important to bear in mind that as many as 65 percent to 95 percent of whites describe any one of these settings as either "all white" or "mostly white." Consider also that the overwhelming majority of "mostly white" responses probably indicate the presence of either a single black or at best only a few blacks. Thus, although the majority of whites are unlikely to experience complete insulation from blacks in any setting other than their neighborhoods, they are also unlikely to encounter more than a token representation of blacks.

The experience for blacks is somewhat different. The lapses in spatial segregation penetrate the relatively small black community more deeply than the larger white community. This is manifested in two main ways. First, blacks are less likely than whites to experience complete racial insulation. The setting in which blacks are the most insulated is in the clubs and organizations to which they belong: 42 percent describe them as "all black." Fewer than one-third of blacks say they live in neighborhoods where all the residents are black, and fewer than one-tenth describe any of the other social settings as "all black." In all, about two-thirds of blacks describe their neighborhoods and their clubs and organizations as either "all black" or "mostly black," and between about 17 percent and 43 percent describe any of the other four social settings in those terms. Second, when blacks do encounter whites, they are more likely than whites to experience either a similar numerical presence of the other group or to be outnumbered by the other group. Between one-fifth and one-half of blacks describe any of the six social settings as being comprised of roughly equal numbers of blacks and whites, and another one-tenth to one-third of blacks describe any of those settings as either "mostly white" or "all white." Thus, blacks are not only more likely to experience contact with whites than are whites with them, but they are also more likely than whites to experience contact in settings where their presence is a token one only, with the other group in clear numerical dominance.

Gender. Outright spatial segregation of groups is patently less of a factor in gender relations, and men and women experience a high degree of proximity in their neighborhoods, schools, and homes. Role segregation is a more pertinent organizing principle in gender relations, but it does spill over into spatial segregation in some social settings. Table 4.2 suggests that each gender group experiences considerable physical insulation from the other in the workplace and some in clubs and organizations as well.

TABLE 4.2.   Respondents' Reported Exposure to Women and Men in Selected Social Settings, by Gender.

| | *Reported Gender Composition* | | | | | | |
	All Own Gender	Mostly Own	Half & Half	Mostly Other	All Other	D.K.	Base N[a]
Men:							
Workplace	22.4%	42.3	28.0	5.6	1.0	0.7	586
Clubs/Orgs.	9.3%	34.6	51.7	3.5	0.7	0.2	460
Women:							
Workplace	6.1%	38.9	38.5	13.3	2.9	0.2	442
Clubs/Orgs.	11.9%	35.9	49.0	3.1	0.0	0.2	582

[a] Excludes respondents with missing data on the pertinent variables.

Men's larger numerical presence in the workplace has afforded them more gender insulation from occupational segregation than women experience. Almost one-quarter of men describe their work environments as comprised entirely of men, while only 6 percent of women say they work exclusively with women. In all, about two-thirds of men say their work environments are entirely or mostly male, and almost half of women report that they work entirely or mostly with women. This asymmetry is also evident in the slightly higher proportion of women (16 percent) than of men (under 7 percent) who report that their workplaces are comprised entirely or mostly of the opposite sex.

Gender segregation in clubs and organizations is less pronounced than in the workplace, and it is experienced by both groups symmetrically. In both groups, about one-tenth describe their clubs or organizations as comprised entirely of their own sex, about one-third describe them as "mostly" made up of their own sex, and about one-half say they are comprised of men and women about equally. The result is that men are more likely to experience physical insulation from women in their workplaces than in their clubs and organizations, whereas for women, their clubs and organizations afford them a slightly greater probability of insulation from men than in the workplace, or at least a somewhat lower likelihood of being outnumbered by men.

Taking both social settings, spatial segregation is neither as pronounced nor as asymmetrical for gender as it is for race. However, given the lesser significance of spatial segregation as a differentiating mechanism in gender relations, the degree to which it is present in gender relations is noteworthy. This is especially true of the workplace, where the pattern of spatial gender segregation approximates (albeit in weaker form) that for race.

TABLE 4.3.   Respondents' Reported Exposure to Various Social Classes in Selected Social Settings, by Subjective Social Class.

	Mostly Own Class	Own + Higher	Mostly Higher	Own + Lower	Mostly Lower	Other[a]	D.K.	Base N[b]
	Reported Class Composition							
Upper-Middle Class:								
Neighborhood	30.6%	2.5	1.9	14.6	48.4	2.0	0.0	157
Clubs/Orgs.	27.1%	0.9	0.9	21.5	44.9	4.7	0.0	107
Middle Class:								
Neighborhood	49.9%	4.7	4.4	11.3	27.7	1.5	0.5	817
Clubs/Orgs.	60.5%	5.6	7.0	9.7	10.9	4.9	1.4	514
Working Class:								
Neighborhood	68.2%	8.4	15.4	2.9	2.3	1.2	1.6	689
Clubs/Orgs.	54.7%	11.2	26.5	0.0	0.6	6.2	0.9	340
Poor:								
Neighborhood	14.2%	26.2	56.0	0.0	0.0	0.0	3.5	141
Clubs/Orgs.	15.9%	27.3	54.4	0.0	0.0	0.0	2.3	44

[a] This comprises responses of "own + higher + lower" classes and "higher + lower" classes.
[b] Excludes respondents with missing data on the pertinent variables.

Class.   Table 4.3 presents data on the degree of spatial segregation experienced along class lines in neighborhoods and in clubs and organizations.[2] Because the questions for class were phrased slightly differently and because the choice of stimuli involves a graded series of five categories rather than a dichotomy, the data are not directly comparable with those for race and gender. However, careful comparison suggests that spatial segregation by class in neighborhoods and in clubs and organizations approaches the level of racial segregation in those settings. The main distinction between race and class is that the physical barriers between adjacent classes tend to fade into each other rather than being as sharply drawn as they are between the races.

The pattern of class segregation is very similar in both social settings. The classes that experience the most physical insulation are the two larger classes, the working class and the middle class. Substantially less physical insulation is experienced by the smaller classes that lie on either side of those classes, the poor and the upper-middle class. In the neighborhood setting, the working class experiences the most physical insulation, with over two-thirds describing their neighborhoods as made up mostly of their own class. About half of the middle class, almost one-third

2. Recall that respondents identifying with the upper class are excluded because there are too few of them to constitute a reliable basis for analysis, but the upper class is retained as a stimulus in questions.

of the upper-middle class, and about one-seventh of the poor report the same degree of class insulation in their neighborhoods. In clubs and organizations, it is the middle class that is the most insulated, with almost two-thirds describing their clubs and organizations as comprised mostly of their own class. In this setting, similar attributions are made by just over one-half of the working class, a little more than one-quarter of the upper-middle class, and only one-sixth of the poor. In evaluating these data, it is important to bear in mind that almost all mentions of exposure to higher or lower classes entail an adjacent class only (data are not displayed here). In keeping with the graded nature of social classes, physical contact with classes more distant in status drops precipitously. Thus, the four classes differ primarily in the degree to which they are physically insulated from adjacent classes.

In comparing these data with those for race and gender, the shading-off in the pattern of class spatial segregation distinguishes it from the single line that divides the groups in the race and gender dichotomies. Even so, the amount of spatial segregation between classes is quite pronounced, especially when one considers that none of the classes approaches the relative size of the white population. Take, for example, the physical insulation experienced by the middle class in their neighborhoods. Fifty percent describe their neighborhoods as mostly middle class, but only a small minority (5.5 percent) report that their neighborhoods include residents from classes other than the two adjacent ones (the working class and the upper-middle class). The figure of 50 percent is substantially smaller than the 95 percent of whites saying their neighborhoods are all white or mostly white, but the insulation of the middle class from the poor (and from the upper class) is very similar to the insulation experienced by whites from blacks. Regarded in the same light, the physical insulation of the working class from higher classes is very similar to, or possibly exceeds, that experienced by blacks from whites. Recall that 67 percent of blacks describe their neighborhoods as all or mostly black: compare that with 68 percent of the working class who describe their neighborhoods as mostly working class, and with the fewer than 4 percent of the working class who report any upper-middle-class or upper-class presence in their neighborhoods. The physical insulation experienced by the two smaller classes, the upper-middle class and the poor, lags considerably behind, but still no more than about 15 percent of the upper-middle class and 24 percent of the poor report having residents in their neighborhoods from nonadjacent classes. Patterns of class spatial segregation are very similar for clubs and organizations.[3]

3. Patterns of class spatial segregation are generally duplicated among both white and black respondents, with one interesting exception—the class-neighborhood segregation

In an effort to ward off exhaustion among my respondents, I did not ask them to report the class composition of their schools, shopping districts, and work environments, but I would expect similar patterns of class segregation in those settings as in neighborhoods and clubs and organizations. Even in work settings where the chain of command dictates a certain degree of physical proximity between different roles for instrumental purposes, that proximity is mostly restricted to contiguous authority levels that may even lie within the same social class.

It would be a mistake, however, to conclude that spatial segregation along class lines has scored social life as deeply as it has along racial lines. This is clear if we consider the extent to which spatial segregation is manifested in family patterns. Families, especially extended families, are more likely to include people from different social classes than from both races. Intergenerational mobility has produced extended families that include people of varying socioeconomic standing, and sometimes that variation is sufficient to make for different class identifications (Jackman and Jackman 1983). At the same time, physical separation of classes in families is considerable, and is not to be likened to gender relations, where both the extended and the nuclear family bring the two groups into close proximity.

The Terms of Intergroup Contact: Role Segregation

Beyond the question of how much contact there is between groups lies the issue of the terms under which contact takes place. To what extent are distinctive roles assigned to groups that invest those groups with different prerogatives and levels of authority?

Because of the high physical proximity of men and women in most spheres of life, this issue is especially pertinent to gender relations, and there has been much empirical research on the pervasive effects of gender role prescriptions on the division of labor in the home and in the workplace (see, for example, Meissner et al. 1975; Walker and Woods

---

experienced by blacks and whites identifying with the middle class. Black middle-class respondents reported considerably less insulation from the poor and working class in their neighborhoods than did their white counterparts. Of the 43 black respondents identifying with the middle class, only 28 percent reported living in a neighborhood that was "mostly middle-class," and as many as 67.5 percent mentioned lower classes, either in combination with their own class or, more often, without any mention of their own class. Among the 755 whites identifying with the middle class, 51 percent described their neighborhoods as "mostly middle class," and only 37.7 percent made any mention of lower classes (usually in combination with their own class). These data help to explain those reported in Jackman and Jackman (1983), which showed that although the affective class bonds of poor and working-class blacks were very similar to those of their white counterparts, blacks identifying with the middle class tended to have stronger affective bonds to lower classes than to their own.

1976; Pleck 1977; Reskin 1984; Ross 1987). Of course, role prescriptions also condition the quality of interactions between social classes and races. For example, data presented in Jackman and Jackman (1983) suggest that there is fairly high consensus among Americans about what kinds of occupational roles belong to each of the social classes; in addition, they found that the varying degrees of authority that are vested in various occupational positions reinforce class distinctions. We also know that occupations at the lower rungs continue to be filled disproportionately by blacks, despite some lessening of racial role segregation in the labor market in the post-World War II era (Farley 1984). However, because of the restricted opportunities for contact between people from different classes or races, the role prescriptions associated with class and race do not have the heightened significance that they do for gender relations. It is only in the latter case that role prescriptions are reiterated in the routine, day-to-day practice of personal life. For these reasons, the data that I present here on role segregation focus primarily on the gender relationship. In tables 4.4 and 4.5, I present some simple information that gives us a glimpse into the workings of role segregation in gender relations, and to a lesser extent, in race relations.

Table 4.4 focuses on the manifestation of gender role segregation in domestic life. This arena of life is central to the division of resources between men and women, and it is the arena in which men and women find themselves repeatedly thrown into contact. Other studies have documented gender role segregation in the household more thoroughly than is possible in these data (e.g., Meissner et al. 1975; Walker and Woods 1976), but the figures in table 4.4 offer a good summary of the differential activities in which husbands and wives are engaged. The first two panels of the table have data on participation in the prescribed female tasks of housework and childcare, the next four panels focus on male breadwinner tasks, and the last panel addresses the domestic stature of husbands and wives.

To measure engagement in designated female tasks, respondents were asked how much of the housework was done by themselves, their spouses, children, and other paid or unpaid help; for each category of persons, response options were "All, most, about half, some, none or very little." The same question was asked about childcare. The measures that are reported in the first two panels of table 4.4 focus on the relative contributions made by husbands and wives. "Equal" contributions were defined generously, to include respondents who used adjacent response-options to describe the contributions of both spouses as well as those who gave identical responses for both spouses. Only about one-sixth of either husbands or wives described their contributions to housework as even approximately equal, and fewer than one-third described their rela-

TABLE 4.4.   Segregation in Domestic Gender Roles, as Reported by Currently Married Men and Women.

| | Who does the housework? | | | |
| | | Husband | | |
	Wife All	Some	Equally	Base N[a]
Men	21.9%	62.0	16.1	576
Women	36.9%	46.2	17.2	651

| | Who takes care of the children? | | | |
| | | Husband | | |
	Wife All	Some	Equally	Base N[a]
Men	7.2%	61.6	31.1	318
Women	21.1%	50.6	28.3	350

| | Proportion of Adult Life Respondent Has Worked | | | |
	All	> Half	≤ Half	None	Base N[a]
Men	58.2%	36.4	3.3	2.1	569
Women	18.0%	27.2	44.0	10.7	656

| | Proportion of Married Life Spouse Has Worked | | | |
	All	> Half	≤ Half	None	Base N[a]
Men	17.4%	20.3	43.4	18.9	562
Women	79.5%	16.6	1.2	2.7	639

| | Current Level of Respondent's Employment (hours per week) | | | |
	35+ hrs.	20–34 hrs.	1–19 hrs.	0 hrs.	Base N[a]
Men	74.8%	3.4	1.9	19.9	588
Women	38.5%	8.2	4.6	58.7	671

| | Current Level of Spouse's Employment (hours per week) | | | |
	35+ hrs.	20–34 hrs.	1–19 hrs.	0 hrs.	Base N[a]
Men	29.1%	8.0	3.6	59.4	588
Women	76.3%	3.4	1.6	18.6	671

| | Who is the head of the household? | | |
	Husband	Both/Neither	Base N[a]
Men	70.1%	29.9	562
Women	81.5%	18.5	631

[a] Excludes respondents with missing data of the pertinent variables.

tive contributions to childcare in this way. Married men appear slightly more likely to claim they make some contribution to domestic labor than married women are to perceive it, but the modal tendency of both is to see the wife as doing most of the household labor with the husband making minor contributions. The prescriptive rather than pragmatic basis of this division of labor is apparent when one observes the minuscule shifts that are achieved when wives join their husbands in the labor market outside the home (see, for example, Meissner et al. 1975; Walker and Woods 1976; Jackman and Jackman 1983; Ross 1987; Hochschild 1989).

To address engagement in the male side of the domestic role arrangement, the next four panels of table 4.4 present data on the continuity of labor-force participation of husbands and wives and their current time commitments to the wage-labor market. Respondents were asked for the total number of years they had worked and for the number of years their spouses had worked since they had been married. Continuity of respondents' labor-force participation was measured as the proportion of their adult lives (that is, between ages twenty-one and sixty-five inclusive) they had worked; continuity of spouses' labor-force participation was measured as a proportion of the years they had been married. Current time commitments to the labor market were measured in terms of the number of hours worked each week by the respondent and spouse, including both main and second jobs. These measures indicate married women's relatively marginal relationship with the wage-labor market. Although most married women had had experience in the labor force, fewer than one-fifth had participated in it without interruption, and well over half were not employed at the time of the survey. These figures contrast sharply with those for married men, among whom the modal experience is continuous, full-time employment. Women's marginal acceptance in the paid labor force is underscored when one considers the extent to which women in the labor force are found in a relatively narrow subset of occupations (Treiman and Hartmann 1981; Beller 1984; Reskin and Roos 1990). Research on occupations that have "turned" female suggests that occupations are more available to women when they are routinized, lack autonomy, and/or offer limited promotion opportunities (Strober 1984; Reskin and Roos 1987, 1990). Such occupations are less attractive to men, offer less financial remuneration, minimize job-market competition between men and women, and do the least violation to prevailing gender-role prescriptions and prerogatives.

Men's and women's distinctive rates of participation in domestic versus breadwinner roles should not be construed as a neutral, "separate-but-equal" arrangement. The unequal amount of authority vested in each role is plainly apparent in people's conceptions of who is the head of the household. Respondents were asked, "Do you think of anyone here as the head of the household?" and, if so, to identify the person or persons. The overwhelming majority of currently married men and women identified the husband as the head of the household (70 percent of husbands and 82 percent of wives). Significantly, these figures are barely altered when both spouses are employed: 62 percent of men and 82 percent of women from such couples still identified the husband as the head of the household.

The issue of the differential authority conferred on different roles is pursued further in table 4.5. I discussed earlier how common understandings about the direction of authority in the chain of command at work condition interaction between various occupational levels in the workplace. Table 4.5 presents data on respondents' exposure to men and women and to whites and blacks at varying levels of responsibility in the workplace. These data underscore the point that information about the degree of spatial segregation tells only part of the story: exposure to different groups in the workplace is not necessarily benign since the quality of the exposure more often reinforces the unequal positions of the respective groups than it neutralizes or undermines them. In this respect, although the patterns of spatial segregation in the workplace by race and gender are somewhat different, the degree of positional segregation by race and sex is very similar.

Respondents who were currently employed were asked a series of three questions:

> Are there any people with *more* responsible positions than you at the place where you work?
> Are there any people with *less* responsible positions than you at the place where you work?
> Are there any people at work in positions with *about the same* amount of responsibility as you?

If they answered "Yes" to any of those questions, respondents were asked several follow-up questions, including items on the racial and gender composition of the pertinent level of responsibility: "Which of the categories on this card best describes how many blacks and whites [men and women] are among the people with. . ."; the five response-options ranged from "All black" ["All women"] to "All white" ["All men"] as in the racial- and gender-composition items reported above.

For both gender and race, the existence of spatial and role segregation in the labor force constrains the amount of exposure people can have to people from other groups at any level of job responsibility. This factor is especially pronounced in limiting whites' exposure to blacks. However, in both cases, the likelihood of encountering members of the subordinate

TABLE 4.5. Reported Gender and Racial Composition of Various Levels of Responsibility at Work, by Gender and Race, Respectively.

Level of Job Responsibility	*Reported Group Composition*				
	All Own Gender	Mostly Own	Half & Half	Mostly/ All Other	Base N[a]
Men					
Higher than R	50.6%	38.3	8.3	2.7	472
Same as R	48.9%	33.3	14.2	3.6	444
Lower than R	27.7%	35.5	23.7	13.1	473
Women					
Higher than R	9.1%	16.5	27.1	47.4	395
Same as R	26.3%	39.5	23.1	11.1	372
Lower than R	19.2%	41.7	24.4	14.7	312
	All Own Race	Mostly Own	Half & Half	Mostly/ All Other	Base N[a]
Whites					
Higher than R	68.0%	26.7	4.1	1.2	752
Same as R	57.4%	32.1	9.7	0.8	704
Lower than R	46.1%	37.4	11.9	4.6	688
Blacks					
Higher than R	7.4%	6.2	21.0	65.4	81
Same as R	11.5%	27.6	34.5	26.4	87
Lower than R	21.7%	30.4	27.5	20.2	69

[a] Excludes respondents who were not employed or who had missing data on the pertinent variables.

group increases noticeably at lower levels of job responsibility. About one-half of employed men describe the authority levels that are higher than or the same as their own as being made up entirely of men, whereas only 28 percent describe lower levels of responsibility as all male. Among employed whites, 68 percent describe higher levels of responsibility as made up entirely of whites, 57 percent describe their own level as all white, and 46 percent describe lower levels as all white. Thus, although whites are more likely to be physically insulated from blacks than men are from women in the workplace, the relationship between level of job responsibility and degree of exposure is similar for both groups. Among both men and whites, there is a difference of 22–23 percentage points in the likelihood of exposure to members of the pertinent subordinate group at higher versus lower levels of job responsibility, and for men, there is the same distinction between their own and lower levels. If we flip the question around and look for the work situations that are most likely to expose dominant-group members to a larger proportion of sub-

ordinates, we find that over one-third of men report that women constitute one-half or more of those who occupy positions lower than their
own, whereas only 11 percent of men report that degree of representation of women in positions higher than their own. Among whites, about
17 percent report that half or more of those at lower authority levels
than their own are blacks, whereas only about 5 percent describe authority levels higher than their own as having half or more blacks.

These experiences have their counterpart on the subordinate side.
Blacks are somewhat less insulated from whites than women are from
men in the workplace, but both groups experience more exposure to
dominant-group members at levels of responsibility higher than their
own. Almost one-half of employed women report that those at higher
levels of job responsibility are all or mostly men, whereas only 11 percent
and 15 percent, respectively, describe the gender composition of their
own or lower levels as so overwhelmingly male (these are differences of
about 35 percentage points). Among employed blacks, about two-thirds
describe higher levels of job responsibility as entirely or mostly white,
whereas 26 percent and 20 percent, respectively, make this description
of their own or lower levels (these are differences of about 39 and 45
percentage points).

In short, within the constraints set by role and spatial segregation in
the labor force, both men and whites experience the least insulation from
their respective subordinates when viewing those with less responsibility
than themselves in the workplace. On the other side, subordinates are
the least insulated from members of the dominant group when they
observe those in positions of higher responsibility at work. These patterns are consistent with the prerogatives of advantaged or disadvantaged group membership.

The data in tables 4.4 and 4.5 have illustrated how the points of contact
between unequal groups tend to be structured by rules that confer unequal prerogatives on the respective groups. Such rules invade the experiential quality of the relationship between men and women at a more
personal and intimate level than is the case with either class or race
relations.

Affiliative Behavior

The volume and quality of personal interaction across group lines can
be seen as a product of both physical availability and role constraints.
Spatial segregation and role segregation each creates barriers to personal
interaction by preventing its occurrence, restricting the locations where
it may occur, constraining the behaviors of the individuals concerned,
or limiting the substantive content of interactions. In this section, I assess
evidence of barriers that prevent or constrain the development of affilia-

TABLE 4.6. Reported Informal Interaction with Members of
Different Groups in the Neighborhood and/or Workplace, by Race,
Gender, and Class.

| | *Frequency of Interaction with Other Group* | | | |
	Never	Occasionally	Very Often	Base N[a]
In Neighborhood				
Whites (w/blacks)	73.5%	21.4	5.0	461
Blacks (w/whites)	58.8%	29.8	11.4	114
In Workplace				
Whites (w/blacks)	37.3%	38.4	24.3	474
Blacks (w/whites)	26.7%	38.4	34.9	86
Men (w/women)	43.1%	31.4	25.5	392
Women (w/men)	36.8%	33.9	29.3	389
Upper-Middle Class (w/lower resp. levels)	7.0%	40.7	52.3	86
Middle Class (w/lower resp. levels)	13.9%	34.8	51.3	359
Working Class (w/lower resp. levels)	12.5%	31.5	56.1	305
Middle Class (w/higher resp. levels)	14.2%	35.1	50.7	373
Working Class (w/higher resp. levels)	19.3%	36.5	44.2	373
Poor (w/higher resp. levels)	40.0%	24.0	36.0	25

[a] Excludes respondents who reported no physical presence of the pertinent group in the specified setting or who had missing data on either physical presence of the group or personal interaction with group members.

tive ties across group lines in race, gender, and class relations. I begin by examining the frequency of informal interaction between members of different racial groups in the neighborhood and between members of different racial, gender, and authority groups in the workplace. I then compare the extent to which people's friends and acquaintances are contained within the boundaries of various groups. After considering those data, I evaluate the extent and quality of personal interactions across group lines in the conduct of each relationship.

Informal Interaction. Table 4.6 presents data on the frequency of personal, informal interaction across racial lines in the neighborhood and across racial, gender, and authority lines in the workplace. When people are exposed to members of other groups in those settings, how much

personal, informal interaction takes place? Measures come from a series
of items. Respondents who had indicated that there were members of
the other racial group in their neighborhoods were asked, "Do you and
any of your black [white] neighbors ever do anything like talk informally
over coffee or in the street, lend each other things, or help each other
out with babysitting or chores?" To gauge informal interaction across
group lines in the workplace, employed respondents who had indicated
that there were any members of the other racial or gender group in their
workplaces were asked, "Do you and any of the blacks [whites/women/
men] at work ever have lunch together or talk informally over coffee
about things not related to work?" This question was also asked with
reference to people at higher, the same, and lower levels of job responsibility, if respondents had indicated there were such people in their workplaces. If respondents said "Yes" to any of these items, they were
asked,"How often do you do this—very often or not too often?"

I begin with the first two panels in table 4.6, which present data on
the frequency of informal interaction across racial lines in neighborhoods and workplaces. Observe that exposure to people of the other
race is by no means a guarantee that any personal interaction will take
place. However, interracial contact in the workplace is considerably more
likely to lead to personal interaction than it is in the neighborhood. And
a somewhat higher proportion of blacks than of whites report interacting
with members of the other race in either setting. Only about one-quarter
of whites who have black neighbors have ever chatted with them, and
only 5 percent say they have done this often; in the workplace, almost
two-thirds of whites have chatted over coffee or lunch with their black
co-workers, and one-quarter say they have done this often. Over 40 percent of blacks have interacted with their white neighbors (and about 11
percent have done so frequently), and about three-quarters have interacted with their white co-workers (and over one-third have done so frequently).

These figures speak most directly to the issue of physical availability.
Blacks are somewhat more likely to experience personal interaction with
whites than vice versa because (since they are outnumbered by whites)
they are more likely to find themselves in an interracial setting where
the other group comprises a substantial proportion of those present.
And intergroup contact in the workplace is more productive of personal
interaction because (1) interracial workplaces are likely to involve a
higher proportion of blacks than interracial neighborhoods, and (2) the
workplace is a more finite locale that presents more opportunities for
casual chit-chat than in the neighborhood. Neighbors whose homes do
not lie immediately adjacent to one another may rarely or never cross
each other's path (Festinger et al. 1950), whereas the organization of

work often encourages or necessitates some degree of personal inter-action.

Of course, entrenched norms about racial separation may also inter-vene, creating a social reticence on both sides because of inexperience in such situations and anxiety about the likely outcome of personal inter-action, even when whites and blacks find themselves in the same physical space. In this respect, the neighborhood may represent a more sensitive territorial bastion in which there are stronger psychological barriers to personal interaction across racial lines as well as fewer opportunities for such interaction. Data presented in Jackman and Crane (1986) show that whites' likelihood of interacting personally with the blacks in their neighborhoods or workplaces increases substantially both as the propor-tion of blacks who are present increases and when whites have previously had black neighbors or co-workers. This suggests that both present avail-ability and past interracial experience work to break down barriers to personal interaction across racial lines.

The third panel of table 4.6 gives comparable figures for personal interaction between men and women in the workplace. The most notice-able thing about these figures is their strong similarity to those for racial interaction in the workplace. As many as 43 percent of men and 37 percent of women say they have never chatted over coffee or lunch with their co-workers of the other sex. These figures are notable because generalized physical avoidance has not been a factor in gender relations as it has in race relations in the past few decades. This suggests that the high level of personal interaction that exists between men and women within the context of family life is closely circumscribed. When women appear in male-dominated domains outside those bounds, personal in-teraction between the sexes appears subject to the same pressures as it does between the races.

The last panel of table 4.6 gives data on the informal interaction of respondents from the upper-middle, middle, and working classes with people at lower levels of responsibility at work, and of respondents from the middle class, working class, and poor with people at higher levels of responsibility at work. These data are not directly comparable with those for race and gender, because many of the cross-level interactions do not involve people from other classes, and few of them are likely to involve people from classes that are not proximate to one's own. The line of command at work is generally segmented, so that adjacent levels of re-sponsibility often do not involve a shift in social class and they are most unlikely to involve nonproximate classes. For example, the factory line-worker and the foreman may both be considered working class or the foreman may be considered, at most, middle class; similarly, the supervisor in the office is likely to be a member of the middle class, and those he or she supervises may be either middle class or working class.

Informal interaction with those at lower or higher levels of responsibility at work appears to be the prevailing experience of employed people from all social classes, with the possible exception of the poor (and we have no data on the upper class). Only a small minority of people from the upper-middle, middle, and working classes (between 7 and 19 percent) have had no informal interaction with those at different levels of job responsibility. It is only among the poor that an appreciable number (40 percent) say they have had no informal interaction with people at higher levels of job responsibility. The last figure should be treated with caution since it is based on an N of only 25 people, but it is plausible that the occupational roles filled by the poor are more socially isolating. Relations between other levels in the chain of command tend to be escorted by personal chit-chat and social niceties. Far from undermining the chain of command at work, such factors humanize immediate authority figures and thus make their authority on the job more personally compelling. Although this often does not involve people from different social classes and rarely involves people from nonadjacent classes, this pattern also works to segment and soften somewhat the physical and social gulf that separates classes that lie further apart.

Friends and Acquaintances. Tables 4.7, 4.8, and 4.9 present data on the restrictions that race, gender, and class impose on the development of friendships. Using a "Friends Sheet," respondents were asked to list the first names of all the people they considered their "good friends" and then to indicate the race, sex, and occupation of each friend. These questions were introduced in the interview as follows:

> I would like to ask you some questions about the people you consider your good friends—by good friends I mean adults you enjoy getting together with at least once a month or so and any other adults who live elsewhere that you try to keep in close touch with by calling or writing.

Parents, spouses, and children were excluded from the sheet, in order to restrict it to affiliative behavior outside the immediate family. Eighty-eight respondents (4.6 percent) said they had no good friends; among those who did, the median number of friends was 6, with the highest emuneration of friends being 20.[4] Following the questions about friends, respondents were asked, "Are there any other people you keep in touch with or get together with occasionally?"; if they said "Yes," they were

---

4. The "Friends Sheet" and the data and composite measures derived from it are described in detail in Jackman and Jackman (1983, 173–178).

TABLE 4.7.   Affiliative Ties between Races, Reported
by Whites and Blacks.

	Whites	Blacks
Friends:		
All Own Race	90.2%	65.2%
One Friend Other Race	6.4	19.0
Two + Friends Other Race	3.4	15.8
Base N[a]	1520	158
Acquaintances:		
All Own Race	74.1%	47.9%
Mostly Own Race	23.9	40.3
Half + Other Race	1.9	11.8
Base N[b]	1332	119

[a] Excludes respondents with no friends or with missing data on either number of friends or race of any friends.
[b] Excludes respondents with no acquaintances or with missing data on either existence of acquaintances or racial composition of acquaintances.

asked about the racial and gender composition of those acquaintance circles, with five response-options ranging from "All black [women]" to "All white [men]," as in the spatial-segregation items presented above. Again, the data for class are not directly comparable with those for race and gender, since they present friends' occupational status (in terms of the Duncan socioeconomic index) rather than their attributed class membership. However, we may conclude from the data in these three tables that the most severe social rift between groups exists in race relations, where spatial segregation has found its strictest application, whereas the rift is weakest in the gender relationship, where role segregation prevails. Class relations show a social rift as marked as that for race between highly disparate socioeconomic levels, but the rift is less marked between proximate socioeconomic levels.

Racial segregation in the social circles of whites and blacks is pronounced but lopsided in its experiential impact on the respective groups. Blacks are usually absent from whites' friendship circles and they appear among whites' acquaintances only somewhat more frequently. Fewer than 10 percent of whites include any blacks among their good friends, and in most cases the referent is a single black friend. Just over one-quarter of whites include blacks among their acquaintances, and in most of these cases "mostly white" is the way the acquaintances are described, which probably indicates only one black acquaintance or possibly two. Thus, although whites are almost twice as likely to include one or two

TABLE 4.8.   Affiliative Ties between Sexes, Reported
by Men and Women.

	Men	*Women*
Friends:		
All Own Gender	29.1%	32.0%
70%–99% Own Gender	23.3	21.4
50%–69% Own Gender	38.6	41.4
More than Half Other Gender	9.6	5.2
Base N[a]	720	1021
Acquaintances:		
All Own Gender	3.6%	7.3%
Mostly Own Gender	28.9	30.3
Half + Other Gender	67.5	62.3
Base N[b]	634	858

[a] Excludes respondents with no friends or with missing data on either
number of friends or gender of any friends.
[b] Excludes respondents with no acquaintances or with missing data on
either existence of acquaintances or gender composition of
acquaintances.

blacks among their acquaintances as among their more intimate friends,
the penetration of blacks into either circle is very limited.

Blacks' social circles are less likely to be racially exclusive than are
those of whites; again, because of whites' numerical advantage, there is an
asymmetry in the degree to which each group penetrates the experiential
world of the other. About 35 percent of blacks include whites among
their friends, and these cases are almost as likely to involve two or more
whites as they are to involve a single white. About one-half of blacks
include whites among their acquaintances, and over 10 percent say that
at least half of their acquaintances are white.

Table 4.8 presents the proportion of men's and women's friends and
acquaintances who are of the same sex. People's social circles are considerably less segregated by gender than by race, but gender segregation
is still fairly marked, especially in people's friendship circles. Because
women's presence in men's friendship circles goes well beyond the minuscule number of blacks found in whites' circles, gender representation
is measured in terms of the proportion of friends who are the same sex
as the respondent, rather than the bare number.

Almost one-third of both men and women include no members of
the other sex among their good friends, and the overwhelming majority have more friends of their own sex than of the other sex. This
again suggests that the relatively high personal interaction experienced
between the sexes in family life is somewhat circumscribed. Outside those

bounds, the close affiliative ties of men and women are more likely to involve their own sex. Interestingly, additional analyses (not presented here) indicate that men who are married are somewhat more likely than unmarried men to have friends who are exclusively or disproportionately of their own sex. For example, 33 percent of married men versus 19 percent of unmarried men have exclusively male friends. This pattern is not duplicated among women, but it suggests that, for men, once the business of finding a sexual mate is removed from the social agenda, men retreat somewhat from women's company outside the family. Sex segregation is less in evidence in acquaintance circles: about two-thirds of both sexes say that half or more of their acquaintances are of the other sex, and acquaintance circles that completely exclude the other sex are a rarity.

To assess the impact of class on the pattern of affiliative ties, I examine data on the socioeconomic status of respondents' friends. Respondents gave the occupation of each friend, and this information was used to assign a Duncan Socioeconomic Index (SEI) score to each friend. The SEI is an estimated prestige ranking of occupations that ranges from 0 to 96 (Duncan 1961). These data provide two different measures. First, I calculated the mean SEI score for the friends of each respondent, in order to have a summary measure of their socioeconomic composition. These mean SEI scores are broken into four categories, and the percentages of each class with friends in each category are presented in the first panel of table 4.9. Second, I calculated the average absolute size of the deviations of friends' SEI scores from that of the respondent (the respondent's score was based on the occupation of the head of the household), in order to measure the extent to which people have friends who are similar to them in socioeconomic status. The mean deviations are expressed in SEI points and are broken into five categories, ranging from very small mean deviations (10 SEI points or less) to large ones (30 points or more). The percentages of each class with friends in each category are presented in the second panel of table 4.9.

I begin with the first panel of table 4.9, which shows a marked association between the class of respondents and the average socioeconomic status of their friends. The percentage distributions of the upper-middle class and the poor are almost the obverse of each other, although the tendency of the poor to have low-status friends is somewhat more pronounced than the tendency of the upper-middle class to have high-status friends. Almost three-quarters of the upper-middle class have friends whose mean SEI scores fall in the top two categories (with 44 percent falling in the top category alone); and at the other end, only 5 percent of the upper-middle class have friends whose mean SEI scores fall in the lowest category. Among the poor, over 80 percent have friends whose

TABLE 4.9.   Socioeconomic Status of Affiliative Ties Reported by the
Upper-Middle Class, Middle Class, Working Class, and Poor.

	Upper-Middle Class	Middle Class	Working Class	Poor
Mean Socioeconomic Status of Friends:				
SEI ≤ 28 (low)	4.9%	14.1%	27.9%	44.2%
SEI 29–47	23.1	38.6	47.3	38.4
SEI 48–58	28.0	22.1	17.0	8.1
SEI ≥ 59 (high)	44.1	25.2	7.8	9.3
Base N[a]	143	750	588	86
Mean Deviation of Friends' SEI from Respondent:				
Deviation ≤ 10 points	21.4%	21.2%	23.1%	23.4%
Deviation 11–15 points	25.2	19.2	16.8	10.4
Deviation 16–20 points	26.7	20.1	20.5	26.0
Deviation 21–30 points	19.3	24.6	24.7	20.8
Deviation ≥ 30 points	7.4	14.9	15.0	19.5
Base N[b]	135	712	567	77

[a] Excludes respondents with no friends or with missing data on either number of friends or socioeconomic status of friends.
[b] Excludes respondents with no friends or with missing data on either number of friends, socioeconomic status of friends, or socioeconomic status of respondent.

mean SEI scores are in the lowest two categories, with 44 percent falling in the lowest category alone. The figures for the middle and working classes fall in a gradual progression between the upper-middle class and the poor. Among middle-class respondents, almost two-thirds have friends whose mean SEI scores lie in the two middle categories, and of the two more extreme categories, their friends are more likely to be in the highest than the lowest. Among the working class, three-quarters have friends whose mean SEI scores lie in the two lowest categories, with the largest proportion (47 percent) falling in the second-lowest category.

The second panel of table 4.9 approaches the issue in terms of the status homogeneity of people's friends, and these data lend a similar picture to that suggested by the first panel. People from all social classes tend to have friends whose socioeconomic status resembles their own, although the pattern is loose rather than tight. Only about one-fifth to one-quarter of the people in any class have friends whose socioeconomic status is *very* close to their own (that is, within 10 SEI points), but about three-quarters of the upper-middle class and about 60 percent of each of the other classes have friends whose status lies within an average of 20 SEI points of their own.

The data in both panels of table 4.9 reinforce the picture of class contact that was suggested by the class data in tables 4.3 and 4.6. People's friendship circles indicate considerable "bunching" of individuals with similar socioeconomic characteristics and a strong tendency for people of widely divergent socioeconomic status to lead separate social lives. However, this is obscured somewhat by the fact that classes lie in a graduated series rather than a dichotomy. The social circles of the upper-middle class and the poor rarely overlap, but in between lie the middle and working classes, whose own localized social tendencies work to segment the social ravine between the more disparate classes. This pattern is exacerbated by the fact that the specific location of the boundaries between classes is less rigidly specified than it is for race or gender, with the effect that social boundaries between the classes tend to fade into each other rather than being sharply marked by a single line.

SUMMARY

As dominant-group members differentiate themselves socially from subordinates, they are faced with a dilemma. On the one hand, differentiation is inevitable and necessary in practicing expropriation from subordinates. But on the other hand, social differentiation erects barriers to communication with subordinates, making it more difficult to integrate subordinates within the unequal relationship. In this chapter, I began by considering the distinctions between two major forms of intergroup differentiation—*role (or social) segregation* and *spatial (or physical) segregation*. I discussed the factors that shape the prevalence of one or the other form of segregation, the various manifestations that each form may take, the experiential impact of each, and the implications of each for communication patterns between groups.

Unequal relationships between groups are likely to embroil more than one type of social differentiation, but the specific form that prevails is conditioned by the functional mechanics of the expropriation that undergirds an intergroup relationship. Dominant groups practice exclusionary behavior within those constraints. When the functional mechanics of the expropriation require sustained, intimate contact between groups (as in gender relations), the dominant group develops a more highly elaborated system of role segregation to demarcate the boundaries between groups. When the expropriation involves a more aggregated use of subordinates, the dominant group turns to spatial segregation as the primary symbolic marker between groups.

Both role and spatial segregation may be implemented with greater or less scope and intensity, and each form of segregation has several faces. Role segregation may specify activities and occupations for each group, interpersonal behaviors (both within and across group lines), and dress codes. In each area, role presciptions may be loose or strict, and they may have a narrow scope or a broad reach over different domains of social, economic, and political life. Spatial segregation may involve a fairly rudimentary physical separation of groups within common sites (as when whites and blacks were seated in different sections of the same buses in the Jim-Crow South), it may mean the allocation of each group to separate, sometimes adjacent, facilities, or it may entail the allocation of each group to different residential locations. Each of these elaborations steps up the physical distance between groups, and contemporary urban residential segregation in the United States has injected a spatial rift between whites and African Americans that is unprecedented in its scope and pervasiveness.

These different forms of segregation vary greatly in their experiential impact and in the opportunities they offer for communication between groups. The rigid application of role segregation produces ingrained expectations about appropriate personal behaviors and activities for the members of each group, and those expectations perpetuate status distinctions between the groups as their members interact with one another. In the close-knit relations between groups, there is ample opportunity for the members of the dominant group to reinforce those expectations on a daily basis. In systems of spatial segregation, restraints are not placed on the personal behaviors or activities of subordinates, but instead status boundaries are built into the allocation of space to each group. High symbolic value is attached to the physical separation of the groups and to the allocation of space to each group according to the desirability and material attributes of that space. Because subordinates are placed at a greater physical distance from the members of the dominant group, this complicates communication across group lines. Relations that rely on role segregation embed status distinctions in reiterated, personal, day-to-day interactions between individuals from each group. Relations that rely on spatial segregation, however, must turn to more impersonal, aggregated, and distal communications to reach subordinates who have been given the opportunity to draw more freely on the social resources of their own group.

In the second part of the chapter, I turned to a comparison of data on the structure of intergroup contact in the three cases in this study. Race, gender, and class relations were compared in terms of the physical insulation of groups, the degree to which intergroup contacts are conditioned by role prescriptions, and the amount of affiliative behavior across group lines. Those data offer some insight into the distinctive ways in which intergroup contact is structured in race, gender, and class relations. I summarize the most salient points about each intergroup relationship in turn.

Race.   Race relations are marked by pervasive spatial segregation that has served to keep most whites socially insulated from blacks most of the time. At the same time, blacks experience less racial insulation than whites because the lapses in spatial segregation affect a larger proportion of the smaller black community. Interracial contact is also most likely to take place in situations in which blacks are a token presence among an overwhelmingly white majority. Thus, whites have been able to penetrate the black community to some extent while keeping the white community relatively insulated from blacks. In addition, the points of personal contact between whites and blacks are quite likely to be engraved with role prescriptions that uphold the white position of status dominance: for example, whites are more likely to encounter blacks at work as their status-inferiors than as their equals or superiors. Overall, whites' numerical dominance has afforded them the opportunity to insulate themselves from blacks without severing their communication lines with blacks commensurably. Nonetheless, whites' indulgence in pervasive residential segregation by race has resulted in their personal communication lines with blacks becoming much curtailed.

Gender.   Gender relations are governed by role segregation more than spatial segregation, but the role prescriptions themselves generate some spatial segregation which, in turn, experientially reinforces the message carried in the role prescriptions. Within the bosom of the family, men have repeated opportunities to communicate personally with women, and the communication channels are nested in clear role positions that unobtrusively reaffirm the power differential between the two groups. In addition, women learn that their intimacy with men is circumscribed. In spheres of activity outside the conduct of family life, women experience a noticeable degree of spatial separation from men; and when they do enter male-dominated domains, they are likely to be assigned tasks that leave gender role prerogatives inviolate.

Class.   Class relations are visibly marked by both role segregation and spatial segregation, although neither form of differentiation is specified as sharply as it is for gender and race, respectively. Classes perform different roles in the economic production of society, and the physical aggregation of those roles in industrial production has engendered considerable spatial segregation by social class, both in and out of the workplace. The social contacts experienced by the members of each class are centered in their own class and do not usually extend far beyond the boundaries of adjacent classes. Because the classes lie in a graded series rather than a dichotomy, and because the boundaries between classes are relatively ragged, the resulting pattern of class contacts is a seg-

mented one, with the contacts of each class centered on a different point
and fading out over different spans.

Thus, in both the workplace and the conduct of social life, the wide
chasm that separates the highest classes from the lowest is partially
bridged, in segments, by the classes that lie in between. This does not
afford the highest social classes the same direct, personal communication
channels with the lowest classes that men have with women. At the same
time, it means that the social rift between the top and bottom of the class
structure, wide though it is, is sketched in ragged lines rather than being
sharply engraved as it is between the races.

The Communication Grid.   Race, gender, and class relations each present distinct patterns of intergroup contact. These differences have profound implications for the kinds of communication lines that are laid
down in each case. In the next part of the book, I explore the intergroup
ideologies that are articulated in the three intergroup relationships. We
may then assess the extent to which the ideologies that groups espouse
are shaped by the structure of their contact with their would-be protagonists.

PART III

Dialogues of Dominance and Subordination

CHAPTER FIVE

Intergroup Feelings and the Definition of Group Interests

> *It is expedient to hate the adversary with whom one fights (for any reason), just as it is expedient to love a person whom one is tied to and has to get along with. . . . The mutual behavior between people can only be understood by appreciating the inner adaptation which trains in us feelings most suitable to a given situation. . . . By means of psychological connections, these feelings produce the forces which are necessary to execute the given task and to paralyze inner countercurrents.*
>
> GEORG SIMMEL, *CONFLICT* (1955, 34)

Simmel's reasoning exemplifies the logic that has prevailed in the literature on intergroup attitudes—that love for our own and hatred for our adversaries are the natural pivots in one group's orientations toward another, providing the necessary energy for the conduct of their unequal relationship. I discussed that reasoning in Part I and found it wanting. I argued that the ongoing, relational basis of the inequality between groups demands that one must get along with rather than fight with one's "adversaries," and, indeed, it is problematic whether the other group will even be defined as an adversary. Ironically, this means that the feelings that dominant groups find "most suitable" to the "given situation" of their relationship with subordinates may not be hatred, but instead affection or at least temperance. These pressures should mitigate against the expression of disparity and hostility and instead draw the dialogue between groups toward more amicable declarations.

In this part of the book, I appraise the part played by hostility and affection in the shaping of the dialogue that takes place between groups who are bound together in different kinds of unequal relationships. Over the next few chapters, I will be examining data on different elements of the intergroup attitudes that accompany race, gender, and class relations in the United States.

I begin, in this chapter, at the most fundamental level: do contending, unequal groups express negative or positive feelings toward one another, and do they view their interests as adversary or unified? The character of intergroup feelings is basic because it sets the tone of the relationship between groups: before we can interpret any other elements of people's intergroup attitudes, we need to delineate their emotional packaging. The perception of group interests tells us about the cognitive understandings that accompany intergroup feelings: do unequal groups believe they are separated by a deep divide in their interests or do they see each other as having a shared community of interests?

I start by assessing the differing meanings attached to intergroup feelings and the perception of group interests in traditional conceptions of prejudice, tolerance, and group consciousness. I then discuss problems involved in the measurement of intergroup feelings and the perception of group interests, for despite their intrinsic conceptual significance, these two elements have rarely been directly measured. With those issues in hand, I outline my approach to the meaning of intergroup feelings and the perception of group interests. The second part of the chapter proceeds with an examination of my data on these two key elements of intergroup ideology.

Two broad sets of questions govern that analysis. First, to what extent do the feelings expressed by dominant and subordinate groups reflect basic currents of hostility or warmth? How sharply do people express an affective preference for their own group, and how much is hostility a factor in their feelings toward the other group? How does the element of hostility vary across the three intergroup relationships, and is there any consistent tendency for the expression of hostility to come more from one side of a relationship than the other?

Second, to what extent are group interests defined in conflictive or integrative terms? Do the members of unequal groups tend to perceive existing social arrangements as serving the interests of all the affected groups, as serving the interests of the dominant group at the expense of subordinates, or as detrimental to the interests of all groups? How does this vary according to the nature of the intergroup relationship and the position of the group within that relationship?

Answers to these questions will uncover the elementary thrusts of the ideologies that distinguish race, gender, and social class relations in the United States. Are those ideologies framed, emotionally and perceptually, by a sense of disparity or unity between groups?

THE ISSUES

Despite their centrality, intergroup feelings and the perception of group interests have had different specific meanings attached to them from one body of literature to another. That variation reflects two main factors: primarily, whether intergroup attitudes are thought to have a rational or an irrational basis; and second, different ideas about the natural attitudinal expression of rational or irrational forces. I briefly consider the different ways that intergroup feelings and the perception of group interests have been treated in traditional conceptions of prejudice, tolerance, and group consciousness: as we move from one concept to the next, rationality assumes a larger presence. I then turn to measurement issues that have hampered the assessment of intergroup feelings and the perception of group interests. Finally, I discuss my theoretical approach, and I draw out the primary empirical questions that confront us.

Prejudice

Prejudice has usually been conceived as an intrinsically psychological phenomenon, in which negative feelings constitute the hot core. Recall that Allport's widely accepted definition of prejudice is "an antipathy based upon a faulty and inflexible generalization" ([1954] 1979, 9). The centrality of negative feelings to the concept of prejudice has been restated many times (see, for example, Williams, Jr. 1947, 36–42; Harding et al. 1969, 3–6; Newcomb et al. 1965, 430–431; Simpson and Yinger 1972, 24; Berry and Tischler 1978, 235; Kinder and Sears 1981, 416; Pettigrew 1982, 1–5; Sniderman and Tetlock 1986, 186; Marger 1994, 74–75). The meaning attached to those feelings is somewhat different than in the literature on group consciousness. Most analysts of prejudice have paid almost exclusive attention to the attitudes of dominant-group members within a framework that seems to view all of the energy as coming from the members of the dominant group as they unleash their personality or cultural deficiencies on subordinate victims. Thus, the feelings that drive prejudice are not usually linked to the rational interests of a group within a relationship. Instead, things are seen as more of a one-way tirade: the members of the dominant group are the actors, and their feelings emanate from factors endogenous to their own ranks.

Within this perspective, negative intergroup feelings are seen as destructive, and theories have concentrated on how to change negative feelings into positive ones, in order to convert rejection into acceptance. In this endeavor, the locus of energy is clearly within the ranks of the dominant group: they initiate the hostility, and social change can only be accomplished by altering the emotional proclivities of dominant-group members toward subordinates.

And because intergroup feelings have not usually been linked with the tangible interests of the group, the way group members perceive their interests has not been regarded as critical in most analyses of prejudice. Of course, analysts in the realistic group-conflict school have argued that negative feelings are founded in a sense of threat that people feel vis-à-vis subordinates, and that sense of threat derives from their group's "realistic" interests (see, for example, LeVine and Campbell 1972; Bobo 1983; Giles and Evans 1986). Similarly, Sherif (1965) emphasized the importance of establishing competitive or cooperative group interests in instigating or de-escalating intergroup hostility. The most common governing assumption, however, has been that it is not disparate interests that are ultimately responsible for dividing racial groups (see, for example, Allport [1954] 1979, 229–233), but rather that prejudice embroils an *erroneous* belief that the groups have incompatible interests. Thus, although analysts working on the effects of intergroup contact have repeatedly stipulated that contact situations must not contain competitive group interests if there is to be a positive effect on intergroup attitudes (see, for example, Williams, Jr. 1947; Wilner, Walker, and Cook 1955; Allport [1954] 1979; Amir 1969; Cook 1984; Miller and Brewer 1984), the import of that stipulation has been that policies designed to eradicate prejudice must be structured so as to expose the participants to the "common interests and common humanity" that exist between their own and the other group. In this way, policies may break down the artificial barriers that prejudiced people have erected between the groups (Allport [1954] 1979, 281; Wilner et al. 1955: 3–6).

Students of prejudice regard the antipathy that is the core of the concept as a complex puzzle. Some ambiguity hangs over the issue of whether negative feelings derive logically from "faulty and inflexible generalizations" that have been formulated in the absence of accurate information about a group or whether the faultiness and inflexibility of those generalizations are themselves conditioned by preexisting negative feelings (see, for example, the discussions of prejudice in Williams 1947, especially pages 40–41; and Allport [1954] 1979, chapters 1 and 2). Theories emphasizing personality or socialization factors (for example, Adorno et al.'s theory of the "authoritarian personality," 1950) have promoted the latter view. Theories focusing on personal contact with the object-group (for example, Wilner et al. 1955; Stephan and Stephan 1984) have put more emphasis on the idea that the initial negative beliefs derive primarily from ignorance but that once established they become the logical basis for negative feelings toward the object-group. Analyses done in the minimal-group paradigm (see, for example, Tajfel 1969, 1978; Brewer 1979) imply that antipathy toward other groups springs from cognitive and emotional biases that are elicited simultaneously by any intergroup situation, no matter what, or how flimsy, the basis of the division.

In any event, students of prejudice view negative feelings as a destructive force that is hurled upon subordinate groups and that must be eradicated in order to progress toward a more egalitarian society. Those feelings have sometimes been linked to the perception of disparate group interests, but since most students of prejudice regard such a perception as misplaced rather than rationally derived, the source of negative feelings toward subordinates remains a puzzle—the solution to which holds the key to the problem.

Tolerance

Like other students of intergroup attitudes, analysts of tolerance have assumed that negative feelings toward other groups provide the motivational basis for negative behavioral dispositions toward those groups. However, those feelings are neither irrationally based, as most students of prejudice would have it, nor rationally escalatory, as students of group consciousness would have it. Instead of seeing the existence of negative intergroup feelings as a puzzle that needs to be solved (like students of prejudice) or as an ultimate state that needs to be attained (like students of group consciousness), analysts of tolerance have assumed that such feelings are a constant and unremarkable feature of relations among contending groups in democratic societies. This relegates both intergroup feelings and the perception of group interests to a latent, rather than an active, presence—they are neither the obstacle to intergroup harmony nor the key to constructive conflict.

Contending groups are assumed to represent different interests, and intergroup antipathy is regarded as a natural outgrowth of those differing interests. However, unlike students of group consciousness, students of tolerance do not seem to regard those contending interests as irreconcilable. Instead, they are committed to the utility of a continuing democratic choice among contending political alternatives. Thus, although they view intergroup antipathy as an inevitable outcome of social diversity, they also, like analysts of prejudice, view intergroup antipathy as destructive, or at least potentially so, rather than rationally constructive (see, for example, Stouffer 1955; Nunn, Crockett, and Williams 1978; McClosky 1964; Sullivan et al. 1982; McClosky and Brill 1983, chapter 1).

This line of thinking leads students of political tolerance away from any direct focus on the affective or perceptual boundaries that they assume exist between contending groups. Those boundaries are seen as potentially dangerous, but not subject to eradication. The pertinent empirical problem has been defined as how people learn to override their negative feelings toward contending groups and abide by "the rules of the game" that grant full civil and political rights to the groups they dislike. And because of a primary concern with the danger of a "tyranny of the majority," analysts have focused on the tolerance expressed by politically dominant groups toward "nonconformists" or other minorities.

The difficult attitudinal task of tolerance has been regarded as unattainable when intergroup antipathy is intense (Dahl 1956, especially 75–80; Sullivan, Pierson, and Marcus 1979, 1982). Mild feelings and

perceptions of intergroup disparity are regarded as optimal for the con-
tinuance of democratic procedures—enough to ensure a political choice
but not enough to fragment society irreconcilably.

Group Consciousness

Analysts of group consciousness have viewed intergroup attitudes as rationally derived: groups are generally expected to espouse attitudes that
are consistent with their interests. The class literature, in which the analysis of group consciousness is rooted, has implied this in drawing a clear
link between the fundamental nature of socioeconomic inequality and
the state of class consciousness. The primary concern has been the state
of awareness of subordinate groups, with the question of dominant-
group consciousness receiving less attention. The result has been a lack
of clarity about what form a rational expression of dominant-group interests should take. This, in turn, has led to some confusion about subordinate attitudes: after all, the rational response of subordinates cannot be
ascertained precisely without an understanding of the political reality
that they confront. The literature on group consciousness offers several
possible scenarios.

The picture that comes most immediately to mind is that of emotional
and cognitive polarization between groups. This was the picture con-
veyed by Marx and Engels, as when they wrote in "The Manifesto of the
Communist Party" ([1888] 1959, 8) that "the epoch of the bourgeoisie . . .
has *simplified the class antagonisms.* Society is more and more splitting up
into *two great hostile camps*, . . . bourgeoisie and proletariat" (emphasis
added). Marx's central thesis about the inevitability of increasing class
polarization under capitalism rests on the expectation that as capitalism
develops, it reveals its workings more and more sharply: the mutually
opposed interests of exploiting and exploited classes become manifested
unmistakably to both sides, and this engenders feelings of solidarity
within groups and disparity and hostility between them.

Within this framework, two elements have been regarded as basic in
identifying subordinates' level of consciousness. First, do they identify
emotionally with their group and distance their feelings from the dominant group? Indeed, do they hold negative feelings toward those against
whom they must fight for social change? Second, do subordinates perceive their group as an entity that has distinct interests that lie opposed
to those of the dominant group and that cannot be served within the
status quo? These two elements have been considered essential to a sense
of "shared fate" that binds subordinates together in opposition to the
dominant group (see, for example, Centers 1949, chapter 2; Landecker
1963; Morris and Murphy 1966; Olsen 1970; Oberschall 1978; Tilly
1978; Fireman and Gamson 1979; Gurin, Miller and Gurin 1980; Miller

et al. 1981). Thus, unlike most students of prejudice, analysts of group consciousness have viewed intergroup disparity and hostility as rational expressions of a group's interests that provide the necessary energy for conflict and change.

Although this general expectation provides the backdrop for the analysis of group consciousness, it is not clear how such a state is reached. In particular, there is disagreement about which side is expected to initiate the path to conflict. Some analysts have seemed to assume that subordinates routinely encounter hostility and derogation from dominant groups. This assumption has been especially prominent among those studying ethnic identification (see, e.g., Brand et al. 1974). Many such scholars appear to have accepted the prevailing viewpoint of the prejudice literature that dominant groups are unable to contain their irrationally founded negativism toward minority ethnic groups. Other scholars follow the assumption employed in the realistic group-conflict school that the negativism of dominant groups is the rational expression of their privileged interests. In either case, the issue has been whether subordinates can distance themselves sufficiently to develop a positive sense of group identity in the face of that derogation, assert their interests, and counter with hostility for hostility. Whether or not the presumed negativism of dominant groups is thought to have a rational basis, signs of intergroup negativism among subordinates are interpreted as a constructive and rational response to the barrage that they receive from the dominant group.

Many analysts, however, have argued that it is in the interests of those in command to mask their privileged receipt of benefits. To that end, dominant groups are expected to represent their interests in universalistic terms as being at one with those of society as a whole (see, for example, Marx and Engels [1846] 1970; Dahrendorf 1959, 280–289; Genovese 1968; Parkin 1971, chapter 3; Gramsci 1971; Huber and Form 1973; Giddens 1979, 193–197). This changes the nature of the task for subordinates, putting the onus on them to raise the voice of disparity.

The manifest appeal of universalism to dominant groups, with the self-satisfaction and integrated view of life that it provides, is illustrated in the following excerpts from two essays by Stringfellow in Eliott's collection of proslavery arguments (1860). Tracts such as these show the seemingly boundless breadth of the claims that can be made by a system's beneficiaries about the universality of those benefits.

> It is or ought to be known to all men, that African slavery in the United States originated in, and is perpetuated by a social and political necessity, and that its continuance is demanded equally by the highest interests of both races. . . . The guardianship and control of the black race, by the

white, in this Union, is an indispensable Christian duty, to which we must as yet look, if we would secure the well-being of both races. (Stringfellow 1860*a*, 521)

The facts which have been reviewed prove with equal clearness, that where slavery exists, the white race, and the black, have prospered more in their religious, social and moral condition, than either race has prospered, where slavery has been excluded. We see that an increased amount of poverty and wretchedness has to be borne in New England by both races. Ecclesiastical statistics will show an increased amount of prosperity in religion that is overwhelming.

Such is the prostration of moral restraint at the North, that, in their cities, standing armies are necessary to guard the persons and property of unoffending citizens, and to execute the laws upon reckless offenders. This state of things is unknown in the slave States.

The census shows that slavery has been a blessing to the white race in these slave States. They have prospered more in religion, they have more homes, are wealthier, multiply faster, and live longer than in New England, and they are exempt from the curse of organized infidelity and lawless violence.

A comparison of the slave's condition at the South, with that of his own race in freedom at the South, shows with equal clearness, that slavery, in these States, has been, and now is, a blessing to this race of people in all the essentials of human happiness and comfort. Our slaves all have homes, are bountifully provided for in health, cared for and kindly nursed in childhood, sickness, and old age; multiply faster, live longer, are free from all the corroding ills of poverty and anxious care, labor moderately, enjoy the blessings of the gospel, and let alone by wicked men, are contented and happy. (Stringfellow 1860*b*, 538–539)

With such arguments as these, dominant groups promote their own cause without stooping to the level of appearing self-interested. Their appeal is made in the name of moral righteousness, and at the same time, the potentially damaging issue of group interests is neutralized.

This implies that, if there is to be conflict, it is subordinates who initiate it. The way that subordinates respond to dominant claims of universalism, however, has been the subject of some disagreement. One argument has been that the political task of subordinates is to reveal the mutually opposed interests that divide the groups and to withdraw their emotional support from the modus vivendi. Dominant groups prefer to deny that there are opposed group interests, but they are eventually forced to accept that interpretation as a result of the concerted political efforts of subordinates. Indeed, Mannheim (1936, 229–235) has argued that dominant groups remain blissfully unaware of their special interests until the matter is rudely brought to their attention by subordinates. Appealing as it may be to view the world from which one benefits as one happy family, this view may become increasingly difficult to maintain when confronted with repeated shrill denials of happiness from the other "family members."

Another well-known argument is that when subordinates mount a challenge, they are as liable as dominant groups to opt for the language of universalism. That was the argument made by Marx:

> Each new class which puts itself in the place of one ruling before it, is compelled, merely in order to carry through its aim, to represent its interest as the common interest of all the members of society, that is, expressed in ideal form: it has to give its ideas the form of universality, and represent them as the only rational, universally valid ones. The class making a revolution appears from the very start, if only because it is opposed to a *class*, not as a class but as the representative of the whole of society. (Marx and Engels 1970, 65–66)

This suggests that both established and insurgent groups avoid characterizing society in terms of narrow, adversary interests, as they make competing claims to be the sole representatives of the common good. In this vein, Gamson (1968, 53–54) has argued that all contending solidary groups tend to represent their interests in universalistic terms. Indeed, if dominant groups eschew hostile assertions of their own interests and instead claim that current arrangements are to everyone's benefit, this may condition the moral framework so that any challenge is also couched in universalistic rather than "selfish" terms. In that spirit, socialist doctrine claims that redistributive measures would benefit the well-being and fulfillment of all elements of society, not just the working class, and the liberal doctrine of racial integration depicts segregation as a universal evil that works to the cultural detriment of whites as well as African Americans.

Other analysts have argued that subordinates' responses to the universalistic claims of dominant groups fall short of any outright challenge. Subordinates grapple with the reality of their day-to-day experience juxtaposed against the constant ideological onslaught of the dominant group. As they cope with these inconsistent stimuli, they may succumb to abstract representations of dominant ideological principles but formulate concrete micro-interpretations that are more in keeping with their personal experience (Mann 1970; Parkin 1971, chapter 3; Huber and Form 1973, chapter 9; Abercrombie et al. 1980, 140-155).

For scholars committed to a conflict perspective, subordinate attitudes that do not display some form of challenge are characterized as "false consciousness" (see, for example, Mills 1946; Mann 1970). As I discussed in chapter 1, this phenomenon poses an awkward puzzle for such analysts. Indeed, this is the only point at which students of group consciousness have toyed with the idea of irrationally founded attitudes. A distinction is drawn between what people in a group "ought" to think and what they do think—a distinction that is rather tenuous, especially within a general framework that presupposes rationality in people's intergroup attitudes.[1] Indeed, this line of explanation credits the dominant class with a rational pursuit of its interests, as it dupes the masses with a glossy picture of the status quo: it is only subordinates who, in allowing themselves to be duped, fail to demonstrate the rational awareness of their condition that is so urgently expected of them. Thus, in the attempt to define away the empirical problem of the lack of any sharp political challenge among subordinates, some conflict-oriented scholars have cut into the very building-block on which the expectation of conflict rests—that is, the assumption that individuals comprehend and respond rationally to the conditions that they experience. Analysts have attempted to resolve the contradiction by relegating false consciousness to the status of a temporary lapse over which rational political organization will eventually triumph, but the ideas that I have reviewed do not offer any sound basis for expecting the development of such an organization from grassroots that are so devoid of rational consciousness.

This is especially true of the literature on cultural hegemony, which represents the most sustained attempt to grapple with the issue of false consciousness. Marx and Engels' famous discussion in *The German Ideology* provides the basis for ideas on hegemony: "The ideas of the ruling class are in every epoch, the ruling ideas, i.e. the class which is the ruling *material* force in society is at the same time its ruling *intellectual* force" (Marx and Engels 1970, 64). Building on that argument, Gramsci (1971) posited a process whereby the dominant group gains the consent of subordinates by infiltrating their system of values. Williams gives a good description of the process:

> [Hegemony is] an order in which a certain way of life and thought is dominant, in which one concept of reality is diffused throughout society in all its institutional and private manifestations, informing with its spirit all taste, morality, customs, religious and political principles, and all social relations, particularly in their intellectual and moral connotations. (Williams 1960, 587)

From this perspective, dominant groups succeed in imposing a single interpretation of social reality, in which all parties embrace the status quo as representing the common interest. Genovese has argued that

1. See Mann (1970) for an interesting attempt to make an empirical determination of "false consciousness." Ultimately, however, the "falseness" of someone's consciousness is a definitional rather than an empirical problem, resting on prior assumptions about what someone's "true" interests are (see Connolly 1972) and about the rational course of action to pursue those interests.

hegemony depends on much more than consciousness of economic interests on the part of the ruling class and unconsciousness of such interests
on the part of the submerged classes. The success of a ruling class in establishing its hegemony depends entirely on its ability to convince the lower
classes that its interests are those of society at large—that it defends the
common sensibility and stands for a natural and proper social order. (1968,
407)

The idea of cultural hegemony poses a contradiction within the conflict framework. In order for hegemony to work, subordinates must be
relatively passive ideological consumers, which makes them improbable
agents of ideological challenge. Subordinates are left wallowing in a state
of false consciousness without any structural process being posited that
might counter the effects of hegemony and instigate the path to emotional and perceptual estrangement from the status quo.[2] At the same
time, conflict scholars continue to uphold such estrangement as the catalyst for a political initiative to attain a more egalitarian society, and thus
it is seen as the ultimate rational course for subordinates.

Measurement Issues

Despite their pivotal conceptual status, intergroup feelings and the perception of group interests have rarely been measured directly in analyses
of prejudice, tolerance, or group consciousness. Direct measurement of
intergroup feelings has largely been confined to the "thermometer
scales" used in the National Election Studies (NES 1952–1990 Cumulative Data File Codebook), and those measures have been employed occasionally to make rudimentary assessments of feelings toward other social
groups or one's own group in studies of prejudice or group consciousness
(see, for example, Campbell 1971; Jackman 1978; Gurin, Miller, and
Gurin 1980; Miller et al. 1981; Bobo 1983).[3] Direct measurement of the
perception of group interests is even more unusual; a rare example is
found in Landecker (1963).

2. Gramsci was writing as a political activist as much as an analyst, and his interest in
the concept of hegemony appears to have been motivated in large part by the implications
it held for the Communist party political agenda. His ideas about cultural hegemony led
him to advocate that, in order to accomplish a complete overthrow of capitalism, in all its
manifestations, it was essential to foster a working-class cultural hegemony (Williams 1960;
Cammett 1967, 204–206; Anderson 1976). However, as Scott (1985, 316) has observed,
it is difficult for the analyst to divine how, given one hegemony, there can simultaneously
be the latitude to cultivate a counter-hegemony: the two ideas are logically inconsistent.

3. The community studies conducted by Williams, Jr. (1964, 280–281) included a rare,
early attempt to measure blacks' feelings toward whites directly. Two items were used:
"Sometimes I hate white people [agree/disagree]," and "In general, how friendly or unfriendly are your feelings toward whites? Would you say you are very friendly, fairly
friendly, rather unfriendly, or not friendly at all?" The first of these items was used again
by Paige (1972) in a study of blacks' racial attitudes in the 1960s.

The minimal measurement of these concepts is paradoxical, but it is probably attributable to the compounding of two factors. First, ironically, assumptions about these phenomena have been so deeply embedded in various conceptual positions that there has not been much pressure to measure them directly: their importance has been so confidently assumed that empirical validation has rarely entered the research agenda. Students of prejudice and group consciousness have assumed that people's emotional dispositions toward other groups are artlessly manifested in every aspect of their intergroup attitudes, especially in stereotypical attributions of personality traits, social-distance dispositions, and policy views. Meanwhile, students of tolerance simply assumed that people's feelings toward minority groups were negative—and they then concentrated on measuring people's policy dispositions toward a group to assess whether they had attained a state of political tolerance (see, for example, Stouffer 1955). Inferences about people's perception of group interests have frequently been made in studies of class consciousness, but those inferences have generally been drawn from measures of people's policy views—it was presumed that the latter constituted a clear reflection of the perception of group interests.

Second, those proclivities have been compounded by the fact that intergroup feelings and the perception of group interests are relatively difficult to measure directly. Analysts have found other attitudinal elements, such as stereotypes, social-distance dispositions, and policy views, more susceptible to measurement. The inclination to measure indirect manifestations of the attitudinal core rather than the core itself was perhaps encouraged by the influence of Freudian thinking among some early empirical researchers. Some researchers felt that direct measures of people's feelings in particular would be invalid because respondents would be unable to retrieve or reflect clearly on such a deeply embedded and sensitive matter. This kind of concern is apparent in the widely influential California F-scale, whose creators (Adorno et al. 1950) deliberately relied on projective rather than direct questions. But one does not need to be a Freudian to acknowledge the difficulties that confront the survey researcher in measuring intergroup feelings and the perception of group interests.

Feelings are intrinsically nonverbal, and our culture gives us little experience in articulating our feelings verbally. In our everyday efforts, we usually find speech a clumsy instrument to convey the rich texture of felt emotions, and we often rely on nonverbal cues (posture, facial expression, tone of voice, body movements) to transmit the emotional coloration of our words. We may expect, then, that people would find it difficult to retrieve and convey their feelings in the somewhat stilted verbal back-and-forth of the survey interview.

The perception of group interests presents fewer intrinsic measurement difficulties, but because public political discourse rarely portrays political issues explicitly in those terms, the mass public is unschooled in the concrete attribution of group interests. Thus, they may have trouble understanding or responding to questionnaire items that ask about the specific policy interests of their own and other groups, because they are unused to the process of sizing up social life explicitly in that light.

These various difficulties are substantial, but not insurmountable. Indeed, it is essential to develop direct measures of these phenomena if we are to develop more specific expectations about their place in the mapping of intergroup attitudes. I return to these issues when I present my measures in the Data section below.

An additional consideration has probably discouraged researchers from measuring feelings toward social groups especially, and that is concern about social desirability pressures. On a topic as sensitive and personal as one's feelings toward social groups, some researchers may feel that respondents would be reluctant to reveal themselves openly, especially when asked about groups that have been the topic of heated public-policy debate. The potential for social desirability pressures must be respected in designing survey items on sensitive issues, but the significance of such pressures may have been overestimated.

Evidence suggests that people tend to assume that others hold similar views to their own (Schuman and Kalton, 1985, 655), a phenomenon that has been termed "looking-glass perceptions" (Fields and Schuman, 1976) or the "false consensus effect" (Ross, Greene, and House, 1977). Although that may seem surprising, most people are caught up in their own networks of information and experiences: because their own feelings and opinions have been formed within that context, they generally find that their own reactions are consistent with those of others in their social environment. This leaves them unself-conscious about their own reactions. Individuals whose feelings and opinions are out of step with the normative proclivities of their group might be expected to be especially susceptible to social-desirability pressures, but such people generally come from pockets that have been bypassed by the primary information channels that flow through the group, and hence they may also be oblivious to the "social undesirability" of their views. In other words, the same factors that shaped their unusual reactions also buffer them from an acute awareness of their unusual nature. Thus, for example, Fields and Schuman (1976) report that only 2 percent of Detroit whites believed that white and black children should be prevented from playing with one another even at school, but this tiny minority believed overwhelmingly that their own attitude was shared by the majority of Detroit whites. And even when people are aware that their feelings are in the minority for their group, it is probably more compelling to them that others in their local network share their reactions than are the relatively distant reactions of others who lie outside their day-to-day lives.

On a more fundamental level, the concept of social desirability is less straightforward than it first seems. The problem is that if social desirability exerts pressure on how people reveal themselves, it may not be a narrow problem of measurement error confined to the survey interview, but a general phenomenon affecting the way people express their attitudes to their friends and associates, and even affecting the way they form those attitudes in the first place. If attitudes are seen primarily as the personal, private property of individuals, it is somewhat easier to conceive of pressures outside the individual as a contaminant. If, however, we see intergroup attitudes as being shaped by the exigencies and information that emanate from the group, the notion of the culture of the group exerting an extraneous pressure on its individual constituents' attitudinal expressions no longer makes sense. My argument is that people do not develop their attitudes independently and then lie about them when they believe they are out of step with the predominant cultural values of the group. Instead, the individual's attitudes are acquired without originality from the array provided by the group, and that array is itself shaped by the pressures to which the group is subject: in this unselfconscious process, the distinction between private dispositions and public ones becomes more difficult to maintain. Thus, although it is essential to construct measures that minimize any artifactual pressures in the interview situation itself, the notion of social desirability is not necessarily a simple issue of measurement alone, but entails broader questions about the forces that shape the attitudes we are trying to measure.

Dispensable Hostility

All the arguments I have outlined from past literature on prejudice, tolerance, and group consciousness pivot, for different reasons, on the notion of intergroup disparity and hostility. But I contend that dominant groups, far from having negative feelings toward subordinates, gravitate toward positive, or at least neutralized emotional dispositions. By the same token, I expect dominant groups to maintain an integrated view of the interests of their own and subordinate groups. If this is correct, it changes the nature of the game dramatically from any of the scenarios that have framed past discussions.

First, it means that subordinates do not have to distance themselves from the dominant group in order to have positive feelings about themselves. Second, it means that if subordinates are to take a hostile disposition toward the dominant group, they cannot simply reciprocate with venom for venom. Instead, it is incumbent upon them, from their weaker political position, to renounce amicable feelings and inject hostility into the relationship—a dangerous game, since the dominant group has the resources to reciprocate more than generously. Third, if the amicability of the dominant group is packaged with an interpretation of social reality that binds the interests of the groups together, subordinates may have a difficult time prying those two items apart, and thus the acceptance of the amicability carries a price tag.

I assume that groups gravitate to an ideology that is rationally consistent with their interests. But I also assume that the rational actor does not naively pursue goals on the basis of their desirability alone, but is sensitive to constraints. Occasional mistakes and miscalculations are to be expected, but groups do learn from their mistakes. Most of the time, the articulated attitudes of unequal groups reflect responses that strive to maximize their control over resources *within the conditions that they confront*. This does not lead me to expect a great deal of hostility from either side of an intergroup relationship. Indeed, even the literature on group consciousness, for all its endorsement of intergroup hostility as the ultimate rational outcome, does not specify an avenue by which such hostility may be realized. None of the ideas articulated in that literature can be reconciled with the expectation of an eventual conflict, such as that envisioned by Marx and Engels, in which both sides attain an understanding of their mutual relationship and draw a sharp affective boundary between each other.

If, as many students of group consciousness have argued, dominant groups are engaged in establishing the common interest as the moral guideline, it would seem more in keeping for them to espouse the spirit of friendship toward subordinates than to adopt hostile feelings toward them. It is not in the interests of the dominant group to introduce or encourage feelings of hostility because that would (1) expose the inequality in the harshest possible light, and (2) remove their most potent weapon of social control—the offer of amicable relations, on their terms. On subordinates' part, it is hard to see how they can break completely free of such a sticky moral framework and push it to one of sharp mutual disparity and hostility.

At the same time, the totality of the concept of hegemony seems too unyielding and unidirectional to take account of the varying opportunities that different kinds of unequal intergroup relationships offer for dominant groups to invade the perceptions and feelings of subordinates. Subordinates are not passive recipients of dominant ideology, and their frame of mind is much affected by the opportunities that are afforded them to alienate their thinking from that of the dominant group. The dominant group, in turn, is sensitive to the kinds of communication channels that are available and attentive to the mood of the group over which it seeks to maintain control. In other words, the thinking on both sides responds to the specific constraints that are presented.

In relations that are structured with frequent personal contact across group lines, dominant groups have more opportunity to infiltrate the lives of subordinates. Under these circumstances, there are escalated costs to individual subordinates of emotional and cognitive estrangement from the prevailing arrangements. When relations are structured more distally, warm intergroup feelings are more difficult for the dominant group to maintain and less personally costly for subordinates to abandon—but even here, there is good reason for the dominant group to strive to avoid disparity and for subordinates to approach it with circumspection.

To begin to address these issues, we need to delineate the emotional and perceptual currents that flow back and forth from one group to another in different intergroup relations. Three pieces of information are central. First, is there an emotional rift between one group and another, such that the members of each group feel emotionally attached to their own and separated from the other group(s) in the relationship? In other words, is there a sense of affective solidarity within groups and disparity between them? Second, to what extent is hostility present in people's feelings toward the other group(s) in the relationship? The degree of affective differentiation between groups and negative feeling directed toward the other group(s) represent the two elementary pieces of information that we need to assess one group's emotional disposition toward another. How those dispositions are exchanged between unequal groups throws light on their use and meaning in the interplay of dominance and subordination. Of particular importance is the question of which group—dominant or subordinate—seems more wedded to intergroup amicability or further advanced into the realms of hostility. Third, how do the contending groups define their interests? Do dominant groups tend to portray status quo arrangements as being in the common good, or do they identify distinct group interests? Do subordinates accede to the views of the dominant group? And if they mount a challenge, what form does it take? As we examine the admixture of feelings and perceptions that characterize race, gender, and social class relations, we can identify the place of hostility and amicability in the conduct of different kinds of unequal relations.

DATA: INTERGROUP FEELINGS

I begin by examining the intergroup feelings that characterize race, gender, and class relations. After describing my measures, I examine the data for each intergroup relationship, in turn, and I then draw out the general patterns across the three cases.

Measures

I measured people's feelings toward their own and other groups with two sets of questions that were contained in a booklet that respondents filled out privately during the interview. Interviewers introduced the booklet as follows:

> The questions in this booklet ask about various feelings people might have toward different groups. On the first page, you are asked generally how warm or cold you feel toward different groups. The warmer you feel toward a group, the *higher* the number you should select from the scale at the top of the page. The *colder* you feel, the *lower* the number you should select. Don't feel you have to spend a lot of time on this. Again, we're just interested in your first reactions.

Interviewers were instructed to hand the booklet and a pencil to the respondent, to busy themselves with other tasks while the respondent filled out the booklet, and to put the booklet in an envelope when the respondent handed it back.

On two separate pages in the booklet (back to back) were two sets of questions of the following form:

> In general, how warm or cold do you feel toward ———?
> In general, how close do you feel to ———?

The stimulus-objects were *poor* people, *working-class* people, *middle-class* people, *upper-middle-class* people, *upper-class* people, *women, men, blacks,* and *whites,* in that order for the warm/cold questions, and rearranged as gender, race, and then class groups for the closeness questions. For both sets of questions, subordinate groups preceded dominant groups as stimulus-objects within each relationship, so that respondents would use subordinate groups as the anchor. The scales that accompanied these questions at the top of the page were marked in single digits from 1 to 9 going across the page: 1 was identified as VERY COLD and NOT AT ALL CLOSE for the respective sets of questions, 5 was identified as NEITHER COLD NOR WARM or NEITHER ONE FEELING NOR THE OTHER, 9 was identified as VERY WARM or VERY CLOSE, and the other numbers were left unmarked.

These questions are modeled, with several modifications, on the thermometer questions used repeatedly in the National Election Studies conducted by the Inter-University Consortium for Political and Social Research at the University of Michigan (NES 1952–1990 Cumulative Data File Codebook). Like the thermometer items, these questions rely on numbers rather than words as the vehicle to communicate feelings, thereby avoiding the difficulty that respondents might have in using words to articulate their feelings accurately. The use of numbers seems to require a less complex transliteration of a nonverbal phenomenon. The thermometer scale relies on the analogy with a thermometer to assist the respondent, but I used a shorter numerical scale because I feared that the use of 100 points might convey an expectation of precision that would lead the respondent to become more self-conscious and guarded. A relatively crude numerical scale, with higher numbers corresponding in the intuitively easiest way with warmer or closer feelings, should maximize respondents' ability to express their feelings with as little self-consciousness as possible.

The questions have four features to alleviate possible social-desirability pressures. First, and most important, the presentation of the questions in a self-administered booklet made people's responses private from the interviewer, thus removing the most immediate potential stimulus for social-desirability responses. It is hard to assess how much or what the respondent assumes about the attitudes of the female stranger who interviews him or whether the respondent cares, but whatever pressures exist to impress another should be more potent when face-to-face with a live person than vis-à-vis an anonymous researcher at the other end of a computer somewhere. Second, reliance on numbers rather than words for responses avoids the social overtones that adhere to many words associated with emotions. By intercepting responses without using the language of social discourse, any pressures stemming from that source are kept more at bay. Third, by asking respondents about their feelings toward each group separately, they are spared the invidious task of drawing explicit comparisons between different groups. Although comparisons are still implied in the sets of questions (and are of primary interest in our analysis), they are broached with more delicacy than would be the case with explicit comparisons. This, too, should make respondents more relaxed in answering the questions. Finally, I used balanced questions with graduated response-options in order to avoid loading the questions in one direction or the other.

In their content, my measures focus on the two affective responses that are most fundamental to discussions of intergroup attitudes—feelings of like or dislike, and feelings of closeness or distance. Although the former presents clear positive and negative poles (warm versus cold), the latter has no clearly negative pole but instead strikes at the degree of affinity someone feels for her own and other groups. These two kinds of feelings are very similar, but their particular nuances may elicit subtle differences. In particular, if people tend to avoid the expression of hostility, they may be more inclined to give responses that suggest a feeling of closer affinity to their own group than an outright preference for their own group on a positive-negative dimension.

With both kinds of feelings, I am interested in two aspects of their expression. First, and most important, I gauge the extent to which affective boundaries are drawn between groups. Are groups solidified by emotional bonds within ranks and ruptured from other groups by affective disparity? This is measured by examining the difference between the feelings respondents express for their own group and for the other referent group. Each respondent's warmth- or closeness-score for the other group was subtracted from her score for her own group. With 9-point scales, difference-scores could range from +8 (strong preference for one's own group) through 0 (same score for both groups) to −8 (strong preference for the other group).[4] These scores are collapsed into three categories in tables 5.1 (for race), 5.3 (for gender), and 5.5 (for class), to show the percentages of each group who (1) feel warmer or closer to their own group, (2) do not differentiate in their feelings toward the two referent groups, and (3) say they feel warmer or closer to the other group.

Second, I look behind the issue of affective differentiation at the absolute level of feeling respondents express for other referent groups. This gauges the way their emotional dispositions toward other groups are cast. The 9-point scales for warmth and closeness were each collapsed into three categories: negative feelings (scores of 1–4), neutral feelings (score of 5), and positive feelings (scores of 6–9). Those data are presented in tables 5.2 (for race), 5.4 (for gender), and 5.6 (for class).[5]

Results

For each intergroup relationship, there are two tables presenting data on, first, the affective boundaries that lie between groups and, second, the degree to which hostility or affection is the emotional currency that is being tendered. I examine race, gender, and class, in turn, before drawing out general patterns.

Race.   Race relations present our best evidence for reciprocated hostility between groups. Even here, however, the hostility is muted. Table

---

4. The difference-scores for warmth and closeness are highly correlated. The Pearson's r's (with missing data excluded) are as follows: for race, .77; for gender, .59; and for class, they range from .42 to .67 across the ten possible class comparisons.

5. In tables 5.1 through 5.6, respondents with missing data or who said "don't know" are excluded. Such respondents comprised about 3–5 percent of the total sample on any given measure.

TABLE 5.1.   Affective Differentiation between the Races Made by
Whites and Blacks: Percentages and Mean Scores.

	Warmth		Closeness	
	Whites	Blacks	Whites	Blacks
Prefer Own Group	44.7%	55.8%*	59.9%	62.0%
Neutral	53.9	44.2	38.8	38.0
Prefer Other Group	1.4	0.0	1.3	0.0
Mean Score[a]	1.23†	1.82†	1.79†	2.10†
Base N	1582	190	1569	187

[a] Mean scores are based on the full scale: range $= -8$ (prefer other group) to $+8$ (prefer own group).
* Difference between groups in percentage distributions is statistically significant (p = .01).
† Mean score is significantly different from zero (p < .01).

5.1 presents the percentages of whites and blacks making different kinds of affective distinctions between the races, as well as the mean difference-scores for each group. Table 5.2 presents the percentages of whites and blacks expressing negative, neutral, or positive feelings toward each other, along with the mean warmth and closeness scores.

Whites and blacks almost mirror one another in the affective distinctions they draw along racial lines. No blacks and virtually no whites express greater warmth or closeness toward the other racial group: affective differentiation ranges from neutrality to preference for one's own group. In feelings of closeness, own-group preference predominates, with about 60 percent of both whites and blacks saying they feel closer to their own group.[6] In terms of warmth, where the scale contains a clear negative pole, there is a little more reticence about expressing a preference for one's own group, especially among whites: 45 percent of whites and 56 percent of blacks feel warmer toward their own racial group.

Expressions of own-group preference are unlikely to be fulsome, however, on either side, and whites are especially inclined to confine their expressions of preference to modest levels. More detailed data for the uncollapsed scales (not presented here) indicate that about half of the whites who express a preference for their own group on either scale are drawing a distinction of only one or two points, and the percentages drawing larger distinctions drop off rapidly. Blacks are just as unlikely to draw gaping distinctions (that is, to have difference-scores of 5–8

6. Middle-class blacks are slightly more likely than blacks in the poor and working class to say they feel closer to their own race. In the poor and working class, blacks express about the same degree of own-race preference as do whites, but in the middle class, 72 percent of blacks and 64 percent of whites say they feel closer to their own race.

TABLE 5.2.   Percentages of Whites and Blacks Expressing Negative and Positive Feelings toward Each Other.

	Warmth		Closeness	
	Whites	Blacks	Whites	Blacks
Negative Feelings (1–4)	25.0%	13.7%*	39.1%	19.8%*
Neutral (5)	43.1	38.9	40.3	36.4
Positive Feelings (6–9)	31.9	47.4	20.5	43.9
Mean Score[a]	5.2	5.9	4.5	5.6
Base N	1584	190	1572	187

[a] Mean scores are based on the full scale: range = 1 (most negative) to 9 (most positive).
* Difference between groups in percentage distributions is statistically significant (p < .01).

points), but they are a bit more inclined to draw moderately large distinctions: about 80 percent of the blacks who prefer their own racial group have difference-scores of 1–4 points, with differences of 3–4 points occurring with about equal frequency to differences of 1–2 points.

When we look at the absolute feelings that are exchanged between groups (table 5.2), we find that outright negative feelings are expressed by a minority on either side. However, negativism is a little more likely to be expressed in terms of not feeling close than in terms of feeling cold toward the other group, and it is found more among whites than among blacks. Among whites, as many as 25 percent say they feel cold toward blacks and 39 percent say they do not feel close to blacks. Among blacks, only 14 percent say they feel cold toward whites and 20 percent say they do not feel close to whites.[7] The balance of responses is tilted slightly toward neutral expressions among whites and slightly toward positive expressions among blacks. The result is that among whites, professions of warmth still slightly outweigh professions of coldness toward blacks, but expressing a lack of closeness outweighs some degree of closeness by about two to one; among blacks, positive dispositions outweigh negative ones by more than three to one in terms of warm versus cold and by more than two to one on the close/not-close dimension.

The data in tables 5.1 and 5.2 indicate that whites and blacks roughly mirror each other in an exchange of muted hostility. Blacks are somewhat more likely than whites to express a preference for their own group, but a larger minority of whites invokes negative feelings toward the other

7. Black women express a little more negativism than do black men in their feelings toward whites: 6.5 percent of black men and 17.2 percent of black women say they feel cold toward whites; 8.1 percent of black men and 25.6 percent of black women say they do not feel close to whites.

TABLE 5.3.   Affective Differentiation between the Sexes Made by Men and Women: Percentages and Mean Scores.

	Warmth		Closeness	
	Men	Women	Men	Women
Prefer Own Group	4.5%	19.6%*	14.1%	31.6%*
Neutral	60.3	65.5	55.8	52.0
Prefer Other Group	35.2	14.9	30.1	16.4
Mean Score[a]	−0.72†	0.13†	−0.42†	0.30†
Base N	775	1066	772	1062

[a] Mean scores are based on the full scale: range = −8 (prefer other group) to +8 (prefer own group).
* Difference between groups in percentage distributions is statistically significant ($p < .01$).
† Mean score is significantly different from zero ($p < .01$).

group. These small differences aside, the prevailing feelings on both sides range from neutrality to restrained affective disparity.

Gender.   The affective character of gender relations contrasts sharply with that of race relations. Although men and women also tend to mirror each other's feelings, the tenor of the exchange is markedly more positive. The pertinent data are presented in tables 5.3 and 5.4.

The data in table 5.3 show that few men express an emotional preference for their own sex, in terms of either warmth (under 5 percent) or closeness (14 percent). Instead, most men either draw no affective distinction between the sexes (56–60 percent) or actually state a preference for women (30–35 percent). Thus, men's gender feelings tend to cluster around the neutral point, and deviations from affective neutrality are more likely to extend in the direction of preferring the other sex. In addition, men are likely to draw slightly larger affective distinctions when their feelings favor women: among men favoring their own sex, difference-scores are almost never larger than 2 points, but among men favoring the other sex, the differentiation generally falls in a range from 1–4 points.

Women more or less reciprocate men's feelings, although they are slightly more likely than men to feel warmer toward their own sex (20 percent) or closer to their own sex (32 percent), and they are a bit less inclined to express a preference for the other sex (15–16 percent). Nor do women share men's slight proclivity to draw larger affective distinctions in favor of the other sex than their own: among women, affective distinctions that favor either their own or the other sex tend to fall in the range from 1–4 points.

Not surprisingly, the data in table 5.4 indicate that in the affective

TABLE 5.4.   Percentages of Men and Women Expressing Negative and Positive Feelings toward Each Other.

	Warmth		*Closeness*	
	Men	Women	Men	Women
Negative Feelings (1–4)	3.1%	3.8%*	8.3%	8.3%
Neutral (5)	25.4	32.7	29.6	33.4
Positive Feelings (6–9)	71.5	63.5	62.1	58.3
Mean Score[a]	6.9	6.5	6.3	6.1
Base N	775	1070	774	1062

[a] Mean scores are based on the full scale: range = 1 (most negative) to 9 (most positive).
* Difference between groups in percentage distributions is statistically significant (p < .01).

dispositions of each sex toward the other, positive feelings abound. About two-thirds of men and women have positive emotional dispositions toward each other, and negative feelings are expressed by only 3–8 percent of either group.

Thus, the overwhelming tenor of gender feelings is a lack of affective differentiation along group lines and a positive emotional disposition toward the other sex. Feelings of closeness are slightly less likely than feelings of warmth to evince such inclusive feelings toward the other sex, and women are a little more hesitant than men, but the general pattern stands in sharp contrast to race relations.[8]

Class.   Because class relations do not involve a simple dyad, assessment of the exchange of feelings among social classes is necessarily more complex. Table 5.5 presents data on the affective differentiation made by members of the upper-middle class, middle class, working class, and poor between their own class and each of the other classes. Table 5.6 presents data on the level of warmth/coldness and closeness expressed in people's feelings toward each of the other classes. Upper-class identifiers are excluded from these tables because there is an insufficient num-

8. Black men and women are more likely than their white counterparts to express an affective preference for and positive feelings toward the other sex, but this tendency is especially pronounced among black men. Most notably, among black men 63 percent feel warmer toward women than toward their own sex, and 65 percent feel closer to women (as compared with 33 percent and 27 percent of white men expressing those feelings). Among black women, 25 percent feel warmer toward men than toward their own sex (as opposed to 13 percent of white women) and 33 percent feel closer to men (as compared with 14 percent of white women). Thus, black women do not display the slight tendency observed among white women to prefer their own sex over men; but, at the same time, the asymmetry between black men and black women in the degree to which they favor the other sex is considerably larger than it is among whites, with black men leading even more in the expression of inclusive feelings.

TABLE 5.5. Affective Differentiation between the Classes, Made by the Upper-Middle Class, Middle Class, Working Class and Poor: Percentages and Mean Scores.*

	Warmth					Closeness				
	vs. Upper	vs. Upper-Middle	vs. Middle	vs. Working	vs. Poor	vs. Upper	vs. Upper-Middle	vs. Middle	vs. Working	vs. Poor
Upper-Middle Class										
Prefer Own Class	32.9%	—	12.9%	20.0%	27.3%	42.5%	—	20.9%	34.6%	45.1%
Neutral	63.2	—	71.0	58.7	44.8	55.6	—	61.4	49.7	40.5
Prefer Other Class	3.9	—	16.1	21.3	27.8	2.0	—	17.6	15.7	14.4
Mean Score[a]	0.57†	—	−0.08	−0.04	−0.05	0.81†	—	−0.02	0.50†	0.93†
Base N	155	—	155	155	154	153	—	153	153	153
Middle Class										
Prefer Own Class	49.3%	36.4%	—	14.5%	28.3%	57.6%	43.8%	—	21.5%	40.8%
Neutral	47.3	59.1	—	70.7	49.8	38.6	51.7	—	67.6	45.0
Prefer Other Class	3.3	4.4	—	14.8	22.0	3.9	4.6	—	10.9	14.1
Mean Score	1.08†	0.61†	—	−0.02	0.13††	1.35†	0.77†	—	0.17†	0.61†
Base N	811	810	—	811	810	808	809	—	805	806
Working Class										
Prefer Own Class	59.8%	53.0%	34.9%	—	26.8%	62.5%	57.0%	37.6%	—	32.3%
Neutral	37.1	43.2	60.9	—	60.0	35.7	40.4	58.5	—	58.2
Prefer Other Class	3.1	3.8	4.3	—	13.2	1.8	2.7	3.9	—	9.5
Mean Score	1.66†	1.18†	0.57†	—	0.31†	1.87†	1.39†	0.64†	—	0.53†
Base N	676	676	677	—	680	673	674	675	—	677
Poor										
Prefer Own Class	58.2%	55.4%	44.7%	21.4%	—	62.3%	57.7%	49.6%	23.6%	—
Neutral	36.4	36.9	49.2	69.5	—	33.6	36.6	42.4	65.4	—
Prefer Other Class	5.6	7.7	6.1	9.2	—	4.1	5.7	8.0	11.0	—
Mean Score	2.05†	1.62†	1.11†	0.25	—	2.12†	1.77†	1.08†	0.34†	—
Base N	129	130	132	131	—	122	123	125	127	—

[a] Mean scores based on the full scale: range = −8 (prefer other class) to +8 (prefer own class).
* Differences between all reciprocal pairs of classes in percentage distributions are statistically significant (p < .05), with the following three exceptions: in Warmth differentiation, Working Class versus Poor; in Closeness differentiation, Working Class versus Poor, and Middle Class versus Poor.
† Mean score is significantly different from zero (p < .01).
†† Mean score is significantly different from zero (p < .05).

ber of them to allow for reliable inferences (see chapter 3), but the upper class is retained as a stimulus for those who identified with other classes.

The amount of affective disparity expressed between classes and the level of warmth/coldness and closeness expressed toward other classes are both highly variable, being dependent on two main factors. First, affective distinctions and negative feelings are more in evidence when people are contemplating classes higher than their own than when they regard those lower than their own. Second, such feelings come more to the fore as the status-distance of the referent class increases. These effects are compounded in the overall pattern of class feelings, to which

I now turn. Examples are drawn from the warm-cold data, but note that affective disparity and negative feelings are both more likely to be evinced in terms of degree of closeness than in terms of coldness versus warmth, especially when the referent class is lower than one's own.

The heightened sensitivity of people to the gap that separates them from higher classes than from the gap between their own and lower classes is illustrated neatly in the affective distinctions drawn by the middle class. When the upper class is the referent, about one-half of the middle class express warmer feelings toward their own class and virtually no one states a preference for the higher class; but in relation to the poor (an equally distant, lower class), only 28 percent of the middle class express a preference for their own class, and this is almost matched by 22 percent who express warmer feelings toward the lower class. The more generalized display of this phenomenon is in the marked asymmetry between the intergroup feelings expressed by lower and higher classes in relation to one another. Lower classes express greater affective disparity from higher classes than is reciprocated, and this asymmetry is more pronounced than that observed between unequal racial or gender groups. For example, only 27 percent of the upper-middle class feel warmer to their own class than to the poor, and this is matched by 28 percent of their class-compatriots who profess warmer feelings toward the poor. But among the poor making the same affective comparison, 55 percent feel warmer to their own class, and fewer than 8 percent express greater warmth toward the upper-middle class.[9]

This asymmetry is also evident in the exchange of feelings between

9. The asymmetry in the feelings exchanged between higher and lower classes is more sharply pronounced among blacks, even though their class identifications effectively span only the distance from the poor to the middle class. In the exchange of feelings among those three classes, blacks in the working and middle classes are less likely than their white class-peers to express own-class preference vis-à-vis lower classes, and are more likely to prefer the lower class; in addition, there is a (weaker) tendency for blacks in the poor and working class to be more likely than their white class-peers to feel warmer and closer to their own class than to higher classes. For example, in differentiation in feelings of closeness between the poor and the middle class, only 17 percent of the black middle class prefer their own class whereas 43 percent prefer the poor (as compared with 42 percent of the white middle class who prefer their own class and 12 percent who prefer the poor); among the poor, 58 percent of the blacks and 43 percent of the whites prefer their own class over the middle class. These distinctive class feelings among blacks are most readily interpreted in terms of the intensity of racial identity combined with the overrepresentation of blacks among lower classes and their marginal presence in the middle and upper-middle classes: blacks in all classes may feel more distant from the middle and upper-middle classes because these classes are predominantly white, whereas they feel closer to the poor and the working class because they have a stronger black contingent and because they identify their historical roots in those classes (these issues are discussed in greater detail in Jackman and Jackman 1983, 46–53).

proximate classes, where class feeling is weakest. Between any pair of proximate classes, own-class preference is generally expressed by about one third of the lower class, whereas affective neutrality prevails much more heavily in the higher class (only between the poor and the working class do feelings of warmth fall closer to the neutral point on both sides). Expressions of affective disparity increase steadily among both lower and higher classes as the status-distance of the referent class increases, with lower classes maintaining greater affective distinctions than are reciprocated.

Thus, affective differentiation between the classes encompasses a wide range. In some class comparisons, there is a virtual absence of affective disparity (as when higher classes regard proximate lower ones). This is akin to men's feelings vis-à-vis women, except that men's feelings show more of a tilt toward an actual preference for the subordinate group. At the other extreme are the class feelings expressed by the poor and working class vis-à-vis the upper and upper-middle classes: here, the extent of affective disparity exceeds that expressed by blacks vis-à-vis whites. The response of the upper-middle class, however, is more tempered than the response blacks get from whites. The size of the affective distinctions that are drawn between the classes also varies widely, in tandem with their frequency: the smallest distinctions are comparable to those expressed by men vis-à-vis women and the largest are about as large as or larger than the racial distinctions drawn by blacks.

The absolute level of people's affective dispositions toward other classes reflects the same mixture of elements (see table 5.6). In feelings toward the upper and upper-middle classes expressed by the working class and the poor, feelings of warmth generally outweigh feelings of coldness by a factor of two or three to one, with about one-third to one-half holding positive dispositions. This is similar to blacks' level of warmth toward whites. However, in the emotional dispositions of the upper-middle class toward the working class and poor, there is an even stronger positive bent: well over half of the upper-middle class profess feelings of warmth toward the working class and poor, and only a negligible percentage (5–9 percent) express negative feelings. Positive feelings are generally heightened between more proximate classes, although they usually fall short of the level of positive feeling expressed by men toward women.

General Patterns. Two general patterns are present to a greater or lesser degree across all three intergroup relationships. I discuss each pattern in turn and then consider the sources of their varied expression from one relationship to another. Figure 5.1 provides a quick reference for this discussion, by summarizing the differentiation in feelings of

TABLE 5.6.   Percentages of the Upper-Middle Class, Middle Class, Working Class, and the Poor Expressing Negative and Positive Feelings toward Each of the Other Classes.[a]

	Warmth toward . . .*					Closeness toward . . .*				
	Upper	Upper-Middle	Middle	Working	Poor	Upper	Upper-Middle	Middle	Working	Poor
Upper-Middle Class										
Negative (1–4)	16.8%	—	3.9%	4.5%	9.1%	22.9%	—	7.8%	17.6%	32.0%
Positive (6–9)	40.0	—	53.5	54.2	55.2	37.9	—	58.8	42.5	34.6
Mean Score[b]	5.5	—	6.1	6.1	6.1	5.3	—	6.1	5.6	5.2
Middle Class										
Negative (1–4)	21.6%	12.1%	—	3.6%	9.6%	28.5%	17.2%	—	8.3%	20.1%
Positive (6–9)	34.4	44.4	—	60.9	56.2	27.6	39.9	—	57.0	44.5
Mean Score	5.4	5.8	—	6.5	6.3	5.0	5.5	—	6.1	5.7
Working Class										
Negative (1–4)	29.1%	16.1%	4.1%	—	6.6%	32.1%	22.1%	7.0%	—	11.9%
Positive (6–9)	33.1	41.0	57.9	—	62.6	26.3	34.9	55.4	—	56.2
Mean Score	5.3	5.7	6.3	—	6.6	4.9	5.4	6.1	—	6.2
Poor										
Negative (1–4)	21.7%	13.1%	9.8%	0.8%	—	22.0%	17.7%	7.1%	3.9%	—
Positive (6–9)	47.3	53.8	64.4	79.4	—	46.3	52.4	66.7	76.6	—
Mean Score	5.7	6.1	6.6	7.5	—	5.5	5.9	6.6	7.3	—

[a] Percentages sum to less than 100% because the percentage giving the mid-point response ("5") is not displayed. Base N's are the same or slightly larger than those given in table 5.5.
[b] Mean scores based on full scale: range = 1 (most negative) to 9 (most positive).
* Differences between reciprocal pairs of classes in percentage distributions are statistically significant (p ≤ .01), except for the following cases: in WARMTH toward each other, Working Class versus Middle Class, Poor versus Middle Class, and Poor versus Upper-Middle Class; in CLOSENESS toward each other, Working Class versus Middle Class, and Working Class versus Upper-Middle Class.

warmth expressed between whites and blacks, men and women, and the poor and the upper-middle class.

First, and most important, there is a general avoidance of hostile feelings by both dominant and subordinate groups. Even in the staunchest examples of affective disparity (as in the feelings of the poor and working class vis-à-vis the upper-middle and upper classes, and in the feelings exchanged between blacks and whites), one-third to one-half of the members of those groups refrain from socially divisive feelings. In addition, the affective distinctions that are made are most likely to be small or moderate in size—gaping affective distinctions are rare. By the same token, most respondents stay away from the negative side of the two scales in expressing their affective dispositions toward other groups.

The general avoidance of inflammatory feelings is further demonstrated in the amplified expressions of own-group preference and slightly freer use of the negative side of the scale for other groups when respondents were asked about degree of closeness to each group rather than feelings of warmth versus coldness. The lack of a clear negative pole in the former scale gave respondents an opportunity to express a feeling of closer affinity to their own group without seeming to disparage the other group. The pattern of responses in all groups was affected at

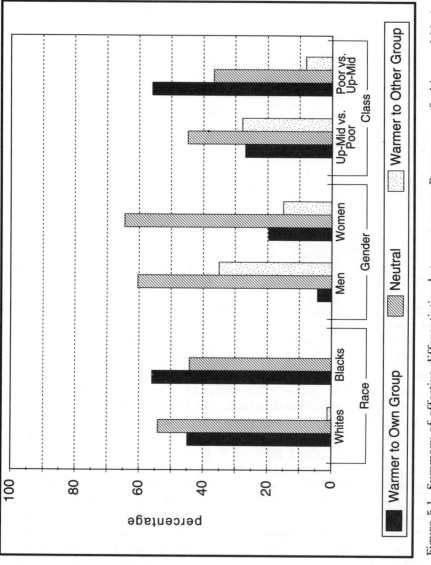

Figure 5.1. Summary of affective differentiation between groups: Percentages of whites and blacks, men and women, and the upper-middle class and the poor expressing warmer feelings toward their own group, neutral feelings, and warmer feelings toward the other group. Based on figures from tables

least slightly by that delicate distinction (even in the gender relationship), but dominant groups appear somewhat more sensitive to this than do subordinate groups.

The second general pattern that holds to some degree across all three intergroup relationships is a slight asymmetry between the feelings of dominant and subordinate groups. Subordinate groups run a little ahead of dominant groups in expressing a feeling of preference for their own, and the affective distinctions they make are likely to be a bit larger than those made by dominant groups. This asymmetry is never dramatic—the feelings that are exchanged between contending groups are generally in the same vein—but dominant-group members seem slightly more reticent than subordinates about drawing affective boundaries along group lines. Interestingly, the asymmetry is more noticeable on the warm-cold scale (with its clear negative pole) than it is on the closeness scale: in the safer context of affinity-without-disparagement, dominant-group members come nearer to matching subordinates in expressions of intergroup disparity.

The general restraint that is shown in the expression of intergroup feelings suggests that pressures on both sides of unequal relationships mitigate against flagrant emotional divisiveness. That dominant groups show particular restraint probably reflects a slightly different balance of pressures to which they are subject. To begin, dominant groups may be less sensitive than subordinates to the experiential disparity that exists between the groups. The experience of deprivations may be a more compelling nudge to awareness of disparity than is the enjoyment of benefits. It is easier to overlook or minimize the rude division between unequal groups when the arrangement delivers benefits rather than deprivations. By the same token, as dominant groups enjoy the sweet benefits of harmony within the status quo, divisiveness looms more unequivocally as a risk that could lead to a narrower circumscription of those benefits or even their loss. For subordinates, however, the costs of conflict (which are still considerable in view of their weaker position) are weighed against the daily price they pay for their integration in the status quo as incumbents of an inferior position.

This discrepancy in the pressures felt on either side of an unequal relationship is exacerbated in class relations, where the upper-middle class has been the tardiest in reciprocating the affective disparity expressed by the poor and working class. I suggest two main factors are at work here. First is the importance of self-identification, rather than imposed group definitions, for the existence of social classes as status groups. Dominant groups should be especially aversive to reciprocating affective disparity vis-à-vis groups whose very existence they would prefer to obscure. A second factor is the step-wise structure of class relations, which has important implications for interclass contact and communication. People in the upper-middle class live far removed from the day-to-day existence of those in the poor and working class; this gives those distant subordinates the same opportunity as blacks to develop separate affective bonds, at least vis-à-vis classes located at the more distant extremes. But the feelings of the poor and working class toward higher classes are fragmented, with less disparity felt vis-à-vis more proximate classes, with which they are more likely to have interclass contact. For their part, those in the upper-middle class also have relatively frequent contact with more proximate subordinates in the middle class, which conditions that relationship more amicably. The limited reach of their downward exposure to those whose interests are only slightly estranged from their own may leave them less keenly aware of the depth of disparity felt by people in classes that are further removed. The buffering action of the middle class leaves the upper-middle class less directly exposed to the more divisive feelings that lie further below and thus it obscures their perception of those feelings. And at the same time, people in the upper-middle class are prevented from allying their feelings unequivocally against those beneath them because they still turn to face a class yet higher than their own, from whom they also harbor a feeling of disparity.

The exchange of intergroup feelings comes closest to reciprocated disparity in race relations, where physical separation of the groups is the sharpest, and where the dyadic structure leaves communication between groups uncomplicated. Because of the pervasive spatial segregation of racial groups, whites have forfeited the opportunity to penetrate and condition the emotional vulnerabilities of blacks. At the same time, the dyadic structure of the race relationship leaves the members of the dominant group with no buffer between them and restive subordinates. Thus, strict physical separation of the groups gives subordinates more opportunity to disentangle their emotions from the grasp of the dominant group; and because there are no buffering groups, the dominant group receives direct delivery of subordinates' feelings and may also feel beleaguered more quickly when confronted with feelings that are less than amicable. In such a context, whites have come closer to reciprocating the affective disparity expressed by subordinates and have slightly outstripped blacks in expressing negative feelings.

The most amicable exchange of feelings is found between men and women, where intimate intergroup contact is the norm, and where the dyadic structure of the relationship makes communication between groups straightforward. In this situation, men's and women's lives are emotionally intertwined, and without any other pertinent groups to create interference, each side can read the other's mood relatively easily.

Even here, however, there is a slight asymmetry between men's and women's feelings, with men's feelings being a bit more eagerly inclusive across group lines than are women's.

These patterns all suggest that no group in an unequal relationship seems predisposed to hostility, but subordinate groups are a little more inclined to gravitate toward feelings of intergroup disparity, albeit tentatively. As they retreat emotionally behind group lines, subordinates tend to stay away from expressions of outright hostility toward the dominant group and instead curb their feelings to a preference for their own group. Because the data are cross-sectional, they do not offer direct information about which side introduces affective disparity into the relationship, but it is subordinates who seem to be at the vanguard in every case, even in the prevailingly amicable gender relationship. The most plausible interpretation is that it is subordinates who introduce affective disparity and dominant groups who try to prevent or restrain such a movement.

The success of dominant groups in that regard depends on their ability to entangle subordinates emotionally within a social structure that binds the groups together in close physical proximity. That entanglement is severed when the groups are spatially separated. Without repeated physical contact, emotional ties across group lines are harder to maintain on both sides, but it is subordinates, as they experience the daily sting of deprivation, who are more inclined to emotional withdrawal behind group lines. The extent to which dominant groups feel the direct blast of subordinates' change in mood depends on whether their relationship is dyadic or whether there are intermediary groups who buffer communications between top and bottom and fragment the exchange of feelings. But once introduced, hostility changes the tenor of the relationship unavoidably, and dominant groups are shunted fitfully into the game of muted conflict.

DATA: THE DEFINITION OF GROUP INTERESTS

As before, I describe my measures and then proceed to an examination of the way group interests are perceived in race, gender, and class relations, in turn. To what extent do the groups on different sides of those relationships define their interests as mutually opposed? Or do they take a more inclusive view by seeing their interests as either communally served or communally hurt by the status quo? After delineating the exchange of perceived interests in each case, I turn to more general questions about the proclivities of dominant and subordinate groups to portray social arrangements in divisive or integrative terms as they seek to defend or challenge those arrangements.

Measures

To measure the perception of group interests, I used specific policies and practices as the stimuli, rather than asking about the global interests of groups. The latter is a more abstract concept and, in view of the particularistic quality of public political discussion, respondents are most likely to have contemplated the interests of their own and other groups in relation to specific policies and practices. By asking about the implications for relevant groups of well-known, specific policies or practices that have high symbolic value in the conduct of a relationship, it should be easier for the respondent to understand the question and to consider its meaning in concrete terms. In this way, the questions also avoid hazy generalizations by anchoring people's responses to a more tangible reality.

The items focused on two policies or practices for each intergroup relationship, presented as follows:

> People have different opinions about who benefits and who is hurt by certain policies and practices in America today. I am going to read you a short list of such policies and practices and ask you for your opinion about who benefits and who is hurt by each of these.

> If blacks generally live in black neighborhoods and whites live in white neighborhoods, who benefits from this—whites, blacks, everyone, or no one?
> Who is hurt by this—whites, blacks, everyone, or no one?

> How about private ownership—*rather than* government ownership—of business corporations? Who benefits from *private ownership* of business corporations—upper-class people, upper-middle-class people, middle-class people, working-class people, poor people, everyone, or no one?
> Who is hurt by this? [same response-options presented on show-card]

> Who benefits from the practice of women staying home to take care of children and men working to support the family financially—men, women, everyone, or no one?
> Who is hurt by this—men, women, everyone, or no one?

> If blacks generally go to some schools and whites go to other schools, who benefits from this—whites, blacks, everyone, or no one?
> Who is hurt by this—whites, blacks, everyone, or no one?

> Who benefits from the tax policy that reduces taxes for some types of business investments—upper-class people, upper-middle-class people, middle-class people, working-class people, poor people, everyone, or no one?
> Who is hurt by this? [same response-options presented on show-card]

> There are more women in certain kinds of jobs such as nurses and secretaries while there are more men in other kinds of jobs such as engineers and doctors. Who benefits from this—men, women, everyone, or no one?
>
> Who is hurt by this—men, women, everyone, or no one?

All these policies and practices are highly salient to the conduct of the intergroup relationship in question. Five of them have also been the focus of considerable public discussion; the only one that has not is private ownership in industry, but since this is the core tenet of capitalism, it is implicated in much public discussion of subsidiary economic issues and is too central to our system of economic organization to be omitted from any inquiry into perceptions of class interests. At the same time, the wording of all the items was kept as neutral as possible, avoiding such value-loaded terms as "racial segregation" that might trigger defensive or pat responses. The purpose was to focus on the prime substance of specific arrangements without appearing to cast them in a negative or positive light.

For similar reasons, the question of who, if anyone, is hurt by each arrangement was separated from the question about beneficiaries. I wanted to leave respondents with as many degrees of freedom as possible in answering the questions. Responses to the items in each pair were combined afterwards to assess the degree to which people's perceptions of group interests fall into categories that have been discussed most often in the literature. Respondents who think the dominant group benefits and the subordinate group is hurt are taking the classic view of mutually opposed group interests in which the status quo serves the interests of the dominant group at the expense of subordinates. Those who think everyone benefits and no one is hurt are interpreting group interests as being communally served by the *status quo*. People who think no one benefits and everyone is hurt are of the logically contrary opinion that the status quo universally hurts all the groups involved. Many other combinations of responses are also possible, which may suggest a partially formed view of distinct group interests (such as "the dominant group benefits but no one is hurt"), a neutral view of the matter (such as "no one benefits and no one is hurt" or "everyone benefits and everyone is hurt"), or an idiosyncratic view that is less readily interpretable.

Results

The pertinent data are presented in tables 5.7 (for race), 5.8 (for gender), and 5.9 (for class). Responses to each pair of questions about who benefits and who is hurt by each policy or practice were combined to yield the categories listed down the left side of each table, with the "who-benefits" response given on the left of the pound-sign (#) and the "who-is-hurt" response given on the right of the pound-sign. The list begins with the most divisive perception, that the dominant group benefits and the subordinate is hurt by a specific policy or practice—that is, that the interests of the groups are mutually opposed. For class relations, the existence of multiple groups means there is no single place to draw the line, and so three different kinds of responses are presented as alternative expressions of mutually opposed interests: (1) that the upper and/or the upper-middle class benefit and the poor and/or the working class are hurt; (2) that the upper and/or the upper-middle class benefit and the poor, the working class, and/or the middle class are hurt; and (3) that the upper class benefits and "everyone" is hurt (I assume that, since the upper class constitutes such a tiny minority of the population, "everyone" in this context was shorthand for "everyone else").

The next row presents a muted version of a zero-sum view, which is that only the dominant group benefits, but no one is hurt. The next three categories involve different ways of denying special group interests: in turn, that the policy is detrimental to everyone's interests ("no one benefits and everyone is hurt"), that it is beneficial to everyone's interests ("everyone benefits and no one is hurt"), or that it is neutral in its impact (almost all of these responses were that "no one benefits and no one is hurt"). The next category ("don't know who benefits and don't know who is hurt") involves a more passive kind of neutrality, stemming from uncertainty or ignorance about the issues.

The final category, labeled "Other," incorporates an amalgam of dispersed responses. Most of these responses represent slightly different twists of the main categories already listed (for example, "no one benefits and blacks are hurt" or "everyone benefits but women are hurt"), which make sense in their own terms but which do not fall neatly into any of the classic positions. Most of the specific combinations of responses incorporated under the "Other" label were articulated by only a handful of respondents, but a few of them (such as the examples given above) were expressed by a sufficient number of respondents to merit separate recognition: these will be mentioned in context.[10]

Race. Table 5.7 presents whites' and blacks' views of how racial group interests are served by racially segregated neighborhoods and schools.

10. The number of different "Other" response-combinations in each intergroup relationship was as follows. For race, there were 21 separate other combinations on each item-pair. For gender, the sex-role items elicited 27 other response-combinations, and the occupational-segregation items elicited 20. For class, where there are many more possible permutations, the private-ownership items elicited 86 separate other combinations of responses and the tax-policy items elicited 75. In each case, no more than 2–8 of the separate combinations attracted more than 15 respondents.

TABLE 5.7.   Beliefs about Who Benefits and Who Is Hurt by Racial Segregation in Neighborhoods and Racial Segregation in Schools, by Race.

	Neighborhood Segregation		School Segregation	
	Whites	Blacks	Whites	Blacks
Whites # Blacks[a]	6.8%	18.3%*	8.7%	24.4%*
Whites # No One	1.5	0.5	1.2	0.5
No One # Everyone	19.5	27.7*	21.9	23.8
Everyone # No One	38.4	14.1*	34.3	8.3*
Neutral[b]	14.2	16.2	15.3	15.5
Don't Know # Don't Know	5.7	5.8	6.3	6.2
Other	13.9	17.3	12.4	21.2
Base N	1623	191	1614	193

[a] Notation is "Who Benefits # Who Is Hurt."

[b] Neutral consists of the following responses: No One # No One; Everyone # Everyone; and DK # No One.

* Difference between groups in percentage giving this response is statistically significant ($p < .01$).

The two sides differ in the degree to which they take a critical view of racial segregation, but plainly divisive interpretations are not popular in either group.

The view that has the plurality among whites (34–38 percent) is that racial segregation in neighborhoods and schools benefits both racial groups and hurts no one. When one takes account of the additional 15 percent or so who think that racial segregation is neutral in its impact and the 6 percent who don't know who benefits or is hurt by it, well over one-half of whites espouse a view of racial segregation that denies that it harms anyone or that it serves any special group interests. Very few whites (7–9 percent) see racial segregation as something that benefits whites and hurts blacks, and even the muted view of special group interests that whites alone benefit but no one is hurt is espoused by only another 1 percent of whites. About 20 percent of whites view racial segregation as harmful to the interests of both groups, and another 5 percent (incorporated in the "Other" category) take the slightly different view that blacks alone are hurt by it, but that no one benefits from it.

Blacks are more likely to see the two racial groups as having mutually opposed interests, but still only about one-fifth to one-quarter take that view. Equally popular among blacks is the less divisive criticism of segregation as detrimental to both groups' interests: about one-quarter or more of blacks believe that racial segregation benefits no one and hurts everyone. Most blacks who gave responses in the "Other" category be-

TABLE 5.8.   Beliefs about Who Benefits and Who Is Hurt by Traditional Sex Roles and Sex-Typing of Occupations, by Sex.

	Domestic Sex Roles		Sex-Typing of Occupations	
	Men	Women	Men	Women
Men # Women[a]	5.3%	4.7%	8.8%	11.2%
Men # No One	3.5	3.3	1.8	1.7
No One # Everyone	4.5	3.9	8.2	10.0
Everyone # No One	50.9	54.0	50.7	43.0*
Neutral[b]	7.9	7.4	15.6	17.9
Don't Know # Don't Know	4.4	4.0	4.8	7.9
Other	23.4	22.7	10.1	8.3
Base N	795	1088	793	1085

[a] Notation is "Who Benefits # Who Is Hurt."
[b] Neutral consists of the following responses: No One # No One; Everyone # Everyone; DK # No One.
* Difference between groups in percentage giving this response is statistically significant (p < .01).

lieve that segregation is harmful, either to blacks solely or to everyone, with the combination that no one benefits and blacks are hurt being given by about 10 percent. Blacks are about as likely as whites to see segregation as neutral in its impact on racial groups (15–16 percent) or to say "don't know" on the issue. But blacks are considerably less likely than whites to go as far as to believe that segregation bestows benefits in a color-blind way—only 14 percent of blacks think neighborhood segregation benefits both groups and hurts no one, and as few as 8 percent think this about school segregation.

Gender.   The muted conflict of race relations stands in sharper relief against the amicable consensus that permeates gender relations. There are no important differences between men and women in the way they see, or rather do not see, gender-group interests.

Approximately one-half of both sexes believe that everyone benefits from and no one is hurt by traditional domestic sex-roles or the sex-typing of occupations. When one also takes account of the respondents who said these gender arrangements have no impact on the interests of either group or who said they did not know (11–12 percent on sex-roles and 20–26 percent on the sex-typing of occupations), a total of about two-thirds of men and women either view gender arrangements as a communally positive good or fail to see any involvement of group interests. Only a small minority see men's and women's interests as mutually

TABLE 5.9. Beliefs about Who Benefits and Who Is Hurt by Private Ownership of Business Corporations and Tax Reductions for Business Investment, by Class.

	Private Ownership				Tax Reductions for Investment			
	Upper Middle	Middle	Working	Poor	Upper-Middle	Middle	Working	Poor
U.UM # P.W.[a]	14.1%	23.2%	30.6%	25.9%*	29.0%	32.8%	41.8%	32.9%*
U.UM # P.W.M.	5.1	7.8	5.3	9.4	16.1	19.4	13.7	10.7
U # Everyone	5.8	4.8	6.0	5.8	9.0	8.0	7.0	7.1
U.UM # No One	8.3	5.9	4.3	3.6	6.5	5.4	2.9	0.7
No One # Everyone	0.0	0.1	0.1	1.4	0.0	0.6	0.6	0.0
Everyone # No One	37.2	26.9	18.6	8.6*	12.3	6.5	4.7	5.0*
Neutral [b]	1.9	1.4	1.6	2.9	2.6	1.6	1.8	0.7
Don't Know # Don't Know	2.6	7.3	10.4	20.1	5.8	8.2	10.2	21.4
Other	25.0	22.6	23.0	22.3	18.7	17.6	17.3	21.4
Base N	156	810	682	139	155	803	684	140

[a] Notation is "Who Benefits # Who Is Hurt."
[b] Neutral consists of the following responses: No One # No One; Everyone # Everyone; DK # No One.
* Difference by class in percentage giving this response is statistically significant (p < .05).

opposed (5–11 percent) or even view gender arrangements as harmful to both groups (4–10 percent).

The amalgamated "Other" responses display the same tendencies toward consensual inclusiveness. The items on traditional domestic sex-roles elicited a larger number of responses that fell into the "Other" category (about 23 percent), which in part reflects respondents who named children as beneficiaries of traditional domestic sex-role arrangements. The majority of the "Other" responses to this item-pair involved perceptions either that no one is hurt by traditional domestic sex-roles or that if women are hurt, they are also among the beneficiaries. A slightly larger portion of the "Other" responses to the occupational-sex-typing items involved allegations that it is harmful to either women or everyone, but only 8–10 percent of all responses fell into the "Other" category on this item-pair.

Class.   There is more evidence of conflictive views of class interests than there is of either gender or race interests. The specific pattern of responses varies, however, across the two issues of private ownership of business corporations and tax reductions for investments.

Both class issues elicited the perception of mutually opposed group interests with considerably more frequency than did either gender or race issues. The first two rows in table 5.9 give the percentages of respondents with unambiguous views of class interests as mutually opposed, while the third row presents separately the relatively small percentage of respondents who offered the slightly less clear-cut zero-sum response that upper-class people are the sole beneficiaries and everyone [else] is hurt. When contemplating private ownership, respondents from different social classes vary somewhat in their tendency to perceive mutually opposed class interests: just over 40 percent of the poor and the working class see private ownership as benefiting higher classes and hurting lower ones, whereas 36 percent of the middle class and 25 percent of the upper-middle class take that view. Correspondingly, the more integrative view that everyone benefits and no one is hurt by private ownership gains in popularity with ascending social class, with the percentages increasing monotonically from under 9 percent of the poor up to 37 percent of the upper-middle class. On the issue of tax-reductions for business investments, more than one-half of every social class see class interests as mutually opposed; and the more integrative perception that everyone benefits and no one is hurt is taken by only 5–6 percent of the poor, working class, and middle class, and by just 12 percent of the upper-middle class. Virtually no one in any social class espouses the view that either private ownership or investment tax-credits are harmful to the interests of all classes.[11]

Consistent with the greater polarization that characterizes the perception of class interests, almost no one in any class sees either of these policies as neutral in its effects. However, as many as one-fifth of the poor and one-tenth of the working class take a more passively neutral position by saying "don't know." And between one-sixth and one-quarter of each class gave responses that were amalgamated in the "Other" category. A substantial minority of the latter (about one-sixth) involved the perception of mutually opposed class interests in which the middle class was named as a beneficiary rather than being aligned with the poor and working class, and there were many other responses that drew slightly different cut-points in identifying specific classes that benefit or are hurt by these economic practices. As with the patterns in interclass feelings, these data suggest the importance of the step-wise structure of class relations in fragmenting and scattering the ingredients for polarization.

General Patterns.   Two general patterns mark the perception of group interests in race, gender, and class relations, and these patterns parallel

11. On both of the class issues, blacks are somewhat more likely than their white class-peers to take the position that the classes have mutually opposed interests and less likely to take the benign view that everyone benefits and no one is hurt. In people's views of private ownership, it is primarily among the middle and working classes that blacks are more caustic than whites (with differences of about 14–22 percentage points). In people's views of investment tax-credits (where perceptions in general have a more divisive cast), it is among the poor that blacks differ most from whites in their adoption of a class-divisive interpretation (among the poor, 59 percent of blacks and 45 percent of whites take the view that class interests are mutually opposed, whereas no blacks and 9 percent of whites take the position that everyone benefits and no one is hurt). These patterns are discussed in greater detail in Jackman and Jackman (1983, 66).

those observed for intergroup feelings. First, sharply divisive perceptions of group interests are far from being the order of the day. This holds even in class relations, where they put in their strongest appearance. Second, subordinate groups tentatively lead the way in drawing divisive distinctions between the interests of contending groups. Dominant groups show more of a preference for the inclusive view that current arrangements serve the needs of all pertinent groups. As with intergroup feelings, both sides appear to tread cautiously, with subordinates showing slightly less reluctance to express divisiveness.

The presentation of these patterns varies from one intergroup relationship to another. In gender relations, which are marked by intimate contact between groups and permeated by role segregation, divisive perceptions are the farthest removed from everyone's mind. Both sides tend to embrace gender arrangements as serving communal interests.

In race relations, which are pervaded by physical separation of the groups, blacks show more indication of seeing status-quo arrangements in a critical light. But they are as likely to include whites along with their own group as being ill-served by racial segregation as they are to accuse whites of benefiting from segregation at blacks' expense. The prevailing response among whites is to persist with an inclusive view of racial segregation as being communally beneficial or at least neutral in its effects.

The perception of class interests is the most polarized, but the polarization is fragmented and dispersed by the step-wise structure of class relations and the ensuing pattern of communication among social classes—there is no single rift to clarify polarization. That aside, the pattern of responses in class relations suggests that economic interests have a tangibility that is harder to obscure than are interests based on cultural distinctions (such as in race). This is particularly noticeable on the concrete issue of tax reductions for business investments, with respect to which a majority of every class sees class interests as mutually opposed. On the more abstract issue of private ownership, ascending social class is associated with an increasing proclivity to the integrative view that it serves the interests of all classes, but those in the poor and working class do not see mutually opposed class interests quite as readily as they do on the more explicitly distributive issue of investment tax-credits.

CONCLUSIONS

In this chapter, I have addressed the rudimentary questions of how contending groups in the unequal relationships of race, gender, and social class define the boundaries between them, emotionally and perceptually. What part is played by hostility and affection in the definition of group boundaries, and do groups perceive their interests as opposed or shared?

Past research on racial prejudice, political tolerance, and group consciousness has overwhelmingly emphasized hostility and the perception of mutually opposed interests as the key germs in intergroup ideology. Contrary to that emphasis, my contention has been that hostility is dispensable—indeed, an encumbrance—in the dynamics of intergroup inequality. The members of dominant groups are inclined to strike an inclusive tone as they orient themselves toward those from whom they derive everyday benefits. And subordinates restrain themselves from a costly expression of negative affect.

The data in this chapter on intergroup feelings and the perception of group interests suggest there is a strain toward inclusiveness in the emotional and perceptual delineation of intergroup ideology. Most significantly, the pattern of results suggests that the expression of inclusive feelings toward subordinates cannot be construed as an abandonment of the unequal terms of the relationship. Indeed, it appears that dominant groups lean toward inclusive intergroup feelings as part of an effort to integrate subordinates within status-quo arrangements. Their success in molding the feelings and cognitions of subordinates is never complete, but their efforts do not meet with absolute failure in any of the three intergroup relationships. Whether one encounters the near-incorporation of subordinates or their contained estrangement depends on the opportunities for ideological incursion that are offered by the structure of the relationship.

When the normal conduct of the relationship provides frequent one-to-one contact between groups, conditions appear most conducive for luring subordinates into mutual affection and the perception of shared interests. In this paternalistic nest, dominant-group members express affection for subordinates and they define subordinates' needs as being met by current arrangements. Their efforts appear to meet with success. Unsullied by hostility, such a relationship depends on mutual good feeling and shared perceptions of communal interests to embrace the role segregation that sustains the inequality.

When the conduct of an intergroup relationship separates the groups physically, the dominant group forfeits the opportunity to infiltrate the feelings and awareness of subordinates. Under these circumstances, subordinates become more inclined to withdraw their good feeling and to separate their interests from those of the dominant group. However, through sporadic trial and error, they grasp that radical confrontation is not efficacious in changing the system in which they are the weaker party. They come to couch their withdrawal of support in terms that minimize its alienating effect on the more powerful party while providing themselves with an adaptive (rather than a frustrating) interpretation of the world in which they live. Confronted with recalcitrant subordinates, the dominant group learns that the least costly response is to contain the damage by restraining the element of hostility and continuing to reach out to subordinates with an inclusive appeal. Each side opts to engage the other with persuasion rather than to resort to open hostilities.

However, even as subordinates tread wearily, they still step a little ahead of dominant groups on the path to divisiveness. For subordinates, there is a trade-off between their implicit understanding of the need for restraint and their discomfort with the costs they bare under present arrangements. This formula works in all three intergroup relationships to lure subordinates to the fragrance of challenge. Always with caution and with varying ardor, subordinate estrangement ranges from the tempered recalcitrance of women to reciprocate men's proffered affection to the stronger expressions of group bonds and group interests among the poor and working class and among blacks.

For dominant groups facing challenge, their satisfaction with present arrangements and their understanding of the costs of divisiveness both work to restrain confrontation in their response and to steer them toward an inclusive, persuasive appeal. The specific form their restraint takes depends on the exigencies of the relationship. For example, the tangibility of material differences in interests between social classes makes them more difficult to obscure, but the step-wise fragmentation of class relations makes it easier for the upper-middle class to stay away from negative feelings toward lower classes. Whites, caught in a dyadic relationship from which many members of the other group have withdrawn emotionally, find it more difficult to contain their emotional response, but the cultural basis of their unequal relationship makes it easier to cling to the inclusive perception that racial arrangements do not injure the interests of either group. In both instances, however, the dominant group takes reluctant leave of the comfortable ideological system that was built on an exchange of good feeling and shared perceptions of communal interests. It is prodded into the forum of muted conflict.

CHAPTER SIX

The Articulation of Policy Goals

Views about policies that affect the relationship between groups are a first-order expression of grassroots political alignments. The choice between egalitarian and expropriative policies defines the fundamental issue of contention between unequal groups. To what extent do groups align themselves on contending sides and pursue policy goals that promote their control over resources?

Policy goals are articulated as part of the dialogue that evolves between unequal groups. In that dialogue, the political posture of each group is not formulated freestyle. Groups maneuver within constraints. Those constraints arise from two sources. First, the day-to-day practice of the relationship with another group generates specific pragmatic and moral exigencies that mold the formulation of policy goals. The institutional means by which the expropriation is practiced and the communication channels that are thus created between groups generate varying opportunities and risks for each of the participating groups. Second, at the same time broader societal pressures bear down on the relationship and steer the moral parameters of discussion. The society in which the intergroup relationship resides is enveloped by a broad moral climate that is the product of the various intergroup relations and institutional arrangements that have shaped its history. Those pressures lend moral credibility to certain ideas at the expense of others and hence steer the direction of policy discussion in each intergroup relationship.

Intergroup policy goals in the contemporary United States are shaded by the normative climate of capitalist democracy, a climate in which egalitarianism has interfaced with individualism. This has had the dual effect of transmogrifying the popular understanding of egalitarianism and of lending a special moral significance to individualism. The specific pressures generated by the practice of race, gender, and class relations are each nested within that broader ideological context.

The chapter opens with a discussion of the meaning and significance of people's intergroup policy views. Those views have been the subject of repeated deliberation in research on racial prejudice, tolerance, gender attitudes (especially "sex-role attitudes"), and class consciousness. And unlike the attitudinal elements under examination in the last chapter, they have also been subjected to extended empirical analysis. I start by considering, briefly, the various concerns that have guided past research and the measurement issues that have confounded that research. I then delineate my theoretical approach, in which I emphasize the pursuit of resources within pragmatic and moral constraints, and I consider the significance of individualism as an overarching moral principle that shapes contemporary policy debates. With those issues delineated, I out-line the empirical questions that confront my analysis, before turning to an examination of my data.

The measurement of intergroup policy goals has been snared by a number of issues. In particular, many analysts have drawn a distinction between people's articulation of abstract policy principles and their posi-tions on specific, concrete policy issues. Uncertainty about the resilience and meaning of that distinction obstructs our understanding of inter-group policy goals. Accordingly, the analysis of my data proceeds in two stages. I begin by asking about patterns of support for abstract policy principles. To what extent is there consensual endorsement of egalitarian (or individualistic) policy principles, and how does this vary across the three intergroup relationships of race, gender, and social class? Second, I assess views that are articulated about specific governmental policies. What are people's beliefs—both prescriptive and existential—about gov-ernmental intervention to promote affirmative change on behalf of sub-ordinate groups? That is, how much affirmative activity do people think should be taking place on behalf of blacks, women, and lower social classes—and how much activity do they believe is already taking place? How much of a rift is there between dominant and subordinate groups in their beliefs about what should be, and what already is, the thrust of governmental policy?

THE ISSUES

Analysts of prejudice, tolerance, gender attitudes, and class conscious-ness have each pursued and interpreted people's articulated policy views within their own distinctive framework of concerns. I briefly discuss the varying meaning and significance attached to people's policy views in past research, along with the measurement issues that have snagged that research. My theoretical approach is then delineated, and I draw out the primary empirical questions that inform my analysis.

Prejudice

For students of prejudice, who have always been motivated by a strong social-problems orientation, whites' behavioral predispositions toward blacks have been a continual target of investigation. When physical segregation remained virtually unchallenged, researchers' policy concerns were primarily occupied by the question of how whites would react to intrusions by blacks in their personal lives—with acceptance or antagonism. But as the nation began to grapple legislatively and legally with racial segregation and the issue assumed increasing public visibility in broad policy terms, scholars enlarged their focus. Increasingly, whites' orientation toward racial integration and blacks' civil rights, in terms affecting blacks as a whole, became an absorbing policy question of immediate practical import. After the violent eruption of black urban discontent in the late 1960s, some scholars also began to ask about the racial-policy views of blacks (G. Marx 1967; Campbell and Schuman 1968; Aberbach and Walker 1972; Schuman and Hatchett 1974; Schwartz and Schwartz 1976; Turner and Wilson 1976; Schuman et al. 1985; Sigelman and Welch 1991). But the primary focus has been on the degree to which whites—the status-dominants—have resolved the "American dilemma" by retracting their support for established patterns of racial discrimination and endorsing affirmative change on behalf of blacks' civil rights.

At a deeper level, whites' responses to survey items about racial segregation have also been monitored as a barometer of the underlying level of racial antipathy. Because of the urgent significance attached to both the policy goals themselves and the deeper antipathies thought to lie beneath, there has been intense debate among scholars about the extent to which whites have abandoned support for segregation. Numerous studies have documented a marked decline in whites' support for racial segregation, in principle, over the past few decades (for example, Greeley and Sheatsley 1971, 1974; Jackman 1978; Schuman et al. 1985). And yet this has not been accompanied by a comparable change in whites' enthusiasm for the idea of specific governmental interventions to promote racial integration (for example, Jackman 1978; Fairchild and Gurin 1978; Sears et al. 1979; Kinder and Sears 1981; McConahay et al. 1981; Schuman et al. 1985; Taylor 1986; Sigelman and Welch 1991). This apparent gap between principle and implementation has left students of prejudice divided and uncertain about both the state of whites' dispositions toward blacks and the future of legislated racial integration.

Tolerance

Policy prescriptions have been the attitudinal element of prime interest to students of tolerance. Indeed, with the exception of Jackman (1977, 1978) and Sullivan, Piereson, and Marcus (1979, 1982), policy prescriptions have been the sole empirical target of research on tolerance. Questions address support for civil liberties and civil rights, and people's responses have been interpreted as indicating the degree to which they adhere to the democratic norm of tolerance. As with studies of racial prejudice, the problem has been couched as one involving dominant predispositions toward minorities, but the construction put on those predispositions is very different from that found in research on prejudice. Far from being a barometer of underlying feelings toward target groups, such feelings are instead presumed to be less than positive, and policy prescriptions are taken to reflect the extent to which people can override their affective dispositions in the way they orient themselves toward political minorities. Thus may people demonstrate their graduation to democratic citizenship.

The norm of tolerance occupies such a vital role in theories of democratic legitimacy and stability that observations of its weak presence have struck scholars as a daunting puzzle. Different assaults on that puzzle have roughly paralleled the lines of debate in the literature on prejudice. Prothro and Grigg (1960) found consensual endorsement of the guiding principles of majority rule and minority rights, when those principles were stated in their most general form, but they found sharply diminished levels of adherence when people were asked about specific policy-situations that embroiled those principles. Discouraged, they ironically concluded that the solvent that stabilizes the democratic system is mass apathy. They and other scholars offered the reassurance that those most actively engaged in the democratic endeavor—social or political elites—were the most likely to apply the norm of tolerance consistently to specific policy-contexts (Stouffer 1955; Prothro and Grigg 1960; McClosky 1964; Converse 1964). Some analysts have optimistically observed increasing levels of tolerance over the past few decades (Davis 1975; Nunn, Crockett, and Williams 1978), but Sullivan, Piereson, and Marcus (1979, 1982) found tolerance was still largely wanting, even among social elites, when they explicitly built affective reactions into their measure and asked people about their policy dispositions toward groups they personally disliked. They concluded that democratic stability is left undisturbed primarily because of the diversity of personal targets among the citizenry.

Gender Attitudes

The division of labor between the sexes is the most visible symptom of gender inequality. Like spatial segregation in race relations, the specifics of role segregation between men and women have assumed high symbolic significance, and analysts of gender attitudes have had a primary interest in measuring support for that traditional division of labor, in its various manifestations (for example, Mason and Bumpass 1975; Mason, Czajka, and Arber 1976; Thornton and Freedman 1979; Spitze and Huber 1980; Cherlin and Walters 1981; Helmreich, Spence, and Gibson 1982; Thornton, Alwin, and Camburn 1983; Mason and Lu 1986; Simon and Landis 1989). Questions about endorsement or rejection of traditional sex-roles and equality of opportunity for women are often interspersed with, and not sharply distinguished from, questions on people's beliefs about the traits of women and the needs of children. All of these indicators are seen as parts of the psychological nexus that bolsters or opposes the traditional gender division of labor, and, indeed, they have commonly been termed sex-role attitudes.

As I discussed in chapter 1, the prime and sometimes exclusive interest has been in the views of women. This contrasts sharply with research on racial prejudice and tolerance, where it is the views of dominant-group members that are treated as the focal concern. Research on sex-role attitudes has not generally assumed any necessary power relationship between the sexes. Instead, the underlying presumption seems to have been that, since women have participated in the roles that differentiate them from men, those roles must be consistent with their preferences, in a power-neutral sense (for an extended discussion of this point, see Kane 1989). With women held as responsible at least in part for their own fate, the question becomes whether they indicate a ground swell for change or satisfaction with traditional gender arrangements. Empirical studies have suggested decreasing support for traditional sex-roles over the past few decades, and this has usually been treated as an important indicator of contemporary social currents.

Class Consciousness

Policy views are the most common empirical focus in analyses of class consciousness, where they are treated as an indicator of the rational perception and pursuit of class interests. The question has been whether different classes, and especially lower classes, take policy stances that suggest they understand and pursue their interests on distributive issues. This information is assumed to be vital to assessments of the fundamental organizational properties of class, including whether classes exist as social entities. Like women, the working class is asked to demonstrate an open sense of dissatisfaction with current arrangements, but, unlike women's views, the views of the working class are almost always assessed in comparison with those of higher classes. The goal has been to show evidence of either class conflict or benign consensus.

Because of the underlying concern with the existence of politically opposed classes based in distinctive social communities, analysts have attended not only to articulated policy goals but also to existential perceptions about the degree of equality and openness that already holds within the status quo (for example, Mann 1970; Parkin 1971; Huber and Form 1973; Abercrombie and Turner 1982). It is assumed that privileged classes will portray the status quo in benign terms as unbiased and open as they articulate conservative policy goals, whereas lower classes, if anything is amiss in the dominant portrayal, will indicate so with more jaundiced perceptions of current policies as they frame goals that call for affirmative change.

Studies have generally shown modest differences between classes in their perceptions of and prescriptions for socioeconomic policy, leaving analysts to argue about the implications of such differences for the viability of class conflict, and therefore of class itself. A repeated observation has been that when asked about policies as broad abstractions, socioeconomic policy views are more consensual and conservative than they are for specific, concrete issues (Mann 1970; Parkin 1971; Huber and Form 1973; Abercrombie and Turner 1982). Analysts have concluded that at an abstract level, there is a pervasive dominant ideology, but that subordinate classes are more inclined to pull away from the dominant interpretation of social reality when dealing with concrete issues that have definite experiential correlates. Whether the latter tendency heralds incipient class conflict or merely reflects minor quibbling on the fringes of a broad consensus about governing principles of distribution is a matter that hangs unresolved over the literature.

This failure of subordinates to deviate decisively from the dominant view has been interpreted by some as evidence of "false consciousness" (see, e.g., Mann 1970). But, as Mann's article demonstrates, the task of distinguishing empirically between false consciousness and spontaneous consensus is fraught with ambiguities. Besides, if the working class is judged to have fallen short of a rational awareness of its "true" interests, analysts are left with the theoretical problem of explaining how such a lapse in rationality could occur without at the same time undermining the long-term prediction of confrontational politics growing out of a rational processing of class experiences. The injection of false awareness among subordinates raises a theoretical inconsistency that weakens the long-term prognosis of rationally based class conflict.

Overview

Despite their urgent significance for research on race, gender, and class attitudes, people's articulated policy views have been interpreted quite variously from one body of research to another. At one extreme are policy dispositions taken as a reflection of prejudice, where whites' views are examined to assess their readiness to relinquish irrational, parochial opposition to blacks' civil rights. At the other extreme are class policy views, where different classes (if they exist) are expected to reveal themselves in the articulated pursuit of rationally opposed goals: policy views are scrutinized to ascertain the extent to which classes manifest their Marxian-ordained destiny for head-on conflict. Between these extremes lie the analyses of sex-role attitudes and political tolerance, each of which incorporates idiosyncratic combinations of elements from either extreme. Sex-role attitudes have generally been examined as barometers of a benignly changing climate of opinion about women's roles in society—a climate in which women are presumed to take the lead by indicating freely any changing aspirations. And tolerance is measured to assess the degree to which society has elevated itself above narrow group interests to embrace the concept of universally equal political and civil citizenship—an elevation that is regarded as lying critically in the hands of dominant groups.

All analyses of articulated policy goals seem to share an understanding that what is at stake is the allocation of valued resources. But only analysts of class consciousness treat that allocation in clearly relational terms that recognize that if disadvantaged groups get more, then currently advantaged groups must give something valuable up. This perspective on policy goals casts them as a contest between the have's and the have-not's rather than as a test of the dominant group's readiness to advance itself to a higher moral state or of subordinates' benignly spontaneous election of change. What analysts of class consciousness have also assumed, however, is that *if* the have-not's are being exploited by the have's, the only rational course ultimately for the have-not's is to issue a head-on challenge to the unequal arrangement. In this framework, only one set of policy goals for subordinates is recognized as a rational expression of their interests: uncompromised confrontation.

Measurement Issues

Although people's policy views have probably been measured more frequently than any other aspect of intergroup attitudes over the last twenty years, doubts have beleaguered that research about what kinds of measures are most appropriate and how to interpret people's responses to various measures. Those doubts generally spin out from one or more of the following three issues.

Abstract Principles and Applied Policy Goals.   The distinction between abstract policy principles and specific policy implementation has been a centerpiece of empirical debate in research on intergroup policy views.

The focus of disagreement is about which level of analysis provides the more valid indication of people's policy views. And as with many other measurement debates, the substantive implications are profound: indeed, the discussion turns more on conceptual and interpretive issues than on methodological issues per se.

Prothro and Grigg (1960) were the first to comment on the significance of the distinction between abstract principles and applied policy views. In their well-known article, they found widespread popular support for the abstract democratic principles of majority rule and minority rights, but the level of support dropped precipitously when respondents were asked to react to specific policy situations that involved an application of those principles. The nonequivalence of abstract and applied policy principles has continued to intrigue students of public opinion, especially in the contexts of racial policy attitudes and class consciousness, where scholars have struggled to explain the meaning of this distinction.

Students of racial policy views have repeatedly observed that whites exhibit higher levels of support for the general principle of racial integration than they do for specific governmental policies that would implement integration. Further, whites' opposition to the general principle of racial segregation has been steadily increasing over the past few decades to near-consensual levels while their support for specific governmental policies to implement integration has languished with virtually no change over the same time-period (Jackman 1977; Schuman, Steeh, and Bobo 1985). This persistent gap between abstract and applied policy principles among whites has been a central puzzle that has been the focus of considerable research, speculation, and debate (see, for example, Jackman 1977; Kinder and Sears 1981; McConahay, Hardee, and Batts 1981; Jackman and Muha 1984; Pettigrew 1985; Schuman, Steeh, and Bobo 1985; McConahay 1986; Schuman and Bobo 1988; Kuklinski et al. 1991; Sigelman and Welch 1991).[1] The assessment of the current state of whites' racial attitudes and the prognosis for their trend-line and future direction have been seen as hinging critically on the interpretation of the discrepancies between abstract and applied views.

Various interpretations have been offered. Jackman (1977) argued that whites' commitment to racial integration is sincere but superficial: in specific contexts, the commitment to racial integration is not deep enough to override other values or interests that come into play. Several other scholars have argued that whites do have a serious commitment to racial integration but that in the applied context, the injection of the

---

1. This discrepancy in whites' racial attitudes was the subject of an article in *Research News*, published for general dissemination by the University of Michigan (Katterman 1987). The article's title captures the state of the literature: "The Attitudes Gap: White Americans Endorse Racial Equality, Yet Show Little Support for Policies to Achieve It."

federal government as the proposed agent of change causes many whites to back off: many citizens lack confidence in the federal government and are unable to endorse policies that rely on that agency for implementation (Margolis and Haque 1981; Kuklinski and Parent 1981). Empirical analyses by Jackman (1981a, 1981b) turned up no evidence to support that optimistic interpretation. Others have argued that it is the mechanics of some racial policies, such as school busing, that make them distasteful to many whites: whites' genuine desire to see racial integration implemented does not find a satisfactory outlet in existing policy options (Greeley and Sheatsley 1974). Yet another interpretation that puts a relatively good face on whites' racial attitudes is that many whites resist specific intervention by the federal government because they resent the coercive power of government in general or they resent any intrusions on individual liberties (for example, Lipset and Schneider 1978; Stinchcombe and Taylor 1980; Sniderman and Hagen 1985; Taylor 1986; Merriman and Carmines 1988).

Several more skeptical arguments have also been made. Some have argued that the positive sentiments elicited from whites on survey questions about abstract support for racial integration reflect only lip service to democratic platitudes: the underlying resistance to racial equality is manifested as soon as one starts talking about specific policies that would implement racial integration (Crosby, Bromley, and Saxe 1980; Dovidio and Gaertner 1986). Scholars in the "symbolic racism" school have argued that the old, more blatant expressions of racism (such as overt support for segregation) have become socially unacceptable, but the racism itself is deep-seated and finds expression in objections to specific policies that are designed to redress racial inequalities (Kinder and Sears 1981; McConahay et al. 1981; Kinder 1986; McConahay 1986). Finally, I have argued (Jackman and Muha 1984) that many whites oppose racial segregation as a general principle because it violates their reverence for individualism—but, by the same token, they are unable to support governmental policies that would enforce integration, since those too would trample on individual rights. And the commitment to individualism is an integral part of the defense of racial privilege, not an orthogonal value that merely collides accidentally with racial policy goals.

At the same time as students of racial attitudes have debated about whether the abstract or the specific level is the more valid reflection of people's policy views, students of class consciousness have used the discrepancy between abstract and applied policy views as a wedge to identify the limits of consent in the working class. Focusing on the degree to which different social classes show consensual or conflicting views of the social order, they have observed the dissipation of conservative consensus as one moves from the abstract to the specific level in both perceptions of how the system operates and in economic policy goals. In this research, the dominant class reveals itself fairly constantly across abstract and specific contexts, but subordinates slip from an abstract endorsement of the regime to specific views indicating disaffection. Mann (1970) uses the discrepancy between abstract and specific views to infer that working class endorsement of the status quo reflects a "false consciousness," imposed from above, rather than an internalized set of values. He reasons that dominant values are absorbed by the working class at only the abstract level: in concrete applications, the divergent experiences of the working class lead them to take a more critical view of how the system operates and a more assertive position on economic policies. Without entangling himself in the question of what constitutes "true" or "false" consciousness, Parkin (1971) makes a similar attribution to a "subordinate value system" which he describes as accommodative: although working-class people unthinkingly soak in the broad moral precepts of the dominant value system, the milieu of the local working-class community provides the source for specific perceptions and normative judgments that are more jaundiced. The disjuncture between the two levels of abstraction is left unresolved within working-class culture. Other analysts too have emphasized the duality of working-class political beliefs, in which abstractions endorsing the status quo reside next to specific views and moral judgments that are far more cynical about how the system actually works (Huber and Form 1973; Abercrombie and Turner 1982).

Two questions are suggested. First, is the discrepancy between abstract principles and applied policy views a constant, or does it vary with different kinds of policies or in different intergroup contexts? Second, is there anything in the patterns of discrepancy that can throw light on which level of abstraction carries more significance? Is the specific application confounded with idiosyncratic factors that make it a messy test of policy commitments, or is the abstract level too vague to be meaningful? Perhaps it is only in the abstract that policy principles are unsullied by particulars that create interference. Or is it only when we get to specifics that the logical implications of conflicting interests are manifested?

Agents and Methods of Change.   This issue intersects with the one above: what are the legitimate agents of change and the desirable methods of change? Some analysts have argued that, in asking people about their specific policy views, idiosyncrasies about the proposed agent or method of change may determine people's responses, irrespective of their views about the general target of change. This issue has been discussed above, and I will not reiterate the various arguments here. The crux of the matter is whether people's disaffection from the agency of change or fears about the disruption or inconvenience associated with the method of change are confounding our inferences about their preferred policy outcomes.

But what are the policies that can alter the patterns of discrimination that are built into our way of life without at the same time disrupting elements of that way of life? Inconvenience to the more privileged parties seems intrinsic to any effective policy, since the only way to eradicate socially patterned discrimination is to circumvent or counteract it with the introduction of socially "artificial" measures. Policies that are not socially disruptive will by the same token fail to alter the discrimination that is the "natural" product of established social practices.

By the same token, to what agency of change might we turn if we deprive the federal government of that role? No other governmental body has the same breadth of authority or the same powers of enforcement. For that reason it is hard to digest the plea that some people would be more comfortable if local governmental agencies had the responsibility for blacks' civil rights: a preference for local government connotes a preference not just for another governmental agency but for a weaker one. Indeed, in the context of the history of blacks' civil rights, the federal government has been indelibly associated with any moves for affirmative change (from the Emancipation Proclamation on), and any argument that a more local government agency could do the job better flatly contradicts the experience of history. I suggest that what most whites find objectionable in the proposition of federal government enforcement of racial integration is the prospect of *enforcement*. That flies in the face of individualism and free choice and implies an imposed uniformity of standards from which personal or local deviation is impossible.

Tangible Policies and the Framing of Policy Debate.   This measurement issue is more elusive, buried in the depths of our conceptual approach. As empirical analysts, we prefer to focus on policies that have found some tangible expression in the extant political arena—and we ignore those that lie outside. This means that our empirical thinking about policy issues is directed by the way those issues are framed on the political agenda that is the site of our analyses. Examples of this slant can be found in research bearing on class, race, and gender policy views. In analyses of class policy views, there is a plentitude of questionnaire items on support for welfare policies but very few items asking about radical redistribution of income or about the elimination of private ownership. Items about racial policy focus almost exclusively on racial integration and equal opportunity, bypassing the question of racial equality in economic resources, status, or power. And in research on gender policy views, there has been a repeated focus on opinions about the particulars of gender-role definition along with a dearth of items on male status or power prerogatives.

It is unlikely to be productive to ask people about their support for policies that are completely hypothetical and removed from the realm of everyday political reality. Respondents would have no real-world framework in which to place such questions and hence would have no reality-based cues to interpret their meaning. Under such circumstances, responses would tend to be unstable, the stimulus would fail to have a standardized referent, and for many respondents it would have no referent at all, leaving the researcher with a harvest of haphazard reactions and "don't know's" in lieu of valid information about their policy goals.

For these eminently sensible reasons, empirical analysts contain their attention to issues that have been given life in the extant political arena. And yet, as Bachrach and Baratz (1970) have pointed out (in the context of the empirical debate on how to analyze community power structures), this strategy creates a slippery path whereby we allow our conceptual definition of the range of policy options to be captured within the net of those that already exist. Polsby has rightly argued that we cannot observe that which does not exist (1980), but we must nonetheless apply the conceptual corrective that what exists is but a restricted subset of a much wider theoretical range, a subset created by non-neutral political pressures. The only practical empirical strategy is to devise measures of people's policy goals that draw on known policy options being aired on the public agenda. But as we allow the existing political agenda to determine the focus of our empirical inquiry, we must resist the pressure to define our theoretical parameters within the same narrow scope. As we interpret responses to the policy options that are the necessary focus of our measures, our inferential framework should also incorporate those unmeasured policy options that lie outside the bounds of public political discussion.

The Constrained Pursuit of Resources

The sustained, unequal distribution of resources creates groups that are bound to each other by their mutual relationship. Dominant groups depend on the compliance of subordinates for the continuation of the way of life that they enjoy, and subordinates are obliged to pay heed to their more powerful protagonists if they wish to hold on to whatever limited control over resources they have attained. What this implies is that groups on both sides are bound by the constraints imposed by their mutual relationship as they formulate their policy goals.

Within this framework, the members of both dominant and subordinate groups seek to maximize their control over resources. At the same time, neither side puts all or even part of its current holdings at risk in the attempt to gain more. The central goal is to maximize: neither side will invest energy in quests for advancement that have few or no prospects of success, and there will be an even greater aversion to goals that may overstep the moral latitude of the relationship and thus incur the wrath of the other group. The malevolent interdependence created by the relational basis of the inequality forces the participating groups to be cognizant of their protagonists as they formulate their political goals.

I view the policy goals that are articulated by the members of unequal groups as the rational expression of their desire to control resources. And because I assume that the rational person avoids danger as much as he or she seeks to improve his or her condition, I cannot pronounce what goals are in the "true" interests of a group without attention to the constraints that are operative. Indeed, I assume that people seek to improve their lot only to the extent that it can be done without jeopardizing what they already have. Thus, I expect that over the long haul, barring occasional miscalculations and mistakes (which become part of the group's corporate history and knowledge), the articulated policy goals of group members will reflect their desire to improve their control over resources, limited by an implicit cognizance of the operative constraints. Those constraints emanate not only from pressures indigenous to their specific relationship with another group but also from broader societal pressures that bear down on the relationship from without. Those pressures affect both the formulation of policy goals themselves and the particular expression those goals take.

Within the confines of the debate between functionalists and conflict-oriented scholars, analysts were obliged to assert prima facie whether a group's "true" interests are served better by support for or opposition to inequality. Anything short of opposition to inequality among subordinates was in danger of being taken as evidence that inequality is benign rather than exploitative—with the only escape hatch being offered by the tenuous interpretation of "false consciousness." But by disentangling conflict from expropriation, we can avoid the bind of interpreting the absence of conflict as either the sign of benign consensus or as an incorrigible puzzle. We are freed from the imperative to make an assumption about whether the true interests of a group lie either in seeking complete equality or in embracing inequality. As Connolly (1972) has convincingly demonstrated, determining a group's ultimate, true interests remains a complicated philosophical issue that presents no ready solution. With the question of expropriation separated from the expectation of conflict, we can view the political goals of unequal groups in a less exalted light.

As people muddle through their daily lives in a reality that holds much uncertainty, they grope to maximize their control over resources that ease the business of living. In that unmeditated endeavor, the knowns in life that are imposed by the institutional structures and the moral climate within which the person is born provide the guides as to what is possible and what is safe. Attitudes are not contrived actively through the independent thought of individuals, but instead evolve unself-consciously through the collective experience of a group that is bound to another group in an unequal relationship. The individual members of those groups are trying to maximize their control over resources while avoiding danger. It follows that the political goals of individuals will be molded by the pragmatic and moral reality that surrounds them.

In this light, the limits placed on subordinates' goals by the culture and morality that infuses their lives are not a block to their perception of their true interests (as Gramsci would have it). Instead, those limits are an affirmation of the link between pragmatic and moral constraints. The morality that is promoted by dominant groups is not an artificial phenomenon—it springs from the pragmatic reality in which the members of dominant groups find themselves and over which it casts a delicate veil. And, further, that morality itself dominates the political climate within which subordinates grapple for resources, setting bounds that are at once pragmatic and normative on what kinds of proposals have political credibility.

Martin Luther King, Jr.'s recollections of the Montgomery bus boycott provide an interesting example of how these pressures operate to constrain the substance and tone of subordinate challenge. In their initial meeting with the city fathers and bus officials in December 1955, the Montgomery Improvement Association limited itself to three fairly modest proposals:

> (1) a guarantee of courteous treatment; (2) passengers to be seated on a first-come, first-served basis, the Negroes seating from the back; and (3) employment of Negro bus operators on predominantly Negro routes. (King, Jr. 1958, 109)

Each of these proposals was explained to the Montgomery city fathers and bus officials, drawing on arguments that might appeal to their specific moral sensibilities:

> I made it clear, for instance, that our request for a first-come, first-served seating arrangement, with Negroes loading from the back and whites from the front, was not something totally new for the South; other Southern cities—such as Nashville, Atlanta, and even Mobile, Alabama—followed this pattern, and each of them adhered as rigorously to a pattern of segregation as did Montgomery... (King, Jr. 1958, 110)

Despite the modest nature of the proposals, the representatives of the white community remained intransigent:

The commissioners and the attorney for the bus company began raising questions. They challenged the legality of the seating arrangement that we were proposing. They contended that the Negroes were demanding something that would violate the law. We answered by reiterating our previous argument that a first-come first-served seating arrangement could exist entirely within the segregation law, as it did in many Southern cities. (King, Jr. 1958, 111)

Ultimately, segregated seating in buses was completely overthrown by a Supreme Court decision imposed on the community from outside. But within the context of locally based negotiations, the leaders of the African-American community in Montgomery were mindful of the mentality of their white opponents as they formulated their initial demands. Those are the pressures that operate, on a more diffuse scale, in the general formulation of subordinates' policy goals. The issues that are addressed in the public forum are a constrained subset of the full range of possibilities, and that subset then frames policy awareness at the grassroots level.

The morality that infuses an intergroup relationship derives from the specific exigencies imposed by the expropriative basis and structural form of that relationship. In addition, the broad moral climate of the society in which the intergroup relationship is nested is likely to wield some influence. As I discussed in chapter 3, within a particular society each intergroup relationship does not operate in isolation but is affected—sometimes tangentially, sometimes critically—by events in other intergroup relationships that cohabit in the same society. In this sense, there is the potential for cultural diffusion from one unequal relationship to another when they exist in the same society and embroil the same people. The diffusion could take place directly, as individuals apply lessons learned in one intergroup setting to their orientation toward another intergroup relationship. Or the diffusion might take place indirectly, as when a particular intergroup relationship plays an important part in the historical development of a society and thus shapes the general moral code of that society. A potent example of such a process is the unfurling of individualism as a governing principle of the American moral code.

Individualism and Egalitarianism.   The principle of individualism is an undisputed bedrock of American morality and, indeed, of the Western capitalist-democracies in general. The centrality to Western ethics of the associated norms of individual liberty, achievement based on individual merit, and "free" competition has been observed by such disparate social analysts as Edmund Burke ([1775] 1954), Alexis de Tocqueville ([1850] 1969), Karl Marx ([1857–1858] 1971, 70–73, 128–131), and Max Weber (1946b; [1930] 1958). Its pertinence has repeatedly been stressed in analyses of class consciousness (for example, Parkin 1971; Huber and Form 1973; Abercrombie and Turner 1982; Jackman and Muha 1984), racial attitudes (for example, Kinder and Sears 1981; Jackman and Muha 1984; Sniderman and Hagen 1985; Bobo 1984; Kluegel and Smith 1986; Kluegel 1990), and contemporary American culture (for example, Bellah et al. 1985; Gans 1988).

The Western democracies also put a high stake on egalitarianism, or so it would seem, but the pervasive influence of individualistic values has worked to twist the popular meaning of equality to make it consistent with individualism. The "egalitarian" distribution of the vote in the Western democracies has been cast in terms of providing everyone with the same *right* to vote, not in terms of ensuring that everyone's voice is actually heard (Parkin 1971, 185). People do not have the equal distribution of public goods as their normative ideal—what is instead upheld, in the name of equality, is equality of opportunity. And as Schaar (1967) has deftly observed, equality of opportunity ironically presupposes a competitive world in which resources are allocated unequally. The morality of inequality hangs on the rules by which the race is conducted, on whether all competitors are given an equal chance in the race:

> The doctrine of equality of opportunity is the product of a competitive and fragmented society, a divided society, a society in which individualism. . . is the reigning ethical principle. It is a precise symbolic expression of the liberal-bourgeois model of society, for it extends the marketplace mentality to all spheres of life. It views the whole of human relations as a contest in which each man competes with his fellows for scarce goods, a contest in which there is never enough for everybody and where one man's gain is usually another's loss. . . . The fundamental character of the social-economic system is unaltered. All that happens is that individuals are given the chance to struggle up the social ladder, change their position in it, and step on the fingers of those beneath them. (Schaar 1967, 237)

The same sentiment is expressed in a more glowing light by Morris Abram (appointed as vice-chairman of the United States Commission on Civil Rights during the Reagan presidency):

> Civil rights have a unique meaning in this country. Elsewhere, in some of those societies where engineering a certain distribution of wealth and goods is part of the state's mission, people have economic rights—the right to housing, health care, and other goods. But civil rights have a different meaning in this country. We live in a constitutional democracy built not on the proposition that each [individual] has a fundamental entitlement to a particular piece of the economic pie, but rather on the concept that it is up to each individual to compete for economic goods, constitutionally protected from interference by guarantees of equal protection under the

law, due process, the Bill of Rights and, most fundamentally, the ballot. (Abram 1984, quoted in Taylor 1986, 203)

In this moral code, competition is hallowed. Indeed, the contractual, competitive work relations that mark capitalism have created a framework in which "freedom" takes on the individualistic meaning, "freedom to compete."

This shift in the meaning of equality to connote equality of opportunity is captured in the term "discrimination," which is the term that recurs most frequently in popular discussions (and in many scholarly discussions) of inequality. It is discrimination that collects all the feelings of moral disapprobation associated with the systematic disadvantages experienced by subordinate groups as a result of inequality. The term "discrimination" conceives of the problem as a violation of individual rights—that individual members of subordinate groups are not given the same opportunity to compete for public goods because they are treated categorically rather than on the basis of their individual attributes. With this normative emphasis, any ideological tendencies that encourage the categorical treatment of group members (most notably stereotypes) are seen as damaging, because they lower the probability that group members will be treated on an individual basis. By the same token, if discrimination is conceived as a violation of individual rights, so too is "reverse discrimination" (Gamson and Modigliani 1987). The speed with which this relatively new term was adopted in common usage reflects the moral precedence of individualism: it is regarded as morally equivalent to give a categorical preference to the members of either dominant or subordinate groups.

Scholars have made different arguments about the means by which individualism enters into the articulation of egalitarianism. Some have taken the more optimistic view that the prominence of individualism is just an unfortunate happenstance that gets in the way of support for specific egalitarian policies (for example, Merriman and Parent 1983; Sniderman, Brody, and Kuklinski 1984; Sniderman and Hagen 1985; Merriman and Carmines 1988). This view has been especially prominent in discussions of whites' lackluster support for interventionist policies on behalf of blacks' civil rights. It is argued that whites' objection to specific racial policies, such as quota systems, is based on the fact that these policies violate individualistic principles: the commitment to individualism is seen as a coincidental obstacle driven by factors independent of racial inequality. Indeed, Sniderman and Hagen (1985, 22) go so far as to say:

Individualism. . . undercuts efforts to realize racial equality not out of hostility to the idea of equality but for just the opposite reason: Individualism is itself a species of egalitarianism. . . . Even were this a world free of preju-

dice and meanness of spirit and ignorance, there would still be opposition
to racial equality—an opposition rooted in egalitarianism in the form of
individualism.

Other scholars have taken a less benign view of the role of individualism in popular responses to egalitarianism. Students of class have been
especially likely to see individualism as an intrinsic part of the defense
of inequality in the contemporary Western world (for example, Parkin
1971; Jackman and Muha 1984). Parkin (1971) has argued that the individualistic goals fostered by equality-of-opportunity issues have provided
a convenient distraction from core redistributive issues, and that the
political agendas of left-wing parties in Western democracies have shifted
more toward equality-of-opportunity issues because they are less threatening to established groups and thus present a more fruitful avenue for
contention. And some students of racism have also identified the morality
of individualism as something that is actively invoked in the defense of
racial inequality (for example, Kinder and Sears 1981; Jackman and
Muha 1984; Gamson and Modigliani 1987). Kinder and Sears have argued that the traditional American values of individualism and self-reliance form the moral basis for racism and also provide a "safe" outlet for
voicing objections to affirmative action programs. For these scholars, the
popular whine of "reverse discrimination" reflects the moral envelop-
ment of racism in individualism. The tone of principled moral outrage
in the "reverse discrimination" argument is drawn out clearly by Gamson
and Modigliani (1987), and they show how exponents of that argument
sanctimoniously defended the rights of individuals against incursions on
behalf of groups. For example, they quote Cohen (1979, 44) as saying,
"Injuries are suffered. . . by individual persons. . . . The sacrifice of fundamental individual rights cannot be justified by the desire to advance
the well-being of any ethnic group," and Glazer (1975, 220) is quoted
as saying that affirmative action abandons the "first principle of a liberal
society, that the individual and the individual's interest and good and
welfare are the test of a good society" (quoted in Gamson and Modigliani
1987, 146). In this way, antiracist and "equality" symbolism were adroitly
summoned to oppose affirmative action on behalf of blacks (Gamson
and Modigliani 1987, 169–170).

I have argued that individualism has been the hallmark cry of dominant groups under challenge in the capitalist-democracies, precisely because it offers a principled way of denying the moral legitimacy of egalitarian demands made on behalf of groups (Jackman and Muha 1984).
As Gamson and Modigliani (1987) point out, the symbolism that is thus
invoked sounds conveniently like egalitarianism, and it also makes a
trenchant appeal to "fairness" norms. Individualism has been especially

appropriate for the defense of class inequality in the "free-market" era because dominant classes have no incentive to emphasize the boundaries between classes. The practice of the expropriation does not require an emphasis on the "groupness" of the arrangements, and, indeed, as I argued in chapter 3, dominant classes prefer to encourage the notion of unsegmented socioeconomic differentiation where people's placement from one generation to the next is seen as fluid. Industrial economies require the recruitment of talent into skilled positions, and individualistic, meritocratic principles are consistent with that requirement.

The shift to equality of opportunity has had such overriding significance in the conduct of political life in the capitalist democracies that it should influence the articulation of policy issues even in relationships in which there is less indigenous pressure for individualism. Ideas that have worked in one context drift comfortably into another: they are the ideas that are the most readily available, and they have demonstrated credibility. However, it is in relationships marked by prolonged challenge from subordinates that individual rights become established as a bedrock moral tenet. This has a profound effect on the shaping of subordinate demands and the tenor of political debate between groups.

Empirical Questions.   My argument is that unequal groups pursue resources under constraints. Those constraints emanate from the specific pragmatic and moral exigencies that are posed by the intergroup relationship of which they are a part, as well as from the broad moral code of the society in which the relationship resides. By examining the policy goals of unequal groups in relationships where different constraints are operative, we can assess the degree to which those goals do appear to reflect an ongoing endeavor to maximize, within constraints, control over resources. I have argued that the more distally relations are structured in the day-to-day exchange between unequal groups, the more opportunities there are for subordinates to disentangle themselves from the dominant group cognitively and emotionally and to frame policy goals that aim at affirmative change. However, one set of constraints is traded for another. When the dominant group is faced with institutional arrangements that deliver benefits to them in a cruder, more aggregated fashion and with subordinates who are more restive about those arrangements, dominant-group members move to contain the damage by redirecting people's moral sensitivities into more individualistic channels. The moral emphasis is shifted from the group to the individual, and subordinates are pressed to transform their group demands into individual aspirations. With the political credibility of groups undermined, those demands that continue to be issued by subordinates shift away from the redistributive issues that lie at the core of the intergroup relationship to the safer moral ground of individual rights and equal opportunity. Indeed, those pressures have been such a central feature of American social history that we may find the morality of individualism is omnipresent in the articulation of policy views in all three intergroup relationships.

This argument directs us to the following empirical questions. What are the policy goals that are voiced by groups as they face each other under different kinds of constraints, and what refrains, if any, are found in all three intergroup relationships? To what extent do the members of each of the groups attempt to increase their group's control over resources or restrict their goals to more of a holding operation? And in their dialogue back and forth, what concessions, if any, do groups on either side appear to grant to their protagonists?

On the dominant side of the relationship, is there a tendency to pursue reactionary policies that would enlarge the inequality, to maintain a conservative stance that aims at keeping things as they are, or to make concessions to subordinates by acknowledging the need for some affirmative change? What kinds of concessions are most likely to be offered, and to what extent do dominant groups attempt to satisfy demands from subordinates with concessions that are symbolic or that involve only minor readjustments, enough to shave off the most offensive aspects of the inequality while leaving the main thrust of arrangements intact?

And on the subordinate side, how much of a tendency is there to demand affirmative changes or to hold on conservatively to current arrangements? How moderately or radically do subordinates compose their demands, and what direction is followed in the shaping of their policy goals? Is there any evidence of a readiness among subordinates to yield some ground to their protagonists by supporting reactionary changes that would further diminish their control over society's resources? Are there circumstances under which subordinates are prepared to suffer some additional symbolic indignity or to advocate some small tangible loss in order to stave off greedier assaults on their resources?

As we evaluate the policy goals of unequal groups, we should differentiate abstract principles from more specific policy views. Are there systematic differences in the way people think about general policy principles on the one hand and specific policy issues on the other? And it is important to assess people's specific policy goals against the existential perceptions of governmental policy that frame those goals. Without knowing the subjective existential framework through which people see ongoing public policy, it is impossible to assess the meaning of their prescriptions about how much activity they think the government ought to be promoting on behalf of various groups. It is also important to assess the extent to which group membership determines political perceptions.

Do the members of a group share the same perception of their fate at the hands of the government? And does the experiential quality of the intergroup relationship create a common estimate across group lines of the current level of governmental activity, or does it lead to sharply disparate existential views between the contending groups?

DATA: ABSTRACT POLICY PRINCIPLES

I begin with the abstract principles that are espoused by contending groups in race, gender, and class relations, and then in the next section move to people's views—both existential and prescriptive—about specific policies. At each level, I start by assessing the opinions that are exchanged between groups in each intergroup relationship, and I then draw out the general patterns that are suggested by comparing the three cases. These data allow us to assess the way policy goals are shaped as unequal groups face each other under constraints.

Measures

Race.   I use two items to reflect abstract racial-policy principles. Both items are modeled on those used repeatedly in the National Election Studies:

> Generally speaking, are you in favor of racial integration, racial segregation, or something in between? (IF NECESSARY: By integration we mean when things are racially mixed, and by segregation we mean when races are separate.)[2]

> Which of these two statements do you agree with more?:
> Blacks have a right to live wherever they can afford to.
> *or*
> White people have a right to keep blacks out of their neighborhoods if
>   they want to.

These items have been frequently used in the past and need little comment here. Both items clearly address the general principle of racial integration, which has had high visibility and symbolic importance over the past few decades. Note, however, that they do not address the principle of racial equality per se—that principle has been relatively distant from public discussion about racial policy and is thus absent from these items. The second item even idealizes the concept of economic inequality

---

2. This item was worded a little differently in the National Election Studies: "Are you in favor of desegregation, strict segregation, or something in between?" (National Election Studies 1991, 274). I modified the wording to reflect the terms that had more currency in the 1970s.

with the qualifier, "Blacks have a right to live *wherever they can afford to*": that phrase gives voice to the assumption that not everyone can or should be able to afford the same quality housing, and more obliquely, it also leaves unmolested the expectation that blacks lie considerably behind whites in what they can afford. As I have argued elsewhere (Jackman and Muha 1984), both items implicate the norm of individualism rather than equality. During the height of the civil rights movement, Southern-style segregation of facilities was repeatedly depicted by the media as a serious violation of individual rights; and the right of individuals to buy and sell freely on the housing market without neighborhood interference is another premise of individual freedom in an economy ruled by private ownership.

Gender.   There are three items to reflect abstract gender-policy principles, and they focus on the issues that have been aired the most in public discussion of gender policy. The first two items address the classic division of domestic responsibilities between men and women, and the third item focuses on equality of job opportunity for both sexes:

> Generally speaking, do you think that doing the housework and taking care of the children should be *mainly* the woman's responsibility or that it should be the man's responsibility *as much as* the woman's?

> Generally speaking, do you think that the man should have the responsibility for providing financial support for the family, or that the woman should *also* have some responsibility for providing financial support?

> Which of these two statements do you agree with more?:
> A woman should be considered just as seriously as a man for any job that fits her interests.
> *or*
> Certain jobs should be open to men only.

As with the race items above, these items are straightforward and deal with familiar topics, but a few points are in order. First, the two items on domestic gender-roles necessarily deal with a more personal and privatized aspect of life than do the items for race or class. This is in keeping with the conduct of gender relations, in which home and family comprise the prime theater. But by the same token, this means that many of the central symptoms of gender inequality lie in a zone that has been exempted from the normal purview of public, governmental policy. Thus, they are not as susceptible to policy manipulation. This is intrinsic to the structure of gender relations and indicates yet again the advantages that accrue to dominant groups when they establish social control over subordinates through paternalistic arrangements that hinge on personal, one-to-one contacts.

Second, the two gender-role questions focus on the delineation of gender-appropriate responsibilities rather than whether certain tasks are beyond the ken of either sex. The purpose was to gauge opinions about basic principles of role definition rather than about whether one spouse may *help* another with gender-defined activities. For example, someone may consider it fine for the wife to take paid employment if she wishes and even to supplement the family pot with her earnings but at the same time consider the financial provision of the family to remain the husband's *responsibility*. Similarly, someone may think it appropriate for the husband to help his wife wash the dishes or the baby's bottom, but still believe that the cleanliness of house and family is the wife's worry. Public discussion of these issues usually presents them in terms of individual freedom of choice to deviate from prescribed norms if circumstances permit rather than in terms of how responsibilities should be assigned. Some respondents may not have been able to break out of that pattern of thinking, despite the stricter wording used on those items.

Third, the question on housework and childcare poses an egalitarian division of responsibility as one option, while the question on the family's financial support does not pose a completely egalitarian arrangement as an option, just *some* diffusion of responsibility. Pretesting indicated only minuscule support for an egalitarian division of financial responsibility between husbands and wives: the "egalitarian" response option was diluted to its present wording in order to capture whatever leanings away from traditional male role-definitions could be found.

Finally, the item on equality of opportunity is closer in spirit to the racial-policy items above: it deals with a public sphere more within the purview of government, and at the same time it implicates the principle of individual rights rather than equality. In this regard, note that the item only asks whether women should be *considered* for any job, not whether they should be hired. This distinction is important: the wording makes it plain that the focus is on procedures rather than outcomes, and endorsing the principle of an open procedure is of course not tantamount to expecting an egalitarian outcome. Indeed, such prominent theorists as Emile Durkheim ([1897] 1951, 385) and John Stuart Mill ([1869] 1970) were moved to advocate open procedures for women's employment opportunities while at the same time reassuring their readers that such procedures would not lead to any serious competition between the sexes in the job market—because, they argued, women's natural aptitudes would steer them into different occupations than men without any imposition of discriminatory rules.

Class.   The general policy principle that is most central to class is economic inequality. I have two measures reflecting that principle, both phrased in terms of occupational inequality in earnings:

Thinking about the amount of money people in different occupations earn, do you think there *should be* a great deal of difference, some difference, or almost no difference in how much people in different occupations earn?

We're interested in getting people's opinions about how much money people in different occupations should make. Please look at these occupations and tell me how much money you think people in each one *should* make, regardless of how much they *do* make. Just tell me what you think would be best.

Now, how about a school teacher? How much money do you think an *average school teacher should* make in a year?

How much money do you think an *average assembly-line factory worker should* make in a year?

How much money do you think an *average doctor should* make in a year?

How much money do you think an *average business executive should* make in a year?

How much money do you think an *average janitor should* make in a year?

The first of these measures is the simpler test of support for income inequality as an abstract principle. Note that it does not include a response option for complete income equality: as with the item on the gender division of financial responsibility, pretesting indicated that complete income equality is outside the moral bounds of American society.

The second measure relies on a set of questions about desired incomes for a range of occupations to construct a general recommended ratio of incomes of low-level occupations to high-level occupations. Each respondent's concept of how much income inequality there should be was calculated by taking the mean of four recommended-income ratios: janitors to doctors, janitors to business executives, assembly-line factory workers to doctors, and assembly-line factory workers to business executives.[3] The closer the ratio to 1.0, the smaller the desired income gap. Note that the occupations chosen as stimuli do not represent extremes in the occupational distribution (as, say, between migrant farmworkers and corporation presidents), but are intended to capture opposing poles in the *mainstream* of the labor force. This measure addresses general notions of the optimal income-gap by asking about concrete salary preferences: it thus allows us to validate the first measure, which relies on broader language to capture the same concept.

Results

Race. Racial segregation is largely repudiated by both blacks and whites—and yet there is a divergence between the two groups in their

3. Respondents with missing data on two or more of the four individual ratios were excluded from analysis. (Application of a more stringent decision-rule excluding those with missing data on one or more of the individual ratios resulted in a slightly smaller *N*, but yielded virtually identical distributions.)

TABLE 6.1.   Percentages of Whites and Blacks in Favor of Racially
Open or Exclusive Housing, and Racial Integration or Segregation.*

	Whites	Blacks
Residential Rights		
Blacks have a right to live wherever they can afford	80.5%	96.9%
Whites have a right to keep blacks out if they want to	14.0	0.0
Depends, Other	0.8	0.0
Don't Know	4.7	3.1
Base N	1,632	195
Racial Integration/Segregation		
Racial integration	35.3%	72.9%
Something in between	44.4	14.6
Racial segregation	15.7	7.3
Depends, other	0.5	0.0
Don't know	4.1	5.2
Base N	1,632	192

* Differences between groups in the percentage giving the primary responses are
statistically significant (p < .01).

enthusiasm for what would seem to be the most obvious alternative, racial
integration. That divergence reveals itself suggestively rather than starkly.
Table 6.1 displays the percentage distributions of responses given by
whites and blacks to the two items on racial integration.

Only about 15 percent of whites endorse either the right of whites to
exclude blacks categorically from their neighborhoods or an overall policy of racial segregation; this is not very different from the near-complete
lack of support for segregation among blacks. For many whites, however,
rejection of segregation is not tantamount to endorsement of racial integration. When forced to choose between the right of whites to exclude
blacks categorically from their neighborhoods and the right of blacks to
live wherever they can afford, about eight out of ten whites endorse the
latter right. But on the other item, which offers the option of "something
in between" racial segregation and integration, fully 44 percent of whites
are drawn to that response, leaving only 35 percent supporting unmodi-
fied racial integration. By contrast, only 15 percent of blacks find "something in between" racial segregation and integration an attractive proposition: 73 percent of blacks support racial integration and 97 percent
support blacks' residential rights. Thus, overall, the principle of racial
integration receives overwhelming support from blacks, whereas among
whites it has frequent but guarded support.[4]

4. Data from the American National Election Studies reported in Schuman, Steeh,
and Bobo (1985, 74–75, 95–96, 144–145) suggest even higher levels of attraction to the
"something in between" response among whites (and also among blacks) than is indicated

One might well ask what "something in between" racial segregation and integration could be. What it probably conjures up for most people is the idea of racial integration or segregation being decided on the basis of individual free will, without any external interference—so-called "voluntary integration." Taylor maintains that the principal issue of contention in whites' orientation to policies of racial integration since the 1950s has been over mandatory versus voluntary compliance (Taylor 1986, 24–38, 191–204). As though to underscore that point, Herrnstein (1990, 6) carefully distinguishes between "desegregation" (by which racial segregation is made illegal) and "integration" (by which equal proportionate representation of groups is mandated). It is well known that Northern whites who opposed slavery in the 1860s did not generally have racial equality in mind as the obvious alternative; likewise in the latter half of the twentieth century, it seems that many Northern whites who opposed the de jure segregation of the Jim-Crow South did not object to the de facto segregation that characterized the neighborhoods and schools of Northern cities.

The attraction of whites to "something in between" segregation and integration suggests that their support for racial integration might most generously be described as soft. Indeed, it may not reflect support for the rights of blacks so much as the rights of individuals to live their lives as unencumbered as possible by the stipulations of others. Individuals should be able to buy and sell in a free housing market and they should

---

in my data. In the NES data, whites' support for "something in between" increased from 46 percent in 1970 to 60 percent in 1978, and blacks' support for this option increased from 18 percent to 39 percent over the same time period. Schuman, Steeh, and Bobo provide evidence from a split-ballot experiment that the NES's placement of the item in the interview schedule immediately after an item on federal school intervention (a particularly sensitive issue) was contaminating responses to the "general principle" item and increasing the number of "something in between" responses. In my interview schedule, the item on general support for racial integration *preceded* the item on federal school intervention; the only racial items asked immediately before were on respondents' personal preferences for interracial contact in the workplace and neighborhood, which I judge to be relatively innocuous.

The figures in Schuman, Steeh, and Bobo (1985) indicate that the percentage of blacks to be drawn to the "something in between" response has also increased, although it still trails behind the percentage of whites giving that response. This pattern suggests that blacks may have backed away from the goal of racial integration in the face of unrelenting white opposition to racial integration in specific policy contexts, especially in public schools. Blauner (1989) argues that blacks have become disillusioned with the goal of racial integration, and the growing interest in Afrocentrism among blacks in the late 1980s and early 1990s lends support to that view. Confronted with unyielding white opposition, the goal of seeking more contact with whites may have lost its appeal as a means of attaining racial equality. This may be especially true in the context of public schools, where the prospect of sending one's children to learn in a hostile white environment may seem an unsatisfactory outcome.

also be able to decide whether they want to have contact with another racial group. No one should be prevented from selling his house to whoever can afford it, and by the same token no one should be forced to have contact with another racial group. Such a view falls considerably short of an abandonment of the racial status quo and implies a larger gap between the racial policy principles of whites and blacks than a cursory inspection of the data might suggest.

Gender. The views of men and women on gender policy principles reveal two important contrasts with the racial policy principles expressed by whites and blacks. First, rejection of discriminatory gender-policy principles lags considerably behind the repudiation of racial segregation found among both blacks and whites. Second, men and women do not differ markedly from each other in the gender policy principles they espouse. Men and women exhibit a roughly parallel division of opinion on the subject. The percentage distributions of men's and women's responses to the three items on gender policy principles are presented in table 6.2.

When asked about responsibility for housework and childcare, there is an almost even division of opinion within each gender group. Close to half of each sex endorses the principle of an egalitarian division of domestic labor; almost as many men and just as many women maintain that domestic labor is primarily the woman's responsibility. When asked about whether women should share *some* of the financial responsibility for the family (recall the conservative phrasing of this question), the distribution of responses from women is very similar to that elicited from them by the item on housework and childcare. Men lag a little behind, with only about one-third supporting even some diffusion of financial responsibility to women and just over one-half seeing the financial support of the family as the man's responsibility alone.

On both of these items, a small minority of each sex (11–16 percent) broke away from the absolutes that were posed and volunteered conditional answers (such as, for the first item, saying it depended on whether the woman worked, for the second item, on whether the husband's income was sufficient, and for both items, on whether there were children). That some respondents were moved to volunteer such statements without any encouragement from the question itself suggests that such considerations feature prominently in people's thinking. Their effect is largely conservative, and their insertion into the issue implies that others' support for egalitarian principles of labor-division may also be fragile, crumbling easily in the face of specific objections that might be raised in individual cases. Few men or women may believe in an egalitarian division of labor between the sexes as a first-order right of women, but

TABLE 6.2. Percentages of Men and Women in Favor of Egalitarian or Traditional Division of Responsibility in Housework/Childcare and in Provision of Financial Support.

	Men	Women
Responsibility for Housework and Children		
Man's as much as woman's	48.4%	42.6%
Mainly woman's	39.8	43.8*
If woman works, both	7.4	9.6
Depends, Other	3.9	3.7
Don't Know	0.4	0.3
Base N	801	1,108
Responsibility for Financial Support		
Woman should also have some	33.6%	41.9%
Man only	51.5	40.2**
If income sufficient, man only	4.3	7.2
Woman shouldn't work if small children	2.1	3.8
Woman equally responsible	0.9	0.8
Depends, Other	7.2	5.3
Don't know	0.5	0.5
Base N	800	1,107
Equal Job Opportunities		
Woman should be considered	57.2%	64.2%
Some jobs for men only	40.3	33.4**
Depends, Other	0.5	0.7
Don't Know	2.0	1.7
Base N	797	1,106

* Difference between men and women in the percentage giving the primary responses is statistically significant (p < .05).
** Difference between men and women in the percentage giving the primary responses is statistically significant (p < .01).

rather as something that is permissible, if individual circumstances are favorable or if it can be done without violating the primary obligations of either gender.

The third item on gender policy principles directly broaches an issue that is hallowed in the Western capitalist democracies—equality of opportunity—and in this respect its focus parallels the race item on equal housing opportunity. This gender item elicits more affirmative responses than either of the other two items on gender principles, but equal job opportunity for women still does not receive as much support as the principle of equal housing opportunity for blacks receives from both blacks and whites. And as with the other two gender items, this issue does not elicit very different responses from women than from men: 57

TABLE 6.3.   Percentages of the Upper-Middle Class, Middle Class, Working Class, and Poor in Favor of Income Equality or Inequality.*

	Upper-Middle	Middle	Working	Poor
Preferred Income Gap				
Almost No Difference	7.6%	8.0%	11.2%	17.1%
Some Difference	42.7	58.0	58.7	50.7
Great Deal of Difference	47.8	31.2	25.9	24.3
Don't Know	1.9	2.7	4.2	7.9
Base N	157	820	698	140
Preferred Income Ratio of Janitor/Factory Worker to Doctor/Executive[a]				
Below .25 (largest gap)	29.9%	19.9%	14.0%	17.0%
.25–.33	30.7	21.2	18.6	16.0
.34–.43	20.4	21.9	21.9	18.0
.44–.57	14.6	19.5	20.7	24.0
.58–1.0 (smallest gap)	4.4	17.5	24.7	25.0
Base N	137	708	570	100

[a] Respondents with missing data on two or more ratios were excluded.
* Differences by class (with Don't Know's excluded) are statistically significant (p < .01).

percent of men and 64 percent of women endorse the principle that a woman should have an equal opportunity to be considered for any job that interests her.

Class.   Egalitarian principles seem even further removed from most people's thinking when confronted with the topic of how incomes should be distributed. And although there is some disagreement by social class, the vast majority of people in all social classes subscribe to the principle of income *inequality* to some degree. The percentage distributions of people's responses about income inequality, by social class, are given in table 6.3.

When asked in the most general terms about whether there should be a great deal of difference, some difference, or (as the timidly egalitarian option) almost no difference in how much money people in different occupations earn, the variation in responses by social class is limited. The main distinction is that, with descending social class, there is some retraction of support for a great deal of income inequality; the position to which people in lower classes remove themselves, however, is most likely to be support for *some* difference in income. Among those identifying with the upper-middle class, there is a roughly even division of opinion between those favoring a great deal of difference and some difference in incomes. Among the three lower classes, opinion shifts slightly to favoring some income difference over a great deal of difference by a ratio of about 2 to 1. The idea of almost no income difference remains largely out of bounds in all social classes: that idea is supported by only about 8–11 percent of the upper-middle, middle, and working classes, and 17 percent of the poor. Data from an open-ended probe asking respondents why they took the positions they did indicate that the overwhelming majority of people in all social classes subscribe to some version of an individualist-achievement rationale (those data are discussed in detail in Jackman and Jackman 1983, 206–213).

The pattern of responses to the income-ratio measure replicates responses to the more global item above. Again, we observe a general aversion to the idea of a very small income gap. Note that the most egalitarian ratio-score category in the table is set very inclusively at merely .58 and above, and even so, it attracts very little support. Again, there is a mild relationship between social class and conceptions of the optimal size for the income gap. With descending social class, there is some retreat from the idea of a very large income gap and a timid lead in favoring a small gap. About 60 percent of the upper-middle class and 40 percent of the middle class advocate an income gap in which the highest occupations earn *at least* three times as much as the lowest occupations, whereas about one-third of the poor and working class support such a large income gap. Conversely, about one-quarter of the poor and working class favor an income gap in which the highest occupations earn less than twice as much as the lowest occupations, compared with only 4 percent of the upper-middle class.

General Patterns. The general policy principles that are espoused in these three intergroup relationships betray only limited support for egalitarian goals and only restricted disagreement between unequal groups on this score. Egalitarianism in the shape of income equality elicits the least support overall, and there is modest disagreement among social classes only in the *extent* of their *rejection* of the principle of income equality. In gender relations, both men and women are divided almost evenly between egalitarian and discriminatory principles on the division of labor between the sexes. It is in the context of racial segregation/integration that one finds the strongest endorsement of affirmative principles, but the race items invoke equality of opportunity rather than racial equality per se. Blacks assert their right to equal treatment more clearly than do women or the poor or working class. Whites also reject the idea of the categorical separation of the races more vehemently than men (or women) reject the categorical separation of tasks between the sexes or than the upper-middle class rejects the notion of wide income differentials. But, nonetheless, whites lag behind blacks in their enthusiasm for the principle of racial *integration*, resulting in a larger rift in general policy principles between the races than exists between the sexes or classes.

These patterns suggest that subordinate challenge of categorically unequal treatment may push the dominant group away from a stance that morally endorses such treatment, but the position to which the dominant group retreats is likely to be one of equal opportunity rather than egalitarianism pure and simple. Thus, although whites have largely repudiated racial segregation, they have not embraced racial integration either. Many whites appear to be drawn to an alternative that leaves the rights of individuals confined as little as possible. In a similar vein, the arena of gender relations that shows the highest rejection of unequal treatment is that of employment opportunity, the arena that most directly invokes the principle of individualism. Note, however, that the rights of individuals are not enunciated as vehemently in the context of gender as they are in the context of race. Finally, the almost total absence of support for the concept of income equality is explained by the respondents themselves as stemming from a belief in individualistic-achievement principles.

DATA: SPECIFIC POLICY GOALS

To explore the substance of people's specific policy beliefs, I begin with their ideas about the appropriate course for governmental action, along with the existential beliefs that subjectively anchor those prescriptions—their perceptions of the current level of governmental activity. In the second part of the analysis I build that anchor into my assessment of specific policy goals. I measure the extent to which people advocate affirmative change over the perceived current state of affairs, no change (that is, conservatism), or reactionary change back to a lowered level of governmental intervention on behalf of subordinates' rights.

Measures

Given the importance of the federal government as the most powerful institution in American politics, my measures of specific policy goals all focus on federal government intervention. And in keeping with my concern that people's prescriptions be anchored in their subjective perceptions of the current status of policy activity, respondents were asked about both their perceptions of and prescriptions for governmental action.

Specific policy goals for race, gender, and class were measured with a series of item-pairs: for each policy issue, a question about respondents' existential perceptions of governmental activity was followed by a question about what level of governmental activity they would prescribe. The pairs of items for policies relevant to race, gender, and class were interspersed among one another, and the series was introduced as follows:

People have different opinions about how much the federal government is doing about various things. People also differ about how much they think the federal government *should* be doing about these things.

First of all, how much do you think the federal government *is* doing to make sure blacks and whites go to the same schools? Just look at the card and tell me what you think [A lot, Quite a bit, A little, Nothing].

Now, how much do you think the federal government *should be* doing about this?

The pairs of questions covered the following policy issues for race, gender, and social class:

(RACE)
... to make sure blacks and whites go to the same schools?
... to make sure that blacks can buy any house on the market that they can afford?
... to make sure blacks have the same job opportunities as whites?

(GENDER)
... to make sure women have the same job opportunities as men?
... to make sure laws are applied in the same way to women and men?
... to provide daycare centers for the children of working mothers?

(CLASS)
... to make sure that everyone who wants a job can get one?
... to give welfare benefits to people who don't have very much money?
... to make sure that everyone has at least a minimum income?

To interpret these items, two factors need to be considered: (1) are they straightforward applications of the abstract principles addressed in the earlier questions?; and (2) to what extent do they address the enforcement of individual rights or equality of opportunity versus group rights or the redistribution of resources from one group to another? I consider these issues for race, gender, and class, respectively.

The specific policy questions for race all involve straightforward applications of the general principle of racial integration. These items address three alternative, highly visible policies that seek to implement racial integration. As with the abstract principle of racial integration itself, these policies do not broach the issue of racial equality, but instead are aimed at the protection of individual rights. But, unlike the questions on abstract principles, these questions do ask about enforcement, and as such, they automatically remove some of the laissez-faire connotations that notions of individual rights and personal freedom have for many people. In addition, two of the items (on jobs and schools) do deviate somewhat from the abstract principles in that they implicitly entangle redistributive issues. Of the three items, that on equal housing opportunity has the closest correspondence with at least one of the abstract-principle items and it is the most oriented toward individual rights. The item on equal job opportunity also broaches the enforcement of individual rights, but for many whites the issue of *enforcing* equal job opportunity may conjure up visions of racial quotas or preferential treatment of blacks (cutely termed "reverse discrimination" because they violate whites' individual rights), and to the extent that this is the case, this item embroils a significant redistributive element. Finally, the item on school integration undoubtedly elicits thoughts about school busing: school busing was designed to create equality of educational opportunity for blacks and whites, but the implementation clearly involves some redistribution of valued educational resources from whites to blacks.

The items on specific gender policies are tangential to the basic principles of gender-role definition, but one item corresponds quite closely to the abstract principle of equal employment opportunity for women. As I noted earlier, the principal sphere for the enactment of gender-roles is in intimate personal relationships, conveniently beyond the reach of normal governmental activity. Thus, the question of how to enforce any change in gender-role definitions becomes moot. Instead, these items focus on policies that address some of the fallout from gender differentiation: women's inferior employment opportunities, women's inferior legal rights, and women's need for daycare for their children so that they can participate in the paid labor force. The first two of these issues involve the enforcement of individual rights (with the same proviso as noted for the comparable racial-policy items), whereas the third item involves the redirection of resources to assist women's participation in society on the same terms as men.

The three specific class-policy items are essentially soft applications of the general principle of income equality—to the policies of full employment, welfare, and minimum income. The item on guaranteed employment is the most moderate of the three: although full employment has traditionally been a higher priority of the left-wing, it is regarded as desirable by both the left and the right, especially insofar as it is associated with a healthy economy rather than with governmental intervention through public work-programs. The item on welfare programs probably has the most cogently redistributive meaning, both because of the frequent public discussion of welfare programs and because such programs are generally assumed to connote the direct redistribution of resources at the government's disposal. Note, however, that in keeping with the boundaries of public discussion of economically redistributive measures,

TABLE 6.4. Prescriptive and Existential Beliefs of Whites and Blacks about Government Action to Promote Racial Equality.*

	Whites	Blacks	Whites	Blacks
	How much SHOULD gov't be doing?:		How much IS gov't doing?:	
Integrated Schools				
A Lot	14.3%	66.8%	35.8%	13.6%
Quite a Bit	25.6	18.4	42.2	28.3
A Little	27.4	5.3	16.5	46.6
Nothing	27.1	3.2	1.3	5.8
Don't Know, Other	5.5	6.3	4.2	5.8
Equal Housing Opportunity				
A Lot	17.9%	71.6%	20.0%	6.3%
Quite a Bit	32.1	23.2	29.2	19.4
A Little	22.0	0.0	27.1	45.0
Nothing	18.9	0.0	6.0	19.9
Don't Know, Other	9.2	5.3	17.8	9.4
Equal Job Opportunity				
A Lot	24.3%	79.1%	29.7%	5.8%
Quite a Bit	42.0	14.1	44.5	18.3
A Little	21.2	0.5	18.8	55.5
Nothing	7.1	0.5	0.8	14.7
Don't Know, Other	5.4	5.8	6.2	5.8
Base N (ranges)	1,612–1,623	190–191	1,624–1,627	191

* All differences between groups (with Don't Know's excluded) are statistically significant (p < .01).

none of the specific policies addressed in these items does more than raise the possibility of minimal safety-net measures. Such measures merely aim to soften the harshest punishments of economic inequality: they fall far short of any attempt to eliminate or even to reduce significantly the gap between rich and poor.

Results: Prescriptive and Existential Beliefs

Race. The disagreement between whites and blacks that showed itself only suggestively in the articulation of abstract policy principles becomes a marked and systematic rift when we examine people's prescriptive beliefs about how active the federal government should be in pursuing specific racial policies and also in their existential perceptions of the current level of governmental activity. The relevant percentage-distributions are presented in table 6.4: the first two columns give the percentages of whites and blacks who advocate that the federal government should be doing "a lot," "quite a bit," "a little," or "nothing" to ensure racially integrated schools, equal housing opportunity, and equal job opportunities for blacks; the second two columns give comparable distributions for whites' and blacks' existential beliefs about how much the federal government is currently doing on those same racial policy issues.

Whites' support for governmental intervention to promote blacks' civil rights tends to be lackluster—blacks are much more likely than whites to think that the federal government should be intervening vigorously in this area. The gap between the races widens still further when one considers that whites also tend to see the current level of governmental intervention on behalf of blacks' civil rights as much more vigorous than do blacks. I begin with the prescriptive beliefs of each racial group.

The policy that elicits the least support from both racial groups is that of racially integrated schools; equal job opportunity elicits the highest levels of support from both groups. But there the similarity between the two groups ends. Among blacks, about two-thirds to three-quarters think the federal government should be doing a lot to promote these policies, and virtually all the remaining blacks think the government should be doing quite a bit. Among whites, only 14 to 24 percent think the government should be doing a lot on any of these policies. On the issue of equal job opportunity, only slightly over one-quarter of whites go to the opposite extreme of advocating little or no governmental activity, but 40 percent of whites would like to see little or nothing done to promote equal housing opportunity, and on the issue of racially integrated schools, over one-half of whites think the government should be doing only a little or nothing.

These data give us an indication of the different directions that the two racial groups take when they apply their abstract policy principles to specific issues. What looks like a reasonably high, albeit guarded, endorsement of the principle of racial integration among whites is unlikely to manifest itself in a desire for strong governmental measures to bring integration about. But among blacks, endorsement of the abstract principle of racial integration is highly likely to be manifested in a strong commitment to specific policies to achieve that goal. Thus, for example, although 80 percent of whites believe blacks have a right to live wherever they can afford, only 18 percent think the government should be doing a lot to ensure that right. Among blacks, however, 97 percent endorse the same abstract principle and 72 percent think the government should be doing a lot to make it happen. Thus, what appear at face value to be relatively modest differences between blacks and whites at the level of abstract support for racial integration translate into a serious rupture in real policy terms.

When we consider people's existential beliefs about the same three racial policies, the rift between the racial groups deepens. Governmental activity is most likely to be seen on the issue of integrated schools, with equal job opportunity close behind and the least activity being perceived on the issue of equal housing opportunity. This rank ordering is found in the perceptions of both whites and blacks, and it corresponds reasonably well with the relative public attention that each issue has received in the media (note also the relatively large number of whites—18 percent—who say they don't know how much the government is doing to promote blacks' housing rights). All this might suggest that people's existential beliefs about racial policies are cleanly grounded in a common reality. However, on each issue, whites and blacks diverge sharply in their perceptions of *what* the current level of governmental activity is.

Among whites, the most frequent perception is that the federal government is currently doing "quite a bit" to promote blacks' civil rights, with "a lot" of governmental activity being the second-most frequent perception on two of the three issues. In all, as many as three-quarters of whites believe the federal government is already doing either quite a bit or a lot to ensure integrated schools and equal job opportunity; about one-half of whites see that degree of governmental activity on the issue of equal housing opportunity. Against this existential backdrop, whites' policy prescriptions are revealed in a yet meaner light.

Blacks' estimates of the current level of governmental activity tend to fall far short of whites': only about one-quarter of blacks think the government is already doing a lot or quite a bit to ensure equal housing opportunity or equal job opportunity for blacks, and even on the highly visible issue of school integration, only about 40 percent think that a lot or quite a bit is being done. The most frequent perception among blacks is that the government is doing only "a little," with about one-half of blacks having that perception; over the three policy issues, the perception that the government is doing little or nothing to ensure blacks' civil rights is held by over one-half to over two-thirds of blacks. With these existential beliefs as the backdrop, blacks' advocacy of governmental intervention is revealed even more urgently. The rift that separates their policy views from those of whites gapes open to a chasm.

These existential beliefs also provide, less directly, contextual information by which we may reinterpret the abstract policy principles of whites and blacks that were reported in table 6.1. If many whites believe that much is already being done to ensure racial integration, this suggests that their conception of what constitutes racial integration is much less far-reaching than what many blacks have in mind. This is consistent with my earlier argument that the large proportion of whites who favor "something in between" segregation and integration (when they are given such an option) suggests that many whites endorse a vaguely conceived, laissez-faire situation of "voluntary integration" that would protect whites' personal freedom of choice without "forcing" them to conform to the requirements of either racial segregation or integration. Such an arrangement would of course fall seriously short of any guarantee of racial integration, but this shortcoming is doubtless less apparent to whites than to blacks.[5]

In this regard, bear in mind that the urban residential segregation that characterizes race relations in the contemporary United States has a de facto quality that leaves most individual whites feeling personally blameless. The policies and practices that have brought about residential segregation have had low visibility and they are buried in history, lost behind such positive terms as "suburban growth" and "urban renewal." Most whites are blissfully unaware of the policies pursued by federal and local governments and by the banking and real estate industries that established racially segregated neighborhoods. And whereas the racial segregation of the Jim-Crow South required the active involvement of the white population in order to maintain it, contemporary residential segregation achieves a pervasive separation of the two groups without individual whites having to take any active steps. Thus, much as most whites express a clear personal preference for neighborhoods that are all-white or mostly white (Jackman and Jackman 1983, 197), they are rarely called upon to act on their preferences. Segregation is so well entrenched that most whites can enjoy its benefits without exerting any personal effort. Blacks reside in different locations, and segregation in schools and jobs follow "naturally" from that. In such a situation, a laissez-faire approach by whites is sweetly convenient.

Thus, the so-called gap or inconsistency between whites' racial policy principles and their specific policy views may be illusory. At both the abstract and the applied level, many whites gravitate to a policy solution that puts a priority on individual freedom of movement with as little governmental intervention as possible. With an initially weak conception of what constitutes racial integration, whites are consistently following through (rather than inconsistently backing off) when they oppose specific policy proposals that would accelerate governmentally enforced racial integration.

Gender.   Men and women do not differ markedly from one another in their views about governmental gender policies. Table 6.5 presents the percentage distributions of men's and women's prescriptive and exis-

---

5. The wishful thinking that is manifested in whites' support for "something in between" racial integration and segregation might be likened to Walter Laqueur's analysis of German citizens' cognizance of the holocaust: "while many Germans thought that the Jews were no longer alive, they did not necessarily believe that they were dead" (Laqueur 1980, 201, quoted in Elster 1983, 152).

TABLE 6.5.   Prescriptive and Existential Beliefs of Men and Women about Government Action to Promote Gender Equality.

	Men	Women	Men	Women
	How much SHOULD gov't be doing?:		How much IS gov't doing?:	
Equal Job Opportunity				
A Lot	26.3%	29.9%	18.0%	13.6%
Quite a Bit	40.0	37.3	42.0	36.4
A Little	19.2	18.0	31.8	35.3
Nothing	10.4	7.6	2.4	5.1*
Don't Know, Other	4.1	7.2	5.8	9.6
Equal Legal Treatment				
A Lot	38.1%	37.3%	18.1%	13.2%
Quite a Bit	43.1	38.0	38.4	32.6
A Little	9.8	9.8	28.8	30.4
Nothing	2.7	3.0	3.3	3.9*
Don't Know, Other	6.3	11.9	11.3	19.8
Daycare Centers for Working Mothers				
A Lot	24.3%	31.0%	5.9%	7.9%
Quite a Bit	30.3	31.3	15.7	22.1
A Little	19.9	14.7	34.0	30.8
Nothing	13.8	10.4**	12.5	12.0
Don't Know, Other	11.8	12.7	31.9	27.2
Base N (ranges)	790–792	1,089–1,090	794–795	1,091–1,095

* Difference between men and women (with Don't Know's excluded) is statistically significant (p < .05).
** Difference between men and women (with Don't Know's excluded) is statistically significant (p < .01).

tential beliefs about governmental intervention to ensure equal job opportunity for women, equal legal treatment for women, and daycare centers for the children of working mothers.

Of the three issues, it is equal legal treatment for women that elicits the strongest support from both sexes. Almost 40 percent of both sexes think the government should be doing "a lot" and about another 40 percent think the government should be doing "quite a bit" to make sure that laws are applied in the same way to women and men. Both of the other two policy issues elicit somewhat less support from both gender groups, with women's level of support only a shade ahead of men's.

Both men and women are less likely to think the government *is* currently doing a lot or quite a bit than that the government *should* be doing that much. On the issues of equal job opportunity and equal legal treatment for women, this tendency is slightly more marked among women, with 46 to 50 percent of women and 56 to 60 percent of men believing that quite a bit or a lot is currently being done by the government. The issue of daycare centers is less likely to be seen by either men or women as a target of governmental activity, with only about 20 percent of men and 30 percent of women believing that a lot or quite a bit is already being done.[6]

These figures contrast sharply with those for race. Most notably, women do not deviate seriously from men in their views about governmental intervention in women's civil rights. And although men appear to be slightly less withholding than whites in their prescriptive policy beliefs, this difference is not nearly as large as the difference between women and blacks in the degree to which they advocate affirmative change. Indeed, on the issues of equal job opportunity for blacks and for women, respectively, whites and men exhibit virtually the same levels of support—they differ only in that men are somewhat less likely than whites to believe that the government is already engaging in "a lot" of affirmative activity. Women, however, lag considerably behind blacks in the strength of their support for governmental activity on behalf of their group, and they also display considerably less jaundiced perceptions of the current level of governmental activity on their behalf than do blacks. Whereas almost all blacks advocate either a lot or quite a bit of governmental action to ensure equal job opportunity for blacks and only one-quarter believe that level of activity is already happening, about two-thirds of women advocate a lot or quite a bit of governmental activity to ensure equal job opportunity for women and one-half believe that level of activity is taking place already. The net effect is that only a hint of the rift found between racial groups is to be found between women and men.

Another contrast with the data for racial policy views is that, for gender, the move from abstract principles to specific government policies is not associated with any clearly interpretable changes in the data. In both realms, men's and women's views parallel one another fairly closely, and neither realm elicits systematically more or fewer affirmative prescriptions from either group. Of course, comparison of the two realms is less straightforward because the issues that come into focus are not directly comparable: the most central abstract principles for gender deal with egalitarianism in the conduct of people's "private" lives, whereas governmental intervention is usually raised in relation to the enforcement of individual rights in the public sphere. The former broaches redistributive goals at the sensitive core of the relationship; the latter

6. But this issue also elicits a large number of "don't know" responses (about 30 percent). Daycare centers cater to a relatively narrow constituency, and the issue may not be very salient or visible to those who do not have preschool-aged children.

TABLE 6.6.   Prescriptive and Existential Beliefs of the Upper-Middle Class, Middle Class, Working Class, and Poor about Government Action to Promote Economic Equality.*

	Upper-Middle	Middle	Working	Poor	Upper-Middle	Middle	Working	Poor
		How much SHOULD gov't be doing?:				How much IS gov't doing?:		
Guaranteed Jobs								
A Lot	36.4%	44.6%	54.0%	65.0%	8.3%	8.4%	10.4%	10.6%
Quite a Bit	36.4	37.3	30.9	20.0	28.8	25.0	19.2	11.3
A Little	18.8	9.2	6.5	3.6	45.5	47.9	46.3	41.1
Nothing	7.1	5.4	4.0	0.7	12.8	12.1	16.6	25.5
Don't Know, Other	1.3	3.5	4.6	10.7	4.4	6.6	7.6	11.3
Welfare Benefits								
A Lot	21.7%	25.7%	36.2%	51.1%	39.9%	33.1%	30.4%	20.6%
Quite a Bit	37.5	37.3	32.9	26.6	41.2	42.2	34.9	27.7
A Little	30.9	26.2	20.7	11.5	14.4	16.4	25.2	32.6
Nothing	8.6	6.2	5.1	1.4	2.0	3.7	4.2	7.8
Don't Know, Other	1.3	4.7	5.1	9.4	2.7	4.7	5.3	11.3
Guaranteed Minimum Income								
A Lot	30.6%	33.9%	44.3%	58.3%	13.4%	13.1%	12.1%	6.5%
Quite a Bit	34.4	36.0	32.8	24.5	31.8	30.7	21.9	19.4
A Little	20.4	18.5	11.9	2.9	36.9	36.8	40.7	34.5
Nothing	10.8	6.5	4.6	1.4	11.5	10.9	15.0	20.9
Don't Know, Other	3.8	5.0	6.4	12.9	6.3	8.4	10.2	18.7
Base N (ranges)	152–157	810–818	686–693	139–140	153–157	816–817	689–694	139–141

* All differences by class (with Don't Know's excluded) are statistically significant (p < .01).

raises the threatening specter of enforcement but on issues involving individual, rather than group, rights, and away from the nerve center of family relations. In my study, there are just two items that allow for a fairly clear-cut comparison: those on abstract support for equal job opportunity for women and on support for governmental intervention to ensure that opportunity. On this issue, approximately 60 percent of both sexes support the abstract principle whereas about 30 percent think the government should be doing "a lot" to guarantee the principle and about 40 percent think the government should do "quite a bit."

Class.   Social classes present a similar pattern of disagreement to that found between whites and blacks—but in muted form. As with whites and blacks, lower classes are more likely to advocate governmental intervention whereas higher classes are more likely to perceive that such intervention is already taking place. However, existential beliefs are less disparate by class than are prescriptive beliefs, and the pattern of class differences in general is not as dramatic as it is for race. The data for class are presented in table 6.6.

Descending social class is associated with a gradual increase in advocacy for these economic policies, and there is a difference of about 30 percentage points between the upper-middle class and the poor in their propensity to advocate "a lot" of governmental intervention. The magnitude of this class difference is constant across all three issues, even as the absolute levels of support shift. It seems that the more directly a policy carries redistributive goals, the less support it receives from any class. Thus, the provision of welfare benefits receives the lowest endorsement from any class, with fewer than one-quarter of the upper-middle class and about one-half of the poor advocating "a lot" of governmental action on that issue, whereas the provision of guaranteed jobs receives the highest levels of endorsement, with just over one-third of the upper-middle class and about two-thirds of the poor supporting "a lot" of governmental intervention on that issue. Virtually no one among the poor believes the government should do only "a little" or "nothing" to guarantee jobs or a minimum income and about 13 percent of the poor take such a position on the more sensitive issue of welfare benefits. Among the upper-middle class, between 26 and 40 percent advocate little or no government action on the three issues, with welfare benefits exciting the strongest exhortations to inaction.

These figures (both in the pattern of disagreement among classes and in the absolute levels of support for egalitarian goals) are broadly consistent with those for abstract economic policy principles. If anything, there seems to be slightly less resistance in all classes to specific redistributive governmental policies than to economic egalitarianism in the abstract. As I noted earlier, however, these policies encompass only modest safety-net provisions, and thus they do not broach the issue of economic equality as boldly as did the items on the abstract principle of income equality.

In existential beliefs, the largest class differences occur in perceptions of the government provision of welfare benefits. The upper-middle class is almost twice as likely as the poor to believe that the government is already doing "a lot" or "quite a bit" to provide welfare benefits: among the upper-middle class, about 40 percent think a lot is being done and another 40 percent think quite a bit is happening, whereas only about 20 percent of the poor believe a lot is happening and fewer than 30 percent of the poor think even quite a bit is being done. On the other two economic policy issues, class differences in perceptions are in the same direction but smaller. And as with economic policy prescriptions, the gap between the poor and the upper-middle class is bridged in stepwise increments by the classes that lie in between. In this way, the political rift among classes is fractured rather than presenting alignments on either side of a simple, dichotomous cleavage.

These class divisions in economic policy views fall short of the gaping chasm that exists in both prescriptive and existential beliefs between whites and blacks. At the same time, the differences among classes are persistent and systematic, and far exceed the mere hint of disagreement found between men and women. This muted rift is reflected in the absolute levels of support for affirmative policies that are displayed by the various classes. The upper-middle class demonstrates about the same degree of support for affirmative economic policies as do men for affirmative gender policies. The degree of support gradually increases from one class to the next until, at the other end of the class structure, the poor's advocacy of redistributive economic policies is almost as strong as blacks' advocacy of governmental action on behalf of blacks' rights.

General Patterns.   Overall, these data yield very similar patterns to those that obtain for abstract policy principles. It is only in the relationship between whites and blacks that the rift between groups is revealed much more sharply in the context of specific governmental policies. And this shift is solely attributable to one group—whites—whose policy goals appear considerably less affirmative in the context of specific governmental policies. In gender and class relations, the policy goals of the respective groups appear fairly consistent in the abstract and specific contexts. In either arena, there is very little rift between men and women, with both groups indicating moderate levels of support for egalitarian and affirmative policies. Among classes, there is a muted rift that follows a step function from modest support for redistributive policies among the upper-middle class to fairly strong support among the poor. There is, if anything, a slight tendency for social classes to express slightly higher levels of support for specific governmental policies than for abstract egalitarian principles.

Thus, there does not seem to be any necessary relationship between the level of abstraction of policy questions and the degree of support expressed for them. Subordinate groups do not systematically reveal more radical goals in the "real" world of governmental policies. And dominant groups do not display any systematic tendency to espouse lofty principles and then abandon them when they move to specifics. Finally, there is no evidence of a general aversion in any group to the federal government intervening in social or economic issues. The oft-cited "gap" between abstract and applied principles in whites' policy views may simply stem from ambiguities that are inherent to items that measure general principles. Abstractions are by definition nonspecific, and it is only in the context of the specific that their meaning is revealed. Investigators may have optimistically read more into people's responses to general items on racial integration than was really there.

Support for a policy instead seems to hinge on three interrelated factors, none of which is related to the distinction between abstract principles and applied policies. First, policies that strike at the core of an intergroup relationship generate more cautious responses than those that aim at the periphery of the relationship. Thus, enforced racial integration in schools generates the least endorsement from both whites and blacks because its sensitivity is recognized by both sides: whites guard their schools with particular ferocity because schools constitute the primary institutions by which cultural values and achievement-related skills are transferred to the next generation, and blacks are less likely to be assertive in an area that is most likely to elicit a backlash (and perhaps especially since it is their children who would be on the frontline). Second, by the same token, policies that have a broader scope elicit less support than policies that seek only small changes. And third, people are more likely to shy away from policies that threaten individualistic values, especially freedom of choice. All of these factors are interconnected, and, indeed, the prevalence of individualism lies in its ideological convenience as dominant groups strive to divert energies away from core redistributive issues to those that lie closer to the periphery of their relations with subordinates.

There seems to be a common understanding between contending groups of the moral framework that binds their disputes. As subordinate groups attempt to enhance their control over society's assets, they cope with the uncertainty of the terrain by avoiding dramatic demands that violate the terms of that framework. Dominant groups continue to proselytize the broad outlines of the moral code as they resist the specific inroads that subordinates attempt to forge. Subordinates have no choice but to be sensitive to the hard spots and soft spots of the dominant group and to calibrate their demands accordingly. In this way, the contending groups get locked in a delicate struggle that is several steps removed from the core redistributive issues that define their relationship. The rights of groups appear to lie beyond the confines of legitimate political contention, and the domain of debate becomes restricted to questions about the extensiveness and enforcement of individual rights.

As the contending groups address those questions, a comparison of their prescriptive and existential policy beliefs reveals that they are divided by both. People's sensitivities—whether to the indignities of deprivation or to the threat of lost benefits—affect not only their advocacy but their perceptions of reality as well. Subordinates are generally more likely to advocate government intervention, whereas dominant-group members are more likely to believe that government intervention on behalf of subordinates is already considerable. In this way, the separate existential worlds of dominant and subordinate groups reinforce the rift created by their differing prescriptive views. The dual-edged divide is most pronounced between whites and blacks, somewhat weaker in class relations, and only whispered in gender relations. Men and women do not differ substantially from one another in their prescriptive views, but women do tend to see somewhat less government activity already in place

than do men. These patterns suggest that the import of the policy goals
that people articulate cannot be fully assessed unless we know the existential context in which they are framed.

Results: Affirmative Change, Conservatism, and Reaction

In order to define the lines of contention between groups more sharply,
I now synthesize the data on specific policy goals by building people's
existential beliefs into the measure of their policy prescriptions. In this
way, each individual's policy prescriptions are measured with a built-in
reality check—against the existential beliefs that frame those prescriptions. This yields a more sensitive indicator of people's policy goals.

Measures. I take the difference between each respondent's belief
about what should be done and her belief about what is already being
done by the government for each policy issue.[7] For each policy measure,
this yields scores ranging from -3 (the government *should* be doing a
lot but *is* doing nothing) through $+3$ (the government *should* be doing
nothing but *is* doing a lot). These scores break down into three distinct
categories: those who advocate affirmative change (that is, they think
the government should be doing more than it currently is), those who
take a conservative position (they think the government is doing about
the right amount now), and those who take a reactionary position (that
is, they would like to see the government do *less* than it currently is).

By using perceptions of the status quo as the anchor for prescriptions,
we can directly assess the degree to which various groups advocate affirmative change. For example, the white who says the government should
be doing "a lot" to ensure equal employment opportunity for blacks takes
on a less glowing pallor if she also thinks the government is already doing
a lot. We can also assess whether resistance to affirmative change takes
the form of conservatism or is outright reactionary. In this way, the
character of the debate between contending groups may be specified
more acutely.

Definition of Policy Domains. I begin by examining the zero-order correlations among the government-policy difference-scores, to check the
extent to which the measures for race, gender, and class, respectively,
fall into distinct domains. Table 6.7 presents correlation matrices (Pearson's r's) for the government-policy difference-scores (below the diagonal), as well as for the original prescriptive government-policy items
(above the diagonal). The correlations for policies within each intergroup

---

7. Respondents who said "don't know" or who had missing data for either item in a
pair were excluded from the calculation of the difference score for that pair.

TABLE 6.7.   Zero-Order Correlations (Pearson's r's) among "Government Should . . ." Items (above Diagonal) and Government Action Difference-Scores (below Diagonal): For the Total Sample, Using Pairwise Deletions of Missing Data.

	Race			Gender			Class		
	R1	R2	R3	G1	G2	G3	C1	C2	C3
Race									
R1 Integrated Schools	—	.49	.45	.39	.21	.31	.26	.31	.28
R2 Equal Housing Opportunity	.60	—	.56	.40	.32	.36	.35	.34	.32
R3 Equal Job Opportunity	.56	.68	—	.37	.37	.34	.39	.39	.37
Gender									
G1 Equal Job Opportunity	.40	.41	.42	—	.41	.40	.36	.29	.31
G2 Equal Legal Treatment	.22	.30	.33	.46	—	.27	.31	.28	.28
G3 Daycare Centers	.29	.34	.38	.39	.31	—	.45	.42	.45
Class									
C1 Guaranteed Jobs	.25	.29	.33	.32	.30	.41	—	.42	.45
C2 Welfare Benefits	.35	.38	.41	.30	.29	.41	.35	—	.44
C3 Guaranteed Minimum Income	.31	.31	.35	.29	.27	.42	.46	.45	—

relationship are in boldface. The difference-scores are in their continuous scoring from −3 to +3, while the original prescriptions are scored from 1 ("A Lot") through 4 ("Nothing"). "Don't Know" responses and missing data are excluded on a pairwise basis.

For gender and class, the two sets of measures display similar correlations. For race, however, the policy difference-scores are more highly intercorrelated than are the uncorrected policy prescriptions. This doubtless reflects the double polarization between whites and blacks that is captured when both prescriptive and existential beliefs are incorporated.

Of the three intergroup relations, the policy goals for race show the sharpest internal convergence. The three race-policy difference-scores are all intercorrelated between .56 and .68. These correlations are not only very high in themselves but they all exceed the correlations between any of the race measures and the measures of gender or class policy goals. Thus, the three race-policy measures demonstrate both high convergence as well as clear separation from the policy domains of gender and class.

The three gender-policy measures do not cluster together as sharply. The difference-scores for equal job opportunity and equal legal treatment are strongly intercorrelated (.46) and this intercorrelation is higher than either measure correlates with measures from race or class (although the correlations of the equal job opportunity measure with the race measures are only a shade lower). The daycare measure does not correlate distinctively with the other two gender issues, and its correlations with the class measures especially suggest that it is seen as a class issue at least as much as a gender issue.

The class-policy issues, not surprisingly, tend to be somewhat entangled with the race issues: interestingly, the welfare issue (the most directly redistributive policy) is also the one that is the most highly correlated with the race issues. Given the disproportionate share of blacks who live in poverty, it seems unrealistic to develop any measures of views about redistributive economic policies that would not be intertwined with views about racial policies. Yet the welfare difference-score still correlates more highly ($r = .45$) with one of the other class policy measures (guaranteed minimum income) than it does with the race issues. The guaranteed minimum income and the guaranteed jobs difference-scores also correlate more highly with each other ($r = .46$) than either does with the race issues. It is only the correlation between welfare and guaranteed jobs (.35) that fails to exceed the correlations of welfare with the race issues.

These data indicate that the issues surrounding policies that are aimed at a specific intergroup relationship tend to fan out to other intergroup relationships. Insofar as race, gender, and class all involve alternative manifestations of inequality in the same society, it is perhaps inevitable that there will be spillover effects from policy views in one area to those in another. The intergroup relationship that has had the most sustained policy visibility—race—should be expected to generate the tightest set of policy views, as people get more experience in using contextual information from that intergroup relationship to cue their reactions to any new policy issue that arises. Indeed, habits of thinking coming out of that intergroup relationship then take on psychological primacy and are especially likely to permeate the way people think about policy issues arising in other intergroup relationships as well.

The Lines of Debate.   I now evaluate the lines of policy debate between groups. What are the blends of affirmative advocacy, conservative resistance, and reactionary opposition that color each intergroup relationship? Table 6.8 presents the percentage distributions by group for the pertinent policy measures, for race, gender, and class, respectively.

The chasm between whites and blacks is revealed starkly with these measures. Whereas the overwhelming majority of blacks (72–89 percent) want affirmative change on each of the policy issues, whites are almost as overwhelmingly conservative—or reactionary. On the issue that generates the staunchest opposition among whites and the least support among blacks (integrated schools), over 70 percent of blacks want to see affirmative change whereas almost 60 percent of whites desire reactionary change. On the other two race issues, almost 90 percent of blacks

TABLE 6.8.   Beliefs of Relevant Groups about How Much the Government Should Be Doing, Relative to How Much It Is Perceived to Be Doing, for Racial Equality, Gender Equality, and Economic Equality.*

	Affirmative Gov't should be doing MORE	Conservative Gov't doing about the RIGHT amount	Reactionary Gov't should be doing LESS	Base N
Racial Equality				
Integrated Schools				
Whites	16.4%	25.1	58.5	1,504
Blacks	71.6%	19.3	9.1	176
Equal Housing Opportunity				
Whites	28.5%	39.1	32.4	1,294
Blacks	87.6%	11.2	1.2	170
Equal Job Opportunity				
Whites	22.6%	45.7	31.6	1,480
Blacks	88.8%	10.7	0.6	178
Gender Equality				
Equal Job Opportunity				
Men	34.2%	40.9	24.9	734
Women	42.6%	37.9	19.5	959
Equal Legal Treatment				
Men	39.6%	52.2	8.2	699
Women	48.4%	42.6	9.0	853
Economic Equality				
Guaranteed Jobs				
Upper-Middle	56.5%	29.9	13.6	147
Middle	65.2%	26.2	8.6	753
Working	71.5%	21.8	6.6	632
Poor	77.0%	20.5	2.5	122
Welfare Benefits				
Upper-Middle	19.3%	35.9	44.8	145
Middle	26.0%	35.6	38.4	750
Working	35.9%	35.3	28.8	629
Poor	59.5%	27.3	13.2	121
Guaranteed Minimum Income				
Upper-Middle	43.1%	38.9	18.1	144
Middle	50.0%	34.0	16.0	730
Working	62.2%	28.4	9.4	609
Poor	79.3%	18.0	2.7	111

* All differences between groups are statistically significant (p < .01).

advocate affirmative change, whereas about one-third of whites take a reactionary position and about 40–45 percent are conservative.

For gender, I restrict attention to the two issues that reflect gender concerns relatively cleanly, equal job opportunity and equal legal treatment for women. The opinions of men and women almost parallel one another on these issues: both groups are predominantly divided between conservatism and affirmative advocacy, with women leaning slightly more in the affirmative direction and men's views weighted more toward conservatism. Reactionary views are less frequent, although the issue of equal job opportunity generates stronger resistance than does the issue of equal legal treatment: fewer than 10 percent of either sex take a reactionary position on the question of equal legal treatment, but about one-quarter of men and one-fifth of women take a reactionary position on the issue of equal job opportunity. The general tenor of opinion on these gender policy issues is thus more moderated than for racial issues and involves much less disagreement across group lines. But, nonetheless (as with whites' racial policy goals), support for affirmative change in gender policies is considerably lower than was inferred when people's prescriptive views were considered separately from their existential beliefs. Only slightly over one-third of men favor affirmative change, and women have just nudged ahead of men in advocating such change.

With the class policy measures, one issue—guaranteed jobs—generates fairly high levels of affirmative advocacy from every class, but the other two issues—welfare benefits and guaranteed minimum income—are more divisive. The clear majority of every class (ranging from 57 percent of the upper-middle class to 77 percent of the poor) wants to see the government do more to guarantee jobs, and most of the balance of opinion is conservative rather than reactionary. More governmental effort to guarantee a minimum income is advocated just as strongly by the poor (79 percent), but with ascending social class support gradually slips away to only 43 percent of the upper-middle class. And although most of the balance of opinion in each class is again conservative rather than reactionary, ascending social class brings a steady increase in reactionary opinion, from only 3 percent of the poor to 18 percent of the upper-middle class. The most sharply divisive issue is that of welfare benefits. On this issue, the stance of the upper-middle class is almost as withholding as that of whites on school integration (only 19 percent of the upper-middle class supports affirmative change and 45 percent is reactionary); opinion shifts slightly in the direction of affirmative change from the middle class to the working class, but among the poor there is a pronounced shift in opinion, with 60 percent of the poor advocating that more be done and only 13 percent taking a reactionary stance. In all, the class rift in policy goals is pronounced, although it still does not equal the rift between whites and blacks.[8]

These data thus portray rather disparate dialogues across the three intergroup relationships as the contending groups articulate their policy goals. Although subordinates consistently take the lead in the direction of affirmative change, the depth of their rift from their dominant-group counterparts varies dramatically. Between blacks and whites there is a searing disparity, among social classes there is a large but graduated disagreement, and among women there is only a hinted departure from the policy goals of men.

CONCLUSIONS

This chapter has been directed by one central question: to what extent do contending groups in an unequal relationship seek to increase their control over resources? Although the question sounds straightforward, the answer is necessarily layered beneath a series of considerations.

Intergroup policy goals have been the object of repeated empirical inquiry, but scholars have varied widely in their assumptions about whether policy goals reflect underlying, irrational, intergroup antipathies (prejudice), the apolitical quest for altered lifestyles ("sex-role attitudes"), the overriding of conflicting interests and intergroup antipathies (political tolerance), or the rational pursuit of group interests (class consciousness). Investigators have also disagreed about how to interpret various measures of policy goals. Attempts to measure intergroup policy goals have been waylaid repeatedly by an observed gap between the views expressed about abstract principles and applied policy goals. In research on prejudice and class consciousness, scholars have debated fretfully about the meaning of that gap. This has led to arguments about what agents and methods of change are most appropriate to achieve particular goals. And throughout, the measurement of policy alternatives has been restricted to those that have been given life in the public debate. Scholars have generally lost sight of the broader spectrum of issues that lies outside the realm of public discourse.

My approach calls for the examination of intergroup policy goals as the rational pursuit of group interests, within constraints. As people attempt to further their interests, they do not operate freestyle. They ma-

---

8. Within each class, blacks are more likely to advocate affirmative change in these economic policies than are whites. Further, among blacks there is no systematic relationship between class and class policy goals. Although whites' support for these economic policies gradually diminishes with ascending social class, blacks' support remains at a high level, making the racial difference larger as one progresses from the poor to the middle class. This underscores the intersection of race and class issues in American society.

neuver within pragmatic and moral conditions that render some routes plausible and others futile or even dangerous. The society that houses an intergroup relationship is infused by a general moral climate that has grown out of the various intergroup experiences that have dominated its history: that climate limits the kinds of demands and appeals that have moral credibility. Within that societal context, specific constraints are posed by the internal structure and politics of the relationship itself. The parameters of public policy discussion are set by the conditions that are fused from those two sources.

Out of the growth pains of capitalist democracy, individualism has become established as a bedrock moral tenet. The norm of individualism has infused popular conceptions of intergroup policy goals and twisted the meaning of equality into something more accommodative—equality of opportunity. Attempts to assess popular sentiment for an egalitarian redistribution of resources have repeatedly run aground on the shoal of individualism. The patterns displayed in my data underscore the pervasiveness of individualism as a guiding principle in the articulation of intergroup policy goals. Indeed, the so-called gap between abstract and applied policy views that has persistently intrigued empirical analysts may be nothing more than segmented reflections of the layering of individualism beneath egalitarianism. The silent transformation of egalitarianism to incorporate individualism is masked in many survey questions, leading to apparent inconsistencies in responses to various questions.

On the issue of racial integration, questionnaire items measuring abstract principles have elicited more support from whites because they leave the rights of individuals untrammeled, whereas questions about government intervention to enforce racial integration uncover the conflict between individual rights and group rights. Many whites then back away from enforced racial integration as they opt for the protection of (their own) individual rights. In gender policy goals, the degree of support elicited for different abstract principles varies according to their link with individualistic principles. A general question on equal employment opportunity for women invokes individualistic principles and it elicits much stronger support than do general egalitarian principles for the division of labor between the sexes. And once the unsullied individualism of the general principle of equal job opportunity for women is harnessed to governmental enforcement, support for stepping up that enforcement drops to about half the level garnered for the general principle. In class policy goals, it is the abstract principles of egalitarianism that elicit less support than do questions about specific governmental policies, because in this case it is the abstract principles that state the goal of equality more boldly whereas specific governmental measures merely cast safety nets to cushion the deepest ravines of inequality. And among questions that

ask about various specific governmental policies, the degree of support
for those policies is elevated or depressed as a direct function of the
extent to which such policies are respectful of individual rights or tilted
more toward an egalitarian redistribution of resources between groups.

Hedged in by the pervasive morality of individualism, the contending
groups in race, gender, and class relations formulate their policy goals.
The issues that are thus breathed into life in the public arena do not call
for radical changes in the established division of resources but involve
readjustments at the margins. Even those issues, however, do not gain
easy acceptance. As dominant groups resist intrusions by subordinates,
contending groups become locked in disputes—at times heated, at times
mild—about potential alterations to arrangements at the periphery of
their relationship.

Within these boundaries, do contending groups seek to increase their
control over resources, simply maintain their current holdings, or make
concessions to their protagonists? On what kinds of issues do contending
groups yield concessions or press harder to advance their control over
resources? Are these proclivities affected by the position of the group
in the relationship (dominant or subordinate) or by the structure of the
relationship between groups? To address these questions, I examined
people's prescriptions for policy against their existential beliefs about the
current state of governmental intervention. In this way, we can distinguish those who favor affirmative change, those who wish to maintain
things as they are (the conservatives), and those who would like to reduce
the amount of government intervention (the reactionaries).

To begin, we can observe that in all three intergroup relationships,
subordinate groups show little tendency to give up their current holdings: their energies are primarily divided between preserving what little
they have and pressing for more control over resources. That is to say,
very few members of subordinate groups voice the reactionary view that
the government should reduce its intervention on their behalf. Women
are the only subordinate group to evidence such a propensity among
more than a handful of their members, and even here, it is distinctly a
minority view within the group. The policy goals of subordinates generally range between conservative and affirmative, with blacks showing an
overwhelming preference for affirmative change, the poor and working
class leaning almost as strongly toward affirmative change, and women
showing only a slight preference for affirmative change over conservatism.

Among dominant groups, affirmative change usually finds less support than do conservative or reactionary policy goals, but the aversion
to affirmative change among dominant groups is less extreme than is
subordinates' aversion to reactionary policy views. It might thus seem

that dominant groups are more susceptible to relinquishing resources than are subordinates, but recall that the policies under discussion have already been molded by the time they reach the public arena so that none of them threatens flagrant redistribution. By steering discussion away from the most threatening issues, members of the dominant group can afford to have occasional concessions wrung out of them on the more peripheral issues that become the focus of public debate. Among those issues that do surface, dominant-group intransigence increases as specific policies come closer to touching core redistributive issues. On the issues that are more threatening (governmental intervention to ensure equal job opportunities for women and blacks, racially integrated schools, and provision of welfare benefits), the responses of dominant groups are largely torn between holding on to present arrangements and increasing their control over resources in a reactionary bid. The reactionary spirit is most in evidence in the racial policy goals of whites and least evident in the gender policy views of men. Among men, preserving current policies is the prevailing disposition. In the upper-middle class, the prevailing weight of opinion ripples from affirmative to reactionary, depending on the specific policy at hand. And among whites, the prevailing policy stance is lodged between conservative and reactionary, with the specific tilt dependent on the policy at hand.

There is clearly an interplay between the policy goals of dominant and subordinate groups. Within each intergroup relationship, the issues on which dominant groups are more intransigent are also the issues on which subordinates are less likely to push forcefully for affirmative change. Subordinate groups learn to throw more energy into issues that keep a safer distance from core redistributive concerns. And so the game goes on, with contending groups apparently torn between preserving current holdings and gingerly seeking to increase their control over resources. Subordinates generally yield to their more powerful protagonists by shying away from issues that are more threatening to the relationship. When more assertive policy proposals slip into the public arena, they meet with stiff resistance, or even reactionary counterproposals. But on more peripheral issues subordinate investment is more likely to be rewarded with occasional minor concessions—after exhaustive debate.

This pattern holds across all three intergroup relationships, but it is played out with varying ferocity, according to whether communication channels between groups are personal or aggregated. Between men and women, where the structure of intergroup contact is the most intimate, each group arrives at its mutually negotiated position with only a hinted rift between them. Between whites and blacks, where the physical separation of the groups is the most extreme, the negotiations between groups take the severest form. As the groups communicate across a great divide, messages must be shouted to be heard. Each group must react to the demands and vulnerabilities of the other in full public view. Finally, in class relations, the physical separation of disparate classes is broken by a step-wise pattern of restricted personal contact between adjacent classes. Both of these channels of communication affect the negotiated policy position of each class. The result is a graduated but resilient rift between contending classes in their articulated policy goals.

In these variants, it is the policy position of subordinates that is more vulnerable. Dominant groups retain the upper hand and they do not stray far from a general proclivity to resist change. At the same time, it should be remembered that it is generally the dominant group's hold over resources that is under more immediate threat in these policy discussions. A defensive position, backed by the full weight of established institutions and their supporting morality, is easier to maintain than is the assertive position of visualizing, demanding, and justifying affirmative change.

The opportunities that are offered to subordinates to advocate affirmative change are never great. They gravitate to causes that do not pose deep risks and that offer some promise of success. That steers the mainstream of subordinate effort inexorably toward less radical issues. But the ability of subordinates to chip away at even the periphery of their relationship with the dominant group is constrained by the structure of that relationship. As the structure imposes increasing physical distance between the groups, subordinates are afforded more opportunity to coalesce around demands for moderate, affirmative change.

CHAPTER SEVEN

The Ideological Molds of Paternalism and Conflict

The prevailing approaches to intergroup attitudes and group consciousness anticipate "consistency" in people's attitudes as the emblem of coherence, constraint, and crystallization in the way people think about their relations with another group. In particular, the policy dispositions of dominant group members toward subordinates should be a direct reflection of how positive or negative their feelings are toward subordinates. The latter, in turn, are thought more likely to assert their political rights when they feel hostile toward those who assert dominance over them. The only "inconsistent" attitude structure that has been the object of sustained scholarly attention is tolerance, that is, the advocacy of equal rights for another group despite negative feelings toward the group.

In this chapter, I explore the relationship between people's intergroup feelings and their policy dispositions. My approach to intergroup ideology does not anticipate a pivotal role for feelings of intergroup hostility. Nor does it anticipate that the magnet that binds attitudes and lends them coherence is "consistency" in the conventional sense. The extent to which groups pursue their interests must be disentangled from the issue of whether feelings of hostility pervade the relationship. The intersection of intergroup feelings and policy views holds considerably more subtlety and implicit finesse on the part of both dominant and subordinate groups than conventional approaches have anticipated.

My thesis is that the beacon to which dominant groups are drawn is the "inconsistent" attitudinal mold of paternalism—the combination of conservative or reactionary policy dispositions with positive feelings toward subordinates. How much paternalism is manifested in the three different relationships under investigation in this book? To what extent is paternalism displaced by "consistent" attitudes comprising negative feelings and conservative policy views or positive feelings and affirmative policy views? And how empirically viable is the alternative form of attitudinal inconsistency, the configuration of tolerance?

The ideology of paternalism is geared toward eliciting deference from subordinates—warm intergroup feelings and conservative policy dispositions that comply with the dominant design. How successfully do the different dominant groups elicit such deference from their subordinates? What blends of feelings and policy goals are interlaced by subordinates to deal with the rigors of inequality, and how does this vary from one type of intergroup relationship to another?

I begin the chapter by discussing the featured role of consistency in the literature on attitudes and public opinion. This includes a brief discussion of the single empirical concept that has posited an inconsistent attitude structure—political tolerance—to assess its bearing on the prevailing preoccupation with attitudinal consistency. I then consider the factors that have contributed to the binding significance of consistency in attitude theory, and I challenge the underlying assumptions on which that significance rests. Following this, I address two different theoretical concepts that imply attitudinal inconsistency, but which have developed without reference to that issue. The first of these is "hidden" or "everyday" resistance, which depicts the attitudes of subordinates. The second concept is paternalism, which addresses the attitudes of dominant-group members. With those issues delineated, I turn my attention to the intersection of intergroup feelings and policy goals in my data for race, gender, and social class.

I begin that analysis by examining the ways in which positive and negative intergroup feelings are converted into policy goals by people in different kinds of dominant and subordinate groups. I then present a simple empirical scheme that allows us to identify broad configurations of intergroup feelings and policy views. As I address the meaning of each of the categories in the scheme, it becomes apparent that there is not a straightforward equivalence between dominant and subordinate attitudes and that the meaning of particular attitudinal compounds depends on the position of the person's group in an unequal relationship.

This scheme is used to make a baseline empirical assessment of the prevalence of alternative attitudinal configurations in the exchange of ideologies between dominant and subordinate groups in race, gender, and class relations. These data also suggest broader inferences about the dynamics that pervade the articulation of intergroup ideologies by unequal groups. In this way, we can delineate the intersection of the two basic parameters of intergroup ideologies—the expression of hostility or friendship and the pursuit of group interests.

THE ISSUES

Attitudinal Consistency and Ideological Constraint

An assumption has run like a deep dye through public-opinion research that the hallmark of constraint, coherence, and crystallization in people's belief systems is consistency. Since Philip E. Converse's seminal article, "The Nature of Belief Systems in Mass Publics" (1964), students of public opinion have taken it as a given that consistency is the key indicator of whether attitudes have substance and meaning. A number of factors have conspired to foster the preoccupation with consistency in analyses of attitudes and public opinion.

The work that riveted the attention of political-opinion analysts on attitudinal consistency was Converse's 1964 article. His argument was located squarely within the context of mass political opinion in liberal-conservative partisan politics. He contended that most members of the mass public in the United States have only a hazy understanding of the terms *liberal* and *conservative* and that they have poorly formulated political opinions of their own. The issue stance of the average citizen fluctuates on the liberal-conservative axis, both over time and from one policy issue to another. Converse demonstrated empirically that correlations were weak between people's issue-stances on the same issues over time and between different specific issues at the same point in time. From this evidence, he argued that belief systems in the mass public generally lack constraint. He reasoned, further, that this lack of constraint derived from the low salience of political issues to most members of the mass public, as well as from poor information about both those issues and the broader political principles that could lend them coherence. This public-opinion muddle was contrasted with the political opinions of political elites: the latter were portrayed as having considerably more constrained belief systems and as being better schooled in the principles that bind specific issues together.

Converse's argument was very compatible with earlier work on voting and public opinion which had already decried the ideological confusion and lack of coherent political thought that reigned in the mass public. For example, the main conclusions of a major empirical study of political opinion by Berelson, Lazarsfeld, and McPhee (1954) were that the average democratic citizen lacks political interest, motivation, or knowledge and casts his vote in a way that is unconstrained by principles and without reference to considered thought about political issues. A similar argument was made in 1960, in a much-cited article in the *American Political Science Review* by McClosky, Hoffmann, and O'Hara. In an empirical comparison of the policy views of a sample of the mass public and a sample of the participants in the national conventions of the Republican and Democratic parties in 1958, McClosky, Hoffman, and O'Hara argued that the mass public contrasted sharply with political leaders in having poorly formulated political ideologies and in being poorly informed and having low interest in politics.

Converse's research completed the indictment of the American mass public. This dismal depiction of nonattitudes withering the grassroots of democracy inevitably drew fire. Converse's paper was the lightning rod for a crop of articles that sprang up over the years from scholars who found the picture offensive or unpalatable, or who sought to defend or elaborate Converse's original argument. The ensuing debate has been catalogued by others (see especially Smith 1989). One line of research took off on the question of whether the level of (in)consistency has changed over time (e.g., Bennett 1973; Nie and Anderson 1974; Hagner and Pierce 1983; Kirkpatrick 1976; LeBlanc and Merrin 1977; Nie, Verba, and Petrocik 1976; Piereson 1978; Smith 1989), or whether changes in survey question-wording in the National Election Studies were responsible for the observed changes in consistency (e.g, Bishop, Oldendick, and Tuchfarber 1978*a*, 1978*b*; Bishop et al. 1979; Brunk 1978; Sullivan, Piereson, and Marcus 1978; Sullivan, Piereson, and Marcus 1979). Another line of research raised statistical questions about how best to measure consistency, pursuing such concerns as measurement unreliability, the idiosyncratic properties of various measures of association, and the statistical confounding of true change in attitudes with mindless fluctuations in political views (e.g., Butler and Stokes 1974, 276–295, 316–337; Achen 1975; Weissberg 1976; Krosnik 1991). Meanwhile, Converse continued to develop and buttress his original argument with further empirical work, most notably with two articles titled (meaningfully) "Attitudes and Nonattitudes: The Continuation of a Dialogue" (1970) and, with Gregory B. Markus, *"Plus ça change . . .* The New CPS Election Panel Study" (1979).

In short, the publication of Converse's article in 1964 provoked an enduring research agenda and molded the way public-opinion analysts continue to think about attitudes. For all the energy that has been absorbed by the questions of how much consistency there is in the mass public and how to measure it, no one has paused to ask whether consistency is such a vital concept in the first place. It has been accepted intrinsically that consistency is the benchmark by which we judge whether attitudes have meaningful substance and whether they may reasonably be considered to belong to a coherent belief system. Indeed, *consistency* and *constraint* have been treated as equivalent terms.

There is only one form of attitudinal inconsistency that has engaged empirical analysts of mass political opinion, and that is political tolerance. This construct has been the subject of sustained empirical inquiry, but, perversely, that research has done nothing to undermine the prevailing conception of attitudes as governed by the pressure toward consistency. The concept of political tolerance, as it emerged in empirical research on democratic norms, is concerned with the ability of democratic citizens to grant full civil liberties to groups with whom they disagree or whom they dislike. In other words, the concept posits a logically inconsistent attitude structure: can people override their negative feelings toward out-groups and support affirmative policies toward them? The concept is central to empirical democratic theory, and it has generated a substantial body of public-opinion research, starting with Stouffer's classic study, *Communism, Conformity, and Civil Liberties* (1955), and continuing actively to the present (e.g., Kuklinski et al. 1991). I have discussed that research in chapters 1, 5, and 6. What is of relevance here is that, despite the central position of that research in the literature on public opinion, it has not undermined the prevailing conception of attitude structure as bound by the pressure to be consistent.

There are probably three main reasons for this apparent disconnection. First, although tolerance was conceived as an inconsistent attitude structure, empirical measures initially focused on policy dispositions entirely, without heed to respondents' feelings toward the target groups. Respondents' feelings were simply assumed to be negative. But because feelings were not incorporated in measures of tolerance, the specific composition of the tolerant attitude was not acknowledged explicitly. This element was not highlighted in empirical work until Jackman (1977, 1978) and Sullivan, Piereson, and Marcus (1979, 1982) developed measures of tolerance that incorporated both feelings and policy dispositions. Second, tolerance was initially conceived as a difficult state to attain, something uniquely required and fostered by democratic political systems. The problem was posed in terms of whether people could overcome their natural tendency to express their negative feelings in negative policy dispositions and instead develop the restraint necessary to sustain political tolerance. Tolerance was thus thought of as the exception that proved the general rule of attitudinal consistency. Third, empirical research on tolerance showed that it was, indeed, a difficult state to attain. Although scholars have disagreed about the extent of its dearth (see, for example, Sullivan, Piereson, and Marcus 1979, and Abramson 1980), studies have generally found political tolerance to be present in no more than a minority of the population. By default, then, the consistency rule was reaffirmed by empirical analyses of tolerance.

The intuitive reliance on consistency as the cement of attitudes is not restricted to the literature on political opinion. Students of prejudice have conceived of that phenomenon as a lock-step of negative beliefs, negative feelings, and negative policy dispositions. The unprejudiced person converts those negative values into positive ones: just as negative feelings fuel discrimination, positive feelings undermine it. Similarly, students of class consciousness have expected a proletarian "class-for-itself" to show its ripened political consciousness by adopting negative beliefs about and hostile feelings toward the dominant class, along with assertive policy goals and combative strategies. In the cases of both prejudice and working class consciousness, feelings feed policy dispositions.

In another variant of the consistency approach, Abercrombie and Turner (1982) reflexively use the presence or absence of a consistently applied moral code as a yardstick to assess the fiber of dominant ideology. Their reasoning is that if the dominant class propagates an ideology as a broad moral code to induce the compliance of subordinates, the same moral precepts will be used consistently to dictate the social behaviors of all members of society. They argue that dominant classes in history have not held their subordinates to the same moral code as they apply to themselves and that this means that dominant classes do not in fact have coherent ideologies that would qualify as viable instruments of social control. As I argued in chapter 2, however, this implicit reliance on consistency as the yardstick for the salience of an ideology is misplaced. Dominant groups are not in a contest for consistency: in the day-to-day business of eliciting compliance from subordinates, rigid consistency may be more of a political liability than an asset. Belief systems that are unerringly consistent are vulnerable to attack from all angles: the demolition of a single segment would cause the entire edifice to crumble. Additionally, there seems little practical compunction to apply the identical moral precepts to the group from whom one desires compliant behaviors as to the group whose design it is to govern: divergent roles in life would seem to call instead for flexibility in the application of an abstract moral code.

The common reliance on consistency in these different variants of research on attitudes, belief systems, and ideology is not a coincidence. It can be traced back to the way attitudes were initially conceived in classic attitude theory. An attitude is a purely theoretical construct that is not susceptible to direct empirical observation or measurement. What can be observed in human behavior is sporadic expressions of beliefs, feelings, and behavioral predispositions: in order to tighten their conceptual grip on such an unwieldy class of phenomena, attitude theorists relied on consistency as a key building block. Most definitions of attitudes have given a central place to an evaluative or affective disposition: the feelings that lie at the core of an attitude are thought to be supported by consistent perceptions and, in turn, to drive a stable predisposition to respond to the object of the attitude (see, for example, Allport 1935; Doob 1947). In this way, some order and predictability were carved out of a complex web of empirical phenomena.

The theme of consistency was to be replayed in a range of theories about the structure and characteristics of attitudes. Heider's balance theory (1946) posited that people press their cognitions into consistent configurations. A state of cognitive balance exists when an entity is perceived as having the same dynamic character in all respects (as when a person both admires and likes an object), when all parts of a unit are perceived as having the same dynamic character (as when they are seen as all positive or all negative), and when entities with different dynamic character are segregated from one another. A state of imbalance produces tension that creates pressure to reshape incongruent cognitions so that they come into line with the perceptual *gestalt*.

These postulates laid down a framework that was explored, developed, and elaborated in theoretical and empirical work by a large and influential school of researchers (see, for example, Newcomb 1953; Osgood and Tannenbaum 1955; Cartwright and Harary 1956; Rosenberg 1956; Festinger 1957; Abelson 1959; McGuire 1960; Cohen 1960; Abelson et al. 1968). Some of the most influential ideas to come out of this school of thought have been that incongruent perceptions cause dissonance in individuals that they are driven to resolve (Festinger 1957); that the affect an individual feels toward an object is tied logically to specific positive or negative perceptions of the object (Rosenberg 1956); that changes in evaluation are always in the direction of increased congruity with the existing frame of reference (Osgood and Tannenbaum 1955); that the greater the salience of a topic, the less tolerance the individual has for attitudinal inconsistency about that topic (Cohen 1960); and that the more directly two issues are connected with one another, the less the individual is able to tolerate inconsistent cognitions across those issues (McGuire 1960).

It thus became a theoretical maxim that attitudes can be identified by their internal consistency: the more salient a topic, the more the individual thinks about it and the more internally consistent the attitude becomes. A lack of consistency signifies the lack of an attitude. Research on political ideology, prejudice, and class consciousness simply built on that theory. Consistency became the standard currency of that research. People's attitudes are thought to manifest increasing internal consistency as they become more crystallized. Indeed, the standard procedure for testing the validity of specific questionnaire items is to check their consistency with other items on the same topic.

Consistency clearly has intuitive appeal to scholars as a magnet to organize the tangled web of beliefs, feelings, and behavioral dispositions that are observed in human expression. Two assumptions underlie this appeal. First, there is an implicit assumption that attitudes are self-contained and individually driven. This creates the theoretical imperative to find the source of someone's policy dispositions toward an object within the structure of the attitude itself. Thus, discriminatory policy dispositions are driven by negative feelings, whereas positive feelings remove the individual's motivation for discriminatory policy goals and lay the foundation for affirmative policy dispositions. The feelings, in turn, are logically fed by the person's beliefs about the object. Second, there is an assumption that people have a need to be consistent when they think about something. As a topic becomes more salient, the individual thinks about it more often and more intensely: the pressures increase to mold the various idea-elements into a consistent mass. Inconsistency can only be tolerated on topics that receive little attention and are not salient to the individual.

Both of these assumptions are problematic. To begin, the assumption that attitudes are primarily the property of individuals is questionable. Although individuals are the bearers of beliefs, feelings, and behavioral dispositions, they do not hatch these thoughts and feelings independently. Instead, they borrow from the cultural repertoire that is available to them. This book is premised on the idea that the intergroup attitudes that individuals espouse are not formulated discretely out of their personal experience, but are the communal property of the group to which they belong. Second, as people grapple to understand the world in which they live, they do not work according to the principles of either originality or logic. Instead, they reach for ideas from those that float past them on a daily basis, ideas that are espoused convincingly by others, and that have the ring of truth that only familiar things can have. Various thoughts and feelings are borrowed as needed.

The principles that guide the adoption of specific beliefs, feelings, and behavioral dispositions are convenience and efficiency. People tend to think and feel whatever is convenient, and they tend to deal with an issue as efficiently as possible, thinking about it only as much as is necessary to satisfy the political and practical exigencies of the moment. As the political reality changes, the members of a group will adjust their views and feelings, gradually, in a piecemeal fashion. How those exigencies are seen and interpreted can vary within the group: individual variation could stem from variation in personal experiences or pressures, and from differential exposure to information flows. Thus, for example, the well-educated members of a dominant group may espouse a slightly different variant of their group's intergroup ideology: their prolonged experience in educational institutions molds them into an especially individualistic way of thinking and it also exposes them more directly to information flows that contain the latest ideas (Jackman and Muha 1984). But the prevailing force that shapes an individual's intergroup attitudes is his or her membership in a group that has interests to defend or advance. The specific interests of the group and the history of its collective experience always limit the range of ideological options available to the individual actor.

Intergroup attitudes that are shaped by political exigencies are not perversely static. If political conditions remain unchanged, the prevailing intergroup attitudes will likewise remain in place. But as people respond to the political dynamics of the intergroup relationship in which they participate, old ideas are abandoned, gradually, if they are found to be less serviceable. New ideas drift into their place. At any single point in time, examination of a cross-section of attitudes in a group most likely uncovers a variety of elements, old and new, surrounding the prevailing theme. Similarly, individuals in the group have amalgams of thoughts and feelings that may contain residues from an earlier era along with the currently adopted line. As new information and ideas disseminate through the community in irregular flows, new patterns of ideological response emerge. An interesting example of this process is provided by Gamson and Modigliani (1987) in their analysis of the various packages of ideas that emerged in the unfolding public debate on affirmative action from the 1960s to the 1980s. In response to the policy initiatives of the federal government in the 1960s, a welter of competing ideas in the media were gradually reduced to an identifiable set of packages, out of which one emerged as dominant—the "reverse discrimination" argument. As I discussed in chapter 6, the "reverse discrimination" argument caught on because it resonated with the morality of individualism, and thus it provided whites with a basis for opposing affirmative action that felt comfortably principled and unbiased.

In such a dynamic and political process, the expectation of a clean consistency at either the individual or the group level defies political or common sense. The structure of intergroup attitudes conforms, not to what is consistent, but to what is politically expedient. Indeed, political expediency may dictate an inconsistent attitude structure.

Inconsistent Attitudes in Ideology

In the theoretical literature on intergroup attitudes and group consciousness, two different ideological modes have been posited that imply technically inconsistent attitudes. One of these, known as "hidden" or "everyday" resistance, is described as politically expedient for subordinate groups. The other is paternalism, and it applies to the politics of domination. The concepts of hidden resistance and paternalism have developed without reference to the empirical literature on attitudes, but each of these concepts has important implications for the structure of attitudes in intergroup ideology. The first of these, hidden resistance, has attracted a good deal of attention from scholars of group consciousness, but it is problematic, with serious measurement ambiguities. The concept of paternalism has attracted less interest, and scholars have been wary of its subtleties. I discuss each concept in turn.

Hidden Resistance. An idea that has gained increasing currency among scholars of group consciousness is that a common, stable response to subordination is "hidden resistance," masked by visible acts of compliance (Genovese 1974; Cloward and Piven 1979; Anyon 1984; Scott 1985; 1990). The essence of the argument is that there is more resistance and alienation among subordinates on an everyday basis than a superficial observation of their behavior would suggest. This approach emerged out of the consternation of scholars as to why there has been little sign of an assertive conflict-orientation among subordinates. The argument is that we just were not looking hard enough. The major acts of compliance that are readily observable are depicted as politically expedient acknowledgments by subordinates of the superior might of their oppressors. Underlying such apparent conservatism are definite feelings of alienation from the dominant group which are expressed openly "in house" and which bubble up in acts of petty sabotage, dissembling, and minor infractions of the dominant will. This everyday resistance lies behind the grand theater of compliance (see, especially, Scott 1990, 1–16, 45–69). The expression of resistance is restricted to individual behavior, and it is channeled into hidden outlets that are safe from the scrutiny of the dominant group, or else it is disguised in such behaviors as fawning, feigned stupidity, or incomprehension.

This argument is interesting in that it highlights the subtleties that are nested in the interactions that take place between unequal groups. It also breaks free of the all-or-nothing approach to intergroup conflict. It is still, however, bound by the general parameters of the conflict model, seeking to bring the search for intergroup conflict to a fruitful conclusion by redefining the nature of conflict. In so doing, it introduces some serious definitional ambiguities that sometimes cloud the delineation of resistance beyond recognition. Major acts of compliance are discounted whereas petty acts of noncooperation or sabotage are given predominant weight in the assessment of subordinates' state of mind. Resistance becomes something individual (rather than a group action) and something private or camouflaged (rather than openly combative). Further, scholars acknowledge that acts of hidden resistance often also function as accommodative acts, buffering their practitioners from the worst indignities of subordination as they comply with its requirements (Genovese 1974, 597–598; Anyon 1984). Many acts of day-to-day "resistance" are safe precisely because they conform to the dominant group's expectations (such as beliefs that subordinates are childlike, irresponsible, emotional, or stupid), and such acts thus also function to reaffirm dominant ideology and legitimize the regime. Indeed, the line between accommodation and resistance becomes faint, and sometimes evaporates altogether (see, especially, Anyon 1984). Malleable rules about which behaviors are valid reflections of the underlying consciousness of subordinates and about how to read specific behaviors turn the observation of human behavior heavily into a matter of interpretation. This makes it difficult to verify or falsify the concept of hidden resistance.

Despite the ambiguities of the concept, we can extrapolate expectations for the structure of subordinate-group attitudes. It implies that subordinates refrain from threatening the dominant group on issues that embroil the conduct of their mutual relationship, but beneath this conservatism lie feelings of estrangement and alienation from the dominant group. These feelings are a part of everyday discourse among subordinates and are thus a part of their consciousness. What this implies, then, is that subordinates have conservative policy views that comply with the dominant will, but that they retain negative feelings toward the dominant group. Any negativism in their behavioral dispositions is restricted to safe areas that are petty or hidden from view.

Paternalism.   Dominant attitudes that are paternalistic combine positive feelings toward subordinates with discriminatory policy dispositions. By taking over the definition of subordinates' interests, dominant groups bring themselves to believe that the inequalities that they seek to perpetuate are actually to everyone's benefit. This frees them to practice the inequality without any sense of unpleasantness or hostility. Instead, they can discriminate against subordinates while professing warm feelings toward them and indulging in a gratifying sense of duty and obligation. It is a central premise of the book that this ideological system is a favorite with dominant groups.

Yet paternalism has received remarkably little attention from scholars. Genovese's rich and sensitive (and controversial) portrayal of slavery in the American South features paternalism as the central organizing principle of that system of oppression (Genovese 1974), and Newby has used the concept with effect to analyze both rural labor relations in Britain (Newby 1977*a*) and historical changes in the control of industrial labor (Newby 1977*b*). There have also been a few scholars who have made use of the concept of paternalism to throw light on race relations or labor relations (e.g., Blumer 1951; van den Berghe 1967; Burawoy 1984).

There is a strain that runs through these discussions of paternalism, as scholars try to reconcile the dominant group's espousal of positive feelings toward subordinates with the presence of exploitation in the intergroup relationship. The subtle but shattering difference between paternalism and benevolence lends itself both to a misconstruction of the dynamics of paternalism and to an edginess or defensiveness in using the concept. Analysts are torn between assimilating the many expressions of positive affect that emanate from the dominant group and contemplating the brutalities that are also manifested in such a system of inequality. It would seem that analysts experience some disbelief or puzzlement as they are confronted with these apparently contradictory phenomena. Warm feelings seem incongruous with a discriminatory intent, even in the minds of scholars who work with the concept of paternalism.

Indeed, both Genovese (1974) and Newby (1977b) have argued that a paternalistic system of control gives subordinates a wedge to extract more concessions from the dominant group than they could otherwise obtain. In essence, they believe that the dominant group's espousal of warm feelings toward subordinates poses an internal contradiction in paternalistic systems of control. This contradiction causes a strain that clouds the relationship and leaves the dominant group vulnerable. They argue that subordinates can take advantage of the dominant group's sanctimonious casting of their relationship in terms of a sense of duty and mutual obligation to make a moral claim on some small transfer of resources. Both scholars see dominant groups who espouse paternalism as being vulnerable to giving away more than they bargained for, in order to preserve the legitimacy of their system of inequality. At the same time, the intrinsically demeaning character of paternalism is noted by these scholars, and Genovese is at pains to point out that paternalistic ideology did not prevent white slave-owners from practicing routine violence against their subordinates. These different themes are not integrated, however, and an ambiguity hangs over these analyses.

But it is precisely this ambiguity and subtle deception that makes paternalism such an insidious form of social control, and that generates the lure that it holds for dominant groups. Paternalism offers a way for them to have their cake and eat it too, a way to enjoy the fruits of expropriation without feeling they are taking anything, without having to wrest it away. Far from causing dissonance, expressing affection toward those whom one exploits comes as naturally as retracting your finger from a flame—as long as subordinates are duly compliant and loyal. If analysts sometimes trip up in the morality of paternalism, even as they are observing it from a distance, imagine how well that morality captures the awareness of the hapless participants who are living by its precepts.

In any system of power relations, it is an implicit rule that the dominant party must give some resources to subordinates. In order to facilitate social control, it is important to make sure that subordinates have something to lose. Groups who have nothing to lose pose a dangerous threat, since they have no stake in the system, no resources to protect. The trick is to keep the exchange of resources as unequal as possible, that is, to extract as much as possible from subordinates while giving as little as possible in exchange. Paternalism, far from lessening the dominant group's control, actually makes it easier for the dominant group to obtain a more favorable exchange. First, paternalism presents the inequality less harshly and thus masks the inequality of the exchange. This leaves subordinates less offended and therefore less guarded. Second, in a paternalistic system, the dominant group has seized more control over the way subordinates' needs are defined. This makes it less likely that subordinates will demand something that the dominant group does not want them to have. And finally, as its trump card, paternalism trades a distinctly invaluable commodity in return for compliance: friendship. If subordinates are dependent on members of the dominant group for the fulfillment of their emotional needs and for their full acceptance in organized social life, the dominant group has an extremely potent weapon with which to extract their compliance.

The coercive potency of paternalism thus draws vitally on the "inconsistent" attitude structure that lies at its core. In order to grasp fully the special dynamics of this ideological system, it is critical to acknowledge this rudimentary point. Feelings toward a group are important, but not in the conventionally understood way of dictating logically consistent policy dispositions. Instead, feelings that are logically inconsistent can enhance the dominant group's ability to practice discrimination. For this reason, I argue that paternalism can become a highly crystallized ideological form that is hard to dislodge. Thus, attitudinal coherence and constraint should not be measured in units of consistency. Dominant groups have every reason to crystallize their thinking in the form of positive feelings toward subordinates and discriminatory policy dispositions.

DATA

I begin my analysis by examining the extent to which people's intergroup feelings seem to influence their policy goals in the conventionally expected, logically consistent direction. Next, I investigate the various ways that feelings and policy goals can intersect, first by considering a simplified empirical scheme, and then by examining how the data for race, gender, and class fall into that scheme.

The Relationship between Intergroup Feelings and Policy Goals

How consistent are the data with the expectation that feelings drive policy dispositions, as dominant and subordinate groups face each other in their ongoing relations? Tables 7.1, 7.2, and 7.3 present data that address that question, for race, gender, and social class, respectively. These tables show the percentages of each group with affirmative, conservative, and reactionary policy goals, according to the distinctions they draw between their own and the other group in their feelings of warmth.

Intergroup feelings are measured in terms of the distinctions people draw between groups, since they are a more sensitive and cogent indicator of affective boundaries than are people's absolute feelings toward the other group. In addition, recall from chapter 5 that people are generally much more likely to express an affective rift between their own and another group than to express outright negative feelings toward the other group. Thus, use of measures of affective differentiation between groups draws out feelings of rift where no absolute feelings of hostility may be present. They make a less exacting indicator of intergroup negativism than would absolute feelings.

Intergroup feelings are categorized slightly differently across the three tables, since the distribution of feelings varies somewhat from one intergroup relationship to another (see chapter 5). And feelings of warmth (rather than closeness) are presented, since the former seem more pertinent to the rudimentary issue of the presence or absence of intergroup hostility.[1] Similarly, the analyses in chapter 6 indicated that policy goals are reflected more sensitively when they are measured against people's existential perceptions. Policy goals are defined as in chapter 6: *affirmative* goals are those that advocate the government should be doing *more* than it currently is doing, *conservative* goals are those that urge *no change*, and *reactionary* goals are those that advocate the government should do *less* than it currently is doing.

Conventional conceptions of intergroup attitudes anticipate a substantial difference between the policy goals of those who draw intergroup affective distinctions and those who do not. If feelings drive policy goals, we should expect the percentage supporting affirmative policy goals to shift substantially and systematically as one moves from those who draw affective distinctions to those who do not. However, across the three tables, the data fall considerably short of that. Overall, the relationship between intergroup feelings and policy goals might most generously be described as loose. I discuss the data for race, gender, and social class, in turn, before drawing out the general patterns.

Race.   Table 7.1 displays the figures for whites and blacks. Among whites, intergroup feelings range primarily between degrees of prefer-

---

1. Intergroup feelings of closeness and warmth are in fact very highly correlated (see chapter 5, footnote 4). And when tables 7.1, 7.2, and 7.3 were reestimated, substituting feelings of closeness for warmth, the results were highly comparable.

TABLE 7.1.   Percentages of Whites and Blacks Taking Alternative Policy Stances on Race Issues, According to Their Affective Differentiation between the Races.

	Whites				Blacks		
	Much Warmer to Own Group[a]	Slightly Warmer to Own Group[b]	Neutral	Warmer to Other Group	Much Warmer to Own Group[a]	Slightly Warmer to Own Group[b]	Neutral
Integrated Schools							
Affirmative	9.0%	16.5%	19.9%	47.4%*	78.7%	81.8%	61.5%
Conservative	21.9	23.8	27.4	26.3	12.0	13.6	28.3
Reactionary	69.1	59.7	52.7	26.3	9.3	4.5	10.3
Equal Housing Opportunity							
Affirmative	15.2%	32.4%	35.5%	66.7%*	91.7%	90.9%	82.7%
Conservative	33.1	38.9	43.0	27.8	6.9	9.1	16.0
Reactionary	51.7	28.6	21.5	5.6	1.4	0.0	1.3
Equal Job Opportunity							
Affirmative	12.1%	23.2%	27.6%	59.1%*	96.1%	95.6%	79.2%*
Conservative	42.4	45.9	48.7	18.2	3.9	4.3	19.5
Reactionary	45.5	30.9	23.7	22.7	0.0	0.0	1.3
Base N (ranges)	402–456	185–206	660–785	18–22	72–77	22–23	75–78

[a] Race-Warmth difference-scores = 2–8.
[b] Race-Warmth difference-score = 1.
* Association between intergroup warmth and policy disposition is statistically significant (p < .05).

ence for their own group and affective neutrality, with just a tiny minority of whites (1.4 percent) saying they feel warmer to blacks than to their own group. Among blacks, intergroup feelings vary between degrees of preference for their own group and affective neutrality. In neither group does this variation in intergroup feelings bear distinctly on racial policy dispositions.

Among whites, the relationship between feelings of intergroup warmth and racial policy goals is nonmonotonic and of only moderate strength. There are only modest shifts in the percentage supporting affirmative policy goals (shifts of 10 to 20 percentage points) and somewhat larger shifts in the percentage advocating reactionary goals (15 to 30 points) between those who feel much warmer toward whites and those who draw no affective boundary. Policy goals shift more sharply among those few whites who go so far as to prefer blacks to whites: among those whites, the percentage supporting affirmative goals shifts about another 30 points beyond those who draw no affective boundary. Such an abundance of good feeling, however, is not only rare but it is more than should be required to remove any affective basis for racial discrimination. The three lefthand columns in table 7.1 represent a wide range of intergroup feelings, and yet the shifts in policy goals that accompany that range of feelings are fairly limited.

Whites who express affective neutrality are, indeed, more likely than those who prefer their own group to take an affirmative stance on racial policies, but these differences are modest. And unless they go so far as to express an affective preference for blacks, it remains only a minority of whites who can bring themselves to support affirmative racial policy goals. The effect of feelings is consistently more pronounced in drawing whites away from reactionary policy opinions. But dislodgement from a reactionary position does not translate into a comparable increase in support for affirmative change.

Among blacks, the overwhelming preference for affirmative racial policies is budged only a little by their interracial feelings. Between those who draw larger and milder affective distinctions, there is no difference in their policy dispositions. And the move from making slight affective distinctions to making no distinctions in feelings of warmth between the two races brings but a moderate shift (of 8 to 20 percentage points) away from affirmative policy goals.[2]

Gender. Table 7.2 presents the data for gender. Recall from chapter 5 that feelings between men and women span a smaller range than for race or class. In general, neither gender draws an affective boundary between the groups, and feelings do not stray far in either direction. Although women show a stronger tendency than men to prefer their own gender group, women's gender feelings have no bearing on their policy goals. Among men, gender feelings have a modest effect on their policy goals: between men who feel warmer to their own group and warmer to women there is a shift of 11 and 21 points, respectively, in the percentage supporting affirmative policies to provide equal job opportunity and equal legal treatment for women. Most of that difference occurs between those who prefer their own group and those who draw no affective distinctions.[3]

Class. The data for class are presented in table 7.3. For ease of presentation, interclass feelings are dichotomized into those who feel

2. Measures of association for the cross-tabulations in table 7.1 tell the same story of only moderate associations between interracial feelings and racial policy goals. For whites, Goodman-Kruskal gammas range from .27 to .40, and Kendall's tau-b's range from .16 to .26 (recall that these measures of association include those whites who express an affective preference for blacks over whites). For blacks, gammas range from .29 to .34, and tau-b's range from .12 to .20. Gammas are of course sensitive to the presence of cell N's that are zero or small; the more stable tau-b's range from small to modest.

3. Measures of association for the cross-tabulations in table 7.2 are uniformly trivial: for men, gammas range from .08 to .13, and tau-b's range from .05 to .08; for women, gammas range from .01 to −.04, and tau-b's range from .00 to −.02.

TABLE 7.2. Percentages of Men and Women Taking Alternative Policy Stances on Gender Issues, According to Their Affective Differentiation between the Sexes.

	Men			Women		
	Warmer to Own Group	Neutral	Warmer to Other Group	Warmer to Own Group	Neutral	Warmer to Other Group
Equal Job Opportunity						
Affirmative	18.2%	32.8%	39.1%	49.7%	39.0%	49.3%*
Conservative	54.5	41.1	39.1	35.5	39.8	31.5
Reactionary	27.3	26.1	21.9	14.8	21.1	19.2
Equal Legal Treatment						
Affirmative	33.3%	38.2%	41.8%	53.4%	45.2%	55.7%
Conservative	54.5	53.6	51.0	36.8	46.3	34.4
Reactionary	12.1	8.2	7.2	9.8	8.4	9.9
Base N (ranges)	33	403–433	251–256	163–183	546–610	131–145

* Association between intergroup warmth and policy disposition is statistically significant (p < .05).

TABLE 7.3. Percentages of the Upper-Middle Class, Middle Class, Working Class, and Poor Taking Alternative Policy Stances on Economic Issues, According to Their Affective Differentiation between Their Own and Other Classes.

	Upper-Middle		Middle		Working		Poor	
	Warmer to Own Class[a]	Neutral/ Other	Warmer to Own Class[a]	Neutral/ Other	Warmer to Own Class[b]	Neutral/ Other	Warmer to Own Class[b]	Neutral/ Other
Guaranteed Jobs								
Affirmative	39.0%	63.5%*	66.5%	65.1%	75.7%	65.6%*	79.1%	70.2%
Conservative	36.6	26.9	24.2	26.8	18.3	27.1	19.4	25.5
Reactionary	24.4	9.6	9.3	8.2	5.9	7.3	1.5	4.3
Welfare Benefits								
Affirmative	12.2%	21.6%	23.1%	27.1%*	38.4%	32.4%	65.2%	52.2%
Conservative	36.6	35.3	30.8	37.8	34.1	37.7	21.7	37.0
Reactionary	51.2	43.1	46.2	35.1	27.6	30.0	13.0	10.9
Guaranteed Minimum Income								
Affirmative	37.5%	46.1%	50.7%	49.6%	64.8%	58.0%*	86.6%	65.8%*
Conservative	42.5	36.3	29.1	35.8	24.9	34.0	10.4	34.2
Reactionary	20.0	17.6	20.2	14.6	10.3	8.0	3.0	0.0
Base N (ranges)	40–41	102–104	213–221	508–527	362–371	238–247	67–69	38–47

[a] Referent classes are the Poor and Working Class.
[b] Referent classes are the Middle, Upper-Middle, and Upper classes.
* Association between intergroup warmth and policy disposition is statistically significant (p < .05).

warmer toward their own class and those who make no affective distinction or who prefer other classes; recall from chapter 5 that most people
falling in the latter category have neutral interclass feelings (rather than
preferring the other class). For respondents in the upper-middle and
middle classes, the referent classes are the poor and the working class;
for those in the latter two classes, the referent classes are the middle,
upper-middle and upper classes. In both cases, people's feelings between
their own and the referent classes are averaged.

Interclass feelings have only a modest impact on policy goals. Among
the upper-middle class, there is a difference of 24 percentage points
between those who prefer their own class and those who do not in their
likelihood of taking an affirmative position on the issue of government-
guaranteed jobs; but on the other two issues, the comparable percentage
difference is only about 9 points. Among the middle class, interclass
feelings show even less connection to people's policy goals. The impact
of feelings is virtually restricted to drawing people away slightly from
reactionary goals on two of the issues (providing welfare benefits and
guaranteeing a minimum income)—and the percentage difference there
is only about 11 points and 5 points, respectively.[4]

Among the working class, the effect of feelings is again quite modest:
between those who express warmer feelings toward their own class and
those who do not, there are percentage differences of just 6 to 10 points
in the likelihood of taking an affirmative position on any of the three
policy issues. Among the poor, the effect of feelings is just a notch
stronger than in the working class.[5] Regardless of their interclass feelings, very few poor people endorse reactionary policy positions, but they
are slightly more likely to move away from conservative policy positions
to affirmative ones (by 9 to 21 percentage points) when they have warmer
feelings toward their own class.[6]

4. Data from tables that trichotomize interclass feelings indicate that, in the upper-
middle class, there is little difference in policy views between those who prefer lower classes
and those who have neutral feelings. In the middle class, however, those who prefer lower
classes are more likely to take an affirmative policy stance whereas those with neutral
feelings are little different from those who prefer their own class.

5. Because so few members of the poor and working class express warmer feelings for
higher classes than for their own class, an attempt to cross-tabulate policy goals with a
trichotomized version of interclass feelings resulted in cell N's that were too low to yield
reliable data for those who preferred higher classes.

6. Measures of association for the class cross-tabulations in table 7.3 are as follows: for
the upper-middle class, gammas range from .13 to .44 and tau-b's range from .07 to .23;
for the middle class, gammas range from −.02 to .16 and tau-b's range from −.01 to .08;
for the working class, gammas range from .08 to .22 and tau-b's range from .05 to .10;
and for the poor, gammas range from .19 to .50 and tau-b's range from .10 to .23. The
occasional higher gammas are attributable to the presence of empty or near-empty cells
in those cross-tabulations. The more stable tau-b's remain in a range from zero to modest.

,General Patterns.   Overall, the relationship between intergroup feelings and policy goals ranges from zero to moderate. The policy dispositions of whites show more of a connection to their intergroup feelings than is the case for other groups, but even among whites, the relationship is only moderate. Nor does the relationship between intergroup feelings and policy goals fall into a straightforward monotonic pattern that affects the main body of responses in a single thrust. In addition, there is no systematic tendency for the relationship between feelings and policy dispositions to be affected by the position of the group to which the person belongs (that is to say, dominant or subordinate), or by the type of policy issue at hand (that is, moderate versus more redistributive policies).

Instead, the impression these tables convey is that the prevailing preference of subordinate groups for affirmative policies and aversion of dominant groups to those same policies is buffeted only a little by the intergroup feelings that individuals hold. Clearly, people's intergroup feelings are too loosely coupled with their policy goals to be construed as the force that is driving the formulation of those goals.

Alternative Attitudinal Compounds

The analysis thus far has conceived of the relationship between intergroup feelings and policy goals in the conventional way—that is, in terms of the "consistency" between the two. That approach looks for positive feelings to go with affirmative policy goals and negative feelings to go with conservative or reactionary policy goals among the members of dominant groups and for the opposite relationship to hold among subordinate group members. I ask the reader now to abandon that mold of thinking. It restricts our thinking about intergroup attitudes to a narrow track that bypasses the very types of attitudes that are, I argue, the primary draw for groups. I suggest a new approach that delineates the various ways that intergroup feelings and policy goals may intersect.

An Empirical Scheme.   In order to clarify the issues, figure 7.1 presents a simplified scheme that depicts the main ways that intergroup feelings and policy goals can intersect, for people in dominant and subordinate groups, respectively. Each axis is dichotomized. On the horizontal axis, *intergroup feelings* are divided into (1) those making no distinction between groups or even showing a preference for the other group (labeled *inclusive* feelings), and (2) those expressing a preference for their own group over the other (labeled *estranged* feelings). On the vertical axis, *policy goals* are divided into (1) those advocating *affirmative change* (that is, that the government should do more than it currently is doing), and (2) those taking *conservative or reactionary* positions (that is, that the government should do no more, or less than it is currently doing). Four

Policy Goals	DOMINANT GROUP: *Feelings toward subordinate group* — Inclusive	DOMINANT GROUP: *Feelings toward subordinate group* — Estranged	SUBORDINATE GROUP: *Feelings toward dominant group* — Inclusive	SUBORDINATE GROUP: *Feelings toward dominant group* — Estranged
Affirmative Change	*REVISIONIST*	*TOLERANT*	*INTEGRATIONIST*	*CONFLICTIVE*
Conservative or Reactionary	*PATERNALISTIC*	*CONFLICTIVE*	*DEFERENT*	*ACCOMMODATIVE*

Figure 7.1 Paternalism and conflict: Alternative configurations of intergroup feelings and policy goals for dominant and subordinate groups.

distinct compounds of feelings and policy goals may thus be identified in dominant and subordinate groups.

The first thing that is highlighted by this scheme is that the meaning of particular configurations is altered entirely according to whether one is examining the attitudes of dominant-group members or subordinates. Among the members of dominant groups, those configurations that fall on the diagonal going from top left to bottom right (*revisionist* and *conflictive* attitudes) are the "consistent" ones that have been the target of scholarly scrutiny. They combine inclusive feelings with support for affirmative policy change or estranged feelings with conservative or reactionary policy goals. These are the attitudinal configurations that are commonly termed "unprejudiced" and "prejudiced," respectively.

Of the two "irregular" cells, one—the compounding of estranged feelings with affirmative policy dispositions (*tolerant*)—has received considerable attention from students of political tolerance. The other formally inconsistent cell—the compounding of inclusive feelings toward subordinates with conservative or reactionary policy goals (*paternalistic*)—has been bypassed in conventional approaches to public opinion and has fallen by the wayside as an awkward anomaly. It is this configuration, however, that holds the most promise for scholars in unraveling the dynamics of intergroup ideologies.

Among the members of subordinate groups, it is the configurations that fall on the opposite diagonal, going from top right to bottom left (*conflictive* and *deferent* attitudes), that have conventionally been treated as consistent. Subordinates are logically expected either to take a conflictive approach by expressing estranged feelings from the dominant group and demanding affirmative change, or to be deferent toward the dominant group by espousing inclusive feelings toward them (possibly even showing a higher regard for the dominant group than for their own) and adopting conservative or reactionary policy views.

Neither of the two "irregular" cells has been the object of investigation in public-opinion research on subordinate group consciousness. However, the *accommodative* cell (that combines estranged intergroup feelings with conservative or reactionary policy dispositions) is certainly implied by theories that postulate that subordinates express "hidden resistance" (Genovese 1974; Cloward and Piven 1979; Anyon 1984; Scott 1985, 1990). Such theories imply that although subordinates generally comply with dominant group demands, their compliance is nothing more than a tacit acknowledgment of the superior power of the stronger group that masks an underlying alienation in spirit that is manifested in small, hidden acts of resistance. If the compliance of subordinates is merely a veneer, we would expect them to populate the accommodative cell, espousing conservative or reactionary policy views but retaining alienated feelings from the dominant group. Accommodation among subordinates might be regarded as the logical counterpart to tolerance in the dominant group: in each case, estranged feelings must be overridden to behave in a supportive way toward the other group.

The opposite "irregular" cell—the combination of inclusive feelings toward the dominant group with calls for affirmative change—I have labeled *integrationist*, because it reflects the spirit of the movement for racial integration in the United States in the 1950s and 1960s, as advocated by Dr. Martin Luther King, Jr. Despite the prominent position of the civil rights movement in recent U.S. history, this attitudinal compound has had no place in conventional analyses of group consciousness, since it is logically inconsistent. This configuration of feelings and policy goals might be regarded as the subordinate counterpart to paternalism in dominant groups: subordinates might find it strategic to moderate their demands for change with assurances that they feel no hostility toward those from whom they wish to extract concessions.

The simplified scheme that I have outlined identifies four main ways that dominant-group members and subordinates may blend their intergroup feelings and policy goals. The meaning of any specific compound of feelings and policy dispositions cannot be interpreted out of context but depends on whether the exponent is a member of a dominant or a subordinate group. Only one term is applicable to both kinds of groups—*conflictive* attitudes—but note that it is constructed quite differently, depending on whether one occupies a dominant or a subordinate position in an intergroup relationship. All the other terms are unique to dominant or subordinate groups. For example, it is not germane to ask whether subordinates are willing to override their estranged feelings and grant equality to the people who exceed them in status and perquisites. Similarly, the attitudinal state of deference is a prospect that members of dominant groups are spared.

Fitting the Data.   The next step is to apply this empirical scheme to the data for race, gender, and class. To that end, figures 7.2, 7.3, and 7.4 present the percentages of the pertinent dominant and subordinate groups expressing each of the four possible attitudinal compounds, for race, gender, and social class, respectively. Intergroup feelings are measured in terms of warmth or coldness. And recall that since feelings are measured in terms of affective differentiation (rather than absolute feelings toward other groups), the effect is to create more respondents who are categorized as having "negative" feelings, since more people draw affective distinctions between groups than express outright negative feelings toward the other group. Policy goals are reported separately for each specific policy, in order to capture the variant reactions that

WHITES[c]

	REVISIONIST	TOLERANT
Integrated Schools	11.2%	5.1%
Equal Housing Opportunity	19.5%	9.6%
Equal Job Opportunity	15.8%	6.8%

	PATERNALISTIC	CONFLICTIVE
Integrated Schools	43.6%	40.1%
Equal Housing Opportunity	34.1%	36.8%
Equal Job Opportunity	39.7%	37.6%

BLACKS[d]

	INTEGRATIONIST	CONFLICTIVE
Integrated Schools	27.4%	44.0%
Equal Housing Opportunity	36.7%	50.9%
Equal Job Opportunity	34.4%	54.3%

	DEFERENT	ACCOMMODATIVE
Integrated Schools	17.2%	11.5%
Equal Housing Opportunity	7.7%	4.7%
Equal Job Opportunity	9.1%	2.3%

[a] Intergroup feelings are categorized into (a) feeling equally warm toward both groups or warmer to the other group, and (b) feeling warmer toward one's own group.

[b] Policy goals are categorized into (a) affirmative and (b) conservative or reactionary.

[c] Base N's for whites: 1,466 (Integrated Schools), 1,265 (Equal Housing Opportunity), 1,446 (Equal Job Opportunity).

[d] Base N's for blacks: 175 (Integrated Schools), 169 (Equal Housing Opportunity), 177 (Equal Job Opportunity).

Figure 7.2 Paternalism and conflict: Percentages of whites and blacks with alternative configurations of intergroup feelings[a] and policy goals.[b]

WOMEN[d]

	INTEGRATIONIST	CONFLICTIVE
Equal Job Opportunity Equal Legal Treatment	33.0% 38.1%	9.7% 10.4%
	DEFERENT	ACCOMMODATIVE
Equal Job Opportunity Equal Legal Treatment	47.5% 42.5%	9.8% 9.0%

MEN[c]

	REVISIONIST	TOLERANT
Equal Job Opportunity Equal Legal Treatment	33.5% 37.7%	0.8% 1.6%
	PATERNALISTIC	CONFLICTIVE
Equal Job Opportunity Equal Legal Treatment	61.9% 57.5%	3.7% 3.2%

[a] Intergroup feelings are categorized into (a) feeling equally warm toward both groups or warmer to the other group, and (b) feeling warmer toward one's own group.

[b] Policy goals are categorized into (a) affirmative and (b) conservative or reactionary.

[c] Base N's for men: 722 (Equal Job Opportunity), 687 (Equal Legal Treatment).

[d] Base N's for women: 939 (Equal Job Opportunity), 840 (Equal Legal Treatment).

Figure 7.3 Paternalism and conflict: Percentages of men and women with alternative configurations of intergroup feelings[a] and policy goals.[b]

UPPER-MIDDLE/MIDDLE[c]

	REVISIONIST		TOLERANT	
	Upper-Middle	Middle	Upper-Middle	Middle
Guaranteed Jobs	45.5%	46.2%	11.0%	19.3%
Welfare Benefits	15.4%	19.1%	3.5%	6.8%
Guaranteed Minimum Income	33.1%	35.0%	10.6%	15.0%

	PATERNALISTIC		CONFLICTIVE	
	Upper-Middle	Middle	Upper-Middle	Middle
Guaranteed Jobs	26.2%	24.8%	17.2%	9.7%
Welfare Benefits	56.0%	51.3%	25.2%	22.8%
Guaranteed Minimum Income	38.8%	35.5%	17.6%	14.6%

WORKING/POOR[d]

	INTEGRATIONIST		CONFLICTIVE	
	Working	Poor	Working	Poor
Guaranteed Jobs	26.2%	28.9%	45.5%	46.5%
Welfare Benefits	13.0%	20.9%	23.0%	39.1%
Guaranteed Minimum Income	23.0%	23.8%	39.1%	55.2%

	DEFERENT		ACCOMMODATIVE	
	Working	Poor	Working	Poor
Guaranteed Jobs	13.7%	12.3%	14.6%	12.3%
Welfare Benefits	27.1%	19.1%	36.9%	20.8%
Guaranteed Minimum Income	16.7%	12.4%	21.2%	8.6%

[a] Intergroup feelings are categorized into (a) feeling equally warm toward one's own and other classes or warmer to other classes, and (b) feeling warmer toward one's own class. For the upper-middle and middle classes, the referent classes are the poor and working class; for the poor and the working class, the referent classes are the middle, upper-middle, and upper classes.

[b] Policy goals are categorized into (a) affirmative and (b) conservative or reactionary.

[c] Base N's for upper-middle class: 145 (Guaranteed Jobs), 143 (Welfare), 142 (Guaranteed Minimum Income). Base N's for middle class: 742 (Guaranteed Jobs), 745 (Welfare), 721 (Guaranteed Minimum Income).

[d] Base N's for working class: 618 (Guaranteed Jobs), 617 (Welfare), 599 (Guaranteed Minimum Income). Base N's for poor: 114 (Guaranteed Jobs), 115 (Welfare), 105 (Guaranteed Minimum Income).

Figure 7.4 Paternalism and conflict: Percentages of the upper-middle class, middle class, working class, and poor with alternative configurations of intergroup feelings[a] and policy goals.[b]

different policies elicit. Thus the patterns of attitudes can be mapped in the form in which they find expression in the evolving policy debate—around specific policy issues.

The construction of these figures focuses our attention on the structure of intergroup attitudes in a different way than the conventional approach. Instead of asking what percentage of a group with particular intergroup feelings support logically "consistent" policy goals, we now catalog the varying ways that intergroup feelings and policy goals intersect. The concern becomes, what percentage of each group compound their intergroup feelings and their policy goals in various alternative ways?

Two tiers of questions await us. First, what proportion of responses are logically consistent or inconsistent, and does that vary between dominant and subordinate groups or across the three intergroup relationships? Second, we move to the more important set of questions, which are unconstrained by concerns with logical consistency: What kinds of attitudinal compounds prevail among dominant and subordinate groups? What are the attitudinal blends by which dominant groups rule or concede and by which subordinate groups comply or resist? And what is the fit between the attitudinal compounds that are favored by dominant groups and the subordinates they seek to control?

Consistency.   First, what percentage of responses fall into the logically consistent cells?[7] About 51 to 56 percent of whites, about 40 percent of men, between 41 and 63 percent of the upper-middle class, and 42 to 56 percent of the middle class espouse feelings and policy dispositions that are either consistently positive or consistently negative. Among subordinate groups, the comparable figures for those taking either a consistently conflictive or consistently deferent position are about 60 percent of blacks, about 55 percent of women, 50 to 59 percent of the working class, and 58 to 68 percent of the poor.

In general, then, the proportion of responses that could be considered conventionally consistent falls in the range from somewhat below one-half to just over one-half. The proportion giving consistent responses is somewhat less in the context of gender relations than for either race or

---

7. Scholars have conventionally relied on measures of association to assess attitudinal consistency, but, as Weissberg (1976) has suggested, a more direct measure of attitudinal consistency is the percentage of respondents giving consistent responses—that is, the percentage giving responses that fall on the main diagonal when two attitude items are cross-tabulated. As Weissberg points out, measures of association can be depressed when there is restricted variance on the items (even if responses are very consistent), and two items can be strongly associated in the absence of consistency if responses on two items fall in the same rank-ordering.

class relations. And in all three intergroup relations, dominant groups show a slightly greater aversion to logically consistent responses. However, the proportion of logically consistent responses does not vary greatly from one intergroup relationship to another, or between dominant and subordinate groups.

Alternative Compounds.   Overall consistency may not vary dramatically across groups or intergroup relationships, but there is substantial variance in the *types* of consistent responses that prevail. We turn now to the second tier of questions: What blends of feelings and policy goals are espoused by dominant and subordinate groups in the three intergroup relations? I start by comparing the prevalence of alternative types of "consistent" responses, and I then consider the prevalence of alternative "inconsistent" compounds. Finally, I evaluate the way dominant and subordinate attitudes dovetail with one another to form a patterned exchange in each intergroup relationship.

Among whites, consistently conflictive responses far outweigh consistently revisionist responses, by a ratio of at least two to one. And on the issue of integrated schools, conflictive responses outnumber revisionist responses among whites by almost four to one. Among men, however, consistently revisionist responses outnumber conflictive responses by more than ten to one: almost no men take a conflictive stance in gender relations. In the upper-middle and middle classes, the ratio of revisionist to conflictive responses fluctuates, depending on the extent to which the specific policy is redistributive. On two of the policy issues, revisionist responses outnumber conflictive ones in both the upper-middle and middle classes, by ratios between two to one and four to one. But on the issue of welfare benefits, conflictive responses either equal or slightly outnumber revisionist responses.

On the subordinate group's side, consistently conflictive responses far outnumber consistently deferent ones among blacks and the poor and working class. Among blacks, conflictive responses prevail by more than two to one on the issue of school integration (the most sensitive of the three race policy issues) and by more than five to one on the other two race policy issues. Only between 8 and 17 percent of blacks assume a deferent orientation in their racial feelings and policy goals. Among the poor and working class, the margin favoring conflictive responses over deferent ones is slightly smaller than for race. And on the most sensitive class policy issue (welfare benefits), the margin in favor of conflictive responses drops to about two to one among the poor, and it disappears completely among working class respondents. The poor and working class thus manifest just slightly more deference than do blacks, with the figures ranging from 14 to 27 percent among the working class and 12 to 19 percent among the poor. Among women, the ratio of deferent responses to conflictive ones flips around completely from that observed for blacks and the poor and working class. For women, deferent responses outnumber conflictive ones by more than four to one, with almost one-half of women taking a deferent position.

Thus, over the three intergroup relations, conflictive orientations are most heavily in evidence among whites and blacks: approximately 40 percent of whites and 44 to 54 percent of blacks take a conflictive stance. Gender relations manifest the smallest evidence of conflictive orientations: fewer than 4 percent of men and about 10 percent of women take this stance. In class relations, the poor manifest about the same proclivity as blacks for a conflictive orientation, and the working class lag just slightly behind them. The upper-middle and middle classes, however, do not match the propensity of whites for a conflictive orientation: among the upper-middle class, about 17 to 25 percent take a conflictive stance, and among the middle class, conflictive responses drop to between 10 and 23 percent. Note that in all three intergroup relations, even in gender relations, subordinates are more drawn to conflictive responses than are the members of dominant groups. I return to this point below.

The response pattern that draws dominant groups more than any other is a technically inconsistent one: paternalism. Paternalistic attitude blends are most in evidence among men, of whom about 60 percent evince such a response pattern. Among the upper-middle and middle classes, paternalism accounts for about 25 to 56 percent of responses, with the sensitive welfare-benefits issue drawing the most paternalistic responses. Finally, even among whites, whose propensity for conflictive responses exceeds that of any other dominant group, still between 34 and 44 percent take a paternalistic position—roughly the same percentage as take a conflictive position.

The alternative inconsistent attitude blend for dominant groups—tolerance—is the one that has received much more attention from students of intergroup attitudes, but it is the least common response pattern among dominant groups in all three intergroup relationships. Only about 5 to 10 percent of whites and a minuscule 1 to 2 percent of men indulge in affirmative policy dispositions with feelings that are estranged from the other group. Among the upper-middle and middle classes, as many as 10 to 20 percent take a tolerant position on the two relatively tame policies of guaranteed jobs and guaranteed minimum income, but only 4 to 7 percent ascend to a tolerant position on the more threatening issue of welfare benefits. It seems that it is far easier to discriminate against groups one likes than to give equal treatment to groups from whom one feels estranged.

A similar but less extreme phenomenon occurs among subordinates. In general, it seems to be easier to demand affirmative change from a group one likes (the integrationist response) than to accept the status quo from a group from whom one feels estranged (the accommodative response). Among blacks, integrationist responses sharply outnumber accommodative ones, with about one-third of blacks taking an integrationist position and only between 2 and 12 percent taking an accommodative stance. Interestingly, it is on the explosive issue of integrated schools that blacks yield the most. The figures are similar for women, with about one-third or more of women taking an integrationist position and about one-tenth taking an accommodative posture. Among the poor, integrationist responses have a smaller edge over accommodative ones, with about one-quarter of the poor expressing integrationism and about one-tenth being accommodative on the two tamer policy issues and about 20 percent taking each position on the tougher issue of welfare benefits. Among the working class, integrationism loses its edge over accommodative responses. On the two less demanding issues, about one-quarter of the working class take an integrationist stance, with either a smaller percentage or the same percentage taking an accommodative stance. And on the tougher issue of welfare benefits, integrationist responses are far outweighed by accommodative ones in the working class, with only 13 percent being integrationist and 37 percent being accommodative. Thus, overall, subordinates find it more difficult to be accommodative than to be assertively upbeat—but on issues that find stronger resistance among dominant groups, subordinates are somewhat more likely to yield, despite estranged feelings.

Finally, I consider how dominant and subordinate response-patterns dovetail with one another. Surely the response pattern that dominant groups crave from subordinates is deference—the willing and friendly accession to the modus vivendi. To that end, dominant groups drift easily into paternalism, extending the hand of friendship as they withhold resources. How successful are they in their endeavor? Is paternalism rewarded with deference, or is it met with rebuff?

It is in gender relations that paternalism has its fullest flowering, with about 60 percent of men expressing a paternalistic compound of warmth and discrimination. Consistently positive responses are the only other compound to be expressed by any significant number of men, with about one-third being revisionist and only minuscule numbers taking either a tolerant or a conflictive approach. In short, men's gender attitudes commonly include discriminatory policy goals, but estranged feelings from women are virtually absent. And it is in gender relations that deference is most in evidence: close to half of women reward men's paternalism with deference. Some women seek affirmative change, but when they do so they are much more likely to take the route that is the subordinate counterpart to dominant paternalism—integrationism—than to be flagrantly conflictive. About one-third of women are integrationist. Only about 10 percent of women venture into a conflictive mode, and another 10 percent take the accommodative route. Note, however, that much as deference is the prevailing mode among women and conflictive attitudes uncommon, still deference is less in evidence among women than paternalism is present among men. And, by the same token, a few more women than men launch into a conflictive approach. It seems that the paternalistic-deferent mode of interaction holds somewhat more appeal for men than for women.

In class relations, the upper-middle and middle classes appear primarily as either revisionist or paternalistic, depending on the policy issue at hand. On the two more moderate issues, revisionists tend to equal or outnumber paternalists, but on the tougher issue of welfare benefits paternalists lead the way, with over half of these classes taking a paternalistic line on the issue of welfare benefits and only 15 to 19 percent venturing into revisionism. The poor and working class are much less likely to show deference than are women, although deference is slightly elevated on the sensitive issue of welfare benefits. And as in gender relations, fewer subordinates exude deference than seems called for by the rate of paternalism among dominant group members—indeed, this imbalance is stronger than in gender relations. Over the three policy issues, between 12 and 27 percent of the poor and working class express deference. Matching the class imbalance between paternalism on the one hand and deference on the other, the poor and working class are also considerably more likely than the upper-middle and middle classes to engage in a conflictive approach. Note, however, that on the tougher issue of welfare benefits, the conflictive tendencies of the upper-middle and middle classes are somewhat heightened and the temerity of the poor and working class slips somewhat. Over the three policy issues, between one-tenth and one-quarter of the upper-middle and middle classes take a conflictive stance, whereas the comparable figures for the poor are about 40 to 55 percent and for the working class about 23 to 46 percent.

The exchange of attitudes between blacks and whites is especially revealing. As whites face blacks, they find a group that is more combative than any other subordinate group. Among blacks, conflictive responses are at about the same high level as among the poor (44 percent on the sensitive issue of integrated schools and 51 to 54 percent on the other two issues). In addition, the level of deference among blacks is lower than in any other subordinate group (17 percent on the issue of school integration and less than 10 percent on the other two issues). The response among whites is that a higher percentage is drawn to the conflictive mode than is the case for dominant class or gender groups—approximately 40 percent of whites assume a conflictive orientation. At the same time, however, it is interesting that whites still do not match the level of conflictive orientation found among blacks. In addition, despite the low levels of deference and high levels of conflictive attitudes among blacks, still about 40 percent of whites cling to a paternalistic mode—just as many whites as take a conflictive approach. Despite the failure of paternalism to elicit any significant level of deference from blacks, many whites still cling to this comforting ideological mode.

In each case, then, it is subordinates who seem to lead the way on the path to conflict—albeit with caution. In gender relations, this is manifested in women's slight lag in returning deference for paternalism and in their timid lead in venturing into conflictive dispositions. In class and race relations, where paternalism has less of a grip, these asymmetries between dominant and subordinate groups are more pronounced. The middle and upper-middle classes remain more likely to express paternalism than outright conflictive dispositions, and whites are as likely to express paternalism as conflictive dispositions, even as these dominant groups are confronted with subordinates who generally fail to be deferent and who seem more drawn to the conflictive path.

CONCLUSIONS

Consistency has been the centerpiece of theory and empirical research about attitude structure, mass political opinion, prejudice, and class consciousness. Attitudinal expressions that reflect something tangible have been routinely expected to follow the precepts of consistency. Only one attitudinal construct that involves a logically inconsistent configuration has been subjected to sustained inquiry, and that is tolerance—the extension of equal rights to subordinates despite negative feelings toward them. This construct has generally been regarded as the exception that proves the rule, a testament to the power of democratic norms to reshape humans' basic proclivity to form policy dispositions toward a group on the basis of their feelings toward the group.

Outside the bounds of attitude research, two concepts have been introduced that have important implications for the way intergroup attitudes should be conceived, but these implications have not been fully realized. The two concepts are hidden resistance and paternalism. Hidden resistance implies that subordinates retain negative feelings toward the dominant group as they yield to its will. Paternalism implies that dominant groups fuel their discriminatory dispositions toward subordinates, not with negative feelings, but with positive ones.

My approach, abandons the underlying premise on which rests the commonly held tenet that consistency is the glue of well-formed attitudes. Instead of portraying attitudes primarily as a property of individuals, I treat them primarily as the property of groups. The attitudes that prevail in a group are shaped by its collective experience: the moral framework imposed by societal institutions, and the political pressures and opportunities emanating from the structure of the intergroup relationship and the behavior of the other group or groups in that relationship. Individual group members are the agents of ideological forms, not the autonomous creators of those forms. Attitudes are selected from the available repertoire, not for their tidy logic, but for their political utility. As exigencies shift, so too does the array of attitudes in a group: new patterns of response work their way through information channels and gradually supplant older forms that no longer prove serviceable.

The data in this chapter indicate that, in all three intergroup relationships, and among both dominant and subordinate groups, the direction of intergroup feelings has only a moderate influence on policy dispositions. Like many other students of public opinion, I have found that consistency is not the hallmark of popular attitudes. However, I do not infer from this that popular attitudes are unwieldy or incoherent. Instead, I have argued that the question of how feelings and policy goals intersect should be laid open empirically. I outlined a simple empirical scheme that identified alternative configurations of intergroup feelings and policy goals. Each configuration holds a distinct meaning for the ideological messages that flow back and forth through an intergroup relationship.

An examination of the data through this lens demonstrates that formal consistency does not mechanically stamp the intersection of people's intergroup feelings and their policy goals. Instead, the importance of consistency appears stronger or weaker, as a function of the direction of people's feelings. Among both dominant and subordinate groups, negative intergroup feelings are more likely to find expression in logically consistent policy dispositions than are positive feelings.

Thus, the members of dominant groups find it very difficult to maintain affirmative policy dispositions toward subordinates unless they hold inclusive feelings toward them. The inconsistent attitudinal compound of tolerance does seem to stretch most people's capabilities too far: estranged feelings from subordinates are hard to repress when dominant group members formulate their policy goals. Conservative and reactionary policy dispositions, however, do not require estranged feelings to fuel them, and, indeed, they are more often fueled by inclusive feelings. The inconsistent attitudinal compound of paternalism draws as many whites as does a flagrantly conflictive approach, and it occupies a slight lead over conflictive attitudes in the upper-middle and middle classes and an overwhelming lead over conflictive attitudes among men. Overall, inclusive intergroup feelings are more likely to accompany discriminatory dispositions than are estranged feelings, and holding inclusive feelings toward subordinates is more likely to result in discriminatory policy dispositions than in affirmative ones.

Among subordinate groups, alienated feelings from the dominant group are more likely to produce a consistent pattern of advocating affirmative policy change than they are to be found simmering quietly behind conservative acceptance of the status quo. It seems to be almost as difficult for subordinates to keep their negative feelings tamed in the formulation of their policy goals as it is for dominant group members, and unhappy accommodation to the dominant will is almost as unusual among subordinates as is tolerance in dominant groups. But, as with dominant groups, inclusive intergroup feelings provide less of a guide than do estranged feelings as to the way policy goals will be formulated. Inclusive feelings toward the dominant group sometimes lead to a deferent acceptance of the status quo and sometimes accompany a call for change. Indeed, in race relations, integrationist responses resoundingly outnumber deferent ones, and in class relations, integrationism usually predominates over deference. In gender relations, where deference is more common than in either of the other two intergroup relationships, integrationist responses are clearly outnumbered by deferent ones, but still a substantial minority of women (one-third or more) match inclusive feelings toward men with the advocacy of affirmative change.

We may think about integrationism as the subordinate counterpart to paternalism in dominant groups, whereby each group packages the pursuit of its interests with the expression of positive feelings toward the other group. Just as paternalism is an intuitively shrewd way to soften the presentation of dominant group interests, integrationism relies on the expression of affective inclusiveness toward the dominant group to sweeten the advocacy of affirmative change. It is interesting that dominant groups seem more drawn to such an ideological strategy than are subordinate groups.

We know from the data in chapter 5 that subordinates are more likely to withdraw emotionally behind group lines than are the members of dominant groups. The experience of underprivilege is more of a stimulant to the development of emotional boundaries between groups than is the experience of privilege. When subordinates develop estranged feelings from the dominant group, they find it more difficult to contain those feelings and continue endorsing the status quo than to translate them into an assertion of affirmative policy goals. Subordinates seem more inclined to engage in open resistance than hidden resistance. But even though the dominant group is getting less compliance from subordinates than it seeks, dominant-group members generally resist the pull toward either affirmative change or intergroup conflict. Confined by their unwillingness either to grant concessions or to engage in flagrant conflict, the members of dominant groups find refuge in the haven of paternalism.

In an intergroup relationship that is structured with frequent, intimate, one-to-one contacts across group lines, paternalism holds the day. Almost two-thirds of men are paternalistic, and they are rewarded with deference from almost half of women, considerably more deference than is found in any other subordinate group. In race and class relations, the structure of interaction across group lines is less favorable to paternalism. The extreme spatial segregation of blacks from whites has seriously restricted whites' opportunities to invade the cognitive and emotional sensibilities of blacks, and blacks show less inclination to be deferent than does any other subordinate group. Yet even as about half of blacks take a conflictive orientation and only a tiny minority are deferent, still whites lag behind blacks in their readiness to be openly conflictive, and they are as inclined to cling to paternalism as they are to be conflictive. The structure of class relations is marked primarily by spatial segregation and aggregated communication channels between classes, especially between the highest and lowest social classes, but this pattern is broken by limited opportunities for personal contacts across the boundaries of adjacent classes. The former factor undercuts the suitability of class relations for the practice of paternalism, but the latter introduces some opportunities to penetrate the awareness of at least those subordinates who are most adjacent to one's own class in the step-wise chain of class contacts. These dual factors work to mitigate the tendencies toward conflict: even as the poor, and to a lesser extent the working class, manifest a pronounced proclivity for conflictive attitudes and only slightly more deference than do blacks, the upper-middle and middle classes retain a greater propensity for paternalism than for conflictive attitudes.

In the ongoing political game between dominant and subordinate groups, it is subordinates who lead the way to conflict, but even their efforts in that direction are wary. As each side attempts to engage the other while trying to avoid a strong counterreaction that could jeopardize current holdings, bold moves are a rarity. Dominant and subordinate groups demonstrate their mutual sensitivity in the way they shift their positions in step with each other as they move from one policy issue to another that is more, or less, threatening to the core of their relationship. On those issues that have less redistributive implications, such as guaranteed jobs in the class arena, dominant-group members are more inclined to be revisionist and subordinates push a little harder. On issues that are more threatening, such as the class issue of welfare benefits, dominant group members move from tolerance to conflict and from revisionism to paternalism: subordinates retreat accordingly from conflict to accommodation and from integrationism to deference. By responding differentially to the various policy issues that are raised in an intergroup relationship, dominant groups can thus steer their attentive subordinates away from those issues that pose the greatest threat to dominant interests.

As the game continues, flexibility and differentiation are more common traits on both sides than is an unerring consistency. Far from indicating a lack of coherence or salience, these traits reflect the acute political sensitivities of both sides as they pursue their interests with intuitive care. For the same reasons, the ideological patterns that prevail are not flagrantly conflictive. Both dominant and subordinate groups show an inclination to package the pursuit of their group's interests in positive, rather than negative, feelings. This task is more difficult for subordinates, who must bear the daily offenses of underprivilege, and who are thereby often provoked into feelings of estrangement from the dominant group. But for the members of dominant groups, who can usually contemplate their daily experiences with greater equanimity, paternalism holds a magnetic lure that lingers on even as they are jostled by the wary and fitful ventures of subordinates into conflict. It proves difficult to abandon the trappings of an ideological system that so delicately obscures the raw pursuit of your own group's interests.

CHAPTER EIGHT

The Cognitive Embroidery of Intergroup Relations

The way people portray the vital characteristics of their own and other groups has drawn the attention of scholars of prejudice, gender ideology, and class and race consciousness. Two kinds of cognitive attributions have received particular attention. First, there is a large and venerable literature on personality trait attributions to groups, commonly termed *stereotypes*. Second, there has been a growing literature on the way people explain the relative standing of contending groups, with particular interest in whether people locate the causes in the internal characteristics of the affected groups (such as inherent biological attributes or subcultural mores) or in biases of the social structure (such as the structure of rewards and opportunities).

Research on stereotypes has been tied most closely to the analysis of racial and ethnic prejudice. Recall that research on prejudice has been guided by Allport's classic definition of that phenomenon as "an antipathy based on a faulty and inflexible generalization" (Allport 1954, 9), thus giving stereotypes a pivotal role in the generation of prejudice. This role for stereotypes has been absorbed into their intrinsic conception, even when they are studied in other contexts, such as in attitudes toward women or the poor.

The way people *explain* differences between groups has been regarded as critically important by a growing number of scholars in predicting policy dispositions toward the respective groups. Research on popular causal attributions to groups has been directed primarily to the explication of racial ideology and opinions about poverty. The classic archracist or class elitist is expected to believe in immutable, biological differences between the pertinent groups, whereas the person who seeks change is thought to draw on a cognitive scheme that posits a critique of the way structural arrangements disburse resources to contending groups.

The recurrent concern has been the extent to which subordinates are set apart, categorized, and derogated in popular beliefs. The underlying purpose has been to distinguish "good" beliefs from "bad" ones, to assess the extent to which people indulge in beliefs that are irrational, untrue, exaggerated, negative, simplistic, and inflexible. The identification of these elements in popular beliefs is deemed critical because they are thought to play a pivotal causal role in the endorsement of discriminatory practices. It is held that among dominant-group members, cognitions that are derogatory and categorical fuel hostile feelings and discriminatory dispositions; among subordinates, the acceptance of such beliefs undermines self-esteem and thus renders them passively uncritical of discriminatory arrangements. In short, specific kinds of beliefs are identified as damaging to the subordinate group—if those beliefs could be erased, the cognitive basis for the inequality would be dissolved.

I approach intergroup attributions from a different perspective. Although individuals' beliefs about groups surely serve to justify their behavioral predispositions and to frame their expectations about group members, I hold that it is a mistake to attach any genuine causal significance to those beliefs. People's intergroup policy goals are not driven by the kinds of intergroup beliefs they hold—instead, policy goals derive directly from the pursuit of group interests within a specific political context. Intergroup beliefs serve as cognitive props to explain, justify, and perpetuate those goals. In this framework, the significance of intergroup cognitive attributions is as cultural artifacts that embellish the way one group orients itself toward another. Cultural beliefs about the salient characteristics of unequal groups symbolize each group's attempts to define and explain social reality—they embroider the ideological representations that are exchanged between groups. The beliefs that unequal groups have about each other are subject to the same constraints as other aspects of their intergroup attitudes, and, thus, self-serving beliefs do not inevitably translate into hostile beliefs. Indeed, the pernicious quality of intergroup beliefs does not lie in any fixed, constantly identifiable quality—but rather in their malleability.

The focus of past literature on categorical, derogatory beliefs has misdirected our attention from more subtle and insidious forms of cognitive attribution that can pervade cultural interpretations of inequality. The problem is not whether the members of dominant groups categorize and derogate subordinates and whether subordinates accept or reject their assigned image as inferior and less worthy. History should have taught us that the reasoning that supports systems of inequality rarely follows such a straightforward design. Instead, the cognitive struts of inequality follow various and often convoluted paths, as people grope for stories that address the sundry tensions pervading an intergroup relationship.

Stories are framed in terms that conform to the current moral code and they shift to keep up with altered exigencies. In this ongoing process, those stories are more notable for their slippery variegation than for their rigidity, constancy, or logical tightness of reasoning. After all, there is more than one way to skin a cat. As we sift through the tangle of popular narratives about the pertinent characteristics of unequal groups, we must treat those narratives for what they are—interpretive stories about the modus vivendi that reveal the underlying pressures and strains demanding popular explanation.

What are the alternative modes of cognitive attribution that dominant groups develop, under different constraints, to interpret their unequal relations with another group, and how effectively can they limit the cognitive reactions of subordinates? As we move from paternalistic to more conflictive relations, what kinds of definitions and explanations of group differences gain popular credence among members of dominant groups, and how persuasive are those messages with subordinates?

In this chapter, I assess the cognitive attributions that shade different kinds of intergroup relationships. This begins with a discussion of the concerns, assumptions, and measurement strategies that have governed past work on cognitive attributions to groups, and I then delineate my approach. With those issues in hand, I turn to my data. The ensuing analysis of the cognitive props of race, gender, and class relations focuses on two sets of questions. First, I examine the ways in which people describe the salient personality characteristics of their own and other groups. Specifically, I examine the extent to which such descriptions entail derogation, sharp intergroup distinctions, and categorical imagery. Second, I investigate the perception of intergroup differences, more broadly conceived, and the popular causal attributions that are adduced to explain such differences. These two kinds of data inform us about the types of cognitive representations that prevail among dominant and subordinate groups as they face one another under varying constraints. What does the cognitive embroidery of an intergroup relationship tell us about the specific sensitivities and moral proclivities of the affected groups? More generally, what can we learn about the quicksand of folk wisdom as it absorbs the problematics thrown up by different forms of social inequality?

THE ISSUES

Stereotypes of subordinates and folk explanations of perceived group differences have both been assumed to play a portentous role in motivating negative feelings and discriminatory policy dispositions toward subordinates. The intimate conceptual link between stereotypes and prejudice continues to impel much research on stereotyping among students of prejudice as well as in some applications to gender and class attitudes. More recently, interest in intergroup beliefs has broadened to include folk explanations of group differences, and there has been a growing body of research on how people account for the differences they perceive between unequal groups.

The exact role played by intergroup beliefs in people's attitudes toward a target group has not usually been specified, and some unacknowledged and unresolved ambiguity hovers over this issue. The prevailing theme has been that such beliefs arise out of ignorance and parochialism and that, once installed in the person's mind-set, they establish expectations about the members of the target group and they thus function to motivate the person's feelings and dispositions toward the group. This theme is consistent with Allport's definition of prejudice as "an antipathy based on a faulty and inflexible generalization" (Allport 1954, 9). The term *prejudice* itself is derived from the notion of prejudgment and carries a strong connotation of a preexisting bias based on a prejudgment. Some scholars have attempted to test specific models based on this conception (for example, Rosenberg 1956; Rokeach, Smith, and Evans 1960; Stephan and Stephan 1984; Kluegel and Smith 1986), but more commonly this conception of the causal dynamics has simply underwritten empirical research on prejudice.

For example, the two most widely suggested policy interventions for eradicating or diminishing prejudice are built on that causal conception. The contact theory of prejudice postulates that with high levels of personal, equal-status contact between groups, dominant-group members learn the invalidity of their stereotypes and thus shed their prejudice (for example, Deutsch and Collins 1951, 1965; Wilner, Walkley, and Cook 1955; Miller and Brewer 1984; Stephan and Stephan 1984; Hewstone and Brown 1986; Hewstone 1989). And a policy that has been rapidly gaining attention in college campuses throughout the United States is the introduction of required ethnic studies courses in undergraduate liberal arts curricula: here the purpose is again to eradicate stereotypical thinking about minority ethnic groups in order to undermine prejudice. In short, stereotypes are considered the direct product of ignorance and parochialism: by reeducating people, stereotypes can be dispelled and thus the cognitive basis for intergroup hostility is removed.

At the same time, there has been a secondary theme that intergroup beliefs are rationalizations, adduced by the individual to justify preexisting discriminatory feelings and policy dispositions. This secondary theme is sometimes injected into discussions of stereotypes. If taken literally, it contradicts the primary theme noted above, since it suggests that intergroup feelings and policy dispositions temporally precede, rather than follow, beliefs about the group. This, in turn, has distinctly different implications for theories of prejudice. However, this conception of the causal direction is not usually introduced as an alternative to the primary conception, but rather as a supplement. For example, in *The Nature of Prejudice*, Allport credits stereotypes with a pivotal role in causing intergroup antipathy in his basic definition of prejudice in chapter 1 (quoted above), but in his subsequent discussion of stereotypes in chapter 12 he proceeds with the following elaborations:

> . . .a stereotype is an exaggerated belief associated with a category. Its function is to justify (rationalize) our conduct in relation to that category.
> In chapter 2 we examined the nature of categories; in chapter 10 we explored the cognitive organization that builds itself around categories. In the preceding chapter we stressed the importance of the linguistic tag that designates our categories. At the present time we are completing the story by talking about the ideational content (the image) that is bound in with the category. Thus category, cognitive organization, linguistic label, and stereotype are all aspects of a complex mental process.
> . . . .A stereotype is . . . a fixed idea that accompanies the category.
> The stereotype acts as both a justificatory device for categorical acceptance or rejection of a group, and as a screening or selective device to maintain simplicity in perception and in thinking. (Allport 1954, 191–192)

Perhaps the best way to reconcile these contradictory causal conceptions is to extrapolate a model in which negative beliefs are given a primary causal role but in which there is some feedback from feelings and policy dispositions that reinforces the negative beliefs. In such a model, negative beliefs foster negative feelings and policy dispositions: once the latter are enacted, the person then reaches for the beliefs to provide the justification for his feelings and policy dispositions. In this way, a loop is set up in the person's mind that can perpetuate itself indefinitely, resulting in beliefs becoming rigidified as they become emotionally invested. This model captures the various strands that have been emphasized by analysts (see, for example, Myrdal 1944, 101–112; Rose 1964, 36–42; Williams, Jr., 1964, 36–38; Tajfel 1969, 1982; Pettigrew 1979).

In any event, both stereotypes and folk explanations of group differences are seen as critically important in the formulation of prejudice. Although some murkiness surrounds the exact role in these cognitions in prejudice, most research has proceeded on the assumption that negative images and explanations are the product of ignorance, and that, once installed, such cognitions rigidly feed intergroup hostility. Both forms of cognition involve the delineation of images of groups and causal attributions about them, although stereotypes involve the latter more implicitly and folk explanations invoke imagery more implicitly. In either case, the primary concern has been with the degree to which the members of dominant groups indict subordinates by portraying them as deficient in the personal attributes that are associated with success in life. I turn now to a brief discussion of the ways in which that theme has been pursued in research on first, stereotypes, and then, folk explanations of group differences. I then present my conception of the nature of intergroup beliefs in ongoing relations of inequality.

Stereotypes

Stereotypes occupy a venerable position in research on prejudice. Their invidious character has been so well established that the term immediately conjures up trait attributions to groups that are categorical, rigid, and invective. Stereotypes have been inextricably bound to the concept of prejudice—they are "the language of prejudice" (Ehrlich 1973, 21).

In identifying those aspects of stereotypes that are especially damaging to intergroup relations, analysts have focused primarily on the following: the categorical attribution of personality traits to a group, the sharp setting-apart of a subordinate group from the dominant group, the derogation of subordinates, and the reliance on erroneous information (folk knowledge) rather than rational, scientific information about a group. These properties have been regarded as so endemic to stereotyping that researchers have felt no compunction to assess their presence empirically in standard measures of stereotypes. Instead, these properties were simply loaded into the two prevailing measures of stereotypes (stereotype checklists and agree-disagree categorical statements) rather than providing subjects with the opportunity to express more modified intergroup beliefs. I briefly discuss analysts' concern with each of the key properties of stereotypes, in turn, and then outline how the standard measures of stereotypes have served to reinforce, rather than to test, common assumptions about the content and form of damaging intergroup beliefs.

Categorical Attributions.   For many scholars, the description of groups in categorical terms is perhaps the most fundamentally damaging feature of stereotypes. Most definitions of stereotypes emphasize categorical attributions as a critical element (for example, Allport 1954; Fishman 1956; Richter 1956; Vinacke 1957; Secord 1959; Koenig and King 1964; Williams, Jr. 1964; Sherif 1966, 38–41; Campbell 1967; Harding et al. 1969; Tajfel 1969, 1982; Cauthen, Robinson, and Krauss 1971; Brigham 1971; Mackie 1973; Hamilton 1981; Hamilton and Trolier 1986). The tendency to simplify and classify the world is often regarded as a basic perceptual operandum as well as a functional coping mechanism for bringing some order to the confusion of reality (Lippmann 1922; Allport 1954; Tajfel 1969; Ehrlich 1973, 38; Hamilton and Trolier 1986). In the context of intergroup beliefs, however, this process is believed to become emotionally invested, exaggerated, and rigidified.

Use of the term *stereotype* to denote trait attributions to groups is borrowed from the printing industry where it means "a one-piece printing plate cast in type metal from a mold taken of a printing surface, as a page of set type" (*Webster's New World Dictionary* 1968). Stereotypes thus preempt raw perception with a rigidly fixed stamp. The categorical perception of groups "provides the mold which gives shape to intergroup attitudes" (Tajfel 1969, 91).

A frequent line of reasoning has been that any perception that unequivocally lumps all the members of a group into one unvaried category is intrinsically damaging because it credits group membership with an overwhelming role in determining individual personality characteristics, and because it provides the perfect grounding for discriminatory policies and practices. Most important, the categorical description of a group represents a closed and insensitive perception that routinely pigeonholes group members and leaves the perceiver unreceptive to contrary evidence, which is either overlooked or dismissed as a mere "exception." Categorical descriptions of groups are thus seen as inherently inaccurate and irrational (Lippmann 1922; Allport 1954; Richter 1956; Williams, Jr. 1964, 36; Ehrlich 1973; Mackie 1973; Tajfel 1969, 1978; Prager 1982). Thus, although there has been more interest in categorical attributions that are explicitly derogatory, any kind of categorical attribution is regarded as damaging, whether the specific traits are positive, negative, or even vague. An extreme example of a belief item that reflects this perspective is found in Wilner et al.'s study (1955, 62): "There may be a few exceptions, but in general, Negroes are pretty much alike." A similar item is found in the ethnocentrism scale of Adorno et al. (1950).

It is frequently assumed that such categorical attributions are more probable when people are describing groups other than their own, especially groups with which the individual has little or no personal familiarity (for example, Allport 1954; Pettigrew 1982; Hamilton and Trolier 1986; Linville, Salovy, and Fischer 1986; Miller and Brewer 1986; Hewstone 1989). This assumption ties in with the recurrent theme that prejudice is a product of ignorance. It is assumed that familiarity would yield the inescapable observation of variation within the target group, and categorical attributions would thus crumble.

Setting Groups Apart and Derogating Subordinates.   A second feature of stereotypes that has been regarded as damaging is the attribution of *positive* traits to one's own group and *negative* qualities to other groups. Such attributions set groups apart and assert the superiority of one group over another in a single maneuver (Vinacke 1957; Allport 1954; Williams

1964, 40; Sherif 1966, 37–38; Campbell 1967; Harding 1968; Tajfel 1969, 1978; Eldridge 1979, 23–27). In Tajfel and Turner's theory of social identity and social comparison, it is postulated that individuals seek to enhance their self-esteem by comparing themselves favorably to other individuals and their group favorably to pertinent out-groups: this poses a problem for subordinated groups, whose self-esteem is damaged by their position as the object of consensual dominant derogation (Tajfel and Turner 1979).

The extent to which people distinguish between the basic personality attributes of their own and other groups provides the meaning for group labels. In addition, such distinctions carry an implicit evaluation of each group's worth and serve as part of an attributional process that accounts for the varying fates of different groups. A positive self-image is believed to come easily to dominant groups as a product of their privileged position in society; besides, assertions of their superior endowment of personality traits constitute a convenient rationale for their privileged position. Thus, the common assumption has been that dominant groups will assert large and invidious distinctions between their own and subordinate groups as part of a logical attempt to vindicate the status quo unequal relations between them.

The extent to which subordinate groups accede to or deny dominant group assertions of superiority has been regarded as more problematic. This is a critical question, since the former implies a consensus about fundamental perceptions that bolster the status quo, whereas the latter implies a rift between groups that would provide a force for social change. It is generally assumed that the dominant view, because it emanates from the group with more power and prestige, has the advantage, and that it is difficult for subordinate groups to counter with claims of their own superior or even equal endowment of personal attributes. The extent to which a subordinate group does challenge the dominant group's definition of the distinctions between them gives a fundamental indication of their development of positive group consciousness as well as of the dominant group's ideological control over the relations between groups.

Erroneous Beliefs.   A common but often unspoken assumption is that stereotypes are erroneous, and that a good part of the damage they wreak comes from their unscientific, irrational genesis. Students of prejudice generally place implicit faith in rational, scientific knowledge as the enlightened replacement for parochial folk knowledge. In Allport's initial delineation of prejudice, he illustrates the problem by drawing a pivotal distinction between two different types of avoidance behaviors: his first case is the anthropologist who does not allow his children to have contact with the American Indian tribe he is studying, and his second case is the hotel proprietors who refuse accommodation to "Mr. Greenberg" because of his Jewish name. Allport reasons that the anthropologist's behavior is untainted by prejudice because it is based on a realistic assessment of the risk of his children contracting tuberculosis from the Indian children in the village, whereas the hotel proprietors are acting out of prejudice because their behavior is based on an irrational, categorical rejection.

> If the innkeepers were basing their rejection on facts (more accurately, on a high probability that a given Jew will have undesirable traits), their action would be as rational and defensible as the anthropologist's. . . . Certainly they had not consulted scientific studies concerning the relative frequency of desirable and undesirable traits in Jews and non-Jews." (Allport 1954, 5–6)

Allport's exposition is consistent with the reigning assumption that prejudice is born out of ignorance. Although there is some ambiguity as to the source of such ignorance (that is, whether it is imposed on the individual by circumstances beyond her individual control, or whether the individual fails to seek out available information about the target group), ignorance itself is regarded as a key to the problem of prejudice. In 1944, Myrdal wrote:

> The race prejudice of the typical Northerner . . . is based mainly on ignorance, both simple and opportune. . . . The Northerner seldom gets a chance to see the Negro's good points, and he does not understand the social background of the Negro's bad points. The Southerner's prejudice also has much ignorance in it, but the Southerner's ignorance is more opportune because it is tied to fundamental motives. (Myrdal 1944, 1142)

The theme has persisted: stereotypes contradict knowledge and reason (see, for example, Harding et al. 1969; Selznick and Steinberg 1969; Simpson and Yinger 1972; Pettigrew 1982; Stephan and Stephan 1984).

Despite this emphasis, the verity of stereotypes has been a troublesome issue that has thrust an uncomfortable wedge into scholarly inquiry from time to time. Some scholars have wrestled with the "kernel of truth" hypothesis that stereotypes are exaggerated attributions based on a germ of truth (Allport 1954, 189–196; Mackie 1973). Others have pondered the distinction between incorrect beliefs and negative beliefs (Schuman and Harding 1964). Discussions of Jensen's argument (1969) that ethnic groups vary in IQ also have hinged on whether his argument is true or false. And moral judgments about Jensen's line of research have hinged on whether it is scientifically motivated or racially motivated, as though science automatically cleanses human observation. This issue has been troublesome because stereotypes have been regarded as the antithesis of science and "rational" knowledge.

Measurement of Stereotypes.   Two measures of beliefs about group traits became the standard, the *stereotype checklist* and *agree-disagree categorical statements about a group's attributes.* Both measures reflected analysts' assumptions about the hallmark characteristics of stereotypes. Rather than testing the properties of people's intergroup beliefs, analysts instead relied on measures that had the expected properties loaded into them. Reliance on these measures thus served to perpetuate analysts' preconceptions about the specific properties that go into the manufacture of discriminatory intergroup beliefs.

The most frequently replicated research on trait attribution to groups has used the stereotype checklist, usually administered to small samples of select subgroups (generally college undergraduates). This measure presents respondents with a long list of traits and instructs them to assign the traits to specific groups; the positive or negative values attached to the traits are often obtained from another group of respondents (see, for example, Katz and Braly 1947; Meenes 1943; Gilbert 1951; Sherriffs and McKee 1957; Karlins, Coffman, and Walters 1969; Broverman et al. 1972; Smedley and Bayton 1978).

In cross-sectional, public-opinion surveys, the measure that has been used most frequently presents respondents with categorical statements about the trait attributes of a group (such as "poor people are lazy," "blacks are musical"), and respondents can express agreement or disagreement with those statements (see, for example, Adorno et al. 1950; Deutsch and Collins 1951; Wilner, Walkley, and Cook 1955; Marx 1967; Selznick and Steinberg 1969).

These two standard measures share one important feature—they both force respondents to express themselves in categorical, all-or-none terms, thereby precluding the expression of more qualified beliefs.[1] Because of this constraint, these measures cannot reflect the degree to which people do in fact think about groups in a categorical or qualified way. The concern of analysts with this specific issue has exacerbated the problem by encouraging interpretations that far outstrip the information yielded by these measures. Thus, it is commonly assumed that respondents who agree with the statement "blacks are lazy" think *all* blacks are lazy. Similarly, the very name of the "stereotype checklist" carries the clear assumption that, in requiring respondents to label groups with

---

1. Procedures used by Broverman et al. (1972) did allow respondents to make finer distinctions between men and women, but these distinctions were ignored in the variables that were constructed from the data.

traits, the analyst has captured stereotypical thinking. Indeed, one analyst has made this assumption explicit: Ehrlich argues that "the statement 'Atheists are cynical' may be correctly transliterated 'All Atheists are cynical'" (Ehrlich 1973, 21).

The categorical phrasing of the measures not only restricts the information they can yield, but it may also make them more susceptible to response-bias effects. The blatant character of the task may cue some respondents (especially the well-educated) to social-desirability pressures, and make them unwilling to present their beliefs in an unfavorable light.[2] Meanwhile, other respondents with simpler cognitive styles (especially the poorly educated) may be trapped by the loaded and unbalanced construction of the measure into saying "yes" or into labeling groups with traits because these response options are "near enough." Thus, these measures may be seriously confounded with response sets caused by varying cognitive styles or susceptibility to social-desirability pressures (Campbell et al. 1960; Ehrlich 1964; Jackman 1973; Jackman and Muha 1984).

Several analysts have registered dissatisfaction with these measures of stereotypes. As early as 1951, LaViolette and Silvert noted that "the attributes of stereotypes have not been examined critically by social psychologists" (1951, 260). In 1954, Harding et al. pointed out that standard stereotype measures do not differentiate between respondents who are indeed ignoring individual differences and those who are merely making a statistical generalization. These complaints have been reiterated over the years (Hyman 1969, 10; Brigham 1971; Jones 1972, 70; Jackman and Senter 1980, 1983; Ashmore and Del Boca 1981). Ehrlich (1964) experimented with the introduction of response options to the standard public-opinion measure that allowed for the expression of strong or mild agreement or disagreement, indecision, and "don't know": he reported that the standard format overstates the degree of acceptance of prejudiced statements. Ehrlich and Rinehart (1965) experimented with a variant of the stereotype checklist that used an open-ended format: they reported that the standard format elicited the assignment of more traits to groups and more consensus among respondents, and that the two formats produced different listings of traits. Brigham (1971) suggested that respondents should be asked to assess what percentage of a group has a particular trait, in order to get a more valid measure of the form of people's attributions to groups. McCauley and Stitt (1978) and McCauley, Stitt, and Segal (1980) have suggested that the standard stereotype check-

---

2. Some evidence of this is provided by the replications of the original Katz and Braly design among Princeton undergraduates. Gilbert (1951) and Karlins, Coffman, and Walters (1969) report that many subjects protested the unreasonableness of making such simplistic generalizations.

list oversimplifies human perception and that stereotypes can be understood better as probabilistic predictions that distinguish one group from another. More recently, the General Social Survey (Davis and Smith 1990; Bobo and Kluegel 1991) measured stereotypes of whites, blacks, Hispanics, and Asians with 7-point bipolar scales in which respondents indicated whether they thought each group was characterized more by one trait (for example, *hardworking*) or by its opposite (for example, *lazy*). But despite the criticisms and suggested revisions over the years, the standard measures of stereotypes have not been seriously discredited. Studies using the traditional measures continue to be cited as classic evidence of the pervasiveness of stereotyping, and, as Ashmore and Del Boca (1981) report, the Katz and Braly checklist has continued to be the reigning measure in the prolific literature on stereotypes.

As a consequence, the complaint made by LaViolette and Silvert in 1951 that "we may call their [stereotypes'] characteristics 'claims' rather than established attributes" (1951, 260) remains as true today. First, as already noted, the standard measures do not yield direct evidence on the extent to which people's images of social groups are indeed categorical or qualified. Second, we lack critical information on the *pattern* of categorical thinking. Is categorical thinking more evident when people are describing groups other than their own, or do people tend to describe their own group in positive categorical terms and other groups in negative categorical terms? In other words, are categorical descriptions used to differentiate the homogeneity of another group from the individual variance within one's own group ("*they* are all alike"), or to maximize the difference between the bad qualities of the other group and the good qualities of one's own group ("they are all bad, we are all good")? Third, by the same token, the standard measures cannot give information on the degree to which people draw distinctions between groups. Do people tend to draw large or small distinctions between their own and other groups? Do people tend to minimize within-group variance among outgroups and exaggerate between-group differences, as Tajfel and others have claimed? Fourth, the stereotype checklist is often accompanied by an evaluative scale for the traits on the list, but the standard measure used in public-opinion surveys makes no direct assessment of the derogatory or flattering intent of a person's beliefs.

Folk Wisdom about Group Distinctions

As students of prejudice began to focus increasingly on whites' policy dispositions toward blacks (and especially support for policies of racial integration and affirmative action), their interest in intergroup beliefs broadened to include people's causal attributions about the differences they perceive between groups (Tajfel 1969; Schuman 1975; Pettigrew

1979; Apostle et al. 1983; Sniderman and Hagen 1985; Kluegel and Smith 1986; Kluegel 1990). At the same time, there has been a parallel and sometimes overlapping interest in how people account for the socio-economic condition of the poor (Feagin 1972, 1975; Williamson 1974*a*, 1974*b*; Nilson 1981; Kluegel and Smith 1981, 1986; Kluegel 1987). In both cases, the essential quest has been to find something in the individual's package of beliefs that could explain why he took a position for or against policy intervention on behalf of a specific group.

This research developed as an application and extension of attribution theory from social psychology. Pettigrew (1979) drew on the idea of "the fundamental attribution error" (Heider 1958; Ross 1977) that observers consistently underestimate the effects of situational factors and overestimate the influence of personal, dispositional factors on actors' behavior. A logical parallel in intergroup relations would be the propensity of dominant group members to attribute the unhappy fate of subordinates to personal, dispositional factors rather than to situational factors beyond the control of subordinates. Pettigrew dubbed this proposed phenomenon the "ultimate attribution error."

Various studies have employed somewhat different terminologies and have highlighted slightly different distinctions among competing popular attributions. However, the central issue has been whether the individual explains group differences in a way that lays the blame for those differences on biases in the social structure (thereby facilitating support for affirmative policy interventions) or on the subordinate group itself (thereby alleviating the dominant group of responsibility for affirmative policy intervention).

Two other themes are reiterated in much of this research. First, several analysts have discussed the pervasive effects of individualism on the way dominant-group members explain group differences. Whether the American commitment to individualism and self-reliance is depicted as a merely technical obstacle to equality (Sniderman and Hagen 1985) or as a deeply entrenched value-system that runs directly counter to the concept of equality (Kluegel and Smith 1986), analysts have argued that individualism further encourages Americans to hold subordinates responsible for their own fate. Second, a key distinction is often drawn between two alternate ways that subordinates may be held responsible for their own fate: are group differences attributed to immutable, biological factors or to distinctive cultural mores and values? The former view is the one traditionally treated as the hallmark of racism and prejudice (Myrdal 1944, 97–99; Rose 1964, 37; Sherif 1966, 39; Tajfel 1969, 94; Schuman 1975; Apostle et al. 1983; Pettigrew 1985, 343): it unambiguously explains the current position of the subordinate group as fixed by the group's inborn characteristics. The invocation of cultural differences is more ambiguous and complex: subordinates are still burdened with the primary responsibility for their fate, but their culture and values may be amenable to change with appropriate resocialization. For this reason, analysts have usually regarded this view as less venomous or hopeless than the invocation of immutable differences between groups.

Attributions as Embroidery

I view intergroup attributions in a different light. Dominant groups' beliefs about the vital attributes of subordinates have their genesis in political exigencies rather than in ignorance per se. The importance of these beliefs is not as a causal force impelling negative feelings and discriminatory policy dispositions. Instead, intergroup beliefs are the embroidery of intergroup attitudes, and they are important for what they tell us about the sensitive spots in the relationship and the values that infuse and protect the inequality.

Ideas about the characteristics of subordinates emerge out of the political demands imposed by the need to justify and clothe the rude facts of expropriation. Thus, the perceptual distortions and lacunae that are manifested in the intergroup beliefs of dominant groups should not be expected to follow any one prescribed pattern or to be locked into any particular configuration. They are more likely to have a chameleon quality, with various ideas and modes of attribution flourishing or fading, dependent upon the demands of the relationship at any given time and the broad moral themes that have contemporary currency.

In this process, logical inconsistencies abound. As with other aspects of people's attitudes, the essentially political nature of intergroup beliefs means that they do not need to fulfill any logical consistency requirements to be satisfactory to those who hold them.[3] Indeed, rigidity and consistency turn out to be poor political weapons. As Myrdal (1944) and Rose (1964) long since observed, the overwhelming requirement of intergroup beliefs is that they address the various stress points that exist in the intergroup relationship. Inconsistencies may lie quietly unresolved and untroublesome to their adherents as balm is offered to the complicated sources of stress in an unequal relationship.

Frederickson's essay (1988) on white slave-owners' beliefs about their slaves in the Old South provides a pointed illustration of the way inconsistent beliefs can cohabit comfortably within a single culture, and, indeed, within a single mind. On the one hand, slave-owners depicted slaves as

---

3. Interestingly, Adorno et al. (1950, 75–76) note an inconsistency between the anti-Semitic images of Jews as both intrusive and seclusive. But they interpret this inconsistency as evidence for the irrational basis for stereotypes: that stereotypes fulfil the warped personality needs of the individual.

Sambo (happy-go-lucky, lazy, content, friendly, warmhearted, childlike), and on the other hand they drew a more menacing image of the black savage (threatening, violence-prone, emotionally volatile, sexually aggressive). The inconsistency in these images apparently mattered little to those who held them, since both images addressed the sensitive spots in their relations with slaves. The former image assuaged slave-owners' half-dormant fears about black resistance to slavery by declaring blacks to be contented, and it also justified slavery by declaring blacks to be in need of white tutelage to take care of them. This all contributed to the general goal of portraying the master-slave relationship in benevolent terms. Nevertheless, residual fears about the dangers posed by having an exploited labor force in residence on the premises of the master's own home surfaced in simultaneous accounts of the black savage. The latter image also worked to justify the institution of slavery by claiming that it protected whites (as well as blacks themselves) from blacks' underlying savagery. Slavery was thus deftly recast from an institution of exploitation into a benign institution that elevated blacks from savagery and gave them a chance to travel the long road to civilization.

If consistency is not the glue that makes certain beliefs stick together, what is? To elucidate the inherently political nature of intergroup belief systems, I now reconsider each of the qualities that have traditionally been identified as the hallmarks of discriminatory intergroup beliefs: that they attribute traits to subordinate groups in ways that are erroneous, derogatory, categorical, and sharply differentiated from the dominant group, and that such beliefs draw an immutable, genetic boundary between the groups. I argue that dominant groups are rarely at liberty to manifest all of these qualities in their intergroup beliefs. As they fashion their stories about the attributes of their own and other groups, they are buffeted by the daily pressures that they encounter in their attempts to govern and explain the relationship from which they benefit.

Science, Folk Knowledge, and Human Error.   The traditional distinction between beliefs that are rational or "scientific" and those that are irrational or false is irrelevant. It requires only cursory reflection to recall the venerable history of science in the propagation of harmful beliefs about various social groups. Consider, for example, the beliefs about women that were vigorously promoted by American physicians and medical researchers in the last quartile of the nineteenth century—that women's reproductive function placed such stringent demands on their energy that attempts on their part to engage in sustained intellectual work would impair their health and weaken or destroy their reproductive capacity (Rosenberg 1982). These ideas, emanating as they did from legitimate scientific sources, were taken very seriously in educational circles. Consider also the beliefs that were espoused at the turn of the century by prominent scientists about head size, brain size, and genetic intelligence among various ethnic groups. Such respected figures in the British scientific community as Francis Galton (Darwin's half-cousin) and Karl Pearson did not hesitate to issue scientific judgments about the relative physical and intellectual capabilities of various ethnicities (Hirsch 1973). More recently, in World War II, Nazi racist ideology in Germany employed scientific delineations of Aryan facial and body features and their relationship to personality attributes; and many scientists, academics, and physicians participated voluntarily and actively in the persecution of Jews, Gypsies, the mentally ill, and gay men, both in delineating "theoretical" materials and enacting policies (see Burleigh and Wippermann 1991, especially pages 51–56, for a chilling account of scientific and medical complicity in Nazi policies of racial purity). Meanwhile, on the other side of the war, psychiatrists in the United States' armed forces actively promoted the definition of homosexuality as a mental illness, and they devoted vigorous effort to the scientific detection of homosexuality, including such procedures as examining recruits' physiques, analyzing their urine, administering psychological tests and "tongue depressor tests," and developing a profile of the homosexual "personality type" [stereotype?] (Berube 1990, 128–174). And in the present era, respected scientific figures such as Arthur Jensen and William Shockley have asserted the scientific basis of their claim that IQ test scores provide a valid measure of intellectual capacity and that various ethnic groups differ in their average, genetically determined, intellectual capacity (for example, see Jensen 1969; Shockley 1971, 1972a, 1972b).

Would Allport's infamous hotel proprietors have been cleansed of impure thoughts if they had consulted any of those scientific studies to get their "facts"? Reflection on the history of scientific thought hardly makes one sanguine about the ability of science to withstand either the foibles of human perception or the political pressures to which all other participants in an unequal intergroup relationship are subject. Folk knowledge may be articulated with less polish but it seems no more vulnerable to the political exigencies of the moment.

Malevolent intergroup beliefs are popularly validated by drawing on sources that carry contemporary credibility as independent fonts of knowledge and morality. The possessors of such beliefs reach for validation from whichever source offers the surest authority. When religion held sway, dominant groups drew on religious precepts and beliefs to validate their claims about ethnic group attributes. For example, the American proslavery apologists of the mid-1800s relied heavily on Christian theology to validate their claims about the attributes and needs of enslaved Africans (see Fitzhugh 1854; Elliott 1860), and Jordan's detailed account of the historical genesis of English attitudes toward Africans in the 1500s and 1600s indicates the central role of religious beliefs in the formulation and justification of those beliefs (Jordan 1968). With the demise of religious authority and the advent of science, the preferred source of validation for intergroup beliefs likewise shifted. Both religion and science have proved to be rich and conveniently malleable sources of validation. Both offer a set of precepts and a method of viewing the world that are authoritative at the same time as they are sufficiently broad and encompassing as to lend themselves conveniently to a variety of interpretations.

More generally, it is misleading to try to evaluate intergroup beliefs by their apparent verity. It is not so much whether beliefs are true or false or contain a "kernel of truth"—it is more a matter of which factors are selected for emphasis and what values are attached to those factors. For example, in contemporary Western achievement-oriented society, it is hardly surprising that intelligence is a highly salient personal attribute and that groups who have experienced more socioeconomic success should find themselves in possession of more of the golden attribute than less "successful" groups. For similar reasons, dominant classes and races have historically had a penchant for describing the lower orders as lazy. Is this attribution made because subordinates have a bad habit of contributing their labor to the dominant group with less alacrity than the dominant group deems appropriate, or because it is convenient to regard one's comparative well-being as a hard-earned success rather than the spoils of a biased reward structure?

Another interesting intergroup comparison that has been reiterated through history is the depiction of subordinates (peasants, lower classes, blacks in slavery, and, in contemporary America, women) as more emotional or volatile than the members of dominant groups. Presumably, those in a position of command find it necessary to curb their emotional expressiveness, since such expressiveness would be more self-revealing and hence make them more vulnerable (Henley and Freeman 1979). For these reasons, it might be advantageous to dominant groups to have subordinates reveal their emotions (thus making them more vulnerable) while controlling their own emotional expressiveness. This is somewhat akin to the power differential between one person being clothed and the other naked. Are there "real," systematic behavioral differences between dominant and subordinate groups in emotionality? Or do groups find different avenues for emotional expression—for example, open expression of anger may be more acceptable for dominant-group members whereas open expression of warmth or laughter or emotional distress may be more acceptable for subordinates? Or do both groups exhibit the same range of emotional expression, but dominant group members are unduly sensitive to "inappropriate" emotional displays from subordinates (such as anger) that are threatening to authority relations between the groups? Or, finally, is the group difference portrayed in order to establish an ideal to guide each group's behavior?

Ultimately, it matters little whether the imputed differences between groups are "real" or false. It is not self-evident how one would "scientifically" measure alleged differences between groups in any case. One would need to incorporate and observe all manifestations of a specific trait (for example, the many forms of "emotionality"). Further, observations of that trait would need to be weighted within the full range of personality attributes on which individuals and groups might potentially be compared. Such a task is not only daunting—it is beside the point. What is more revealing is which traits are popularly selected as salient comparison-points between groups and the way in which those traits are used to delimit the place of each group in society. Attention to these issues can direct us to both the stresses and the moral basis of an unequal relationship.

The Derogation Game: Flattery and Social Control.   The traditional emphasis on the derogation of subordinates is also misleading. Derogation of subordinates has indeed been a frequent recourse of dominant belief systems, but this recourse is not always politically convenient. And even when derogatory distinctions are drawn, they are unlikely to comprise the complete picture that the dominant group draws of subordinates. More likely, invidious distinctions are softened with other distinctions that credit subordinates with the advantage in some positive attributes.

The derogation game is further complicated by two other factors. To begin, certain traits can be portrayed in alternative ways to turn them into assets or detriments, or as impediments or advantages in the fulfillment of particular roles in life. Gloria Steinem's clever article, "If Men Could Menstruate" (1978), illustrates this point well. As Steinem adroitly observes:

> Male human beings have built whole cultures around the idea that penis-envy is "natural" to women—though having such an unprotected organ might be said to make men vulnerable, and the power to give birth makes womb-envy just as logical.
>   In short, the characteristics of the powerful, whatever they may be, are thought to be better than the characteristics of the powerless—and logic has nothing to do with it.

In this spirit, do we depict a group as lazy or as laid-back, as hardworking or uptight, as consistent and rational or rigid and cold, as emotional and temperamental or warm and expressive, as absentminded or flakey?

A second and more elusive point is that traits may sometimes be regarded as an asset when they are possessed by a person from one group but as a detriment when exhibited by someone from the other group. Such conditional value-shifts are to be particularly expected in intergroup relationships that are governed by role segregation. Thus, for example, individual women are praised for being warm and expressive (designated role-appropriate female traits) but criticized for being detached and authoritative (designated male traits). This leaves women who seek positions of authority with an awkward choice: either fulfill the classic female attributes (and thus retain one's feminine identity but fail to command authority), or mimic the classic male traits (and command more authority but incur disapproval as a "cold bitch"). And the unhappy possibility remains that women may not be able to command authority even when they forfeit their "femininity" and mimic male traits: women behaving in this way run the risk of being regarded as such deviant personalities that their claim to authority is undermined.

These considerations suggest that derogation often takes a more roundabout route that camouflages the invidious character of intergroup distinctions and nestles them softly into the pattern of everyday life. When groups are at war, blatant derogation of one's opponents serves a useful political purpose, for the overriding task then is to incite one's own ranks to unbridled animosity. But the maintenance of peaceful expropriation requires attention to the sensibilities of both groups, and the purpose of intergroup attributions then is to weave a case for the modus vivendi that will be persuasive to *all* the participants. Blatant derogation is hardly up to the task.

The overwhelming pressure exerted on dominant groups is to mold the attributed characteristics of each group to be consistent with the organization of everyday life. In this endeavor, it is preferable to weave a story that melts naturally into the setting it seeks to preserve rather than to draw starkly invidious contrasts that might jar the senses. Of course, the superiority of the dominant group must be worked into the story, since the dominant group has an obvious interest in promoting its higher status—but there is no need to overdo it. Indeed, there is every reason to credit subordinates with a superior endowment of certain attributes that are consistent with the tasks or the position assigned to subordinates and inconsistent with the tasks or position claimed by the dominant group for itself.

As with other manifestations of hostility, derogation of subordinates is fraught with risk. The members of groups that benefit from relationships of inequality are aversive to strategies that carry a high risk of alienating the very people whose continued cooperation is essential to the perpetuation of that relationship. In relationships based on role segregation, flagrant derogation is likely to be particularly counterproductive. In such relations, the high level of interpersonal contact across group lines increases the political pressure to sweeten the exchange with a little flattery. As any job supervisor ought to know, the alienating effects of insults are revealed especially swiftly in interpersonal interactions, whereas the impact of the derogation is less immediately and less vividly felt when the object of the derogation is spatially separated from the subject. In any case, the primary need in relations organized around role segregation is to distinguish clearly the attributes of the respective groups to match the segregated tasks to which they have been assigned.

How sweet it is to praise subordinates warmly for their enviable possession of those personality traits to which one's own group makes no claim. Thus, women may be praised copiously for their abilities and achievements as mothers or as family cook or housekeeper. Status distinctions between the two groups can be maintained unobtrusively but securely by assigning greater prestige, power, and material rewards to the tasks for which the dominant group appears more aptly fitted. And besides, what more gratifying way is there to achieve a feeling of comfortable superiority than by making it your business to define the needs and attributes of your subordinates? And then to provide for their defined needs furnishes an incomparable opportunity for amiable condescension. The result: a cozy feeling of magnanimous superiority without a single derogatory stone being cast. How much more subtle and effectual is this strategy than would be the clumsy excesses of direct derogation.

Unequal relations marked by spatial segregation do not pose the compelling interpersonal constraints against direct derogation that exist in relations that have high one-to-one contact across group lines. In addition, spatial segregation affords subordinates more opportunity to distance themselves from the warm clutches of the dominant group and hence to begin to mount more opposition. In such circumstances, not only are there fewer constraints against derogation, but as subordinates introduce some conflict into the relationship the good old paternalistic way of sweet praise for the successful execution of narrowly defined tasks no longer quite works. Besides, what more natural response is there to groups who get uppity than to remind them of their deficiencies? When subordinates challenge arrangements, it becomes necessary to put them in their place—however regretfully. But even here, the dominant group is unlikely to rush headlong into derogation—ways will be found to soften the blow even as it is administered. After all, the dominant group has no interest in heightening hostilities, but rather in putting a stop to them.

The Politics of Setting Groups Apart.   The common assumption has been that harmful intergroup beliefs set groups apart sharply and attribute traits categorically to the subordinate group. As with derogation, this assumption is misleading, and for similar reasons. Although it is important for dominant-group members to maintain group boundaries, there are a variety of ways of accomplishing this end without invoking exaggerated descriptions of the groups. And it is not always opportune to categorize the members of a group flatly or to draw abrupt distinctions between groups in their attributed characteristics. Indeed, as McCauley, Stitt, and Segal (1980) have pointed out, probabilistic attributions should be less subject to everyday disconfirmation than are flatly categorical attributions. This should make probabilistic attributions more resilient than categorical ones, and thus more serviceable politically.

Malevolent intergroup thinking does not express itself irrepressibly in sharp distinctions and categorical attributions. Such attributions will surface only when they meet the demands of the situation—otherwise, popular thinking will travel along other more convenient routes. In order to be politically serviceable, attributions to groups need only to conform to the demands of the relationship and be formulated in a language that is culturally compelling at the moment. This permits intergroup attributions to assume a variety of specific forms.

In relations based on role segregation, there is a pressing need to differentiate the traits of the participating groups sharply: a benign explanation must be established for the inflexible way tasks are allocated to each group. In addition, the high degree of interpersonal contact across group lines that often accompanies role-segregated relationships might pose some risk of muddying group boundaries if the participants were not reminded of the boundary that exists between them on the basis of their group membership. As I outlined above, there is also pressure in such relationships to avoid outright derogatory attributions, and so the combined effect is to encourage evaluatively neutral but sharp distinctions to be invoked between the groups—"we are good at this, you are good at that." Finally, an essential element of the paternalistic ideology that emerges under these conditions is the presumptive definition of the subordinate group's needs—and in order to define the group's needs, one must first define the group's attributes. All these constraints push the dominant group toward categorical descriptions of subordinates and sharp differentiation of subordinates from the dominant group in their personality traits.

In relations based on spatial segregation, a different set of constraints is operative. In such relations, the inequality does not rest on the groups performing categorically different tasks in life that must then be justified. Nor do such relations present much threat of the members of the unequal groups crossing over group lines: the spatial separation of the groups effectively rids the relationship of opportunities for confusion about which individuals are in which group. Instead, strong systems of spatial segregation pose a different problem for the dominant group—how to maintain links between the groups so that the relationship does not rupture completely. Without the existence of a complementary, group-based task structure that instructs the participants in how their group is related to the other, the prevailing risk is that subordinates might drift away from dominant control entirely. There are not daily opportunities for the dominant group to invade the consciousness and emotional vulnerabilities of subordinates, and the latter are thus able to begin formulating an independent interpretation of their experiences. To compound the problem, the spatial separation of the groups reveals the accompanying disparities in status, power, and economic well-being more rudely than when they were nestled in the intimate daily lives of the participants.

Under these constraints, the dominant group would be ill advised to heighten group distinctions by describing subordinates as categorically different. As subordinates decry the group basis of social life, ways must be found to deny and obscure it. And since spatial segregation effectively ensures that the groups will remain separate, there is little risk that the ideological softening of the group basis of social life will result in a wholesale breakdown of group distinctions—especially if the strategy is pursued with care. Under these constraints, it behooves the members of the dominant group to assert the principle of individualism.

As I argued in chapter 2 and chapter 6, individualism provides an effective, principled way of undermining the moral credibility of claims and grievances made on behalf of groups while at the same time reaffirming a competitive norm that works quietly to preserve inequalities. The individualistic goal of equality of opportunity preempts egalitarianism, making outright redistribution of social assets a dead issue and morally endorsing the idea of a competition—in which there will be winners and losers (Schaar 1967). What implications does this have for the shape of intergroup beliefs?

Individualism spawns discomfort both with blanket categorizations of subordinate group members and with attributions that draw impermeable distinctions between groups. Categorical thinking becomes a liability. Instead, the pressures are toward emphasizing individual variation: distinctions between groups must still be made, but they must be couched in the language of individualism. Dominant group members drift toward muted differentiation between groups—individual variation within groups is readily acknowledged at the same time as *average* or *modal* distinctions between groups are reaffirmed. This more probabilistic mode of differentiation is also consistent with scientific methods and lanaguage, and this adds to the credibility of such attributions. Arthur

Jensen's discussion of differences in IQ between ethnic groups (1969) epitomizes this approach. The essential process of group attribution is retained, allowing people to make the critical distinctions they are impelled to make, while seeming like the product of careful, objective observation—what could seem more reasonable or undeniable? Thus, the political dynamics of spatial segregation push dominant-group members more toward the derogation of subordinates, but the same dynamics also force them to retreat from categorical attributions and to edge toward the more guarded delineation of group differences within a framework of individual variability.

Fingering the Causes of Group Differences: The Political Uses of Equivocation.   As with other aspects of intergroup beliefs, folk wisdom about the causes of group differences is likely to veer away from the blatant, the definite, or the unremitting disparagement of subordinates. Several scholars have noted the ambiguity of some popular explanations of group differences and the tendency of many people to espouse seemingly contradictory explanations of group differences (Apostle et al. 1983; Sniderman and Hagen 1985; Kluegel and Smith 1986). Although the classic, dyed-in-the-wool racist has been expected to show himself by a belief in immutable, genetic differences between groups, unequal relations may rarely present circumstances where such a flagrant position is politically opportune. The invocation of cultural differences between groups, although usually treated by scholars as less invidious than the allegation of immutable differences, may actually fulfil the political requirements of group domination much more satisfactorily.

Cultural explanations still lay the blame for group differences squarely in the subordinate camp—such explanations make it clear that subordinates lack the requisite values and attributes for success because their culture fails to instill them. And cultural explanations still assert dominant superiority over subordinates, as well as extolling dominant culture and values as the ideal. Thus, cultural attributions achieve the most important goals of a discriminatory belief, but in a way that has less edge to it than the assertion of genetic differences. Indeed, the reaffirmation of dominant culture and values that is built into such attributions is more likely to entrap subordinates' thinking. The assertion of cultural deficiencies in the subordinate group takes it as a given that the dominant culture is indeed the superior and desirable one. The terms of debate are then set in terms of whether and to what extent subordinate-group members manage to manifest the cultural attributes of the dominant group—and kept safely at bay is the prospect of any direct challenge to the reigning cultural values of the dominant group.

At the same time, cultural attributions sound much more reasoned, reasonable, and open to falsification than does the rigid assertion of genetic differences between groups. Cultural explanations imply that if change occurs in the subordinate group's culture or if some individuals from the subordinate group manifest the appropriate dominant values, it will be noticed and there will then be no further obstacles to success and integration into the dominant stream. And yet the lack of specificity of cultural attributions and their reference to such intangibles as personal motivation and willingness to defer gratification actually renders them immune to any threat of falsification. In addition, such attributions astutely concede the possibility of change in the future while simultaneously making such change seem arduous, remote, and improbable.

Cultural explanations of group differences also offer more versatility of application to different kinds of intergroup relationships, precisely because they are more vague and less flatly disparaging than is the assertion of immutable, biological distinctions. Within a cozy paternalistic framework, the impact of biological attributions is softened: dominant-group members can feel confident about defining the needs of their immutably inferior subordinates and they may magnanimously assume control of a group that has been defined as weaker by nature than themselves. But in a more conflictive political context, the assertion of immutable, genetic differences between groups is too rigid and harsh to carry much political value—such assertions would only serve to heighten hostilities when the primary game-plan for the dominant group is to curb conflict.

Cultural attributions, on the other hand, can be tailored for either paternalistic or conflictive relations. Allusions to cultural deficiencies among subordinates fit comfortably into a paternalistic framework. Such explanations depict subordinates as requiring the benefit of a proper education in the dominant values in order to "civilize" them or resocialize them. With supercilious generosity, the dominant group may then take that burden upon itself. When stripped of a paternalistic support system and thrown into a more conflictive setting, cultural attributions retain their political value, as the dominant group reaches for stories that seem universalistic, open-minded, and reasonable. How can you expect to do as well as us when you don't speak proper English, you don't defer gratification for long-term benefits, you are unlawful, and you fail to maintain a decent family life? Be more like us!

Interestingly, the proslavery tracts of the mid-1800s in the South were as likely to allude to potentially correctable cultural deficiencies in their African-American slaves as to refer to biologically immutable attributes (see, for example, Fitzhugh 1854; Elliott 1860). The attribution of cultural deficiencies to African Americans allowed the defenders of slavery to define a singularly satisfying role for that institution: slavery could be represented as a vehicle for teaching people who were less culturally developed in the ways of Western civilization while protecting them from full participation in a society for which they were deemed as yet culturally ill-equipped. In a similar vein, white South Africans have often been heard in the past few decades arguing that the blacks are "not ready" for democracy and that further time (left gloriously unspecified just how long) would be needed to socialize them into the norms and values of Western democracy.

In short, the assertion of cultural differences between groups offers the dominant group all the advantages of genetic assertions—and more. As with other aspects of their intergroup beliefs, the members of dominant groups may display more political acumen than analysts have credited to them.

The Agility of Intergroup Beliefs.   The most enduring feature of malevolent intergroup beliefs is not their rigidity, negativism, persistence, or consistency—it is their elasticity. Dominant groups gravitate toward this or that explanation of the vital attributes of their own and other groups according to the political exigencies of the moment. Their beliefs must serve a political purpose, and they are continually molded, reformulated, and reshaped to meet that purpose. The particular ideas that have prominence in a given era and the way they are expressed and validated have no intrinsic meaning or significance. They are a patchwork of thoughts, accumulated from an aggregate of people, past and present, who are continually responding to the pressures of the unequal relationship in which they participate.

Various personality traits and values gain or lose salience. Different modes of attribution flourish and decline. Different factors gain or lose credibility in popular explanations of group differences. Alternative sources of validation are called into service. As the members of dominant groups reach for persuasive explanations of their privilege, they glide easily into patterns of thinking that fit the needs of the moment. Dominant groups focus automatically on those personal attributes that seem to bear meaningfully on their relationship with subordinates. They allude to values that strike a cord in themselves and their contemporaries. They express themselves in ways that are persuasive and compelling in the light of contemporaneous pressures. And they draw on sources of validation for their stated beliefs that carry authority in their era.

In this ongoing process, the behavior and reactions of subordinates feed into the ideas mill. Through trial and error, the members of the dominant group learn what kind of stories not only are persuasive within their own ranks but also produce the desired response from subordinates. Thus, the part played by subordinates is not as mere passive victims. Subordinates react in one way or another to the stories they are told, depending upon the opportunities posed by the structure of their daily interaction with the dominant group and the degree to which the dominant group has fashioned a story that fits the contingencies. Of course, subordinates are no more at liberty than are members of the dominant group to be freely expressive in their reactions, but the dominant group has every reason to be finely attuned to their mood. Accordingly, the nature of the subordinate response shapes the unfolding storytelling efforts of dominant-group members.

And because the line of defense is constantly shifting, the amalgamated ideas at any one time contain internal inconsistencies and a deliberate lack of clarity. Precision and consistency are only important if one wishes one's ideas to be potentially falsifiable, but popular intergroup beliefs are of more use to their proponents if they are not falsifiable. Thus, the language of intergroup beliefs will tend more toward the slippery and imprecise than toward the extreme or definite. And the package of beliefs to which people adhere will conveniently contain inconsistencies. Loose-jointed belief systems are less vulnerable to attack, since one component can be given up or reformulated, if politically convenient, without jeopardizing other components that still prove serviceable.

The resultant mix of intergroup beliefs that exists at a particular historical moment has accumulated artlessly from the reactions of the individual participants. And yet, because individuals' perceptions are molded by the pressures that bear on them, the emergent composite proficiently addresses the stress points in the relationship.

DATA: TRAIT ATTRIBUTION TO GROUPS

We may now assess the content and form of the intergroup beliefs that embroider race, gender, and class relations in the United States. The analysis begins by examining the way salient personality traits are ascribed to the unequal groups, for race, gender, and class. In the next section, I take up the issue of how distinctions between these three sets of unequal groups are popularly explained.

To what extent do dominant groups invoke categorical imagery of subordinates and draw large and invidious distinctions between their own group and subordinates? And do subordinates accede to the images, distinctions, and values that are set by the dominant group? If subordinates succeed in breaking away from the dominant story, what kinds of moves do they make and what aspects of the dominant story are most likely to be rejected? As we compare data from the three different intergroup relationships, what do they suggest about how patterns of dominant assertion and subordinate reaction are affected by the structure of contact between groups?

For race, gender, and class, respectively, I assess how key personality traits are attributed to groups. I examine the extent to which cognitive distinctions are drawn between groups in salient personality attributes and the prevalence of categorical imagery in trait attributions to groups. I also evaluate the extent to which cognitive attributions involve the derogation of subordinate groups.

This analysis addresses questions at two levels. First, what is the general character of intergroup trait attributions? Are stereotypes, as traditionally conceived, an important feature of intergroup imagery, or are intergroup perceptions more qualified and malleable? Second, with these broad issues resolved, I turn to the shifting character of intergroup trait attributions as we move from one intergroup relationship to another. How are popular beliefs about the salient attributes of unequal groups molded by the specific exigencies of an intergroup relationship?

Measures

Trait Attributions.   My measure of trait attributions was designed to maximize information on the degree to which people describe their own and other social groups in categorical or qualified terms, while minimizing social desirability and other response-set pressures. During the interview, respondents were handed a booklet with the following introduction by the interviewer:

> There are many groups in America and people have different opinions about what these groups are like. This booklet contains a list of some of the ways groups are described. In each case, you are asked how many people in various groups you would say are like this. The more people you think are like this, the *higher* the number you should choose from the scale at the top of the page—the fewer people you think are like this, the *lower* the number you should choose.
>
> This doesn't need to take much time. We're just interested in your first reaction to these questions.

There were thirty-two questions of the following form in the booklet: "How many (*group*) would you say are (*trait*)?" For example, "How many women would you say are emotional?" Questions were grouped by trait, with the question about the subordinate group preceding the parallel question about the respective dominant group (a given question about blacks preceded the one about whites, and so on). Each trait was introduced by a subheading and a definition of the trait in parentheses. Respondents selected their responses from a 9-point scale extending from left to right and printed at the top of each page of the booklet, and they recorded responses in the box next to each question.[4] The lefthand pole of the scale was labeled 0-NONE, and the righthand pole was labeled 8-ALL. The intervals between were marked 1 to 7; no labels were attached to them. Attention was drawn to the midpoint of the scale by short vertical lines above and below the 4. Respondents were also provided explicitly with a "don't know" response-option: to the right of the scale was written "X = DON'T KNOW."

As with the measurement of intergroup feelings, questions about trait attributions to groups were presented in a self-administered booklet in order to maximize the respondent's sense of privacy and reduce social pressures.[5] The construction of the items also presents no obvious source of bias, since a variety of response options (including "don't know") are presented in an equally balanced way.[6]

The specific traits that were used in the questions were selected for their pertinence to each relationship of inequality and their prominence in research on race, gender, and class stereotypes. At the same time, traits could only be used if they could be comprehended readily and interpreted commonly by a cross-section of the population which includes people with widely varying levels of education and life experiences. In this way, we selected the following traits. First, the trait *INTELLIGENT (or bright)* was included for all three intergroup relationships: in a society obsessed with IQ tests and individual achievement, the trait of intelligence seems centrally significant to popular discussion of any form of inequality. Other traits varied across the three intergroup rela-

4. Brigham (1971) has suggested that respondents be asked to indicate what *percentage* of a group they think has some trait. However, we found in a pretest that this format elicited a large number of response-set answers where respondents repeated the same percentage throughout the booklet. Apparently, the implication of precision in the use of percentages scared some respondents away from the task.

5. To increase the respondents' sense of privacy and to reduce social pressures further, interviewers were instructed to keep busy with other editing tasks while the respondent was completing the booklet and to put the booklet into an envelope as soon as the respondent was finished with it.

6. The administration of the trait-attribution booklet went smoothly. Of the 1,914 people in the sample, only 42 (2.2 percent) did not answer the booklet at all. The median time spent on the booklet was five minutes. No response-set problems were apparent. In a check for blatant response-set, we counted the number of times each numerical response was repeated throughout the booklet. The middle category on the scale (the 4's) was used most often, but even here only 5 respondents used this response exclusively and only 68 respondents used this response twenty-one times or more over the thirty-two questions. The "don't know" response was chosen for all thirty-two items in the booklet by only 20 respondents; 69 respondents gave this response twenty-one or more times. No other points on the scale were used more than twenty-three times by any respondent. We may assume these counts constitute an upper-bound estimate of this kind of response-set since we cannot separate out content-free repetition from "true" responses.

tionships. For race, the two additional traits of *LAZY (or not hardworking)*, and *DEPENDABLE (or reliable)* were included. Both of these traits have figured centrally in whites' beliefs about blacks from slavery to the present. For gender, the two additional traits were *EMOTIONAL (or quick to show feelings)*, and *TALKATIVE (or talk a lot)*. Both of these classically "feminine" traits relate centrally to the expressive role that has been assigned to women. For class, three additional traits were included, all of them relating in some way to the business of individual socioeconomic achievement : *LAZY, THRIFTY (or careful with money)*, and *SELFISH (or concerned only with one's own problems)*. The trait lazy has featured prominently in popular discussions of the poor much as blacks have been labeled with that trait, and a lack of thrift is another deficiency that has been commonly attributed to the poor. The trait selfish was added to the set on class since that attribute has variously been attributed to the working class (selfishly pursuing their own interests rather than the common interest of society) or the upper class (selfishly ignoring the economic plight of the remainder of society).[7]

These measures permit two different kinds of assessments of the way in which people attribute key personality traits to social groups. First, each respondent's attribution of a specific trait to a subordinate group was subtracted from his or her attribution of that trait to the pertinent dominant group. This allows us to assess the degree to which the respondent draws a difference between the two groups being compared, and the resulting difference-scores can range from -8 (all of the subordinate group and none of the dominant group have the trait) through 0 (no difference drawn between the groups) to $+8$ (all of the dominant group and none of the subordinate group have the trait). Second, people's responses to each trait item are examined singly to ascertain the nature of their imagery about each group: of particular interest is the extent to which people describe a group in categorical terms or see internal variation within the group.

Evaluative Overlay of Trait Attributions.   In addition to the trait attributions themselves, I gathered data on the evaluative connotations of the traits involved, with an independent measure of the respondent's evaluation of each of the traits used in the booklet. This information is critical to the assessment and interpretation of trait attributions. The items on the evaluative overlay of the traits were administered thirty-four pages after the beliefs booklet in the interview schedule.

7. Other traits were pretested, but they proved unsatisfactory, either because of poor respondent comprehension (e.g., *logical* for gender) or because they seemed to produce discomfort/evasiveness (e.g., *musical* for race.)

TABLE 8.1.   Mean Evaluations of the Seven Traits Used in the Trait Booklet, in Rank Order from Most Positive to Most Negative.[a]

Trait	Mean	Standard Deviation	Base N
Dependable (*Race*)	8.20	1.16	1881
Intelligent (*Race, Gender, Class*)	7.24	1.56	1884
Thrifty (*Class*)	6.84	1.69	1884
Talkative (*Gender*)	5.64	1.84	1882
Emotional (*Gender*)	4.71	1.61	1886
Lazy (*Race, Class*)	2.31	1.57	1886
Selfish (*Class*)	2.23	1.49	1885

[a] Items scored on a 9-point scale from 1 ("dislike very much") through 5 ("neither like nor dislike") to 9 ("like very much"); don't know's scored 5.

I am going to read a list of things people use to describe each other. For each one, I am going to ask how much you generally like or dislike people like this. Here is a scale that ranges from 1 for "dislike very much" to 9 for "like very much." For each characteristic I read, please tell me the number that comes closest to how you feel.

How much do you like or dislike *lazy* people?

The question was repeated for the remaining six traits used in the trait booklet. The poles of the scale that was shown to respondents were labeled as described above, and the midpoint of the scale (5) was labeled "neither dislike nor like."

The mean evaluations of the traits are presented in table 8.1. The traits vary considerably in how they are valued, with dependability being rated considerably more positively than any other trait, and selfishness and laziness being valued considerably more negatively than any other trait. Although the data are not presented here, these traits are valued in much the same way by different groups and by people who attribute the traits differently to the pertinent groups. These data highlight the values that are at stake, on both sides of the relationship, when people are comparing different types of dominant and subordinate groups. Race comparisons carry strong value-connotations, since they involve the two most highly valued traits (dependable and intelligent) and one very negatively valued trait (lazy). Similarly, class comparisons involve two positively valued traits (intelligent and thrifty) and the two most negatively valued traits (lazy and selfish). Gender comparisons involve one positively valued trait (intelligent) and two fairly neutral traits (talkative and emotional).

Results

Tables 8.2, 8.4, and 8.6 report the cognitive distinctions that are drawn between groups, for race, gender, and class, respectively. Each table gives the percentage distributions, by group, of the trait difference-scores in collapsed form, as well as the mean trait difference-scores (based on the full scales). For race and gender, the scales are collapsed into 7 points, whereas for class they are collapsed into 3 points (to spare the reader's eyesight). Tables 8.3, 8.5, and 8.7 report the manner in which the traits are assigned to each group for race, gender, and class, respectively. These tables give the percentage distribution and mean score for each trait as it is attributed to each group, by group. For class, the data are again presented in reduced form because of space limitations: for class, only the tails of the distributions are presented, along with the mean scores for the full scale.

A quick perusal of the data reveals two general points. First, it is rare for large trait distinctions to be drawn between groups, in any of the three intergroup relationships. Instead, people who differentiate between groups in salient personality traits tend to portray those distinctions as small or moderate. Second, in the same vein, categorical images of groups are also far from commonplace. Although categorical descriptions of groups are more in evidence than the attribution of large differences between groups, there is considerably more popular recognition of internal variation within groups than the literature on stereotypes might lead us to expect. Thus, the beliefs that accompany these three relationships of inequality do not seem to be scored very deeply by two of the most central conceptual elements of stereotypical thinking—the attribution of extreme differences between groups and the categorical description of groups.

What, then, are the characteristics of the intergroup trait attributions that accompany race, gender, and class relations? I turn to each of those now, in turn, before assessing the general patterns that are suggested by these data.

Race. Two main factors distinguish the trait attributions that accompany racial inequality. First, it is in the race context that the classic elements of stereotypical attributions are least in evidence. Trait distinctions are less likely to be made between racial groups than between gender groups or classes, imputed trait distinctions are the smallest, and categorical imagery is the least likely to be invoked to describe either racial group. Second, the race context is also marked by more disagreement between groups than one finds for either gender or class in the way traits are attributed to the pertinent groups. Whites tend to draw small to substantial, but invidious, distinctions between the races, whereas blacks tend either to deny that there are differences between them or to make counterclaims that blacks have a superior trait endowment to whites. The combination of clear disagreement between the races and restrained

TABLE 8.2. Perception of Differences between Blacks and Whites in Personality Traits: Percentage Distributions and Means by Race.*

	Trait Difference Score	Intelligent		Dependable		Lazy	
		Whites	Blacks	Whites	Blacks	Whites	Blacks
More Blacks	−8/−5	0.0	2.4	0.1	0.6	2.1	0.0
Have Trait	−4/−2	0.1	8.5	0.5	13.3	20.3	3.8
	−1	0.6	4.8	1.7	10.3	14.9	7.6
	0	42.4	66.1	46.9	55.8	49.7	63.3
	+1	20.0	13.3	14.7	12.7	6.6	12.0
More Whites	+2/+4	35.1	4.8	33.4	6.7	6.3	10.8
Have Trait	+5/+8	1.8	0.0	2.8	0.6	0.1	2.5
	Base N	1417	165	1430	165	1406	158
	Mean Score	1.19†	−.17	1.14†	−.16	−.56†	.38†

* Differences between groups in percentage distributions are statistically significant (p < .01).
† Mean score is significantly different from zero, p < .05.

TABLE 8.3. Attribution of Personality Traits to Blacks and Whites: Percentage Distributions and Means for Whites and Blacks.

Trait Item Score	Blacks Intelligent*		Whites Intelligent*		Blacks Dependable*		Whites Dependable*		Blacks Lazy		Whites Lazy*	
	Whites	Blacks	Whites	Blacks	Whites	Blacks	Whites	Blacks	Whites	Blacks	Whites	Blacks
None	0.5%	0.0%	0.0%	0.5%	1.3%	0.5%	0.1%	1.1%	0.3%	1.6%	0.4%	0.0%
1	1.4	0.0	0.0	1.1	3.2	0.0	0.1	2.6	1.4	1.1	1.8	2.1
2	7.0	0.5	0.7	0.5	9.6	3.2	1.1	2.1	6.8	8.0	9.7	5.3
3	16.2	1.6	1.8	2.7	15.6	6.8	3.9	7.9	13.5	14.4	16.7	10.2
4	33.9	18.3	23.5	18.2	35.4	25.3	32.6	21.6	31.0	32.6	39.5	29.4
5	14.2	10.8	22.2	10.2	12.1	15.8	21.4	15.8	12.0	13.4	13.2	15.0
6	11.2	28.5	28.0	26.2	9.1	20.5	25.2	21.1	12.3	8.0	7.0	11.2
7	2.9	21.0	12.5	21.4	2.4	8.9	7.4	7.4	7.6	6.4	2.1	9.6
All	1.6	9.7	3.3	8.0	0.8	7.9	2.3	7.4	3.9	2.7	0.4	2.7
Don't Know	11.0	9.7	8.0	11.2	10.6	11.1	6.0	13.2	11.2	11.8	9.2	14.4
Base N	1594	186	1598	187	1601	190	1605	190	1596	187	1595	187
Mean Score[a]	4.17	5.85	5.37	5.69	3.89	5.12	5.03	4.98	4.48	4.22	3.91	4.58

* Difference between groups in percentage distributions (with Don't Know's excluded) is statistically significant (p < .01).
[a] Means calculated with Don't Know's excluded. Scale ranges from 0–8.

cognitive expressions on the part of whites suggests that as contending groups diverge in their cognitive attributions, dominant-group members become self-conscious and cautious about the way the subordinate group is portrayed.

Whites are more likely than blacks to think there are trait differences between the races, and whites who see race differences generally say there are fewer intelligent or dependable blacks and more lazy blacks. Between 37 and 57 percent of whites make these invidious distinctions between the races. Interestingly, whites indicate greater reluctance to distinguish blacks on the negative trait lazy (37 percent) than to credit whites with the positive traits intelligent and dependable (57 and 51 percent, respectively). It may seem less blatantly inflammatory to give one's own group the advantage in positive attributes than to depict the other group as prevailing in negative traits. In keeping with that cognitive caution, fewer than 3 percent of whites draw extreme differences between the races (that is, differences of 5 to 8 points), although the majority of whites who draw racial distinctions do describe those differences as substantial—that is, as 2 to 4 points apart. And as further evidence of caution in whites' racial trait attributions, virtually all whites refrain from describing blacks categorically: fewer than 4 percent of whites say that all blacks are lazy or that no blacks are intelligent or dependable. Trait attributions tend to be anchored around or above the middle of the scale (with the negative trait lazy being attributed to fewer members of both groups than are the two positive traits), indicating that whites are careful to acknowledge internal variation within each group, even if they draw distinctions between them.

The racial trait attributions of blacks differ from those made by whites in three main respects. First, blacks are less likely to believe there are any differences between the races in their personality traits: between 56 and 66 percent of blacks assert that there are no differences between the races in intelligence, dependability, or laziness (as compared with 42 to 50 percent of whites who say there are no racial differences in those traits). Second, when blacks do see racial differences in personality traits, they are somewhat more likely to assert opposite differences from those claimed by whites than to concur with the views of whites. This tendency is most pronounced with the negative trait lazy, where blacks are about twice as likely to assert that laziness is more characteristic of whites as they are to concur with the more common white claim that laziness is more characteristic of blacks. With the two positive traits, blacks are about equally likely to assert differences that favor their own group as they are to concur with the prevailing white portrayal of racial differences, but blacks whose perceptions favor their own group tend to assert larger differences between the groups. The net result is that only 11 to 20 percent of blacks accept the invidious trait distinctions that are drawn by 37 to 57 percent of whites. Third, blacks do not avoid categorical or near-categorical descriptions of either racial group quite as assiduously as do whites. Almost 10 percent of blacks categorically attribute the two positive traits, intelligent and dependable, to all whites and blacks; another 21 percent claim that almost all whites and blacks are intelligent and about another 8 percent say that almost all whites and blacks are dependable. Thus, blacks seem less aversive to making sweeping trait

TABLE 8.4.   Perception of Differences between Women and Men in Personality Traits: Percentage Distributions and Means, by Gender.

Trait Difference Score		Emotional		Talkative		Intelligent	
		Men	Women	Men	Women	Men	Women
More Women	−8/−5	2.4	4.0	1.3	1.7	0.0	0.1
Have Trait	−4/−2	49.1	48.9	36.2	30.1	2.0	3.0
	−1	21.8	19.8	18.3	18.9	8.8	7.8
	0	21.5	22.7	34.9	39.5	72.3	68.8
	+1	3.5	2.5	5.3	5.2	12.3	13.9
More Men	+2/+4	1.6	2.1	3.7	4.5	4.5	6.1
Have Trait	+5/+8	0.0	0.0	0.3	0.1	0.0	0.3
	Base N	743	1018	759	1041	737	993
	Mean Score	−1.53*	−1.62*	−1.05*	−.91*	.09*	.14*

* Mean score is significantly different from zero, $p < .05$.

attributions to racial groups, but these sweeping attributions are as likely to be made to either racial group.[8]

Overall, blacks diverge less sharply from whites in their racial trait attributions than they do in their intergroup feelings or in their racial policy goals, but the differences between the trait attributions made by the two groups are still pronounced. Only 11 to 20 percent of blacks accept the invidious racial trait distinctions that are drawn by 37 to 57 percent of whites. Between 56 and 66 percent of blacks deny that there are any trait distinctions between the races, and another 16 to 25 percent make the more assertive claim that the trait distinctions favor blacks rather than whites. Faced with this opposition, whites appear to proceed cautiously rather than to launch into more extreme claims. Whites avoid categorical attributions or the assertion of extreme differences, and yet a sizable proportion of whites claim that there are small-to-substantial differences between the races in their endowment with key personal traits. Thus, whites respond to blacks' challenge by phrasing their comparisons of the two groups with care, moderating their claims of invidious intergroup distinctions with acknowledgments of *intra*group variation. In this way, whites are able to interject qualifications without yielding their claims of critical, invidious distinctions between the groups.

Gender.   Trait attributions to gender groups contrast with racial trait attributions in four main ways. First, women and men do not differ from each other in their trait attributions to gender groups. Second, trait distinctions between the sexes are made more frequently, and these

8. The tendency is somewhat more pronounced among black women than among black men. Indeed, black women are more likely than black men to make categorical attributions to all race, gender, and class groups.

TABLE 8.5.   Attribution of Personality Traits to Women and Men:
Percentage Distributions and Means for Men and Women.

Trait Item Score	Women Emotional		Men Emotional		Women Talkative		Men Talkative*		Women Intelligent*		Men Intelligent	
	Men	Women	Men	Women	Men	Women	Men	Women	Men	Women	Men	Women
None	0.0%	0.1%	0.1%	0.6%	0.1%	0.2%	0.3%	0.5%	0.0%	0.1%	0.0%	0.1%
1	0.3	0.1	1.2	1.2	0.3	0.2	0.5	0.5	0.0	0.2	0.0	0.1
2	1.2	0.6	5.0	4.2	1.4	0.7	2.8	2.7	0.6	0.8	0.3	0.5
3	2.2	1.7	10.6	11.0	3.5	2.5	10.6	6.7	3.8	1.4	2.1	1.8
4	11.5	11.2	31.9	31.3	24.0	20.7	40.6	36.2	26.0	22.7	25.1	21.6
5	10.2	10.4	22.4	20.9	12.7	14.0	20.0	18.5	19.6	20.9	20.0	17.4
6	24.4	24.3	15.0	15.5	24.8	23.4	14.0	15.2	28.7	29.1	30.9	29.3
7	31.2	29.6	5.4	6.3	16.5	18.2	5.6	8.4	11.8	13.0	13.1	16.8
All	14.5	17.8	3.7	3.7	13.8	17.3	2.9	7.9	4.0	4.5	3.3	5.3
Don't Know	4.6	4.4	4.7	5.2	2.9	2.8	2.7	3.3	5.4	7.3	5.3	7.2
Base N	782	1,079	781	1,077	782	1,081	784	1,082	780	1,074	780	1,075
Mean Score[a]	6.15	6.25	4.62	4.63	5.64	5.84	4.59	4.94	5.30	5.42	5.39	5.55

* Difference between groups in percentage distributions (with Don't Know's excluded) is statistically significant (p < .05).
[a] Means calculated with Don't Know's excluded. Scale ranges from 0–8.

distinctions also tend to be larger than those made between the races. Third, women are considerably more likely to be described categorically than are blacks. And fourth, although both men and women differentiate between gender groups fairly sharply, these attributions do not carry invidious overtones.

Table 8.4 shows that few people think there is any difference between the sexes in intelligence: about 70 percent of both women and men see no difference here (roughly comparable to the percentage of blacks who see no race difference in that trait). However, 50 to 60 percent of both sexes think there are more talkative women than men, and over 70 percent believe there are more emotional women. Although extremely large distinctions (of 5 to 8 points) are as uncommon between the sexes as between the races, moderately large differences (of 2 to 4 points) are seen by about one-third of both sexes in the trait talkative and by about one-half of both sexes in the trait emotional. These trait distinctions are, respectively, as large as and larger than the race differences seen by whites alone in the most differentiating race traits, dependable and intelligent.

The data in table 8.5 indicate that the images of each gender group that underlie the imputed distinctions between them are that men vary a good deal in their personal attributes whereas women tend to be fairly homogeneous. The trait intelligent elicits few categorical attributions, and between half and three-quarters of both sexes are commonly described as intelligent. But the traits emotional and talkative are attributed to all women by about one in six respondents. And about one-third of both sexes believe that all or almost all women are talkative (scale values of 7 and 8), and almost one-half of both sexes make such sweeping statements about the proportion of women who are emotional. Consistent with these results is the low amount of uncertainty ("don't know's") expressed by either men or women when they are asked to describe the sexes—lower than one finds for either race or class attributions.[9] All indications suggest that both men and women feel a high degree of confidence in describing the trait attributes of gender groups.

The trait distinctions that are so sharply drawn between women and men do not carry invidious value implications. The mean evaluations of the traits emotional and talkative hover around the neutral point (see table 8.1), and most respondents who draw a distinction between the sexes on these traits are implying an evaluation of women that is mildly negative, neutral, or mildly positive (data not shown here). Differentiation between the sexes in the trait intelligent does carry more invidious implications, but only a small minority draw such a distinction. In the paternalistic setting of gender relations, the definition of large, neutrally valued distinctions between the groups in personal attributes serves both to validate the group basis of social life and to neutralize it: the features that are alleged to distinguish the two groups are presented in a positive, rather than a negative, light. The success of this presentation can be gauged by its near-consensual endorsement by both groups.

Class.   Trait attributions to social classes involve a more complex set of comparisons, since there are five, rather than just two, groups. To sharpen the focus, table 8.6 presents only those trait comparisons made between one's own class and other classes, rather than all possible class comparisons. Table 8.7 presents the images that are held of each class by the members of each class. These data reveal several features in the way people portray the salient personality attributes of different social classes.

First, trait distinctions are drawn frequently between classes, especially between classes from opposite ends of the continuum, where distinctions are sometimes larger and more frequent than between race or gender groups. As with interclass feelings, the frequency and size of distinctions that are drawn between classes increase incrementally as one moves from adjacent classes to classes that are further apart. Both the direction and the evaluative connotations of these attributed trait distinctions vary. Second, categorical attributions are also made relatively frequently, although it is the two *highest* social classes that are most likely to be described

9. Uncertainty about how to describe a group might be seen as diametrically opposed to the categorical description of a group. Indeed, certainty is sometimes explicitly included in definitions of a stereotype (Lippmann 1922; Richter 1956; Harding et al. 1969).

TABLE 8.6. Perception of Differences between Own and Other Classes in Personality Traits: Percentage Distributions and Means, by Subjective Social Class.*

Trait Difference Score	Upper-Middle Class				Middle Class				Working Class				Poor			
	vs. Upper	vs. Middle	vs. Working	vs. Poor	vs. Upper	vs. Upper-Middle	vs. Working	vs. Poor	vs. Upper	vs. Upper-Middle	vs. Middle	vs. Poor	vs. Upper	vs. Upper-Middle	vs. Middle	vs. Working
Intelligent																
Lower Class More	11.3%	4.2%	2.1%	2.9%	6.5%	4.5%	5.2%	3.4%	9.3%	7.7%	9.2%	6.5%	12.6%	13.6%	13.4%	9.9%
No Difference	57.7	45.1	18.2	12.9	33.7	46.5	39.5	19.7	21.0	26.3	48.6	29.2	15.3	16.4	24.1	31.5
Higher Class More	31.0	50.7	79.7	84.2	59.8	49.0	55.3	76.8	69.7	66.0	42.2	64.3	72.1	70.0	62.5	58.6
Mean Score[a]	.27†	.63†	1.53†	2.39†	.90†	.56†	.68†	1.70†	1.30†	1.00†	.44†	1.11†	1.58†	1.40†	1.14†	.85†
Selfish																
Lower Class More	9.0%	17.8%	19.1%	20.6%	13.9%	12.6%	13.5%	16.9%	10.2%	10.4%	10.5%	17.8%	20.4%	19.1%	23.4%	20.0%
No Difference	59.7	45.9	34.4	31.7	35.3	42.8	52.6	33.4	25.0	27.7	46.0	40.1	27.8	28.2	27.9	34.8
Higher Class More	31.3	36.3	46.6	47.6	50.8	44.7	33.8	49.7	64.8	61.9	43.5	42.1	51.9	52.7	48.6	45.2
Mean Score[a]	.28†	.22†	.53†	.89†	.84†	.50†	.26†	.70†	1.59†	1.11†	.51†	.41†	1.27†	1.13†	.73†	.35†
Thrifty																
Lower Class More	36.6%	30.8%	33.8%	26.2%	49.4%	42.5%	25.9%	23.6%	46.3%	47.1%	39.0%	19.9%	34.6%	29.9%	28.1%	23.9%
No Difference	45.1	35.0	20.4	12.8	18.4	29.1	36.2	16.2	14.1	15.4	35.1	25.0	15.9	15.0	19.3	24.8
Higher Class More	18.3	34.3	45.8	61.8	32.2	28.4	37.9	60.2	39.6	37.5	25.9	55.1	49.5	55.1	52.6	51.3
Mean Score[a]	-.35†	.08†	.19	1.24†	-.55†	-.34†	.17†	1.06†	-.46†	-.41†	-.31†	.93†	.55	.76†	.59†	.64†
Lazy																
Lower Class More	18.8%	30.2%	37.7%	50.4%	28.1%	22.6%	26.0%	47.9%	28.0%	25.9%	19.9%	49.6%	34.6%	35.8%	37.1%	39.4%
No Difference	51.4	46.0	35.5	28.1	36.9	51.0	47.1	25.1	29.7	34.5	50.6	26.9	22.1	21.7	22.9	28.4
Higher Class More	29.7	23.7	26.8	21.5	35.0	26.4	26.9	27.0	42.3	39.6	29.4	23.5	43.3	42.5	40.0	32.1
Mean Score[a]	.17	-.09	-.18	-1.03†	.24†	.12†	.03	-.54†	.48†	.35†	.16†	-.69†	.34	.02	.03	-.31
Base N (ranges)	134–142	135–144	131–143	126–141	717–755	725–764	724–773	700–753	599–624	603–637	611–656	606–637	101–111	106–110	105–114	109–117

[a] Scale ranges from −8 (lower class more) through 0 (no difference) to +8 (higher class more). Don't know's and missing data excluded.

† Mean score is significantly different from zero, p < .05.

* Differences between reciprocal pairs of classes in percentage distributions are statistically significant (p < .05), except for the following cases: in INTELLIGENT, Upper-Middle vs. Middle, Working vs. Poor; in SELFISH, Upper-Middle vs. Middle, Upper-Middle vs. Poor, Middle vs. Poor, Working vs. Poor; in THRIFTY, Upper-Middle vs. Poor, Middle vs. Working vs. Poor; in LAZY, Upper-Middle vs. Middle, Working vs. Poor.

TABLE 8.7.   Attribution of Personality Traits to the Five Social Classes: Tails of Percentage Distributions and Mean Scores for the Five Subjective Social Classes.

Intelligent

Trait Item Score	Upper Intelligent*				Upper-Middle Intelligent*				Middle Intelligent*				Working Intelligent*				Poor Intelligent*			
	UpMid[a]	Middle[b]	Work[c]	Poor[d]	UpMid	Middle	Work	Poor	UpMid	Middle	Work	Poor	UpMid	Middle	Work	Poor	UpMid	Middle	Work	Poor
None/1	0.6%	0.0%	0.6%	1.5%	0.6%	0.1%	0.3%	0.7%	0.0%	0.0%	0.0%	0.0%	0.0%	0.2%	0.4%	1.5%	7.7%	5.3%	5.3%	4.4%
All/7	42.9	46.2	50.1	50.0	27.2	31.2	38.1	45.5	12.3	15.4	17.4	28.7	5.2	8.4	14.1	27.4	2.6	4.8	7.2	14.0
D.K.	6.5	6.8	8.5	13.2	5.2	5.5	7.0	12.7	5.8	5.9	6.2	14.0	6.5	6.9	5.0	14.1	9.0	9.7	8.5	15.4
Mean score[e]	6.17	6.26	6.37	6.25	5.86	5.92	6.06	6.11	5.26	5.37	5.49	5.79	4.40	4.70	5.09	5.53	3.55	3.68	3.96	4.64

Selfish

Trait Item Score	Upper Selfish*				Upper-Middle Selfish*				Middle Selfish*				Working Selfish				Poor Selfish*			
	UpMid	Middle	Work	Poor	UpMid	Middle	Work	Poor	UpMid	Middle	Work	Poor	UpMid	Middle	Work	Poor	UpMid	Middle	Work	Poor
None/1	1.3	3.1	2.9	8.1	0.6	3.0	2.3	6.7	0.6	3.8	2.2	5.1	1.3	4.6	5.3	5.9	3.3	12.2	14.1	13.2
All/7	22.7	21.8	32.5	26.7	13.6	10.3	16.1	23.0	8.4	4.7	7.5	13.2	5.8	3.8	4.8	9.6	7.2	5.4	6.2	11.8
D.K.	13.0	11.2	10.6	18.5	11.7	10.1	10.3	17.0	11.7	9.6	10.1	16.2	13.6	9.9	8.1	14.7	17.0	12.3	10.9	12.5
Mean score[e]	4.95	4.91	5.40	4.99	4.68	4.56	4.90	4.80	4.44	4.07	4.30	4.39	4.15	3.82	3.79	3.88	3.81	3.38	3.39	3.58

Thrifty

Trait Item Score	Upper Thrifty*				Upper-Middle Thrifty*				Middle Thrifty*				Working Thrifty*				Poor Thrifty*			
	UpMid	Middle	Work	Poor	UpMid	Middle	Work	Poor	UpMid	Middle	Work	Poor	UpMid	Middle	Work	Poor	UpMid	Middle	Work	Poor
None/1	7.7	9.6	11.2	10.9	0.6	3.1	3.2	2.2	0.6	0.6	1.2	0.7	0.6	0.9	0.9	2.2	9.6	8.2	8.0	7.4
All/7	19.9	23.8	27.0	37.2	18.6	15.4	18.0	30.9	9.0	13.8	12.0	23.5	9.6	12.6	19.5	28.5	7.1	9.7	13.1	26.5
D.K.	8.3	6.6	7.6	17.5	7.1	5.5	5.7	16.2	7.1	3.8	2.9	11.8	7.1	4.3	2.2	8.8	8.3	6.4	5.6	9.6
Mean score[e]	4.55	4.43	4.66	5.23	4.90	4.63	4.71	5.29	4.83	4.98	4.81	5.22	4.70	4.81	5.13	5.33	3.67	3.93	4.23	4.76

Lazy

Trait Item Score	Upper Lazy*				Upper-Middle Lazy*				Middle Lazy*				Working Lazy*				Poor Lazy			
	UpMid	Middle	Work	Poor	UpMid	Middle	Work	Poor	UpMid	Middle	Work	Poor	UpMid	Middle	Work	Poor	UpMid	Middle	Work	Poor
None/1	11.7	10.2	10.1	9.0	8.4	5.6	7.6	8.9	3.2	5.3	6.8	6.7	1.9	5.6	9.5	11.8	3.2	3.8	5.4	6.7
All/7	7.1	10.2	13.2	16.4	3.9	5.7	8.1	8.9	1.3	3.0	3.7	6.7	0.6	1.1	5.7	9.6	13.5	9.0	13.2	11.1
D.K.	10.4	8.9	10.0	20.9	9.1	8.4	8.4	19.3	8.4	5.7	6.3	20.0	9.0	5.9	4.5	16.2	11.0	8.1	7.0	14.8
Mean score[e]	3.62	3.84	4.05	4.32	3.46	3.73	3.92	4.05	3.58	3.61	3.75	4.03	3.68	3.57	3.57	3.75	4.43	4.15	4.29	4.03

[a] Upper-middle class N ranges from 153–156   [b] Middle class N ranges from 805–815   [c] Working class N ranges from 678–683   [d] Poor N ranges from 134–137
[e] Means calculated with Don't Know's excluded. Scale ranges from 1–7.
* Differences by class in percentage distributions (with Don't Know's excluded) are statistically significant ($p < .05$).

categorically. The upper class is described categorically about as frequently as are women, with the upper-middle class not too far behind. Further, the class context is unique in that categorical exclusions of traits from a class (for example, "no poor people are selfish") are also made by more than a handful of respondents. Third, the amount of disagreement among the social classes is not pronounced, although it is more in evidence than it is between gender groups. Across all classes, the same general patterns of trait attributions are made, but there is some tendency for distinctions to be asserted more frequently in the class that is reflected favorably in the comparison and less frequently in the class that is reflected unfavorably.

Americans commonly believe that both intelligence and selfishness are found increasingly with ascending social class. Differences in intelligence are attributed more frequently than are differences in selfishness, but note that although the former belief puts higher classes in a more favorable light the latter belief puts lower classes in a more favorable light. Class distinctions in the traits thrifty and lazy are just as likely to be seen as in the traits intelligent and selfish, but there is less convergence within each class as to the direction of these differences. The prevailing attributions in each class are that the poor have the most lazy and the fewest thrifty people, with the *upper* class ranked next, followed by the upper-middle class and then the other two classes. These two trait attributions both cast the poor in a more negative light than other classes. At the same time, they ironically characterize the upper class almost as negatively as the poor, whereas the working class and middle class are portrayed in a relatively positive light.

Classes are portrayed as differing sharply in intelligence. Indeed, differences in this trait are drawn more frequently between classes from opposite ends of the continuum than race differences in this trait are asserted by whites. With decreasing social class, there is a gradual drop in the percentage of people subscribing to this belief, but even in the poor and working class, the ascription of greater intelligence to higher classes is widespread. Thus, in the upper-middle class, 84 percent assert that their class has more intelligent people than does the poor and 80 percent compare their class as favorably vis-à-vis the working class. Among the poor, 70 percent concur with the upper-middle class's assertion of the difference between them in intelligence, and 66 percent of the working class concur with the upper-middle class's asserted superiority over them in intelligence. The negative trait selfish is also attributed more frequently to higher classes (although not as overwhelmingly as is intelligence)—this attribution reflects less well on higher classes, and in this case it is the higher classes that tend to minimize the distinction.

There is considerably less agreement, both within and across classes, about which classes are more characterized by the traits thrifty and lazy. Again, the clearest distinction is made between the poor and other classes: in comparisons between the other classes, people from each class are almost as likely to see differences in one direction as in the other, although there is a slight tendency for self-flattering attributions to prevail and for attributions that reflect negatively on one's own class to be minimized. In the upper-middle, middle, and working classes, the prevailing assertions are that the poor have the most lazy and the fewest thrifty people, with the upper class ranked next. In addition, there is a slight tendency for people in these three classes to see their own class as having the fewest lazy and the most thrifty people. Note that, in comparing their own class with the poor, about one-half of the people in each of these three classes assert that the poor are more likely to be lazy—considerably more than the percentage of whites (37 percent) who distinguish blacks from whites on this negative trait. Among the poor, there tends to be concurrence with the view that higher social classes have more thrifty people than does their own class (although with less vigor than this distinction is asserted by higher classes), but the poor tend to reject the portrayal of their class as the most characterized by laziness. Although most poor people do see a difference between their own class and higher classes in laziness, they are divided almost evenly about whether it is the higher class or their own that is more characterized by this negative trait.

Table 8.6 does not display data on the size of asserted class differences, but large distinctions are drawn more frequently between the classes than between racial or gender groups (and this is reflected in the size of the mean difference-scores). Indeed, although extremely large distinctions (± 5 to ± 8) are made infrequently, they are made more often than with race or gender, and moderate-to-substantial distinctions (± 2 to ± 4) are more likely to be seen between classes from opposite ends of the continuum than between the races or sexes. For example, when comparing the poor and the upper class on the trait intelligent, more than 12 percent of each class see extreme differences, and as many as 48 to 59 percent of each class see moderate-to-substantial differences (data not presented here).

Table 8.7 indicates that the images of each class that underlie these trait distinctions include a relatively high incidence of categorization. It is the upper and upper-middle classes that are most likely to be described categorically. The upper class is described categorically about as often as are women, with the upper-middle class not far behind. Poor people are slightly more likely than people from other classes to attribute traits categorically to *all* classes (including their own), especially positive traits. As with blacks' images of blacks and whites, poor people's categorical descriptions of classes do not seem to be part of an attempt to differentiate between them. And the stronger proclivity of the poor to make categorical trait attributions is offset by their considerably higher expression of uncertainty. When asked to describe any class, about one-tenth to one-fifth of the poor say "don't know," whereas people from other classes give this response with approximately the same infrequency as in the race context.

Intelligence is thought to characterize all or almost all of the upper class by fully one-half of the poor and working class and by almost as many people from the middle and upper-middle classes. The other positive trait (thrifty) is attributed categorically to the upper class by over one-third of the poor, whereas the negative traits selfish and lazy are attributed categorically to the upper class by about one-quarter and one-sixth of the poor, respectively.[10] The proportion of the poor making such sweeping attributions to the upper-middle class is only somewhat lower. People from other social classes are as likely or almost as likely as the poor to attribute these traits to all or almost all of the upper class,[11] but considerably less likely to make such sweeping attributions to the upper-middle class. A markedly smaller proportion of people from any class perceives the other three classes in categorical terms. In this regard, note that the negative trait lazy is attributed categorically or near-categorically to the poor with about the same infrequency as it is attributed in this way to blacks (between 9 and 14 percent of each class). The positive trait intelligent, however, is attributed categorically to the upper class much more often than it is attributed categorically to whites (by about one-half of each class, compared with about 16 percent of whites and 29 percent of blacks who attribute that trait categorically to whites).

General Patterns.   Portrayals of the trait attributes of unequal groups seem to be characterized more by moderation and caution than by unrestrained assertions. Extreme trait distinctions between groups are made by only a small minority of respondents, and categorical attributions to specific groups are also the exception rather than the rule. In addition, these assertions do not always carry value connotations that are either strong or negative toward the subordinate group. Indeed, the size of the distinctions that are made and their positive or negative value connotations vary independently of one another. Although the gender context is marked by the relatively frequent perception of substantial trait distinc-

10. Discussion here is based on belief-scale values of 7 and 8. As with race and gender, "pure" categorical thinking (scale values of 8 or 0) is generally less prevalent than "almost all" or "almost none" statements (scale values of 7 or 1).

11. In fact, people from all classes are about equally likely to attribute the two traits intelligent and selfish to the upper class.

tions between the sexes, these distinctions rarely imply a negative evaluation of women. In the race context, the perception of trait distinctions is considerably less frequent and imputed distinctions tend to be moderate rather than extreme—but the evaluative connotations of the distinctions that are made by whites are sharply negative toward blacks. Trait differences among the social classes are seen frequently and they are often substantial distinctions, but the evaluative connotations are mixed rather than uniformly positive or negative. Thus, intergroup attributions do not seem to conform to the specifications of the stereotype concept in any of these three intergroup relationships.

In addition, none of the intergroup relationships is marked by dramatic disagreement between groups about their distinguishing characteristics. In no case is the rift between groups such as to produce radically different portrayals. Subordinate groups do appear to find it relatively difficult to challenge dominant group definitions of the distinctions between them. It seems that dominant groups are generally quite successful (although to varying degrees) in defining the way in which the contending groups are distinguished in salient personal attributes.

The infusion of subordinate thinking with dominant beliefs is most successful in gender relations. An amicable consensus appears to envelop gender groups about their defining characteristics. Men assert that there are substantial but evaluatively neutral differences between the sexes, and women do not disagree. A challenge to dominant assertions is most likely to be made in the race context. Most blacks deny white assertions about black inferiority and assert their equality with (and sometimes their own superiority to) whites. Faced with this challenge, whites become skittish about making dramatic assertions of racial distinctions: some whites disclaim racial differences altogether, and the majority who do draw distinctions do so with care. In class relations, substantial personality-trait distinctions are widely perceived and they more often favor higher classes over lower ones. These differences tend to be minimized somewhat by lower social classes or even refuted with minor competing claims of their own superior endowment, but the dissent is modest.

These differences across the three intergroup relationships reveal the variability and the malleability of stories that are woven to characterize unequal groups. In the sticky web of paternalism that envelops gender relations, men praise women for their distinctive personality attributes and women graciously accept the confining compliments. In the more conflictive political environment of race relations, whites have met the challenge from blacks by retreating from sharply categorical distinctions as they attempt to preserve a blurred definition of group attributes that does not violate their heightened commitment to the norm of individualism. In class relations, shaped by a dual history of muted conflict and paternalistic domination, subordinate classes are both derogated and flattered. Sharp class distinctions in key achievement-related attributes have been embossed on the public consciousness with only petty dissent from the less-favored classes. At the same time, subordinates are granted superiority on an attribute that is irrelevant to the business of socioeconomic achievement. Class images are further muddied by the fact that class relations involve multiple groups in which people in all classes except the poor and the upper class schizophrenically experience deprivation and privilege as their vision swivels upwards or beneath them. Even those who enjoy the safehouse of upper-middle-class privilege are not immune to occasional moments of resentment against a class higher than their own. Images of the low and the mighty classes are thus torn by these competing pressures.

DATA: POPULAR EXPLANATIONS OF GROUP DIFFERENCES

I turn now to the folk wisdom that accompanies group attributions. To what extent do people think there are important differences between their own and other groups, and how do they account for those differences, for race, gender, and social class?

Measures

Immediately following the administration of the beliefs booklet, respondents were asked the following set of questions, beginning with gender, followed by race, and then class:

> *Apart from differences in appearance* between men and women, do you think there are *many* important differences between men and women, *some* important differences, a *few* important differences, or *no* important differences?

If respondents gave one of the first three response-options, they were asked the follow-up:

> People disagree about *why* there are differences between *men and women*. Which of the statements on this card comes closest to what you think? Just tell me the letter of your answer. (Interviewer instruction: READ CARD. MARK ALL LETTERS MENTIONED.)
>
> X. Most differences are there because they're born different.
> Y. Most differences come from the way they're brought up at home.
> Z. Most differences come from the different opportunities they have in America.

The wording for the comparable questions for race and class was identical, except that the lead-in for the class questions began:

Remember I asked you about the poor, the working class, the middle class, the upper-middle class, and the upper class. Do you think there are *many* important differences between these classes, *some* important differences, . . . [and so on].

The first item in each set takes a broader gauge of the potential group distinctions that people might see than do the personality-trait attributions analyzed in the previous section. The respondent was free to draw on any characteristics that she felt were variant across groups: this might include personality attributes, socioeconomic differences, crime rates, or anything else that the respondent considered salient.

The second question in each set provides for three primary explanations of perceived group differences: groups are inherently or biologically different (*born different*), groups are raised with different cultural values (*home upbringing*), and groups have unequal opportunities in society (*opportunities*). These three response-options cover the essential distinctions about which analysts have been concerned. The first explanation (*born different*) is the one associated with a classic racist position: it makes the group's condition immutable and therefore beyond the reach of public policy. The second explanation (*home upbringing*) alludes to differences in culture and values between groups, but it takes on a slightly different meaning for gender than for race and class. Since both gender groups are raised in the same homes by the same people, reference to the way people are brought up at home has more discriminatory implications. (Note, however, that the critique is at best ambiguous, since it is the subordinates—women—who have primary responsibility for bringing up children of both sexes, and private homes have been defined as safely outside the domain of public policy.) For race and class, the meaning of the second proffered explanation is more clear-cut, since the pertinent groups are brought up within their own ranks: thus, any differences in their upbringing at home are the responsibility of the group itself. This explanation casts the blame for any differences between race or class groups on the subordinate group, and it implies that any policy intervention would have to include such paternalistic measures as resocialization of subordinates or developing special programs that would counteract subordinates' unfortunate values. The third explanation (*opportunities*) casts the blame for any group differences on the social system, and it implies that to eliminate group differences, biases in the structure of society must be eradicated.

Results

Table 8.8 presents the percentages of each group who believe there are no important differences, a few, some, or many important differences between contending groups, and table 8.9 presents the percentages of

TABLE 8.8.   Number of Important Group Differences Perceived by Groups, for Race, Gender, and Class.

Number of Differences	Race Differences*		Gender Differences		Class Differences			
	Whites	Blacks	Men	Women	Upper-Middle	Middle	Work	Poor
None	14.1%	30.4%	12.9%	11.8%	7.1%	6.7%	10.5%	9.1%
A Few	18.9	18.0	19.3	19.5	19.9	19.3	16.6	18.2
Some	37.5	33.0	40.5	43.1	42.9	48.5	44.3	35.0
Many	26.7	17.5	25.7	22.6	28.8	24.6	26.5	31.5
Don't know	2.8	1.0	1.6	3.0	1.3	0.9	2.0	6.3
Base N	1638	194	798	1104	156	822	697	143

* Difference between groups in percentage distributions (with Don't Know's excluded) is statistically significant (p < .01).

TABLE 8.9.   Folk Explanations for Group Differences, among Those Seeing at Least a Few Important Differences, by Group.

Explanations for Differences	Race Differences		Gender Differences		Class Differences			
	Whites	Blacks	Men	Women	Upper-Middle	Middle	Work	Poor
Born Different	18.0%	11.3%*	27.8%	21.0%*	7.7%	7.3%	6.6%	5.8%
Home Upbringing	36.9	28.6*	42.8	52.2*	37.3	34.3	33.5	23.1
Opportunities	28.9	42.1*	15.4	14.1	35.2	46.8	48.5	57.0*
Born + Home	2.1	0.8	3.1	3.3	2.8	0.4	1.2	0.8
Born + Opportunities	1.3	8.3	0.9	0.7	1.4	0.7	1.0	2.5
Home + Opportunities	8.4	5.3	5.4	4.4	11.3	6.6	5.4	5.8
Born + Home + Opportunities	3.4	3.8	3.2	2.9	1.4	2.9	2.5	1.7
Don't Know	1.2	0.0	1.3	1.4	2.8	1.1	1.3	3.3
Base N	1358	133	680	941	142	758	606	121

* Difference by group in percentage giving this response is statistically significant (p < .05).

the respective groups who endorse various explanations of those differences.

In all three intergroup relationships, the overwhelming view is that there are at least a few important differences between the contending groups. And in every group except one (blacks), at least two-thirds claim that there are more than just a few important differences between the pertinent groups. Blacks are the only group to diverge from this generally held view, and they diverge only slightly. About 30 percent of blacks think there are no important differences between the races, as compared with 14 percent of whites who hold this view, about 12 percent of men and women who think there are no important gender differences, and about 7 to 10 percent of the four social classes who think there are no important class differences.

The folk explanations that are adduced to account for these alleged differences do show more variance across the three intergroup relationships. Table 8.9 presents the percentage of each group who espouse each of three alternative explanations for group differences: that the groups are "born different," that there are differences in "the way they're brought up at home," or that they have "different opportunities." A few respondents preferred to cite more than one explanation, and those responses are recorded in the bottom rows of the table, along with the "don't know's."

Group differences are not generally seen as inherent. The explanation that the groups are "born different" is particularly out of favor in class relations, where fewer than 8 percent of any class endorses this view. In race relations, it is also the least favored of the three possible explanations, but it gains more credence than in the explanation of class differences, especially among whites: 18 percent of whites and 11 percent of blacks see race differences as inherent. It is in gender relations that this explanation has most credence, especially among men: 28 percent of men and 21 percent of women say that most important gender differences are inherent.

The explanation of important group differences in terms of "different opportunities" is found most frequently in class relations, although endorsement of this view varies by class, decreasing gradually from 57 percent of the poor to 35 percent of the upper-middle class. Blacks are less likely to attribute race differences to this cause than are poor, working-class, and middle class people to explain class differences this way, but blacks are still somewhat more likely to blame differences in opportunities than are whites: 42 percent of blacks and 29 percent of whites take this view (making whites just slightly less likely than the upper-middle class to blame opportunities). Differences in opportunities are least likely to be cited in the gender context, where this explanation has less credence than either of the other two possibilities. Only about 15 percent of either men or women adduce this explanation for the important gender differences that they see.

Attributions to "the way they're brought up at home" as the main cause of group differences are found most frequently in gender relations, where this explanation is also cited more often than either of the other two possibilities by both sexes: 43 percent of men and 52 percent of women take this view. As noted earlier, this explanation has a somewhat more critical ring in the context of gender relations, since men and women are not brought up in separate homes, but, even in this context, it is considerably less critical than the allusion to opportunities, since it is the subordinate group—women—who are assigned the main responsibility for how children are brought up. In race and class relations, this explanation is cited almost as often by whites and by the upper-middle class as it is by men, but blacks and the poor are less likely to accede to this explanation. About 37 percent of whites and 29 percent of blacks say that home upbringing is the cause of most important race differences, and it is cited as the cause of most important class differences by 37 percent of the upper-middle class, 34 percent of the middle class and working class, and 23 percent of the poor.

Thus, the repertoire of folk wisdom about the causes of group differences varies somewhat across the three intergroup relationships. In the explanation of class differences, the dialogue is almost exclusively about whether it is the cultural socialization that takes place within each group or the societal structure of opportunities that bears primary responsibility. Opinion in the upper-middle class is split pretty evenly between those two views, but with descending social class, opinion gradually shifts more in the direction of blaming opportunities: among the poor, the opportunities explanation is favored over home upbringing by almost three to one.

In the explanation of race differences, the same two alternative explanations are again the most commonly cited, but these two explanations do not hold such a near-exclusive reign as they do in class relations. A significant minority of whites (almost one-fifth) subscribe to the view that racial differences are immutable, and, although blacks are less likely than whites to share this view (just over one-tenth), they are more likely than the poor to attribute pertinent group differences to inherent causes. Of the two main explanations that are adduced in the race context, whites lean somewhat more toward cultural attributions whereas blacks lean more toward explaining race differences in terms of the structure of opportunities. Whites and blacks differ less sharply in their racial explanations than do the social classes in their explanations of class differences. It seems that whites have been more successful than the upper-middle class in steering the thrust of folk wisdom away from explanations that challenge structural arrangements and toward interpretations that lay the blame outside the purview of public policy. The economic basis of class distinctions appears to have a tangibility that is more difficult to obscure (as we found with the perception of class interests).

In the folk explanation of gender differences, structural factors are further obscured, and the stories told by the two groups are more closely allied than in race relations. Gender differences are attributed to the structure of opportunities with about the same infrequency as race differences are attributed to inherent causes, and this holds for women's explanations as much as men's. Popular discussion of gender differences is centered primarily on whether they are inherent or caused by differences in socialization, with the latter interpretation carrying overtones that are ambiguously critical of societal arrangements while still being outside the scope of public policy. Both men and women favor the latter view over the attribution of inherent differences, although the margin of preference is slightly greater among women than among men. In the context of gender relations, where paternalism holds the strongest sway, causal allusions to the structure of opportunities have been relegated to a fringe status, whereas the attribution to inherent causes remains a respectable option. As long as hostility is kept at bay, the dominant group may claim inherent and indelible differences between the groups with relative impunity, and the framework of popular discussion is shifted away from the ogre of outright challenge. Women's mild digression from the prevailing path is to venture slightly ahead of men into an interpretation that alludes to social rather than biological causes but which also lays the responsibility for group differences as much with women themselves as with men.

CONCLUSIONS

Cognitive attributions about social groups have been a focal point of research on intergroup attitudes. A particular kind of intergroup belief, the stereotype, has occupied a venerable place in that research. Intimately linked to the concept of prejudice, the stereotype has been the template used to assess the quality of intergroup attitudes. Researchers have targeted cognitive attributions that are categorical, sharply differentiating, derogatory, inflexible, and untrue as the kind of beliefs that damage subordinate groups. Ignorance and parochialism are thought to provide the breeding ground for such beliefs, which then set the mold for hostile feelings and discriminatory dispositions toward subordinates while eroding the self-esteem of subordinates themselves. The stereotype has so dominated scholarly thinking about intergroup cognitive attributions that researchers have felt little compunction to validate the concept through measurement. Instead, the prevailing measures of intergroup trait attributions have been phrased so as to constrain responses to simplified, categorical terms.

There has also been growing interest in the popular explanations that are adduced to explain the differences people perceive between groups. Folk wisdom about group differences has been measured in a variety of ways, but researchers have been especially concerned with distinguishing among popular explanations that treat subordinate groups as biologically distinct, as culturally different, or as the victims of biased social arrangements. The primary purpose has been to ascertain the extent to which people have a cognitive basis for supporting policies geared toward affirmative change. In this endeavor, the cultural type of explanation has occupied a relatively ambiguous middle-ground, one that still casts blame within the subordinate group but with less rigidity than the biological view, which is seen as the clear hallmark of the bigot.

My approach to intergroup attributions takes a different course. Instead of being the fuel for discrimination, individuals' intergroup beliefs are molded by the system of inequality that links their own group with another. Rather than being the naive driver of inequality, intergroup cognitive attributions are themselves driven by the political exigencies arising from the system of inequality. These beliefs are the cognitive embroidery of intergroup relations, with the patterns tacked in to meet the demands imposed by the pursuance of group interests within a specific set of constraints.

The perennial search of scholars for a specific type of intergroup belief as the bane of intergroup relations has diverted us from the variegated forms that such beliefs may assume, as the beneficiaries of inequality tell stories that advance their self-serving interpretation of their privilege. Various traits may be credited to or debited from groups, and various modes of attribution may be employed, depending on the political exigencies that are operant and the moral code that holds sway. Intergroup beliefs are of interest for what they reveal about the points of tension in an intergroup relationship and the moral umbrella that is unfurled over the inequality.

These constraints are unlikely to produce unmitigated hostility. As the members of the dominant group attempt to explain expropriative arrangements as fair and reasonable, they are channeled into perceptions that seem compelling from their own perspective and that also seem to appease subordinates. Insofar as dominant-group members continue to seek the compliance of subordinates in expropriative arrangements, they can ill-afford to be impervious to subordinates' sensibilities. Various stories and variants of stories circulate: through trial and error, some are relegated to a marginal position or cast off altogether, and others become broadly accepted. The diversity or singularity of opinion within and across the ranks of each group gives an indication of the extent to which stories have evolved that "work" for all the participants, or whether alternative packages of ideas are vying for primacy.

As the beneficiaries of inequality seek to promote their cognitive attributions, they draw on recognized fonts of knowledge and established moral tenets to validate their claims. In the contemporary era, science has largely displaced religion as the legitimate basis of knowledge, and individualism has become the governing moral precept. Both of these factors influence the content and language of intergroup beliefs. As the specific exigencies of an intergroup relationship shape the contours of dominant stories, scientific and individualistic principles infiltrate their language and expression.

As various stories circulate, the beliefs that gain the broadest acceptance are those that seem to flow most naturally from the constraints of the relationship and the prevailing morality. Such beliefs have credibility because they seem to be substantiated by the daily "facts" that the relationship creates. Thus, the beliefs that develop with the most ease are also the beliefs that offer the most compelling explanation of current arrangements. For this reason, it is misleading to ask whether dominant portrayals of subordinates are "true" or "false." It is more significant to ask why certain personal attributes are emphasized in intergroup beliefs and how much consensus there is within and between groups in those ascriptions. In relations marked by high personal contact across group lines, the two groups are daily presented with the same set of stimuli and they are exposed to the same communication channels. Thus, both groups are routinely presented with the same "confirmation" of dominant beliefs. In relations marked by spatial segregation, the lives of the two groups diverge into separate daily spheres, and the way is opened for subordinates to develop communication networks that are less tied to those of the dominant group. In this context, the unequal groups are more likely to differ in both the stimuli they encounter and the way those stimuli are interpreted.

Thus, the way unequal groups depict their vital attributes is both political and interactive, as the members of each group react to the circumstances in which they find themselves and the claims of the other participants. Dominant beliefs cannot be understood without an assessment of the political climate that pervades the intergroup relationship, and subordinates' views are an important element of that climate. At the same time, the structure of the relationship provides subordinates with varying opportunities to break loose from the symbolic framing of the relationship that is imposed by the privileged participants.

When role segregation constitutes an important basis of group differentiation, it is convenient for dominant-group members to depict the affected groups as sharply distinctive in their vital attributes in order to make the role divisions seem natural. The more central role segregation is to the conduct of the relationship, the more the dominant group feels moved to depict subordinates as sharply and categorically distinct and to explain group differences as self-perpetuating, either through biological or cultural processes. And when the groups are in frequent personal contact, as is the case in relations that are governed by role segregation, it is convenient to describe subordinates in distinctive terms simply in order to brace the boundaries between groups. In the paternalistic atmosphere that is encouraged by the practice of role segregation with high one-to-one contact across group lines, the clear delineation of the subordinate group's attributes also serves the dominant group's interest in defining subordinates' *needs*. By describing subordinates as distinctively different from the dominant group in their personal attributes, the way is cleared to define subordinates' needs as distinct from those of the dominant group as well.

In this endeavor, however, there is every reason to avoid the hostile derogation of subordinates. By avoiding derogation while sharply distinguishing the subordinate group, the role segregation is sustained in the cozy spirit of "Vive la difference!" As subordinates comply with the demands of the relationship and the groups thus routinely perform distinctive tasks and behaviors in life, it does not take any contrivance for the members of the dominant group to believe that the groups are indeed distinctive in their personal attributes. Subordinates, too, need only to look at the behaviors of those around them for daily confirmation of the dominant beliefs.

When spatial segregation is the primary differentiating mechanism, there is less need for the categorical differentiation of the subordinate group's personal attributes. The spatial boundary alone accomplishes the clear separation of the groups, and the dominant group thus feels less of an imperative to underscore the boundary line between groups. In addition, the spatial separation of the groups permits subordinates to break away from the dominant group's cognitive and emotional grip and to incubate a challenge to the modus vivendi. Dominant-group members are thus pushed into a defensive position, in which they feel impelled to assert their superiority more overtly, but in which continued emphasis on the group basis of social life has become incendiary. In this more unwieldy situation, dominant-group members prefer to shift the moral tenor of debate away from groups to individuals, even as they are pressed to portray subordinates in a more negative light.

In the contemporary era, the morality of individualism has already evolved and ripened from the competitive *praxis* of the capitalist economy: individualistic principles govern economic life, and they fall conveniently to hand when they are needed for the exegesis of other intergroup relations. As the members of the dominant group reach for the moral umbrella of individualism to undermine the credibility of group-based demands and complaints, categorical attributions become a liability and they atrophy. Categorical attributions are reshaped into probabilistic ones, even as dominant-group members are pushed by subordinate challenge to assert their superiority more overtly. The language of science, with its emphasis on such methodological principles as variability, precise measurement, and central tendencies, provides a credible and prestigious basis for probabilistic intergroup comparisons. In the context of spatial segregation, such comparisons are perfectly serviceable for explaining the differential experiences of the unequal group. At the same time, probabilistic comparisons combat an incendiary atmosphere with a language that seems reasoned, moderate, and unbiased.

The patterns of intergroup beliefs observed for race, class, and gender relations illustrate the politically adaptive quality of those beliefs. When we rely on more refined measures than have generally been used in the past and we compare across three intergroup relationships marked by different structural exigencies, we find a distinctive pattern of intergroup beliefs in each case. The prevalence of categorical descriptions, large cognitive distinctions, derogatory characterizations, and biological, cultural, and structural explanatory schemes varies substantially across the three intergroup relationships. Further, these various elements of intergroup beliefs are not locked together, as the stereotype concept would lead us to assume. Instead, they vary flexibly to create configurations of beliefs that are uniquely adapted to the political context in which they are formulated.

In gender relations, the lives of men and women are intricately bound together within the rigid confines of role segregation. Here, the contending groups manifest the strongest convergence in their intergroup beliefs, and the categorical differentiation of subordinates occupies a central place in those beliefs. At the same time, the evaluative overtones are kept on a positive note. Women are warmly congratulated for their distinctiveness in personal traits that are appropriate to the tasks and behaviors assigned to them and to which men have no aspirations. And although biological attributions are generally out of favor in all three intergroup relationships, gender differences are attributed to immutable, biological causes by over one-quarter of men and one-fifth of women—more than for race or class, and more often than differential opportunities are invoked to account for gender differences. The most common explanation of gender differences is to allude to the way people are brought up at home. Thus, the overwhelming majority of both men and women believe women are clearly different from men—in positive ways—and that those differences are caused by factors outside the domain of governmental intervention: responsibility is generally attributed to either the physical makeup or behavioral proclivities of women themselves.

Class relations are marked by an intermixture of role and spatial segregation, with a step-wise pattern of contact that brings people into considerable personal contact with those in adjacent classes but little or no

contact with people in more distant classes. Class is also distinct in that
there is an absence of rigid, social rules for group ascription: instead,
there has been an emphasis on the importance of individual, achievement-related factors as the basis for socioeconomic standing. In the resulting hierarchy of self-defined classes, people who are at neither the
pinnacle nor the base alternately occupy a dominant or a subordinate
position, depending on whether they cast their vision beneath or above
them.

In this context, large and invidious differences are drawn among the
classes in the vital achievement-related trait of intelligence. This attribution prevails in all social classes, although its popularity decreases slightly
with descending social class. Categorical attributions are invoked as frequently as in gender relations, but, interestingly, the brunt of those attributions is softened by describing the two *highest* classes in *positive* categorical terms rather than portraying the lowest classes as categorically
deficient in this vital trait. This use of categorical attributions thus pays
homage to individualism both by crediting higher classes with a clearly
superior endowment of this achievement-related trait and by acknowledging individual variability in the ranks of the lower classes. To soften
the sting of this invidious class comparison further, the lower classes are
simultaneously credited with *superiority* in another trait—selfish—that is
not pertinent to the justification of socioeconomic inequality. On two
other achievement-related traits—thrifty and lazy—the poor are once
again compared unfavorably to higher classes, but in these traits people
in the working, middle, and upper-middle classes also tend to portray
higher social classes as less well endowed than their own. Thus, a variegated pattern of trait attributions emerges among the social classes, in
which categorical attributions, positive and negative evaluative connotations, and various class distinctions are intermixed.

Although lower classes have absorbed much of the unflattering portrayal of them in achievement-related personal traits, by and large they
have not been asked to see themselves as biologically inferior. The reluctance of dominant classes to declare rigid class groupings makes it awkward for them to draw immutable, biological differences between classes.
In the folk explanations that are invoked to account for class differences,
biological factors are barely mentioned, and the debate instead centers
on cultural factors versus the opportunity structure. Among the poor,
there is a strong preference for the argument that the opportunity structure is to blame for class differences. With ascending class, the popularity
of that argument diminishes as more people are drawn to the position
that responsibility lies with the cultural attributes of classes—a factor
that is potentially subject to change but which remains beyond the scope
of any obvious governmental intervention.

In race relations, the widespread residential segregation of blacks from whites in urban America has accomplished a pervasive spatial separation of the two groups. Past policies and practices by the federal government, local governments, and the banking and real estate industries have made residential racial segregation such an embedded feature of contemporary urban life that it now requires little active engagement on the part of individual whites to maintain it. Thus, most whites do not feel pressed to explain the residential segregation that insulates them from blacks—it is conveniently a fait accompli. But the lower socioeconomic achievement of the subordinate racial group presents itself as a glaring issue that requires explanation. Indeed, the spatial segregation of the two groups highlights the socioeconomic differences between them, as well as offering blacks more opportunity to break loose from dominant communication channels and articulate a grievance.

In these circumstances, the primary symbolic task for whites is to draw distinctions between the two groups in personal attributes that can account for the differences between them in achievement. As whites accord superiority to themselves in such achievement-related attributes as intelligence, dependability, and laziness, they are generally careful to differentiate the average characteristics of the two groups without making sharp or categorical distinctions. Rather than pouring venom into an already endangered relationship by describing blacks as categorically deficient in achievement-related traits, whites simply credit themselves with a somewhat greater endowment of those traits. And although a significant minority of whites claim the differences between the races are immutable, whites are more likely to allude to cultural factors in accounting for racial differences.

The moral umbrella of individualism is unfurled squarely over the relationship and encases the challenge that is articulated by blacks. Blacks are unlikely to challenge the values attached to achievement-related personal attributes. A minority asserts superiority to whites in those attributes, but blacks' challenge to whites' symbolic portrayal of racial differences is largely confined to denying racial differences in key personal traits and to explaining racial differences in terms of the structure of opportunities more often than do whites. Overall, blacks' cognitive attributions diverge on their own path more notably than do those of other subordinate groups in this study, but they are necessarily contained within the same symbolic framework as that put forward by whites.

These variant patterns of intergroup beliefs in gender, class, and race relations demonstrate the malleability of those beliefs in the face of political pressures. As people try to pursue their interests and as they grope to interpret the circumstances in which they find themselves, they succumb to the relentless pressure of the stimuli that press on them. The

structural arrangements that shape their lives lend credibility to alternative cognitive attributions. Various stories circulate to address the exigencies that people face. In their ongoing interest in communicating with
and persuading others, the bearers of those stories are obliged to heed
the stories and the morality that others espouse and to frame their own
assertions in a common language. The resulting commonality or diversity
of stories within and across groups reveals the extent to which structural
arrangements create common, interrelated, or divergent conditions of
life and lines of communication. Intimate relations based on role segregation nourish paternalistic consensus, and one finds the simple categorization of subordinates, rendered in benign terms. In relations based on
spatial segregation, the members of the dominant group retreat from
simple group differentiation as they feel the sting of subordinate dissent
and hostility creeps into the relationship.

Thus, the cognitive attributions that are formulated by the members
of the dominant group are not fixed but are continually reshaped in an
interactive process with other members of their own group, with subordinates, and in response to any alteration in circumstances. In this way,
dominant-group members retain the upper hand in framing the symbolic portrayal of their relationship with subordinates. In relations with
high spatial separation of the groups, the dominant group's communication lines do not envelop subordinates as effectively, but even here, subordinate dissent from the main symbolic themes is contained. Stories
are advanced that seem credible, and those stories flourish, fade, or are
remodeled, according to their fitness in addressing the stresses that beset
the various participants in the relationship.

PART IV

Threads of Paternalism and Conflict

CHAPTER NINE

Ideology and Coercion

The term "intergroup relations" refers to the relations between two or more groups and their respective members. . . . The appropriate frame of reference for studying such behavior includes the functional relations between the groups. Intergroup situations are not voids. . . . The behavior by members of any group toward another group is not primarily a problem of deviate behavior. . . . *The crux of the problem is the participation by group members in established practices and social distance norms of their group and their response to new trends developing in relationships between their group and other groups.*

SHERIF (1965, 695)

In a dramatic series of field experiments, Sherif and his colleagues created a boys' camp from hell and then transformed it into a model of harmony and mutual good feeling (Sherif and Sherif 1953; Sherif 1965, 1966; Sherif et al. 1961, 1988). Those experiments quickly became established as the definitive demonstration of the way in which intergroup attitudes reflect the relations from which they spring (see, for example, Turner 1981; Worchel and Austin 1986; Campbell 1988). Indeed, the behavioral dynamics in Sherif's experiments became broadly accepted as the prototype for intergroup relations, even among scholars whose own approach emphasized individual-level rather than structural factors.

Sherif's experiments created two kinds of functional relations between groups. First were "negative functional relations," in which the boys were divided into groups whose sole basis for interaction was competitive sports events:

A series of situations was introduced in which one group could achieve its goal only at the expense of the other—through a tournament of competitive events with desirable prizes for the winning group. . . . During interaction between groups in experimentally introduced activities which were competitive and mutually frustrating, members of each group developed hostile attitudes and highly unfavorable stereotypes toward the other group and its members. In fact, attitudes of social distance between the groups became so definite that they wanted nothing further to do with each other. This we take as a case of experimentally produced "social distance" in miniature. Conflict was manifested in derogatory name-calling and invectives, flare-ups of physical conflict, and raids on each other's cabins and territory. Over a period of time, negative stereotypes and unfavorable attitudes developed. (Sherif 1965, 698)

Second, Sherif created "positive functional relations" by introducing common, "superordinate goals" that required cooperation across group lines for their attainment:

> The introduction of a series of such superordinate goals was indeed effective in reducing intergroup conflict: (1) when the groups in a state of friction interacted in conditions involving superordinate goals, they did cooperate in activities leading toward the common goal and (2) a series of joint activities leading toward superordinate goals had the cumulative effect of reducing the prevailing friction between groups and unfavorable stereotypes toward the out-group. . . . The series of superordinate goals produced increasingly friendly associations and attitudes pertaining to out-group members. (Sherif 1965, 700)

Thus, Sherif's conception of the variability in intergroup structure was limited to a dichotomy between competitive relations with opposed, all-or-nothing interests and cooperative relations with common interests. On the basis of these experiments, Sherif reached the following conclusions about the ideological dynamics of intergroup relations:

> In the process of interaction among members, an in-group is endowed with positive qualities which tend to be praiseworthy, self-justifying, and even self-glorifying. . . . To out-groups and their respective members are attributed positive or negative qualities, depending on the nature of functional relations between the groups in question. The character of functional relations between groups may result from actual harmony and interdependence or from actual incompatibility between the aspirations and directions of the two groups. A number of field studies and experiments indicate that, if the functional relations between the groups are positive, favorable attitudes are formed toward the out-group. If the functional relations between the groups are negative, they give rise to hostile attitudes and unfavorable stereotypes in relation to the out-group. . . . In time, the adjectives attributed to out-groups take their places in the repertory of group norms. The lasting, derogatory stereotypes attributed to groups low on the social distance scale are particular cases of group norms pertaining to out-groups. (Sherif 1965, 696)

In this way, hostility was equated with "negative functional relations" and favorable attitudes with "positive functional relations." This is the model that has reigned over research on intergroup ideology.

My purpose in this book has been to take up anew the question of how the functional relations between groups shape intergroup ideology. Rather than accepting the dichotomous distinction between "positive" and "negative" relations as capturing the effective range, I have sought to enlarge our conception of the variability in functional relations between groups. Expropriative relations may be structured in a variety of ways that lend themselves to different avenues of communication. By examining three different intergroup relationships involving long-term inequalities—race, class, and gender in the contemporary United States—I have traced the ideological processes that are set in motion by variant political exigencies. In that endeavor, I have sought to demonstrate that hostility is not routinely paired with "negative functional relations," indeed, that hostility is the option of last resort.

I have no quarrel with the demonstrated verity of Sherif's maxim that competitive relations with all-or-nothing stakes produce open expressions of hostility between groups. Further, the boys' camp prototype can be applied to many empirical examples of intergroup relations. Nations at war approximate the conditions fairly well. Similarly, many cases of ethnic relations are competitive with all-or-nothing stakes, as when ethnic groups with no functional interrelationship vie for political and economic control of states in which they unwillingly share citizenship.

But Sherif's model has been mistakenly applied to the intergroup attitudes associated with longstanding relations of inequality, in which one group expropriates continuing benefits from another. Here, his model does not fit. In such relations, individuals are not confronted with uncertainty about which group (their own or another) is dominant, and the stakes are neither dichotomous nor winner-take-all. Further, the mutual dependence and cooperation that were intrinsic and exclusive to Sherif's "positive functional relations" are usually found as elements of "negative" relations in expropriative systems of inequality. In short, long-term relations of inequality between groups present considerably more complex configurations of elements than is captured by Sherif's experimental conditions.

In long-term relations of inequality, one group clearly occupies the dominant position—indeed, one group is institutionally embedded in the dominant position. In the ensuing exchange relations between the unequal groups, those groups do have mutually opposed interests, for each group's benefits and losses are drawn from the same finite pool of resources. However, their long-term, mutual relationship binds the groups in a web of interdependence that makes all-or-nothing calculations inappropriate. Unlike sports contests, in which victory or defeat in one event has no direct bearing on the outcome of future contests, in relationships of inequality the gains or losses experienced by either group are carried over to future interactions. To begin, in order to maintain their elevated stature in life, dominant-group members remain dependent on subordinates for a continuing transfer of benefits. If subordinates lose too much or have no prospect of maintaining or improving their holdings in the future, their cooperation may be harder to elicit. Discontent among subordinates raises the costs of governance and threatens to remove or diminish some of the privileges that dominant-group members have incorporated into their lives. It thus behooves the dominant group to provide subordinates with incentives to cooperate with current arrangements. By these means, subordinates are granted some small stake in current arrangements—and thus noncooperation on their part becomes potentially costly. This point is illustrated clearly in the following account of how the control of slaves evolved in Martinique in the early 1800s:

> [P]hysicial coercion alone provided insufficient motivation for the slaves. It produced sullen and recalcitrant slaves who worked only because of the threat of punishment and did only enough work to avoid punishment. . . . Some sign of encouragement or favor or small rewards of food or clothing from the plantation's stores for obedience or good work were necessary to temper fear of the lash and obtain some degree of goodwill and cooperation from slaves. . . . [B]y the 1830's a growing number of planters were attempting to move beyond overt physical coercion and develop more effective means of labor discipline and social control. . . . [O]ne planter testified . . . "When . . . one of my Negroes [acquires] some savings, he is in my control from then on. . . . [T]he desire to protect what is his makes him more careful and rarely at fault." (Tomich 1990, 244)

The same point was made earlier by Fogel and Engerman in their discussion of the mixed use of physical punishments and pecuniary incentives in slave-owners' relations with their slaves in the antebellum South:

> While whipping was an integral part of the system of punishments and rewards, it was not the totality of the system. What planters wanted was not sullen and discontented slaves who did just enough to keep from getting whipped. They wanted devoted, hard-working, responsible slaves who identified their fortunes with the fortunes of their masters. . . . Such an attitude could not be beaten into slaves. It had to be elicited.
>
> Much of the managerial attention of planters was focused on the problem of motivating their hands. To achieve the desired response they developed a wide-ranging system of rewards. (Fogel and Engerman 1974, 147–148)

Although subordinates' assets may be vastly unequal to those enjoyed by the dominant group, they are not zero, and therefore subordinates do have something to lose. The uncertainty that hangs over established relations of inequality is not over which group will dominate, but over whether current holdings are to be maintained, enlarged, or diminished, and by how much. This array of potential outcomes is infinitely more complex and variegated than the winner-take-all stakes in Sherif's experiments. Sherif used the beacon of common interests to induce cooperation between his competitively matched groups. But in relations between unequal groups, the cooperation of subordinates with institutionalized, expropriative arrangements is coerced by the dull reality of their weaker command over resources as they seek to protect their distinct group interests. In order to protect their current holdings from incursions by a stronger party, it is restraint and caution that are operative, rather than bold advocacy. Cooperation in this light takes on a more diminished hue than the bright luster that it is generally accorded.

The incentive for cautious and cooperative strategies is reinforced by three additional factors that distinguish long-term relations of inequality from Sherif's model. First, sports contests are discrete events, but interactions in relationships of inequality are embedded in an iterative pattern that continues indefinitely. Second, sports contests are run according to a finite set of published rules, and impartial referees interpret potential violations of the rules and call the score. But the rules in relations of inequality are subject to negotiation and are neither fixed nor free of ambiguity: the exact boundaries of the rules must often be tested and there is no impartial referee to cry foul. Third, by virtue of their simplified rules, the presence of an impartial referee, and the discrete definition of contests, sports events have clear outcomes. In relationships of inequality, however, the lack of either published rules or impartial referees, the existence of a broad and continuous array of possible outcomes, and the continuous nature of interaction, all combine to reduce the clarity of outcomes. The outcomes of contests become subject to conflicting interpretation as well as to both material and symbolic manipulation. Apparent gains may be eroded by counterclaims or by enactments that fall short of promises. These factors multiply the uncertainty that infuses relations of inequality, giving both dominants and subordinates reason to tread with care. The terrain is dotted with pitfalls. And the game knows no end.

Sherif demonstrated that individuals act in ways to further their interests and that they develop belief systems in accord with those interests. When interests are structured as competitive, finite, and winner-take-all along group lines, people close ranks within groups and incite their fellow group-members to vanquish the opponents by glorifying their own cause and slinging insults at their opponents. Scholars have treated Sherif's experimental condition of "negative functional relations" as the microcosm of all negative intergroup relations. I treat it as the limiting case.

Groups engaged in long-term relations of inequality are not at liberty to close ranks and scream abusively at each other. Their functional interrelationship binds them and obliges them to communicate with each other in ways that are mindful of their mutual sensibilities. Screaming is fine for war, when each side needs to rally its own ranks to endure the hardships of open hostilities. But until then, those on each side are mindful of their protagonists, as they seek to further their interests without putting their current holdings at risk. Cooperation is not the exclusive bedfellow of either equality or common interests. When groups are bound by an ongoing relationship of inequality, they are driven by their mutually opposed interests to engage in cooperative transactions with one another. The ideological exchanges that evolve between them follow accordingly.

Sherif's insight was to direct our attention to the structure of intergroup relations as the key to intergroup ideology. As the members of unequal groups seek to protect and further their interests, their ideological positions are constrained by the organizational forms that have been imposed by the functional requirements of their relationship with one another. But those functional requirements do not fall into a simple dichotomy. Configurations are various, and each creates different opportunities for communication within and across group lines. I briefly outline my model and my strategy of inquiry, and then review the evidence from race, class, and gender relations in the United States. What are the principles that drive ideology in systems of inequality?

THE POLITICS OF INTERGROUP IDEOLOGY

Like Sherif, I begin with the premise that people pursue their interests and that their ideology is shaped accordingly. In order to understand the beliefs, feelings, and goals that people weave out of their existence, we need to understand the constraints to which they are subject and the opportunities that fall in their path.

As people negotiate through life's uncertainties, they attempt to preserve what they already have and, where possible, to enhance their control over resources. In short, people seek to maximize their control over resources, and this makes them both protective and acquisitive. Theoretical discussions of interests as a motivator of human action (especially in theory about class interests) have generally focused overwhelmingly on the acquisitive aspect of self-interest and have given insufficient weight to the protective concerns of humans. It is the latter that drives people to be conservative rather than rash, as they accommodate their goals to the realm of the possible. Thus, the privileged members of society might be expected to aspire to an expanded control over resources—except for their dim realization that they need to elicit the continuing accedence of subordinates in order to maintain their existing benefits. And although some political activists have wishfully urged that the working class has nothing to lose but its chains, provisions have been made to give the working class reason to judge otherwise.

People's ambitions rise and fall in accordance with the opportunities and constraints they encounter. Ever wary of the uncertainty that lies beyond, people make use of whatever resources they command to consolidate and strengthen their position. Those with an initial advantage in their control over resources utilize that advantage to establish expropriative relations with weaker members of the community. Those who are weaker confine their ambitions to the meager opportunities that come their way. Such opportunities are constricted by the strategies pursued by their more advantaged peers. The latter collaborate with one another to institutionalize expropriative arrangements. These institutions create a pattern of social life comprised of distinct groups, formed according to their position in the exchange relations that are managed within the institutions. Patterns of thinking are also engendered by the institutional structure of the expropriative relations between groups, and ideologies emerge that reflect the distinct existential worlds and political pressures to which the different parties are subject.

Men's greater physical strength than women put them at an initial advantage in the control of sexual access and sexual reproduction. That initial advantage was capitalized in institutions and systems of thought that consolidated men's control over sexuality so successfully that the initial asset of greater physical strength can usually be kept in reserve in the day-to-day.practice of expropriation between men and women. Power relations between men and women have not only shaped the most pertinent institution of marriage and family: differentials in interpersonal power, status, and economic standing have been so intricately attached to gender that they have permeated every niche of organized social life and the deepest recesses of people's beliefs, feelings, and personal goals in life.

European colonists in need of cheap labor to exploit the New World took advantage of their superior technology (especially in transportation and weaponry) to abduct African blacks to fulfill their labor needs. What began as abduction became a firmly entrenched institution fortified by law, social custom, and ideology. And with the demise of slavery, whites tenaciously sought alternative institutional forms and drifted into adapted ideological arguments that would allow them to continue their long-established practice of expropriating labor, status, and power from African Americans.

And in class relations, those with more material assets have used those assets to expropriate the labor of their less fortunate peers who are obliged to work for others in order to acquire the necessities of life. Material assets are invested in economic institutions that organize pro-

ductive work and harness the labor of others to the economic enhance-
ment of those who began in an advantaged position. People's opportunity
to extract personal gains from those institutions hinges on their control
over material resources or their possession of skills that have material
value in the functioning of those institutions. These economic arrangements are buttressed by power and status distinctions and upheld by
ideological arguments that promote their moral rectitude. The raw economic expropriation is buried in a network of social rules, habits, and
patterns of thinking.

In such ways, the stronger members of the community seek to consolidate their advantaged position. They invest their material, status, or
power advantages in ventures that seem to assure the stable receipt of
long-term benefits. This interest in the conservation of existing benefits
and in long-term investment for the future constrains the strategies of
dominants and their way of thinking about the subordinates on whom
they depend for their benefits.

First, the dominant members of society cannot afford to put subordinates in a position where they have nothing to lose. Thus, the institutions
they establish are not designed to strip the weaker members of the community of *all* their resources. The purpose of expropriative institutions
is to perpetuate exchange relations that are profitable to their dominant
members. The continued potency of those institutions depends intrinsically on their ability to set the terms by which valued resources will be
delivered to or withheld from those whose compliance provides social,
political, and economic benefits to the dominant members. If subordinates had nothing to lose, there would be no basis on which to rest the
capacity to wield potent threats over them. The capacity for power depends inescapably on the control of resources that are valued by the
weaker party. Thus, the task for dominant members of the community
is to institutionalize exchange relations with their weaker peers that give
the latter a vested interest while delivering the lion's share of resources
to themselves. The accomplishment of this task is the first step toward
securing a stable flow of benefits.

Second, insofar as their benefits are extracted from the weaker members of the community, dominants can ill afford to develop social arrangements that exclude them entirely. This elementary point compounds the one already noted, and it imposes limits on the shape of
expropriative institutions and the ideology to which dominants gravitate.
It poses a delicate dilemma for dominants that haunts them perennially.
On the one hand, expropriative institutions must differentiate subordinates from dominants sufficiently well to spell out the allocation of tasks
and benefits unambiguously. This generally necessitates the definition
of social groups with clear rules of differentiation. On the other hand,

strong ties must be nurtured between groups, so that they are bound together and subordinates are contained within expropriative institutions. This generally necessitates inclusive behaviors that encircle subordinates within the social web. These two opposing goals of differentiation and inclusion beget an intrinsic tension in expropriative relations.

Dominants follow strategies that are geared to resolving these problems and thus to securing their benefits. They establish and maintain institutions that manage exchange-relations between themselves and subordinates, making sure to leave subordinates with some limited opportunities for personal gain. They reinforce those institutions in two ways. On the one hand, they engage in exclusionary behaviors that demarcate the different social parties. They do not generally indulge in extremist behaviors on this score, differentiating themselves from subordinates only as much as required to carry out the expropriation. And at the same time, they gravitate to a pattern of thought that is directed inclusively toward subordinates. As they explain the differentiation between groups that is engendered by expropriative institutions, they are drawn to lines of reasoning that are persuasive rather than alienating and that emphasize binding ties between groups rather than casting them apart.

In short, dominants seek to befriend subordinates, even as they differentiate themselves from them, in order to lubricate their continued compliance with expropriative arrangements. Dominants have the capacity to exact subordinates' compliance through threats or outright force, and, indeed, their advantaged position in society rests on that capacity. But those avenues of control are more costly than the sweeter approach, and they are likely to be considerably less lucrative. Hence, such options are reserved as a last resort for troublesome individuals who have balked at social expectations or for moments of lapse in social arrangements when subordinates appear to be in need of a sharp reminder of the potency of the dominant group. Otherwise, that potency lies discreetly submerged beneath the social niceties that pervade everyday transactions.

In these activities, dominants are constrained by the technological limits of the expropriation that undergirds their relationship with subordinates. That sets the structure of expropriative institutions, and those in turn steer dominants to particular kinds of exclusionary behaviors. These factors alter subordinates' opportunities to insulate themselves from dominants and thus affect the political exigencies that dominants confront as they try to explain their relations with subordinates in a way that will prove satisfactory to all the participants.

The technological limits of sexual access and sexual reproduction have meant that control over that resource requires institutions that manage intimate, one-to-one relations between individuals. Those institutions define gender groups sharply and dictate intimate rules about personal behaviors and activities according to gender-group membership.

In class and race relations, the method by which subordinates' labor has been expropriated depends on the technology of productive work. For example, in the agrarian economy of feudal society and in the plantation economy of the Old South, it was economically convenient to control labor through long-term relations with individual subordinates. One member of the dominant group expropriated the labor of a fairly small number of individuals with whom he usually had enduring personal relationships. In contemporary industrial economies, the large scale of efficient production has dictated an aggregated use of labor. Industrial technology has thus severed or drastically limited the possibilities for personal contact between those who provide capital investment and those who labor for them. Personal contact across class lines is generally restricted to adjacent levels in the line of command in work relations. In addition, the technological requirements of industrial production encourage individual competition and achievement, and the expropriation of labor in such a system can take place effectively without reifying group boundaries, so long as there are clear rules governing relations between dominants and subordinates in the conduct of productive work. Thus, in accordance with the principle that differentiation should be kept to the minimum necessary to maintain expropriation, class dominants have avoided the sharp specification of class boundaries.

In race relations, white Americans have maintained their urgent interest in expropriating status as well as labor from African Americans. To achieve this goal, institutionalized racist practices have followed the pattern laid out by the reigning technology of economic relations, within which blacks have been held as a subjugated pool of labor. Thus, racial differentiation has slowly changed from a system based on detailed rules about appropriate behaviors and activities for each group to one based on deeply entrenched rules about the spatial separation of the groups.

In dominants' endeavor to maintain a precarious balance between differentiation from and inclusion of subordinates, they meet with the least hazard when the technology of expropriation incubates intimate relations between groups. In intimate relations, dominants are able to invade subordinates' day-to-day lives with institutional arrangements and ways of thinking that are profoundly coercive. Friendship and affection are offered to subordinates on the strictly imposed condition that they comply with expropriative arrangements. Institutional arrangements ensure that the weaker party has no other source from which these precious social resources might be obtained. Through such means, women yield control over sexual access and reproduction to men in return for their affection and protection. These negotiations are nestled in the bosom of personal day-to-day relations and submerged beneath an ornate ideological edifice that effectively permeates the thinking of both parties.

In intimate relations, differentiation is reiterated and reinforced in daily, personal contact through the imposition of strict rules of role segregation. Inclusion is accomplished through the transmission of beliefs, feelings, and values in communication channels that are shared by both groups and through the insidious practice of love to tie an intricate bond between individual dominants and subordinates. By the strict specification of role behaviors and activities according to group membership, dominants are able to define the ideal personal traits for subordinates and then warmly congratulate and reward them when they manifest those traits. Dominants are thus able to define the needs of subordinates and then gallantly offer to provide for those needs. Expropriation is symbolically transformed into affection, kindness, and good will.

These conditions prove too much for the defenses of the subordinate group. Subordinates are engulfed by the total and softly coercive grip of paternalistic institutions. They are trapped by the conditional practice of love into cooperating in their own subordination. Their failure to issue a flagrant challenge to prevailing arrangements is not "false consciousness" but an implicit recognition of the constraints that define their reality. Restricted by bonds of love with individual dominants and shared communication channels, subordinates pursue what options are left to them to maximize their control over resources. Because their opportunities for interaction with dominants are generally confined to one-to-one relations and their command over resources in those interactions is very limited, they are largely reduced to individual acts of petty recalcitrance or manipulation. Manipulative behaviors, whereby another party is duped into yielding resources without his full comprehension, are the last remaining ploy for those who are resource-poor to elicit some desired resource from those whom they have no ability to threaten, and interpersonal interactions present an easy context for safe manipulative strategies. Caught in a paternalistic grip that makes simple compliance the safest normal strategy to maximize their control over resources, individual subordinates use what limited opportunities come their way to carve out some small discretionary latitude.

In this cozy environment, dominants enjoy the richest fruits of expropriation. The group basis of social life is lauded and made the cornerstone for personal relations of mutual affection. Dominants are granted almost unlimited access to the services of individual subordinates, in privacy, without intervention from outside agencies. The compliance of subordinates in these arrangements is generally without question. And the bonds of conditional love are not only insidiously coercive but they lend a positive glow to the entire transaction.

Expropriative technologies that foster distal relations between groups pose a more serious hazard to dominants' ability to keep subordinates entwined as they conduct the differentiation necessary for expropriation. The aggregated mode of expropriation is harder to camouflage and the group basis of social life is revealed in a ruder light, unprotected by the disarming individuation of personal relations. Spatial distancing of the groups robs dominants of the near-exclusive control of precious social resources that they enjoy in intimate relations. Separated from the personal, day-to-day lives of subordinates, dominants' communication channels no longer flow naturally into the subordinate community, and dominants lose their ability to infiltrate subordinates' perceptual and emotional vulnerabilities.

In this setting, subordinates are granted greater personal latitude. They generate their own sources of emotional support and indigenous communication networks. Indeed, were it not for the advanced systems of mass communication and transportation that exist in contemporary industrial society, the extreme form of spatial segregation that is currently practiced to separate blacks from whites in the United States would pose a perilous threat to whites' control over race relations. As it is, the technologies of mass communication and transportation make it feasible for dominants to conduct expropriative business, even from a physical distance, and to transmit ideological messages into the subordinate community.

But the cloying grasp of dominants is loosened. Subordinates begin to articulate a challenge and they too avail themselves of the technology of mass communication to convey their grievances to the dominant group. Communications across group lines in both directions are thus channeled primarily through an impersonal, public, aggregated medium, and this affects the tenor of such communications. Bolstered by their indigenous capacity for mutual personal support and unhampered by individuated, personal relationships with dominants, subordinates have more latitude to withdraw emotionally behind group lines and to test the possibilities for change. Through trial and error, they learn the limits of dominants' indulgence and they are reminded, sometimes painfully, of dominants' superior control over resources. The public nature of all communications, including dominants' responses to their demands, ensures that information about opportunities and constraints is widely disseminated in the subordinate community. The goals and strategies of subordinates are reshaped accordingly.

In what direction are subordinates' bolder claims to resources pushed? Their introduction of hostility into the intergroup relationship disturbs rather than excites the members of the dominant group. In their ideological response, dominants thus endeavor to reduce the hostility and redirect the attendant claims. They try to meet hostility with reason. Finding that the group basis of social life has become an incendiary issue, they proceed to divert attention away from it. Individual rights are elevated as a guiding existential and moral principle. Subordinates are exhorted to strive as individuals and promised that individual achievement will be acknowledged and rewarded. Claims made on behalf of the whole group are decried as illegitimate and contrary to human freedom. The principle of individual competition and achievement is also highly compatible with the requirements of the industrialized economy that spawned the spatial separation of the groups. Subordinates learn that grievances confined to the domain of individual rights are within moral bounds and thus constitute a basis for legitimate negotiation with the dominant group. The specter of intergroup conflict is thus reduced to interminable disputes about the degree to which the system has perfected the principle of individual rights. As both sides become absorbed with the flashpoint of intergroup contention, equality is quietly transmogrified into equality of opportunity. Intergroup debate remains lodged there, leaving untrammeled the basic machinery of intergroup expropriation.

The processes by which particular ideological forms are adopted and modified by dominants and subordinates are neither planned nor conscious. As the members of contending groups go about the business of making the most of their lives, they unthinkingly absorb the constraints and opportunities that make up their separate realities. As they seek to understand and interpret the pattern of their lives, they fall in with the currents of thought to which they are exposed and which seem to square with the realities of their existence. Both of these factors are conditioned by the technology of the intergroup expropriation, by way of its effects on the structure of intergroup differentiation and the character of the communication channels that are thus thrown out within and across group lines. These set the pragmatic constraints and opportunities to which individual dominants and subordinates are subject.

Subordinates, from the vantage point of their weaker position, are usually vividly aware that things could be worse, and this is a constant prompt to proceed with care. Young adults have the smallest stake in the present system and the poorest appreciation of their group's historical experience, and they are thus the most inclined to be reckless. Once beyond this brief life-stage, subordinates show little inclination to risk whatever small degree of latitude and security they have carved out for themselves in an all-or-nothing bid for greater control over society's resources. Dominants, for their part, have no wish to upset subordinates, who after all provide them with the benefits of their existence. Participants on each side of the relationship thus gravitate toward ideologies that promote their cause without offending or unnerving those in the contending group. On each side, the modus operandum is persuasion rather than shock.

Within these constraints, various beliefs, values, feelings, and political goals circulate within and across group lines. What individuals think, feel, and strive to attain is a synthesis of their personal day-to-day experiences, the currents of thought to which they are exposed, and their knowledge of the behaviors and experiences of others, both past and present. All these sources are highly salient as people try to comprehend their lives and formulate their goals and strategies. Their implicit fear of uncertainty means that people's antennae are forever cocked for new information. As a result, ideologies should not be conceived as either static or neatly integrated. Instead, they are fluid, disjointed, ad hoc, and adaptable.

Individuals adopt various ideological elements that float their way according to the exigencies that bear on them and the information at their disposal about the behaviors and experiences of other participants in the intergroup relationship. Fragments that become inconvenient are dropped, and new ideas that are compelling because of altered exigencies gain currency. In this way, various ideological packages are constructed and reconstructed as they are transmitted through dominant and subordinate groups. Those packages are spread eagerly or they fail to gain a following, they persist over a long period of time or they fade quickly, depending on their success in addressing the political problematics that beset the relationship.

STRATEGY OF INQUIRY

To explore the empirical plausibility of my model, I have embarked on a comparative analysis of the ideologies that are exchanged between dominant and subordinate groups in race, class, and gender relations in the United States. My data are drawn from a national probability survey of adults aged eighteen and over in the United States in 1975. From this camera-shot of the patterns of intergroup contact and the ideologies that characterize these three systems of inequality, I have sought to cull evidence about the structure of intergroup relations and the ideological forms that are thus incubated.

The logic of my analysis departs from conventional empirical analyses of intergroup ideology. Most scholars have sought to unravel the causes of intergroup attitudes by focusing on variance among individuals—in their education, the region of the country in which they live, their economic security, their social status, their religious beliefs, their childhood socialization, their personalities, their general knowledge, their cognitive sophistication, or their personal contact with members of their own and other groups, to name the most prominent foci of inquiry. Some analysts have included group membership as one individual attribute to help explain intergroup attitudes, but many analysts have restricted their inquiry entirely to the individual variance that can be found within a single group, as in studies of whites' racial attitudes or women's gender attitudes. It is commonly assumed that if a theory is valid, one must be able to demonstrate its effects at the individual level. Empirical tests of key theories of intergroup ideology have thus been routinely reduced to the realm of individual differences in experiences and behavior.

I do not dispute the existence of individual variability in experience or its pertinence to the intergroup attitudes that people espouse. Since no system of inequality works with perfect rigidity as it engraves social experiences, individuals within broad social groups may be exposed to somewhat varying stimuli, some of which follow systematic, predictable lines and some of which result from personally idiosyncratic compounds of experience. Analyses that focus on individual variance capture the systematic differences in individual experience, although of course the personally idiosyncratic compounds of experience are largely out of analytic reach or interest (except for occasional inquiries into the way two or more explanatory variables interact to produce special effects). However, such analyses leave a major portion of the genesis of human behavior unexplored and unexplained. In a sense, the last step in the process is analyzed with a magnifying glass but the broad structural forces that condition the collective experience and frame individual decision making are either outside the line of vision or left nebulously in the periphery. The individual is thus implicitly given primacy as an autonomous, even atomized actor, whereas the broad institutional arrangements that sweep up individuals and shape their collective history are either dismissed or relegated to a secondary role.

I have shifted the focus of inquiry. In my analysis, the realm of individual variability slips out of focus and I concentrate instead on how broad structural forces impinge on human behavior. My explanatory lens has been moved away from the variance that exists across individuals and refocused on the variance that exists among different relationships of inequality. This broadens our conception of the pertinent social environment of individual actors and opens up fresh explanatory opportunities. I cede causal primacy to the institutionalized relations between groups: those relations set the general parameters of experience and frame the way it is interpreted. Even aberrant experiences and information are interpreted in the light of the general institutionalized arrangements that govern an expropriative relationship.

I assume that institutionalized relations between groups create sufficient commonalities of experience within the affected groups to provide the basis for systematic comparison. Those commonalities of experience not only directly reflect the conditions of life of many people, but they also set people's expectations for themselves as they observe the experiences of others who are similarly placed in social institutions. As people try to reduce uncertainty and make inferences about their prospects and their best course of action, they draw on information from the experiences and interpretations of others as well as from their personal experience. People are not inclined to block out valid sources of information coming from the experiences of pertinent others; nor do they function autonomously as they generate ideological responses to their direct experiences. People instead borrow from their group as they appraise their circumstances and reach for ideas that explain those circumstances. In the ongoing process of information gathering, the experiences and interpretations that are reiterated wield a stronger influence than those that are occasional or exceptional. I thus assume that the commonalities of experience that are generated by expropriative arrangements are important, both for their direct impact on human lives and for the indirect effects they exert through information-gathering processes.[1]

My analytic approach raises its own set of methodological issues. Before we assess the pattern of evidence from my data, we should take brief cognizance of the limitations that circumscribe the analysis. My three comparative cases are drawn from a single society at a single point in history, and thus they are not independent. This has several implications. First, individuals occupy positions in more than one, and usually in all three, of the intergroup relationships. Second, the propinquity and simultaneity of the three cases means that there are numerous opportunities for cultural diffusion from one intergroup relationship to another. Third, features observed in common across the three cases may reflect the specific pressures of an advanced industrialized, capitalist democracy, not universal features of relations of inequality. I briefly consider each of these issues in turn.

Because this analysis is directed at the dynamics of intergroup relationships and not the multiple varieties of individual experience, I have not traced the various ways in which group memberships may intersect to create idiosyncratic experiences for individuals. For the reader's interest, I have inserted footnotes throughout the analysis whenever particular combinations of class, race, or gender group memberships produced

---

1. For this reason, analyses focusing exclusively on individual-level variance should not be expected to explain more than a modest portion of the variance in ideology. If individuals are informed by the experiences of others as well as by their own experiences, and if they indeed interpret their own experiences in the light of information from others, models are misspecified if they restrict attention to effects emanating solely from the individual's own experience and psyche.

noticeable deviations in attitudes. Such occasions were infrequent. The only intersection that seems to have some systematic effect is that between race and class: strong feelings of racial identity among blacks combined with their historically persistent experience of poverty have made blacks generally more sensitive to the plight of the poor, even when they do not personally live in economic want. A detailed investigation of such effects does not lie within the scope of this analysis. I have proceeded on the assumption that when people respond to a specific intergroup relationship, the pertinent stimuli are those emanating from their position in that intergroup relationship. Apart from the partial exception just noted, the data do not violate this assumption. Most important, no instance was uncovered of inferences about the general effects of race, gender, or class memberships being undermined by internal subgroup variations.

The issue of cultural diffusion across cases is potentially serious since my analysis depends on being able to trace the impact of structural variation among intergroup relationships on their intergroup ideologies. To the extent that there is cultural diffusion, variance across cases in the object of my investigation—ideology—would be constricted. Further, my model of how people acquire their attitudes lends plausibility to the concept of cultural diffusion. Specifically, I assume that when people are presented with an issue that needs resolution, they do not autonomously fabricate or consciously search for ideas: they merely reach for the ideas that come most readily to hand. I expect people to borrow freely from the various ideas that they encounter, especially if those ideas have proved serviceable in other intergroup relationships. However, I also expect that ideas are dropped promptly if they do not work in a particular context. Thus, the totality of ideas that exist in a society constitute the pool from which people draw as they formulate their responses to specific situations—but pragmatics and politics come first, and what does not work will be dropped or modified in its new application. My data indicate that three intergroup relationships coexisting within a single society can indeed manifest ideological patterns that are quite distinctive from one another, despite the fact that a few ideas find at least some application in all three intergroup relationships.

The social context of all three cases is an advanced industrial society with a capitalist economy and a democratic form of government. Its institutions have also been shaped from its inception by a sharp racial divide between whites of European extraction and blacks of African extraction, by deep-seated social distinctions between men and women, and by an evolving pattern of expropriation in class relations. These factors have jointly forged the social fabric of the contemporary United States. To what extent are my empirical observations bound by this constellation of societal pressures? Clearly, this question cannot be answered without comparable data from societies that are formed differently.

The United States' institutional history and present form do not differ critically from the other advanced industrial nations, and thus we may generalize to those nations with a minimum of discomfort. The broad influence of such moral precepts as personal freedom, competition, and individual rights and liberty may have become especially pronounced in the course of the United States' breakaway colonial history, but they doubtless wield strong influence in the other industrialized capitalist democracies as well.[2] But what of societies shaped by different pressures? For example, in medieval Europe, with its lower standard of living, reduced prospects for individual mobility, poor life expectancy, and more limited command of knowledge, did dominants feel the same compunction to befriend their subordinates? Or were expectations of life so foreshortened and the sense of personal autonomy so diminished that expropriation required fewer niceties? Because of the improved standard of living and the more ambitious goals of economic production that are associated with economic development, has the necessity increased for systems of expropriation to seek legitimacy by eliciting the active consent of subordinates?

These questions are beyond the scope of my study. For the present, it seems safest to remain cognizant of the attributes that distinguish industrialized capitalist democracies. As with Sherif's experimental conditions, the three expropriative relations that are the subject of this study do not constitute the universe of possibilities. The significance of the analysis rests, not on claims of its infinite generality, but on the social pertinence of the specific cases and their ability to demonstrate meaningful structural variation. As we extract the principles that seem to guide the exchange of ideologies in these three cases, we must reserve judgment about their generality.

Two other methodological issues deserve comment here. First, like most other empirical studies of attitudes, I rely on data from a static snapshot to make inferences about dynamic processes. The logic of the analysis is based on the familiar principle that the examination of comparative data from critically distinct cases allows us to extrapolate the

2. Some suggestive figures are offered by a cross-national survey that was conducted by Gallup International Research Institute in 1987–1988 and reported in *The Economist* (September 5–11, 1992: 19–21). For example, in response to the question, "Which is more important, equality or freedom?," freedom figured prominently in all the industrialized nations. Americans and the British overwhelmingly valued freedom higher, and the French were also more likely to endorse freedom, although less overwhelmingly. In Italy, West Germany, Japan, and Spain, citizens were more evenly divided in the relative importance they attached to freedom or equality.

underlying dynamic processes that have thrown up the patterns we observe in the snapshot. Second, and finally, it bears explicit recognition that the number of cases on which my analysis relies is very small—too small for a standard causal analysis. Because the number of potential explanatory variables is considerably larger than the number of cases, there is no definitive way to isolate empirically the effects of various factors in producing the differences in ideology that are observed across the cases. Viewed in this light, the cases' confinement to a single society is an advantage, since it limits the number of potential explanatory factors among the cases. Nonetheless, my analysis should be regarded as a demonstration rather than a test: my purpose has been to establish the empirical plausibility of my model.

THE PATTERN OF EVIDENCE

The Three Cases

The three cases of expropriative relations differ substantially in the way they are socially defined and in the structure of contact between groups. These distinctive arrangements are accompanied by equally distinctive ideological patterns.

Race.   Whites of European extraction have maintained a rigid social distinction between themselves and blacks of African extraction. This dichotomous classification has relied on a simplified rule for assignment to groups—the so-called one-drop rule by which one drop of African "blood" makes a person black. In this way, racial group membership has been rendered immutable, and membership in the more numerous white group has been made extremely exclusive. For blacks, group membership is also absolutely heritable, but whites pass their privileged racial standing to their children only if they refrain from sexual unions with blacks.

Relations between these two groups are marked by pervasive spatial segregation that serves to keep most whites socially insulated from blacks most of the time. Blacks are not afforded quite as much racial insulation as whites because lapses in spatial segregation affect a larger proportion of the smaller black community. The lapses that occur are also likely to involve a token presence of blacks among an overwhelmingly white majority. Thus, whites' numerical dominance has enabled them to penetrate the black community to some extent while keeping the white community relatively insulated from blacks. In addition, the points of personal contact between whites and blacks, such as the workplace, are also quite likely to find whites occupying the status-dominant role. Nonetheless, whites' practice of pervasive residential segregation by race has dramatically restricted the number of personal contacts and friendships across the racial boundary. Whites' personal communication lines with blacks are much curtailed.

Race relations are marked by the sharpest ideological rift between groups. To begin, blacks and whites display the strongest mutual emotional disaffection. Blacks run a little ahead of whites in their emotional retreat behind group lines, but their intergroup feelings are closely reciprocated by whites. About 60 percent of blacks and 45–60 percent of whites express feelings of greater warmth or closeness for their own racial group. Indeed, whites express more outright racial hostility (as opposed to own-group preference) than do blacks, and although only a minority of whites express such outright hostility, it is a larger minority than is found in other dominant groups.

The policy goals of whites and blacks are also the most divergent in the study: a deep chasm lies between the racial policy goals of the two groups. Although the members of both groups usually reject the abstract concept of racial segregation, the overwhelming majority of blacks (70–90 percent) want more governmental intervention to promote affirmative change on behalf of blacks, whereas whites' views on governmental racial policy are almost as overwhelmingly conservative—or reactionary.

In the way people compound their feelings and policy goals, race relations again manifest the sharpest evidence of conflictive attitudes. About one-half of blacks express the conflictive compound of affirmative racial policy goals underlaid by feelings of estrangement from whites, and only about one in ten blacks defers to whites by expressing inclusive feelings toward them and acceding to conservative or reactionary racial policy goals. Among whites, a larger percentage than of any other dominant group (about 40 percent) express the conflictive attitudinal compound of emotional disparity from subordinates combined with conservative or reactionary policy dispositions, whereas only 10 to 20 percent (a smaller percentage than of any other dominant group) take the revisionist position of inclusive feelings combined with affirmative policy views.

Finally, race relations also manifest the sharpest divergence between groups in the way vital personal traits are attributed to the groups. Although categorical distinctions are generally avoided, one-half or more of whites depict their own group as superior in the key achievement-related attributes of intelligence and dependability, and over one-third believe that blacks are more likely to be lazy. Blacks rarely accede to these views. They are more inclined to counter with claims that the two groups do not differ in these personal attributes, and the small number who accede to the dominant white attributions are more than offset by the number who claim that it is blacks who have the superior endowment.

Gender. As in race relations, gender-group membership is based on a simplified rule that results in the rigid social definition of two groups. On the basis of genitalia, and without regard to individual sexual preference or subjective feelings of gender identification, two gender groups of approximately equal size are created. Gender-group membership is generally immutable, but it is the least heritable of the three types of groups in the study—both men and women have only 50–50 odds of transmitting their own gender-group membership to their children.

Gender relations are governed by role segregation, although the gender-specific domains of activity that are prescribed by gender roles do introduce some spatial segregation of the groups as well. Within the bosom of the family, men have repeated opportunities to communicate personally with women, and the communication channels are nested in clear role-positions that unobtrusively reaffirm the power differential between the two groups. In spheres of activity outside family life, gender roles have introduced a noticeable degree of spatial separation between the sexes; when women do enter male-dominated domains, such as the workplace, they are likely to be assigned tasks that leave gender role prerogatives inviolate.

The ideological patterns that mark gender relations contrast sharply with those observed for race. Between men and women there is generally an amicable exchange of feelings and only small hints of rift to break the prevailing pattern of conservative consensus across group lines. Most men draw no affective distinction between the sexes (56–60 percent), or actually express a preference for women (30–35 percent). Neutral gender feelings are about as common among women, although they are a little less likely than men to express a preference for the other gender group and a little more likely to prefer their own group. Accompanying these positive feelings, a majority of both men and women express the belief that traditional gender roles are for the mutual benefit of both sexes.

The policy goals of men and women also parallel one another fairly closely, with women leaning slightly more in the affirmative direction and men weighted more toward conservatism. In both groups, there is a roughly even division between support for and opposition to traditional gender arrangements in domestic life (although men retain a somewhat stronger commitment to their role as breadwinner), and a clear majority of both sexes supports the principle of equal job opportunity for women. In their opinions about governmental intervention on behalf of women, men are more likely to take a conservative position (40–52 percent) than an affirmative position (34–40 percent), and women are slightly more likely to be affirmative (43–48 percent) than conservative (38–43 percent). Reactionary views are much less in evidence than in race relations, but they are found about as often among women as among men.

In the way gender attitudes are compounded, the snug duo of paternalism and deference holds sway. Almost two-thirds of men—more than in any other dominant group—express the paternalistic blend of inclusive intergroup feelings and conservative policy goals. They are rewarded with deference (inclusive feelings combined with accedence to conservative policy goals) from almost half of women, considerably more deference than is found in any other subordinate group. By the same token, conflictive attitudes are almost absent from gender relations: they are virtually nonexistent among men (about 3 percent) and only slightly more in evidence among women (about 10 percent).

The paternalistic mold is supported by the categorical attribution of distinctive personality traits to women. The overwhelming majority of both sexes believes that women's personal attributes are sharply different from men's—in positive ways. Women are more likely than any other subordinate group to be described in categorical terms and the accompanying evaluative implications are also the most positive. Women are warmly congratulated for their distinctiveness in personal traits that are appropriate to the role they have been assigned.

Class. Class relations are bereft of any rigidly imposed rules for group membership since those who expropriate economic resources of production and consumption have little reason, either technologically or politically, to heighten socioeconomic boundaries. Instead, the social definition of classes has arisen out of the subjective feelings of identification that are prompted by the keen experiential impact of inequalities in such tangible items as educational and occupational attainment, income and wealth, job authority, and material standard of living. People form communities with others whose socioeconomic attributes cluster close to their own. The resulting classes have ragged boundaries and are neither immutable nor completely heritable, although class membership is usually stable over people's adult lives and is strongly related to parents' social class. The social classes that find common expression in popular discourse fall into a loosely arranged hierarchy: poor, working class, middle class, upper-middle class, and upper class.

Class relations are visibly marked by both role segregation and spatial segregation, although neither form of differentiation is enacted as sharply as it is for gender and race, respectively. Classes perform different roles in economic production, and the physical aggregation of those roles in industrial production has engendered considerable spatial segregation by social class, in the workplace as well as in residential patterns and affiliative networks. The social contacts experienced by the members of each class are centered in their own class and do not usually extend far beyond the boundaries of adjacent classes. The resulting pattern of class contacts is segmented over the class hierarchy, with the contacts of each class centered on a different point and fading out over different spans. Thus, in both the workplace and the conduct of social life, the wide chasm that separates the highest classes from the lowest is partially bridged, in segments, by the classes that lie in between. This does not afford the highest social classes the same direct, personal communication channels with the lowest classes that men have with women. At the same time, it means that the social rift between the top and bottom of the class structure, wide though it is, is sketched in ragged lines rather than being sharply engraved as it is between the races.

The features that characterize the structure of class relations are reflected in the patterns of class ideology. There is clear evidence of divisive feelings, perceptions, and policy goals along class lines, but they are fragmented along the step-wise structure of class relations and muted by an underlying consensus on the general equity and morality of economic differentiation. People's feelings of disparity from other classes increase as those classes become more distant from their own in the hierarchy, and they also express more estrangement from higher classes than from lower ones. For example, among the poor, almost 60 percent express emotional estrangement from the upper and upper-middle classes (about the same as the level of racial disaffection expressed by blacks), but fewer than 25 percent express the same estrangement from the adjacent working class. People in the upper-middle class are considerably less likely to indulge in divisive feelings as they orient themselves to lower classes, but they make the same distinctions among classes according to their proximity. People in lower classes are also more likely than those in higher classes to define their interests as mutually opposed, but they disagree about where exactly to draw the boundary-line between those classes that benefit from economic arrangements and those classes that are hurt.

There is broad support across classes for the general principle of economic inequality, although people in lower classes tend to favor a more moderated degree of inequality. There is also broad endorsement of the principle that societies should dispense rewards in accordance with individual differences in ability and achievement. However, there is a graduated disagreement among classes in their views about governmental intervention in social welfare measures. With ascending social class, the level of support for affirmative change gradually gives way to conservative or (less commonly) reactionary views. For example, about

60–80 percent of the poor advocate affirmative change in the various social welfare policies; the level of support for these policy goals declines steadily with ascending class until reaching a low of about 20–55 percent in the upper-middle class. In all, the class rift in policy goals is pronounced, although it does not equal the policy rift between blacks and whites.

In the way class attitudes are compounded, patterns fall in between those found for race and gender. People in the upper-middle and middle classes are more likely than are men to display conflictive attitude blends (emotional disparity from lower classes mixed with conservative or reactionary policy views), but they are less drawn to conflictive responses than are whites. Paternalistic blends (conservative or reactionary policy views undergirded with inclusive class feelings) draw the middle and upper-middle classes more than do conflictive blends. On the most demanding social-welfare issue, that of welfare benefits for the poor, about one-quarter of the middle and upper-middle classes take a conflictive stance and over one-half take a paternalistic approach. Among the poor and working class, the level of deference (inclusive class feelings blended with accedance to conservative or reactionary policy views) remains at a low level and conflictive blends are generally considerably higher, especially among the poor, for whom this pattern is almost as pronounced as it is among blacks. A significant minority of the poor and working class (more than among blacks or women) express accommodative attitude blends, whereby they accede to conservative or reactionary policy views despite feelings of estrangement from higher social classes.

The way vital personal traits are attributed to classes reflects the continuing importance of role distinctions along class lines and the hierarchical organization of classes. Categorical attributions in achievement-related traits are invoked as frequently in class relations as traits pertinent to gender roles are invoked in gender relations. However, the tendency is manifested primarily in the categorical attribution of *valued* traits to the *highest* social classes. And to compensate for the invidious differentiation of the poor in achievement-related traits such as intelligence, laziness, and thriftiness, the poor are also complimented as being the least selfish of the classes. There is more disagreement among classes in these trait attributions than there is between men and women, but the extent of disagreement does not match that found between blacks and whites.

The Dynamics of Intergroup Ideology

Race, gender, and class relations each manifest distinctive patterns of intergroup ideology, as the configuration of exigencies thrown up by each relationship has steered the responses of the contending groups. What do these patterns suggest about the dynamics that shape intergroup ideology? I begin by reviewing the general proclivities manifested in all three intergroup relations, and I then consider the systematic differences that exist.

Dispensable Hostility and Muted Conflict. The data indicate that, in the ideologies of all three intergroup relations, flagrant hostility is a minor actor. And conflict between groups follows a bounded and circuitous path that avoids the core areas of expropriation and skirts around the periphery of the relationship. These tendencies are manifested in several ways.

Most fundamentally, people generally refrain from expressing outright negative feelings toward contending groups: emotional boundaries between groups are usually confined to expressions of preference for one's own group. This is especially true for the measure of warm-versus-cold, where the polar ends of the scale carry sharper positive-versus-negative connotations than does the measure of closeness. Even in race relations, where intergroup feelings are the most divisive, only 25 percent of whites and 14 percent of blacks express feelings of outright coldness toward one another. Feelings of preference for one's own group, or estrangement from the other group, in warmth or closeness is more common, but the percentage gripped by such feelings ranges from a high of over 60 percent among blacks to a low of about 5 percent among men.

In addition, people's feelings of estrangement from or inclusiveness toward other groups are weak predictors of their policy dispositions toward those groups. Feelings of estrangement from a contending group are indeed more likely to be associated with policy positions that oppose the other group than with positions that support the other group. However, inclusive intergroup feelings do not portend policy positions that support the other group. Although it is apparently difficult for those with estranged intergroup feelings to take a policy stance that supports the other group, it does not seem at all difficult for those with inclusive intergroup feelings to pursue policies that oppose the other group's advancement.

In the same vein, people are unlikely to define group interests in sharply divisive ways. Even in class relations, where the concrete material distinctions encourage the strongest tendencies toward the perception of conflicting group interests, the percent of each class defining class interests as mutually opposed ranges from a high of about 60 to a low of 25. And, of course, this potentially explosive perception of class interests is fragmented by the lack of popular agreement about where to draw the cutoff between beneficiaries and losers. In race and gender relations, there is more of a tendency to depict current arrangements as affecting both groups in the same way, whether those effects are seen as beneficial or harmful, and even in class relations the upper-middle class prefers to depict private ownership as universally beneficial rather than as something that benefits higher classes at the expense of lower ones.

People's trait attributions to groups also seem to avoid the inflammatory. Dominant groups have discovered more subtle ways of differentiating subordinates from themselves. And subordinates, even when they challenge dominant portrayals, do not generally seem any more inclined than their stronger contenders to hurl insults. There is little evidence of hostile stereotyping in any of these intergroup relations. Dominants either refrain from invidious attributions (when they describe subordinates categorically) or they refrain from categorical attributions (when they make more invidious distinctions between groups). Subordinates do not stray far from the mold cast by dominants: when they do challenge dominant attributions, it generally takes the form of claiming equality with dominants, not superiority over them, in their personality attributes. Folk wisdom about the causes of group differences also shows only a modicum of flagrant hostility. Dominants are more likely to attribute group differences to potentially malleable cultural factors than to immutable biological causes, and a significant number of subordinates are drawn away from blaming the structure of opportunities to the more ambiguous invocation of cultural differences.

Finally, the policy goals voiced by contending groups also show a moderated pattern. The general policy principles that find broad acceptance do not endorse equality but individual rights and equality of opportunity. And the specific policy measures that become the focus of public debate call for neither radical affirmative change nor radical reactionary change. Subordinates' demands have been pressed inexorably in the direction of moderate affirmative change, and disputes with dominants have become locked on safety-net social-welfare measures and guarantees of equality of opportunity and individual rights rather than on comprehensive programs that would redistribute resources between groups. Dominants usually counter subordinates' proposals for affirmative policies with conservative objections. But on those proposals that strike a deeper nerve in the expropriative relationship (such as school busing in race relations and welfare benefits in class relations), a larger proportion of dominants is drawn to reactionary counterproposals. Thus, the issues that sustain the most prolonged public attention are those that call for moderate affirmative change. These policies do not meet with easy acceptance among dominants, but at the same time they do not violate the moral principles that frame the debate and they do not incite a significant reactionary response from defensive dominants.

Ideology Constrained. It is subordinates who seem to take the lead in introducing conflict. Subordinates are a little more inclined than dominants to gravitate toward feelings of intergroup disparity, and they tentatively lead the way in drawing divisive distinctions between the interests of the contending groups. Subordinates nudge policy discussion in the direction of affirmative change, whereas dominants generally restrict themselves to a defensive, conservative position in policy debate. Even when dominants advocate reactionary change, that seems to be in response to affirmative policy proposals that are too threatening, not on their independent initiative.

The scant showing of conflict is no doubt associated with the fact that it is subordinates—the weaker party—who are obliged to introduce it. Dominants find themselves in the felicitous position of merely having to defend existing institutional arrangements. Inertia is on their side. Existing arrangements strike dominants as quite satisfactory, and, unless provoked, they have no reason to dislike or disparage the subordinates who thus enhance the quality of their lives. Until provoked, it is enough for dominants to depict subordinates as different and to celebrate those differences ("Vive la différence!"), and then sit back and enjoy the benefits. When provocation comes, dominants' conservative goals direct them to deflect and dissolve the grievances and demands that are brought into the political arena rather than to excite things further.

From the subordinate perspective, however, things are stacked differently. Existing arrangements deliver some resources but also many deprivations. To improve their fortunes, subordinates must take an assertive role. As the ones who bear the costs of current arrangements, there is more incentive for them to envision change. At the same time, change is more difficult to accomplish than simple conservation. The weight of organizational inertia works against them. In addition, change involves more uncertainty than does the present: more ideological imagination and personal courage are required to visualize change than to maneuver within the familiar terrain of present arrangements. Finally, change is particularly difficult to achieve, and risky to attempt, when present arrangements restrict one's control over resources and make one vulnerable to backlash from stronger parties. Subordinates are reluctant to arouse the sleeping giant.

The net effect for subordinates is that the costs of compliance with present arrangements are delicately balanced against the risks of advocating change. Change smells sweeter when one bears the costs of present arrangements, but because of the attendant weaker control over resources, attempts at change carry serious risks. Subordinates are thus drawn to strategies that might improve their lot, but they operate with extreme caution. Dominants, for their part, are quick to remind subordinates of the downside risks if they become too assertive, but they are unlikely to take the initiative in trying to exact more resources from subordinates. That would present the hazard of undermining subordinates' small vested interest in current arrangements and thus altering their calculus of the costs of compliance versus the risks of revolt. Dominants prefer to let sleeping dogs lie. The surest strategy for dominants is to sit tight and to celebrate and defend current arrangements.

As subordinates introduce the germ of conflict into their relationship with dominants, they feel their way along, alert to opportunities and hazards. In intimate relations, such as those between men and women, dominants are able to hold relations in a paternalistic grip that leaves subordinates with precious little room to maneuver. In distal relations, such as those that have evolved between whites and African Americans and to a lesser extent among social classes, subordinates have a bit more room to breathe, and the sting of their complaint swells accordingly. Thus, although subordinate grievances are never exhibited lavishly, blacks and the poor and working class have traveled considerably further down the tortuous path to conflict than have women.

The sensitivity of subordinates' antennae is further manifested, in all three intergroup relations, by the pattern of their articulated policy goals. Women are more likely to assert their rights in the more impersonal domain of the workplace and in the more morally acceptable terrain of equality-of-opportunity issues: the sacrosanct domain of home and family is more likely to be left inviolate. Blacks are more likely to assert their rights on equality-of-opportunity issues than on more fundamental issues of racial equality. And the poor and working class are also more likely to galvanize around equality-of-opportunity issues, or around minimal safety-net measures, leaving the core issue of economic inequality virtually untouched. Even within these more acceptable domains, subordinates learn keenly which specific policies touch a raw nerve amongst dominants, and they retract their energies from those proposals, concentrating instead on milder policy initiatives that carry less risk. There is a consistent pattern in the data of subordinates showing lower levels of support for policies that elicit the lowest support—and the highest reactionary response—from dominants.

This general pattern of subordinates gingerly nudging opportunities to introduce conflict and dominants resisting those attempts is encapsulated neatly in the way the two kinds of groups compound their feelings and policy dispositions toward one another. In gender relations, dominants show the strongest proclivity to the paternalistic blend of inclusive feelings toward subordinates and conservative policy goals, and subordinates manifest the strongest tendency toward deference—inclusive feelings toward dominants and an acceptance of conservative policy goals.

Race and class relations indicate considerably more evidence of conflictive attitudes on the part of both dominants and subordinates, and this exchange of estranged feelings and conflicting policy goals is most pronounced in race relations. But beneath these gross differences across the three intergroup relations, dominants and subordinates dance to the same beat. In each case, even in gender relations, subordinates run slightly ahead of dominants in expressing conflictive attitudes, and the degree to which subordinates manifest deference lags slightly behind the degree to which dominants espouse paternalism.

For dominants, paternalism continues to hold an allure, even when subordinates have broken free of its grip. Thus, in race relations, where about half of blacks have conflictive racial attitudes and only about 10 percent manifest deference, about 40 percent of whites respond with a conflictive stance—but another 40 percent still cling to paternalism. Dominants rouse themselves from the delights of paternalism only reluctantly, and by degrees. John Stuart Mill sardonically described the paternalistic vision that entices dominants to yearn for the "good old days" as they face subordinates who have broken off on a more discordant path:

> According to the [theory of dependence and protection], the lot of the poor, in all things which affect them collectively, should be regulated *for* them, not *by* them. They should not be required or encouraged to think for themselves, or give to their own reflection or forecast an influential voice in the determination of their destiny. It is supposed to be the duty of the higher classes to think for them, and to take the responsibility of their lot, as the commander and officers of an army take that of the soldiers composing it. This function, it is contended, the higher classes should prepare themselves to perform conscientiously, and their whole demeanour should impress the poor with a reliance on it, in order that, while yielding passive and active obedience to the rules prescribed for them, they may resign themselves in all other respects to a trustful *insouciance,* and repose under the shadow of their protectors. The relation between rich and poor, according to this theory (a theory also applied to the relation between men and women) should be only partly authoritative; it should be amiable, moral, and sentimental: affectionate tutelage on the one side, respectful and grateful deference on the other. The rich should be *in loco parentis* to the poor, guiding and restraining them like children. Of spontaneous action on their part there should be no need. They should be called on for nothing but to do their day's work, and to be moral and religious. Their morality and religion should be provided for them by their superiors, who should see them properly taught it, and should do all that is necessary to ensure their being, in return for labor and attachment, properly fed, clothed, housed, spiritually edified, and innocently amused.

This is the ideal of the future, in the minds of those whose dissatisfaction with the present assumes the form of affection and regret towards the past. Like other ideals, it exercises an unconscious influence on the opinions and sentiments of numbers who never consciously guide themselves by any ideal. (Mill [1848] 1970, book 4, 119)[3]

Subordinates, for their part, do not rush headlong into conflictive attitudes. As they begin to formulate goals for affirmative policy change, they take their cue from dominants and retain inclusive feelings toward them rather than jumping straight into conflictive attitudes. Thus, most of the women who are drawn to affirmative policy goals retain their inclusive feelings toward men rather than taking a more conflictive tack that would jar unproductively in the paternalistic context of gender relations. The poor and working class and blacks have had the opportunity to venture further into conflictive attitudes, but even here more than a third of those pursuing affirmative policy goals suffuse those goals in inclusive feelings toward those they would like to persuade.

And so the game endures. Subordinates gingerly test the limits of the expropriative rules that bind their existence, and dominants work to contain the incipient threat to their privileges. In that cause, the coercive gentility of conditional love remains their first-choice strategy, but as circumstances erode its efficacy, dominants reluctantly convert to an ideology based on reasoned persuasion. In the advanced industrial economy of the United States, dominant groups who have found their paternalism rebuffed have turned to the principle of individualism to divert and restrain subordinates' demands.

LOVE AND ENMITY

The data in this book demonstrate the varying trails along which intergroup ideology may wind as groups with unequal resources negotiate with each other in the face of various constraints. As people try to make the best of their lot, they seek to protect what they have and, if the opportunity arises, to enhance their situation. Subordinates tread warily as they ask for more, alert to both opportunities and hazards. They show little inclination for a head-on fight with those who have the power to intrude further on their meager resources. For dominants, the opportunity rarely arises to exact more from subordinates: their main effort is directed to a holding action, with threats to exact more reserved for

3. Mill's description of the paternalist's ideal is quoted out of context by Newby (1977b, 64–65), who paradoxically represents it as Mill's own view. However, Mill was at pains to dissociate himself from that euphemistic portrayal of "the patriarchal or paternal system of government" (Mill [1848] 1970, book 4, 121), observing that "no times can be pointed out in which the higher classes of this or any other country performed a part even distantly resembling the one assigned to them in this theory" (Mill [1848] 1970, book 4, 120).

those moments when subordinates' demands have become too invasive. In the cause of preserving the modus vivendi, dominants have little wish to enter into battle with subordinates over the distribution of resources. They prefer to hold them in a coercive embrace, and failing that, they endeavor to contain subordinates' incipient challenge with principles and reason.

Paternalism has occupied a marginal and nebulous position in past research on intergroup relations because of the overriding significance attached to conflict and hostility as the emblem of exploitation. I have sought to demonstrate that such an emphasis is misplaced. Paternalism beckons the members of dominant groups with a radiant beacon as they seek to preserve the expropriative arrangements on which they depend for their privileged stature in life. In this abiding endeavor, love and affection offer a coercive energy and a soothing balm that cannot be matched. In the words made famous by Doris Day:

> Love makes the world go 'round.
> Love makes the world go 'round,
> Somebody soon will love you,
> If no one loves you now.
> High in some silent sky,
> Love sings a silver song,
> Making the earth whirl softly,
> Love makes the world go 'round. 'round.
> Bob Merrill, theme from *Carnival,* 1961

Sung with blissful confidence, the dark side of these words remains far from the thoughts of either the singer or those who listen and hum along.

REFERENCES

Abelson, Robert T. 1959. "Modes of Resolution of Belief Dilemmas." *Journal of Conflict Resolution* 3(4): 343–352.

Abelson, Robert T., Elliot Aronson, William J. McGuire, Theodore M. Newcomb, Milton J. Rosenberg, and Percy H. Tannenbaum. 1968. *Theories of Cognitive Consistency: A Sourcebook*. Chicago: Rand McNally and Company.

Aberbach, Joel D., and Jack L. Walker. 1972. "Political Trust and Racial Ideology." In *Black Political Attitudes: Implications for Political Support*, ed. Charles S. Bullock, III, and Harrell R. Rodgers, Jr., pp. 133–162. Chicago: Markham Publishing Company.

Abercrombie, Nicholas, Stephen Hill, and Bryan S. Turner. 1980. *The Dominant Ideology Thesis*. London: Allen and Unwin.

Abercrombie, Nicholas, and Bryan S. Turner. 1982. "The Dominant Ideology Thesis." In *Classes, Power, and Conflict: Classical and Contemporary Debates*, ed. Anthony Giddens and David Held, pp. 396–416. Berkeley, Los Angeles, London: University of California Press.

Abram, Morris. 1984. "What Constitutes a Civil Right?" *New York Times Magazine*, 10 June.

Abramson, Paul R. 1980. "Comments on Sullivan, Piereson, and Marcus." *American Political Science Review* 74 (September): 780–781.

Achen, Christopher H. 1975. "Mass Political Attitudes and the Survey Response." *American Political Science Review* 69 (December): 1218–1231.

Adorno, T. W., Else Frenkel-Brunswik, Daniel J. Levinson, and R. Nevitt Sanford. 1950. *The Authoritarian Personality*. New York: Harper and Row.

Allport, Gordon. 1935. "Attitudes." In *Handbook of Social Psychology*, ed. C. Murchison, pp. 798–844. Worcester, Mass.: Clark University Press.

—— [1954] 1979. *The Nature of Prejudice*. Reading, Mass.: Addison-Wesley.

—— 1962. "Prejudice: Is It Societal or Personal?" *Journal of Social Issues* 18 (2): 120–134.

Almond, Gabriel A., and Sidney Verba. 1963. *The Civic Culture: Political Attitudes and Democracy in Five Nations*. Princeton: Princeton University Press.

Amir, Yehuda. 1969. "Contact Hypothesis in Ethnic Relations." *Psychological Bulletin* 71 (May): 319–342.

Anderson, Margaret L., and Patricia Hill Collins, eds. 1992. *Race, Class, and Gender: An Anthology*. Belmont, Calif.: Wadsworth Publishing Company.

Anderson, Perry. 1976. "The Antinomies of Antonio Gramsci." *New Left Review* 100 (November-January): 5–78.

Anyon, Jean. 1984. "Intersections of Gender and Class: Accommodation and Resistance by Working-class and Affluent Females to Contradictory Sex Role Ideologies." *Journal of Education* 166 (1): 25–48.

Apostle, Richard A., Charles Y. Glock, Thomas Piazza, and Marijean Suelzle. 1983. *The Anatomy of Racial Attitudes*. Berkeley, Los Angeles, London: University of California Press.

Apter, David E., ed. 1964. *Ideology and Discontent*. New York: Free Press.

Ashmore, Richard D. 1970. "Prejudice: Causes and Cures." In *Social Psychology: Social Influence, Attitude Change, Group Processes, and Prejudice*, ed. B. E. Collins, pp. 245–339. Reading, Mass.: Addison-Wesley.

Ashmore, Richard D., and Frances K. Del Boca. 1981. "Conceptual Approaches to Stereotypes and Stereotyping." In *Cognitive Processes in Stereotyping and Intergroup Behavior*, ed. David L. Hamilton, pp. 1–35. Hillsdale, N.J.: Lawrence Erlbaum Associates.

Atkinson, Ti-Grace. 1984. "Radical Feminism and Love." In *Feminist Frameworks*, 2d ed., ed. Alison M. Jaggar and Paula S. Rothenberg, pp. 403–405. New York: McGraw-Hill.

Bachrach, Peter, and Morton S. Baratz. 1970. *Power and Poverty: Theory and Practice*. New York: Oxford University Press.

Baer, Hans, and Yvonne Jones, eds. 1992. *African Americans in the South: Issues of Race, Class, and Gender*. Athens: University of Georgia Press.

Baker, Donald G. 1983. *Race, Ethnicity and Power: A Comparative Study*. London: Routledge and Kegan Paul.

Barry, Kathleen. 1979. *Female Sexual Slavery*. Englewood Cliffs, N.J.: Prentice-Hall.

Bartlett, John. 1968. *Familiar Quotations*, 14th ed. Boston: Little, Brown.

Bayton, James A., Lois B. McAlister, and Jeston Hamer. 1956. "Race-Class Stereotypes." *The Journal of Negro Education* 25 (Winter): 75–78.

Bell, Colin, and Howard Newby. 1976. "Husbands and Wives: The Dynamics of the Deferential Dialectic." In *Dependence and Exploitation in Work and Marriage*, ed. Diana Leonard Barker and Sheila Allen, pp. 152–168. London and New York: Longman.

Bell, Daniel. 1973. *The Coming of Post-Industrial Society*. New York: Basic Books.

Bellah, Robert N., Richard Madsen, William M. Sullivan, Ann Swidler, and Stephen M. Tipton. 1985. *Habits of the Heart: Individualism and Commitment in American Life*. Berkeley, Los Angeles, London: University of California Press.

Beller, Andrea H. 1984. "Trends in Occupational Sex Segregation by Sex and Race, 1960–1981." In *Sex Segregation in the Workplace: Trends, Explanations, Remedies*, ed. Barbara F. Reskin, pp. 11–26. Washington, D.C.: National Academy Press.

Bennett, Stephen. 1973. "Consistency among the Public's Social Welfare Policy Attitudes in the 1960s." *American Journal of Political Science* 17 (August): 544–570.

Berelson, Bernard R., Paul F. Lazarsfeld, and William N. McPhee. 1954. *Voting: A Study of Opinion Formation in a Presidential Campaign.* Chicago: The University of Chicago Press.

Berry, Brian, and Henry L. Tischler. 1978. *Race and Ethnic Relations,* 4th ed. Boston: Houghton Mifflin.

Berube, Allan. 1990. *Coming Out Under Fire: The History of Gay Men and Women in World War Two.* New York: The Free Press.

Bettelheim, Bruno. 1984. "Fathers Shouldn't Try to Be Mothers." In *Feminist Frameworks,* 2d ed., ed. Alison M. Jaggar and Paula S. Rothenberg, pp. 306–311. New York: McGraw-Hill.

Bielby, William T., and James N. Baron. 1986. "Men and Women at Work: Sex Segregation and Statistical Discrimination." *American Journal of Sociology* 91 (January): 759–799.

Billig, Michael. 1976. *Social Psychology and Intergroup Relations.* London: Academic Press.

Bishop, George F., Robert W. Oldendick, and Alfred J. Tuchfarber. 1978a.. "Change in the Structure of American Political Attitudes: The Nagging Question of Question Wording." *American Journal of Political Science* 22 (May): 250–269.

—— 1978b. "Effects of Question Wording and Format on Political Attitude Consistency." *Public Opinion Quarterly* 42 (Spring): 81–92.

Bishop, George F., Alfred J. Tuchfarber, Robert W. Oldendick, and Stephen E. Bennett. 1979. "Questions about Question Wording: A Rejoinder to Revisiting Mass Belief Systems Revisited." *American Journal of Political Science* 23 (February): 187–192.

Blalock, Hubert M. 1967. *Toward a Theory of Minority-Group Relations.* New York: John Wiley and Sons, Inc.

Blau, Francine, and Wallace Hendricks. 1979. "Occupational Segregation by Sex: Trends and Prospects." *Journal of Human Resources* 14 (Spring): 197–210.

Blau, Peter M., and Otis Dudley Duncan. 1967. *The American Occupational Structure.* New York: John Wiley.

Blauner, Bob. 1989. *Black Lives, White Lives: Three Decades of Race Relations in America.* Berkeley, Los Angeles, London: University of California Press.

Blea, Irene. 1992. *La Chicana and the Intersection of Race, Class, and Gender.* New York: Praeger.

Bledsoe, Albert T. 1856. *An Essay on Liberty and Slavery.* Philadelphia: J. B. Lippincott.

Blumer, Herbert. 1951. "Paternalism in Industry." *Social Process in Hawaii* 15: 26–31.

—— 1958. "Race Prejudice as a Sense of Group Position." *Pacific Sociological Review* 1 (Spring): 3–7.

—— 1965. "Industrialisation and Race Relations." In *Industrialisation and Race Relations: A Symposium,* ed. Guy Hunter, pp. 220-253. New York: Oxford University Press.

Bobo, Lawrence. 1983. "Whites' Opposition to Busing: Symbolic Racism or Realistic Group Conflict?" *Journal of Personality and Social Psychology* 45 (December): 1196–1210.

—— 1984. "Racial Hegemony: Group Conflict, Prejudice, and the Paradox of American Racial Attitudes." Ph.D diss., University of Michigan.

—— 1988. "Group Conflict, Prejudice, and the Paradox of Contemporary Racial Attitudes." In *Eliminating Racism: Profiles in Controversy*, ed. Phyllis A. Katz and Dalmas A. Taylor, pp. 85–116. New York: Plenum Press.

Bobo, Lawrence, and James R. Kluegel. 1991. "Modern American Prejudice: Stereotypes, Social Distance, and Perceptions of Discrimination toward Blacks, Hispanics, and Asians." Paper presented at the Annual Meeting of the American Sociological Association, Cincinnati, Ohio.

Bobo, Lawrence, and Frank Licari. 1989. "Education and Political Tolerance: Testing the Effects of Cognitive Sophistication and Target Group Affect." *Public Opinion Quarterly* 53 (Fall): 285–308.

Bocock, Robert. 1986. *Hegemony*. London and New York: Tavistock.

Bogardus, E. S. 1925. "Measuring Social Distances." *Journal of Applied Sociology* 9 (March-April): 299–308.

Bonacich, Edna. 1972. "A Theory of Ethnic Antagonism: The Split Labor Market." *American Sociological Review* 37 (5): 547–559.

—— 1973. "A Theory of Middleman Minorities." *American Sociological Review* 38 (October): 583–594.

—— 1975. "Advanced Capitalism and Black/White Relations in the United States: A Split Labor Market Interpretation." *American Sociological Review* 41 (February): 34–51.

—— 1976. "Abolition, the Extension of Slavery, and the Position of Free Blacks: A Study of Split Labor Markets in the United States, 1830–1863." *American Journal of Sociology* 81 (3): 601–628.

Bourdieu, Pierre. 1977. *Outline of a Theory of Practice*. Cambridge: Cambridge University Press.

Brand, Elaine S., Rene A. Ruiz, and Amada M. Padilla. 1974. "Ethnic Identification and Preference: a Review." *Psychological Bulletin* 81 (11): 860–890.

Brewer, Marilynn B. 1979. "In Group Bias in the Minimal Intergroup Situation: A Cognitive-motivational Analysis." *Psychological Bulletin* 86 (March): 307–324

Brigham, John C. 1971. "Ethnic Stereotypes." *Psychological Bulletin* 76 (July): 15–38.

Broverman, Inge K., Susan Raymond Vogel, Donald M. Broverman, Frank E. Clarkson, and Paul S. Rosenkrantz. 1972. "Sex-role Stereotypes: A Current Appraisal." *Journal of Social Issues* 28 (2): 59–78.

Brunk, Gregory G. 1978. "The 1964 Attitude Consistency Leap Reconsisdered." *Political Methodology* 5 (3): 347–359.

Burawoy, Michael. 1984. "Karl Marx and the Satanic Mills: Factory Politics under Early Capitalism in England, the United States, and Russia." *American Journal of Sociology* 90 (2): 247–282.

Burke, Edmund. [1775] 1954. "On Conciliation with the Colonies." In *Edmund Burke: Speeches and Letters on American Affairs*. London: J. M. Dent and Sons Ltd, 76–141.

Burleigh, Michael, and Wolfgang Wippermann. 1991. *The Racial State: Germany 1933–1945*. Cambridge: Cambridge University Press.

Butler, David, and Donald Stokes. 1974. *Political Change in Britain: The Evolution of Electoral Choice*, 2d ed. New York: St. Martin's Press.

Cammett, John M. 1967. *Antonio Gramsci and the Origins of Italian Communism.* Stanford: Stanford University Press.

Campbell, Angus. 1971. *White Attitudes Towards Black People.* Ann Arbor: Institute for Social Research.

Campbell, Angus, Philip E. Converse, Warren E. Miller, and Donald E. Stokes. 1960. *The American Voter.* New York: Wiley.

Campbell, Angus, and Howard Schuman. 1968. *Supplemental Studies for The National Advisory Commission on Civil Disorders.* Washington, D.C.: U.S. Government Printing Office.

Campbell, Donald T. 1967. "Stereotypes and the Perception of Group Differences." *American Psychologist* 22 (October): 817-829.

—— 1988. "Introduction to the Wesleyan Edition," In Muzafer Sherif, O. J. Harvey, B. Jack White, William R. Hood, and Carolyn Sherif, *The Robbers Cave Experiment: Intergroup Conflict and Cooperation*. Middletown, Conn.: Wesleyan University Press, xiii–xxi.

Cancian, Francesca M. 1985. "Gender Politics: Love and Power in the Private and Public Spheres." In *Gender and the Life Course*, ed. Alice S. Rossi, pp. 253–264. New York: Aldine Publishing Company.

—— 1987. *Love in America: Gender and Self-Development.* Cambridge: Cambridge University Press.

Cartwright, Dorwin, and Frank Harary. 1956. "Structural Balance: A Generalization of Heider's Theory." *Psychological Review* 63 (September): 277–293.

Cauthen, Nelson R., Ira E. Robinson, and Herbert H. Krauss. 1971. "Stereotypes: A Review of the Literature 1926–1968." *Journal of Social Psychology* 84 (June): 103–125.

Centers, Richard. 1949. *The Psychology of Social Classes*. Princeton: Princeton University Press.

Cherlin, Andrew, and Pamela Barnhouse Walters. 1981. "Trends in United States Men's and Women's Sex-role Attitudes: 1972–1978." *American Sociological Review* 46 (August): 453–460.

Clark, Kenneth B., and Mamie P. Clark. [1947] 1958. "Racial Identification and Preference in Negro Children." In *Readings in Social Psychology*, 3d ed., ed. T. M. Newcomb and E. L. Hartley, pp. 602–611. New York: Holt, Rinehart, and Winston.

Cloward, Richard A., and Frances Fox Piven. 1979. "Hidden Protest: The Channeling of Female Innovation and Resistance." *Signs* 4 (Summer): 651–669.

Cohen, Arthur R. 1960. "Attitudinal Consequences of Induced Discrepancies between Cognitions and Behavior." *Public Opinion Quarterly* 24 (2): 297–318.

Cohen, Carl. 1979. "Why Racial Preference Is Illegal and Immoral." *Commentary* 67 (6): 40–52.

Cohen, Lawrence E., and Richard Machalek. 1988. "A General Theory of Expropriative Crime: An Evolutionary Ecological Approach." *American Journal of Sociology* 94 (November): 465–501.

Connolly, William E. 1972. "On 'Interests' in Politics." *Politics and Society* 2 (Summer): 459–477.

Conrad, Robert Edgar. 1983. *Children of God's Fire: A Documentary History of Black Slavery in Brazil.* Princeton: Princeton University Press.

Converse, Philip E. 1964. "The Nature of Belief Systems in Mass Publics." In *Ideology and Discontent*, ed. David Apter, pp. 206–261. New York: Free Press.

—— 1970. "Attitudes and Nonattitudes: The Continuation of a Dialogue." In *The Quantitative Analysis of Social Problems*, ed. Edward Tufte, pp. 168–169. Reading, Mass.: Addison-Wesley.

Converse Philip, E., and Gregory B. Markus. 1979. *"Plus ça change . . .* The New CPS Election Panel Study." *American Political Science Review* 73 (March): 32–49.

Cook, Stuart W. 1984. "Cooperative Interaction in Multiethnic Contexts." In *Groups in Contact*, ed. Norman Miller and Marilynn B. Brewer, pp. 155–185. Orlando, Fla.: Academic Press.

Coser, Lewis A. 1956. *The Functions of Social Conflict.* New York: Free Press.

Cronan, Sheila. 1984. "Marriage." In *Feminist Frameworks*, 2d ed., ed. Alison M. Jaggar and Paula S. Rothenberg, pp. 329–333. New York: McGraw-Hill.

Crosby, Faye, Stephanie Bromley, and Leonard Saxe. 1980. "Recent Unobtrusive Studies of Black and White Discrimination and Prejudice: A Literature Review." *Psychological Bulletin* 87 (3): 546–563.

Dahl, Robert A. 1956. *A Preface to Democratic Theory.* Chicago: University of Chicago Press.

—— 1961. *Who Governs?* New Haven: Yale University Press.

—— 1968. "Power." In *International Encyclopedia of the Social Sciences*, vol. 12, ed. David L. Sills, pp. 405–415. New York: Macmillan.

Dahrendorf, Ralf. 1959. *Class and Class Conflict in Industrial Society.* Stanford: Stanford University Press.

—— 1964. "Recent Changes in the Class Structure of European Societies." *Daedalus* 93 (Winter): 225–270.

Davis, F. James. 1991. *Who Is Black?: One Nation's Definition.* University Park, Pa: The Pennsylvania State University Press.

Davis, James A. 1975. "Communism, Conformity, Cohorts, and Categories: American Tolerance in 1954 and 1972–73." *American Journal of Sociology* 81 (3): 491–513.

Davis, James A., and Tom W. Smith. 1990. *The General Social Survey: Cumulative Codebook and Data File.* Chicago: National Opinion Research Center.

Davis, Kingsley, and Wilbert E. Moore. 1945. "Some Principles of Stratification." *American Sociological Review* 10 (April): 242–249.

de Beauvoir, Simone. [1953] 1973. "The Second Sex." In *The Feminist Papers: From Adams to de Beauvoir*, ed. Alice S. Rossi, pp. 674–705. New York: Columbia University Press.

Degler, Carl N. 1971. *Neither Black nor White: Slavery and Race Relations in Brazil and the United States.* New York: Macmillan.

de Queiros Mattoso, Katia M. 1986. *To Be a Slave in Brazil: 1550-1888*, trans. by Arthur Goldhammer. New Brunswick, N.J.: Rutgers University Press.

Deutsch, Morton, and Mary Evans Collins. 1951. *Interracial Housing: A Psychologi-*

cal Evaluation of a Social Experiment. Minneapolis: University of Minnesota Press.

—— 1965. "The Effect of Public Policy in Housing Projects upon Interracial Attitudes." In *Basic Studies in Social Psychology*, ed. Harold Proshansky and Bernard Seidenberg, pp. 646–657. New York: Holt, Rinehart, and Winston.

Dollard, John. 1937. *Caste and Class in a Southern Town*. New Haven: Yale University Press.

Doob, Leonard W. 1947. "The Behavior of Attitudes." *Psychological Review* 54 (May): 135–156.

Dorn, Edwin. 1979. *Rules and Racial Equality*. New Haven: Yale University Press.

Dovidio, John F., and Samuel L. Gaertner. 1986. "Prejudice, Discrimination, and Racism: Historical Trends and Contemporary Approaches." In *Prejudice, Discrimination, and Racism*, ed. John F. Dovidio and Samuel L. Gaertner, pp. 1–34. New York: Academic Press.

Downs, Anthony. 1957. *An Economic Theory of Democracy*. New York: Harper & Row.

Duncan, Otis Dudley. 1961. "A Socioeconomic Index for All Occupations" and "Properties and Characteristics of the Socioeconomic Index." In *Occupations and Social Status*, ed. Albert J. Reiss, pp. 109–161. New York: Free Press.

Durkheim, Emile. [1897] 1951. *Suicide*. New York: Free Press.

—— [1895] 1964. *The Rules of the Sociological Method*. New York: Free Press.

—— [1893] 1965. *The Division of Labor in Society*. New York: Free Press.

The Economist. 1992. "American Values: Life, Liberty and Try Pursuing a Bit of Tolerance Too." September 5–11: 19–21.

Edelman, Murray. 1964. *The Symbolic Uses of Politics*. Urbana: University of Illinois Press.

Ehrlich, Howard J. 1964. "Instrument Error and the Study of Prejudice." *Social Forces* 43 (December): 197–206.

—— 1973. *The Social Psychology of Prejudice*. New York: Wiley-Interscience.

Ehrlich, Howard J., and James W. Rinehart. 1965. "A Brief Report on the Methodology of Stereotype Research." *Social Forces* 43 (May): 564–575.

Eldridge, Albert F. 1979. *Images of Social Conflict*. New York: St. Martin's.

Elkins, Stanley M. 1968. *Slavery: A Problem in American Institutional and Intellectual Life*, 2d ed. Chicago: University of Chicago Press.

Elliott, E. N. 1860. *Cotton Is King and Pro-Slavery Arguments: Comprising the Writings of Hammond, Harper, Christy, Stringfellow, Hodge, Bledsoe, and Cartwright, on This Important Subject*. Augusta, Ga.: Pritchard, Abbott, and Loomis.

Ellyson, Steve L., and John F. Dovidio, eds. 1985. *Power, Dominance, and Nonverbal Behavior*. New York: Springer-Verlag.

Elster, Jon. 1983. *Sour Grapes: Studies in the Subversion of Rationality*. Cambridge: Cambridge University Press.

Engels, Friedrick. [1884] 1972. *The Origin of the Family, Private Property and the State*. New York: International Publishers.

Fairchild, Hal H., and Patricia Gurin. 1978. "Traditions in the Social-psychological Analysis of Race Relations." *American Behavioral Scientist* 21 (5): 757–778.

Farley, Reynolds. 1984. *Blacks and Whites: Narrowing the Gap?* Cambridge, Mass.: Harvard University Press.

—— 1993. Personal Communication about the Spring 1992 Detroit Area Survey.

Feagin, Joe R. 1972. "America's welfare stereotypes." *Social Science Quarterly* 52 (March): 921–933.

—— 1975. *Subordinating the Poor: Welfare and American Beliefs.* Englewood Cliffs, N.J.: Prentice-Hall, Inc.

Femia, Joseph. 1975. "Hegemony and Consciousness in the Thought of Antonio Gramsci." *Political Studies* 23 (March): 29–48.

Festinger, Leon. 1957. *A Theory of Cognitive Dissonance.* Evanston, Ill.: Row, Peterson.

Festinger, Leon, Stanley Schachter, and Kurt Back. 1950. *Social Pressures in Informal Groups: A Study of Human Factors in Housing.* New York: Harper and Brothers.

Fields, James M., and Howard Schuman. 1976. "Public Beliefs about the Beliefs of the Public." *Public Opinion Quarterly* 40 (Winter): 427–448.

Firebaugh, Glenn, and Kenneth E. Davis. 1988. "Trends in Antiblack Prejudice, 1972–1984: Region and Cohort Effects." *American Journal of Sociology* 94 (September): 251–272.

Fireman, Bruce, and William A. Gamson. 1979. "Utilitarian Logic in the Resource Mobilization Perspective." In *The Dynamics of Social Movements,* ed. Mayer N. Zald and John D. McCarthy, pp. 8–44. Cambridge, Mass.: Winthrop Publishers, Inc.

Firestone, Shulimith. 1970. *The Dialectic of Sex.* New York: William Morrow.

Fishman, Joshua A. 1956. "An Examination of the Process and Function of Racial Stereotyping." *Journal of Social Psychology* 43 (February): 27–64.

Fitzhugh, George. 1854. *Sociology for the South, or the Failure of Free Society.* New York: Burt Franklin.

Fogel, Robert William. 1989. *Without Consent or Contract: The Rise and Fall of American Slavery.* New York: W. W. Norton.

Fogel, Robert William, and Stanley L. Engerman. 1974. *Time on the Cross.* Boston: Little, Brown and Company.

Fredrickson, George M. 1988. "White Images of Black Slaves in the Old South." In *The Arrogance of Race: Historical Perspectives on Slavery, Racism, and Social Inequality,* ed. George M. Fredrickson, pp. 206–215. Middletown, Conn.: Wesleyan University Press.

Gamson, William A. 1968. *Power and Discontent.* Homewood, Ill.: Dorsey Press.

Gamson, William A., and Andre Modigliani. 1987. "The Changing Culture of Affirmative Action." *Research in Political Sociology* 3: 137–177.

Gans, Herbert J. 1988. *Middle American Individualism: The Future of Liberal Democracy.* New York: The Free Press.

Genovese, Eugene D. 1968. *In Red and Black: Marxian Explorations in Southern and Afro-American History.* New York: Random House.

—— 1974. *Roll, Jordan, Roll: The World the Slaves Made.* New York: Random House.

Giddens, Anthony. 1979. *Central Problems in Social Theory: Action, Structure and Contradiction in Social Analysis.* Berkeley and Los Angeles: University of California Press.

Gilbert, G. M. 1951. "Stereotype Persistence and Change among College Students." *Journal of Abnormal and Social Psychology* 46 (April): 245–254.

Giles, Micheal W., and Arthur Evans. 1986. "The Power Approach to Intergroup Hostility." *Journal of Conflict Resolution* 30 (September): 469–486.

Glazer, Nathan. 1975. *Affirmative Discrimination*. New York: Basic Books.

Goffman, Erving. 1956. "The Nature of Deference and Demeanor." *American Anthropologist* 58 (June): 473–502.

Goldberg, Philip. 1968. "Are Women Prejudiced against Women?" *Transaction* 5: 28–30.

Goldman, Emma. [1910] 1969. *Anarchism and Other Essays*. Port Washington, N.Y.: Kennikat Press.

Goldthorpe, John H., David Lockwood, Frank Bechhofer, and Jennifer Platt. 1969. *The Affluent Worker in the Class Structure*. London: Cambridge University Press.

Goode, William J. 1982. "Why Men Resist." In *Rethinking the Family: Some Feminist Questions*, ed. Barrie Thorne and Marilyn Yalom, pp. 131–150. New York: Longman.

Gramsci, Antonio. 1971. *Selections from the Prison Notebooks of Antonio Gramsci*, ed. and trans. Quintin Hoare and Geoffrey Nowell Smith. New York: International Publishers.

Greeley, Andrew M., and Paul B. Sheatsley. 1971. "Attitudes toward Racial Integration." *Scientific American* 225 (December): 13–19.

—— 1974. "Attitudes toward Racial Integration." In *Social Problems and Public Policy: Inequality and Justice*, ed. Lee Rainwater, pp. 241–250. Chicago: Aldine.

Griffin, Susan. 1980. "Rape: The All-American Crime." In *Issues in Feminism*, ed. Sheila Ruth, pp. 300–313. Boston: Houghton Mifflin.

Gross, Harriet E., Jessie Bernard, Alice J. Dan, Nona Glazer, Judith Lorber, Martha McClintock, Niles Newton, and Alice Rossi. 1979. "Considering 'A Biological Perspective on Parenting.'" *Signs* 4 (Summer): 695–717.

Gurin, Patricia. 1985. "Women's Gender Consciousness." *Public Opinion Quarterly* 49 (Summer): 143–163.

Gurin, Patricia, and Edgar Epps. 1975. *Black Identity and Achievement*. New York: Wiley.

Gurin, Patricia, Arthur H. Miller, and Gerald Gurin. 1980. "Stratum Identification and Consciousness." *Social Psychology Quarterly* 43 (March): 30–47.

Hacker, Helen M. 1951. "Women as a Minority Group." *Social Forces* 30 (October): 60–69.

Hagner, Paul R., and John C. Pierce. 1983. "Levels of Conceptualization and Political Belief Consistency." *Micropolitics* 2 (4): 311–348.

Hamilton, David L. 1979. "A Cognitive-attributional Analysis of Stereotyping." *Advances in Experimental Social Psychology* 12: 53–84.

——, ed. 1981. *Cognitive Processes in Stereotyping and Intergroup Behavior*. Hillsdale, N.J.: Lawrence Erlbaum.

Hamilton, David L., and Tina K. Trolier. 1986. "Stereotypes and Stereotyping: An Overview of the Cognitive Approach." In *Prejudice, Discrimination, and Racism*, ed. John F. Dovidio and Samuel L. Gaertner, pp. 127–263. Orlando, Fla: Academic Press, Inc.

Hamilton, Richard F. 1972. *Class and Politics in the United States*. New York: John Wiley & Sons.

Harding, John. 1968. "Stereotypes." In *International Encyclopedia of the Social Sciences*, vol. 15, ed. David L. Sills, pp. 259–262. New York: Macmillan.

Harding, John, Harold Proshansky, Bernard Kutner, and Isidor Chein. 1954. "Prejudice and Ethnic Relations." In *Handbook of Social Psychology*, vol. 2, ed. Gardner Lindzey, pp. 1021–1061. Reading, Mass.: Addison-Wesley.

—— 1969. "Prejudice and Ethnic Relations." In *The Handbook of Social Psychology*, 2d ed., vol. 5, ed. Gardner Lindzey and Elliot Aronson, pp. 1–76. Reading, Mass.: Addison-Wesley.

Heider, Fritz. 1946. "Attitudes and Cognitive Organization." *Journal of Psychology* 21:107–112.

Helmreich, Robert L., Janet T. Spence, and Robert H. Gibson. 1982. "Sex-role Attitudes: 1972–1980." *Personality and Social Psychology Bulletin* 8 (December): 656–663.

Henley, Nancy M. 1977. *Body Politics: Power, Sex, and Nonverbal Communication*. Englewood Cliffs, N.J.: Prentice-Hall, Inc.

Henley, Nancy M., and Jo Freeman. 1979. "The Sexual Politics of Interpersonal Behavior." In *Women: A Feminist Perspective*, 2d ed., ed. Jo Freeman, pp. 474–486. Palo Alto: Mayfield Publishing Company.

Herrnstein, R. J. 1990. "Still an American Dilemma." *The Public Interest* 98 (Winter): 3–17.

Hewstone, Miles. 1989. "Changing Stereotypes with Disconfirming Information." In *Stereotyping and Prejudice: Changing Conceptions*, ed. D. Bar-Tal, C. F. Graumann, A. W. Kruglanski, and W. Stroebe, chap. 10. New York: Springer-Verlag.

Hewstone, Miles, and Rupert J. Brown, eds. 1986. *Contact and Conflict in Intergroup Encounters*. Oxford: Blackwell.

Hill, Kim Quaile, and Jan E. Leighley. 1992. "The Policy Consequences of Class Bias in State Electorates." *American Journal of Political Science* 36 (May): 351–365.

Hirsch, Jerry. 1973. "Behavior-Genetic Analysis and Its Biosocial Consequences." In *Comparative Studies of Blacks and Whites in the United States*, ed. Kent S. Miller and Ralph Mason Dreger. New York: Academic Press.

Hochschild, Arlie, with Anne Machung. 1989. *The Second Shift*. New York: Avon Books.

Hodge, Robert W., and Donald J. Treiman. 1968. "Class Identification in the United States." *American Journal of Sociology* 73 (March): 535–547.

Horner, Matina S. 1972. "Toward an Understanding of Achievement-related Conflicts in Women." *Journal of Social Issues* 28 (2): 157–175.

Huber, Joan, and William H. Form. 1973. *Income and Ideology: An Analysis of the American Political Formula*. New York: Free Press.

Huber, Joan, and Glenna Spitze. 1981. "Wives' Employment, Household Behaviors, and Sex-role Attitudes." *Social Forces* 60 (September): 150–169.

Hyman, Herbert H. 1969. "Social Psychology and Race Relations." In *Race and the Social Sciences*, ed. Irwin Katz and Patricia Gurin, pp. 3–48. New York: Basic Books.

Hyman, Herbert H., and Paul B. Sheatsley. 1956. "Attitudes toward Desegregation." *Scientific American* 195 (December): 35-39.

—— 1964. "Attitudes toward Desegregation." *Scientific American* 211 (July): 16–23.

Inglehart, Ronald. 1977. *The Silent Revolution: Changing Values and Political Styles Among Western Publics*. Princeton: Princeton University Press.

—— 1990. *Culture Shift in Advanced Industrial Society*. Princeton: Princeton University Press.

Jackman, Mary R. 1973. "Education and Prejudice or Education and Responseset?" *American Sociological Review* 38 (June): 327–339.

—— 1977. "Prejudice, Tolerance, and Attitudes toward Ethnic Groups." *Social Science Research* 6 (June): 145-169.

—— 1978. "General and Applied Tolerance: Does Education Increase Commitment to Racial Integration?" *American Journal of Political Science* 22 (May): 302–32.

—— 1981a. "Education and Policy Commitment to Racial Integration." *American Journal of Political Science* 25 (May): 256–269.

—— 1981b. "Issues in the Measurement of Commitment to Racial Integration." *Political Methodology* 7 (nos. 2 & 3): 160–172.

Jackman, Mary R., and Marie Crane. 1986. "'Some of My Best Friends Are Black . . .' Interracial Friendship and Whites' Racial Attitudes." *Public Opinion Quarterly* 50 (Winter): 459-486.

Jackman, Mary R., and Robert W. Jackman. 1973. "An Interpretation of the Relation between Objective and Subjective Social Status." *American Sociological Review* 38 (October): 569–582.

——. 1983. *Class Awareness in the United States*. Berkeley, Los Angeles, London: University of California Press.

Jackman, Mary R., and Michael J. Muha. 1984. "Education and Intergroup Attitudes: Moral Enlightenment, Superficial Democratic Commitment, or Ideological Refinement?" *American Sociological Review* 49 (December): 751–769.

Jackman, Mary R., and Mary Scheuer Senter. 1980. "Images of Social Groups: Categorical or Qualified?" *Public Opinion Quarterly* 44 (Fall): 341–361.

——. 1983. "Different, Therefore Unequal: Beliefs About Trait Differences Between Groups of Unequal Status." *Research in Social Stratification and Mobility* 2:309–335.

Jackman, Robert W. 1972. "Political Elites, Mass Publics, and Support for Democratic Principles." *Journal of Politics* 34 (August): 753–773.

—— 1993. "Rationality and Political Participation." *American Journal of Political Science* 37 (February): 279-290.

Jacobs, Jerry A. 1989. "Long-term Trends in Occupational Segregation by Sex." *American Journal of Sociology* 95 (July): 160–173.

Jaynes, Gerald David, and Robin M. Williams, Jr. 1989. *A Common Destiny: Blacks and American Society*. Washington, D.C.: National Academy Press.

Jencks, Christopher, and Paul E. Peterson, eds. 1991. *The Urban Underclass*. Washington, D.C.: The Brookings Institution.

Jensen, Arthur R. 1969. "How Much Can We Boost IQ and Scholastic Achievement?" *Harvard Educational Review* 39 (Winter): 1-123.

Johnson, Charles S. 1943. *Patterns of Negro Segregation*. New York: Harper and
    Brothers.
Jones, James M. 1972. *Prejudice and Racism*. Reading, Mass.: Addison-Wesley.
Jordan, Winthrop D. 1968. *White over Black: American Attitudes Toward the Negro,
    1550–1812*. Chapel Hill: The University of North Carolina Press.
Judd, Dennis R. 1991. "Segregation Forever?" *The Nation*, December 9.
Kane, Emily W. 1989. "Ideological Consensus in Gender Relations." Ph.D. diss.,
    The University of Michigan.
Kane, Emily W., and Laura Sanchez. 1992. "Pushing Feminism Out?: Family
    Status and Criticisms of Gender Inequality at Home and at Work." Unpub-
    lished paper, Department of Sociology, University of Wisconsin.
Karlins, Marvin, Thomas L. Coffman, and Gary Walters. 1969. "On the Fading
    of Social Stereotypes: Studies in Three Generations of College Students."
    Journal of Personality and Social Psychology 13 (1): 1–16.
Katterman, Lee. 1987. "The Attitudes Gap: White Americans Endorse Racial
    Equality, yet Show Little Support for Policies to Achieve It." *Research News*
    (November-December), The University of Michigan.
Katz, Daniel, and Kenneth W. Braly. 1947. "Verbal Stereotypes and Racial Preju-
    dice." In *Readings in Social Psychology*, ed. T. M. Newcomb and E. L. Hartley,
    pp. 204–210. New York: Holt, Rinehart, and Winston.
Katz, Phyllis A. 1976. *Toward The Elimination of Racism*. New York: Pergamon
    Press.
Keith, Verna M., and Cedric Herring. 1991. "Skin Tone and Stratification in
    the Black Community." *American Journal of Sociology* 97 (November): 760–778.
Kinder, Donald R. 1986. "The Continuing American Dilemma: White Resistance
    to Racial Change 40 Years after Myrdal." *Journal of Social Issues* 42 (Summer):
    151–172.
Kinder, Donald R., and David O. Sears. 1981. "Prejudice and Politics: Symbolic
    Racism versus Threats to the Good Life." *Journal of Personality and Social Psy-
    chology* 40 (March): 414–431.
Kinder, Donald R., and Tali Mendelberg. 1991. "Cracks in Apartheid? Prejudice,
    Policy and Racial Isolation in Contemporary American Politics." Paper pre-
    sented at the Annual Meeting of the American Political Science Association,
    Washington, D. C.
King, Jr., Martin Luther. 1958. *Stride Toward Freedom: the Montgomery Story*. San
    Francisco: Harper and Row.
Kirkpatrick, Samuel A. 1976. "Aging Effects and Generational Differences in
    Social Welfare Attitude Constraint in the Mass Public." *Western Political Quar-
    terly* 29 (March): 43-58.
Klein, Herbert S. 1967. *Slavery in the Americas: A Comparative Study of Virginia and
    Cuba*. Chicago: University of Chicago Press.
Kluegel, James R. 1987. "Macro-economic Problems, Beliefs about the Poor and
    Attitudes toward Welfare Spending." *Social Problems* 34 (February): 82–99.
—— 1990. "Trends in Whites' Explanations of the Black-White Gap in Socioeco-
    nomic Status, 1977–1989." *American Sociological Review* 55 (August): 512–525.
Kluegel, James R., Royce Singleton, Jr., and Charles E. Starnes. 1977. "Subjective

Class Identification: A Multiple Indicator Approach." *American Sociological Review* 42 (August): 599-611.

Kluegel, James R., and Eliot R. Smith. 1981. "Beliefs about Stratification." *Annual Review of Sociology* 7: 29–56.

———. 1986. *Beliefs about Inequality: Americans' Views of What Is and What Ought to Be.* Hawthorne, N.Y.: Aldine de Gruyter.

Koenig, Frederick W., and Morton B. King, Jr. 1964. "Cognitive Simplicity and Out-group Stereotyping." *Social Forces* 42 (March): 324–327.

Krosnik, Jon A. 1991. "The Stability of Political Preferences: Comparisons of Symbolic and Nonsymbolic Attitudes." *American Journal of Political Science* 35 (August): 547-576.

Kuklinski, James H., and Wayne Parent. 1981. "Race and Big Government: Contamination in Measuring Political Attitudes." *Political Methodology* 7 (numbers 2 & 3): 131–159.

Kuklinski, James H., Ellen Riggle, Victor Ottati, Norbert Schwarz, and Robert S. Wyer, Jr. 1991. "The Cognitive and Affective Bases of Political Tolerance Judgments." *American Journal of Political Science* 35 (February): 1–27.

Landecker, Werner S. 1963. "Class Crystallization and Class Consciousness." *American Sociological Review* 28 (April): 219–229.

Lane, Robert E. 1962. *Political Ideology: Why the American Common Man Believes What He Does.* New York: Free Press.

Laqueur, Walter. 1980. *The Terrible Secret.* Boston: Little, Brown.

Lasswell, Harold D. 1936. *Politics: Who Gets What, When, How.* New York: McGraw-Hill.

LaViolette, Forrest, and K. H. Silvert. 1951. "A Theory of Stereotypes." *Social Forces* 29 (March): 257–262.

Lears, T. J. Jackson. 1985. "The Concept of Cultural Hegemony: Problems and Possibilities." *American Historical Review* 90 (June): 567–593.

LeBlanc, Hugh L., and Mary Beth Merrin. 1977. "Mass Belief Systems Revisited." *Journal of Politics* 39 (November): 1082–1087.

Leggett, John C. 1968. *Class, Race, and Labor.* New York: Oxford University Press.

LeVine, Robert A., and Donald T. Campbell. 1972. *Ethnocentrism: Theories of Conflict, Ethnic Attitudes and Group Behavior.* New York: Wiley.

Lieberson, Stanley. 1980. *A Piece of the Pie: Blacks and White Immigrants Since 1880.* Berkeley, Los Angeles, London: University of California Press.

——— 1991. "Small *N*'s and Big Conclusions: An Examination of the Reasoning in Comparative Studies Based on a Small Number of Cases." *Social Forces* 70 (December): 307–320.

Lijphart, Arend. 1971. "Comparative Politics and the Comparative Method." *American Political Science Review* 65 (September): 682–693.

Lindblom, Charles E. 1977. *Politics and Markets: The World's Political-Economic Systems.* New York: Basic Books.

Linville, Patricia W., Peter Salovey, and Gregory W. Fischer. 1986. "Stereotyping and Perceived Distributions of Social Characteristics: An Application to In-group-outgroup Perception." In *Prejudice, Discrimination, and Racism*, ed. John

F. Dovidio and Samuel L. Gaertner, pp. 165–208. Orlando, Fla.: Academic Press, Inc.

Lippmann, Walter. 1922. *Public Opinion*. New York: Harcourt, Brace.

Lipset, Seymour Martin. 1960. *Political Man: The Social Bases of Politics*. London: Heinemann.

—— 1981. *Political Man: The Social Bases of Politics*, 2d ed. Baltimore: Johns Hopkins University Press.

Lipset, Seymour Martin, and William Schneider. 1978. "The Bakke Case: How Would It Be Decided at the Bar of Public Opinion?" *Public Opinion* 1 (March/April): 38–44.

Lipsky, Michael. 1968. "Protest as a Political Resource." *American Political Science Review* 62 (December): 1144–1158.

Litwack, Leon F. 1979. *Been in the Storm So Long: The Aftermath of Slavery*. New York: Knopf.

Lockwood, David. 1966. "Sources of Variation in Working Class Images of Society." *Sociological Review* 14 (November): 249–267.

Lukes, Stephen. 1974. *Power: A Radical View*. London: Macmillan.

McCauley, Clark, and Christopher L. Stitt. 1978. "An Individual and Quantitative Measure of Stereotypes." *Journal of Personality and Social Psychology* 36 (September): 929–940.

McCauley, Clark, Christopher L. Stitt, and Mary Segal. 1980. "Stereotyping: From Prejudice to Prediction." *Psychological Bulletin* 87 (1): 195–208.

McClosky, Herbert. 1964. "Consensus and Ideology in American Politics." *American Political Science Review* 58 (June): 361–382.

McClosky, Herbert, and Alida Brill. 1983. *Dimensions of Tolerance: What Americans Believe about Civil Liberties*. New York: Russell Sage Foundation.

McClosky, Herbert, Paul J. Hoffmann, and Rosemary O'Hara. 1960. "Issue Conflict and Consensus among Party Leaders and Followers." *American Political Science Review* 54 (June): 406–427.

Maccoby, Eleanor E., and C. N. Jacklin. 1974. *The Psychology of Sex Differences*. Stanford: Stanford University Press.

McConahay, John B. 1986. "Modern Racism, Ambivalence, and the Modern Racism Scale." In *Prejudice, Discrimination, and Racism*, ed. John F. Dovidio and Samuel Gaertner, pp. 91–125. Orlando, Fla.: Academic Press, Inc.

McConahay, John B., and Joseph C. Hough, Jr. 1976. "Symbolic Racism." *Journal of Social Issues* 32 (Spring): 23–45.

McConahay, John B., Betty B. Hardee, and Valerie Batts. 1981. "Has Racism Declined in America?: It Depends on Who Is Asking and What Is Asked." *Journal of Conflict Resolution* 25 (December): 563–579.

McGuire, William J. 1960. "Cognitive Consistency and Attitude Change." *Journal of Abnormal and Social Psychology* 60 (3): 345–353.

Mackie, Marlene. 1973. "Arriving at the 'Truth' by Definition: The Case of Stereotype Inaccuracy." *Social Problems* 20 (Spring): 431–437.

Mann, Michael. 1970. "The Social Cohesion of Liberal Democracy." *American Sociological Review* 35 (June): 423–439.

Mannheim, Karl. 1936. *Ideology and Utopia*, trans. Louis Wirth and Edward Shils. New York: Harcourt Brace Jovanovich.

Mansbridge, Jane J., ed. 1990. *Beyond Self-Interest*. Chicago: University of Chicago Press.

Marcuse, Herbert. 1964. *One-Dimensional Man: Studies in the Ideology of Advanced Industrial Society*. Boston: Beacon Press.

Marger, Martin N. 1994. *Race and Ethnic Relations: American and Global Perspectives*, 3d ed. Belmont, Calif.: Wadsworth.

Margolis, Michael, and Khondaker E. Haque. 1981. "Applied Tolerance or Fear of Big Government? An Alternative Interpretation of Jackman's Findings." *American Journal of Political Science* 25 (May): 241–255.

Martin, Patricia Yancey, and Robert A. Hummer. 1989. "Fraternities and Rape on Campus." *Gender and Society* 3 (December): 457-473.

Marx, Gary T. 1967. *Protest and Prejudice*. New York: Harper and Row.

Marx, Karl. [1869] 1959. "Excerpts from *The Eighteenth Brumaire of Louis Bonaparte*." In *Marx and Engels: Basic Writings on Politics and Philosophy*, ed. Lewis S. Feuer, pp. 318–348. New York: Anchor.

——— 1964. *Selected Writings in Sociology and Social Philosophy*, ed. T. B. Bottomore and Maximilien Rubel. New York: McGraw Hill.

——— [1857–58] 1971. *The Grundrisse*, ed. and trans. David McLellan. New York: Harper and Row.

Marx, Karl, and Friedrich Engels. [1888] 1959. "Manifesto of the Communist Party." In *Marx and Engels: Basic Writings on Politics and Philosophy*, ed. Lewis S. Feuer, pp. 1–41. New York: Anchor.

———. [1846] 1970. *The German Ideology*, ed. C. J. Arthur. New York: International Publishers.

Mason, Karen Oppenheim, and Larry L. Bumpass. 1975. "U.S. Women's Sex-Role Ideology, 1970." *American Journal of Sociology* (March) 80: 1212–19.

Mason, Karen Oppenheim, John L. Czajka, and Sara Arber. 1976. "Changes in U. S. Women's Sex-role Attitudes, 1964–1974." *American Sociological Review* 41 (August): 573–596.

Mason, Karen Oppenheim, and Yu-hsia Lu. 1986. "Attitudes toward Women's Familial Roles: Changes in the United States, 1977–1985." *Gender and Society* 2 (March): 39–57.

Massey, Douglas S. 1990. "American Apartheid: Segregation and the Making of the Underclass." *American Journal of Sociology* 96 (September): 329–357.

Massey, Douglas S., and Nancy A. Denton. 1987. "Trends in the Residential Segregation of Blacks, Hispanics, and Asians: 1970–1980." *American Sociological Review* 52 (December): 802–825.

———. 1989. "Hypersegregation in U. S. Metropolitan Areas: Black and Hispanic Segregation along Five Dimensions." *Demography* 26 (August): 373–391.

———. 1993. *American Apartheid: Segregation and the Making of the Underclass*. Cambridge: Harvard University Press.

Massey, Douglas S., and Mitchell L. Eggers. 1990. "The Ecology of Inequality: Minorities and the Concentration of Poverty, 1970–1980." *American Journal of Sociology* 95 (March): 1153–1188.

Meenes, Max. 1943. "A Comparison of Racial Stereotypes of 1935 and 1942." *Journal of Social Psychology* 17 (May): 327–36.

Meissner, Martin, Elizabeth W. Humphreys, Scott M. Meis, and William J. Scheu. 1975. "No Exit for Wives: Sexual Division of Labor and the Cumulation of Household Demands." *Canadian Review of Sociology and Anthropology* 12 (4): 424–439.

Merelman, Richard M. 1968. "On the Neo-elitist Critique of Community Power." *American Political Science Review* 62 (June): 451-461.

Merriam, Charles E. 1934. *Political Power*. New York: McGraw-Hill.

Merriman, W. Richard, and T. Wayne Parent. 1983. "Sources of Citizen Attitudes toward Government Race Policy." *Polity* 16 (Fall): 30–47.

Merriman, W. Richard, and Edward G. Carmines. 1988. "The Limits of Liberal Tolerance: The Case of Racial Policies." *Polity* 20 (Spring): 518–526.

Merrill, Bob. 1961. "Love Makes the World Go 'Round." Miami, Fla.: Columbia Pictures Publications.

Mill, John Stuart. [1848] 1970. *Principles of Political Economy, with Some of Their Applications to Social Philosophy,* books 4 and 5, ed. Donald Winch. New York: Penguin.

———. [1869] 1970. "The Subjection of Women." In *Essays on Sex Equality: John Stuart Mill and Harriet Taylor Mill,* ed. Alice S. Rossi, pp. 123-242. Chicago: University of Chicago Press.

Miller, Arthur H., Patricia Gurin, Gerald Gurin, and Oksana Malanchuk. 1981. "Group Consciousness and Political Participation." *American Journal of Political Science* 25 (August): 494-511.

Miller, Norman, and Marilynn B. Brewer. 1984. *Groups in Contact: The Psychology of Desegregation.* Orlando, Fla.: Academic Press, Inc.

———. 1986. "Categorization Effects on Ingroup and Outgroup Perception." In *Prejudice, Discrimination, and Racism,* ed. John F. Dovidio and Samuel L. Gaertner, pp. 209–230. Orlando, Florida: Academic Press, Inc.

Millett, Kate. 1970. *Sexual Politics*. New York: Doubleday.

Mills, C. Wright. 1946. "The Middle Classes in the Middle-sized Cities." *American Sociological Review* 11 (October): 520-529.

Moore, Barrington. 1966. *Social Origins of Dictatorship and Democracy: Lord and Peasant in the Making of the Modern World.* Boston: Beacon Press.

Morris, Richard T., and Raymond J. Murphy. 1966. "A Paradigm for the Study of Class Consciousness." *Sociology and Social Research* 50 (April): 297–313.

Mullins, Elizabeth I., and Paul Sites. 1984. "The Origins of Contemporary Eminent Black Americans: A Three-generation Analysis of Social Origin." *American Sociological Review* 49 (October): 672–685.

Myrdal, Gunnar. 1944. *An American Dilemma: The Negro Problem and Modern Democracy.* New York: Harper & Bros.

National Election Studies. 1991. *National Election Studies 1952–1990 Cumulative Data File Codebook.* Ann Arbor: Center for Political Studies, University of Michigan.

Newby, Howard. 1977a. *The Deferential Worker: A Study of Farm Workers in East Anglia.* London: Allen Lane.

——— 1977b. "Paternalism and Capitalism." In *Industrial Society: Class, Cleavage and Control,* ed. Richard Scase, pp. 59–73. London: Allen and Unwin.

Newcomb, Theodore M. 1953. "An Approach to the Study of Communicative Acts." *Psychological Review* 60 (November): 393–404.

Newcomb, Theodore M., Ralph H. Turner, and Philip E. Converse. 1965. *Social Psychology: The Study of Human Interaction.* New York: Holt, Rinehart and Winston.

Nie, Norman H., Sidney Verba, and John R. Petrocik. 1976. *The Changing American Voter.* Cambridge: Harvard University Press.

Nie, Norman H., with Kristi Anderson. 1974. "Mass Belief Systems Revisited: Political Change and Attitude Structure." *Journal of Politics* 36 (August): 541–591.

Nilson, Linda Burzotta. 1981. "Reconsidering Ideological Lines: Beliefs about Poverty in America." *The Sociological Quarterly* 22 (4): 531–538.

Nisbet, Robert A. 1970. "The Decline and Fall of Social Class." In *The Logic of Social Hierarchies*, ed. Edward O. Laumann, Paul M. Siegel, and Robert W. Hodge, pp. 570–574. Chicago: Markham.

Nunn, Clyde Z., Harry J. Crockett, and J. Allen Williams. 1978. *Tolerance for Nonconformity.* San Francisco: Jossey-Bass.

Oberschall, Anthony. 1978. "Theories of Social Conflict." *Annual Review of Sociology* 4: 291–315.

Olsen, Marvin E. 1970. "Social and Political Participation of Blacks." *American Sociological Review* 35 (August): 682–697.

Osgood, Charles E., and Percy H. Tannenbaum. 1955. "The Principle of Congruity in the Prediction of Attitude Change." *Psychological Review* 62 (January): 42–55.

Paige, Jeffery M. 1972. "Changing Patterns of Anti-white Attitudes among Blacks." In *Black Political Attitudes: Implications for Political Support*, ed. Charles S. Bullock, III, and Harrell R. Rodgers, Jr., pp. 97–114. Chicago: Markham Publishing Company.

Parelius, Ann P. 1975. "Change and Stability in College Women's Orientations toward Education, Family, and Work." *Social Problems* 22 (February): 420–432.

Parkin, Frank. 1971. *Class Inequality and Political Order.* New York: Praeger.

Parsons, Talcott, and Robert F. Bales. 1955. *Family, Socialization and Interaction Process.* Glencoe, Ill.: Free Press.

Pettigrew, Thomas F. 1958. "Personality and Sociocultural Factors in Intergroup Attitudes: A Cross-national Comparison." *Journal of Conflict Resolution* 2 (1): 29–42.

—— 1979. "The Ultimate Attribution Error: Extending Allport's Cognitive Analysis of Prejudice." *Personality and Social Psychology Bulletin* 5 (no. 4): 461–476.

—— 1980. "Introduction." In *The Sociology of Race Relations: Reflection and Reform*, ed. Thomas F. Pettigrew, pp. xiii-xxxiii. New York: The Free Press.

—— 1982. "Prejudice." In Thomas F. Pettigrew, George M. Fredrickson, Dale T. Knobel, Nathan Glazer, and Reed Ueda, *Prejudice*. Cambridge, Mass.: The Belknap Press, 1–29.

—— 1985. "New Black-white Patterns: How to Best Conceptualize Them?" *Annual Review of Sociology* 11: 329-346.

Piereson, James E. 1978. "Issue Alignment and the American Party System." *American Politics Quarterly* 6 (July): 275–307.

Pleck, Joseph H. 1977. "The Work-family Role System." *Social Problems* 24 (April): 417–427.

Polsby, Nelson W. 1980. *Community Power and Political Theory*, 2d ed. New Haven: Yale University Press.

Powdermaker, Hortense. [1939] 1968. *After Freedom: A Cultural Study in the Deep South*. New York: Russell and Russell.

Prager, Jeffrey. 1982. "American Racial Ideology as Collective Representation." *Ethnic and Racial Studies* 5 (January): 99–119.

Prothro, James W., and Charles M. Grigg. 1960. "Fundamental Principles of Democracy: Bases of Agreement and Disagreement." *Journal of Politics* 22 (May): 276–294.

Przeworski, Adam, and Henry Teune. 1970. *The Logic of Comparative Social Inquiry*. New York: Wiley-Interscience.

Ransford, H. Edward, and Jon Miller. 1983. "Race, Sex, and Feminist Outlooks." *American Sociological Review* 48 (February): 46–59.

Reskin, Barbara F., ed. 1984. *Sex Segregation in the Workplace: Trends, Explanations, Remedies*. Washington, D. C.: National Academy Press.

Reskin, Barbara F., and Patricia A. Roos. 1987. "Status Hierarchies and Sex Segregation." In *Ingredients for Women's Employment Policy*, ed. Christine Bose and Glenna Spitze, chap. 1. New York: SUNY Press.

——, 1990. *Job Queues, Gender Queues: Explaining Women's Inroads into Male Occupations*. Philadelphia: Temple University Press.

Rich, Adrienne. 1980. "Compulsory Heterosexuality and Lesbian Existence." *Signs* 5 (4): 647–650.

Richter, Maurice N., Jr. 1956. "The Conceptual Mechanism of Stereotyping." *American Sociological Review* 21 (October): 568–571.

Robertson, David B., and Dennis R. Judd. 1989. *The Development of American Public Policy: The Structure of Policy Restraint*. Glenview, Ill.: Scott, Foresman and Company.

Rokeach, Milton, Patricia W. Smith, and Richard Evans. 1960. "Two Kinds of Prejudice or One?" In *The Open and Closed Mind*, ed. Milton Rokeach, pp. 132–168. New York: Basic Books, Inc.

Rose, Arnold. 1964. *The Negro in America*. New York: Harper and Row.

—— 1967. *The Power Structure: Political Process in American Society*. New York: Oxford University Press.

Rosenberg, Milton J. 1956. "Cognitive Structure and Attitudinal Affect." *Journal of Abnormal and Social Psychology* 53 (3): 367–372.

Rosenberg, Rosalind. 1982. *Beyond Separate Spheres: Intellectual Roots of Modern Feminism*. New Haven: Yale University Press.

Ross, Catherine E. 1987. "The Division of Labor at Home." *Social Forces* 65 (March): 816–833.

Ross, Lee D. 1977. "The Intuitive Psychologist and His Shortcomings: Distortions in the Attribution Process." In *Advances in Experimental Social Psychology, vol. 10*, ed. Leonard Berkowitz, 173–220. New York: Academic Press.

Ross, Lee D., David Greene, and Pamela House. 1977. "The 'False Consensus Effect': An Egocentric Bias in Social Perception and Attribution Processes." *Journal of Experimental and Social Psychology* 13 (May): 279–301.

Rossi, Alice. 1977a. "A Biosocial Perspective on Parenting." *Daedalus* 106 (Spring): 1–31.

—— 1977b. "Sex Equality: The Beginning of Ideology." In *Masculine/Feminine*, ed. Betty Roszak and Theodore Roszak, pp. 173–186. New York: Harper & Row.

Rubin, Lillian B. 1976. *Worlds of Pain.* New York: Basic Books.

—— 1983. *Intimate Strangers: Men and Women Together.* New York: Harper and Row.

Russell, Diana E. H. 1982. *Rape in Marriage.* New York: MacMillan Publishing Co., Inc.

Schaar, John H. 1967. "Equality of Opportunity and Beyond." In *Equality*, NOMOS IX, ed. J. Roland Pennock and John W. Chapman, pp. 228-249. New York: Atherton Press.

Schattschneider, E. E. 1960. *The Semi-Sovereign People.* New York: Holt, Rinehart, and Winston.

Schermerhorn, R. A. 1970. *Comparative Ethnic Relations: A Framework for Theory and Research.* Chicago: University of Chicago Press.

Schlozman, Kay Lehman. 1984. "What Accent the Heavenly Chorus? Political Equality and the American Pressure System." *Journal of Politics* 46 (November): 1006–1032.

Schuman, Howard. 1975. "Free Will and Determinism in Public Beliefs about Race." In *Majority and Minority: The Dynamics of Racial and Ethnic Relations*, ed. Norman R. Yetman and C. Hoy Steele, pp. 375–380. Boston: Allyn and Bacon, Inc.

Schuman, Howard, and John Harding. 1964. "Prejudice and the Norm of Rationality." *Sociometry* 27: 353–371.

Schuman, Howard, and Shirley Hatchett. 1974. *Black Racial Attitudes: Trends and Complexities.* Ann Arbor: Institute for Social Research.

Schuman, Howard, and Graham Kalton. 1985. "Survey Methods." In *Handbook of Social Psychology, vol. 1*, 3d ed., ed. Gardner Lindzey and Elliot Aronson, pp. 635–697. New York: Random House.

Schuman, Howard, Charlotte Steeh, and Lawrence Bobo. 1985. *Racial Attitudes in America: Trends and Interpretations.* Cambridge, Mass.: Harvard University Press.

Schuman, Howard, and Lawrence Bobo. 1988. "Survey-Based Experiments on White Racial Attitudes toward Residential Segregation." *American Journal of Sociology* 94 (September): 273–299.

Schwartz, Sandra Kenyon, and David C. Schwartz. 1976. "Convergence and Divergence in Political Orientations between Blacks and Whites: 1960–1973." *Journal of Social Issues* 32 (Spring): 153–168.

Scott, James C. 1985. *Weapons of the Weak: Everyday Forms of Peasant Resistance.* New Haven: Yale University Press.

—— 1990. *Domination and the Arts of Resistance: Hidden Transcripts.* New Haven: Yale University Press.

Sears, David O., C. P. Hensler, and L. K. Speer. 1979. "Whites' Opposition to 'Busing': Self-interest or Symbolic Politics?" *American Political Science Review* 73 (June): 369–384.

Secord, Paul F. 1959. "Stereotyping and Favorableness in the Perception of Negro Faces." *Journal of Abnormal and Social Psychology* 59 (November): 309–315.

Selznick, Gertrude J., and Stephen Steinberg. 1969. *The Tenacity of Prejudice: Anti-Semitism in Contemporary America*. New York: Harper and Row.

Sherif, Muzafer. 1965. "Superordinate Goals in the Reduction of Intergroup Conflict." In *Basic Studies in Social Psychology*, ed. Harold Proshansky and Bernard Seidenberg, pp. 694–702. New York: Holt, Rinehart and Winston.

—— 1966. *Group Conflict and Cooperation: Their Social Psychology*. London: Routledge and Kegan Paul Ltd.

Sherif, Muzafer, and Carolyn W. Sherif. 1953. *Groups in Harmony and Tension: An Integration of Studies on Intergroup Relations*. New York: Harper and Brothers.

Sherif, Muzafer, O. J. Harvey, B. Jack White, William R. Hood, and Carolyn Sherif. 1961. *Intergroup Conflict and Cooperation: The Robber's Cave Experiment*. Norman: University of Oklahoma Press.

——. 1988. *The Robber's Cave Experiment: Intergroup Conflict and Cooperation*. Middletown, Conn.: Wesleyan University Press.

Sherriffs, Alex C., and John P. McKee. 1957. "Qualitative Aspects of Beliefs about Men and Women." *Journal of Personality* 25: 451–464.

Shockley, William. 1971. "Models, Mathematics, and the Moral Obligation to Diagnose the Origin of Negro IQ Deficits." *Review of Educational Research* 41 (October): 369–377.

—— 1972a. "Dysgenics, Geneticity, Raceology: A Challenge to the Intellectual Responsibility of Educators." *Phi Delta Kappan* 53 (January): 297–312.

—— 1972b. "A Debate Challenge: Geneticity is 80% for White Identical Twins' I.Q.'s." *Phi Delta Kappan* 53 (March): 415–427.

Sigelman, Lee, and Susan Welch. 1991. *Black Americans' Views of Racial Inequality: The Dream Deferred*. Cambridge: Cambridge University Press.

Simmel, Georg. 1955. *Conflict and The Web of Group Affiliations*. New York: The Free Press.

Simon, Rita J., and Jean M. Landis. 1989. "The Polls—A Report: Women's and Men's Attitudes about a Woman's Place and Role." *Public Opinion Quarterly* 53 (Summer): 265–276.

Simpson, George Eaton, and J. Milton Yinger. 1972. *Racial and Cultural Minorities: An Analysis of Prejudice and Discrimination*, 4th ed. New York: Harper and Row.

Smedley, Joseph W., and James A. Bayton. 1978. "Evaluative Race-class Stereotypes by Race and Perceived Class of Subjects." *Journal of Personality and Social Psychology* 36 (5): 530–535.

Smelser, Neil J. 1976. *Comparative Methods in the Social Sciences*. Englewood Cliffs, N.J.: Prentice-Hall.

Smith, A. Wade. 1981. "Racial Tolerance as a Function of Group Position." *American Sociological Review* 46 (October): 558–573.

Smith, Eric R. A. N. 1989. *The Unchanging American Voter*. Berkeley, Los Angeles, London: University of California Press.

Sniderman, Paul M., with Michael Gray Hagen. 1985. *Race and Inequality: A Study in American Values*. Chatham, N.J.: Chatham House Publishers.

Sniderman, Paul M., Richard A. Brody, and James H. Kuklinski. 1984. "Policy Reasoning and Political Values: The Problem of Racial Equality." *American Journal of Political Science* 28 (February): 75–94.

Sniderman, Paul M., and Philip E. Tetlock. 1986. "Reflections on American Racism." *Journal of Social Issues* 42 (no. 2): 173–187.

Sniderman, Paul M., Thomas Piazza, Philip E. Tetlock, and Ann Kendrick. 1991. "The New Racism." *American Journal of Political Science* 35 (May): 423–447.

Spencer, Herbert. [1862] 1958. *First Principles*. New York: DeWitt Revolving Fund.

Spitze, Glenna, and Joan Huber. 1980. "Changing Attitudes toward Women's Nonfamily Roles 1938 to 1978." *Sociology of Work and Occupations* 7 (August): 317–335.

Stacey, Judith, and Barrie Thorne. 1985. "The Missing Feminist Revolution in Sociology." *Social Problems* 32 (April): 301–316.

Staples, William G. 1987. "Technology, Control, and the Social Organization of Work at a British Hardware Firm, 1791-1891." *American Journal of Sociology* 93 (1): 62–88.

Steinem, Gloria. 1978. "If Men could Menstruate." *Ms. Magazine* 7 (4): 110.

Stephan, Walter G. 1985. "Intergroup Relations." In *Handbook of Social Psychology*, third edition, vol. 2. ed. Gardner Lindzey and Elliot Aronson, pp. 599–658. New York: Random House.

Stephan Walter G., and Cookie White Stephan. 1984. "The Role of Ignorance in Intergroup Relations." In *Groups in Contact*, ed. Norman Miller and Marilynn B. Brewer, pp. 229–255. Orlando, Fla.: Academic Press, Inc.

Stinchcombe, Arthur, and D. Garth Taylor. 1980. "On Democracy and School Integration." In *School Desegregation, Past, Present, and Future*, ed. W. Stephens and J. Feagin, pp. 157–186. New York: Plenum.

Stone, Alfred Holt. 1908. "Is Race Friction between Blacks and Whites in the United States Growing and Inevitable?" *American Journal of Sociology* 13 (March): 676–697.

Storr, Anthony. 1968. *Human Aggression*. New York: Atheneum.

Stouffer, Samuel A. 1955. *Communism, Conformity, and Civil Liberties*. New York: John Wiley & Sons.

Stringfellow, Thornton. 1860a. "The Bible Argument: Or, Slavery in the Light of Divine Revelation." In *Cotton Is King, and Pro-Slavery Arguments*, ed. E. N. Elliott, pp. 459–521. Augusta, Ga.: Pritchard, Abbott and Loomis.

—— 1860b. "Statistical View of Slavery." In *Cotton Is King, and Pro-Slavery Arguments*, ed. E. N. Elliott, pp. 522–546. Augusta, Ga.: Pritchard, Abbott and Loomis.

Strober, Myra H. 1984. "Toward a General Theory of Occupational Sex Segregation: The Case of Public School Teaching." In *Sex Segregation in the Workplace: Trends, Explanations, Remedies*, ed. Barbara F. Reskin, pp. 144–156. Washington, D. C.: National Academy Press.

Sullivan, John L., James E. Piereson, and George E. Marcus. 1978. "Ideological Constraint in the Mass Public: A Methodological Critique and Some New Findings." *American Journal of Political Science* 22 (May): 233–249.

—— 1979. "An Alternative Conceptualization of Political Tolerance: Illusory Increases, 1950's-1970's." *American Political Science Review* 73 (September): 781–794.

—— 1982. *Political Tolerance and American Democracy.* Chicago: University of Chicago Press.

Sullivan, John L., James E. Piereson, George E. Marcus, and Stanley Feldman. 1979. "The More Things Change, the More They Stay the Same: The Stability of Mass Belief Systems." *American Journal of Political Science* 23 (February): 176-186.

Sumner, William Graham. 1883. *What Social Classes Owe to Each Other.* New York: Harper & Brothers.

Tajfel, Henri. 1969. "Cognitive Aspects of Prejudice." *Journal of Social Issues* 25: 79–97.

—— 1978. *Differentiation Between Social Groups.* London: Academic Press.

—— 1981. *Human Groups and Social Categories.* London: Cambridge University Press.

—— 1982. "Social Psychology of Intergroup Relations." *Annual Review of Psychology* 33: 1–39.

Tajfel, Henri, and John Turner. 1979. "An Integrative Theory of Intergroup Conflict." In *The Social Psychology of Intergroup Relations*, ed. William G. Austin and Stephen Worchel, pp. 33–47. Monterey: Brooks/Cole.

Taylor, D. Garth. 1986. *Public Opinion and Collective Action: The Boston School Desegregation Conflict.* Chicago: University of Chicago Press.

Taylor, D. Garth, Paul B. Sheatsley, and Andrew M. Greeley. 1978. "Attitudes toward Racial Integration." *Scientific American* 238 (June): 42–50.

Taylor, Shelley E. 1981. "A Categorization Approach to Stereotyping." In *Cognitive Processes in Stereotyping and Intergroup Behavior*, ed. David L. Hamilton, pp. 83–114. Hillsdale, N.J.: Lawrence Erlbaum.

Thompson, John B. 1990. *Ideology and Modern Culture.* Stanford: Stanford University Press.

Thornton, Arland, and Deborah S. Freedman. 1979. "Changes in the Sex-Role Attitudes of Women, 1962–1977: Evidence from a Panel Study." *American Sociological Review* 44 (December): 831-842.

Thornton, Arland, Duane F. Alwin, and Donald Camburn. 1983. "Causes and Consequences of Sex-role Attitudes and Attitude Change." *American Sociological Review* 48 (April): 211-227.

Tiger, Lionel, and Robin Fox. 1971. *The Imperial Animal.* New York: Holt, Rinehart, and Winston.

Tilly, Charles. 1978. *From Mobilization to Revolution.* Reading, Mass.: Addison-Wesley.

Tocqueville, Alexis de. [1850] 1969. *Democracy in America.* New York: Anchor Books.

Tomich, Dale W. 1990. *Slavery in the Circuit of Sugar: Martinique and the World Economy 1830–1848.* Baltimore: The Johns Hopkins University Press.

Treiman, Donald J., and Heidi I. Hartmann, eds. 1981. *Women, Work, and Wages: Equal Pay for Jobs of Equal Value*. Washington, D.C.: National Academy Press.

Truman, David B. 1951. *The Governmental Process*. New York: Knopf.

Turner, Castellano B., and William J. Wilson. 1976. "Dimensions of Racial Ideology: A Study of Urban Black Attitudes." *Journal of Social Issues* 32 (Spring): 139–152.

Turner, John C. 1981. "The Experimental Social Psychology of Intergroup Behaviour," In *Intergroup Behavior*, ed. John C. Turner and Howard Giles, pp. 66–101. Oxford: Basil Blackwell.

van den Berghe, Pierre L. 1960. "Distance Mechanisms of Stratification." *Sociology and Social Research* 44 (January-February): 155–164.

—— 1967. *Race and Racism: A Comparative Perspective*. New York: John Wiley & Sons.

—— 1981. *The Ethnic Phenomenon*. New York: Elsevier Science Publishing Company.

—— 1983. "Class, Race, and Ethnicity in Africa," *Ethnic and Racial Studies* 6 (April): 221–236.

VanDeVeer, Donald. 1986. *Paternalistic Intervention: The Moral Bounds of Benevolence*. Princeton: Princeton University Press.

Vinacke, W. Edgar. 1957. "Stereotypes as Social Concepts." *Journal of Social Psychology* 46 (November): 229–243.

Walker, Kathryn, and Margaret Woods. 1976. *Time Use: A Measure of Household Production of Family Goods and Services*. Washington, D. C.: American Home Economics Association, Center for the Family.

Weber, Max. [1930] 1958. *The Protestant Ethic and the Spirit of Capitalism*, trans. Talcott Parsons. New York: Charles Scribner's Sons.

—— 1946a. "Class, Status, Party." In *From Max Weber: Essays in Sociology*, ed. H. H. Gerth and C. Wright Mills. New York: Oxford University Press, 180–195.

—— 1946b. "Bureaucracy." In *From Max Weber: Essays in Sociology*, ed. H. H. Gerth and C. Wright Mills. New York: Oxford University Press, 196–244.

——. [1947] 1964. *The Theory of Social and Economic Organization*. Trans. A. M. Henderson and Talcott Parsons. New York: The Free Press.

—— 1949. *The Methodology of the Social Sciences*. Glencoe, Ill.: Free Press.

Webster's New World Dictionary of the American Language, College Edition. 1968. David B. Guralnik and Joseph H. Friend (general editors). Cleveland and New York: The World Publishing Company.

Webster's Third New International Dictionary of the English Language. 1965. Philip Babcock Gove, ed. Springfield, Mass.: G. and C. Merriam Company.

Webster's Third New International Dictionary of the English Language. 1975. Philip Babcock Gove, ed. Springfield, Mass.: G. and C. Merriam Company.

Weiner, Marli F. 1985/86. "The Intersection of Race and Gender: The Antebellum Plantation Mistress and Her Slaves." *Humboldt Journal of Social Relations* 13 (1 and 2): 374–386.

Weissberg, Robert. 1976. "Consensual Attitudes and Attitude Structure." *Public Opinion Quarterly* 40 (Fall): 349–359.

Wellman, David T. 1977. *Portraits of White Racism*. New York: Cambridge University Press.

West, Candace, and Don H. Zimmerman. 1983. "Small Insults: A Study of Inter-ruptions in Cross-sex Conversations between Unacquainted Persons." In *Language, Gender and Society*, ed. Barrie Thorne, Cheris Kramarae, and Nancy Henley, pp. 102–117. Rowley, Mass.: Newbury House Publishers, Inc.

Wilensky, Harold L. 1970. "Class, Class Consciousness, and American Workers." In *American Society, Inc.*, ed. Maurice Zeitlin, pp. 450–462. Chicago: Rand McNally.

Willcox, W. F., U. G. Weatherly, John Spencer Bassett, J. W. Garner, Edwin S. Todd, Edwin L. Earp, W. E. Burghardt DuBois, and Alfred H. Stone. 1908. "Discussion of the Paper by Alfred H. Stone, 'Is Race Friction between Blacks and Whites in the United States Growing and Inevitable?' " *American Journal of Sociology* 13 (May): 820–840.

Williams, Gwyn A. 1960. "Gramsci's Concept of *Egemonia*." *Journal of the History of Ideas* 21 (October-December): 585–599.

Williams, Raymond. 1980. *Problems in Materialism and Culture*. London: Verso.

Williams, Robin M., Jr. 1947. *The Reduction of Intergroup Tensions*. New York: Social Science Research Council.

—— 1964. *Strangers Next Door: Ethnic Relations in American Communities*. Englewood Cliffs, N.J.: Prentice-Hall.

Williamson, Joel. 1980. *New People: Miscegenation and Mulattoes in the United States*. New York: Free Press.

Williamson, John B. 1974a. "Beliefs about the Welfare Poor." *Sociology and Social Research* 58 (January): 163–175.

—— 1974b. "Beliefs about the Motivation of the Poor and Attitudes toward Poverty Policy." *Social Problems* 21 (June): 634–648.

Wilner, Daniel M., Rosabelle Price Walkley, and Stuart W. Cook. 1955. *Human Relations in Interracial Housing*. Minneapolis: University of Minnesota Press.

Wilson, Edward O. 1978. *On Human Nature*. Cambridge: Harvard University Press.

Wilson, William Julius. 1973. *Power, Racism, and Privilege: Race Relations in Theoretical and Sociohistorical Perspectives*. New York: Free Press.

—— 1980. *The Declining Significance of Race: Blacks and Changing American Institutions*. 2d. ed. Chicago: University of Chicago Press.

—— 1987. *The Truly Disadvantaged: The Inner City, the Underclass, and Public Policy*. Chicago: University of Chicago Press.

Worchel, Stephen, and William G. Austin, eds. 1986. *Psychology of Intergroup Relations*. Chicago: Nelson-Hall Publishers.

Wright, Erik Olin. 1979. *Class Structure and Income Determination*. New York: Academic Press.

——. 1985. *Classes*. London: NLB/Verso.

Yinger, J. Milton. 1983. "Ethnicity and Social Change: The Interaction of Structural, Cultural, and Personality Factors." *Ethnic and Racial Studies* 6 (October): 395–409.

SUBJECT INDEX

Abstract policy principles. *See* Policy
  principles
Accommodative attitudes. *See also under*
  Class; Gender; Hidden resistance;
  Race
  conception of, 270–271, 280–282
  data on, 283–285, 289–290
  general evidence on, 293, 295, 376
  measurement of, 279–282 passim
Antebellum slavery, 10, 30, 70, 75, 77, 79,
  130, 131, 173–174, 356
Applied policy goals. *See* Policy goals,
  applied
Ascription to groups, 102–109, 124–125
  passim, 348, 371, 373, 374. *See also*
  under Class; Gender; Race
Attitude theory, 266–269
Attitudinal consistency. *See* Consistency,
  attitudinal
Attribution theory, 308
Authoritarianism, 36, 42, 115
  working class, 36, 42

Belief system. *See* Consistency, attitudinal
Beliefs, intergroup. *See* Categorical
  attributions to groups; Causal
  attributions to groups; Trait
  attributions to groups
Biological determinism, theories of
  in research on class, 52–53
  in research on gender, 52–53
  in research on race, 52–53

Case-study analysis, comparative. *See*
  under Methodological issues
Categorical attributions to groups. *See also*
  under Class; Gender; Race
  data on, 325–338 passim, 347–350
  passim, 372, 374, 376, 378
  general evidence on, 326, 336–338,
  345–347, 349, 378
  measurement of, 305–307, 322–325
  passim
  theories about, 18, 35, 92, 301–302,
  315–318, 343–347 passim
Causal attributions to groups. *See also*
  under Class; Gender; Race
  in antebellum slavery, 319–320
  data on, 339–343, 347, 348, 349
  general evidence on, 341–342, 347, 378
  inconsistencies in, 318, 320, 321
  measurement of, 338–339
  relationship to feelings, 297, 299–301
  relationship to policy goals, 297,
  299–301, 308, 309, 339, 343–344
  research on, 296, 299, 307–309,
  343–344
  theories about, 296–297, 298–301,
  308–309, 310, 318–320, 343–347
  passim
Class
  accommodative attitudes: data on, 285,
  289, 376; measurement of, 279–282
  passim
  ascriptive rules for, 102, 104–107, 109,
  124–125, 348, 374

Class (*continued*)
attitudinal consistency: data on,
276–278, 285, 286–287;
measurement of, 274, 279–282
categorical attributions: data on,
331–336, 347–348; measurement of,
322–325
causal attributions: data on, 339–343
passim, 348; measurement of,
338–339 passim
conflict, research on, 24–33, 37, 55–56,
72–73, 172–180 passim, 212–213,
214
conflictive attitudes: data on, 285,
287–291 passim, 294; measurement
of, 33, 279–282 passim
consciousness, 24–33, 37, 51, 53,
55–56, 57–58, 68, 72–73, 114–117
passim, 172–180 passim, 209,
212–213, 215, 216–217, 223,
225–226, 256, 266, 267, 291, 296
deference: data on, 285, 287–291
passim, 376; measurement of,
279–282 passim
distributive basis for, 74–75, 98–99,
102, 109, 124, 359–360
empirical definition of, 33, 106,
109–110, 111
feelings: data on, 189–193, 194,
195–196, 375; measurement of,
183–185
group membership, inheritance of,
106–107, 125, 374
hidden resistance in, 29–30, 56,
270–271, 281, 285, 289, 376
hostility, 24–26, 72–73, 117–118,
172–173, 189–193, 195–196, 348,
377–382 passim
integrationist attitudes: data on, 285,
287–291 passim, 293; measurement
of, 279–282 passim
nomenclature, 109, 111, 125
paternalism: data on, 285, 287–291
passim, 294; measurement of, 273,
279–282 passim
perception of differences, *see* causal
attributions; trait attributions
perception of group interests: data on,
203–204, 205, 375, 377;
measurement of, 197–199 passim
policy goals, applied: data on, 247–249,
251–253 passim, 255–256, 258, 259,

260, 375–376; measurement of,
238–241, 251
policy perceptions: data on, 247–249
passim, 250–251; measurement of,
238–241; research on, 213, 216–217
policy principles: data on, 236–238,
257, 375; measurement of, 230–231
revisionist attitudes: data on, 285,
287–291 passim; measurement of,
279–282 passim
segregation: role, 130, 139, 147,
155–157, 159–161, 163–164, 346,
374; spatial, 132, 135, 144–146,
155–157, 159–161, 163–164,
195–196, 294, 347–348, 374–375
subjective, 33, 105–106, 110–111,
124–125, 195, 374
tolerance: data on, 285, 387–291
passim; measurement of, 279–282
passim
trait attributions: data on, 326,
331–336, 348, 376; measurement of,
322–325
Communication channels
among classes, 75, 163–164, 195–196,
205, 260, 294, 375
intergroup, 17, 60–61, 86, 119–120,
127, 138, 161–162, 164, 179,
181–182, 259, 345, 350, 355,
362–363, 364
between men and women, 75–76,
80–81, 163, 196–197, 259, 373
between whites and blacks, 75, 163,
196, 259–260, 349, 364, 371–372
Competitive intergroup relations, 5–7,
169–170, 353–358 passim
Conflict
and exploitation, 1–2, 23–24, 32–33,
55–57
overriding of, *see* Tolerance
research on, 1–2, 16, 23–58
theories about: in class relations, 24–33,
56, 172–177, 212–213; in gender
relations, 47–55, 57; in general, 1–2,
9, 16–17, 23–24, 43–47, 55–58,
59–64, 91–93, 167–177, 180–182,
205–207, 213–214, 256–260,
353–358, 377–383; in race relations,
33–43, 169–177
Conflictive attitudes. *See also under* Class;
Gender; Race
conception of, 280–281, 282

data on, 283–285, 286, 287–288,
  289–290, 291, 294, 372, 374, 376,
  380–381
measurement of, 279–282 passim
general evidence on, 288, 292–295
  passim, 380–381, 382
Consciousness. *See* Class consciousness;
  False consciousness; Group
  consciousness
Consistency, attitudinal. *See also under*
  Class; Gender; Race
concept of, 261–269
evidence on, 274–279, 282–287,
  291–295, 377
measurement of, 274, 279–282
research on, 263–267, 291
theories about, 69–71, 120, 263–269,
  291–295, 309–310, 366
Constraint, attitudinal. *See* Consistency,
  attitudinal
  Contact, intergroup. *See also*
  Segregation, role; Segregation, spatial
evidence on, 138–161, 162–164
forms of, 17, 127–131, 132–138,
  161–162, 361–363
personal interactions in, 17, 74, 75,
  76–78, 86, 128–131, 146–161,
  163–164, 182, 206, 294, 345,
  347–348, 361–363, 371–372, 373,
  374–375
physical proximity in, 17, 86, 131–138,
  139–146, 163–164, 182, 206, 294,
  346, 347–348, 349, 364, 371, 373,
  374–375
predetermining factors in, 74–78,
  127–128, 129–130, 131–132, 135,
  161, 361–363 passim
Cultural diffusion, 122, 369

Deference. *See also under* Class; Gender;
  Race
concept of, 10, 79, 134, 262, 279–281
data on, 283–285 passim, 286,
  287–288, 289–291, 293–294 passim,
  372, 374, 376
general evidence on, 286, 289, 291,
  293–295 passim, 380–381
measurement of, 279–282 passim
Deferent attitudes. *See* Deference
Derogation
evidence on, 324–326, 328, 330–331,
  334–337, 347–349, 378

theories about, 297, 302–303, 313–315,
  343–344, 346, 350, 354
Differentiation, social, 76–78, 79–80,
  99–109, 124–125, 127–138, 161–164,
  345, 360–363, 371–372, 373,
  374–375. *See also under* Contact,
  intergroup; Segregation, role;
  Segregation, spatial; Status
Discrimination, 10, 16, 34, 36, 40, 43, 46,
  56, 65, 87, 210, 218, 224, 266, 273,
  275, 289, 297, 344
reverse, 224, 225, 240, 269

Education, effects of, 42, 47, 90, 115, 116,
  119, 268, 306, 323
Egalitarianism
in class relations, 212, 230–231,
  236–237, 240–241, 248
concept of, 89, 208, 222–227, 228, 230,
  230–231
versus equality of opportunity, 89–90,
  223–227, 239, 240–241, 257–258,
  317, 378, 380
in gender relations, 230, 234–235
general evidence of, 237–238, 249–250
in race relations, 228
Equality of opportunity
in class relations, 106, 380
concept of, 46, 257
versus egalitarianism, 89–90, 92–93,
  218, 223–227, 228–229, 237–238,
  239–240, 246–247, 257–258, 317,
  378, 380
in gender relations, 212, 229–230,
  235–236, 238, 239–240, 244–247,
  257, 380
in race relations, 218, 228–229,
  231–234, 237–238, 239–240,
  242–243, 380
and social control, 89–90, 92–93, 238,
  365, 378, 380
Existential beliefs about policy. *See* Policy
  perceptions
Exploitation, 2, 10, 24–29 passim, 32, 37,
  54, 56, 214, 271, 383
Expropriation
in class relations, 99, 102, 105–106,
  109, 124–125, 135–136, 359–360,
  362
concept of, 2–3, 45–46, 214, 355–358,
  359

Expropriation (*continued*)
  in gender relations, 101–102, 103,
    108–109, 125, 359, 361–362
  institutionalization of, 4, 7–8, 64–67,
    91, 355, 358–364
  in race relations, 99–102, 104, 108, 125,
    359, 362

False consciousness, 30–32, 56, 93,
    175–177, 213, 217, 220, 363
Feelings, intergroup. *See also under* Class;
    Gender; Race
  general patterns in, 192–197, 206–207,
    377
  measurement of, 177–180, 182–185
  relationship to intergroup beliefs,
    35–36, 170, 265–267, 297, 298–300,
    309
  relationship to policy goals: data on,
    273–291, 292–293, 372, 374, 376,
    377, 381–382; theories about, 10,
    11–16, 35–36, 45, 78–85, 261–262,
    264–273, 295, 297, 382–383
  theories about, 35–37, 39, 167–177,
    205–207
Folk Wisdom. *See* Causal attributions to
    groups
Force, 1, 2, 9, 11, 15–17, 48–51, 57, 59,
    61–64, 66, 74, 85, 87, 91, 361
Friendships, intergroup
  across classes, 159–161, 374–375
  between blacks and whites, 157–158,
    371–372
  between men and women, 158–159
  general patterns in, 157
  measurement of, 156–157
Functionalism
  in class theory, 26–28, 220
  in gender theory, 51–52, 129

Gender
  accommodative attitudes: data on 284,
    289, 290, 376; measurement of,
    279–282 passim
  ascriptive rules for, 102–103, 109, 125,
    373
  attitudinal consistency: data on,
    276–277, 284, 286–287;
    measurement of, 274, 279–282
  categorical attributions: data on,
    325–326, 329–331 passim, 336–337,
    347, 374; measurement of, 322–325

causal attributions: data on, 339–343
    passim, 347; measurement of,
    338–339 passim
  conflictive attitudes: data on, 284, 287,
    288, 289, 374, 381; measurement of,
    279–282 passim
  deference: data on, 284, 288, 374,
    380–381; measurement of, 279–282
    passim
  distributive basis for, 75–76, 101–102,
    108–109, 125, 359
  empirical definition of, 102–103,
    110–111
  feelings: data on, 188–189, 194,
    196–197, 373; measurement of,
    183–185
  group membership, inheritance of,
    106–107, 125, 373
  hidden resistance in, 51, 284, 289, 290,
    376
  hostility, 47–55, 118, 185, 188–189,
    193–195 passim, 196–197, 313–315
    passim, 343, 346, 377–382 passim
  integrationist attitudes: data on, 282,
    284, 286, 289–290, 293;
    measurement of, 279–282 passim
  paternalism: data on, 282, 284, 286,
    288, 289–290, 291, 374, 380;
    measurement of, 279–282 passim
  perception of differences, *see* causal
    attributions; trait attributions
  perception of group interests: data on,
    202–203, 205, 373, 377;
    measurement of, 198–199 passim
  policy goals, applied: data on, 244–247,
    249, 250, 252, 255, 256, 258–259
    passim, 373–374; measurement of,
    238–240, 251
  policy perceptions: data on, 244–246,
    250–251; measurement of, 238–241
    passim
  policy principles: data on, 234–236,
    237–238 passim, 257, 373;
    measurement of, 229–230
  revisionist attitudes: data on, 284, 287,
    289; measurement of, 279–282
    passim
  segregation: role, 131, 146–152, 155,
    157, 158–159, 163, 205, 211–212,
    314, 347, 373; spatial, 132–133,
    139–140, 142–144, 155, 157,
    158–159, 163, 210–211, 373

tolerance: data on, 282, 284, 288, 289;
    measurement of, 279–282 passim
trait attributions: data on, 325–326,
    329–331, 336–337, 347, 374;
    measurement of, 305–307 passim,
    322–325 passim
Group consciousness, 7–9, 24–33, 51,
    53–55, 56–58, 59–61, 81, 91–93,
    114–115, 168–169, 171, 172–177,
    180–182, 192–197, 205–207,
    208–209, 212–214, 216–217,
    218–222, 226–228, 256–260,
    261–262, 266, 269–271, 279–282,
    291–295, 303
Group interests, perception of. *See also
    under* Class; Gender; Race
general patterns in, 192–197, 204–205,
    206–207 passim, 377–378
measurement of, 177–179, 197–199
theories about, 56, 168–177 passim, 182

Hegemony, cultural, 30–32, 176–177, 181
Hidden resistance. *See also under*
    Accommodative attitudes; Class;
    Gender; Race
concept of, 29–30, 56, 262, 270–271,
    280–281
general evidence of, 293, 377
measurement of, 29–30, 270–271,
    279–282 passim
Hostility, intergroup. *See also under*
    Class; Gender; Race
general evidence of, 192–197, 206–207,
    274, 336–337, 343–350 passim,
    377–378
measurement of, 177–180, 183–185,
    274, 324–325
theories about, 1–2, 11, 16–17, 23–58
    passim, 59–93 passim, 117, 118,
    167–168, 169–177, 180–182,
    205–206, 262, 267–268, 270–271,
    295, 296, 297, 302–303, 309,
    313–315, 343, 346, 353–358,
    382–383

Ideology
as communication, 60, 67–69, 71,
    72–74, 114–115, 181–182, 206–207,
    208, 294–295, 344, 349–350,
    357–358, 362–366
definition of, 69–71
political character of, 64–71, 73–74,

92–93, 221–222, 268–269, 294–295,
    297–298, 309, 344–345, 347, 349,
    355, 358–366
as property of groups versus
    individuals, 7–9, 30, 71–73, 115–120,
    180, 221, 267–269, 366–368
as self-expression, 68–70 passim, 73,
    93, 178
as uncontrived, 7–9, 65, 69–70, 91, 93,
    221, 365
Individualism
in capitalism, 208–209, 222–224,
    225–226, 257, 346
in causal attributions to groups, 308,
    344–345
in class relations, 208–209, 226, 348,
    362
concept of, 87–89, 222–224
versus egalitarianism, 89–91, 92–93,
    208–209, 218, 222–227, 228–229,
    237–238, 239–240, 246–247, 250,
    257–258, 317, 378
in gender relations, 208–209, 238, 240,
    257
in policy goals, 41–42, 208–209, 216,
    218, 222–229, 233–234, 237–238,
    239–240, 246–247, 250, 257–258,
    378
in race relations, 41–42, 208–209, 216,
    218, 223–225, 228–229, 233–234,
    239, 269, 337, 349
and social control, 87–91, 92–93,
    208–209, 225–227, 238, 250, 257,
    258, 269, 317, 365, 378, 382
in trait attributions to groups, 317–318,
    337, 344–345, 346, 348, 349
Inequality
different components of, 98
distributive basis for: in class relations,
    74–75, 98–99, 102, 109, 124,
    359–360; in gender relations, 75–76,
    101–102, 108–109, 125, 359; in race
    relations, 75, 99–101, 108, 125, 359
expropriative basis of, 2–3
institutionalization of, 64–67, 358–364
long-term relations of, 5–7
relational basis of, 2–3, 214, 220
Integrationist attitudes
conception of, 280, 282, 293
data on, 283–285, 289, 290, 293, 377
general evidence on, 289, 295, 377
measurement of, 279–282 passim

Intimacy
  in antebellum slavery, 75, 84–85, 130
  in feudal class relations, 75, 362
  in gender relations, 75–76, 83–84, 118,
    163, 294
  and love, 17, 78–85, 92, 206, 363
  and role segregation, 76–78, 161–163,
    350, 363
  and social control, 17, 73–74, 80–82,
    92, 229, 294, 350, 362–364, 380
  and status differentiation, 76–78,
    130–131, 138, 162, 362–363
  and violence, 48–51 passim, 82–85, 87

Love
  in antebellum slavery, 71–72, 83–85
  and coercion, 10, 16, 17, 71–72, 74,
    78–82, 84–85, 86, 87, 92, 167, 363,
    382–383
  conditional, 78–82, 84–85, 86–87, 363,
    382
  in gender relations, 15, 83–85
  versus hate, 167, 382–383
  and intimacy, 17, 78–85, 92, 206, 363
  limits of, 15–16
  in race relations, 15–16, 71–72, 83–85
  romanticization of, 15, 383
  and violence, 82–85

Methodological issues
  in comparative case-study analysis,
    120–124, 126, 368–371
  in standard survey analysis, 115–120,
    367–368, 370–371
  in this study, 111–124, 126, 366–371
Middleman minorities, 6–7n
Minimal group paradigm, 40
Modern racism. *See* Symbolic racism
Morality, 10, 12, 13, 15, 37, 60, 66–71
    passim, 73, 74, 85, 87, 88, 90, 91–93,
    175–176, 181, 208–209, 217,
    221–224, 225–227, 231, 250,
    257–258, 260, 266, 269, 272, 292,
    298, 309, 311, 313, 344–345, 346,
    350, 365, 370, 375, 378, 381

Paternalism. *See also under* Class; Gender;
    Race
  in antebellum slavery, 10, 71–72, 79,
    83–85, 173–174
  versus benevolence, 11–15, 271–272
  concept of, 9–15, 87, 90, 261–262, 271,
    279–281, 291, 315–316

  data on, 206, 288–291, 292, 294–295,
    337, 343, 350, 374, 376, 380, 381
  general evidence on, 288–289, 291,
    292–293, 294–295 passim, 377,
    380–381
  measurement of, 279–282 passim
  research on, 10–14, 49, 262, 269–270,
    271–273, 383
  theory of, 9–15, 78–85, 87, 90, 206,
    271–273, 294–295, 298, 315–316,
    319, 331, 337, 338, 339, 343, 346,
    350, 363, 380–383
  and violence, 82–85, 87
Paternalistic attitudes. *See* Paternalism
Perception of group interests. *See* Group
    interests, perception of
Pluralism, 25, 28, 46, 113, 122
Policy goals, applied. *See also under* Class;
    Gender; Race
  data on, 241–256, 372, 373–374,
    375–376, 378
  general patterns in, 249–251, 256,
    258–260, 378
  interrelations among, 251–253
  measurement of, 209, 214–219,
    238–241, 251
  relationship to intergroup feelings: data
    on, 273–291, 292–293, 372, 374, 376,
    377, 381–382; theories about, 10,
    11–16, 35–36, 43–46, 78–85,
    171–172, 210–211, 261–262,
    264–273, 295, 297, 382–383
  relationship to intergroup beliefs, 35,
    297, 298–301, 302, 308, 309, 339,
    343–344
  relationship to policy principles, 40–42,
    209, 210, 211, 213, 214–217,
    222–226, 227, 242–244, 246, 248,
    249–250, 256, 257, 372, 373–374,
    375
  theories about, 208–209, 210–226
    passim, 256–260 passim
Policy perceptions. *See also under* Class;
    Gender; Race
  data on, 241–249 passim, 250–251
  general patterns in, 250–251
  measurement of, 238–241
  theories about, 213
Policy principles. *See also under* Class;
    Gender; Race
  data on, 228, 231–238, 257–258, 372,
    373, 375

general patterns in, 237–238, 257–258
measurement of, 214–217, 228–231
relationship to applied policy goals,
40–42, 209, 210, 211, 213, 214–217,
222–226, 227, 242–244, 246, 248,
249–250, 256, 257, 372, 373–374,
375
theories about, 209, 210–226 passim,
256, 257–258
Post-industrialism, 25, 28–29
Post-materialism, 25, 28–29
Power
definition of, 61–67, 69
inequalities in, 37, 65, 98, 272–273
interrelation with status and economic
inequality, 98–102, 359–360
relational basis of, 3, 61
Prejudice
concept of, 18, 24, 33–42, 44–46
passim, 47, 50, 55–56, 57, 116–117,
168–171, 173, 178, 180, 206, 210,
211, 213–214, 224–225, 256,
265–266, 267, 281, 291, 296–297,
298–305, 307–309, 343–344
measurement of, 36, 42–43, 47, 53,
177–178, 305–307, 308–309
research on, 33–42, 52–55 passim, 56,
57, 114–115, 116–117, 168–171,
209–210, 212, 213–214, 215–216,
224–225, 256, 267, 296–297,
301–309, 343–344
theories of, 34–42 passim, 56, 115,
116–117, 170, 299, 302, 304
Prescriptive policy beliefs. See Policy goals,
applied; Policy principles

Race
accommodative attitudes: data on, 283,
289; measurement of, 279–282
passim
ascriptive rules for, 102, 103–104, 108,
125, 371
attitudinal consistency: data on,
274–276, 279, 283, 286–287;
measurement of, 274, 279–282
categorical attributions: data on,
325–329 passim, 337, 349, 372;
measurement of, 305–307 passim,
322–325
causal attributions: data on, 339–343
passim, 349; measurement of,
338–339 passim

conflictive attitudes: data on, 283, 287,
372, 381; measurement of, 279–282
passim
deference: data on, 283, 287, 372, 381;
measurement of, 279–282 passim
distributive basis for, 75, 99–101, 108,
125, 359
empirical definition of, 103, 110
feelings: data on, 185–188, 194, 196,
372; measurement of, 43, 183–185
group membership, inheritance of,
106–107, 125, 371
hidden resistance in, 30, 283, 289
hostility, 33–43, 49–50, 118, 185–188,
192–193, 196, 210, 282–297 passim,
302–303, 313–315, 349, 372,
377–382 passim
integrationist attitudes: data on,
282–283, 289, 293; measurement of,
279–282 passim
nomenclature, 110
paternalism: data on, 282–283, 286,
288, 291, 381; measurement of,
279–282 passim
perception of differences, see causal
attributions; trait attributions
perception of group interests: data on,
200–202, 205, 377–378;
measurement of, 197–199 passim
policy goals, applied: data on, 241–244,
249–250 passim, 252, 253–255, 256,
258–259 passim, 372; measurement
of, 238–240, 251
policy perceptions: data on, 241,
242–244, 250; measurement of,
238–241 passim
policy principles: data on, 231–234,
237–238 passim, 257, 372;
measurement of, 228–229
revisionist attitudes: data on, 283, 287,
372; measurement of, 279–282
passim
segregation: role, 130–131, 133–136
passim, 150–155, 156–158, 163;
spatial, 77, 136–137, 138–142,
150–155, 156–158, 163, 196, 205,
210, 294, 349, 364, 371
tolerance: data on, 282–283, 288;
measurement of, 279–282 passim
trait attributions: data on, 325–329,
337, 349, 372–373; measurement of,
305–307 passim, 322–325 passim

Rationality, 3–4, 32, 57–58, 59–61,
    168–169, 172, 175–176, 181–182,
    208, 212–214, 219–222, 226,
    256–257, 358, 365–366
Realistic group conflict theory, 38–39,
    117, 170–171
Response bias, 179–180, 184, 199, 306,
    322, 323, 323n
Response set. *See* Response bias
Revisionist attitudes. *See also under* Class;
    Gender; Race
    conception of, 280–281
    data on, 283–285, 287, 289, 290, 294,
    372
    general evidence on, 294–295
    measurement of, 279–282 passim

Segregation, role. *See also under* Class;
    Gender; Race
    definition of, 128–129
    and derogation, 314–315
    evidence on, 138–139, 146–161
    forms of, 128, 129–131
    predetermining factors in, 74–75,
    127–128, 129–131 passim, 161,
    361–363 passim
Segregation, spatial. *See also under* Class;
    Gender; Race
    and derogation, 315
    evidence on, 138–146, 152–161
    forms of, 128, 132–138
    predetermining factors in, 74–78,
    127–128, 131–132, 135, 161,
    361–363 passim
Self-interest, 3–4, 174, 219–221, 226, 358,
    365–366
Sex-role attitudes
    conception of, 54, 209, 211–212, 214,
    256
    data on, 234–236, 244–247, 250–252,
    255, 258–259 passim, 329–331, 337,
    339–343 passim, 347
    measurement of, 53–55, 212, 218–219,
    229–230, 239–240, 324, 338–339
    research on, 54–55, 115, 209, 211–212,
    214, 218–219
Social comparison, theory of, 40, 303
Social desirability, 179–180, 184, 199,
    306, 322, 323, 323n
Social distance, feelings of, 43, 178, 210

Specific policy goals. *See* Policy goals,
    applied
Status
    interrelation with power and economic
    inequality, 26, 33, 77, 98–102,
    359–360
    relational basis of, 2–3, 76–78, 161–162
    social demarcation of, 14, 16, 76–78,
    104, 124–125, 127–138, 163–164,
    314, 315–318, 359–360, 362, 371,
    373, 374–375
Stereotypes. *See also under* Trait
    attributions to groups; Categorical
    attributions to groups
    in antebellum slavery, 309–310
    concept of, 43, 224, 296, 298–305, 343
    data on, 326–336, 347–350
    general evidence of, 326, 336–337, 347,
    378
    inconsistencies in, 309–310
    measurement of, 178, 305–307,
    322–325, 343
    relationship to discrimination, 35, 297,
    298–301, 302, 343
    relationship to intergroup feelings, 35,
    296–297, 298–301, 343
    research on, 43, 296–297, 298–307,
    353–354
    theories about, 78–79, 224, 298–305,
    345–347, 353–354
Survey data for study, characteristics of,
    109–111, 123–124
Symbolic racism, 41–42, 216

Tolerance. *See also under* Class; Gender;
    Race
    concept of, 43–46, 56–57, 113,
    171–172, 178, 206, 214, 256, 262,
    264–265, 280–281, 291
    data on, 283–285, 288, 289
    general evidence on, 288, 292, 295, 377
    measurement of, 46–47, 178, 211, 265,
    279–282 passim
    research on, 43–47, 56–57, 113, 178,
    206, 211, 264–265, 267
    theories about, 45, 171–172, 211, 265,
    291
Tolerant attitudes. *See* Tolerance
Trait attributions to groups. *See also under*
    Class; Gender; Race

data on, 325–336, 347–350, 372–373,
     374, 376, 378
general patterns in, 336–338, 378
inconsistencies in, 309–310, 320, 321
measurement of, 305–307, 322–325,
     343
relationship to intergroup feelings, 35,
     170, 265–268, 296, 297, 298–301,
     309, 343
relationship to policy goals, 35, 297,
     298–301, 302, 309, 343
research on, 296–297, 298–307

theories about, 297–298, 302–305,
     309–318, 320–321, 343–347, 350

Violence
  in class relations, 47, 87
  in distal relations, 87
  in gender relations, 15, 47–49, 50–51,
     57, 62, 83–84
  in intimate relations, 82–85, 87
  and love, 82–85
  in race relations, 15, 38, 47, 83, 84–85,
     309–310

AUTHOR INDEX

Abelson, Robert T., 267, 385
Aberbach, Joel D., 210, 385
Abercrombie, Nicholas, 30, 68, 70, 175, 213, 217, 223, 266, 385
Abram, Morris, 85, 223–224, 385
Abramson, Paul R., 46–47, 265, 385
Achen, Christopher H., 70, 264, 385
Adorno, T. W., 42, 170, 178, 302, 305, 309n, 385
Allen, Sheila, 386
Allport, Gordon, 35, 40, 42, 116, 169, 170, 266, 296, 299–304, 311, 386, 401
Almond, Gabriel A., 45, 385
Alwin, Duane F., 54, 212, 406
Amir, Yehuda, 170, 386
Anderson, Kristy, 264, 401
Anderson, Margaret L., 122, 386
Anderson, Perry, 31, 386
Anyon, Jean, 51, 270, 271, 281, 386
Apostle, Richard A., 38, 43, 308, 318, 386
Apter, David E., 69, 386, 390
Arber, Sara, 53, 54, 212, 399
Aronson, Elliot, 267, 385, 394, 403, 405
Ashmore, Richard D., 36, 306, 307, 386
Atkinson, Ti-Grace, 82, 386
Austin, William G., 353, 406, 408

Bachrach, Peter, 61–62, 66, 67, 99, 219, 386
Back, Kurt, 154, 392
Baer, Hans, 122, 386

Baker, Donald G., 104n, 386
Bales, Robert F., 52, 129, 401
Baratz, Morton S., 61–62, 66, 67, 99, 219, 386
Barker, Diana Leonard, 386
Baron, James N., 131, 387
Barry, Kathleen, 51, 386
Bar-Tal, D., 394
Bartlett, John, 44, 386
Bassett, John Spencer, 52, 408
Batts, Valerie, 210, 216, 398
Bayton, James A., 34, 305, 386, 404
Bechofer, Frank, 53, 393
Bell, Colin, 79, 131, 386
Bell, Daniel, 28, 386
Bellah, Robert N., 223, 386
Beller, Andrea H., 149, 386
Bennett, Stephen, 264, 387
Berelson, Bernard R., 263, 387
Berkowitz, Leonard, 402
Bernard, Jessie, 53, 381, 393
Berry, Brian, 36, 169, 387
Berube, Allan, 311, 387
Bielby, William T., 131, 387
Billig, Michael, 40, 387
Bishop, George F., 264, 387
Blalock, Hubert M., 7n, 34, 387
Blau, Francine, 131, 387
Blau, Peter M., 107, 387
Blauner, Bob, 233n, 387
Blea, Irene, 122, 387
Bledsoe, Albert T., 79, 387, 391
Blumer, Herbert, 11, 39, 117, 271, 387

Bobo, Lawrence, 38, 39, 41, 42, 43, 117, 169, 177, 210, 215, 223, 232n, 233n, 307, 388, 403
Bocock, Robert, 31, 388
Bogardus, E. S., 43, 388
Bonacich, Edna, 7n, 34, 388
Bose, Christina, 402
Bourdieu, Pierre, 63, 388
Braly, Kenneth W., 43, 305, 306n, 307, 396
Brand, Elaine S., 38, 173, 388
Brewer, Marilynn B., 40, 42, 170, 299, 302, 388, 390, 400, 405
Brigham, John C., 43, 301, 306, 323n, 388
Brill, Alida, 45, 47, 171, 398
Brody, Richard, 38, 42, 224, 405
Bromley, 43, 216, 390
Broverman, Donald N., 53, 54, 305, 388
Broverman, Inge K., 53, 54, 305, 388
Brown, Rupert J., 299, 394
Brunk, Gregory G., 264, 388
Bullock, Charles S., III, 385, 401
Bumpass, Larry L., 212, 399
Burawoy, Michael, 11, 75n, 271, 388
Burke, Edmund, 62–63, 222, 388
Burleigh, Michael, 311, 389
Butler, David, 264, 389

Camburn, Donald, 54, 212, 406
Cammett, John M., 177n, 389
Campbell, Angus, 38, 43, 169, 177, 210, 301, 303, 306, 389, 397
Campbell, Donald T., 38, 353, 389, 397
Cancian, Francesca M., 79, 131, 138, 389
Carmines, Edward G., 216, 224, 400
Cartwright, Dorwin, 267, 389
Cauthen, Nelson R., 301, 389
Centers, Richard., 29, 32, 33, 97, 172, 239, 348, 389
Chapman, John W., 403
Chein, Isidor, 36, 169, 301, 304, 306, 331n, 394
Cherlin, Andrew, 53, 54, 212, 389
Clark, Kenneth B., 38, 389
Clark, Mamie P., 38, 389
Clarkson, Frank E., 53, 54, 305, 388
Cloward, Richard A., 51, 270, 281, 389
Coffman, Thomas L., 43, 305, 396
Cohen, Arthur R., 267, 389
Cohen, Carl, 225, 389
Cohen, Lawrence E., 2n, 389

Collins, B. E., 386
Collins, Mary Evans, 35, 42, 43, 119, 299, 305, 390
Collins, Patricia Hill, 122, 288, 386
Connolly, William E., 32, 176n, 220, 390
Conrad, Robert Edgar, 104n, 390
Converse, Philip E., 35, 70, 169, 211, 263, 264, 306, 389, 390, 401
Cook, Stuart W., 42, 119, 170, 299, 302, 305, 315, 390, 408
Coser, Lewis A., 28, 390
Crane, Marie, 42, 120, 137, 155, 395
Crockett, Harry J., 171, 211, 401
Cronan, Sheila, 50, 51, 390
Crosby, Faye, 43, 216, 390
Czajka, John L., 53, 54, 212, 390

Dahl, Robert A., 28, 44, 45, 69, 171, 390
Dahrendorf, Ralf, 28, 72, 390
Dan, Alice J., 53, 381, 393
Davis, F. James, 103, 104n, 390
Davis, James A., 211, 307, 390
Davis, Kenneth E., 42, 392
Davis, Kingsley, 27, 390
de Beauvoir, Simone, 49, 390
Degler, Carl, 104n, 390
Del Boca, Frances K., 306, 307, 386
Denton, Nancy A., 136, 137, 140, 399
de Queiros Mattoso, Karia M., 104n, 390
Deutsch, Morton, 35, 42, 43, 119, 299, 305, 390
Dollard, John, 34, 391
Doob, Leonard W., 266, 391
Dorn, Edwin, 89, 391
Dovidio, John F., 36, 38, 43, 76, 216, 391, 393, 396–397, 398, 400
Downs, Anthony, 3n, 5, 88, 391
Dreger, Ralph Mason, 394
DuBois, W. E. Burghardt, 52, 408
Duncan, Otis Dudley, 107, 157, 159, 387, 391
Durkheim, Emile, 25–27, 230, 391

Earp, Edwin L., 52, 408
Economist, The, 370n, 391
Edelman, Murray, 89, 391
Eggers, Mitchell L., 34, 399
Ehrlich, Howard J., 301, 302, 306, 391
Eldridge, Albert F., 303, 391
Elkins, Stanley M., 83n, 100, 391
Elliott, E. N., 72, 80, 85, 311, 319, 391, 405

Ellyson, Steve L., 76, 391
Elster, Jon, 244n, 391
Engels, Frederick, 24–25, 30, 72, 76n,
  101, 172, 173, 175, 176, 181, 391, 399
Engerman, Stanley L., 104n, 356, 392
Epps, Edgar, 38, 393
Evans, Arthur, 37, 39, 117, 169, 390, 393
Evans, Richard, 299, 402

Fairchild, Hal H., 38, 210, 391
Farley, Reynolds, 110, 147, 391, 392
Feagin, Joe R., 308, 392, 405
Feldman, Stanley, 264, 406
Femia, Joseph, 31, 392
Festinger, Leon, 154, 267, 392
Feuer, Louis S., 399
Fields, James M., 179, 392
Firebaugh, Glenn, 42, 392
Fireman, Bruce, 172, 392
Firestone, Shulimith, 82, 392
Fischer, Gregory W., 302, 397
Fishman, Joshua A., 301, 392
Fitzhugh, George, 71–72, 84, 311, 319,
  392
Fogel, Robert William, 104n, 356, 392
Form, William H., 29, 31, 33, 53, 173,
  175, 213, 217, 223, 394
Fox, Robin, 52, 406
Fredrickson, George M., 392, 401
Freedman, Deborah S., 53, 54, 212, 406
Freeman, Jo, 76, 103, 131, 312, 394
Frenkel-Brunswik, Else, 42, 170, 178, 302,
  305, 309n, 385

Gaertner, Samuel L., 36, 38, 43, 216, 391,
  393, 397, 398, 400
Gamson, William A., 172, 175, 224, 225,
  269, 392
Gans, Herbert J., 223, 392
Garner, J. W., 52, 408
Genovese, Eugene D., 10, 12, 30, 51, 75n,
  80, 173, 176, 270, 271, 272, 281, 392
Gerth, H. H., 407
Gibson, Robert H., 54, 212, 394
Giddens, Anthony, 173, 385, 392
Gilbert, G. M., 305, 306n, 393
Giles, Howard, 407
Giles, Micheal W., 37, 39, 117, 169, 393,
  407
Glazer, Nathan, 225, 393, 401
Glazer, Nona, 53, 381, 393
Glock, Charles Y., 38, 43, 308, 318, 386

Goffman, Erving, 76, 393
Goldberg, Philip, 53, 54, 393
Goldman, Emma, 51, 393
Goldthorpe, John H., 53, 393
Goode, William J., 54, 393
Gramsci, Antonio, 31, 69, 173, 176, 177n,
  221, 386, 389, 392, 393, 408
Graumann, C. F., 394
Greeley, Andrew M., 42, 43, 210, 216,
  393, 406
Greene, David, 179, 403
Griffin, Susan, 50, 393
Grigg, Charles M., 45, 211, 215, 402
Gross, Harriet E., 53, 393
Gurin, Gerald, 38, 53, 54, 172, 177, 210,
  391, 393, 394, 400
Gurin, Patricia, 38, 53, 54, 172, 177, 210,
  391, 393, 394, 400

Hacker, Helen M., 49, 81, 393
Hagen, Michael Gray, 41, 216, 223,
  224–225, 309, 319, 405
Hagner, Paul R., 264, 393
Hamer, Jeston, 34, 386
Hamilton, David L., 40, 43, 301, 302, 386,
  393, 406
Hamilton, Richard F., 53, 394
Haque, Khondaker E., 216, 399
Harary, Frank, 267, 389
Hardee, Betty B., 41, 43, 210, 215, 216,
  398
Harding, John, 36, 169, 301, 303, 304,
  306, 331n, 394, 403
Hartley, E. L., 389, 396
Hartmann, Heidi I., 131, 149, 407
Harvey, O. J., 353, 404
Heider, Fritz, 267, 308, 389, 394
Held, David, 385
Helmreich, Robert L., 54, 212, 394
Hendricks, Wallace, 131, 387
Henley, Nancy M., 76, 103, 131, 312, 394,
  408
Hensler, C. P., 38, 210, 403
Herring, Cedric, 104, 396
Herrnstein, R. J., 52, 233, 394
Hewstone, Miles, 299, 302, 394
Hill, Kim Quaile, 99, 175, 394
Hill, Stephen, 175, 385
Hirsch, Jerry, 311, 394
Hoare, Quintin, 393
Hochschild, Arlie, 149, 394
Hodge, Robert W., 28, 33, 391, 394, 401

Hoffmann, Paul J., 70, 263–264, 398
Hood, William R., 353, 389, 404
Horner, Matina S., 53, 54, 394
Hough, Joseph C., 41, 398
House, Pamela, 179, 402
Huber, Joan, 29, 31, 33, 53, 54, 173, 175, 212, 213, 217, 223, 394, 405
Hummer, Robert A., 132, 399
Humphreys, Elizabeth W., 146, 147, 149, 400
Hunter, Guy, 387
Hyman, Herbert H., 42, 43, 306, 394, 395

Inglehart, Ronald, 28, 395

Jacklin, C. N., 53, 398
Jackman, Mary R., 1, 33, 41, 42, 43, 45, 46, 47, 53, 90, 99, 106, 111, 119, 120, 137n, 146, 146n, 147, 149, 155, 156n, 177, 191n, 204n, 210, 211, 215, 216, 223, 225, 229, 237, 244, 265, 268, 306, 395, 399
Jackman, Robert W., 3n, 33, 53, 99, 106, 111, 146, 146n, 147, 149, 156n, 191n, 204n, 237, 244, 395
Jacobs, Jerry A., 131, 395
Jaggar, Alison M., 386, 387, 390
Jaynes, Gerald David, 52, 395
Jencks, Christopher, 34, 395
Jensen, Arthur R., 52, 304, 311, 318, 395
Johnson, Charles S., 16, 38, 72, 396
Jones, James M., 122, 306, 386, 396
Jordan, Winthrop D., 100, 103–104, 311, 312, 392, 396
Judd, Dennis R., 134, 136, 396, 402

Kane, Emily W., 53, 54, 212, 396
Karlins, Marvin, 43, 305, 306n, 396
Katterman, Lee, 215n, 396
Katz, Daniel, 43, 305, 306n, 307, 396
Katz, Irwin, 394
Katz, Phyllis A., 38, 388, 396
Keith, Verna M., 104, 396
Kendrick, Ann, 38, 42, 405
Kinder, Donald R., 36, 38, 41, 42, 43, 169, 210, 215, 216, 223, 225, 396
King, Jr., Martin Luther, 62, 134, 221, 222, 282, 396
King, Morton B., 301, 397
Kirkpatrick, Samuel A., 264, 396
Klein, Herbert S., 104n, 396
Kluegel, James R., 33, 42, 43, 223, 299, 307, 308, 318, 388, 396

Knobel, Dale T., 401
Koenig, Frederick W., 301, 397
Kramarae, Cheris, 408
Krauss, Herbert H., 301, 389
Krosnik, Jon A., 264, 397
Kuklinski, James H., 38, 42, 215, 216, 224, 265, 397, 404
Kutner, Bernard, 36, 169, 301, 304, 306, 331n, 394

Landecker, Werner S., 33, 172, 177, 397
Landis, Jean M., 53, 54, 212, 404
Lane, Robert W., 53, 397, 400
Laqueur, Walter, 244n, 397
Lasswell, Harold D., 8, 397
Laumann, Edward O., 401
LaViolette, Forrest, 306, 307, 397
Lazarsfeld, Paul F., 263, 387
Lears, T. J., 31, 397
LeBlanc, Hugh L., 264, 397
Leggett, John C., 53, 397
Leighley, Jan E., 99, 394
LeVine, Robert A., 38, 169, 397
Levinson, Daniel J., 42, 170, 178, 302, 305, 309n, 385
Licari, Frank, 42, 388
Lieberson, Stanley, 121, 140, 397
Lijphart, Arend, 122n, 397
Lindblom, Charles E., 67, 88, 397
Linville, Patricia W., 302, 397
Lippmann, Walter, 43, 301, 302, 331n, 398
Lipset, Seymour Martin, 28, 29, 32, 42, 46, 216, 398
Lipsky, Michael, 89, 99, 398
Litwack, Leon F., 77, 85, 398
Lockwood, David, 11, 53, 118, 393, 398
Lorber, Judith, 53, 381, 393
Lu, Yu-hsia, 54, 212, 399
Lukes, Stephen, 66, 398

McAlister, Lois B., 34, 386
McCarthy, John D., 44, 392
McCauley, Clark, 306, 316, 398
McClintock, Martha, 53, 381, 393
McClosky, Herbert, 45, 46, 47, 70, 171, 211, 263, 264, 398
Maccoby, Eleanor E., 53, 398
McConahay, John B., 41, 43, 210, 215, 216, 398
McGuire, William J., 267, 385, 398
Machalek, Richard, 2, 389

Machung, Anne, 149, 394ʹ
McKee, John P., 53, 54, 305, 404
Mackie, Marlene, 43, 301, 302, 304, 398
McLellan, David, 399
McPhee, William N., 263, 387
Madsen, Richard, 223, 386
Malanchuk, Oksana, 172, 177, 400
Mann, Michael, 31, 32, 33, 175, 176n, 213, 217, 398
Mannheim, Karl, 174, 398
Mansbridge, Jane J., 3n, 399
Marcus, George E., 45, 46–47, 70, 171, 211, 264, 265, 385, 405, 406
Marcuse, Herbert, 31, 399
Marger, Martin N., 36, 104n, 169, 399
Margolis, Michael, 216, 399
Markus, Gregory B., 70, 264, 390
Martin, Patricia Yancey, 62, 132, 221, 282, 391, 396, 398, 399
Marx, Gary T., 38, 81, 210, 305, 399
Marx, Karl, 24–27, 29, 30, 33, 34, 37, 56, 72, 73, 75, 81, 172, 173, 175, 176, 181, 222, 389, 399
Mason, Karen Oppenheim, 53, 54, 212, 394, 399
Massey, Douglas S., 34, 136, 137, 140, 399
Meenes, Max, 305, 399
Meis, Scott M., 146, 147, 149, 400
Meissner, Martin, 146, 147, 149, 400
Mendelberg, Tali, 42, 396
Merelman, Richard M., 67, 400
Merriam, Charles E., 62, 400
Merrill, Bob, 383, 400
Merriman, W. Richard, 216, 224, 400
Merrin, Mary Beth, 264, 397
Mill, John Stuart, 23, 48–49, 53, 81, 230, 320, 381–382, 400
Miller, Arthur H., 172, 177, 393, 400
Miller, Jon, 402
Miller, Kent S., 394
Miller, Norman, 42, 170, 299, 302, 390, 400, 405
Miller, Warren E., 306, 389
Millett, Kate, 50, 51, 82, 400
Mills, C. Wright, 175, 389, 400, 407
Modigliani, Andre, 224, 225, 269, 392
Moore, Barrington, 27, 64, 390, 400
Morris, Richard T., 172, 223, 385, 400
Muha, Michael J., 41, 42, 46, 90, 119, 215, 216, 223, 225, 229, 268, 306, 395
Mullins, Elizabeth I., 104, 400

Murphy, Raymond J., 172, 400
Myrdal, Gunnar, 10, 34, 47, 49, 53, 60, 79, 84, 103, 104, 300, 304, 308, 309, 396, 400

National Election Studies, 177, 183, 228n, 232n, 264, 400
Newby, Howard, 11, 12, 53, 75n, 79, 131, 271–272, 382n, 386, 400
Newcomb, Theodore M., 35, 169, 267, 385, 389, 401
Newton, Niles, 53, 389, 393
Nie, Norman H., 70, 264, 401
Nilson, Linda Burzotta, 308, 401
Nisbet, Robert A., 29, 32, 401
Nunn, Clyde Z., 171, 211, 401

Oberschall, Anthony, 172, 401
O'Hara, Rosemary, 70, 263, 264, 398
Oldendick, Robert W., 264, 387
Olsen, Marvin E., 172, 401
Osgood, Charles E., 267, 401
Ottati, Victor, 215, 265, 397

Padilla, Amada M., 38, 173, 388
Paige, Jeffrey M., 177n, 401
Parelius, Ann P., 53, 401
Parent, T. Wayne, 216, 224, 397, 400
Parkin, Frank, 31, 46, 88, 89, 99, 173, 175, 213, 217, 223, 225, 401
Parsons, Talcott, 52, 129, 401, 407
Pennock, J. Roland, 403
Peterson, Paul E., 34, 392, 395
Petrocik, John R., 70, 264, 401
Pettigrew, Thomas F., 33, 36, 37, 38, 40, 42, 43, 52, 169, 215, 300, 302, 304, 307, 308, 401
Piazza, Thomas, 36, 38, 42, 43, 308, 318, 386, 405
Pierce, John C., 264, 393
Piereson, James E., 45, 46–47, 70, 171, 211, 264, 265, 385, 401, 406
Piven, Frances Fox, 51, 270, 281, 389
Platt, Jennifer, 53, 393
Pleck, Joseph H., 147, 402
Polsby, Nelson W., 28, 29, 122, 219, 402
Powdermaker, Hortense, 16, 402
Prager, Jeffrey, 302, 402
Proshansky, Harold, 36, 169, 301, 304, 306, 331n, 391, 394, 404
Prothro, James W., 45, 211, 215, 402
Przeworski, Adam, 122n, 402

Ransford, H. Edward, 402
Reiss, Albert J., 391
Reskin, Barbara F., 76, 129, 131, 132, 147, 149, 386, 402, 405
Rich, Adrienne, 2, 51, 71, 82, 178, 241, 271, 312, 381, 402
Richter, Maurice N., Jr., 301, 302, 331n, 402
Riggle, Ellen, 215, 265, 397
Rinehart, James W., 306, 391
Robertson, David B., 134, 136, 402
Robinson, Ira E., 301, 389
Rodgers, Harrell R., 385, 401
Rokeach, Milton, 299, 402
Roos, Patricia A., 76, 129, 131, 132, 149, 402
Rose, Arnold, 28, 300, 308, 309, 402
Rosenberg, Milton J., 267, 299, 310, 385, 402
Rosenberg, Rosalind, 267, 299, 310, 385, 402
Rosenkrantz, Paul S., 53, 54, 305, 388
Ross, Catherine E., 147, 149, 402
Ross, Lee D., 179, 308, 402, 403
Rossi, Alice, 53, 81, 381, 389, 390, 393, 400, 403
Roszak, Betty, 403
Roszak, Theodore, 403
Rothenberg, Paula S., 386, 387, 390
Rubin, Lillian B., 50, 79, 138, 403
Ruiz, Rene A., 38, 173, 388
Russell, Diana E. H., 84, 399, 402, 403

Salovey, Peter, 302, 397
Sanchez, Laura, 54, 396
Sanford, R. Nevitt, 42, 170, 178, 302, 305, 309n, 385
Saxe, Leonard, 43, 216, 390
Scase, Richard, 400
Schaar, John H., 46, 89, 223, 317, 403
Schachter, Stanley, 154, 392
Schattschneider, E. E., 59, 67, 403
Schermerhorn, R. A., 37, 403
Scheu, William J., 146, 147, 149, 400
Schlozman, Kay Lehman, 99, 403
Schneider, William, 216, 398
Schuman, Howard, 38, 41, 42, 43, 179, 210, 215, 232n, 233n, 304, 307, 308, 389, 392, 403
Schwartz, David C., 210, 403
Schwartz, Sandra Kenyon, 210, 403
Schwarz, Norbert, 215, 265, 397

Scott, James C., 29, 51, 63, 177n, 270, 281, 399, 402, 403
Sears, David O., 36, 38, 41, 42, 169, 210, 215, 216, 223, 225, 396, 404
Secord, Paul F., 301, 404
Segal, Mary, 306, 316, 398
Seidenberg, Bernard, 391, 404
Selznick, Gertrude J., 38, 42, 43, 304, 305, 404
Senter, Mary Scheuer, 306, 395
Sheatsley, Paul B., 42, 43, 210, 216, 393, 395, 406
Sherif, Carolyn W., 353, 389, 404
Sherif, Muzafer, 7, 169, 301, 303, 308, 353–358, 370, 389, 404
Sherriffs, Alex C., 53, 54, 305, 404
Shils, Edward, 398
Shockley, William, 52, 311, 404
Siegel, Paul M., 401
Sigelman, Lee, 38, 210, 215, 404
Sills, David L., 390, 394
Silvert, K. H., 307, 397
Simmel, Georg, 122, 167, 404
Simon, Rita J., 53, 54, 212, 404
Simpson, George Eaton, 36, 169, 304, 404
Singleton, Royce, Jr., 33, 396
Sites, Paul, 104, 132, 162, 400
Smedley, Joseph W., 34, 305, 404
Smelser, Neil J., 122n, 404
Smith, A. Wade, 39, 117, 404
Smith, Eliot R., 43, 223, 299, 308, 397
Smith, Eric R. A. N., 70, 264, 405
Smith, Geoffrey Nowell, 393
Smith, Patricia W., 299, 402
Smith, Tom W., 307, 390
Sniderman, Paul M., 38, 41, 42, 169, 216, 223, 224–225, 308, 318, 405
Speer, L. K., 38, 210, 404
Spence, Janet T., 54, 212, 394
Spencer, Herbert, 53, 405, 408
Spitze, Glenna, 54, 212, 394, 402, 405
Stacey, Judith, 53, 405
Staples, William G., 11, 405
Starnes, Charles E., 33, 396
Steeh, Charlotte, 38, 41, 42, 43, 210, 215, 232n, 233n, 403
Steele, C. Hoy, 403
Steinem, Gloria, 313, 405
Stephan, Cookie White, 170, 299, 304, 405
Stephan, Walter G., 36, 40, 170, 299, 304, 405

Stephens, W., 405
Stinchcombe, Arthur, 216, 405
Stitt, Christopher L., 306, 316, 398
Stokes, Donald E., 264, 306, 389
Stone, Alfred Holt, 52, 405, 408
Storr, Anthony, 52, 405
Stouffer, Samuel A., 44–45, 46, 47, 171, 178, 211, 265, 405
Stringfellow, Thornton, 173–174, 391, 405
Strober, Myra H., 149, 405
Stroebe, W., 394
Suelzle, Marijean, 38, 43, 308, 318, 386
Sullivan, John L., 45, 46–47, 70, 171, 211, 264, 265, 385, 386, 406
Sullivan, William M., 223, 386
Sumner, William Graham, 53, 406
Swidler, Ann, 223, 386

Tajfel, Henri, 40, 43, 116, 170, 300, 301, 302–303, 307, 308, 406
Tannenbaum, Percy H., 267, 385, 401
Taylor, D. Garth, 43, 136, 210, 216, 224, 233, 405, 406
Taylor, Dalmas A., 388
Taylor, Shelley E., 40, 406
Tetlock, Philip E., 38, 42, 169, 405
Teune, Henry, 122n, 402
Thompson, John B., 69, 406
Thorne, Barrie, 53, 393, 405, 407
Thornton, Arland, 53, 54, 212, 406
Tiger, Lionel, 52, 406
Tilly, Charles, 172, 406
Tipton, Stephen M., 223, 386
Tischler, Henry L., 36, 387
Tocqueville, Alexis de, 122, 222, 406
Todd, Edwin S., 52, 408
Tomich, Dale W., 104n, 356, 406
Treiman, Donald J., 28, 33, 131, 149, 394, 407
Trolier, Tina K., 43, 301, 302, 393
Truman, David B., 122, 407
Tuchfarber, Alfred J., 264, 387
Tufte, Edward, 390
Turner, Bryan S., 30, 68, 70, 175, 213, 217, 233, 266, 385
Turner, Castellano B., 210, 407
Turner, John C., 40, 303, 353, 407
Turner, Ralph, 35, 169, 401

Ueda, Reed, 401

van den Berghe, Pierre L., 6n, 7n, 10, 76, 104n, 128, 129, 271, 407
VanDeVeer, Donald, 12–14, 407
Verba, Sidney, 45, 70, 264, 385, 401
Vinacke, W. Edgar, 43, 301, 302, 407
Vogel, Susan Raymond, 53, 54, 305, 388

Walker, Kathryn, 146, 147, 149, 210, 385, 407
Walkley, Rosabelle Price, 42, 119, 170, 299, 302, 305, 408
Walters, Gary, 43, 305, 396
Walters, Pamela Barnhouse, 53, 54, 212, 389
Weatherly, U. G., 52, 408
Weber, Max, 3, 25, 26, 33, 34, 65, 98, 222, 407
Webster's, 9, 10, 302, 407
Weiner, Marli F., 11–12, 407
Weissberg, Robert, 118, 264, 286n, 407
Welch, Susan, 38, 210, 215, 404
Wellman, David T., 37, 39, 117, 407
West, Candace, 76, 131, 370, 408
White, B. Jack, 389, 404
Wilensky, Harold L., 28, 29, 33, 408
Willcox, W. F., 52, 408
Williams, Gwyn A., 31, 176, 177n, 408
Williams, J. Allen, 171, 211, 401
Williams, Raymond, 31, 408
Williams, Robin M., Jr., 36, 38, 52, 169, 170, 177, 300, 301, 302, 395, 408
Williamson, Joel, 103, 408
Williamson, John B., 308, 408
Wilner, Daniel M., 42, 119, 170, 299, 302, 305, 408
Wilson, William Julius, 34, 37, 52, 210, 407, 408
Winch, Donald, 400
Wirth, Louis, 398
Woods, Margaret, 146, 147, 149, 407
Worchel, Stephen, 353, 406, 408
Wright, Erik Olin, 32, 33, 105, 400, 408
Wyer, Robert S., Jr., 215, 265, 397

Yalom, Marilyn, 393
Yetman, Norman, 403
Yinger, J. Milton, 36, 42, 169, 304, 404, 408

Zald, Mayer N., 392
Zeitlin, Maurice, 408
Zimmerman, Don H., 76, 131, 408

Designer:	U.C. Press Staff
Compositor:	Maryland Composition Company, Inc.
Text:	10/12 Baskerville
Display:	Baskerville
Printer:	BookCrafters
Binder:	BookCrafters

How Stella Learned to Talk

HOW STELLA
LEARNED TO TALK

The Groundbreaking Story of the
World's First Talking Dog

CHRISTINA HUNGER

wm

WILLIAM MORROW
An Imprint of HarperCollins*Publishers*

HOW STELLA LEARNED TO TALK. Copyright © 2021 by Christina Hunger. All rights reserved. Printed in the United States of America. No part of this book may be used or reproduced in any manner whatsoever without written permission except in the case of brief quotations embodied in critical articles and reviews. For information, address HarperCollins Publishers, 195 Broadway, New York, NY 10007.

HarperCollins books may be purchased for educational, business, or sales promotional use. For information, please email the Special Markets Department at SPsales@harpercollins.com.

FIRST EDITION

Library of Congress Cataloging-in-Publication Data has been applied for.

ISBN 978-0-06-304683-2

21 22 23 24 25   LSC   10 9 8 7 6 5 4 3 2 1

For my husband, Jake.
I couldn't have done any of this without you.
I love you so much.

Contents

_____

PROLOGUE *1*

CHAPTER 1: *Presume Competence* *3*

CHAPTER 2: *Ozzie and Truman* *19*

CHAPTER 3: *The Chocolate-Colored Puppy* *29*

CHAPTER 4: *Communication Is Everywhere* *37*

CHAPTER 5: *Three Feet from Gold* *53*

CHAPTER 6: *Now We're Talkin'* *67*

CHAPTER 7: *Independence* *81*

CHAPTER 8: *Project Disconnect* *95*

CHAPTER 9: *Bye, Omaha* *109*

CHAPTER 10: *The Road to California* *123*

CHAPTER 11: *Using Words in New Ways* *133*

CHAPTER 12: *Creative Combinations* *145*

CHAPTER 13: *Help!* *159*

CHAPTER 14: *Becoming Automatic* *173*

CHAPTER 15: *Hunger for Words* *187*

CHAPTER 16: *Language Explosion* *203*

CHAPTER 17: *Hello, World* *221*

CHAPTER 18: *This Is the Beginning* *233*

APPENDIX A: *Helping Your Dog Learn to Talk* *239*

APPENDIX B: *Resources and Recommended Reading* *249*

ACKNOWLEDGMENTS *253*

NOTES *257*

How Stella Learned to Talk

Prologue

———

"Bye, Stella," I said while I ate breakfast at the dining table. "Have fun with Jake."

My fiancé was holding Stella's leash as he waited by the front door. They left together every morning to play at the beach or park while I got ready for work.

"Ready, Stella?" Jake asked.

Stella paused in the kitchen. She turned to look at the door, then she locked eyes with me. I wondered what she was thinking. Normally, she hurries out the door in the morning.

Stella approached her communication board on the floor. It was two feet by four feet, filled with colorful buttons, each programmed with a prerecorded word. She pressed four different buttons in a row.

"Christina come play love you," Stella said. She hopped off her board and stared at me again.

Jake laughed, and I couldn't help but smile. "You want me to come play, Stella?"

She wagged her tail.

I threw on shoes and a coat, then grabbed the leash from Jake.

My dog just invited me to come play with her. How special is that?

CHAPTER I

Presume Competence

———

As I sat on a six-foot-wide swing resembling a giant padded block, I held my breath in anticipation. Oliver, my speech therapy client, was sitting with me holding his tablet-sized communication device. Oliver rarely initiated using his talker without my help. But today he grabbed it as soon as we met. *What did he want to tell me?*

Even though Oliver was only nine years old, he was almost as tall as me, his twenty-four-year-old speech-language pathologist. His basketball shorts and T-shirt made him look like any typical nine-year-old boy. But the braces on his legs, noise-reducing headphones covering his ears, and communication device strapped over his shoulder indicated that something was different. Oliver had autism spectrum disorder. He had been coming to this pediatric clinic in Omaha, Nebraska, for physical therapy, occupational therapy, and speech therapy for years.

Oliver squinted, his finger hovering over the screen. I focused on what Oliver was about to say, blocking out the noise of children swinging, climbing the rock wall, and riding on scooters around us in the gym.

Possibilities ran through my head. Maybe he would say one of the words we had been practicing on the swing for the past couple of weeks. Since Oliver learned best while he was in motion, we spent much of our sessions practicing words such as *go*, *stop*, *fast*, and *slow* while swinging. I loved modeling the word *fast* on Oliver's device and pushing him as high as I could. Oliver would squeal and throw his head back in laughter, savoring every second of the increased speed. It was impossible for anyone to watch him without smiling. His pure joy lit up the entire room.

Oliver tapped one of the sixty icons on his tablet, which opened a new page of word choices. He traced the brightly colored rows with his index finger before pausing over a single square. When Oliver pressed it, the synthesized voice said, "rice."

"Rice?" I paused. Oliver and I were in the middle of a gym, not a kitchen. "Rice" was about the last thing I expected him to say. "Eat rice at lunch?" I asked. After I said each word, I pushed the corresponding button on his tablet. The best way for Oliver to learn how to use his talker was to see other people using it as well.

Oliver grunted and kicked his legs in frustration. That was not what he was trying to say.

I glanced at my watch, 4:35. "Maybe you want rice for dinner after therapy," I said. "Want eat rice?"

Oliver swatted my hand away, then repeated himself, "Rice rice."

Oliver said "rice" in our session last week, too, but I did not really think anything of it. Since there was no rice around, I chalked it up to Oliver exploring new vocabulary. He had only had this communication device for a few months, and it can take a while before kids start using words intentionally on their own. They need time to explore words and to see and hear their communication system in use before they can be expected to talk with it. It's like how babies need to hear people using language for a whole year before they start saying words on their own. Now that I knew Oliver saying "rice" was not an isolated occurrence, I modeled everything I could think of that was related to rice. I used Oliver's device to try a variety of phrases.

Was Oliver trying to tell me he was hungry and wanted to eat rice? Was he trying to say he liked rice? What if he hates rice and was trying to tell me it is bad? I modeled "rice good," "rice bad," "like eat rice," "all done eat rice," "Oliver eat rice," "school eat rice," everything I could possibly think of. Each time I tried a new phrase, I paused to assess his reaction. Oliver understood much more than he could say; his receptive language skills were significantly greater than his expressive language skills. If I said the right phrase he was trying to communicate, he would get excited. It reminded me of how I felt when trying to say a word in French years after I learned it in high school. If I read the word or heard someone say it, I would know what it meant. But it was so much harder for me to come up with the word on my own. That's because my French receptive language skills were much higher than my French expressive language skills.

Oliver ripped his headphones off and threw them to the

ground. He rattled the swing, knocking my clipboard off it while grunting.

"It's okay, it's okay. We're okay. You sound mad, Oliver," I said. I held the device in front of him and modeled, "mad." I needed to redirect him before things got worse. The fastest way to do that was to start swinging. No matter what was going on, Oliver always loved to swing. This is true for a lot of children with autism. The rocking motion helped regulate his sensory system. Within a minute of using all my body weight to propel Oliver as high as possible, he returned to his giggly self. I fixed the situation for now so we could salvage our session but did not truly solve the problem. *Why is Oliver saying "rice"? And why is Oliver getting so mad when I try talking about rice?*

Oliver was one of the many children on my caseload learning how to use a communication device to talk. Communication devices are a form of augmentative and alternative communication (AAC). AAC is a fantastic tool that gives people with severe speech delays or disorders the ability to say words through another medium. Occasionally Oliver verbally repeated single words he heard in a video or from whoever around him was speaking, but at nine years old, that was the extent of his verbal speech abilities. Many people mistakenly believe that verbal speech skills represent a person's intelligence or language abilities. One of my favorite things about being a speech-language pathologist is shattering this misconception. I love introducing AAC to children who had been misunderstood for years and watching great transformations unfold.

In graduate school, one of my clients had been using an AAC device for a couple of years. She primarily communicated in two-word phrases until the day she felt the sleeve of a fuzzy sweater I had not worn there before. She looked at me and said,

"New purple sweater like." I had no idea that she knew how to say the word *sweater* or had been paying attention to my wardrobe this whole time.

At the clinic, I recently increased another one of my clients' number of visible words on his device from about twenty to the full capacity of two thousand words. On the same day that I made the change, the child said "down stairs down stairs green block" then bolted to the door. He pulled as hard as he could on the doorknob but did not have the dexterity to turn it. If he had not said what he wanted, I would not have opened the door. I would have assumed he was trying to escape from the session. In the therapy area downstairs, he walked straight to the game cabinet and pulled out a cardboard box from the middle of the shelf, not even fazed by all the games he knocked down in the process. He flipped open the lid and picked out all the green magnetic shapes, then started stacking them in different ways. Before today, *down* would have been the only word of that phrase he could have said. How long had he been wanting to tell me the exact game he wanted to play? How long had he been pulling on doorknobs trying to lead me to what he wanted, not to try running away? I could not wait to share this great breakthrough with his mom at the end of the session.

Some parents, and even some professionals, assume that kids with significant disabilities know very little or are too difficult to teach. In my experience, many professionals just didn't know how to give them the opportunity to learn and discover their potential or didn't stick something out long enough to give it a real chance. For all children, belief in their potential makes a huge difference in their learning. But for kids using AAC, belief in potential is everything. If the therapist or parent does not truly believe in the child's potential, they physically limit what is possible for the child to say by only giving them a few options. When professionals set the bar low with AAC, the child will be stuck.

This is what happened with Oliver before I took over his case. His communication device was programmed to only say about eight or ten different sentences. He could push one icon that said, "I want more swing" or push another that said, "I need to go to the bathroom." The therapist before me thought that was all he could handle. For entire thirty-minute-long therapy sessions, Oliver would say "I want more swing" repeatedly. I could not blame him, though; he did not really have any other options. He could not say anything else about the swing or talk about any other activities he might participate in throughout his typical day. Oliver did the best he could with what he had.

After getting to know him more and gaining my own confidence, I set up a conference with his mom to show her how Oliver's device could be programmed to have over two thousand words for him to learn to say instead of the same old ten sentences. This was actually the language program's default setting, how it was supposed to be used. His prior therapist went out of her way to remove all the words and replace them with sentences she created. With access to so many words, Oliver could eventually create millions of different sentences, like we all have the privilege to do. But this was only months into my first year as a speech-language pathologist. I had never made such drastic changes to a child's communication system or scrapped a more experienced speech therapist's treatment plan to create my own. In graduate school, we learned how to set up AAC devices and make solid treatment plans from the start. Fixing ineffective plans was a new territory.

I prepared for the meeting, looking over my notes, pulling together articles on the importance of single-word-based AAC systems instead of preprogrammed sentences, communicating for functions other than requesting, and teaching words that could be used in a variety of contexts rather than focusing only on saying nouns. I hoped his mom could not sense how nervous I was. It was important for her to believe me. Oliver could be learning so much more than anyone had given him the chance to say.

"He's done such a great job with what he has," I said to her as we sat together in a small conference room. "He needs more words, though. I know it will be a transition, but Oliver can learn to say so much more than what he has available to him right now." I showed her the AAC articles as I spoke. "This system will set him up for a lifetime of communication opportunities and allow him to grow," I said. "Think about when your daughter was learning to talk. She babbled first, then said words, then started putting words together, and eventually formed her own sentences, right?"

When she looked up at me, I saw a hesitant mother who had been let down by the years of therapy that did not work for her son. This could not have been easy for her. Oliver already had several speech therapists before me, who each had their own visions for his communication progress. It must have been confusing and exhausting to hear so many different professional opinions and have to figure out which made the most sense for her son. "Yes," she said.

"Oliver needs to go through those stages of language development, too, just in a different way."

"I get it. This looks awesome," she said, tapping the pages. "I'm just . . . I'm just nervous. Oliver has been using his device for a while now and his school knows how to use it. We're all used to it."

I nodded. "We can definitely save this language set in case we ever want to go back. And I'll reach out to his speech therapist at school so we can all be on the same page about targeting the same types of words and concepts. She can let me know what's important at school, and I can let her know what we're working on here. I think it will be worth it."

She asked some other questions, then gave me the green light to move ahead. I was thrilled with the idea that Oliver's world would open up to him, not to mention honored his mom placed her trust in me. In that moment, I committed myself to not only helping Oliver be the best communicator he could be, but also to not letting her down. I adjusted the settings on the device and marveled at all the new words we could use in our sessions.

Oliver progressed through stages of learning as I expected he would. First, he spent time "babbling" on his device by pushing random buttons and observing what would happen. He played with his words just like babies play with sounds as they are learning to talk. Then, Oliver quickly started reusing words he already knew such as *more, swing,* and *go* in appropriate situations. Now, Oliver was starting to say new words like *turn* when he wanted me to spin the swing round and round, or *stop* when he wanted to be finished with an activity. This was the first time in his life that Oliver could tell someone to stop by saying a word instead of by screaming, kicking, or scratching. Oliver was not an aggressive child. He was only doing what he could to convey his message. Oliver's other therapists, his mom, and I were all starting to see that Oliver had all these opinions that he had no way to express. I thought Oliver was really getting the hang of the new device setup.

Until today and "rice," everything he said was making sense. I dropped Oliver off at his physical therapist's desk, where I shared which words we targeted today. His physical therapist, occupational therapist, and I all tried to incorporate one another's goals whenever possible. I popped into the waiting room to talk with his mom. Debriefing at the end of each appointment was crucial in putting the pieces of Oliver's communication together. After one session, for example, Oliver's mom's eyes grew when I casually mentioned that he said "dentist" when we were playing a game. She explained that Oliver left school early that day to go to the dentist. Learning that was huge for me. Without this context, I would have completely missed that he was trying to tell me about his day. Using words to share information is an exciting language milestone. This communication function would have been literally impossible for him to achieve with the limited sentences previously programmed into his device. Oliver's mom was so grateful, and we were both thrilled. Oliver could say much more than what he wanted or needed in the moment.

I crouched down next to her in the crowded waiting room and said, "Has Oliver been saying 'rice' at home at all?"

She frowned. "No, not that I can remember. Why?"

"He said it to me this week and last week. Today he was getting pretty upset when I tried figuring out what he meant. Does he eat rice for lunch or dinner?" I said.

"I mean we have it sometimes, but I don't think he has any strong feelings toward it. He's just . . . he's just Oliver." She sighed. "It could mean anything."

"I'm sure we'll figure it out. Let me know next week if you hear it at home at all," I said. "Also, before I forget, Oliver discovered the dinosaur page on his device. He was repeating dinosaur names over and over while we were cleaning up. We ran out of time, but next week I'll bring some dinosaur toys."

Over the course of the next three weeks, Oliver began each session the same way. He continued saying "rice," and I continued saying anything I could think of that had to do with rice. That word haunted me. I printed off pictures of rice, brought in a pretend box of rice from our play kitchen, studied all the other food words on his device to see if the icon looked similar to another. Maybe he was trying to say a different word, but could not find it? I checked in with his occupational therapist and physical therapist, too. Apparently, Oliver was only saying "rice" when he was with me, nobody else. *Why?* I wondered. Oliver also rejected all the different dinosaur toys and books I brought. He displayed absolutely no interest in any of them even though he continued repeating dinosaur names. I was completely flummoxed.

During these three weeks, Oliver became more and more upset when I responded to "rice." He started screaming louder, dug his fingernails into my forearm, desperate for me to understand him. He chucked his device on the ground, and even at me several times. I moved my head just in time for it to land on the mattress on the floor instead of hitting my face. He was doing everything in his power to let me know he was upset. Taking deep breaths and chanting to myself in my head, *He's acting how he's feeling, he's acting how he's feeling,* kept me from losing my patience. Graduate school prepared me for many aspects of my job, but this was not one of them. What was I doing wrong?

Before this "rice" saga, Oliver and I had a great relationship.

He did not always get along well with adults, and he clearly trusted me. We connected through little games that became inside jokes he anticipated every week. Oliver loved directing me to say specific animal sounds. It cracked him up to hear me shout, "Cock-a-DOODLE-DOOOO" after he said "rooster" or to hear me howl at the ceiling after he said "wolf." If I didn't make the animal noise, Oliver would gently tap my arm to remind me of my role in our game. Oliver and I got along so well because I did not try to force him to do what *I* wanted. Instead, I tried as best I could to follow his interests and expand on them. It was not my job to make Oliver say certain things at certain times. It was my job to give him the skills to talk about anything he wanted to talk about and connect with important people in his life.

Now seeing Oliver this upset during our sessions scared me. He was a strong kid. I had no idea what would happen next if this pattern continued. Would he hurt himself? Would he hurt me? It was heartbreaking to see this complete shift in his behavior. I almost didn't recognize him anymore. Our communication and rhythm had broken down. I feared I was losing his trust more and more each week. The longer this continued, the more difficult it would be to gain it back.

The following Saturday morning, my first client of the day was a sweet elementary-aged girl named Anna who always arrived right on time in her pajamas. Each week, she would immediately tell me where she wanted to play that day. Ninety percent of the time, she asked to go to the gym. If I were her age, I would also prefer to be in a room filled with mattresses on the floor to bounce on, ten different swings, a pillow pit to jump in, and a rock wall to climb. The open play area and sensory gym were very popular with the kids.

That morning she asked, "Can we play upstairs?" That was fine with me. We picked out a book and a game from the shelves and went upstairs to the individual treatment rooms. We walked down the hall, flipping on the lights as we went. We must have been the first ones up there that morning.

"In here!" Anna shouted as she opened the second door on the right. She sighed with disappointment when she realized this room only had a child-size table and chairs, nothing exciting. It looked much less fun than the gym.

"This table will be perfect for our book and game! I'm glad we're up here this morning," I said. Anna looked skeptical. She walked around the table and found a small, clear bin on the floor.

"Miss Christina, what's that?" she asked.

"Good question! It's a bin filled with . . . oh my gosh." I jumped out of my chair.

"A bin what?"

"A bin filled with rice," I said.

She joined me on the ground, suddenly very curious about what we would find as I ripped the lid off. "Look, Miss Christina! Dinosaurs in here." She dove her hands through the rice to find the rest of the dinosaurs. "This feels nice!" Kids with sensory differences loved running their hands through the rice. It felt calm and soothing.

I shook my head and laughed. This must have been what Oliver was trying to tell me for the past five weeks. I had exhausted every other option. He did not want to eat rice. He did not want to look at dinosaur books or videos. No wonder he was getting so mad when I was not understanding. He wanted to play with the rice bin filled with toy dinosaurs.

When Oliver came back to the clinic for therapy on Tuesday, I felt like a little kid trying to keep a secret. I even went so far as to hide the bin behind a stack of cones in the gym. I so badly wanted to shout *"I figured it out! I know you've been asking for the rice bin with dinosaurs this whole time"* as soon as I saw him. Instead, I waited to see if Oliver would ask for it again. I led Oliver through the door to the sensory gym with a little more pep in my step than I typically had. Oliver sat down on the swing as usual, tapped his device to turn the screen on, and said, right on schedule, "rice."

"Rice! Yes! Let's play in the rice," I said.

Oliver's eyes followed me as I walked across the gym to pick up the rice bin I had hidden. By the time I reached the swing, Oliver was shrieking with joy, louder than I had ever heard him yell before. Oliver scooped the rice and threw it in the air and dug for the dinosaurs. I did not care how messy he was being; he deserved this celebration after he waited six weeks for me to understand him. In the thirty-minute session, Oliver only paused his ecstatic play once. He took his hand out of the rice bin and gently squeezed my forearm.

After I talked with Oliver's mom and other therapists about the conclusion of the "rice" saga, I learned that months ago Oliver used to play in the rice bin with the speech therapist who no longer worked at the clinic. That's why he was only asking me for it. Oliver's mom was shocked to learn that he was not saying random words for the past six weeks and getting mad for no reason. She looked at Oliver with a newfound pride and relief in her eyes. She and I knew, once and for all, that switching his device setup was the right decision. We had only caught a glimpse of Oliver's knowledge, perseverance, and potential and could not wait to hear what else he was trying to tell us for so long. In every session from there on out, I opened myself up to all the possibilities of what he could know and be trying to communicate. No words, phrases, or sentences were off-limits. I modeled everything I could for him. Oliver went on to create his own two- and three-word phrases every day, use adjectives like "mean" and "nice" to talk about the people in his life, "funny" after watching his favorite videos, and even told me "speech pathologist sick" after I returned to work from being out with the flu.

My graduate school professors instilled the importance of "presuming competence" when working with children who require AAC. Presuming competence means treating from the fundamental understanding that everyone can learn, and everyone has something to say. It is impossible to know a person's communication potential before they are given the tools and interventions they need to succeed. To everyone else, Oliver was a lost cause. He could only push buttons with complete sentences to express a few different desires. If he did not get what he wanted, he often screamed, kicked, and acted out. Underneath all these behaviors was a child who was so misunderstood, someone with so much potential. He just needed a chance to learn, the right tools, and someone to believe in him. It was impossible for me to fully grasp the significance of presuming competence sitting in a classroom. Now, seeing what happened when we gave Oliver a real chance to learn words and believed in him was life changing. I looked at him, and every child on my caseload, through a lens of potential. I never made assumptions about what any child might know, or be capable of learning. We need to give all kids, regardless of impairments, the opportunity to learn. We need to argue for their potential, not their limitations. I loved seeing what kids could say when given a real chance to learn. I loved the transformative power of AAC. I craved more of it.

CHAPTER 2

Ozzie and Truman

———

Ding ding ding. The bell hanging from the front doorknob chimed. Ozzie, one of the two goldendoodles that my boyfriend, Jake, and I were dog sitting, stared at us from the doormat.

Jake squatted down in front of Ozzie to scratch his white, shaggy fur. "You want to go outside again, bud? Weren't you just out?" Jake asked.

Ozzie lifted his paw and swatted at the bell again. He and his partner in crime, Truman, a black goldendoodle, had been trained to ring a bell when they needed to go outside. We hung the bell on our front doorknob to stay consistent with the setup at their house.

"Ozzie really loves ringing that bell. Maybe he wants to go for a walk," I said. "Want to take them together?" As soon as he heard the word *walk*, Truman hopped off the couch to join Jake and Ozzie near the door.

"That looks like a yes to me," Jake said. "Let's get your leashes on."

Omaha was beginning to break out of winter for the year. Mud piles from melted snow lined the edges of the front yards in our neighborhood. Ozzie and Truman panted with their tongues lolling out the sides of their mouths, happy to be out and about exploring a new neighborhood.

Ozzie and Truman belonged to my former speech therapy supervisor, Mandy. When I heard that Mandy and her family were going out of town for the weekend, I jumped at the opportunity to watch her two goofy dogs. I had dog sat them a few months before, and got a kick out of their different personalities. Ozzie went with the flow of what was happening and adjusted to changes pretty well. Besides ringing the bell when he wanted to go outside, he did not really demand much else from us. He just hung around keeping us company. Truman, however, was more energetic and anxious. He seemed a little unsure about everything, like he could not ever fully relax.

Jake was game to watch them, too. We had been dating for the past eleven months and had just moved in together. Originally from a small town in northern Minnesota, Jake moved to Omaha about five years ago to work as a financial analyst for a large agricultural company. When Jake was growing up, his family lived in the country and had a hundred-pound black lab named Kirby. Kirby spent the day outside exploring the woods behind Jake's house and slept in their insulated shed at night. He swam in the pond to chase fish and fetched baseballs Jake's family would hit deep into the forest for him to find. Taking dogs outside to go to the bathroom and to go on walks was new for Jake.

As a child I desperately wanted a dog, but my struggles with asthma prevented that. In lieu of a real-life furry companion, I collected countless stuffed dogs, robotic dogs, and Beanie Baby dogs throughout my childhood. When I was in second grade, my parents surprised me with a box turtle. I would walk Shellie in our front yard, watch her dig holes by my mom's hostas, feed her, give her baths, and pet her red speckled head whenever she emerged from her shell. No matter how much I treated her like a dog and no matter how many toy dogs I collected, though, my desire for a puppy never went away.

Thankfully, when I was ten years old, I received the official health clearance from my doctor to adopt a dog. I immediately started researching puppies and wrote a persuasive essay to convince my parents that we should have one. I had waited years for this possibility; I *had* to bring my parents on board. Shortly after my essay and presentation, we brought home the new member of our family, a sweet, playful boxer puppy named Wrigley.

Living with a dog was magical. This little, wiggly, slobbery creature joined our family and fit right in. Wrigley's intelligence left all of us in awe. Wrigley learned the patterns of when my older sisters would leave for college. As soon as she saw one of them walk a suitcase up from the basement, she stayed right by their side until their departure. Sometimes she would even lie in their suitcases while they packed. After they left, Wrigley always spent the rest of that day curled up in a ball on their beds. It seemed like her ritual to acknowledge that they would not be back for a while.

Wrigley also knew that my mom was the only consistent

enforcer of the "no dogs on couches" rule. If my dad was home with us, Wrigley would freely hop up to cuddle until she heard my mom's car pull up. Then Wrigley fled the scene and lay on her bed as if nothing had happened. We all laughed and cherished this secret between us. My sisters and I loved trying to convince Wrigley to join us on the couch when my mom was upstairs or in another room. We would encourage her by patting on the cushions. "Come on, girl, come on up." Wrigley looked around cautiously several times before determining it was all clear.

Wrigley always wanted to go play or sunbathe in the backyard. If we were watching TV, she would stand right in front of it whimpering until we let her out. I bet if she had a bell to ring when she wanted to go out like Ozzie and Truman did, we would have heard it all the time. She became so excited for her walk every night. As soon as my mom would grab her headphones and put her tennis shoes on, Wrigley would perk up and run to her leash hanging in the back hall. When my mom would finally ask if she wanted to go for a walk, Wrigley shook her whole body in excitement and whined until they left. She was so expressive and intelligent.

Wrigley had passed away a few months before we watched the goldendoodles. I had only been back to my parents' house in Aurora, Illinois, once or twice since she died and noticed a huge difference. For over thirteen years I was used to Wrigley greeting me with kisses every time I walked through the front door, snuggling next to me on my bed, and running through the house with a toy hanging out of her mouth. I did not realize how central Wrigley's role in our family was until I experienced the stillness of our house when she was gone.

When Jake and I and the goldendoodles all arrived back home, the four of us hopped on the couch, ready to relax.

Truman jumped off the couch and stood in the middle of the living room. "What's up, Truman?" I asked. Truman cried. He sounded like a scared child. "Hm. Let's see if you need water," I said. Truman followed me into the kitchen. "Nope, you have water. And we were just outside so you shouldn't need to go to the bathroom. And you ate all your breakfast so you shouldn't be hungry."

He had to be upset for a reason. What was he thinking about and trying to express? Did he want a certain toy that we did not have here with us? Did he want to be back home? Was he stressed?

Truman kept whimpering. *Are you missing your family?* I wondered. I squatted down to Truman's level, petting his face while staring in his eyes. "What's wrong, buddy?" Truman and I walked back to the living room. "I don't know what's going on. I hope he's okay," I said to Jake. I felt so bad for Truman. It is so frustrating to try communicating something and not be understood.

"Oh, he's fine. I bet he just wants to play!" Jake leapt from the couch and chased Truman up the stairs and back down. Before I knew it Jake, Ozzie, and Truman were running laps around the living room, kitchen, hallway, and dining room. Every time Jake turned a corner, the dogs slid across the hardwood floors. I stayed out of the way, enjoying the show, but it still nagged at me. While Jake had diverted them, I still didn't know what Truman really wanted.

The next morning, Jake and I let the dogs out in the backyard while we cooked pancakes.

"You know, this house is perfect for a dog," I said.

"What do you mean?"

"We have a nice fenced-in yard, we have a mudroom, there's plenty of space. It's perfect." Before I moved in with Jake, he lived in this house with two of his friends. I had heard all about how his friends tried to convince Jake to adopt a dog for two years, but he wouldn't budge. I wanted to introduce the concept lightly to assess where he was at with the whole dog topic.

"Yep! It's perfect for dog sitting," he said.

"Yeah . . ." I paused. "What do you think about us having our own dog?"

Jake chuckled. First his roommates and now his girlfriend. He could not escape the question. "It'd be really fun, but there'd be a lot to consider. They take so much work and they're expensive, and it might be more difficult for us to travel," he said. My heart sank. Jake noticed my sudden change in disposition. "I know we'll have a dog someday," he said. "We just moved in together, let's give it some time."

My feelings in that moment told me how ready I was to have a dog again. I did not at all expect to be upset by Jake's perfectly reasonable response. I didn't want to argue, but I also didn't want to end the conversation here. A few minutes later, I changed my approach.

"So, let's just say, hypothetically speaking about someday, what kind of dog could you see us with?" I asked.

"One that's active, but not too big. Ozzie and Truman feel too big for this house," he said. "But they fit perfectly with Mandy's house." The tall ceilings in Mandy's house really did suit them better.

I imagined us adopting a thirty- or forty-pound, playful dog from a shelter. There were so many dogs who needed a good home, and I wanted to help one of them. Both of my older sisters adopted their first dogs from shelters and had great experiences.

Jake brought our pancakes into the dining room.

"I have an idea. Let's look at the Nebraska Humane Society website to see what kinds of dogs they have," I said.

Jake laughed. "Christina, why would we do that now if we aren't looking for one?"

"Because it's fun. Why not look at pictures of dogs and see what we like? There's no harm in that." Without giving Jake a chance to respond, I ran upstairs to grab my laptop. Jake ate his breakfast, barely looking up at the screen until he caught a glimpse of an image of six or seven chocolate lab puppies cuddled together in a shopping cart.

"Look how cute the puppies are. Christina, look!" Jake grabbed my laptop and zoomed in on their faces. What was happening? Jake was supposed to be the practical one.

"Yes, they're very cute, but there's no way we're getting a puppy," I said.

"What do you mean? We'd be missing out on the best phase. Plus, how could you resist that cute little face?" Jake zoomed in even farther.

"Puppies take so much work."

Jake was only four years old when his family had brought Kirby home. I was older when we added Wrigley to our family. I remembered how much time it took to potty train her, how she could not be left alone for more than a couple of hours at a time, how my dad slept by her kennel every night for a couple of weeks, how we always had to keep an eye on her for months.

"I don't even know how we'd do that," I said. "Let's keep looking at the adult dogs." As we scrolled through the pages,

Jake continued pointing out every puppy and I continued staying focused on my mission.

Later that afternoon, Jake and I unpacked some more of my boxes upstairs. My parents were coming to stay with us the next week, so we wanted to finish setting up the house before they arrived. While we were working, we kept hearing *ding ding ding* from downstairs. I would walk down to our living room, see Ozzie sitting next to the bell staring at me, and I would try to take him outside. Instead of going outside, Ozzie walked back to the door and rang the bell again. After the second or third time of this confusing game, I noticed that the water bowl was empty. "Oh, you need water?" Ozzie licked his lips and ran to his bowl. He and Truman took turns taking long drinks.

Ringing their bell was just supposed to mean they wanted to go outside, but I started noticing that Ozzie seemed to ring it for all his needs. I wondered if he used the bell for everything because that was his only option. It intrigued me. I started imagining the potential for all Ozzie and Truman might have been trying to communicate this weekend. *What if they rang the bell to let us know they were hungry or needed water or wanted to play? What if they wanted us to pet them or to take them somewhere specific? If they only had one bell, how could we know what else they might have wanted?* But my mind quickly shifted back to the current task at hand: fitting all my clothes into the closet.

That night after Mandy picked up Ozzie and Truman to take them home, Jake and I sat in the sunroom in silence. My dad always talked about how once you live with a dog, you cannot go back to life without one. When you are used to a dog's unconditional love, playful spirit, and companionship, life seems too boring and incomplete without one by your side. I remember feeling this way within days of our family bringing Wrigley home. Even though I had lived ten years without a dog, I suddenly could not imagine life without one anymore. Did I really used to walk through the door without someone greeting me? Did I really used to play in the backyard by myself? What did we all do together before Wrigley? Since Jake grew up with an outdoor dog, this was the first time he really experienced a home feeling empty.

"So what do we do now?" Jake asked. "It feels so weird without them here."

"I know what we could do," I said, smiling. "We could look at more dogs."

CHAPTER 3

The Chocolate-Colored Puppy

———

The night that Ozzie and Truman left, Jake agreed to start looking around at dogs. I spent nearly every spare moment the next two days scrolling through online listings of adoptable dogs in Nebraska, Iowa, Illinois, and Kansas, and swiping through pet finder apps on my phone. Our perfect match could be anywhere. I did not want to keep ourselves from finding him or her by restricting the distance. We stopped our scrolling when we saw a one-year-old mutt named Colt from a shelter about an hour away. He was well trained but still young, and he smiled in every single picture.

Jake and I answered each question on the shelter's application with confidence and ease. It seemed like we had every criterion necessary for potential dog owners: solid financial situations, experience with dogs while growing up, a large fenced-in back-yard, active lifestyles, plenty of space in our home, and Mandy's contact information to reference how we cared for Ozzie and Truman. The application probably could have been completed in twenty minutes, but Jake and I spent over an hour sitting on the love seat in our sunroom, savoring this vision of a life with a dog.

The last question was the only one to trip me up: "Under what circumstances would you consider relinquishing a pet?" The only situation I could think of was if we had a baby some-day and the dog harmed him or her. But did I really need to express that? I figured it couldn't hurt to be as honest as possi-ble. I jotted my response down, pushed submit, and headed up to bed. As I drifted off to sleep, I thought, *Tonight could be the start of our story of bringing our dog home.* I could not wait to hear back from the shelter and experience the rest of it.

When I woke up the next morning, I already had a response in my in-box. The adoption coordinator said everything looked great. She needed to officially meet with the rest of the adop-tion committee and would reach back out to schedule a time for us to visit over the weekend.

For the rest of the week, Colt was mentally mine. I had no doubt that we would bring him home. I called my parents to share the exciting plans, brainstormed with Jake about where to keep his bed and dishes, and talked about him nonstop to my friends. But on Friday night, I became nervous. The shelter still had not reached out again to schedule our visit. *Could he have already been adopted?* I wondered.

When my parents arrived the next day, it was still radio silence from the shelter, even after I reached out again. It wasn't until Sunday morning when the four of us were putting our coats on to leave for brunch that my phone screen lit up with a notification from Gmail. Mom, Dad, and Jake all huddled around me. I read it out loud:

Our committee members expressed concern over the possibility of relinquishment if a child is added to the home. One of the common reasons dogs are relinquished to shelters is that the family is unprepared to handle the dog's needs—training, time and attention, and socialization with the new family member. We are unable to further consider your application, but thank you for your interest.

I was crushed. This had to be a miscommunication. I wrote the shelter back immediately, clarifying what I meant. I would only *consider* relinquishment if the dog was outwardly aggressive and dangerous to a child. I wasn't expecting that to happen, I was just being honest.

Everything around us matched our moods the rest of the day. The sky poured rain, we waited for close to two hours to eat at the brunch restaurant, the shelter didn't respond back to me, and every other dog Jake and I showed the slightest interest in had already been adopted. This all felt like a lost cause.

Later that evening, my parents, Jake, and I stopped back at our house to change for our dinner reservations. I announced that I was officially done browsing pet finder apps for the weekend. I think I looked at every adoptable dog between the ages of one and four in the whole state of Nebraska. I wanted to enjoy the rest of the time with my parents here and focus on anything else besides the dog pursuit that was leading me to dead end after dead end. Maybe it was not the right time for us.

At one point, I was talking to Dad but he was oblivious, staring down at his phone.

"Dad?"

"You guys gotta see this," he said, grinning. He handed me his phone and walked away. Jake and I exchanged confused glances and looked down at the screen. It was a picture of four adorable puppies standing together, perched on the edge of a blue tub. Three of the four puppies had speckled and patched fur patterns, but one puppy in the middle had a smooth chocolate coat with a striking white chest. That one stuck out from the crowd.

"These are the cutest puppies I've ever seen," I said. "Mom, come look!"

Jake took the phone out of my hands. "Where are they? What is this?" he asked.

"Craigslist," my dad said. "Just searched for dogs in Omaha."

The listing read "Catahoula/heeler puppies. One male, three females." There were four pictures of the puppies and two pictures of the parents. The only other piece of information was a phone number—no price, no description of the dogs, or anything else.

I decided to call. With the way this weekend had played out, I expected there to be no answer, or to find out that all the puppies were adopted already. I paced across the living room, biting my nails until a woman answered on the fourth ring. It turned out that her Catahoula had puppies with her brother's blue heeler. The three female puppies were still available, and she could bring them to the neighborhood Hy-Vee parking lot after dinner to let us meet them. All the despair from the day washed away.

We spent the entire dinner at our favorite restaurant, Stirnella, staring at the pictures of the puppies, and googling "Cata-houlas," "Blue Heelers" and "Catahoula Blue Heeler mixes." The Catahoula is the Louisiana state dog described as "intelligent, energetic, independent, inquisitive, loving, gentle."[1] Their coats are typically spotted, but one variation, the "red Catahoula," can have a brownish-red coat. From the picture on Craigslist, the mom looked like she might be a red Catahoula. Blue heelers, also known as Australian cattle dogs, are herding dogs described as "intelligent, active, alert, resourceful, protective, hard-working."[2] Even though Jake and I were so excited to meet the puppies, we prepared ourselves to act rationally. We had figured out how our lives would look with an adult dog, not with raising a puppy. We wanted to be responsible and figure out if this could ac-tually work before making any decisions. Jake and I convinced ourselves that we would meet the puppies tonight, sleep on it if we liked them, then take tomorrow off work to prepare our house and bring one home. After dinner, the four of us hurried to the car, trying as best we could to stay dry in the March showers.

"Just so everyone is clear, we are *not* getting a puppy tonight. We're going to look and then decide," I said. "We're all on the same page, right?"

My dad laughed from the back seat. "What have I always said, Christina? Nobody ever ends up just looking at puppies." When I glanced in the rearview mirror, I caught my mom looking out the window, trying to cover her grin with her hand. She somehow knew something magical was about to happen.

"Here we are," I said. The giant red Hy-Vee sign on the front of the building lit up the dark, misty parking lot. I pulled into a spot in the back corner of the lot and waited. Within a few minutes, a car drove up and parked directly behind us. Jake squeezed my hand and smiled. The four of us watched out the window. A dark-haired woman came out of the car snuggling three puppies against her bright blue sweatshirt.

The woman handed the chocolate-colored puppy to my mom, a tan-and-white spotted puppy to me, and a puppy with speckled brown fur to Jake.

"Whoa, I can't keep her in my arms," my mom said. The chocolate puppy leaped from her into my chest. She licked my face over and over again.

I laughed. I looked down and locked eyes with this sweet, tiny creature. How could she possibly be so excited to be held by a complete stranger? It looked like she was dancing in celebration of landing on me. But maybe she felt the same way I did, like I was reconnecting with an old friend instead of meeting someone for the first time.

"Jake, watch out, she's coming for you." The chocolate puppy licked my face one more time, then leaped over into Jake's arms.

Jake looked down into her golden eyes. "You are the happiest little girl."

Jake and I instantly bonded with this little chocolate puppy. She bounced back and forth between us, her tail slapping into us as it wagged with joy. She did not care what the other puppies, my parents, or the breeder were doing. She only looked into our faces, and the three of us entered our own little world, only to be interrupted by the need to decide what we were going to do.

"I love her," I told Jake. "What do you think?"

"I love her, too. Let's stick with our plan. We can always get her tomorrow if we're feeling the same way."

I kissed the puppy's head and whispered in her ear that everything would be okay. I handed her back to the breeder. The puppy's eyes drooped when she realized we were leaving.

She extended her front paws out toward us. When the breeder walked back to the car, the puppy kept her eyes on us. My heart sank. "I can't look anymore!" I turned away and jumped in the car. Why did I set the stage that we weren't bringing home a puppy tonight? She was absolutely perfect, and we just let her go. "I think this is why it didn't work out with Colt," I told my parents and Jake. "She's the one."

Jake and I spent the car ride home gushing about the little brown puppy. I wished she was in my lap right now. We walked into our big, empty house and began panicking that someone else would meet her and take her home before we came back tomorrow. I was not going to last the night.

"I don't care how much time it takes to train her or how much work it is. I want her and I know we'll figure it out," I told Jake.

Jake called his parents to sound them out about adopting a dog. The conversation only confirmed the idea. When he was done, he said, "Let's go get her tonight!"

My parents cheered. I frantically texted the breeder asking if we could come back now. It was already after 9:00 so I wasn't sure if she would respond or wait for the morning. The four of us sat around the coffee table watching my phone. Suddenly, the screen lit up. It was an email from the shelter. Right when we decided we wanted a different dog, they wrote back to say they reconsidered my application and we could proceed with the adoption process if we wanted. But that didn't change anything for Jake or me. We were set on the little chocolate puppy.

Within minutes, the breeder responded that we could come pick her up. We all hopped back in the car. This time when we pulled into Hy-Vee, the rain had stopped, and the breeder was waiting outside the car holding our girl. As soon as she saw me, she wagged her tail and reached out to me. "See, I told you it would be okay," I whispered in her ear. "You're coming home with us now."

Jake and I cuddled the puppy together while Dad ran into the store to pick up a dog bed, food, and a few toys.

"Have you thought about names at all?" Mom asked.

"How about Stella?" Jake said.

"That's perfect," I said. "Stella girl, our little star. We love you so much."

We found our newest family member and I couldn't have been happier. She was all ours to raise, to learn about, and to love.

CHAPTER 4

Communication Is Everywhere

———

At work the next day, I sat on the floor, alternating between stacking blocks with the blond two-year-old I was evaluating and talking to her mom about language development. There are many language milestones that occur even before toddlers start saying words. Words are only one form of expressive language. Parents' anxiety can be alleviated when they know which skills their child already demonstrates, recognize all the other ways their child is communicating, and understand which milestones to look for next in their development. Even though this mom's daughter wasn't talking yet, I had already learned so much about her language skills in the past hour we spent together.

"We'll go over all this in much more detail when I score the assessment and write up the report, but I want you to know that I saw a lot of great things today," I said. "She explored these new toys, engaged in play with me, used eye contact and several gestures to communicate during multiple different activities. These are all really important skills for learning words, so we're on the right track in a lot of ways. Do you have any questions for me right now?"

The mom took a deep breath. "I guess I just want to know, when will she start talking?"

Within this first year of practice as a speech therapist, I quickly learned that was the number one question I would be asked when evaluating children with language delays. At first, it flustered me. I didn't know how to effectively articulate that it was impossible to give an exact time frame, but there were a lot of indicators in a child's prelinguistic skills of how developmentally close they were to saying words. I spent many hours in between sessions rehearsing responses. I wanted to be realistic yet encouraging. And I wanted to be serious about the need for intervention, yet optimistic about the child's potential.

"It's impossible to give an exact time estimate, but the great thing about language development is that it's a gradual process filled with milestones along the way," I said. "It's kind of like trying to predict exactly when a flower will bloom. If a stem hasn't sprouted from the ground yet, we know we probably won't see a flower in the near future. We know there are steps that need to happen before a flower would appear. But if there's a closed bud on top of a stem, we know just about everything is in place for the flower to blossom next. When we go over the assessment results, I'll show you exactly where your child is at in her development, and what steps we'll need to see before we can expect her to say words."

After I walked the mother-daughter pair to the front desk to schedule their next visit, I hurried to grab my keys from my desk. Yesterday, on our first day with Stella, Jake stayed home from work. We needed a day to figure out the logistics of how we would let her out every couple of hours with our work schedules. My last appointment of the day didn't end until 7:30 P.M., and Jake worked a typical eight-hour day. He would head into the office earlier now to be done sooner, and we both would come home on our different lunch breaks. Before we had Stella, I was always annoyed that my hours were later than everyone else's. Now, it felt like a gift that our different availabilities fit together to solve this Stella care puzzle.

When I arrived home and opened our bedroom door, Stella was sitting up perfectly straight in her kennel, waiting for me to let her out. "Stella girl, hi!" Her tail wagged frantically. She jumped up to lick my face repeatedly and flopped over on my lap. "Hi, girl. I missed you, too." I used one hand to rub Stella's belly, and the other to pat the towels in her kennel. *Phew*, I thought. They were all dry. I had been worried all morning about how Stella would react on our first day away.

"Yay, Stella, good girl! Let's go outside, come on." I carried Stella down the stairs. "Outside, outside, let's go outside!" I repeated important words for Stella so she would be able to recognize them and respond. When I used to ask our family dog, "Wrigley, want to go outside?" she would run to the back door if she needed to go to the bathroom or wanted to play. With enough repetitions, Stella should be able to associate "outside" with going out to our backyard, too. When Stella squatted down in the grass, I celebrated even more than I did after realizing her towels were dry. "Good girl, Stella!" I scratched behind her ears and kissed her forehead. "Come on, let's go inside now."

I loved watching eight-week-old Stella explore our home like an adventurer stepping onto uncharted land for the first time. She sniffed everywhere she walked, picked up and dropped each toy she passed, and darted her head toward every new sound. She was fascinated by all that surrounded her. Stella approached her dishes and pawed her water bowl. "Oh, you need water? Let's get more water, Stella." In only two days of living here, Stella learned what each dish was for. She even gestured by pawing her dish to let me know that she needed more water. Her communication was already so clear. "Thanks for showing me, girl. Here you go." Stella started drinking before I could even pull my hand away.

Nonverbal communication plays a crucial role in language development. Not only is it a significant milestone on the way to words, but research shows direct correlations between a child's gestural repertoire and subsequent expressive vocabulary.[3] This means children use gestures before they are able to say a word for the given concept. For example, a child who says "up" when he wants to be lifted likely reached his arms up to communicate that desire before he started saying the word *up*.

"Okay, Stella, it's time for another nap," I said. "Jake will be home in a couple hours to play, I promise." Stella trotted into her kennel sniffing to find the treat I tossed in. I closed the door and resumed the playlist of soothing music I made for her. I didn't want Stella to feel alone while we were gone. "Bye, Stella, love you." Stella watched me as I walked out the door. How could I leave that little face?

Back at work, I was reviewing a toddler language assessment I had completed when something struck me. *If Stella is already gesturing at eight weeks old, what other communication skills does she display that overlap with those of toddlers?* I took a closer look at the prelinguistic skills listed across the areas of "Interaction," "Pragmatics," "Play," "Language Comprehension," and "Language Expression." Turning through the pages I quickly realized, there were parallels in each domain. These are just a few examples of milestones that jumped out at me after being with Stella for only two days:[4]

- "Cries to get attention." Stella cried out to Jake and me, especially at night.
- "Turns head to a voice." When Jake and I talked to Stella, she looked back at us.
- "Anticipates feeding." When we walked to her food shelf, Stella stood by her dishes, waiting for her meal.
- "Maintains eye contact." Stella locked eyes with us while we were playing or talking to her.
- "Attempts to interact with an adult." Stella dropped her toy at our feet, whined, and barked to engage with us.
- "Responds to request to 'come here.'" Stella was learning how to "come" on command. If we patted our legs and crouched down to her level, she ran right to us.

- "Shows a desire to be with people." Stella followed us everywhere we went. If she was startled by a loud noise, she would hop in my lap.
- "Vocalizes to gain attention." Stella barked and whined to make us pay attention to her.
- "Searches for the speaker." If Jake or I started talking from the other room, she ran looking for us.
- "Plays fetching game with caregiver." Ironically, one of the first games young toddlers learn to play is running after a ball and bringing it back to their parent. Stella was learning to do the same thing. She chased her ball and brought it back about half the time.
- "Explores toys." Stella tried out every toy we had for her. She was learning which objects were hers, and which ones were not.
- "Gestures to request action." Stella rolls over to request a belly rub. She pawed at her water bowl to tell me to fill it up.

All these subtle behaviors are actually indicators of a child's language development. I saw all these, and more, in Stella. It made me wonder, *What is Stella's potential for learning and using language?*

After work that day I returned home to a frantic Stella, who was playing with Jake. Jake squeezed a pink plastic ball and bounced it across the living room. When she heard the high-pitched squeak, Stella abandoned a tennis shoe she had picked up and pounced on her toy.

"Good girl, Stella! Good girl playing with your toy," I said.

Stella squeaked her ball a couple of times, then dropped it when her eyes landed on our ivy plant on an end table. She jumped toward the plant, pawing at the leaves.

"Stella, no," I said, firmly. She stopped pawing the plant and looked at me.

"Good girl! Play with your toy." I rolled her ball right in front of her to distract her from the plant. She took the bait and ran through the living room with her ball in her mouth.

"Yes, good girl, Stella. Good Stella," I said.

Jake was impressed. I wanted to teach Stella what was hers and what wasn't by positively praising her every time she played with her toys. When she approached a plant, shoe, or pillow, I would say "no," redirect her to what she could play with instead, and show her how excited I was when she chose one of her toys. I thought back to the toddler language assessment. One of the comprehension skills is "responds to 'no' half the time."[5] After two days in our home, she was beginning to respond to "no." I started tallying in my head.

Later, Stella approached the staircase, and Jake and I followed right behind her. She put her right paw on the first stair, then pulled it back to the ground. She hovered her left paw over the first step for a couple more seconds then brought it right back down. Stella turned to look at me, then looked back at the staircase and whimpered.

I scooped her up and walked up the stairs, analyzing what Stella just did. She wanted me to see that she needed help going up the stairs, so she used her eye gaze to direct my attention to the steps. And she even combined that gesture with a vocalization, her whimpering. That's a skill called *joint attention*, a form of communication kids develop before they can say words. I write about it every day at work in my session notes.

Joint attention is a huge component of communication. It's when two people are focused on the same object or activity. One person draws attention to the object verbally or nonverbally, and the other person responds by looking at it. Anytime we tell someone, "hey, look at that" and point, we are engaging in joint attention. When toddlers are developing this shared attention ability, they first communicate with eye contact or other gestures, then they pair a gesture with a vocalization, then they say words to grab attention.[6] Stella just paired a gesture with a vocalization. That typically comes right before we hear first words.

For the rest of the night, I noticed Stella's joint attention in all kinds of situations. She did not only initiate it once on the staircase. She was constantly using eye contact and vocalizations to show me or Jake what she wanted, or how she wanted us to participate in her play. While sitting on the couch with us, Stella dropped her toy to the ground. She looked down at the toy and looked back at me, showing that she wanted me to pick it up.

"You want me to play?" I picked up Stella's toy from the ground and tossed it in the air for her. Stella bit it a couple of times, then dropped it right back down to the floor and looked up to me. She wanted to play the game she created again. It is like when a baby learns how to play "peekaboo" and repeatedly covers his eyes to start the routine again. After the third time, I started responding as if Stella were a child.

Instead of talking to Stella in sentences, I dropped down to using single words at a time. When children are learning language, it's important to spend time speaking to them at the level right above their current expressive capabilities. If a toddler is not talking yet, I say words like *want* when he reaches for a toy, *more* when I am about to activate the toy again, and *all done* when we are cleaning up. When a child starts saying single words, I increase to saying two-word phrases like "want toy," "more play," "all done play," and so on. With this strategy, I model the next level of communication without overwhelming the child with complex sentences to dissect.

Each time Stella dropped her toy and looked at me, I said "play" before picking it up and handing it to her. Stella and I were building a game together and connecting to each other. I watched and listened to her, and she watched and listened to me. If she dropped the toy and did not look at me or vocalize, I would not reach down for her toy. I waited to say "play" again until she communicated by looking down or whining. This way, I was adding the corresponding word to her nonverbal communication. By the end of our five-minute play session, Stella started wagging her tail every time I said "play." After hearing the word so many times and playing with me and her toy, she began to anticipate what would happen next. By pairing the single word *play* with her gestural communication and engaging in this game with her, Stella was starting to understand what the word *play* meant.

Communication is everywhere when you know how to look for it. On one of my very first days of graduate school, my AAC professors instructed us to write down observations while they showed our class a short video of a speech therapy session. When they collected our papers, I panicked. *What was I supposed to be looking for? What should I have observed?* I didn't know anything yet. Embarrassed, I turned my mostly blank paper over before passing it to the end of the row. On the last day of the semester, our professors played the exact same clip for us. Once again, we were to write down everything we noticed. This time, my pencil could barely keep up with my brain. I saw a rich communication exchange unfolding between this teenage boy and his speech therapist. I did not even realize we were watching the same video from the first class until our professors handed back our original papers.

One of my six bullet points from my first day of class was, "This boy uses a communication device to talk." On the last day, I filled the entire page with comments on his gestures, word choice, level of independence, vocalizations, different functions of communication, the clinician's reactions to his words, language facilitation strategies that worked or did not work, how much time he needed to process language spoken to him, when he became distracted, when he appeared focused, when demands appeared to be too easy, and when demands appeared to be too difficult. I stared down at my two lists in shock. There was so much packed into those five minutes. The video clip did not change. My awareness did.

The first couple days taking care of Stella felt like that last day of class in graduate school. I have played with plenty of puppies, but none since I became a speech-language patholo-gist. Stella was not the only puppy exhibiting all these human developmental milestones. My lens had changed since I learned this information and applied it every single day at work. Stella was already bursting with communication. If she were a child, I would expect to hear her first words soon. But, without the ability to develop verbal speech, what could come next for her?

My thoughts swirled. Dogs can understand words. Wrigley recognized all our names, *walk, outside, cheese, treat, kennel, play, toy,* and I am sure many others. Whenever she heard us say one of those words, she turned her head, wagged her tail, and ran to the appropriate location. Like Wrigley, most dogs wait around all day to hear favorite words like, *walk* or *treat.* Stella, a two-month-old puppy, was already exhibiting over half of the pre-linguistic skills that nine-month-old babies demonstrate before they say first words. We have the technology now to say words in different ways, not only with verbal speech. The era of electronic communication devices began in the 1960s. A hospital volunteer noticed that the only way patients who were paralyzed could communicate was by ringing a bell. He created a typewriter that could be activated by inhaling and exhaling into a sip and puff gooseneck switch.[7] By the 1980s, several different large, portable voice output devices were made to help people of all ages with varying impairments talk if they could not rely on verbal speech. And in 2010, with the release of the Apple iPad, AAC language systems became much more widely available and affordable as apps that anyone can purchase. *What if Stella had access to a few different words?* I wondered. *Could she use an AAC device?*

Throughout the night, Jake and I alternated taking Stella outside when we woke to her cries. It was impossible to tell if she was whining because she was scared and wanted to be with us, or if she needed to go to the bathroom. She was trying to tell us something, I just did not know what.

I picked Stella up, "Come on, let's go outside," and carried her down the stairs to the backyard. My slippers crunched on the frosted grass. I stood shivering in the pitch black. "Come on, Stella, go potty."

Stella sat right against my leg and stared up at me. Even she looked confused as to why we were outside in the middle of the night.

"All right, guess you didn't have to go. Come on, back inside."

An hour later we woke to her whimpering again. "Let's see

if she'll stop in a few minutes," I said. "Maybe she'll go back to sleep." Right when I drifted off, Jake woke me up.

"Do you smell that?" he said. "I think she went to the bathroom." Jake hopped out of bed and turned on the lights. "Yep. Let's get some new towels for her."

The next morning at work, I dropped by my coworker and friend Grace's desk. She was also a first-year speech therapist and shared my enthusiasm for AAC. The two of us went to AAC conferences together, experimented with different devices in our spare time, and continuously worked toward all the children on our caseloads being able to express themselves.

"Why can't dogs use AAC?" I asked.

"Who says they can't?"

"I don't know, maybe no one. But don't you think dogs could say at least a few different words with a device? I was looking at these toddler language assessments and noticing how Stella does so many of the same things."

"Totally. I don't see why not. You should look it up, I'm sure there's something somewhere about it," she said.

I agreed. I thought there would be an abundance of research on dog AAC and the most effective practices. In recent years, multiple studies have confirmed that dogs understand words. In 2010, a retired professor, Dr. John Pilley, published a research study showing how he taught his border collie, Chaser, to learn the names of over one thousand different toys.[8] Dr. Pilley used information about how children learn the meanings of words to guide his teaching. He published another paper explaining how Chaser learned to understand sentences containing a prepositional object, verb, and a direct object.[9] Chaser did not just understand single words; she understood what they meant when combined together.

A study in 2016 proved that dogs do not just respond to the human's tone of voice like many have assumed. Dogs can comprehend the meaning of a word, and the intonation separately, like humans do.[10] One of the researchers from the study expressed that "dogs process both what we say and how we say it in a way which is amazingly similar to how human brains do."[11]

I figured with all these research conclusions, giving dogs a chance to say words would be the next logical step. There is so much research on effectiveness of different types of AAC, when to introduce it, why it works, language facilitation strategies to use, expected outcomes, everything for humans. I wanted to read what the research said for dogs and follow their conclusions.

We searched, "dog AAC research," "speech therapy for dogs," "dog communication device," "dog language use." The closest we could find were companies discussing communication devices that could potentially translate a dog's whines, barks, or gestures to words for their human to understand. But that was not what I was looking for. That would be like a device scanning our facial expressions and gestures and translating those into sentences. That would be much different from saying your own words and expressing your individual thoughts. I wanted to give Stella the opportunity to say the words she was hearing us say all day long and already responding to. If she can understand the words, she should be given a way to use them too.

"Darn," I said after clicking through four pages of results, coming up empty-handed. "I really thought there'd be something. I'm sure Stella could use a device if she had one."

"Let's keep brainstorming later," Grace said. "There's all kinds of AAC out there."

The next day when Grace and I had thirty minutes of open time that lined up, we revisited our dog AAC ideas. *What could Stella physically access?* and *What would be easy to test out?* were our two main questions. The icons on the tablets that Grace and I most frequently used with children would be too small for Stella's paw or nose. We briefly discussed the idea of an eye gaze system, which is a device calibrated to say the word for the icon that the user stares at for a few seconds. But eye gaze devices are very expensive and I did not even know what Stella's vision of a screen looked like.

Some children who have more significant motor limitations use a method called *switch scanning*, instead of directly tapping an icon with their finger. Switch scanning involves pushing a large button hooked up to activate the selected icon on a communication device. The user pushes the button to scan through the options on the screen, then double taps the button after landing on the desired word or pushes a second button to select it. The idea of these buttons seemed promising, if we could program them to say individual words.

"Wait, what about a BIGMack?" Grace said. With the capability to record anything into it, the BIGMack closely resembled a Staples "Easy" button. Individual BIGMacks cost more than $100, so I googled "recordable AAC buttons," in hopes of finding a more cost-effective solution. "Hey, look at those," Grace pointed at the screen.

I clicked on a link for Learning Resources "Recordable Answer Buzzers." They came in a package of four buttons, each a different bright color. "Wow, so much cheaper," I said. "I'm going to try them! What's the worst that happens, Stella can't use them? At least I would know."

TAKEAWAYS FOR TEACHING *YOUR* DOG

- **Observe how your dog already communicates.** Keep an eye out for your dog, whining, barking, pawing, wagging her tail, or using her eye gaze to direct your attention to something. Knowing when your dog is trying to tell you something will help you respond to her communication and determine which words to start teaching.

- **Respond as best you can to your dog's communication.** We are all more likely to communicate when we know we will be acknowledged and understood. Responding to your dog's verbal and nonverbal communication are equally as important as responding to words down the line. Build a solid foundation by observing your dog, learning her habits, and responding when she is trying to tell you something.

- **Pair words with your dog's communication.** Just like how I started saying "play" every time Stella looked down to her toy and looked at me, say a word that goes along with what you think your dog is trying to tell you or what your dog is doing. If you're not sure what to say, you can ask yourself, *What is happening right now?*

CHAPTER 5

Three Feet from Gold

———

One week after bringing Stella home, I tore open the box of Recordable Answer Buzzers that were delivered to my doorstep. Each button fit perfectly in the palm of my hand. The plastic black top curved into its wide base, a small red tab for recording was on its side, and the speaker and battery holder were on the bottom. I pressed the black cap down several times in a row. It was easy to push, which was important.

Stella weighed less than ten pounds at the time. She would grow and become much stronger over the next year, but I wanted to set her up for success from the very start. It is important to choose an AAC system that the user can physically access, or learn to access with practice, that will also support any future development. These buttons met that criteria. The force I had seen her use to paw at her toys and water bowl should be more than enough to push down the buzzers. When she reaches her full-grown adult size, they would not be too small for her paws either.

I was filled with the same anticipation and positive expectation I have right before trying a new AAC device with a client. It's a time that holds so much hope and potential for all that is to come. Even if a huge communication breakthrough does not happen immediately (which it normally doesn't), we are starting a path of discovery that can only help us all in the long run. It's like hopping in the car to begin a big cross-country road trip. You know you will not reach the other side of the country on the first day, and the trip will require hours of driving. But you will see signs that you are moving in the right direction along the way. You pass through different states, observe new landscapes out the window, and see landmarks in person that previously you had only ever read about. In the worst-case scenario, you realize you want to take a different route and adjust your GPS to navigate a new course. Even in that situation, you are still closer to your destination than you would have been by staying at home, wondering what the rest of the country looks like.

I found a couple of batteries. We could start with one button for now. The most immediate need we had for Stella's communication was a way for her to let us know when she needed to go to the bathroom. Now that she had been in our house for a week, Stella knew the door in the kitchen led to our backyard. She would not walk to the door on her own to let us know she had to go out yet, but she was starting to head that way when Jake or I would say "outside." Since Stella was starting to respond to "outside," I wanted to give her the opportunity to say it, too. I held down the recording button and said "outside" into the button's microphone.

I placed the green buzzer right next to the back door in the kitchen. The colors of the buttons wouldn't matter for Stella. Dogs have dichromatic vision, which means they do not see the same spectrum of colors that most humans see. Dogs' vision has been compared to a person who experiences red-green color blindness. At Stella's young age, when she showed any signs that she had to go to the bathroom, we had a very narrow time slot before she would go. There was no waiting for us to figure out what she needed. If she started sniffing the ground, she would go to the bathroom a few seconds later. Now, if she would be able to tell us "outside," she could be in the backyard within a couple of seconds. Keeping the button far away from the door might lead to more accidents on the way out.

I was ready to officially start exploring my big question: *What would happen if I implemented speech therapy language interventions with my puppy?* Our kitchen transformed into a treatment room in my mind. I sat down next to the door to be at Stella's eye level. Jake leaned against the counter, like most parents observing their child's speech therapy session for the first time. They are eager to watch, yet hesitant to participate right away.

Stella walked to our pantry, raising her head up to sniff the lowest shelf filled with cereal boxes, bread, and crackers. I crawled over, attempting to redirect Stella away from the food. "Stella, look!" I crawled back to the door and pointed at the button. She looked back at Jake, over to me, back to the pantry, straight ahead to the door. She might have glanced at the buzzer, but she definitely did not look at it intentionally. I slowed down my rate of speech, articulated each and every syllable, and paused in between every word I said.

"Outside," I said both verbally and with her button at the same time. "Outside. Let's go outside!" Stella stared ahead at the closed door, still unaware of the new addition on the floor. I pushed the button to hear "outside," once more and promptly opened the back door. "Come on, girl!" Stella followed me, trotting down the three steps that led to our yard.

"Yay! Stella outside. Outside!"

Jake joined us. "Is that normal?" he said. "It seemed like she wasn't paying attention."

"It's okay. It takes time for kids to pay attention to a device or watch what I'm doing. So I'm sure it'll take time for Stella, too. At the very least, she's still hearing the words I'm saying and making associations between what she hears and what happens next."

Two important parts of teaching words are modifying how I talk to clients and creating a language-enriching environment for them. If children have a language delay or disorder, that means they are not picking up on language concepts by hearing people talking naturally in their environment. They need focused intervention to help them develop specific concepts. The way I talked to Stella in the kitchen is a combination of two of the most effective, evidence-based speech therapy techniques: *aided language input* and *focused language stimulation*.

Aided language input means using the learner's AAC system to talk naturally while saying the same words verbally at the same time. Using both spoken language and the device simultaneously is shown to increase the learner's receptive *and* expressive language skills.[12] This simple strategy improves language outcomes for a couple of big reasons. First, the speaker tends to slow down their rate of speech as they go back and forth between saying a word verbally and with the device. A slower rate of speech gives the learner more time to process the words. Second, aided language input serves as a *model* for the user. The learner hears a word verbally, hears and sees another way to say that same word, and observes the word being used in appropriate contexts.

Focused language stimulation involves repeating target words that are relevant to what is happening at the time. In a single interaction or activity, a word should be repeated at least five times before moving on. When Stella and I were about to go to the backyard, I said "outside" five times between my verbal speech and using her button. When we were in the backyard, I said "outside" another two times. That means, during this thirty-second period of getting ready to open the door and going into the backyard, Stella heard "outside" seven times. If we take Stella outside six times per day, she would hear "outside" around forty-two times. If we took her outside ten times a day, which was more realistic during this potty-training phase, she would hear "outside" seventy times in one day, all during the appropriate contexts.

Simply changing the way we talk to children and how often we model words at the right time makes substantial differences in their language development. One research study published in the *Journal of Speech and Hearing Research* shows how dramatic differences can be between toddlers' language skills before and after receiving focused language stimulation. At the end of the four-month-long study, the group of toddlers in the experiment possessed 400 percent more words in their expressive vocabularies than when they began. They also produced 257 percent more utterances during a typical play session than they did before receiving therapy. These are huge differences. The results for the experimental group were significantly higher than the statistics from the control group of toddlers who did not receive intervention during those four months.[13]

Late-talking toddlers are much more likely to understand new words and say new words when focused language stimulation is a key part of their treatment plan. Also, AAC users are much more likely to learn how to use their device when the adults around them use aided language stimulation.[14] I did not know if Stella would ever learn to say words, but I wanted to give her the best shot I could. If anything would work, the most effective teaching strategies for kids would probably be a great place to start.

At the end of the week, Stella had not shown any progress with "outside." We took Stella on her first walk around the neighborhood and watched her try climbing her way out of her first bath, but Stella did not show any awareness of the button next to the door. I was used to this happening with kids. Sometimes it took weeks for a child to start really noticing the device I was using. Knowing this, I had motivation to keep going when there were truly no signs of progress after several days. If I had not introduced an AAC system to a child or taught language before, I am sure I would have thrown in the towel pretty early on. But Stella's lack of progress actually propelled me to buy more batteries and program two more words for her. (I would have done all four, but the fourth buzzer was broken.) I was excited to see if using three buttons instead of one would make a difference in Stella's learning.

I had encountered a similar situation when a three-year-old boy with autism transferred over to my caseload. He had never said a verbal word. He only ever squealed when he was excited and grunted when he was frustrated. The previous clinician wrote that she trialed a single button programmed to say "more" for five months. He showed no progress, therefore she questioned his ability to learn any AAC at all.

When I started working with him, I incorporated a device with a robust language system. It had the capacity for him to eventually say thousands of words. Within one month of the change, he used his tablet to say single words such as *up*, when he wanted to go upstairs, *like* when he was excited about a toy I brought, *on* while his occupational therapist helped put his shoes on, *get* when he wanted a toy that he could not reach, and *more* when he wanted me to start his favorite toy again. Instead of seeing his device in use only when it was appropriate to say "more," he saw me using his device constantly for a variety of words. Greater exposure leads to greater learning.

I wanted to pick words that would be meaningful to Stella. From observing and interacting with her for just a couple of weeks, it was very clear that Stella loved to play. She was often initiating some type of game with us. Whether it was chasing Jake around the dining room table, dropping her ball off the couch for me to pick up, or running after a toy, she loved having fun with Jake and me. I recorded "play" into the orange button and set it down in the living room next to her basket of toys. A verb like "play" leads to more opportunities for learning than nouns like "ball" or "toy" do. Stella could say "play" to request any type of game rather than a single one. That could come later.

The next concept that I thought would be helpful was "water." I tried my best to notice when Stella's water bowl was empty, but sometimes I would walk past it, realize it was empty, and fill it up. I hoped it had not been like that for too long. If Stella had a way to say "water," I would know right away when she needed more. I could also hear her request more water from another room instead of needing to see her pawing at her bowl.

Stella was already very aware of how I filled up her water dish. She would nudge her dish, keep her eyes glued to me as I carried it to the sink, and stand right where it would land. I programmed the magenta button to say "water," and set it right next to her bowl.

Since children typically start saying words that they already have gestures for, "play" and "water" made sense for Stella. She used gestures to communicate about both those concepts by pawing at her empty water dish, nudging her toys and looking up to me, and using her eye gaze to direct my attention toward a specific toy that she wanted me to pick up. I could not wait to find out if Stella would demonstrate the same gesture to word progression that occurs with kids.

Now that we incorporated three buttons instead of one, Stella definitely received more exposure to language and her AAC in the following days. Anytime we walked by Stella's dishes and saw her drinking water, we would say "water" and push her button on the way out of the room. Jake would chase Stella around the dining room table, then would stop to model "play" before he started another lap. I would hold Stella's toy basket and push "play" every time I pulled a new toy out of it. Before taking Stella on a walk, we modeled "outside." My friend Grace would come over for lunch, and we alternated between eating and modeling "play" or "outside" for Stella. Stella was now hearing the same few words from multiple people, in several contexts each day.

Celebrating small victories is an important part of being a speech therapist. Significant changes in communication take time to see. There are always little steps on the way to a new milestone that show us we are heading in the right direction. Celebrating those successes gives the child encouragement to keep trying, and his treatment team and parents inspiration to continue teaching. About a week and a half after introducing the buttons to Stella, we witnessed our first small victory to celebrate. I was grabbing a snack from the fridge, when I turned to see Stella standing by the back door, looking down at the "outside" buzzer. This was completely unprompted. I was not in the middle of modeling it, pointing to it, or saying "outside." She gazed down at the button for a whole five seconds. I closed the fridge and squatted down next to her.

"Yes! Good girl, Stella." I petted her head. Stella wagged her tail and licked my face. She got so excited when I told her she was doing a good job. "Outside," I said verbally and modeled with her button. "Come outside." This time, Stella watched me closely when I pushed her button.

There was no way for me to know Stella's intention as she stood in front of the buzzer and looking down at it. She might have wanted to get my attention to go outside, or she might have simply been curious about the object on the floor. Either way, I did not care. Providing positive praise showed Stella that I enjoyed what she was doing, which would hopefully lead her to continue exploring the buttons in the future.

When we came back inside, Stella sprinted through the house and dove into her toy basket. She pulled out her favorite yellow squeaky toy, tossed it in the air, then dropped it right at my feet.

"Play!" I modeled with her button.

Stella cocked her head to the side and looked down at the buzzer. That was the second time in a row that she showed any type of awareness of the buttons.

Instead of pushing Stella to try to do more in those moments, I praised her for showing interest in the buzzers and modeled use of them again. For almost two weeks, Stella had not appeared to notice our modeling, or even the presence of the buttons. Before now, she explored every other object in her space except for these. I hoped this was only the beginning.

Unfortunately, at the end of two weeks of modeling each word extensively at nearly every applicable time, the most Stella had done was look at two of the buttons. She had not looked at them again and did not demonstrate any other signs of progress. *How long should I keep trying this idea?* I wondered. We know all kids can talk in some way, no matter how long it takes to get there. There is no question about whether to give up or not. The answer is always to keep going. We do not know this about dogs, though. *Is this something that will take months? Will the results be worth the time I am putting in? Or is it something I will keep trying and get nowhere?*

Maybe this is why there was no research on dogs using AAC. Maybe the similarities between dogs' and humans' language capabilities stop here, at understanding words and communicating concepts with gestures. Over the next few days, I did not model words as much as I had in the beginning. I said "play" or "outside" or "water" once, and then pressed the corresponding button. But I did not provide as many repetitions, nor make sure I modeled language at every appropriate time. Sometimes I would rush Stella out the door without pressing "outside" first. Or I would fill her water bowl up in a hurry without pausing to model "water." At this point, I stopped expecting to see progress and decided it would be a pleasant surprise if anything more would happen. I did not completely quit my pursuit, but it was no longer a top priority for me. *If she hits a button, great. If not, no big deal*, was my official stance.

There's a famous story written in Napoleon Hill's *Think and Grow Rich* about a man named Mr. Darby who dug for gold during the gold rush. He found a vein of gold close to the surface level, went back home to raise the money he needed for the machinery to extract it, then returned to the mine. He extracted the gold he could see, almost enough to pay back the people who lent him money for the machinery. According to his calculations, there was supposed to be much more gold farther beneath the surface. He kept digging and drilling, digging and drilling, but there was no more gold to be found. With no further evidence of the precious metal, Mr. Darby quit his pursuit. He sold his machinery and went back home. A man bought Mr. Darby's equipment and dug three feet farther. He found an entire vein of gold, which resulted in millions of dollars. Mr. Darby had quit, just three feet from a life-changing find.[15]

Hill pointed out, "Failure is a trickster with a keen sense of irony and cunning. It takes great delight in tripping one when success is almost within reach."[16]

A few days later, at the start of week three with Stella's buttons, I had not modeled anything all day long. Stella sat on my lap on the couch, then jumped off and trotted into the kitchen.

I followed her to the back door where she stopped. Stella looked down at the buzzer, then up at me, and back down to her "outside" button. This time, there was no questioning her eye gaze. She was gesturing for me to push it, just like the time when she gestured for me to help her go up the stairs. I immediately pushed "outside" with my foot and ran into the backyard, praising her the whole way. She went to the bathroom as soon as her paws touched the grass.

When some kids are learning to use their AAC devices, they often grab my hand to push an icon for them. In my experience, this has always come shortly before a child uses his own finger to say a word, when he still needs a little more support before getting there on his own. With one meaningful look from Stella, my enthusiasm was back in full swing. Stella knew that I had been pushing the "outside" button before going outside. When she had to go to the bathroom, she directed my attention to her button to let me know what she wanted.

I came home from work the next day to find Jake smiling in the kitchen. "You were right, she's really aware of the buttons now," he said.

"What is she doing? What did I miss?"

"Give her a minute and you'll see for yourself."

I sat down on the kitchen floor and let Stella crawl all over my lap. This was my favorite part about coming home from work at the end of the day. "Hi girl, I'm so happy to see you." I kissed Stella's forehead in between her floppy ears and stood up. Stella walked around the kitchen, sniffing under cabinets and after a few minutes, she marched up to her "outside" buzzer. She stared down at it. When nothing happened, Stella paced past it three times. She stood in front of it again and lowered her front legs to the ground. She barked at the button and looked up at the doorknob.

"She's already done that three or four times tonight. Whenever I push it, she wags her tail and watches me until I open the door."

Stella combined multiple gestures with a vocalization. That is even more impressive than putting one single gesture and one vocalization together, which is what happens with kids right before a word. It reminded me of watching someone play charades. They come up with every possible gesture for a word without actually saying it. Maybe we were just three feet from gold. Maybe this really was going somewhere after all.

TAKEAWAYS FOR TEACHING *YOUR* DOG

- **Narrate what's happening in your dog's environment by saying single words and short phrases.** Talk about what your dog is doing, what you're doing, or what is about to happen.

- **Be repetitive.** Aim to say a word at least five to ten times before moving on to something else. The more often your dog hears a word in the right context, the faster she'll be able to learn its meaning.

- **Program words into your device that are frequently occurring, and relevant to your dog's daily life.** Remember, a more general word like *play* will be more valuable and frequently occurring than the name of one specific toy.

- **Turn your dog's typical activities into teachable moments.** Before you take your dog outside, go for a walk, feed her, play with her, replenish water, or give her belly rubs, take a moment to say what you are doing multiple times.

- **Use verbal speech *and* your dog's buttons to talk to your dog.** Every time you use your dog's button to say a word, you are modeling appropriate use of it for her.

- **Teach more than one word to start.** Greater exposure leads to greater learning.

- **Be on the lookout for small changes in how your dog interacts with the buttons, responds to you, and communicates.** Your dog probably will not learn to functionally communicate with AAC overnight. That is completely normal for both humans and canines. Look for small victories along the way, such as your dog looking at the buttons, watching you use the buttons, standing next to the buttons, or barking at them. Give verbal praise anytime you see her exploring them.

CHAPTER 6

Now We're Talkin'

———

Stella had already changed so much in this first month since we brought her home. She grew a few inches taller, learned how to climb up and down the stairs, started sleeping through the night without Jake lying next to her kennel, made a couple of puppy friends, and began forming different relationships with each of our friends. Stella was so interested in people. She greeted everyone who came to our house with a warm tail wag and body wiggle followed by falling over in their laps, hoping for belly rubs. She watched all of us so closely, fascinated by our every movement. It entertained Jake, our friends, and me alike to see how Stella preferred to interact with each of us in a unique way.

Stella turned absolutely crazy whenever our high-energy, playful friend, Jenna, came over to visit. Stella would run around in circles at Jenna's feet, baiting her to chase her by lunging and sprinting away. When Jenna sat down on the ground, Stella climbed all over her to attack her face with kisses. But every time our calm, gentle friend, Alex, came over, Stella snuggled in her arms, looking as content as could be. When Jenna and Alex visited at the same time, we all cracked up watching Stella switch back and forth between the frantic and sweet sides of her personality. She would ever so gently lick Alex's hand and sit right by her side, then would leap over to Jenna, bark, and run to her toy basket. Stella's worlds were colliding. Watching her navigate this situation reminded me of parties I had with friends from separate eras of my life all gathered in the same place; different aspects of my personality would come out, depending on who I was interacting with at the time.

Wrigley was the same way. She had been excellent at reading people and adjusting her energy levels to match those around her. When I was a scrawny eleven-year-old, my parents were reluctant to let me hold Wrigley's leash on walks. She was strong and energetic, and notoriously pulled hard. She could have easily knocked me over with one bolt toward a squirrel. Much to everyone's surprise, the complete opposite happened. Wrigley slowed down and walked right by my side the entire time I held her leash. She knew she had to be gentler with me. Similarly, one weekend Wrigley stayed at my grandparents' house while we were out of town. My grandpa left to go on a fishing trip, leaving my grandma alone with Wrigley for the night. Wrigley had stayed there plenty of times and always slept on her own bed in the living room. But that night before falling asleep, Wrigley grabbed her bed with her mouth and dragged it all the way to the doorway of my grandma's bedroom. She stayed right there, guarding my grandma, for the whole night. Our entire family fawned over Wrigley's awareness of her environment and independent decisions to adjust her behavior.

Over our first four weeks with Stella, her personality unfolded more each day. She loved being near Jake and me but had no shortage of intrinsic curiosity or independence. She was well-behaved and intelligent, but not blindly obedient to what Jake or I wanted. She was social with strangers, yet wary of many new objects or sounds. I began to realize that it was hard to describe Stella with only one or two adjectives. But I could not summarize any of my friends' or family members' entire personalities with only a couple of words either. Stella is complex, just like we all are. When friends or family members who had not met Stella asked what she was like, the best single word I could use to describe her in a nutshell was "spunky."

Now after seeing Stella's newfound awareness of the buttons, I returned to modeling language for her every day, in nearly every natural opportunity. She no longer appeared absent-minded when I pushed a button and said the corresponding word. She watched my foot or hand intently as it activated the buzzer. She wagged her tail and looked toward the door, water bowl, or a toy depending on which word I said. Stella's wheels were turning. I felt like I could see her connecting the dots through her head turns, facial expressions, and tail wags. I stopped wondering if it would take months for Stella to use a button, or if she would ever be capable of saying a word. Instead, I started acting as though this milestone was bound to happen. It was the next logical step in her development.

While Jake and I ate dinner later that week, Stella lay on the floor, chewing on her rope toy in the living room. We sat facing her to make sure she stayed out of trouble. Suddenly, Stella dropped her toy and stood up. She started walking toward the kitchen. She paused when she reached the dining room table to make eye contact with us. As soon as she grabbed our attention, she continued on her path. She looked like a little kid making sure she had her parents' full attention before trying something new. Jake and I leaned over the table to watch her through the doorway. Stella stopped in front of the "outside" button. She stared down, like a child standing on the edge of the diving board mustering up the courage to jump into the pool. Stella lifted her right paw. I held my breath. She swatted. And she completely missed the buzzer by at least six inches. Jake and I exchanged glances and hopped out of our chairs.

"Good girl, Stella," I said on my way into the kitchen. "You can do it! Good girl."

Stella wagged her tail and lifted her paw again. She swatted three times in a row, again missing the button by a half of a foot with each attempt. "Yes, you're so close. It's right here." I pointed at the button, hoping one small cue to show her where the button was would do the trick.

In AAC therapy, best practice is to use a "least-to-most" cueing system.[17] Researchers developed a hierarchy that shows cues ranging from the most naturalistic to the most prompted. We begin with the most naturalistic cues such as providing an increased wait time of at least ten seconds, then move down to pointing at the device, or tapping the device. If the user still does not respond, then we model the word again and retarget the vocabulary. I never recommend grabbing a child's finger to say a word for him or grabbing a dog's paw to push a button. That would be the equivalent of pulling words out of a person's mouth, which is impossible. AAC users should be given the same amount of control over their own words.

Starting with the most natural ways to encourage communication and gradually increasing the level of assistance when needed is more beneficial than giving too much help right away and trying to reduce your involvement. The latter often causes "prompt dependency," a reliance on being told when to say a specific word instead of being able to communicate independently. The former builds a solid foundation for functional, independent language use.

Stella looked up at me and back to Jake. *Should I take her outside or give her a little more time to try again?* I asked myself. She was so close. I did not want to rush her out the door and cut this learning opportunity short. But I also wanted to reinforce how close she was to activating her button. Teaching language is a dance. It is a constant search for rhythm and balance between giving the right amount of processing time and reacting quickly, between praising progress and pushing to reach the next step, between helping too much and not supporting quite enough. There is not one exact formula to use in every situation. Even when you know all the tools and strategies to pick from, deciding which ones to try in each moment is an art that only improves with practice and reflection.

"Right here, Stella, right here," I said. I tapped the top of the button. Stella inched over next to me and squatted her hind legs down. A puddle formed right beside the button. Jake swooped in to pick Stella up and run her to the backyard.

"Well, that was 100 percent our fault, not Stella's," I said and sighed. *Why did I have to push for more?*

Even though Stella's attempt at saying "outside" ended with

a swing and a miss and her going to the bathroom on the floor, a lot of good came from that situation. Stella showed us that she was not only aware of the buttons' existence, she also was at least starting to understand their purposes. When Stella had to go to the bathroom, she let us know by walking to the button and trying to hit it. She demonstrated clear communicative intent. Seeing Stella attempt to say "outside" in such an appropriate context on her own was a huge step. I did not care that our twelve-week-old puppy had terrible aim. I was thrilled that when she had to go to the bathroom, she knew what to do.

"Christina, Christina, wake up. Stella said her first word!" Jake shook my shoulder the next night. I was tucked under the covers.

"What?" I reached over to my nightstand to turn the lamp on. It was 11:15 P.M. I must have only been asleep for half an hour or so.

Jake was giddy. He shoved his phone screen in front of my face. "Here, I wrote it all down so I could tell you everything," he said. "Wait, no, actually I want to read it to you." He snatched his phone out of my hands.

I couldn't help but smile as I sat up in our bed and listened as Jake told me the greatest bedtime story I had heard in my adult life. After he caught his breath, he began:

Stella was awake at 11 P.M. 4/30/18. She had lots of energy and trotted over to the kitchen door. She sat by it, so I stood and waited, and stared at her. She sat very patiently and kept looking up and down from the door to me then back. After probably 30 seconds of this (not whining or barking) she looked at me, got a little antsy, and then looked down at the button. She raised up her paw and hit the button! I was so shocked I didn't know what to say. She immediately hit it again and looked up at me expectantly. I opened the door, praising her all the way, and she went straight outside and peed! We stayed out for 5 minutes and she also pooped! Then we went back inside. We were inside for no more than two minutes, and she went back over to the door again and barked, and hit the button with her paw! So I took her outside and she SPRINTED around the backyard. She had so much energy. She is making so much progress and I couldn't be prouder of her!

I hugged Jake. That night, I was equally proud of him as I was of Stella. Jake did absolutely everything right, and he had no experience to guide him. This was all brand-new for him. It was late at night, and Jake could have just rushed Stella outside to go to the bathroom one last time, then put her to bed. Instead, he was incredibly patient. He gave Stella the time and chance to speak up for herself. He reacted to her word perfectly by showing excitement, going outside, and having fun with Stella. Part of me wished I would have stayed awake for another thirty minutes to see this happen in person. Mostly, though, I was overjoyed that Jake could experience the awe of watching another being develop a new skill right in front of your eyes and knowing that you helped them. There are few better feelings than that one.

The next night I came home from work, determined to see Stella say "outside" for myself. According to Jake, she had not said it again since last night. For about half an hour after dinner, I repeatedly modeled "outside" and took Stella out to play in the yard. Stella kept looking up at me with a head tilt and confused eyes every time I said "outside" again. We never went out this many times in a row.

At work it always drove me nuts to see parents trying so hard to make their child say something when they wanted him to, only to prove a point. I would gently say, "It's okay. I believe you. I'm sure he'll say it when it's meaningful to him," and then try to redirect the conversation. In this moment, I realized I was spiraling into exactly what I did not want. Stella would say "outside" again when it was meaningful to her. Communication is always a choice.

I joined Jake on the couch in the living room, distracting myself with an episode of *The Office*. Stella played with a plush raccoon then slipped out of the living room and into the kitchen. I did not notice she was gone until I heard a single high-pitched bark, the one Stella uses to call us over when she wants our attention. When I walked into the kitchen, Stella paced back and forth in front of her button. She looked back at me, then down at the buzzer. I paused for five or ten seconds to see if she would say "outside" on her own. Stella walked over to me, then back to the button.

"Outside?" I asked.

Stella barked.

I walked to the button and lightly tapped the top with my toe, cueing her on what she could do next. Stella's eyes met mine before she marched up in front of the buzzer, lifted her paw, and pushed down to say, "outside."

"Yes, let's go outside." I opened the door and called out to Jake before joining Stella in the backyard. "She did it again!"

Stella promptly went to the bathroom in the grass. It was just as I thought, she waited until it was meaningful to her to say "outside." That was so much more impressive and fulfilling than her saying it only to appease me. Jake and I celebrated another successful communication event by chasing her around the patio table. After a few laps, Stella noticed I had left the door open and pranced back into the kitchen. She turned around to meet my eyes again as I followed her. She said "outside" twice more in a row. She hopped back down the staircase to keep playing with Jake in the yard.

She was discovering her power. "This is incredible," I said.

I was absolutely thrilled that Stella had now said "outside" five total times before needing to go to the bathroom or wanting to run around and play. It amazed me how intentional her communication was, even from this starting point. She did not push a button and walk away. She expressed her desire to go outside first through her bark, eye contact, and pacing next to the button. Then she advanced from using gestures to a word right in front of my eyes. Saying "outside" was the cherry on top of an already rich communication sundae.

For a month, Stella had listened to and watched us say "outside." Through our modeling, she learned what always happened immediately after we said "outside." That is the power of providing naturalistic intervention and modeling words at their appropriate times. Knowing a word and knowing *how to use* a word are completely different skills. I was encouraged to see that so far, Stella said "outside" during contexts that made sense. These observations were still so premature, but I was curious to see what would happen next. *Will this skill last? Or will she become less interested after figuring it out?* I wondered. Would Stella use her "outside" button to communicate every want or need, or would she differentiate its meaning from other words? Would she start saying her other words soon, or would it take another month?

To my surprise, I started learning the answers to a few of these questions much quicker than I expected. Stella, Jake, and I returned to our living room, happy and out of breath from chasing one another in the backyard. Stella, with her bottom-less energy supply, shoved her nose into her toy bin. I modeled "play" a few times while she searched for the toy she wanted.

Stella pulled out a ball and froze. She looked up to me on the couch, then looked back down, still clenching the ball in her mouth. With one confident swoop, she swatted her paw to push the "play" button.

"Was that you?" Jake asked.

"Nope, that was all her," I smiled. "Play? Yes, let's play. Good girl!" I popped up from the couch and bounced Stella's ball across the room for her. A couple minutes later, Stella said "play" again after she dropped her ball and picked up her rope toy.

After weeks spent talking to Stella, modeling words, and observing her communication patterns, that night, for the first time, she and I spoke the same language.

Stella needed a language input stage, hearing and seeing words in use, like all children require, before she could reach the language output phase. Now that we made it here, I was hooked. I opened my laptop and typed the details of her communication events. I wanted to remember everything about this night, the first time my puppy said a word to me.

A couple of days after Stella said her first two words, I stood in the kitchen, scarfing down my toast with jam. I was running late for work after I had stayed outside with Stella for triple the amount of our usual time, encouraging her to go to the bathroom in the rain. I knew if she didn't go then, I would be cleaning up an accident in the house. While I threw my plate in the dishwasher, I could hear the familiar slurping of Stella taking a long drink of water.

Suddenly, the sound stopped. She looked at the magenta button to the right of her water bowl. She then glanced at me, then back at the button. I peered over to see the bowl was now empty. After a few more seconds of hanging on to the silence, I tiptoed over and crouched down next to the "water" button. Positioning myself in this way was a gentle cue, meant to remind her of what she could do. Subtle prompts are like giving hints. It's like when you are trying to remember the capital of Montana. You're thinking and thinking, then when someone says, "It stars with H," you immediately say, "Helena." You did not quite come up with it independently, you needed a little hint to remember.

Stella understood my hint. She lifted her paw, and swatted it down to say "water" for the first time when her bowl was empty. I filled up her dish and Stella drank some more. Stella had now officially used all three of her buttons. I left bursting with pride.

At work, I showed my coworkers the videos of little Stella using three different AAC buttons to say "outside," "play," and "water." Grace was elated about the news. She helped me find these buttons, accompanied me on nearly every lunchtime trip to let Stella out, watched Stella's progressions with me in person, and brainstormed with me several times.

I thought everyone else would be excited, or at least interested in the topic too. I envisioned these videos of my adorable puppy communicating so intently with AAC inspiring other therapists to implement communication devices more and to be proud of how powerful speech therapy is.

Aside from a smile or a "cute" or "aww," people were mostly confused or uninterested. One did ask how I got her to push the buttons, and another simply said "cool trick" before swiveling her chair back to her computer.

In retrospect, my coworkers' reactions should have made a lot of sense to me. Unfortunately, it is common for speech-language pathologists to have little to no experience with AAC. That was true for this clinic. Fortunately, I attended a graduate school with an excellent AAC course. Not all graduate programs have comprehensive classes on augmentative and alternative communication. In fact, it's more common for the latter, meaning that speech therapists are left to figure out unfamiliar technology on the job.

Grace and I had spent the last nine months desperately trying to spread our AAC knowledge and enthusiasm to our coworkers. Together, we navigated the complicated process of submitting requests for AAC devices to be funded by insurance. We invited representatives from device companies to come speak to our staff at the clinic. We came into work on our days off to write an entire guidebook and create resources that explained how to use AAC, step by step. We even conducted AAC evaluations for other therapists' clients, wrote up the lengthy reports, handled all the paperwork, all while still treating the children from our full-time caseloads. We were fueled simply by the hope of more kids learning to talk and more therapists becoming reinvigorated by how much of a difference they could make. A few supervisors applauded our work ethic, but unfortunately it seemed like no matter what we did, we could not inspire anyone else to support AAC.

I did not care if anyone else saw the potential I saw yet or understood how exciting this could be for the field of speech therapy. I knew in my heart and in my head that I was witnessing something fascinating with Stella. If anything, my coworkers' confusion showed me how far our field still needed to come. I hoped someday I could be part of a movement toward more understanding and acceptance of AAC for all who need it, even dogs.

TAKEAWAYS FOR TEACHING *YOUR* DOG

- **Expect a language input phase.** Your dog will need to hear words to learn words and will need to see her AAC in use to learn how to use it. Expect that this will take time.

- **Model words when your dog communicates.** When you see your dog gesturing, whining, or barking, model the word for what you think she is trying to communicate. Pairing a word to her communication is powerful.

- **Use naturalistic cues to draw attention to buttons.** If a long pause doesn't work, you can stand by the button, point at it, or tap it. Pause again after giving a cue. If your dog still doesn't explore the buttons, go ahead and model the word and carry on with your activity.

- **Model during natural contexts.** Model words when they are relevant to what is naturally happening.

- **Respond to communication.** If your dog says a word, respond appropriately! In the beginning, try to honor your dog's communication as much as you can. If your dog is not using words, continue responding to all her other forms of communication. Do not withhold food, water, playtime, trips outside, or anything from your dog. Just create a minute or two of opportunity for your dog to try using a word.

CHAPTER 7

Independence

———

For the next few weeks after Stella said her first words, I rode a continuous, natural high. Summer weather arrived in Omaha, Stella said at least one word every day with less and less cueing needed, and I received my letter from the American Speech and Hearing Association (ASHA) granting me my Certificate of Clinical Competence. After four years of undergrad, two years of graduate school, and a yearlong clinical fellowship, I was finally a fully licensed speech-language pathologist, able to practice without a supervisor observing my sessions and reviewing my documentation. I had dreamed of the day when I would be a full-blown clinician, a licensed health professional, and it had finally arrived. I was proud of the career I had chosen, proud of the work I was doing, and proud of where I could go next. I also felt free to work wherever I wanted, and free to provide my professional opinion without someone signing off on it first. There was nothing more to do to prove that I knew what I was doing. With adding just three letters next to my name, my entire mind-set shifted. I sent more emails to kids' school therapists sharing my observations and recommendations, signed up for an AAC continuing education course to attend next month with Grace, and started thinking about where I wanted to work next. I could stay at my current clinic, but the world and all its job possibilities appeared so vast to me.

Stella still frequently walked back and forth past a button, barked at it, or stared down at it. When I saw these gestures, I would sometimes say a verbal prompt, like "What do you want?" Then I stayed silent for at least fifteen seconds to give Stella a chance to respond. Research shows that when communication partners pause for ten to forty-five seconds, AAC users are more likely to respond using their devices.[18] Giving a longer wait time cues the learner that it is their turn to talk. It also gives them more time to process what is happening then choose what to do next.

I stayed still. Stella stood with her back toward me, looking ahead to her button and her dishes. I counted in my head to keep myself from intervening too quickly. "12, 13, 14, 15, 16 . . ."

"Water," Stella said. She licked her lips and wagged her tail immediately, excited for me to replenish her bowl.

This was the most powerful cue we could give Stella to use one of her words now, simply waiting long enough to give her a real chance to say it. It is so natural for adults to want to jump in and help immediately, or to take over to accomplish something quickly. We have to become comfortable with silence and patience before we can expect to see real, significant progress.

One morning, while I was upstairs brushing my teeth, my thoughts wandered about the workday that lay ahead of me. I was mentally picking out the toys I would grab off the shelves when I arrived at the clinic, when my planning came to a sudden halt.

"Outside," I heard from downstairs.

Jake had already left for the day. So hearing "outside" could only mean one thing. Stella said a word completely independently for the first time. I ran down the steps, toothbrush in mouth, to find Stella standing next to her button, staring at the back door.

"Go outside? Yes! Good girl, Stella."

Stella wagged her tail and jumped around in a circle. As soon as I opened the door, she bolted outside, chasing a squirrel sitting on top of our wooden fence.

This was the first time Stella had ever said a word totally by herself, without any cues or modeling right beforehand. It was a huge milestone to celebrate. Before this morning, she needed at least one or two small prompts. This is completely common and natural for all kids, whether they are learning to talk with a communication device or verbal speech. Children need support before they can do something new entirely on their own. It's like when babies are learning to walk. They need to hold on to furniture or their parents before they can take several steps freely.

It was helpful for both Stella and me that I could be upstairs and know exactly what she wanted right when she wanted it. If she had barked, and come up to find me, I would not have known why. If she were standing quietly by the door, I would not have been able to see her from upstairs or even know that she was wanting something. Stella could have her needs attended to much more quickly if she could tell us exactly what she wanted.

After saying her first independent word, Stella reached the groove of saying all three of her words by herself. She said "outside" nearly every time she needed to go to the bathroom or wanted to go out to play. Jake and I were thrilled that this meant way fewer accidents in the house. She said "water" whenever she noticed her bowl was empty.

I was most impressed with how Stella started using "play" on her own. She could play with her toys whenever she wanted. We kept her basket of toys on the ground, easily accessible to her at all times. But Stella started saying "play" during times when Jake and I were focused on other things besides her, like when we were eating dinner, or in the middle of a deep talk, or on our computers. If we failed to drop whatever we were doing when she approached us with a toy dangling from her mouth, she would go say "play" and trot back over to us. Some nights, Stella said "play" between ten and twenty times. Words were becoming one other way she could communicate her point. They were another tool in her expressive repertoire.

One evening in early June, Stella sat in front of the stove watching me cook dinner. I could feel her eyes tracking my every movement. Every few seconds she inched closer to me, making sure I was aware of her presence. Suddenly, a roaring sound came from the front yard. Stella dashed into the living room, leaped onto the couch, and peered out the window to see Jake mowing the front lawn. When he disappeared from her sight, Stella barked three times, then jumped down. She wedged her head between the shade and the window on our front door. As soon as Jake came back into sight, her tail wagged and she barked again. Stella ran back through the kitchen, said "outside," then bolted to the front door. She stood on the doormat and looked back to me, checking to see if I heard her request and followed.

Of course, I was going to drop everything in the kitchen to take her out to the front yard, even though I knew she hated the lawn mower. This was the first time Stella had generalized "outside" to a location other than the backyard. I could not have been happier. If Stella thought that all three of her buttons were the same and she just pressed whichever one was closest to her to grab my attention, she would have chosen to hit the "play" button literally two feet away from the front door. Or she could have picked the "water" button that was on the way to the kitchen. But she did not do either of those. She ran to the opposite end of the house, completely out of her way, to tell me "outside."

Stella charged through the front door. She alternated between barking at the lawn mower and retreating to my legs to protect me. When Jake shut off the horrifying sound-making machine, she wiggled her entire body in celebration. All Stella wanted was to go outside to see Jake (and possibly save his life from the lawn mower). She had no idea that she achieved a huge communication milestone, and I had glimpsed her potential.

When I write speech therapy goals for emerging communicators, I always include at least one goal for the child to use language for a variety of communication functions. Requesting is often the most heavily targeted communication function with young children, but we need to remember *why* we all actually talk in the first place. We communicate to request items and actions, reject or protest, comment on what is happening, share ideas and feelings, ask questions, answer questions, label objects, direct the actions of others, joke, tell stories, and so much more. When I had the initial idea to teach Stella how to say a few different words, I envisioned her using them to make different requests, to let us know what she wanted or needed. It did not even occur to me to think about supporting Stella's different communication functions until later in June, the day before we were leaving for our family vacation.

I watered my houseplants with Stella standing by my side. Ever since she was eight weeks old, Stella was fascinated by this weekly activity. She followed me from room to room, plant to plant, her eye gaze shifting back and forth from the spout of the watering can to the soil. This time, she left after I finished watering the first plant. About five seconds later, I heard, "water." I chuckled to myself. I bet seeing the water reminded her that she was thirsty. I started walking down the hall to see Stella walking back toward me.

"Do you need water, girl?"

As I saw moments later, her water dish was full, and she did not take a drink. Stella returned to the sunroom with me, continuing to watch me give the plants a good soak. She was talking about what was happening, not about something she wanted.

This was the first time Stella said a word without requesting an object or an action from one of us. She walked out of the sunroom, down the hall, and into the dining room all simply to tell me what she observed in the world around her. It certainly was not easy or convenient for her to share her thoughts, but she did so anyway. I texted Grace immediately relaying the story to her. What other communication functions could Stella use? What else was she noticing in her world that she did not have words for?

The next day, Jake, Stella, and I road-tripped to a lake house in Wisconsin for my family's annual summer vacation. My parents rented the same house each year for the now eight adults, two dogs, and one baby in our family. The front door faced the narrow dirt road surrounded by miles of deep woods on both sides of it. The back door opened to a large, grassy yard with stone steps leading to the sandy shore of Lake Michigan. The space was the most serene bubble away from reality. We spent most of our days relaxing, reading, chatting, and enjoying nature. At night, we would play board games then roast marshmallows in a bonfire pit under the stars. There was little to no cell service, and no internet or cable. This week was always a chance for all of us to take a time-out from our busy lives, reconnect with each other, and let our minds recharge and wander.

This year, I had even more to look forward to. Jake would be on this trip with me for the first time, and we would introduce Stella to her first beach. I could not wait to see how she would react to the sand, water, and waves. Plus, I was eager to see how Stella would communicate in a new place. I wondered if being in an unfamiliar house with different people would impact how she used her words. In speech therapy, it can take a while for a child to transfer what he learns in the treatment room to other environments. I set Stella's buttons up right away when we arrived and modeled each of them a couple of times for her. The "outside" button went next to the back door. "Water" went by her dishes in the hall across from the back door, and "play" sat in the living room near her toys. But, after placing them down initially, I did not pay too much attention to using her buttons. I was preoccupied with catching up with everyone, playing with my five-month-old niece, and enjoying the beach.

Jake and I took Stella out for a walk along the shore. The

water level was higher than I had ever seen it. The lake practically swallowed the shoreline, leaving just enough room for two people to walk on the sand.

"Let's let Stella off her leash," Jake said.

I was extremely hesitant to try this. I had no idea how Stella would react. My family used to let Wrigley off-leash here, but she was much older. I could think of a thousand reasons to say no. There were woods in the distance, we had not practiced this even in a normal park, we didn't have any treats with us to lure her back if she sprinted away, there was no cell service to call for help if we lost her, and she was still so young. But somehow, Jake convinced me that he could run faster than Stella if she sprinted away, and that the two of us would keep her safe. Jake unhooked her leash. I took a deep breath in and crossed my fingers. Stella was officially free for the first time out of our backyard.

Much to my surprise, Stella continued trotting along right in front of us. "Good girl, Stella. Good girl." Stella looked back to Jake and me. She smiled and panted, then bolted ahead. She was at least thirty feet in front of us with no signs of slowing down.

"Stella, wait," I shouted. I shot Jake a look, cueing him to go ahead and start running to catch her.

But Jake did not need to sprint ahead. Stella stopped dead in her tracks. She turned her head back to us and continued smiling.

"Good waiting, Stella. Yes, good girl," I shouted. Stella stood still until we caught up to her. She wagged her tail and jumped up to greet us, as if we had been gone for hours.

I was shocked. Stella was a high-energy puppy, on the beach and off-leash for the first time in her life. She cared enough about us to stop exploring her wide-open surroundings, turn around, and wait for us to catch up to her. Stella continued trotting by our side for another few seconds, then ran ahead again. As soon as I called out for her to wait, she did not take a single step farther until we reached her. This became our pattern for the rest of the walk back to the house.

I wondered if she was listening to us so well because we listen to her so much. It's the same way with kids. The more I pay attention to and really listen to their communication, the more they'll notice and listen to mine. Jake, Stella, and I were building a strong relationship together, based on presuming competence, listening to one another, and trying new things. Every time we acknowledged one of Stella's gestures, vocalizations, barks, or words, we were modeling how to react to another's communication. Now, Stella stopped and listened when we talked too.

If it were not for Jake's push, I never would have given Stella the chance to show us how well she could do. We had truly only practiced the word *wait* a few times at home. We would tell Stella to sit, then say "wait" repeatedly while we slowly backed up. We had only made it across the living room before Stella came running over to us looking for a treat I clenched in my hand. This situation on the beach was different. It actually mattered to Stella and made sense why she should wait. We were in a new environment and she was actually pretty far away from us. This was even more proof to me that both dogs and children learn and perform best when it is meaningful to them. There was not a good reason to have Stella sit in the middle of the living room until we disappeared out of sight and called for her again. She knew we were all still in our home, and she was just waiting for a treat.

A couple of days into our vacation, Stella became comfortable with her new surroundings and all the people who could give her lots of playtime and belly rubs. She was truly a ham, soaking up all the attention. My family all gathered to eat lunch around the dining room table. Stella wandered around the first floor, continuously coming in and out of the kitchen. In the middle of our meal we heard "outside" come from the back-door area. Everyone quieted down and looked around the table, taking a quick mental head count. We were all there together. That meant the only one who could have said "outside" was Stella. Sitting closest to the door, my dad laughed when he leaned back in his chair to see little Stella standing patiently by the door, waiting to go outside.

"I'll take her," he said, laughing. "Yes, that's a good girl, let's go outside." His voice trailed as he walked out the door.

Throughout the rest of the week, Stella continued to say "outside," "water," and "play," without missing a beat. Until this trip, I had no idea if Stella would use her buttons in other locations, or if her learning was specific only to our home. The fact that Stella used her words here in the same ways as she would at home encouraged me. It was one more indicator that Stella was demonstrating true, independent communication.

"If you could live anywhere in the country, where would you go?" I asked my sisters, my mom, and Jake. We all sat on a deck overlooking the lake.

Jake and I had begun exploring thoughts about moving. We loved Omaha but felt that it was time to go. We were ready for new jobs, neither one of our families were in Omaha, and several of our close friends had moved away. Most importantly, we had an unfulfilled sense of adventure that kept creeping up to the forefront of our minds whenever we allowed it to.

Something hit me after becoming a fully licensed speech therapist. I had arrived to the stage of my career where there were no more built-in stopping points like there were in school. I had to make my own stopping points if I wanted anything to change. For college, graduate school, and my clinical fellowship, I picked where to go based on the school or job. This time, I wanted to pick where I wanted to live, then find the perfect job. If not now, then when?

"Wherever we go next, I want there to be a body of water," Jake said.

"Maybe we'll move to Milwaukee. The lakefront is beautiful there," I said. Stella sat in the sand, looking out to the waves, her nose sniffing the air around her. "Do you want to be a beach dog, Stella? I bet you'd like that."

Moving somewhere new wasn't the only big thing on my mind. Stella's communication skills were already surpassing where I initially thought they could go. At four months old, Stella was using three words independently, in multiple environments, with several different people. This was incredibly impressive to me. I could not believe how fast she learned. During the process, it seemed like it took so long, but now, looking back, we only had Stella for two months and she was already saying three different words. We could hear her desires from anywhere in the house, and she rarely went to the bathroom inside now. She did not have to wait for me to guess if she wanted to go out. But to me, *how* Stella learned to use these words was so much more impressive than what she was saying at this point.

When I set out to teach Stella words, I asked the question, *What happens when I implement speech therapy language interventions with my puppy?* I did not ask, *How can I get her to push these buttons that say words?* I am sure there are lots of ways someone could train a dog to push three buttons when they want the dog to. But I taught Stella in all the same ways that I teach children. I didn't train her to push a button on my command. I didn't reward her with treats for saying a word. I didn't use my hand to grab her paw and make her say a word. I didn't train the behavior of pushing the button first before I attached meaning to it. Those approaches would not have been in alignment with best practices for teaching children words.

Stella's ability to learn quickly and with such ease shed light on a power of speech therapy that I imagined reached far beyond where others knew it could go. Now the parallels I saw between Stella's and toddlers' prelinguistic skills were continuing into the linguistic phase. Focusing on *how* we arrived here meant that there was so much more potential left to explore. If the communication similarities between puppies and toddlers continued to this point, what other words and concepts could Stella learn? I couldn't stop here. We were just getting started.

I came back to Omaha knowing two things: (1) I was ready to leave and start a new life somewhere else; and (2) Stella needed more words.

TAKEAWAYS FOR TEACHING *YOUR* DOG

- **Provide a long pause.** When you see your dog noticing your modeling or noticing the buttons, turn your routine interactions into language-facilitating opportunities. The greatest cue we can provide is a long, silent pause to give the AAC user a chance to process what is happening and try exploring her words. When you see your dog communicate through a gesture or vocalization, stay quiet for at least ten to fifteen seconds. At the end of fifteen seconds, if your dog looks like she might be walking toward her buttons or is looking at them, continue staying quiet. If you have not seen an indication that she might try saying a word, add a naturalistic cue.

- **Your dog may need cues for a little while before using words independently.** Keep providing a long pause, pointing at the button, asking a general question such as "What do you want?" or standing near the button to support your dog's emerging vocabulary. Even after you've heard your dog's first words, your dog will likely need support before using words independently and regularly.

- **Model words in different contexts to support generalization.** Your dog will learn to use words in different ways if she sees and hears you using words in multiple ways.

- **Remember that your dog is intrinsically motivated to communicate.** Resist the desire to offer a treat for saying a word (unless the word is *treat*). This will keep your dog from learning the actual meaning of the word. Stick to providing the appropriate response to your dog's word.

- **Think about other communication functions besides requesting.** Your dog might be trying to label an object or activity in her environment or talk about what is happening.

CHAPTER 8

Project Disconnect

———

I returned to Omaha feeling refreshed, reinspired, and ready to make some big life changes. I wanted to choose a new city to live in based on what Jake and I wanted out of life, not based on a job. Jake and I could both find work in whichever city we chose. I craved adventure, balance, and free time. I wanted to let my mind explore, wander, and create like I had on vacation instead of constantly consuming television or social media. I looked down at my phone screen to see pages of apps with red notifications shouting at me. I caught myself mindlessly scrolling whenever I had downtime. I automatically turned Netflix on after dinner nearly every night. This is not what I wanted to become. I wanted to be deliberate about how I spent my time. These habits had not bothered me before. I didn't even realize

I had them. Now, after unplugging for a week, I questioned if I even wanted to allow them back in my life at all.

"What about San Diego?" I said. I stared down at the list of criteria Jake and I made for wherever we would move next. We spent this stormy Sunday inside, dreaming about our future together. *How did we want to live? Where did we want to go? What would our ideal place to live look like?* were the most important questions on our minds. "There are tons of outdoor activities, lots of road-trip destinations around it, it's seriously amazing," I said.

San Diego is my definition of paradise. I visited with friends a year before and loved it. It was the first time during a trip that I decided I wanted to stay longer than I had originally planned. San Diego had everything I could want—a fun city, mountains, and beaches, and the weather pretty much stayed in the 60s and 70s all year long. It was nearly always pleasant outside. I imagined taking Stella for walks on the beach after work, going for hikes on the weekend, and taking road trips to explore other parts of California.

"I think it's definitely in the top three," Jake said. We agreed to see what job options existed and go from there.

Three days later I had a video interview with the owner of a speech therapy company in San Diego. This job would be very different from my current position. I would be an early intervention speech therapist, working only with one- and two-year-olds with speech and language delays. I would provide services in each child's home instead of in a clinic like I was in now. It stimulated my sense of curiosity and adventure within my profession, gave me the power to create my own schedule, and I could take more days off than I could now. I had a great feeling about it as soon as I saw the job listing.

"She offered me the job," I said after closing my laptop.

"You're kidding me, right?" Jake was shocked by how quickly I move when I am set on an idea.

"There's no pressure to decide now. She knows it wouldn't be for a couple of months. But if we did move to San Diego, I would totally work for her."

I hoped if we changed jobs and moved, I would have more time to dedicate to teaching Stella. Since coming back from vacation thoughts about her progress and potential kept bouncing around in my head. Before Chaser, the border collie who learned the names of more than a thousand toys, research showed that the average dog understood 165 words.[19] Chaser taught us that dogs may have much greater lexicons than we thought possible. In humans, our receptive language and expressive language skills are typically pretty close to equal. We all usually understand more words than we use, but the two abilities should be in the ballpark of each other. I wondered, *So if dogs could understand hundreds or even upward of a thousand words, does that mean they could potentially say that many words too?*

Stella was learning so quickly, but I could barely contribute any time or mental energy to support her now. By the time I came home from work every night, it was already 8:00. I was exhausted, hungry, and eager to relax. She was receiving the fried version of myself teaching her. What could she achieve if I could really spend a lot of time working with her? What could she say if I could practice new words with her consistently every day? I felt like this was the prime time for her learning, yet I could not fully take advantage of it in my current circumstances. I hoped I wasn't losing my window of opportunity for her to learn new concepts. I resolved to keep teaching and keep learning as best I could. I ordered two more boxes of buttons and eagerly anticipated introducing more words.

The next morning, I sat in the sunroom enjoying a quiet few minutes of reading before I headed upstairs to shower. I could hear Stella's collar jingling and toy squeaking in the living room. She must have been running around playing. Stella's ability to entertain herself independently was increasing as she became a bit older.

The noises stopped. The quiet was always much more concerning than hearing what Stella was doing. She could be getting into anything or going to the bathroom in the house. I closed my book, about to go check on her. A few seconds later, Stella charged into the sunroom. She stopped in the doorway and barked at me.

"What do you want, girl?"

Stella's nostrils flared. She sighed and barked at me again, then ran back into the living room. I followed to see where she was taking me. Stella stood in the middle of the room looking all around, then back to me.

"Play? Stella want play?" I said "play" with Stella's button and tossed a toy across the room for her.

Stella looked unamused. She stayed standing in the center of the room. "No play? Okay, girl."

I returned to my book in the sunroom. I had only made it through about two sentences when I heard a scratching noise coming from the living room. I ran out to see Stella pawing the floor underneath the couch.

"What's under there, Stella? You need help?" I lay on the

ground and reached as far as I could under the couch. Stella shoved her nose right next to my arm. Neither of us found anything. I walked around to the back of the couch and crouched down. I shined my phone's flashlight into the narrow space between the couch and the wall. The corner of Stella's plush pizza toy was sticking out from under the back of the couch. "How did you even get this back here, Stella?" As soon as I pulled it out, Stella grabbed it from my hand and jumped on the couch to happily resume chewing it.

Stella needed my help when her toy slid behind the couch. Since I did not see what Stella was playing with or what happened, I had no idea what I was looking for. It would be so much easier for all three of us if Stella could say "help" when something like this happened. When the two additional boxes of Recordable Answer Buzzers that I ordered arrived, I thought about what Stella communicates to us with her gestures and vocalizations, which words we say to her frequently during routine activities, words that would allow her to communicate for functions other than requesting, and words that could be used across multiple contexts.

Word choice is a big deal in the world of AAC. The words we program or keep available for children are the only words they will be able to say. There are two categories of words: *core* words and *fringe* words. Core words are the most frequently used words in communication. Studies in which researchers analyze language samples from different populations and contexts have shown that there are approximately three hundred to four hundred words that make up about 80 percent of everything we say.[20] Core words are typically verbs, adjectives, pronouns, adverbs, and prepositions. The most effective AAC systems are set up to teach core vocabulary first "because it allows communicators to express a wide variety of concepts with a very small number of words. Since core words make up the majority of spoken language, focusing on core vocabulary allows many opportunities throughout the day to hear the same words being used in a natural environment."[21] Using core words sets the learner up for their best communication success.

I chose to add six buttons with core words and a phrase for Stella: *come, no, love you, help, bye, eat*. We told Stella to "come" all the time. I wanted her to be able to tell us "come" as well if we were in a different room. We said "no" to Stella if she was chewing on a belonging of ours, or doing something we did not want her to do. Stella deserved the opportunity to tell us when we were doing something she does not like too. Communication is a two-way street. Stella's comfort and happiness mattered to me. Jake and I always said "love you" when we cuddled with Stella, rubbed her belly, or kissed her head. I wanted to give Stella the chance to express her affection to us, or to others, as well. "Help" could be beneficial for Stella when she needed us to help her retrieve a stuck toy or even if something more serious happened. Every time we left for work, we told Stella "bye" multiple times. Our leaving on weekdays was a routine for her now. I wanted to give her a way to talk about that part of the day. And Stella already understood the word *eat*. Before feeding her breakfast and dinner, we always said, "eat." Stella licked her lips and ran to her bowl. Hopefully Stella could tell us when she wanted to eat breakfast and dinner instead of us completely creating the routines for her. Maybe she was hungrier earlier in the day, or maybe she was not quite ready to eat when we put food in her dish. We could not know these answers until Stella had a way to tell us herself.

The remaining 20 percent of vocabulary we use, the fringe

words, are more specific. They are typically nouns that can only be used to mean one thing. Everyone needs both core and fringe words to communicate effectively. I always recommend that a solid vocabulary consisting of mostly core words and a few fringe words be established first so the AAC user can communicate throughout all of his day. More fringe words can be added later to help learners be more specific in their communication. *Play* is an example of a core word. It can be used to talk about all toys and games, whereas *ball* and *toy* are fringe words. *Eat* is a core word. It can be used to talk about all foods and mealtimes, whereas *breakfast*, *dinner*, and *peanut butter* are specific fringe words. Stella hears "eat" many more times in any given day than she hears "dinner."

I included one important fringe word to Stella's available vocabulary: *walk*. We took Stella on walks almost every night after dinner. It was a highly motivating activity for Stella and a significant part of her day. Like most dogs, Stella became so excited every time we asked if she wanted to go for a walk. She would bark, jump around in circles, and stalk me until I followed through by putting my shoes on, grabbing her leash, or finding my headphones. She used every type of communication possible to tell me that she wanted to go for a walk. I wanted Stella to be able to request walks instead of having to wait for us to say one of her favorite words.

For now, I did not want to become caught up in the number of words Stella could say. I knew that with a good selection of vocabulary, she could likely communicate about most parts of her day by using core words. There was no way we were going to place hundreds or a thousand buttons on the ground to experiment with every word she might know. Kids have access to thousands of words on their devices and use the same few hundred most commonly. The best AAC systems are arranged so that core words are on the front page, and fringe words are on the second and third pages. This way, kids can have easiest access to the words they need to say most often.

I wondered if Stella would try pressing her new buttons right away, or if it would take a while for her to notice them. Was the monthlong modeling time frame normal, or was it longer because they were her first words? Would Stella use her old words less and be affected by the novelty of her new vocabulary? I had so many questions that I was eager to start exploring.

I programmed six buttons for her new words and found spots for each button. I set "eat" down next to her food dish, and "bye" next to the front door. I lined up "come," "no," "love you," and "help" on the floor in the living room next to our entertainment center.

"Stella, come," I said verbally and pushed her new "come" button.

Stella trotted over to me.

"Look, girl." I pointed to each of the four buttons. "Now you can say, 'come,' 'no,' 'love you,' and 'help,'" I said while pushing one button at a time. Stella stood next to me. She switched between licking my face and looking down at the buzzers.

After figuring out the best placement for her new buttons, I would always keep them in the same spot. Stella would learn fastest if she didn't have to search for the word she needs every time she wants to say something.

The most effective AAC systems are set up by the principles of motor learning and motor memory.[22] Words and phrases should always stay in the same location on the device, so the locations become automatic to the user. It's similar to how we learn to type on a QWERTY keyboard. If the keys were rearranged on every different keyboard, we would have to search for each and every letter. But since the keys have always stayed in the same location, our fingers automatically know where to go as we type. We do not have to think about where a letter is located at the same time as typing. Having to search for words or letters takes up mental energy that could be spent on communicating.

I saved the best word for last. It took me several tries of shouting "walk" into the blue buzzer to make the final /k/ sound audible. Stella came running over to me when she heard me saying one of her favorite words so many times in a row. When I finally recorded it just right, I placed the "walk" button under the hooks next to the front door where Stella's leash hung.

"Look, Stella, walk!" I pushed her button a couple of times in a row. Stella stood hovering over the buzzer. She cocked her head to the left and to the right. She wagged her tail and looked back up to me.

"Are you excited, girl?" I crouched down to Stella's level. She licked me repeatedly and turned around to face her new button again. Stella lifted her right paw, swatted down, and said, "walk," only one minute after I programmed it for her.

"Go for a walk? Okay, let's go."

Stella barked and smiled at me while she watched me put my shoes on and grab my headphones. "Walk," I said one more time verbally and with her button. "Let's go."

It was fascinating to see such a clear difference in her reactions between all her other vocabulary words and "walk." Stella did not push any of the other words right away, not even "eat." She stood near me while I modeled them, but they did not capture her attention like "walk" had. Seeing her so excited to push it made me wonder if she had ever wished for the ability to say "walk" before I programmed it for her.

The next day, Jake and I sat down at the dinner table, exhausted from our days at work. I brushed the piles of mail, papers, and clutter down to a chair to make room for our plates. Stella was lying down in the living room chomping on a chew toy. I was ready to relax with a nice, calm dinner and a glass of wine. We made it through about two minutes of our meal when we heard, "Walk walk walk walk." Stella poked her head around the corner, checking to see our reaction to her request.

"No walk now, Stella. We're eating." I laughed.

Stella maintained eye contact with me, then barked.

"I hear you, Stella. We'll go for a walk later!"

Stella disappeared from our view. A few seconds later we heard, "walk, walk," followed by a bark.

"It's her second day being able to say 'walk.' She's so excited! Should we take her now and finish eating when we get back?" I asked.

Jake chuckled. "Of course she had to choose now to say a new word a bunch of times. Let's go . . ."

After three days of having seven new words, Stella started saying "walk" all throughout the day without any cueing from us at all. I knew she liked walks, but I had no idea how often she wanted to take them. I noticed that Stella started saying "outside" less often after we introduced "walk." She still said "outside" when she needed to go to the bathroom, but this change in frequency made me wonder if some of the times Stella had been saying "outside," she was wanting to go for a walk. Until now, she could not have specified that with a word.

Stella had not used any of her other new words yet. The closest she had come to exploring them was when her toy bounced and landed in between the buttons by our entertainment center. She pawed at her toy, but accidentally pushed "love you" in the process. Stella cocked her head. She looked surprised to hear "love you."

"Aw, love you, Stella!" I kissed her forehead and scratched behind her ears. Stella licked my face. She pawed the button instead of her toy by accident, but it is important to always respond as if it were intentional. That would help her learn what each word means. If I had ignored Stella accidentally saying "love you," she would have learned, "I pushed this button that said, 'love you,' but nothing happened." That would likely decrease her chance of pushing it intentionally in the future. Instead she learned, "After I pushed this button that said, 'love you,' I received scratches and attention."

Accidental hits, mis-hits, and pure exploration are all fantastic opportunities for AAC users to learn their vocabulary.[23] The more Stella sees us respond appropriately after she says a word, the faster Stella will learn what that word means. At work, anytime a child said a word with his device, even if I knew he was looking to say something else or bumped it by mistake, I always responded to the word he said. Mis-hits are valuable. They provide great opportunities for the learner to hear what they said, observe how their communication partner responded, and decide if that is what they actually wanted or not. If it was not what he intended, the AAC user can try a different word. He would then be exposed to the responses of multiple words instead of only one.

Jake and I had officially decided to move to San Diego. I accepted the early intervention position, and Jake was deciding between a couple of different job offers. We handed in our thirty-day notices at work and started looking for apartments in California. Since we had so much to do to prepare for our move across the country, I figured now was as good of a time as any to prune out the habits that I felt were holding me back.

By the end of July, about a month after we returned from vacation, I still fantasized about unplugging from the overly connected world. I had slipped back into my routines of mindlessly scrolling through social media, unintentionally taking up all the idle moments of my day. Ever since high school I had logged on to at least one social media platform nearly every day. It was so ingrained in our culture, so habitual. I never asked myself if I wanted to, I just did. But I rarely felt great after spending time online. It felt like I was filling my brain with the thoughts, ideas, and photos of people I barely spoke to anymore. This could not be healthy. It certainly was not benefiting me in any way that I could see. I kept wondering what it would feel like to not be a part of that anymore. Would I feel like I was missing out? How would I learn about my friends' big life events? How would I share photos with friends and family members if I wanted to?

One night after work, Jake came downstairs to find me trying to lift the fifty-inch TV off the wooden entertainment center that he built.

"Whoa, what are you doing?" he asked.

"I unplugged the TV! And I deleted all social media apps from my phone, too. I'm done wasting time. I'm calling it 'Project Disconnect.' Let's try putting the TV in the basement. Can you help me carry it?"

"Don't you think that's a little extreme? We can just choose not to watch TV," he said. We both loved to watch shows at night.

Jake and I compromised. We placed the TV behind the console. It was out of sight for me, and still easily accessible if we changed our minds.

Deleting so many apps from my phone brought a couple of significant realizations. Now, all the icons were in a different order. I had to visually scan the screen to find what I was looking for. Even though there were many fewer apps and I only had one page of icons instead of three to look through, it took me longer to find each one. Research shows that motor plans are stronger than recognizing a visual cue for an icon.[24] Before now, I never had to think about where my frequently used apps were. My finger just went there automatically. Experiencing this struggle after changing my setup reminded me how important it was to keep words in the same location for AAC users.

Most importantly, after a couple of days without using social media or watching TV, I already felt a huge difference. I had more energy at the end of the day, I realized how much more time I had when I did not take up every spare moment, and I was so excited. Since my brain was not filled with other people's thoughts, I could really listen to my own.

TAKEAWAYS FOR TEACHING *YOUR* DOG

- **When deciding which words to teach, ask yourself these questions.** *What does my dog communicate with her gestures and vocalizations? Which words do I say to her frequently during routine activities? Which words would allow her to communicate for functions other than requesting? Which words could be used across multiple contexts?*

- **Establish a vocabulary with more core words than fringe words.** For the most communication potential, and more complex use later on, teach high-frequency words.

- **Keep your dog's buttons in the same spot.** We all learn how to talk through the principles of motor learning. Verbal speech users learn the motor plan to say each sound and word, sign language users develop a motor plan for each hand movement, and AAC users for each word location. Continuously moving words around will be confusing for your dog. After you find a spot that works well, stick with it.

- **Spend time modeling new vocabulary.** Whenever you add more words, make sure to model them in their appropriate contexts.

- **Respond to accidental hits, mis-hits, and your dog exploring the buttons.** Even if you think you are absolutely positive that your dog pushed a button accidentally or meant to push a different one, respond to the word she said. These are valuable teaching moments. Plus, your dog might surprise you with what she says and when. To help your dog become a deliberate communicator, always respond as though the message was intentional.

- **Give your dog more words than you think she knows.** This allows for language growth and exploration.

CHAPTER 9

Bye, Omaha

———

Most people assume dogs would say "eat" all day long if they could talk. But this has never been the case with Stella.

Even though I knew Stella had much more to say than requesting to eat, I was still surprised when *eat* was not one of the first of the newly programmed words that she started using. I thought *eat* would provide the easiest and strongest correlation between a word and an outcome for her to make. That is one of the main reasons why I purposefully did not select *eat* as one of Stella's first few words. I thought that the food connection would be too powerful, that it would overtake her ability to learn that she could talk for reasons other than wanting food or treats. Or I thought that Stella would think all her buttons were simply a mechanism to gain more food from us. But I could not have been more wrong. I underestimated Stella's motivations and desire to connect with us about many other activities and parts of her environment, not just food.

When Stella did not say "eat" immediately, I started questioning why I thought that would even be true in the first place. Stella certainly enjoyed eating, but she never sat by her bowl, pawing at her dish all day long. If nonverbally she was not communicating this desire constantly, why would I expect her to suddenly switch to only talking about food now that she could use a word to say "eat"? Stella was interested in and driven by much more than food. She loved being outside, going for walks, playing with us, and receiving positive praise. She watched us closely throughout many events of the day, not only mealtimes. And, like all dogs, Stella communicated nonverbally and with vocalizations about much more than wanting to eat.

Stella picked up on "bye" second fastest after "walk." Jake and I said "bye" to Stella every time either one of us left, so she heard that word quite a bit. I wanted to give Stella the chance to tell us "bye" when we were leaving, to acknowledge the familiar event that was about to happen. Kids learn words best when they are incorporated into their typical activities. Routines are predictable, frequently occurring, and functional.[25] Since Stella also thrived with incorporating structure into her daily life, I figured the same might be true for her as well. I also wanted to introduce "bye" because it represented a new category of vocabulary for her: social words. *Hi, bye, uh-oh, please, thank you* are all examples of toddlers' early developing social words. Along with nouns and verbs, social words make up a significant part of toddlers' utterances.

Late one Saturday night, we were in the middle of a stereotypical midwestern good-bye with a few friends who had been hanging out at our house. The midwestern good-bye involves at least a twenty- or thirty-minute-long process of announcing that you are leaving, making the rounds one more time, starting whole new conversations, then talking for another ten minutes by the front door. We all congregated there, had already hugged good-bye, yet continued our conversations. Stella had stayed up way past her typical bedtime playing with us and enjoying all the attention. She hopped off the couch and walked right through the middle of our circle. She looked up at all of us, then swatted her paw to say, "bye." She looked back up at our friends.

Everyone looked at us in shock and looked back down to Stella. "You want us to leave, Stella? Bye, girl!" one friend said. "I can't believe your dog told us 'bye.' This is wild, you guys," another friend said, laughing.

They left and Stella sat looking through the glass door as they walked to their cars. Then she hopped back on the couch, curled up in a ball, and fell asleep. I am not sure if Stella wanted them to leave so she could go to bed, or if she was commenting on what she knew was about to happen. But either way, it was so exciting to see Stella start to use another one of her words and share thoughts about what was going on.

Stella loved standing on the back of the couch and looking out the living room picture windows. Perched on her post, she could see all that was happening in the world in front of her house. She whined when she saw squirrels running up the tree, barked at strangers walking along the sidewalk, and jumped around in circles if she saw one of our cars pull up to the driveway. While I was in the kitchen, I heard the sound of the blinds clanking against the window. I hurried into the living room to see Stella pawing repeatedly at the closed shades. She was gesturing that she wanted the blinds pulled up so she could look out the window.

I joined Stella on the couch and tapped the blinds with my hand. I said "help," then walked over a couple of feet to also say "help" with Stella's button. When I pulled the shades up, I said "help" a few more times and watched Stella's gaze following the blinds sliding up the window. By imitating her gestures, I was showing that I understood what she wanted. Then I added a word to go along with her gestures.

In speech therapy sessions with AAC users, I recognize and accept all forms of their communication, not only to words spoken with the device. The more communication we recognize and respond to, the more the learner communicates overall. If the child points to something she wants, I also point to it, then model the word she could say. I am showing her that I see and understand what she is communicating, then say "want" or "get" or "help" to teach her a word she could use in that situation.

We do this naturally with babies all the time. When a baby waves to you, you likely instinctively wave back and say, "Bye" or "Hi." Or when a baby claps, you probably clap your own hands and say, "Yay!" Without even realizing it, you recognized the baby's gesture, associated a meaning to it, reinforced the gesture by doing it yourself, and modeled the word that goes along with that gesture. This is the heart of teaching language: making a conscious effort to recognize all forms of communication, responding to them, and modeling the next level.

Since *help* is a versatile core word, I modeled it throughout several different contexts—pulling the blinds up, finding a toy for Stella, putting her harness on, moving her dishes to find the one morsel of food that fell behind her bowl. Modeling words in varying ways helps the learner understand that each word can be used to talk about more than one or two different situations.

Stella started using her sixth word, *help*, multiple times a day when she would drop her toy behind the couch or when it rolled under the TV stand. Initially, she said "help" on its own, without pairing gestures with it. Even though we knew she needed help, if Jake or I had not been watching, we would not know where her toy disappeared. Stella would watch us look around, under the couch or under the entertainment center. Then, her tail started wagging and she came to stand right next to us when we were close to it. Soon, Stella started independently combining "help" with a gesture, normally standing where she wanted us to look. She learned that we needed more information to most effectively find her toy.

As Jake and I started seriously preparing for our fifteen-hundred-plus-mile move from Nebraska to California, it was clear right away that we would need to significantly downsize our belongings before we could leave. There was absolutely no way we could take all the furniture and belongings from a four-bedroom, two-story house to a small one-bedroom apartment in California. We considered all the possible moving strategies: driving a U-Haul with one of our cars attached to the back all the way through the mountains and national parks we hoped to visit on the way, shipping boxes of our possessions, or loading up a giant twenty-foot-long POD that someone else would drive out to San Diego. After days of weighing the options, neither Jake nor I felt like we landed on a solution that we loved. All the options were expensive and required a decent amount of planning. We had no idea what would fit in the small apartment waiting for us.

"What if you guys just packed up and drove out in your two cars and bought new furniture when you get there?" Grace asked.

This suggestion came at the perfect time. Jake and I had recently watched a documentary, *Minimalism*, which discussed the benefits of living with fewer material objects. Minimalism is the intentional promotion of the things that we most value and removing the things, mainly material objects, that distract from that.[26] The founders of the minimalism movement preached how letting go of nonessential items could make space for more creativity, inner peace, and purpose.

Learning about this concept opened our eyes to the amount of possessions requiring our continual attention and maintenance. Before now, it had really never occurred to me to purge all the nonessential possessions I carried with me through different stages of life and to stop automatically accumulating more. This could be an incredible opportunity for us to start fresh and let go of whatever did not serve us anymore. Jake and I could pick out furniture and décor that specifically fit in our new space.

Initially, Jake resisted. "Why would we get rid of things that we will just have to buy again?" he asked. But he hopped on board after he calculated how much everything we considered bringing was even worth. It would cost more to move it. "Let's go for it. We can sell our stuff here and use the money to furnish our new apartment," he said.

Now the idea spoke both our languages. It was a new personal growth challenge for me, and a practical, financially sound decision for Jake. Over the course of the next month, all our spare time was spent confronting the belongings we had accumulated and carried with us unintentionally for years. I fed my mind with podcasts, blog posts, and books about living with less and the process of letting go. As everyone recommended, we started with the easy things to part with—college text-books, old DVD cases, clothes we never wore, old roommates' kitchen utensils. Clutter I did not even know we had crept out of the darkness, into the light of day for us to deal with. Then, we reassessed items of any sentimental value—knickknacks we collected throughout our travels, favorite T-shirts from high school, several-year-old gifts from friends or family that we no longer had a purpose for. Every time I resisted letting go, I reminded myself that if I continued on this way, I would never have room for anything new to come into my life or to appreci-ate my favorite belongings.

We took eight carloads of bins and bags filled with random household objects, furniture, and clothes to Goodwill. We sold our TV, four couches, chairs, tables, appliances, and decorations on Facebook Marketplace and Craigslist. Every evening after work, three or four strangers would show up to our front door to look at an item we were selling. Slowly as we stripped away everything, I started feeling relief. I could see more blank wall space, fit all my clothes in my closet, take a water bottle off the shelf without knocking over a mountain of Tupperware in the process, and could actually appreciate the beautiful hardwood floors and structure of the house. With every trip we made to Goodwill, our minds and our house felt lighter. I never had to worry about finding storage space for these random items any longer. I was freeing myself. My emotions swung from shock at how much I owned to the relief of letting it all go.

Stella did not adjust well to the purging. Her environment was being turned upside down right in front of her. With each piece of furniture that we walked out the door, Stella stood in the middle of the room, stunned. When Jake and a few friends carried out the couch, I stayed inside with Stella to make sure she didn't slip out. Stella walked into the bare sunroom and whined right where the couch used to be. Stella left the room, turned the corner, and said, "no." She looked up to me with the saddest eyes before she curled up in a ball on top of an empty grocery bag lying on the ground. This was the first time Stella had ever said "no." She was either commenting on how there was "no" couch there anymore, upset that the couch she grew up snuggling on was suddenly gone, or protesting what we did. Maybe Stella had more awareness and attachment to the items in our home than I had realized.

Jake and I were constantly buzzing around the house, packing up items we were taking with us, and cleaning out emptied shelves and cabinets. We barely had enough time to stop and rest.

One afternoon, I was upstairs listening to music and emptying out the linen closet. Stella was with me for a bit, but she had left a few minutes ago to go downstairs. I turned my music down to keep an ear out for what she might be doing.

"Come, come," I heard.

I went downstairs to see Stella standing in the middle of the living room. As soon as she saw me, she dove on her toy and ran away. She called me down to come play with her.

Later on, Jake and I were in the basement sorting through boxes.

"Come," we heard again. A few seconds later, Stella's head appeared at the top of the staircase.

"You want us to come up?" I said.

Stella wagged her tail while she watched us walk up the stairs. She immediately rolled over, gesturing for a belly rub.

"Is this why you wanted us to come up here, Stella?" Jake laughed.

I liked that Stella had a way to tell us she wanted us nearby, especially now that Jake and I were not hanging out in the same spots for long periods of time. Most of the time, Stella would follow us around, play close to us, or watch whatever we were doing. But sometimes, she wanted us to come to her. I always modeled "come" naturally whenever I called Stella over to us. By saying "come," and using her button for it, Stella learned how and when she could say it to call us over, too. I found it impressive and interesting that when we were in sight of Stella or were already paying attention to her, she would say "play" if she wanted us to engage in a game. But when we were not paying attention, or were out of sight, she said "come" to call us over to her. Stella never used "come" when she already had our attention, or when we were already where she wanted us to be. Observing the contexts in which Stella used each word gave me important information about her understanding of it. If Stella would have said "come" in all the same situations as "play" or any other word for that matter, it would be difficult to know if she understood the different meanings of each individual word.

Paying attention to how Stella used each word is a much more effective way to assess her language capabilities than quizzing her on the locations of each button. For example, testing Stella by asking "Where is come?" or "Where is play?" and waiting to see if she could find the right button does not actually tell us anything about her ability to communicate with it. It is an entirely different skill. It would be the equivalent of someone asking you "Tell me exactly where the letter 'g' is on the keyboard." Knowing that *g* is in the middle of the second row is not the same as knowing which words are spelled with the letter *g* or how to use it appropriately. So if I asked Stella "Where is come?" and she pushed her "come" button, that would not tell me Stella knew the word *come* or knew how to use it. It would tell me that she memorized its location, and possibly was trained to answer that specific question. A much better way of assessing Stella's language acquisition is tracking her word use along with the environment, context, gestures she used, and typical routines. It is always better to assess AAC users' language skills by analyzing their communication patterns.

After Stella had started saying five of her new words, *walk*, *bye*, *help*, *no*, and *come*, I deliberately gave her more pause time before I fed her each meal. It can be easy to go through motions on autopilot and forget to turn activities into language-facilitating experiences. We need to give emerging communicators the chance to speak up for themselves instead of always speaking for them. When Stella walked past her food dish and licked her lips after she woke up one morning, I stayed silent. She walked across the dining room to sniff the drawer her food was in. Stella walked back to the side of her food dish, said "eat," and looked back to me.

"Stella eat! Yes, Stella eat now."

Stella licked her lips and wagged her tail while she watched me carry her cup of food to her bowl. That night, Stella said "eat" again ten minutes before her normal dinnertime. Stella had now used every new word, except for *love you*, independently and consistently in the appropriate contexts.

Having more words available did not stop Stella from using her old vocabulary. She started communicating about even more activities throughout her day. When I introduced this second set of words to Stella, a lot of her learning came from exploring the buttons and watching our reactions. With all the chaos of emptying our house and preparing to move, I did not model language nearly as much as I had over the first few weeks with Stella's first words. But she had a strong foundation and was able to keep learning on her own. Stella knew that the buttons were for communication. After she heard the words and saw what happened when she said each of them a few times, she started using them more confidently.

Our move grew closer and our house emptier and emptier. Now our voices echoed in most of the rooms, and Stella's buttons, toys, and bed were our only décor. I kept Stella's favorite ball, plush toy, and rope toys out for her to play with over the next couple of days and packed the rest in a suitcase. Stella watched me zip up the suitcase, said "help," and curled up in a ball on my lap. Ever since she witnessed us packing up her belongings, she did not leave my side. I hoped she was not afraid we were leaving her. I hated seeing Stella so upset. I wondered what she thought was happening. Even I was feeling nervous about everything, and I knew exactly what was happening. I could not imagine what Stella was feeling while seeing her routines crumbling and all our belongings disappearing without knowing why. I wished I could communicate to Stella that we were going to be in a new home with new furniture and all her toys soon.

Over the course of a month and a half, Jake and I went from

having every cabinet, closet, and room overflowing with objects to small stacks of our suitcases, houseplants, and a few boxes by the front door. It was exhausting.

I went to bed with my stomach in knots. The next morning, we would hop in the car and leave behind entire lives we built here. Omaha was familiar and kind to me. I knew my way around, had favorite restaurants, bars, and plant shops. I had professional connections, a network of people I could reach out to. Jake and I met here. I had found a close-knit group of friends and could easily drive home to see my family in Illinois. I wondered how our lives would change, if we were making a huge mistake. But there was no going back now. We had new jobs to start, a new apartment to move into, a new life waiting for us to come and claim it.

TAKEAWAYS FOR TEACHING *YOUR* DOG

- **Add a word to your dog's gestures.** Model the next level of communication by saying the word that corresponds to your dog's gesturing. Your dog is learning another way she can communicate that concept.

- **Look for patterns in your dog's vocabulary use.** Learn more about your dog by paying attention to the words she uses most frequently and the specific situations in which she most often uses words. Just like people, every dog is different and will have different communication trends.

The Road to California

Stella sat on her bed in the front seat of my car, a smile stretched across her face. She switched back and forth between sitting up, looking out the window to the never-ending cornfields over the rolling hills of Nebraska, and lying down on the patch of sun that hit her blanket. My copilot and I drove into the future with a bright blue sky above us. I have always loved being on the road. I feel my freest when I'm behind the wheel, listening to music, with nowhere else I need to be, or nothing else I could possibly be doing. It's a meditative experience.

Jake packed our cars like a game of Tetris, each object perfectly locked in its place, except for the grocery bag of Stella's buttons on the floor of the front seat. It was the only place we could keep them that we would be able to easily take them out. Whenever I stopped, turned, or hit a bump, I heard a rattling of plastic and "outside water walk love you help" at the same time. Stella looked down, then looked over to me.

"Yep, I heard it, too, Stella." This was going to be a long thirty hours.

We arrived in Breckenridge, Colorado, after our first nine-hour stretch of the drive. Stella was a perfect passenger the whole way, but as soon as we left the car, she exploded with energy. When Jake and I flopped onto the king-size bed, Stella started running laps around the hotel room. She jumped on the bed, barked at us, hopped off, and ran around in circles by the door. So far, Stella's first night ever in a hotel room was complete chaos.

"Oh, jeez, girl, you're so wound up," I said. Jake placed Stella's buttons around the hotel room. I tossed a toy for Stella and she dove across the floor, knocking the buzzers Jake just set up in all directions. I heard the beeps of a few of them resetting after they banged into the wall.

"Well, this is off to a great start," I said. "What if she's this crazy every night? We're never going to get any sleep." I set the buttons back up.

"Outside," I woke up hearing the next morning at 5:30 A.M. I could only see the outline of Stella standing by the door in the pitch-black hotel room. I stayed in bed while Jake took her out for a short walk to go to the bathroom.

We would need to start getting used to this. At our apartment we wouldn't be able to let her out in the backyard like we could in Omaha. Normally, she asked to go "outside" at least ten or fifteen times a day. It was now occurring to me that if she kept up that frequency in San Diego, we would be spending all our spare time taking her out. When Jake and Stella returned, she jumped on the bed and licked my face until I sat up. She hopped off the bed, took a drink of water, then said "eat" like she would at home.

"Stella eat! Okay, let's get your breakfast." Now I was energized for the day. It excited me to see Stella communicating with her buttons so similarly to how she would in Omaha despite the new location and stress we all had been experiencing for the past few days. Her words must have been becoming pretty automatic for her to say. If she really had to think about what to say or how to say it, she probably would not have used her AAC during this hectic time. It would have taken up too much mental energy for her. It's harder for everyone to do something challenging when they are stressed out. Dogs are no exception. Having access to her words seemed to settle Stella down a bit. She still had an abundance of energy, but she was not nearly as frantic as she was when we arrived in the hotel room before placing her buttons out for her.

On the second day of our drive, we traded the cornfields of Nebraska for mountains in Colorado and Utah covered with trees starting to show off their autumn yellow, red, and orange leaves. That night, we stayed in a small town in Utah. The single-story, U-shaped motel had about twenty rooms, each one accessible from the outside. When Jake and I were brushing our teeth, we walked out of the bathroom to see Stella peeing inside next to the front door.

"Shoot, I forgot to bring her buttons in from the car," I said. "That was my fault." Stella had been hanging out by the door and had whined a couple of times, but I was so tired, it didn't even register that I forgot her buttons. Standing next to the door was Stella's best chance at making me notice she needed to go outside. As much as Stella had learned to communicate with words, Jake and I had become used to Stella telling us exactly what she wanted or needed. Normally we didn't have to be on the lookout for Stella's signs that she needed to go to the bathroom. No matter where we were in the house, we could hear if Stella said "outside."

"Sorry, Stella girl, let's go outside and get your buttons." As soon as I laid out Stella's buttons in the most consistent way I could, she walked over and pushed each one lined up against the wall. She cocked her head as she heard each word.

"I think she's checking to see which one is which," I said.

At home, Stella did not need to test out all the buzzers because she learned the location of each word. A few minutes later, Stella said "water," which alerted us that she had run out.

Stella's buttons were important to her. Now two nights in a row, she became calmer and more settled after we set them up. Tonight, she even showed that she wanted to know which one was which. Her words were consistent parts of the way she communicated. Having everything I needed to express myself would make me feel more comfortable too. I thought back to a few of my AAC clients in Omaha I had observed in their classrooms at school. Oftentimes, their communication devices were not out on their desks or were not being used throughout the day. How did those kids feel when a significant part of their communication was just gone? Stella was acting out when we did not have all her tools available for her. Imagine how frustrating it would be for kids. It had not hit me yet that these clients were not mine to think about or worry about anymore. I hoped they were in good hands. I missed seeing them already.

We split up the last day of our drive and booked a last-minute room in Las Vegas. I had never been to Vegas before, so I thought it would be a fun final night of our trip. I imagined us relaxing in a nice hotel room, playing a slot machine or two, having a good meal, drinking a fun cocktail. It would be a great way to celebrate our trip thus far and pause before the chaos of moving in began.

Our hotel on the Las Vegas Strip was even more enormous than I had imagined. There were multiple restaurants inside, different wings of the hotel that all required a separate elevator, and walkways that connected to other hotels. It felt like its own world.

We walked for almost ten minutes through the main floor to reach the center of the hotel to find the right elevator for our room. Walking adjacent to the casino floor, filled with people everywhere we looked, Stella starting pooping on the carpet.

"Oh my gosh, Jake!" I shouted.

"Stella, no! Wait!" he said.

It was too late to stop it from coming out. Jake and I panicked. Jake scooped Stella up from the ground and started running away. "We gotta find the exit before she goes again!" he shouted. I ran behind Jake, with water from my fish's mason jar splashing out like crazy and Stella's buttons all shouting, "bye love you walk help eat" at the same time as they bumped into one another. I flagged down a maintenance worker on the way to help clean it up. Stella looked back to me over Jake's shoulder, smiling, like she was enjoying the thrill of a lifetime. We were officially the people everyone was staring at in Vegas, a city filled with spectacles at every turn.

Several wrong turns and ten minutes later, we finally found a door. When we set Stella down on the turf lawn, she looked up at us and kept walking. She did not need to go to the bathroom any more than she already had in the casino.

The next morning, Stella said, "outside" twice in a row in our eleventh-story hotel room. Jake walked her down the hallway to the elevator, waited a few minutes for it to arrive, and went down to the main floor. By the time he and Stella walked out of the elevator it had been at least five minutes since Stella said, "outside, outside." This time, Jake knew where the door was. He would have to walk through the casino for about five more minutes to get to it. But, as soon as they stepped out of the elevator, and started walking down the hall, Stella started pooping again. Outside was too far away for her puppy self.

At noon, we arrived at our new apartment in sunny San Diego. The wide street lined with palm trees on each side gave us a warm Southern California greeting. We were a ten-minute drive from downtown and from the beach. A small grocery store and a library sat on the end of our block. Bustling streets filled with boutique shops, restaurants, breweries, and bars were all within a half-mile walk. Lizards scattered into the bushes with each step we took. Hummingbirds buzzed past us. Succulents the size of trees grew in front lawns everywhere I looked. Green-and-red parrots squawked as they flew down the street. It felt like we had entered a completely different world.

Our apartment complex was an off-white building with sixteen units, all facing a courtyard in the center. Our unit was on the first floor, right next to the entrance. We walked in to see the refrigerator and stove in the middle of the living room, and two handymen working in the kitchen.

"Wow . . ." Jake said. "This is really . . ."

I saw the panic in Jake's face. "I'm sure it'll look bigger when the appliances are out of the living room," I said. "The listing said it was seven hundred square feet . . ."

"We'll be done in an hour," one of the workers said. "Come back then."

We walked around the neighborhood and stopped to eat lunch. I was shocked at how many restaurants were dog friendly. Back in Omaha, we could bring Stella with us to eat at only a couple spots. Stella trotted up to everyone we passed on the sidewalk, wagging her tail, and smiling. If someone said "hi" to us, but did not look down to Stella, she jumped up in the air to try catching their attention. Stella loved when people acknowledged her individually.

When we returned to our apartment an hour later, seeing the appliances placed back into the kitchen did not make too much of a difference. The long, narrow living room opened to a tiny U-shaped kitchen on the left, and the bathroom and bedroom on the right. We could see pretty much the entire place from the front door. Jake measured the whole space out to be 470 square feet.

"Well, it's a good thing we didn't bring much from Omaha," he said. "Absolutely none of our furniture would have fit." Our sectional would have taken up the entire living room. The old dining table would have blocked the walkway from the kitchen to the bedroom.

Stella ran in and out of each room, sniffing every inch of the floor. Before we started unpacking the car, we set her buttons

out for her in the living room and tossed a ball across the apartment a few times so she could run a bit. When Jake began
carrying boxes inside, Stella stood in the middle of the living
room, smiling in the patch of sunlight that poured in through
the southern-facing window. She wagged her tail every time
we brought our belongings from Omaha inside. She sniffed
and licked each box.

"Yes, Stella! This is our new home, girl."

I thought we had made it through the most stressful period of
our cross-country move. I figured the process of finding new
jobs, shedding our belongings, and traveling thirty hours in the
car would be the uphill stretch for Jake, Stella, and me. I was
certain that when we arrived, it would be a downhill ride the
rest of the way. That was before I realized it would take Stella
far longer to adjust to a new home than I expected.

Stella had used her buttons in the various hotel rooms on the
trip, so I assumed she would continue using them when we set
them out in our new apartment. But besides saying "outside,"
she did not say anything for the first few days. She was uncomfortable and filled with anxiety being in our unfamiliar apartment. She whined through the night and every time Jake and I
stepped out of the apartment, even when we were just carrying
the trash out. We tried leaving Stella at home while we went
to shop for household necessities. As soon as we walked out the
door, we could hear Stella yelping from inside. What if she
didn't stop? What if the neighbors complained? The two of us
could not leave at the same time anymore without her. When
I went to the bathroom, Stella pawed at the door and whined.
She had never been this anxious or attached before, not even as

a young puppy. I wondered, *Did we completely traumatize her by putting her through this move?*

When I saw how uneasy Stella was, it did not surprise me that she was not talking. Her basic needs of feeling secure and comfortable were not being met. Before anyone can reach their fullest potential, their primary needs have to be attended to first. The noted psychologist Abraham Maslow proposed his hierarchy of needs theory to explain that humans have five different levels of needs. The different levels are illustrated in a pyramid with physiological needs—including food, shelter, and rest—at the foundation; security and safety, second; followed by social relationships and belonging, third; then feeling accomplishment, fourth; and finally, achieving one's full potential, fifth.[27] It is difficult to experience the feelings at the top of the pyramid when the foundation is unstable. We have all experienced varying degrees of this concept. It is harder to learn if you are exhausted from a poor night of sleep, and it is more challenging to focus in class when your stomach is growling. We all do our best when we feel our best. Stella was no different.

TAKEAWAYS FOR TEACHING *YOUR* DOG

- **Bring your dog's buttons, whenever possible, while traveling.** Having all forms of communication available may help your dog feel more at ease in new situations and unfamiliar places.

- **Look for your dog exploring her words on her own.** The more your dog explores her buttons and hears which button says which word, the better for her learning.

- **Keep Maslow's hierarchy of needs in mind.** If your dog isn't feeling safe, secure, healthy, or well-exercised, it will likely be harder for her to learn new skills and use them. Tend to your dog's foundational needs first.

Using Words in New Ways

———

After almost a week of Jake and I alternating leaving, creating new routines for Stella, and setting up our apartment, she settled down. One afternoon she walked to the floor space under the built-in shelves in our living room and pawed each of her four buttons, "play" "no," "love you," and "help." She cocked her head to the left and right, like she had in our hotel room, listening to each word. When she heard them all, she walked away and lay down.

"Good girl, Stella. Yes, those are your words," I said. I modeled each of them again a few times in a row. I walked through the rest of the apartment to show her where "walk," "bye," "come," "eat," and "water" were. I came back to say "love you" with her button, then kissed Stella's head and patted her back. "Everything will be okay, girl."

The next day, Stella stared at the same row of her buttons again. She looked back to me, then looked down at the buttons. She timidly lifted her paw, said "no," then immediately turned her head. It looked like that was not what she was expecting to hear. Stella paused for a few seconds, then hit the button next to "no."

"Play," she said. When Stella heard that the button said "play," she pushed it again two more times. She ran away and shoved her nose into her toy bin across the room.

Stella corrected herself when she said the wrong word. When she reached the word she intended to say, "play," she pushed it two more times, like she was letting me know that was really the one she meant. Stella was now developing such strong pragmatic skills along with her vocabulary. Knowing how to use words is much more than understanding their meanings. It is equally as important to know when to use words and how to convey a message with them. I never directly taught her to push a button twice in a row to let me know that was what she really wanted. If I stepped on the wrong button, I might have modeled that idea once or twice by pushing the button I meant to say a couple of times in a row. So either Stella learned that strategy from such limited exposure, or she realized how to emphasize her words on her own.

Later that day, Stella said "water" when her bowl was empty, and "eat" within a half an hour of her normal dinnertime. She initiated play with us more and stayed by herself in the living room for a few minutes if we went into the kitchen or bedroom. Little by little, she was becoming more at ease and secure. Thankfully, I could see glimpses of the old Stella coming back.

Once we settled into our new space and saw that all our

belongings would indeed fit, our small living quarters did not bother me at all. It was clutter-free. Every object had its own place, and cleaning our entire space only took twenty minutes. Jake and I picked out our furniture together and chose not to buy a TV, which all meant that we were experiencing a new way of living together. We had exactly what we needed—no more, no less. Finally, for the first time in over a month, the three of us could fully relax. We made it. We were here, in California, ready to have fun and begin our new lives.

In Omaha, Stella said "outside," "eat," and "walk," consistently every day. Then, she would also typically use one or two other words throughout the course of the day. Now, Stella said six or seven different words each day and used many of them multiple times. She said "outside," "walk," and "eat," each morning and evening, "come" when Jake and I were making dinner and she wanted us to play in the living room with her, "help" when the blinds were closed or the bedroom door was shut, "no" when we told her we were all done playing or were "all done outside," and "bye" right after Jake or I walked out the door to go to the store. She had not only matched her former communication patterns, now she exceeded them.

Stella used her words more now that I modeled them whenever I could. This progress aligns with what I teach, and what the research shows. The more often speech therapists, parents, teachers, siblings, and peers use a child's communication device, the more the child will use it.[28] Now that all the rooms in our apartment were only a few steps away, we were always near her words. Back in Omaha, Stella could only easily say words when she was on the first floor. If she was upstairs or in the basement and really needed to go to the bathroom, she would run to let us know. But otherwise, she rarely traveled across the house to tell us "help," "come," "play," or "no." And we rarely traveled across the house to model words. By the time we reached the button we were looking for, whatever was happening was usually irrelevant. I wanted to model words when they were relevant, not after the fact. Now, pretty much whenever we talked to Stella, we would come into the living room and use her buttons. It was much easier and more convenient for Stella to access them, which led to even more communication success.

Stella paid close attention to what Jake and I were doing. If she was not playing, she was usually standing a few feet away from us, turning her head toward each of us when we talked or walked away. She was a careful observer of us and her environment. One evening after Stella finished eating, she stood between the kitchen and our dining table, watching us carry plates, glasses, and our food to the table. Jake and I sat down.

"Eat," she said and walked away toward the couch.

"Didn't she already eat?" Jake said.

"Yeah, I think she's talking about what we're about to do. Yes, Stella. Jake Christina eat."

Stella listened to my words from the couch and turned her head to the side. She lay there watching us eat for the rest of our meal. At this point, we had never fed Stella food from the table. She did not beg from us or expect us to give her scraps. She would typically sit on the couch or lie on the floor and observe. Tonight, she used the word *eat* to narrate what was happening instead of requesting food. If Stella was wanting more to eat, she likely would have stayed by her bowl or walked to the cabinet where we kept her food and treats. But she did not do that. She continued watching us.

Hearing Stella say "eat" in this new context was really similar to when she said "water" while she watched me tend to my plants. Words can be used for multiple different functions of communication and for several different meanings. The more we remember that words have multiple meanings, the more we can understand emerging communicators' messages.

The next morning at work, I was reminded of this concept again. I was enjoying my new job in early intervention so far. It was an adjustment for the first couple of weeks, as I drove to each appointment and conducted therapy in other people's homes. But I was getting the hang of it now, feeling more at ease each day. I was empowered knowing that my sessions were most families' introduction into the therapy world. It was an incredible opportunity to show them how fun, powerful, and important speech therapy is.

This morning, a curly-haired toddler shouted, "Monkey." He jumped up and down and clapped his hands in front of my face. He and I were surrounded by toys on his living room floor—a train set, blocks, Mr. Potato Head. His mom bounced his baby sister on her hip in the kitchen, within earshot of the therapy. Since starting speech therapy with this boy a few weeks before, this was only the fourth or fifth word I heard him say.

Last week I brought a couple of stuffed monkeys to play with. I left them in my trunk this week and chose other animals instead. *Maybe he wants those again? Or wait, does he want me to sing "Five Little Monkeys"?*

"Sing monkey song?" I asked. "Five little monkeys jumpin' on the bed . . ."

"Oh, no, he's been saying monkey all day long," his mom said. "He's trying to tell you that we went to the zoo yesterday and saw the monkeys. He kept jumping up and down and pointing at them."

"Oh, monkeys at the zoo. Wow!" He smiled again and resumed jumping up and down.

When toddlers are developing language, they often use single words or short phrases to convey entire thoughts. That is a completely normal part of the language development process. Stella also used the same single words to convey multiple different thoughts. She could say "eat" to request food or to comment on us eating. My client could say "monkey" to mean that he saw monkeys at the zoo yesterday or that he wanted to play with toy monkeys. Staying open to possibilities and using all the available context clues helps us figure out the speaker's intention behind each word.

A few weeks into living in San Diego, we threw together a housewarming party. Jake and I hosted my friend Brissa who was visiting us for the weekend, a fun couple we met at a brewery in our neighborhood, a couple of Jake's old friends from high school who happened to live in the area, and a couple of Jake's coworkers. It was a tight squeeze in our small apartment.

"So what are these . . . buttons you have all around your floor?" Jake's friend asked.

Another friend said he was curious, too.

Everyone stared at me, eager for an explanation. Our friends in Omaha had heard me talking about teaching Stella to say words from the very beginning of my pursuit. They understood me and my job and were not crazy surprised to see me trying to combine my two worlds together. But now here I was, reminded that lining a living room floor with talking buttons is not something people see every day.

"Well, so, I'm a speech therapist . . . and I wanted to see if Stella could learn to say words with these buttons."

Silence.

"I work with a lot of kids who are nonverbal and use communication devices to talk. So I wondered if Stella could learn to use a communication device if she had one."

Brissa caught my eye and gave me an encouraging smile. "They each say a different word," she chimed in.

"Right," I said. "Like, outside, play, walk, eat." I walked around the room, stepping on all the buttons to give a demonstration. "So when Stella wants any of these things, she can tell us."

I braced myself for all kinds of questions and skepticism. But I did not receive any.

"Wait, this is so cool."

"That makes so much sense."

"My dog totally understands words and just waits for me to say them."

I sighed with relief. I was happy to find out that I was not coming across as completely crazy to these strangers and acquaintances. My first impression on our new California friends was not shot. They were all so intrigued.

A couple hours into the party, Stella woke up from her nap, said "play," and trotted into the circle showing off her toy to all these new friends.

The next day, we were about to leave to take a walk on the beach. Brissa went into our bedroom to change. Jake grabbed my hand, turned me toward him, and kissed me.

"Love you," Stella said. We looked down to see Stella

squeezing right in between our legs. She wagged her tail, looked up at us, with her ears turned straight back against her head. Her ears always went back like this when she was happy. She looked like a little otter.

"Aw, love you, Stella. We love you, too, girl." Jake and I crouched down immediately. Stella licked our faces, smiled, and rolled over for a belly rub.

"Good girl, Stella. Good Stella, love you."

It was the first time she had ever said "love you" on her own. Any other time had been after I was modeling it for a bit while giving her belly rubs or scratches.

Stella had now officially used all ten of her words independently. I had always modeled "love you" during natural moments of connection with Stella, like a parent would with a child. Parents say "I love you" to their baby or toddler while they are hugging or kissing their child, taking care of them, or are proud of them. Parents do not explain the meaning of love to their baby first, quiz them on what it means, then accept it when the child says "I love you" to them. Children learn the social times and feelings associated with the words they hear. So far, Stella had learned in the same way. She wanted to join in on the love and had a way to tell us.

I did not worry about whether "love you" meant the exact same thing to me as it did to Stella. It's impossible to know if any single word evokes the identical feeling between multiple different people, much less humans and canines.

At the end of the weekend, Jake, Stella, and I dropped Brissa off at the airport. Stella stood in the back seat, watching out the window as Brissa disappeared into the building. When we returned to our apartment, Stella walked straight to the couch

Brissa slept on. She sniffed the blankets and pillows she used, then said "bye," and looked up directly into my eyes.

"You're right, Stella. She went bye."

This was the first time I noticed Stella talking about something that had just happened, not something about to happen or currently happening. Stella understood the concept that this person was here, but now she is not anymore. This reminded me of all the times Wrigley would sulk on my sisters' beds all day when they left for college. That was her ritual to acknowledge they had left. What was she thinking when she was lying there? And what else was Stella thinking about the fact that our friend was here for a few days and now she was gone? I did not know it then, but this would become a pattern every single time we had friends or family stay with us. Stella would ride in the car to the airport with us, sniff the air mattress or couch when we came back, and say "bye."

After work the next week, we drove west fifteen minutes to the Ocean Beach Dog Beach. Every time we pulled into the parking lot, it felt like we had truly entered a new world. Surfers adjusted their wetsuits in the parking lot, then ran off to catch the next wave. People sold art out of their vans they had turned into homes. Skateboarders zoomed past us. And on the right, there was a football field length of sand leading up to the shore where dogs of all sizes ran and played free as could be. I unclipped Stella's leash when our toes touched the shore. Stella ran up to greet every human who crossed her path. Everyone fawned over her.

Stella barked at older dogs who lacked the care or energy to keep up with her seven-month-old self. She dipped her paws in the water and bolted back to the sand when a wave came crashing in toward her.

When I threw Stella's ball down the shore, she glanced at it, then ran in the opposite direction to chase a dog who was chasing another dog. She could not care less about her ball now.

"We're at the beach, Stella! Beach, beach, beach," I kept saying as she played. "Play at the beach!" Stella smiled and sprinted past me.

The sun started to set, and the palm tree silhouettes against the deep purple sky looked like an image from a postcard. I still could not believe we lived here.

We returned from the beach feeling relaxed and happy that this could be a typical weeknight after work. I glanced at the clock to notice that it was just after 7:30.

"Can you believe this?" I said to Jake. "I would have just gotten done working in Omaha." Now it felt like I had a life. Since the end of my last appointment of the day I had already walked Stella, spent time modeling her words, made dinner, gone to the beach, and come back. It was a balanced life, not work work work.

When we finished drying Stella off, she marched inside straight to her dishes. She slammed her paw to say "eat." She turned the corner, walked to her row of buttons in the living room, and said "no." Stella looked up to us. She maintained eye contact, whined, and stomped her right paw. We did not feed Stella before we left for the beach that night. And Stella created her first two-word combination to tell us that she had not eaten dinner.

TAKEAWAYS FOR TEACHING *YOUR* DOG

- **Consider how easy your button setup is to access.** Are all your dog's buttons spread throughout the house? Are her words in a room that you don't spend much time in? If either of these is the case, consider setting up your buttons in an area that will lead to more modeling, and easier access for your dog.

- **Be present.** Limit distractions in your environment and be in the moment when you're teaching your dog. It's easier for everyone to learn in a calm environment. When you're modeling words, try keeping the TV off or turning the music down so your dog can focus.

- **Stay open to possibilities of communication.** Once again, your dog might not always be using words to request an object or action. Spending time getting to know your dog's communication patterns will help you determine when she is using words in unique ways and what else she might be trying to say. Use context clues such as what's going on in the environment, your dog's typical routines, and her gestures/vocalizations to help you.

- **Don't worry about exact translations of abstract concepts like "love you."** It is impossible to know if two humans even feel the same way when saying the same words. Your dog will likely learn to say these concepts in the same types of contexts that she sees and hears them modeled in.

CHAPTER 12

Creative Combinations

———

Was that a crazy coincidence? Did Stella really mean to put two words together to create a phrase? It was just too unreal. Maybe it was a fluke. Maybe it would never happen again. I texted Grace immediately, Stella said "eat no" when she hadn't eaten dinner way past her normal mealtime . . . so intrigued to see if this happens again . . .

It was not a fluke. The next morning, Stella jumped off our bed before us, like usual, and walked into the living room. I lay in bed, patiently anticipating whether I would hear Stella say she wanted to eat breakfast first or go outside first. She always told us what she wanted to do.

"Come," Stella said. Her collar tags jingled. She must be walking somewhere. Where was she going?

"Outside," she said.

I flung the covers off. "Come outside? I'm coming, Stella." Stella stood by the front door wagging her tail. She went to the bathroom as soon as we reached the courtyard.

Back when I had introduced a few buttons to Stella, I remember joking around with Grace about how crazy it would be if Stella ever said two words in a row, like "play outside." We laughed, and I never seriously thought about that wild scenario again. It was the same sort of hypothetical situation as saying, "How cool would it be if we won the lottery tomorrow?" I had never modeled two words together with Stella's buttons. It never seriously crossed my mind that she might reach this significant language milestone. I modeled two-word phrases all the time verbally, unintentionally—"come girl, come outside," "come eat," "Stella no," "play toy." But I was only doing that because it's natural to talk in short phrases to help her understanding, not because I expected Stella to follow my lead.

The more I thought about Stella's new skills, the more it actually made sense. If she was already using single words for multiple meanings in several contexts, why wouldn't she be able to use them together to create new phrases? Toddlers combine words together when they have a solid understanding of their meanings and have practiced using them individually first. So far, Stella had continued sharing language milestones with toddlers. Why would the similarities stop now? Plus, Stella had been combining single words with gestures regularly. She would say "help" then stand where she wanted us to look for her toy, "walk" then paw at the door. Pairing words and gestures occurs before kids use words to say both concepts. Toddlers typically start combining two words together when they are about eighteen months old. Some skills that happen developmentally right before we see word combinations in children include:[29]

- "Uses single words frequently." Stella communicated with single words several times each day.
- "Verbalizes two different needs." Stella used her buttons to tell us when she needed food, water, and to go to the bathroom.
- "Uses words to interact with others." Stella engaged with us by using gestures, vocalizations, and words.
- "Understands the commands 'sit down' and 'come here.'" Stella responded to these, along with a few other commands.
- "Requests assistance from an adult." Stella said "help" when she needed it.
- "Talks rather than uses gestures." Stella used words for the concepts she had available to her.
- "Uses words to protest." Stella said "no" when we were doing something she did not like.

Even with such a limited vocabulary available to her, Stella was still using words in similar ways as toddlers do before they start putting separate words together. For the first couple weeks of combining words, Stella's most common phrases were actions paired with "no" if we had not done something that we usually do.

One evening, I came home from work, wiped out from a few chaotic sessions. Instead of taking Stella outside to go for a walk right away, I flopped on our bed, hoping to rest for a few minutes. Stella walked into the living room, said "walk no," and poked her head into the bedroom. She looked concerned.

"We'll walk later, Stella. Come up." I patted the bed.

Now, by combining words with "no," Stella could talk about what she noticed in even greater detail. This gave me even more insight into how routine-oriented Stella is. I knew she thrived with structure and anticipated what was coming next, but Stella pointing out when something that usually happened had not occurred yet showed me that she was thinking about it even in its absence. What else was she thinking about that was not happening right in the moment? A few minutes later, Stella hopped off the bed.

"Come walk," I heard from the living room.

I could not resist. I would rest later. First Stella pointed out that we were late for our normal walk, and now she is requesting it. "Okay, girl, let's go for a walk." Stella jumped around in a circle then stood by her leash.

Taking Stella to the dog beach quickly became a routine activity for us. A few times per week I would either take Stella when I came home from work, or the three of us would go together after dinner to watch the sunset. Running with Stella down the shore, meeting new dog and human friends, and enjoying the beauty of the Pacific Ocean was the perfect way to end the day.

"Do you want to make a quick dinner then head to the beach?" I asked Jake.

I heard Stella's tags jingle immediately. She pranced into the bedroom and cocked her head up at us.

"She definitely knows that word now," I said.

"Yes, let's go to the beach," Jake said.

Stella turned her head again, then smiled until we put her leash on. As soon as we pulled into the dog beach parking lot, Stella perked up from the back seat of the car. She looked out the window and started whining and wagging her tail when she saw dogs trotting around.

I knew what this meant. Stella needed a "beach" button. After she heard the word *beach*, she always tracked our every move and tried herding us out the door as quickly as possible. If she was understanding "beach," she should definitely have a way to let us know that is what she wants instead of waiting for one of us to mention it.

"Ready, girl? Let's play on the beach!" I said.

The next day, I found our last spare button in a cabinet. While I put batteries in it, Stella stood close to my side and stared up at me. She knew what these buttons were for by now. I held it out for her. Stella sniffed it, then watched intently, as I said "beach" into the speaker. Stella barely waited for me to set it down near the front door before she pawed at it repeatedly.

"Beach beach beach," Stella said.

I had a feeling something like this would happen, just like when we added a "walk" button for her. Stella could not wait another second to say one of her favorite words.

"Okay, Stella. Let's go to the beach," I said. Luckily I programmed the button when I could actually take her. I am sure Stella would have been so disappointed if I had to say "no" the first time she had the chance to tell me she wanted to visit her favorite spot.

A couple of nights later, I woke up to Stella saying "beach, beach" at 3:00 in the morning. Stella rarely talked in the middle of the night. Once or twice she told us "outside" when she really needed to go to the bathroom. And once last month, she said "help" in the middle of the night, which startled me. It was 2:00 A.M., and when I turned on the light, Stella was chasing a cricket in our living room. But other than those instances, she had never woken up to talk in the middle of the night.

"No beach, Stella. Bed now."

It was not always possible to take Stella to the beach exactly when she asked for it. But it's okay to say no. Stella already had a solid understanding of the word *beach*, from us saying it every time we took her there. In AAC therapy, "once the individual has the idea of what a particular word means and understands that there will be a natural response when appropriate, then it's okay to respond by saying 'no more right now,' 'we're finished with that,'" or something else of that nature.[30] Saying no to a request can still provide reinforcement for the learner. For example, if a child asks for cookies all day long, you would at some point probably tell them "it's not time for cookies now," or "we can have cookies later." You would not be afraid that by saying no, the child would lose understanding of the word *cookies*. You still acknowledged and responded to what they said, which provides reinforcement for their learning.

A lot of parents and professionals can be afraid to program highly motivating words into a child's device. I have heard the same comment so many times, "He'll just ask for it over and over again, so I don't want to start that." I am always thinking to myself, *Isn't that the point of communication? To be able to talk about what you want to talk about? And to communicate what's on your mind?* Imagine someone saying the opposite statement, "He'll never want to say this word so we should definitely have it available for him." We would never choose that because it does not make sense.

Even if it is inconvenient for us for a little while as they are learning, everyone deserves to be able to say the words they want to say *when* they want to say them. Communication should not be conditional. I have seen many adults remove words from a child's device or put the child's talker away because they were becoming annoyed by how often the child said something. This

The night Jake and I picked up Stella (in a grocery store parking lot, of all places). We had no idea how our lives would change, and neither did she! *(Right)* Little Stella staring into my eyes minutes after bringing her home. I instantly felt connected to her.

Stella studying her "outside" button three weeks after I introduced it. Based on how frequently she stared at it, I could tell she was close to pushing it on her own.

After Stella started saying her first three words independently, I was hooked on stories of human and animal communication. I loved when Stella would keep me company while I read!

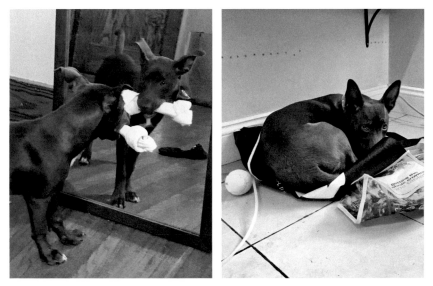

Whenever we gave Stella a new toy or bone, she would go stare at herself in the mirror. I always wondered what she was thinking when she saw her reflection. A few minutes later, she buried that bone in a pile of Jake's clothes. *(Right)* Stella's body language and word use showed us how stressed she was while we packed up our Omaha house. After we removed the last of our couches, Stella said "no" and laid on an empty grocery bag.

On our road trip to California, Stella enjoyed taking in the beautiful new scenery just as much as we did.

About a week after we arrived in San Diego, Stella started using her words consistently again. She told us "eat" every evening without fail at five o'clock on the dot.

Stella adapted well to her new California lifestyle. The dog beach quickly became one of Stella's favorite places, and "beach" became one of her most frequently used words.

Stella looked happy and excited when we responded to her words. She waited for me by the door after she said "walk" and I said "yes."

The first version of Stella's buttons placed together on one board. Once she adjusted to her new setup, Stella loved hanging out on and near her board.

Her left paw on her ball and her right paw saying "play." When Stella's words became automatic for her, she often said them while multitasking.

Stella with two of her best dog friends at the park. She initiated the same games with the same dogs each visit. That reminded me of toddlers initiating the same games I played with them every week.

Stella was a fast learner! Shortly after we switched her buttons to a single board, she was ready for new vocabulary. Every day, Stella generated new word combinations spontaneously.

I thought fifteen words would keep Stella busy for a while, but I was wrong! We transitioned to a larger board with more vocabulary when she used all of her words appropriately and consistently. Stella laid on her old board for a full afternoon before she tried using her new one.

Since we kept all of Stella's buttons in the same order, the switch to a larger board was much easier than when we first grouped her buttons together. Stella's device now took up a big chunk of our living room!

It fascinated me how often Stella would comment "park play" or "park happy" after we returned from the park. I wondered what else she was thinking about her trip, and what more she could say about it if she had the vocabulary available.

Even though she uses words to talk to us, Stella still acts like a dog, and communicates like a dog. The only difference is that she has one more tool to express herself.

With all of her buttons securely fastened to the board, we can travel with it and bring it places without having to set it up every time. Stella always enjoys having her words with her.

would be the equivalent of duct-taping a child's mouth shut if they kept asking for "cookies" over and over again. Instead of removing the word from the device, or hiding the device altogether, it is best to respond by saying "no," "all done," or "later." This gives the AAC user a chance to learn boundaries and understand the meanings of those words, too. It can also provide a good model for how the AAC user could say no to something that they do not want. The point of teaching language is not to hear what we want to hear when we want to hear it. We teach words to empower others to share their own thoughts, whatever and whenever they may be.

With time, practice, and patience, children learn when it is a good idea to ask for something, and when it is not. It is a learning process. Stella did not continue saying "beach" ten times each day forever. Eventually, she learned the patterns of when we typically go and requested "beach" during more appropriate situations.

When Daylight Saving time arrived in November, we turned our clocks back one hour. Stella showed us, once again, how routine based she is. Between 3:30 and 4:00 P.M., she repeatedly requested to "eat." This would have been 4:30 or 5:00 before the time change, which was completely normal for her. But I did not want to feed her dinner so early and throw her off for our workweek ahead. I gave Stella a couple of treats to tide her over but kept saying, "No eat now, eat later."

Fifteen minutes passed.

"Help eat," Stella said then barked.

"I know, Stella, good waiting. Eat later."

Stella sighed. She stood still for about ten seconds.

"Love you, no," she said. Stella walked away, into the bedroom.

Jake's jaw dropped. "Oh my gosh . . ."

I held my hand over my mouth. "I can't believe . . ."

When we were not giving Stella the response she expected, she adjusted her message to say, "help eat." And when we still said no, she let us know that she was not happy with us. She not only combined words and modified her message so appropriately, she also engaged in one of the first actual short conversations we had. Normally, Stella told us what she wanted or what she was thinking, and we would respond. This time, she heard and saw my response that I was not going to feed her right then and replied to it by saying "love you no."

Generating novel utterances is the ultimate goal and purpose of language. According to the American Speech and Hearing Association, "The vast majority of the sentences we use in our daily communication are sentences that we have never used before in our lifetimes. Furthermore, those *sentences have never been spoken by anyone in the history of mankind.*"[31] When we teach single words first, the possibilities for communication are endless.

I had never modeled "help eat" or "love you no." Now Stella was past the point of using words on her own that she saw us model before. She was past the point of combining two words to say a phrase she had heard us verbally say before. She was stepping out to create her own messages and use words in ways unique to Stella. She took pieces of what she had heard and learned and put them together to create something new. This was always one of my favorite parts of teaching language. Seeing a child progress from saying mostly single words that they have heard before to suddenly putting them together to create their own expressions seems miraculous every single time. And now, I was witnessing this with my dog. *What is Stella's actual potential here?* I wondered. *Have I even scratched the surface of what she is trying to communicate to me or what she can learn to say if she has more vocabulary available?*

By mid-November, Stella was generating at least one new two-word phrase each day. Even with only eleven words available, there were still 110 unique two-word combinations possible that she could make. She also used a few of the same phrases throughout daily activities. Some of her frequent messages included "come outside" when she called us over from the bedroom to go out, "bye walk" when she stood by the door ready to leave for her walk, and "love you play" after we spent a longer time than usual playing with her inside. While I did not initially expect Stella to combine words, the words she had available enabled her to reach this milestone. When I selected her vocabulary, I picked mostly core words that I knew she understood and could be used in multiple contexts. If I had selected primarily nouns, Stella would not have had the opportunity to create such functional messages. Verbs are necessary to create phrases. We say phrases like "play outside," not "stick ball." We say, "eat dinner," not "food treat." Providing a solid vocabulary from the beginning paved the way for Stella to achieve these more complex language milestones.

It only took Stella about one month after settling in her new home to explode with language use and combine words. I wondered how quickly she would have reached this breakthrough if her buttons were spread out in one room rather than across the first floor of a house, or if she did not need time to settle

into an entirely new space. Stella had been through a lot over
the past couple of months. But, even with all these changes, she
was still learning so quickly. She was only nine months old and
she talked to us in short phrases every day.

One day while I was washing dishes, I looked out the window to see Jake and Stella returning from their walk. She carried a five-foot-long palm branch in her mouth, looking like
the proudest dog in the world. She loved picking up giant palm
branches on walks. She shredded them and frolicked with a
piece of it for a block or two until she lost interest. Jake let her
bring it through the gate, then had her drop it in the courtyard
before coming inside.

"She's obsessed with this one," he said. "She wouldn't leave
it behind."

Stella took a big drink of water and smiled. She turned the
corner to say "play," then walked over to the door to say, "outside."

"You want to play outside, Stella?" I said. I put Stella's
leash back on and took her to our courtyard. She immediately
pounced on the palm branch, bit it, and shook it back and forth.

She could have only told me "outside" to say that she wanted
to go back out. But she said more than that. She combined
"play" and "outside" to let us know specifically what she wanted
to do. She did not have to go to the bathroom, she did not want
to go for another walk, she wanted to keep playing with the
prized palm branch that she carried all the way home.

Stella's motivation to share her thoughts with us must have
been inherently strong. It was not even easy for her to put
words together. She had to push one button, walk across the
room or around the corner, then push another. Ease of access
to communication devices impacts use. I saw it firsthand with

Stella. Living in our apartment with all her buttons always only steps away was easier for her compared to living in a large house with her buttons spread everywhere. And I witnessed it at work. Some AAC systems require children to navigate through six or seven pages to find specific vocabulary words. When kids use devices that allow them to find every single word by pressing only two or three different icons, it is much easier for them to talk. I wondered how I could make this easier for Stella. Would she communicate even more if her buttons were all in the same place? Or would it be too difficult for her to differentiate between them?

I did not want her to have to walk across the apartment to communicate her entire thought to us. I briefly thought about moving all her buttons close to one another. Maybe I could dedicate one part of the living room to all her buttons. But we were leaving to go back to the Midwest for the holidays in a few weeks. It was not the right time to make any sort of big changes to her button setup. I wanted Stella to be able to communicate with ease while we were gone, and I wanted to be with her to see how she reacted to a new setup. This way I could support her learning and decide if I needed to make adjustments.

The week of Thanksgiving, I caught a terrible bug. The fever and loss of my voice kept me home in bed for an entire week. Stella lay right by me each day, all day long. She curled up in a ball and rested her head on my chest. Every so often she licked my face. This was strange for Stella. She never lay up on the top half of the bed, she almost always stayed near our feet.

On Monday, the worst day of my sickness, Stella did not

request anything from me. She did not ask to go outside or to play, she did not ask me to take her for a walk or go to the beach. She knew I was not going anywhere. She only hopped off the bed once in the middle of the day. I listened while she walked into the living room.

"Love you," she said.

Stella ran back into the bedroom and returned to my side.

"Thank you, Stella. I love you, too, girl."

Later that week, after I finished watching the last Netflix documentary to capture my interest, I sat up on my bed, and looked around at the blank walls. I had read all my books from the library, had watched everything remotely fascinating, and had no idea what to do for the rest of the day. I stared at Stella. *People need to know what she can say*, I thought. *What would happen if the world knew what she could do?*

I opened a blank document on my laptop. I had no idea what I was doing and had no plan for what I was going to write. But somehow it felt like my fingers knew exactly where to start.

Teaching My Dog to Talk, I typed at the top of the page. Looking at those words made me smile.

I had no idea who I was writing this for, or what I would do with it someday, or if I would even finish whatever I was starting. But thoughts were coming to me from all directions. I was remembering what I learned in graduate school, stories from being a speech therapist, reflecting on all that I had seen Stella accomplish so far. I wrote out questions that continuously popped into my head, and ideas for what more I could try with Stella. I typed and typed and typed.

Before I knew it, I had a new folder on my desktop filled with documents of ideas, questions, and explanations of our journey so far. Maybe someday I would write a really cool article about this experience that I could submit to a magazine. Or maybe I could be featured on someone's website or blog. All I knew was how excited I was to be reflecting on Stella's communication skills and thinking about how to share this story when the time was right.

TAKEAWAYS FOR TEACHING *YOUR* DOG

- **Model two-word phrases.** Help your dog learn to combine words by talking in short phrases, and using your dog's buttons as you talk. When your dog starts using single words frequently, be on the lookout for word combinations.

- **Program words that your dog reacts strongly to.** Are there any words that your dog waits around for you to say, or that you have to spell out so your dog doesn't overhear your plans? If your dog understands a word, give her a chance to be able to say it too!

- **Keep all words available for your dog to say.** If you can't say yes to what your dog is asking for, or if your dog is asking for the same thing over and over again, respond with "no," "all done," or "later" instead of taking your dog's buttons away. Give your dog a chance to learn boundaries, and how frequently to ask for something. It takes time to learn the social rules of language.

CHAPTER 13

Help!

———

The morning after we returned from Christmas in the Midwest, Jake and I prepared for a hike. As we packed our backpacks, Stella paced across the living room.

"Come come come come love you," Stella said. Her body language completely changed from being so happy since we reunited with her yesterday, to a concerned, nervous puppy, hoping her owners were not leaving her again. Her tail hid between her legs and she slouched next to the door. She was telling us she wanted to be able to come with us this time.

"Yes, Stella come! I love you, too. We're going for a hike. Jake, Christina, Stella walk."

Stella's tail wagged as I clipped her portable water dish onto my backpack. I scratched behind her ears and gave her a kiss. "We're not leaving you, don't worry, Stella girl."

I had missed her, too. We had not left her for more than a long weekend before. Jake and I logged into the doggy day care webcam every day while we were away to check and see how she was doing. It looked like she was having a blast playing with her dog friends, but I wondered if she was ever worried that we were not coming back. *Did she think about us or her home at all while we were away? Did she think she lived at day care now? Or did she just think about playing with all her new friends?*

Jake and I had spent the flight to San Diego brainstorming how we could arrange Stella's buttons to keep them all in one location. "What if I made a giant AAC device for her? I could get a poster board, set all the buttons down in rows. It would look kind of like the devices I use at work. And we could keep enough space in between the buttons for her to walk through them," I said. If all the buttons were on one board, we could move it to different rooms, or easily bring it with us when we traveled. And Stella would not have to relearn the button locations everywhere we went. They could actually always remain in the same place.

Changing AAC devices can be a challenging time. I have introduced multiple new setups to children, and each one of them had a different reaction. Some kids are intrigued by the new vocabulary available to them right away and start exploring it. Some kids throw the tablet against the wall out of frustration. Some kids switch back and forth between using their old device and their new device, figuring out which one serves them best. I wondered what Stella would do.

I worried, too . . . What if Stella lost all her progress? What if she would no longer be motivated to communicate with words because I made it too challenging for her? What if I had the intention of helping, but ended up taking away her ability to talk? What if this concept only worked by keeping buttons in separate locations for her to distinguish between? It was uncharted territory. The plan seemed sound on the plane ride, but now when I was back home seeing Stella talk so well with her current setup, I did not know if it was the right choice to try to change it all on her.

As a speech therapist, I never quite understood how difficult it would be for parents to hop on board with introducing a new AAC system to their child. I could only see the immense opportunities for learning and communication that it would open up. I expected parents to be thrilled by the potential. But most of the time, they were apprehensive and tentative. They had likely spent years with their current system and had already put so much mental energy into learning it. And they could see firsthand when challenges stressed their child out at home. This is why it is crucial to start out with a great system that will support the child's language growth for years to come. With kids, excellent devices exist where we can set them up for years of development from the beginning. They should not have to undergo major AAC changes. The big difference with Stella was that I did not know what her potential could be or where we were heading. We kept progressing step by step, testing, experimenting, and learning as we went.

I thought back to Oliver and how much language and communication he had access to after we upgraded his device. I could not just sit here and watch Stella continue to progress and not adapt. I had to try something new. I had to give her the chance to thrive. As Grace reminded me, "Worst-case scenario, you can always go back. Might as well give it a shot."

A couple of days later, I picked up a half-inch-thick tan, foam poster board from the store. It seemed thick enough to not slide around or rip, but certainly light enough to carry with ease. When I came home, Jake laid the board down in the dead space on the far side of our living room, a few steps away from the front door. I walked around our apartment, picking up all nine of Stella's buttons. Two of her buttons ("walk" and "bye") broke while we were gone, but two more boxes of buzzers were on the way to us. Stella stood in the middle of the living room, watching my every movement.

The board would fit fifteen buttons while still giving her room to walk between them. I figured that would be plenty of words for a while at least. I placed the buttons down in a three-by-three grid on the left side of the board, leaving space on the right side to add more words when our new buzzers arrived. Stella stood over the board, looking down at her new setup.

"Stella, look. They're your same words," I said. I pressed each one in a row while verbally saying the word again. Stella looked up to me, then ran away. She jumped on the couch and curled up in a ball. She looked stressed out already.

"Love you, Stella," I said while I pushed her "love you" button. "It's okay, girl." Stella jumped off the couch. She lowered her head, put her tail between her legs, and walked into the bedroom. She looked scared of the changes happening out in the living room.

For the rest of the night, I modeled the words. I went back to the frequency of modeling that I started with at the very beginning, repeating each word several times verbally and with her button in its new location. Even though Stella knew and used all these words, this was a relearning period. It reminded me of when I picked up Jake's phone and tried finding an app on it. Even though we had many of the same apps and all the icons looked identical, I had no idea where they were. Jake's organizational system on his phone was completely different from mine. I usually had to ask him where to find the app I was looking for or search the name of it.

Stella watched me from a few feet away, but never came close to the board. She would retreat to her bed, the couch, or to my feet, and keep looking up to me with her big, sad puppy eyes. Her world had just changed drastically. Something she used every single day looked completely different to her now. Her body language called out for love and support. I would give this a few days, then return back to her old setup if it didn't seem to be working out.

The next morning, I walked out of the bedroom with Stella. Normally she told us what she wanted on her own, but now I knew I would need to help her out. She walked straight to her dishes and pawed at the empty space where her "eat" button used to be. I watched as she then walked into the living room, over to her board of buttons, and started pawing at all of them. Each time she activated a word, she cocked her head to the side, and pushed it one or two more times. This is such an important step for AAC users. She was spending time exploring her words to figure out how they now worked.

When she pawed the "help" button once, she continued on to say, "help help help help help help." She asked for help like I would when I could not find something on Jake's phone. Stella hopped off the board and stared up at me.

"You need help, Stella? Here, girl." I sat on the floor to be at her level. I reached my hand to the top row to model "eat" three or four times. Stella wagged her tail, licked my face, and trotted over to her food bowl.

Once again, I saw how strong Stella's intrinsic motivation to communicate was. We all have two types of motivation:

intrinsic and *extrinsic*. Intrinsic motivation is the inner drive someone has to do a specific activity. Extrinsic motivation is the desire to do something for a reward. I was not giving Stella treats or any sort of reward besides the natural response to her communication when she explored her new board setup. Even though extrinsic rewards like treats may seem beneficial, research actually shows that providing external motivation can hinder long-term intrinsic motivation in humans.[32] Recent analyses in the areas of intrinsic and extrinsic motivation has shown that, "128 experiments lead to the conclusion that tangible rewards tend to have a substantially negative effect on intrinsic motivation. When institutions, families, schools, businesses, and athletic teams, for example, focus on the short-term and opt for controlling people's behavior, they do considerable long-term damage."[33]

The entire idea of intrinsic motivation was first discovered in primates who were more motivated to solve puzzles when there was no food reward attached to it. Monkeys who explored the puzzle purely for curiosity and fun consistently outperformed the primates who were given raisins as a reward.[34] I hypothesized that dogs would also have an overpowering intrinsic drive when given the chance to use it. Treats were certainly not everything to Stella.

Stella could have given up. She could have continued pawing at her food dish and water bowl. She could have stood by the door whining whenever she wanted to go outside. She could have nudged the collar she wears when we take her to the beach to let us know she wanted the beach. But she did not do that. Her communication skills had already grown so much beyond simply requesting actions. She was motivated on her own to figure out the new locations of her words, so she could use them again. She needed her words back to share all the thoughts she had about what was happening, what she noticed, and what was missing from her routines.

She was lying on the couch, shredding her plush parrot to pieces, leaving a mess of stuffing. Stella was stressed. This was the second toy she completely destroyed in the last two days. She had not played like this since she was much younger. It looked like she was taking her frustrations out through her play.

She was whining so much more, too. Earlier, I walked into the living room to see Stella standing helplessly by herself, lost and upset. I petted her and threw a ball for her, but she wouldn't settle down.

I hated seeing her so stressed out. I thought about putting her buttons back in their original locations many times throughout those first couple of days. Maybe she would not develop more advanced skills than what she had already showed. Maybe causing her to be so stressed out would not be worth it. But I reminded myself Stella might be able to communicate to her fullest potential. *One more day*, I thought, then I would return the buttons to their original spots.

On day three of the switch, there was hope. Stella showed me that this pursuit was worth our while. She walked to her board and pushed all her buttons again. When she landed on "help," she said it four more times.

"Help help help help." Stella walked to the spot next to the door where her "outside" button used to sit. She pawed the empty space, barked at me, then said "help help" again. I walked over to her board, modeled "outside," a few times, then took her out to go to the bathroom.

Later on, when Stella finished her water, she licked the empty bowl, pawed where her "water" button used to be, then walked across the apartment.

"Help," she said.

"Stella want help?" I walked to her board. "Water, water," I said verbally and with her button. Stella watched my foot closely like a curious student. She was eager to learn where each word was.

This pattern continued with nearly every word, several times over the course of a week. Sometimes Stella would say "help" over and over again without pawing at any of the previous button locations. When this happened, I sat down next to her board with her, and modeled all her words a few times in a row. It felt like the two of us entered our own bubble of communication together.

"Help," Stella said.

I started walking over to her board.

"Love you help." Stella wagged her tail as I approached.

"Love you, too, Stella. You need more help?" I started from the bottom and pushed each button while slowly saying each word. "Love you, play, outside . . ."

Stella wagged her tail, walked to the top of her board, and said "outside" for the first time on her new setup.

"Okay, let's go outside, Stella."

At this point, Stella's language skills, her problem-solving capabilities, and the awareness she had for when she needed our assistance were extraordinary. Stella's intelligence was on full display as, even in this overwhelming situation, she found a creative way to figure out her new setup. "Help" was never one of Stella's most frequently used words. But in this unfamiliar context, she used it over and over again to learn where all her words were.

Day by day, Stella became more comfortable with her buttons again. She spent time on her own pressing different buttons to see what would happen, and she paid close attention when Jake and I modeled her words. Unsurprisingly, Stella learned her favorite words the fastest. At the end of the first week with Stella's board, I stopped home for lunch in the middle of the day when one of my appointments canceled. Stella greeted me with her typical happy self.

"Beach beach beach beach beach," she said.

Maybe she did not mean that. Maybe she was still exploring her buttons, I thought. I rarely came home over lunch, so I was not sure if it would be normal for Stella to ask for the beach in the middle of a weekday. I was still chewing my sandwich and had not yet responded to her.

"Beach beach," she said again. Stella looked back to me. She walked over to the collar she wears on the dog beach, sniffed it, and looked up at me again.

She proved me wrong, and I could not have been happier.

"No beach now, Stella. Sorry, girl. Let's go outside though," I pushed "outside" with my foot a couple of times, then took her out to the courtyard with me. Of course she would learn "beach" again quickly.

Exactly one week after we switched her setup, Stella was talking just like she was before. Her use of each word matched how she typically said it before we moved her buttons. Seeing this consistency showed me that Stella had learned all the new word locations. In addition to being back to her typical chatty self, Stella started using her board almost as a home base. She brought her toys to it, dropped them on the empty space, sat on it, and licked it frequently. Now she sometimes chose to nap lying down on the floor with her head on her board. Before moving her buttons, she never hung out in this area of the apartment. Stella was taking ownership of her device. She knew it was for her and wanted to spend time near it.

Children reach this stage with their devices, too. When kids start taking more ownership and recognizing that the talker is theirs, they carry it around with them if they can, hug it, swat other people's hands away from it. It made me happy to see Stella wanting to spend time by her board and claiming it as hers. In one short week, Stella went from looking continuously stressed out and confused, to exploring words on her own and asking for help, to returning to her same communication patterns and choosing to spend time by her board. I wondered what the next week would bring.

Stella does not cope well with rain. It rarely comes to Southern California, but when it does, Stella is beside herself. When we try taking her out for walks, she runs back toward the door. She would only go to the bathroom under the stairs in our courtyard, where she could avoid becoming too wet. Rainy days meant that Stella would be bouncing off the walls in our apartment. Without taking long walks or running on the beach, she was an unstoppable force of energy. On the third straight day of rain, we had not been on a long walk or to the beach in days.

Stella let out a sharp, high-pitched bark that reverberated off the walls in our apartment. She marched over to her board.

"Beach no," she said. She stared at me, then barked again.

"Yes, Stella, we haven't been to the beach. No beach, it's raining."

Stella whined and looked out the window.

"Come on, girl, let's play with your toy!"

Stella sulked in front of the door.

"It's okay, Stella. Let's play!"

"No," she said. She whined again, then lay down with her head between her paws.

Stella had officially surpassed her previous language use. After a solid week of relearning, she started combining words nearly every time she talked. It must have been so much easier for her to create phrases now that she did not have to walk across the room right in the middle of her thought. She talked much more often and generated even more novel utterances.

Even though Stella knew where all her words were, her hind paws sometimes activated buttons when she walked through her board. Every time this happened, Stella dramatically turned back to look at her paw and back to me. It looked like she was trying to show me she did not mean to say that word. Over the first week, Stella experienced mis-hits like these almost every time she walked through her board. But now, they were starting to decrease as she adjusted and carefully stepped through the rows without bumping into buttons along the way. When given the chance and time to learn, Stella always thrived.

On day ten of her new setup, another rainy day, Stella reached a new milestone.

"Help beach love you," Stella said.

Jake ran out of the kitchen. "Was that her?" he asked.

"It sure was," I said. Stella just said two intentional words and a phrase in a row, when we had not been to the beach in a couple of days due to rain. The only other times Stella had

said three consecutive different words was when she was clearly
exploring buttons. But this time was different. She navigated
to each button so deliberately. And the phrase made sense for
the current circumstances. It was normal for Stella to say "help"
when she appeared desperate. And it was typical for Stella to
use "love you" almost like "please." Stella often added "love
you" to her request if we said "no" the first time.

While Jake and I were still in shock that our dog told us a
three-button phrase, Stella kept talking.

"Love you water," she said. Stella stood next to her beach
collar. Now Stella used "water" as another way to refer to the
beach. Stella found a different way to ask for the beach when
her desires still were not being met. This was an entirely new
level of complexity.

Those first ten days of Stella using her new board inspired
so much hope and encouragement. It furthered my belief that
we have to try new things to see new results. I wondered what
would have happened if I started teaching Stella words with
a setup like this from the very beginning. Every time Stella
reached a new level of word use, more questions and ideas
arose. Would she have combined words faster? Or would it
have taken her longer to learn because the words were not right
next to whatever she was asking for? It was impossible to know
what it would have been like if I had chosen to try this sooner,
or from the start. All I could do was keep progressing forward
one step at a time, observing patterns, asking questions, and
brainstorming solutions. Maybe someday I would have another
dog or someone else would try starting off with a full board of
words to compare learning speeds. Now that Stella excelled
with her new setup, I felt ready to fill up the rest of her board.

TAKEAWAYS FOR TEACHING *YOUR* DOG

- **Be prepared to support your dog if/when you need to change her device setup.** Even if your dog has been independently using words for a while, she will need help from you to reach that stage again with words in new locations.

- **Model words like crazy!** Model words as often as you did in the beginning, when you were introducing each one. The more your dog sees each word in use, the better chance she'll have to learn its new placement.

- **Make communication as easy as possible.** If you choose to keep all buttons on a single board, allow room for your dog to reach each word, walk around the board, or walk in between the rows.

- **Give your dog a chance to learn.** It can be tempting to revert to an old setup or to give up if you haven't seen progress within a couple of days. Adjusting and relearning can take time. Give it at least a week or two before reassessing.

- **Pay attention to your dog's communication patterns.** When your dog starts using words in similar ways to how she did before changing her setup, you'll know she has reached the same level and is ready to progress even further.

CHAPTER 14

Becoming Automatic

———

"Do you think Stella would say our names if she could?" I asked Jake. I sat on our couch staring at the two new boxes of Recordable Answer Buzzers. I already had a list of thirty potential words I was considering adding to Stella's board. But we only had room for six at the time. It was so hard for me to choose. I wanted her to be able to say all the words she possibly could. Once again, I asked myself, *What does Stella hear us say all the time? What words is she already understanding? What words will help her communicate about a variety of experiences?*

One of the first ways toddlers typically combine words is by saying a name with an action or object, like "Mommy drive," "Daddy ball."[35] Since Stella was combining words now, I wanted to give her the opportunity to create phrases that were developmentally appropriate for the skills she was demonstrating. Adding all our names could give Stella a chance to tell us who she wanted, or who she was talking to. I wondered if Stella ever thought about Jake or me when we were gone. Would she ask for one of us if we were not there? Or would she talk only about whoever was home at the time? Would she specify who she wanted to take her outside or for a walk? Would she use her own name to clarify when she wanted to do something rather than when she was commenting on what Jake and I were doing?

I recorded "Stella," "Jake," and "Christina," into three of the six new buttons.

I chose to use "Christina" and "Jake" rather than "Mom" and "Dad." Stella never heard the words *Mom* and *Dad*. Stella had been living with us for almost a year now and had heard us call each other by our names constantly. I also knew that she recognized and understood our different names. After work when I would tell her "Jake's coming," she would run to look out the window for his car. At the dog beach, Jake would tell Stella "go look for Christina." Stella would run around until she found me. We also typically narrated what we were doing with Stella and included our names. Phrases such as "Stella Jake walk" or "Stella Christina play outside" were common for us.

I replaced the "bye" and "walk" buttons that had broken a couple of weeks ago, which meant there was only room for one more word at the time. With her current vocabulary, Stella could tell us what she wanted to do, where she wanted to go, request assistance, protest "no." But she did not have a way to let us know when she liked something we were doing. "We tell her when she's being good all the time. She should have a way to tell us when we're being good in her eyes, too," I said to Jake. I programmed "good" into the sixth button.

Looking down at Stella's words, I thought back to my graduate school AAC class. We had to create communication boards with only nine or twelve words available, then actually try communicating with them instead of using verbal speech. We would know if we selected effective words if we could use the board while interacting with others. If we were repeatedly at a loss for words, we knew that we needed to make changes to it. Now, I spent time by myself testing out how to say common phrases I used on Stella's board. "Good Stella," "Stella play outside," "Christina help Stella," "Jake Christina eat," "Love you Stella," "No beach. Walk," I practiced with my right foot. So far, so good. There were so many functional phrases I could say now.

When communication partners are familiar with the locations of words on the learner's device, they are able to model vocabulary much more efficiently. By practicing now, I was already creating my motor plans so I could model quickly without scanning her board each time I talked to Stella. I learned the importance of this and how fast I could learn the locations of each word after I attended a training for the Language Acquisition through Motor Planning (LAMP) therapy approach. At the workshop, the presenters directed us to say a new word on a communication device five times in a row. The communication devices we used had thousands of words, not only fifteen like Stella's board. After we said the word a few times in a row, they prompted us to close our eyes and try saying the same word again. We could still say the word, or be centimeters off it, with our eyes closed. This was possible because we had all developed the motor plan for where the word was located. Again, this is what happens when we keep word locations in the same place; we become automatic in finding them. Motor planning is not only used in typing or saying words with communication devices. We all motor plan throughout most of our activities, and we don't even realize what our brains and bodies are doing. When we tie our shoes, shift the gears while driving, grab a fork out of the silverware tray without looking, perform a choreographed dance routine, or play an instrument, our bodies are acting automatically after learning the movements from repetition.

"Stella come play," I modeled.

Stella trotted into the living room.

"Stella Christina play," I said before throwing her ball across the room.

Now that Stella was combining two words commonly and three words occasionally, I modeled three- and four-word phrases as much as I could. I talked in these short utterances to Stella and also added on to her words when she said a one- or two-word phrase. This is a common language facilitation technique called "expansions."[36] If Stella said "eat," I responded by saying "Stella eat," or "Jake Christina eat." If Stella said, "Come outside," I responded by saying "Christina come outside" or "come outside play." Providing these expansions of Stella's utterances reinforced what she said and also showed her examples of which other words she could add to her phrases in the future. If every time Stella said "outside," I responded with "Stella outside," it would be more difficult for her to learn that she could pair "outside" with other words to say phrases like "outside good," "play outside," "walk outside," "no outside." I varied my responses as much as possible to help Stella understand how she could use words in many different ways.

On the day that I added Stella's six new words, she continued using her original nine buttons consistently before she started exploring the additions. At first, it seemed like she did not care that her board was filled up. Including more words did not change her usage at all. I was happy to see that we could increase her number of buttons without impacting Stella's motor plans of the original words. That is a hallmark of a functional device setup. If Stella had to relearn how to say words every time we increased her vocabulary size, she would be spending all her mental energy on relearning rather than expanding her current communication.

Stella ran to her board and pawed around at her new buttons, hitting three or four in a row without any pause time in between. She cocked her head to the left and right as she listened to the word each button said. She was babbling on her device. All communicators need time to babble and explore. The only way for AAC users to learn how to use their words appropriately is to start out by pushing random buttons on their devices. They need to hear what each word says and observe what happens around them. So if it looks like an AAC user is "just pushing random buttons," that's completely normal and is actually a great indicator that they are on their way to learning how to say those words appropriately.

"Stella Stella Stella Stella Stella," Jake and I heard from the living room.

I peeked around the corner. Stella stared down at her board. She repeatedly lifted her paw up and pushed it back down. "She's learning how to say her name," I said and smiled.

"Good Stella," I modeled. "Love you Stella."

Stella wagged her tail.

Stella explored her own name first before any of the other new words I added. It was a similar reaction to when she discovered she could say "walk" and "beach." She had the power to say the name she heard us call a hundred times per day. "Stella" was likely the single word she heard Jake and I say the most often. It made perfect sense to me that she would be so quick to say it. Toddlers start referring to themselves by their own names around twenty-one to twenty-four months old when they are consistently saying two-word phrases and occasionally using three-word phrases.[37] Stella demonstrated similar patterns at this time.

"Good bye walk Christina," Stella explored with her right paw. She frantically pawed at different buttons, testing out her different words. She walked through the rows to the left side and hit "Jake Christina" with her back paw accidentally. Stella hopped off her board as soon as she heard words she was not expecting. She circled around her device twice, then walked through it again to say, "outside." Stella continued walking to the door, then looked up to me.

"Stella Christina outside," I modeled. "Let's go!"

For the first time in Stella's learning, I could see a clear divide in her skills. Stella knew the left half of the board well. Those nine words had been with her for months, she had relearned their new locations quickly, and she continued using them every day in unique ways. When she marched up to the left side of the board, she pawed each button with such conviction. She often even looked up to me as she was pawing a button because she did not need to visually scan her board anymore. She looked as automatic as a fluent typist writing a paper.

But the right half of the board was new to Stella. Sometimes her paw slipped off a button as she tried to activate it.

She pushed several buttons in a row, searching for the one she wanted. Her back paws kept activating words unintentionally. I knew exactly what was happening. Stella was at different stages of motor learning for different words on her device.

There are three stages to motor learning. The first is called the *cognitive stage* "marked by highly variable performance. The learner may or may not know what he is doing wrong or how to correct his performance and will need assistance." The second stage is called the *associative stage* where "the learner works on refining his skill. He is more accurate with his responses but occasionally makes errors." The last stage is the *autonomous stage* where "conscious thought is no longer needed. The learner is able to perform the action without assistance and often times while being able to divide attention between tasks."[38] Stella was in the autonomous stage for all her original words. But with her six new buttons, she was still in the first stage of motor learning.

Even though I knew Stella understood all the words I added, she still had to learn how to use them herself. Imagine how it would feel to only have access to the left side of the keyboard when you were learning to type. Then, after you mastered it, the right side of the keyboard became accessible. Even though you know the entire alphabet and how to use each letter, you still have to learn the motor plan for how and when to use the right side of the keyboard. It takes time and practice to move through each stage of motor learning.

While Stella was still in the middle of learning how to use her new words, my sister Sarah and her husband, Stephen, visited us in San Diego over a long weekend. I could not wait to show them the board we had set up for Stella, whom they had not seen since before we moved.

Stella thrived with visitors, soaking up all the attention she could. She wiggled her body like crazy, rolled over for belly rubs at their feet, and smiled constantly when Sarah and Stephen first came over. When they sat on our couch, Stella hopped up in between them so they could take turns petting her and scratching behind her ears.

Suddenly, Stella jumped down from the couch. She walked across the living room and stopped in front of her board.

"Love you," Stella said. She walked back to the couch, staring at Sarah and Stephen, wagging her tail. Stella hopped right back up on the couch in between them.

"Oh my gosh, I think she was talking to us," Sarah said. "We love you, too, Stella."

Stella's ears went straight back against her head. She attempted licking each of their faces. She stayed right there, between Sarah and Stephen, looking happy as could be.

"That's the first time she's ever said 'love you' to someone besides us," I said. "You should feel honored."

Stella was perfectly content with all the attention Sarah and Stephen were giving her. She did not need to say anything to receive what she wanted, but she left the couch anyway to walk across the room to let Sarah and Stephen know how much she cared for them. She literally went out of her way to tell them "love you."

She was also clear in her communication. She did not have a word for anyone besides Jake and me, but she used a word in combination with her eye contact and again joining them to specify she was addressing them. Stella did not limit herself to the words she had available. She combined words with gestures to convey even more specific meanings.

Parents often ask me how I can tell if their toddler is saying a word, or just babbling. It can be tricky to know if sounds are random, or meaningful. According to Dr. Erika Hoff, the director of the Language Development Lab at Florida Atlantic University, a word is "a sound sequence that symbolizes meaning and can stand alone."[39] This means sounds or gestures become official words when the child attaches consistent meanings to them. In determining if a sound or gesture can be considered a word, what's happening around the child is equally as important as what the child said. For example, if a baby said "ba" constantly throughout the day, or randomly, it would not be considered a word. I would say he is babbling or exploring sounds. But if the baby said "ba" every time he played with a ball or pointed to a ball, *ba* would be considered his word for "ball" because there is meaning attached to it. The same reasoning applies to AAC users. When AAC users start saying a word relevant to the context, in multiple scenarios, they are demonstrating their proficiency.

About a week after we filled Stella's board, she started using her new vocabulary in appropriate situations. One weekday morning, when Jake woke up earlier than usual, he took Stella on a much longer walk than they normally took before work. When they returned, Stella walked inside, panting and smiling. As soon as Jake unclipped her leash, she walked over to her board. Instead of trying out different words, she stared down at her array of buttons for a moment, like she was figuring out how to say her thought. Stella stepped forward onto the bottom row of her board with her left paw. She lifted her right paw.

"Good Jake," she said.

"Aww," I said.

"Good Jake walk?" he said. "Love you, Stella."

Stella plopped on the floor, continuing to smile and pant.

Later that morning, I left for work before Jake did. He texted me about five minutes after I had gone. She said "Christina bye" and stared out the window!!!

That was twice in a row that Stella had used our names in such specific ways. I was beginning to learn the answers to some of my questions. Stella did indeed use our names, and she did think about us even when we were not home with her. I was eager to come home at the end of the day and see if Stella would say any more of her new words.

Even when we were out of the apartment, I noticed how intelligent and aware Stella was of her environment. That afternoon, I took Stella to Fiesta Island, a massive dog park with miles of beach and large grassy areas. Stella and I were about a fifteen-minute walk from our car when I felt a couple of raindrops. I looked up to see a dark gray cloud passing right over us. I had not brought a jacket or an umbrella, and there were no trees in sight. I picked up the pace. About a minute later, it completely downpoured. The ground became slick with mud, so I could not run without being at serious risk for wiping out. Stella, meanwhile, was sprinting ahead, leaving me behind. Where the heck was she going? She never ran away this quickly unless she was chasing something.

Stella ran up to a woman about thirty feet away who was walking under an umbrella. Stella carried on walking right under it, keeping dry. The woman stopped and turned around to see where Stella had come from. She waved and waited for me to catch up to them.

"I can't believe she ran all the way over here to stand under an umbrella . . . that's one smart dog you have," she said, laughing.

A few nights later, Stella walked over to her board. "Outside," she said immediately.

I stayed silent. I wondered if she would add any more words to her thought. Stella walked all the way around the top of her board to the opposite corner.

"Stella Stella Stella Stella," she said.

I could tell she was not done. She kept her head down and walked to the bottom of her board.

"Walk," she added.

Stella pawed at the door. "Come outside," she said.

Stella looked up to me and whined, which usually indicated that she had completed her message.

"Okay, come on, girl, let's go outside for a walk," I said.

In total Stella said, "Outside Stella Stella Stella Stella walk come outside." She combined nearly all the words she had available to her that related to going outside for a walk. She said four different words, and eight total words. She even used her gesture of pawing at the door in the middle of her phrase to add to her message, which confirmed that the words she was saying were intentional. This was an entirely new level. She was not only saying one or two words at a time now. She flawlessly used every single form of communication and applicable word available to tell me what she wanted. This happened all the time at work with AAC users. It was so common to see kids say something like "all done no stop off finished bye" when they wanted to be done with an activity. They selected every single word that could convey their meaning to make sure they were understood. I wondered if this happened frequently because many of these children were so used to being misunderstood. Stella said her message loud and clear.

The next morning, Stella hopped off the bed and trotted to the living room.

"Outside," she said.

Jake and I were still tucked in bed, not quite ready to get up yet.

"Stella come," Jake said.

It was quiet for about ten seconds.

"Stella bye," she said.

Jake and I laughed.

"Christina can you take her?" he asked.

It was quiet again.

"Jake," Stella said.

I burst into laughter. "She called you out! You have to go take her outside." Jake rolled his eyes and laughed. He found Stella by the door waiting for him.

Stella had officially progressed to a level far beyond what I ever thought was possible. We had a real conversation, across the apartment, with our one-year-old dog. In the past two days, Stella's extraordinary communication events reawakened the desire I had to share my work. I could not believe that something this revolutionary was happening in my home, yet nobody else knew about it. I wanted to find the right way to introduce this concept to the world so that others could teach their dogs and catch a glimpse of the intelligent and complex thinkers that our pets actually are.

After work, I revisited what I had been writing about Stella when I was home sick the week of Thanksgiving. I picked up where I left off and added more information about her communication advancements since then. I called my best friend from graduate school, Sarah, who also loves AAC.

"I've decided I want to start a blog about this whole experience," I said. "I have no idea how I'm going to do it, but the world needs to know what Stella is saying. Can you help me think of a good name? Maybe something to do with Stella?"

"This is going to be bigger than Stella someday," Sarah said. "What about something with your last name? Like . . . Hunger for Words?"

I knew it as soon as she said it. That had to be it.

TAKEAWAYS FOR TEACHING *YOUR* DOG

- **Add names and other nouns.** This can help your dog communicate more specific messages.

- **Test out your dog's vocabulary.** Spend time using your dog's buttons to try saying the common words and phrases you use. If you're able to use her buttons to say a variety of common phrases, that indicates a solid vocabulary selection.

- **Model three- and four-word phrases.** When your dog starts combining words, keep modeling the next level up. A good rule of thumb is to add one word to whatever your dog said. This helps expand length of utterance.

- **Use the stages of motor learning to help you.** Know that it's possible for your dog to be in the beginning stages of motor learning with some words, and automatic with others. Keep modeling and providing cues for the words that your dog is still learning how to say independently and automatically.

- **Give wait time.** When your dog has shown that she is capable of combining words, give her time to do so. Instead of reacting right away to a single word, wait five to ten seconds to see if she will add to her message. Communicating with AAC takes time. Give your dog a chance to finish her whole thought.

CHAPTER 15

Hunger for Words

———

On my flight from San Diego to Indianapolis for my niece's birthday party, I settled into my seat, expecting my book and music to entertain me for the trip. Instead, I talked to a stranger about my work with Stella, in great detail, for the first time. A friendly, young woman with curly hair and a bright smile sat next to me.

"What's something you're really passionate about? What do you spend your spare time on?" she asked. I could tell this was going to be a great flight. I would much rather engage in a deep conversation than keep to myself for the whole trip. Her warmth and enthusiasm clued me in that she would be receptive to what I was about to tell her.

"I love that question! Well . . . I'm so passionate about speech therapy that I figured out a way to teach my dog how to talk," I said.

Her face froze. I am sure that was the last thing she was expecting me to say. "Here, I'll show you some videos." I explained the concept of AAC and my work as a speech therapist while I rummaged through my bag for my phone. I swiped through several videos of Stella combining words to tell me she wanted to play at the beach, take a walk outside, or wanted to eat.

The two of us spent the rest of the flight brainstorming how I could share my information. She read the articles I had started writing and gave me feedback. On the back of her airline ticket, she wrote down a list of companies and organizations she thought would be interested in this concept of talking dogs. I spent hours with a complete stranger, sharing how excited I was about Stella's communication, where it could go in the future, and how different society would be if we knew our dogs could talk to us. And the concept captivated her enough to spend the duration of the flight brainstorming and dreaming with me.

This was my passion. I wanted so badly to share this information with the world and introduce what was possible. I could not stop thinking about it. I wanted to connect with other professionals who could help me take what I was doing to the next level. I felt like I was walking around with this giant secret, knowing a potential in dogs and a power of speech therapy that others were not aware of yet.

Throughout the spring of 2019, I spent my weekends and evenings figuring out how to create a website. The task sounded easy. People made websites all the time. Surely, if they could do it, I could do it. But I quickly found out it was not easy. Besides creating the actual content that would appear on the website, it required decision after decision about layout, color schemes, font choice, and formatting. And it required competency in a website builder platform, search engine optimization, and a whole host of concepts that sounded like a foreign language to me. I had absolutely no background in any of these areas. I knew my website would not be perfect on my first attempt, but I wanted it to be taken seriously. To me, this was more than a fun side project now. It was my opportunity to introduce a new idea to the world with my professional reputation behind it.

After several weekends spent at my computer, attempting to put something functional and presentable together, I made my blog, www.hungerforwords.com, live on April 25. It had two blog posts, "Teaching My Dog to Talk," which gave an overview of the process from the start of my idea through Stella combining words, and "Stella's Buttons" about the words I chose to teach Stella, several videos dating back to her first words, information about me, and information about Stella. It was simple, colorful, functional, and the first time I had ever created something like this on my own. About one year ago, Stella said her first word. And now, here I was, living in a totally different part of the country, launching a website about her communication skills. So much can change in twelve months' time. I was excited to have a space to share information and inspire myself to keep pursuing this journey. Even though I knew nobody was aware of my blog yet, it still helped me feel a sense of legitimacy and responsibility. This was my vision. I was responsible for bringing it to light and sharing my observations with the world.

First, I only shared my blog with people I knew. I emailed it to my family, friends, professors and supervisors from graduate school, current and former coworkers. Seeing their enthusiastic reactions helped me work up the courage to share it with a slightly wider net of people, the speech-language pathology Facebook community. I had not been on social media in months. Ever since I deleted the apps from my phone before moving to California, I never looked back. I felt so free without social media overtaking my spare moments and time to think. I was hesitant to log in again. I did not want to slip into old habits. But my desire to share Stella's story and the power of AAC was far greater than my fear of becoming addicted to social media again.

A week after the website launch, I posted the link in a couple of SLP Facebook groups with thousands of members in each of them. I had never posted in one of these groups before. I figured this would be a great starting point to gauge reactions. If anyone should understand and appreciate what I was doing, it would probably be the speech therapy community. It was a safe way for me to test the waters and see how others would perceive my work.

"Dogs can use AAC too!" I wrote. "Check out my website to see how my dog, Stella, is saying words." A picture of Stella lying down next to her buttons, smiling, accompanied the caption.

I sat across our dining table with Jake when I clicked "post." I didn't know what to expect. "I hope at least a few people see it," I said. "There are so many posts in these groups. Things can become buried."

"I don't think you have anything to worry about," Jake said. "Look." He turned my laptop screen toward me. In a matter of minutes, hundreds of "likes" and comments swarmed my post.

Over the course of the night, other speech therapists started sharing my link on their own personal pages. A couple of large speech therapy accounts with tens of thousands of followers shared it to their social media platforms. People were signing up to receive blog updates. A community of people interested in my project was forming. The interest was officially there and spreading.

Stella started to learn when to ask for "beach." She used to ask to go constantly, morning, afternoon, and night. But we could never go to the beach in the mornings and make it back in time to go to work. It was the same with my lunch breaks. I could never say yes to taking her if she asked when I stopped home in between clients. The only times we ever could honor her request were after work and after dinner. Stella started adjusting her communication when she realized these patterns. In the mornings and afternoons, she stuck with saying "outside" or "walk." At the end of the day, she would request the beach. As she learned our routines, she adapted.

Every week it seemed like Stella was surpassing the skills she demonstrated the week prior. Three-word combinations became frequent instead of occasional. Stella was averaging approximately thirty different utterances per day, even when we were only home for a couple of hours in the morning and a few hours at night. Something undeniably special was happening and the scientist in me took over. It was time to track and document her progress more thoroughly. Jake and I created charts that we hung on the walls to mark every time she said a word. We recorded stories of her communication, including the context of what was happening at the time, so it would be meaningful to us later on. I jotted down questions I had about her progress and tracked days of her language samples to look for patterns and assess her skills. We took videos with our phones and experimented with having a GoPro camera set up in our living room to catch everything Stella said. We spent hours combing through video footage, splitting clips, and storing them on our computers. I continued writing blog posts about Stella's communication and practicing words with her. In the middle of my speech therapy sessions with toddlers during the day, epiphanies popped into my head about what Stella had possibly been trying to communicate earlier. When I was at home working with Stella in the evenings, I remembered situations from the workday that led me to try new concepts with her. Could she answer simple questions? Could she make choices if I gave her two options? What if I asked, "Stella want play or Stella want walk?" Would she answer with "play" or "walk"? Could she understand the difference in my intonation when asking a question in comparison to telling her what we were doing? There was still so much to discover.

It was a busy time, so Jake and I decided to take a vacation. Since she was too big to fly, Stella stayed with a dog sitter in San Diego for the week. When we met the young woman a few days before dropping Stella off, I listed what we would make sure to bring.

"We'll have her kennel and bed, and her favorite blanket, oh and . . . Stella also has a communication device with buttons on it that she uses to say what she wants," I said.

She frowned. "Okay, yeah, there's plenty of room here for all that."

A few days later, I showed up on her doorstep again, this time holding Stella's leash in one hand and her board of buttons in the other.

"So this is her device," I said. "Stella will tell you what she wants and what she's thinking." I pushed down on a few buttons to show the sitter how it worked.

"Oh . . . wow, okay . . ." she said, scratching her head.

"It should be really convenient. She'll let you know if she's hungry or if she needs to go outside, or where she wants to go." The sitter nodded along while I rambled on about all the things Stella tells us every day.

"Bye, Stella," I said. "Love you, girl. Jake and I will come back soon. Have fun!" I kissed her head and headed out the door. It was so hard to leave her. I hoped she would be happy and feel comfortable while we were gone.

Ten minutes after I left, my phone lit up with a text from the dog sitter: Okay, I'm really spooked . . . Stella just said "Christina bye" . . . I laughed to myself. I wish I could have been there to see the sitter's face in person when Stella marched over to say that I had left. I was glad to hear that Stella was already using her words.

While we were away, we received a video of Stella playing on the dog beach. She kept saying beach, so I figured we had to take her, the sitter texted. We also learned that on the first night of her stay, Stella said "outside" in the middle of the night. The dog sitter heard her from her bed but did not get up. Stella said "outside" a couple more times before she went to the bathroom next to the door. As soon as that happened, I realized she really meant what she was saying, the sitter wrote. That accident was completely my fault.

On the last day of her stay, the sitter packed up Stella's bed, toys, and dishes. Stella watched her compile her belongings, then said "Jake Christina." Apparently, when the sitter told her, "Yes, Jake and Christina are coming back!" Stella waited by the door until we arrived ten minutes later. I wonder if Stella understood her words or had learned that pattern from staying with our friends in the past. They usually packed up her things right before the two of us came back to pick her up. Regardless, Stella's words helped her navigate the situation of staying somewhere new without us. She let the dog sitter know when she realized I was gone. She was still able to communicate all her typical wants and needs. And, with the buttons sticking to her board, she did not have to get used to a new layout or figure out which word was which in a new location. She could carry on, communicating as usual to new people in new places. This all mattered, especially since it had become really hard for Jake and me to leave Stella. She was more like a child than a pet to us. She had her own voice, and thoughts, and had become such an important part of our lives. It comforted me to know that Stella had the ability to voice her thoughts when we were not there.

Back home, I decided to upgrade further, to a larger board. Stella had learned the words on her current device and used all fifteen of them appropriately and frequently. As I've said, when possible, AAC users should always have access to more words than they know how to use. The only way to learn new words is to have access to saying them.

Jake and I took Stella to Home Depot where we picked out a piece of plywood a little over twice the size of her current poster board. Jake measured everything out. "It would fit thirty-two total buttons. I don't know if we'll get to that point but at least we could," he said. Stella trotted next to us, galloping toward any person she saw with a friendly face.

When we returned home, we arranged Stella's fifteen buttons on the larger board, starting again from the top left corner and keeping all her words in the same order. This board was longer and wider. It could fit a fourth row of words on the bottom. I consulted the list I made the last time I expanded Stella's device and selected the six that I thought would be the most impactful and meaningful for her: *want, look, park, happy, mad, bed.*

Jake and I frequently asked Stella "What do you want?" So I know she heard the word *want* often. I unintentionally verbally modeled "want" all the time whenever Stella made a request. When Stella said, "eat," I responded, "Stella want eat?" When she said "beach," I said, "You want beach?" Now I could model these phrases while using her buttons for each word. *Want* is an excellent core word that can apply to many different objects, actions, and people. If Stella learned how to say the word *want*, she could also combine that with a gesture to tell me what she wanted instead of taking up room on her device for several specific toys or activities.

One of Stella's favorite indoor activities was looking out the windows. Whenever I opened the shades for her, I narrated what Stella was doing by saying, "Stella look outside." I wanted to give Stella the chance to talk about looking outside or let us know that she wanted the blinds open. I also said "Stella look" anytime I pointed something out to her. Stella would follow my point and look to whatever I was trying to show her. Research shows that puppies as young as six weeks old respond to human social gestures such as pointing.[40] Maybe Stella would use "look" to point things out to me, too.

Stella and I started adding trips to the local dog park into our mix of evening activities. If I said the word *park*, she ran to the door. She loved running around with her dog friends and teasing them to chase the stick dangling out of her mouth. Since we usually went at the same time of day, we ran into the same people and dogs all the time. Stella greeted everyone happily, and sometimes I wondered if she wanted to see her human friends more than her dog friends.

Stella demonstrated plenty of gestures that indicated if she was happy or upset. When she was happy, she wagged her tail, her ears went back against her head, she jumped around in circles, and she smiled. When she was upset, she barked at us, sighed, turned away, or walked into the other room. Since she was expressing such clear gestures about how she was feeling, I wanted to give Stella the opportunity to tell us more about her emotions.

Every day, we pulled Stella's bed to a variety of locations in the apartment. She liked when we set it under the coffee table for her, by the window, or at the foot of our bed. She often stood where she wanted her bed and whined or barked at us. Once again, since she was already vocalizing and gesturing about this concept, I figured she would have success with using the word *bed* to talk about what she wanted.

I lined up the six new words on the bottom row of Stella's new board. Jake and I added labels under each word like we had on her smaller board. The labels helped visitors and people like the dog sitter identify buttons if they wanted to talk to Stella using them. We decided we would wait to Velcro the buttons down to the board until we knew for sure we were keeping this size. I kept the original poster board between the wall and the desk in case Stella did not do well with the bigger board.

"Look, Stella," I said, modeling with her buttons. "Come look."

Stella walked back and forth through her new board a couple

of times. She sniffed it, looked at me, then walked over to my desk. She started pawing at her old board.

"Want," I modeled.

I pulled her old board out and laid it down on the ground. Would she paw at the spaces where the buttons used to be, to show me which word she wanted to say? Or was she trying to tell me to put her buttons back on this board? Neither, actually. She lay down, sprawled across her old board. She stayed there for the rest of the afternoon. That board was Stella's. She was physically hanging on to it, stopping us from putting it away or throwing it out. She seemed reluctant to let it go, like she needed transition time before she could start making the new board hers.

Once again, I thought back to children switching communication devices. It must be so hard for them to let go of a device that had been their voice for years and try learning a new system. We all need support in times of transition, especially when dealing with something so personal as one's method of communication.

When Stella stood up from her old board, I modeled all Stella's words for her, showing her that all the same words were still there, in their same locations. I modeled the new row of buttons for her as she watched and listened to each word. The transition to this new board looked like it was off to a much better start than before. She did not retreat to the couch or bed like she had the first time we placed all her buttons on a board. She watched me and actually stepped right up to test it out.

"Want," Stella said. She continued walking up the board. "Outside."

"Stella want outside? Okay, let's go outside."

Stella picked up on "want" incredibly quickly. From this very first attempt using it, she continued pairing "want" with her requests to go outside, play, eat, go to the beach. Since Stella had heard us say "want" so frequently, and since Stella already had such strong abilities to combine words, she could incorporate "want" into her vocabulary seamlessly.

Stella walked back inside smiling. "Stella happy," I modeled. "Happy happy." Stella continued smiling and plopped down on her bed. "Stella bed," I modeled. "Love you, Stella." Stella's tail wagged.

Over the next couple of weeks, Jake and I modeled Stella's new words. Before I took Stella to the dog park, I said "park." Every time Stella lay on her bed or on our bed, I modeled "bed." If Stella requested going to the beach when we could not take her, I modeled "mad" when she whined at us. I modeled "look" every time I pointed at one of Stella's toys, or whenever Stella was looking out the window. Stella continued using her old words and started incorporating her new vocabulary into her phrases more and more each day.

Almost every night, Stella let us know when she was heading to bed. Jake and I would be in the living room talking or reading. Stella would say, "bed," then walk past us into the bedroom to fall asleep. And when Jake went out of town for a few days, Stella said, "Jake no bed," before she hopped up on his side of the bed and slept there for the night. If the door to the bedroom door was closed, she would say "bed" or "help bed," then try pawing it open. The word *bed* became instrumental in my awareness that Stella was trying to communicate a sequence of activities to us. She would wake up in the morning, say "bed eat" or "bed outside." In other words, "I'm done sleeping, now I want to eat." She eventually added three words to the sequence to say phrases like "bed eat outside" or "bed outside eat." Or she would come in from me taking her out first thing in the morning then say, "bed outside eat," letting me know all the steps of her morning routine, spontaneously.

Every time I add new words to Stella's board, she exceeds my expectations in many ways. I may think of a few reasons why it would be a good idea to include a certain word, then picture a few different scenarios where I could see it being helpful. But Stella uses words in ways I would not have thought of or combines them to create such unique phrases. This is further proof to me to not direct Stella what to say when. When I focus on modeling words in a variety of contexts, she learns the meanings of them and decides how to use them for herself. She does not need me telling her exactly what to say when. If anything, that stunts her growth more than it helps it.

Stella commented on unique situations that happened in our apartment that I never could have anticipated when I first imagined how she would use words to communicate. One day, our neighbors were dog sitting. When Stella saw them walk past the window with an unfamiliar dog, she barked, said "help no help" and ran to the window to bark again. Stella recognized that our neighbors were bringing a stranger into our complex. She did not bark when they walked with their own dog into their unit. I wondered if Stella was using her words to tell us why she was barking.

Stella's social use of words continued to grow with her vocabulary skills. She started repeating herself if we did not respond to her. One morning, she said, "come come outside." When Jake and I continued our conversation and did not stop to respond to Stella, she repeated "come come outside" and stared at us. I wondered if she learned to do this by observing us repeat a question to Stella if she did not respond. This is such a strong social skill. Stella had the awareness that she said something, we did not respond to it, so maybe she should try again.

Jake and I sat at our table, eating dinner after work. Jake was in the middle of telling me a story when we heard, "Beach eat come eat come," from the living room.

"Yes, we'll go to the beach after we eat, Stella. Eat now, beach later," I said.

"Come come come come," Stella said.

"Just wait a little bit longer, Stella."

Stella stayed by the door, monitoring our meal progress from afar. As soon as we took our dishes over to the sink, she wagged her tail and waited by the door for us. When we came back from the beach, she walked inside and said, "Bye Stella bye good outside." She was using her words to comment on what she just did, not what was happening now or what she wanted.

The next day, I took Stella to the dog park after work. She played with her favorite friends, two Rottweilers who always engaged in tug-of-war with a stick for as long as Stella liked. By the time we came home from the park, Jake was already back from work. Stella ran inside, greeted him, then said, "park play." *Is she trying to tell Jake that was where we were?* I wondered. *Is she trying to share a story about playing at the park, but she doesn't have any more vocabulary to use? Is she saying she wants to go back to the park?* This situation was coming up more and more. I knew we needed a way for Stella to distinguish between something she just did and something that she wanted to do.

TAKEAWAYS FOR TEACHING *YOUR* DOG

- **Give your dog transition time to adjust to a new board.** Even if the words are all staying in the same relative locations, your dog may need time to adjust to a new board. You can make it easier on her by keeping her old board nearby for a little while until your dog claims the new one.

- **Model emotion words when you see your dog exhibiting the emotion.** When your dog is smiling, wagging her tail, jumping in circles, or playing at her favorite place, use these opportunities to model the word *happy*. When you can tell your dog is frustrated or upset, use these times to model the word *mad*.

- **Avoid telling your dog when to say certain words.** Constantly telling your dog "say outside" or "say good" will teach your dog to say what *you* tell them to say, not to use the buttons for what they are thinking. We are teaching our dogs how to use words, not training them to talk on command. Modeling and naturalistic cues are most effective.

CHAPTER 16

Language Explosion

————

"Stella bye play," Stella said. Jake and I were eating dinner. Stella stood next to her buttons, staring straight at us.

"We're going to eat now, Stella. We'll play later," Jake said.

Stella sighed and whined. "Eat eat park."

"Yes, we're eating now, then we can go to the park," Jake said.

Stella lay down in front of the door.

Stella desperately needed a way to communicate about time concepts. Sharing these little sequences of what we were doing now and what Stella wanted to do next were daily occurrences.

The next day, I added *all done*, *now*, *later*, to Stella's board. I modeled *now* right before or during an activity. I would say, "Play now" as she was playing, "eat now" when she was already eating, "park now" when I put her leash on and grabbed her ball. I used *later* to talk about anything happening later than the next ten minutes. I modeled *all done* when Stella finished any activity. Saying "all done eat" when she was finished eating, "all done water" when she stopped drinking water, "all done play" when she dropped her toy to lie down, and "all done park" when we came home from the park all helped Stella understand that *all done* meant the conclusion of something. Even though I just added these three words, I had always used them in my natural vocabulary when I talked to Stella. Stella was no stranger to these words; this was just the first time she had the chance to use them as well.

The combination of time concepts and two emotion words, *happy* and *mad*, caused another language explosion. After only a few days of modeling *all done*, *now*, and *later* whenever possible, Stella started incorporating these concepts into her own phrases.

One evening, I started vacuuming our apartment, which she always hated. She typically ran into the other room and peeked her head around the corner to watch me carefully from a distance. Or she stood on the couch or bed while looking down at the vacuum to stay out of its way. This time, after I was vacuuming the living room for about three or four minutes, Stella ran from the bedroom over to her board. She sped right past me, barely making eye contact with me and avoiding the vacuum.

"All done all done," she said.

I turned the vacuum off.

Stella wagged her tail. Her ears went straight back against her head. "Happy," she said.

"Aw, you're happy it's all done? Good Stella, good girl." I petted Stella and put the vacuum back in the closet. It could wait until Jake took her on a walk later.

This was the first of many times that Stella used "all done" to tell Jake or me when she wanted *us* to be finished with something. She directed us more than she used "all done" to narrate her own activities. If we lay in bed for longer than usual, she told us "all done," and whined from the living room. When we took longer to eat than normal, she said "all done," then walked into the kitchen. It looked like she was trying to cue us to take our dishes into the kitchen like we always did when we finished our meal. If I was writing reports on my laptop and had ignored Stella's play attempts, Stella would tell me, "all done." Almost every time I was talking on the phone, Stella became her chattiest. She would repeatedly say "all done," along with what she wanted me to be doing with her instead. This happened at work with toddlers every single day. As soon as the parent and I would engage in a longer conversation at the end of the session, the child would do whatever he could to grab our attention. Seeing how often Stella told us "all done" made me wonder how else she might be wanting to direct us.

In the summer of 2019, Stella was using over twenty words independently and functionally. She combined words several times each day and continued to make novel phrases. Stella used words to request actions, request places, narrate her morning routine, call out to Jake or me, talk about what just happened, and share how she was feeling. The patterns of language she was using were consistent and predictable. She said words at the times when they made sense. She did not say "eat" in the middle of the day or combine words that did not go together like "beach bed," "good mad," "bye bed," "water park," "walk water," and so on. She had reached the automatic stage with all her words, and it showed. She communicated in several different environments with different people, not only to Jake and me. She first learned to use her buttons on their own, and now on two different-size boards.

Stella's vocabulary was equally as impressive to me as her social skills were. Stella's social use of the buttons matched many of the same social rules we use while we talk. She tried getting our attention first by saying "come" or "look" if we were in the other room before she carried on with her message. She made eye contact with me after she finished her thought, then waited for a response. If we did not understand her, she tried saying what she meant in a different way, or she repeated her message.

Stella rarely interrupted me. When she was emotionally charged, she pressed buttons with more intensity and more repetitions to stress her point. With verbal speech, we can adjust our tone and volume. AAC users, however, do not have that same privilege. AAC users often convey different tones by the way they press buttons, or with the gestures they use in combination with their words. This is similar in American Sign Language. Emphasis is put on words by the speed and force used to make each sign, and the facial expressions of the speaker. When Stella was tired, she stretched along her board, saying words slowly with significant pause time between each one. It reminded me of when I wake up in the morning and yawn and stretch as I talk. When Stella was frantic, she ran to her board and slammed on each button, just like someone who is so excited that they're blurting the words out. Language is so much more than knowing the meaning of words or knowing which button says which word.

One day, Stella's toy landed on our built-in bookshelves. She stood on her hind legs to grab it, accidentally knocking down a sign in the process. Stella looked to me and became submissive. Her tail tucked down between her legs and she lowered her head. She walked to her board.

"No," she said. Stella looked at the sign she knocked over and back at me again. She walked over to me, slowly wagging her tail.

It was her way of saying she didn't mean to do it. "It's okay, Stella! Everything is okay." After some verbal reassurance and petting, Stella perked up again and continued to play.

Stella listened when Jake and I talked between the two of us. One night, we sat on the couch talking about if we wanted to go outside again or if we were done for the night. "I think we can stay in," Jake said. "She's probably good." Stella hopped off her bed and walked over to her board.

"Mad outside come come outside," she said. When we did not jump up from the couch immediately to go outside, Stella barked, then said, "Walk mad Jake outside." Stella did not want to wait for us to decide what we were doing. She spoke her mind, letting us know her say in the matter.

Stella even came up with her own ways to talk about concepts she did not have a specific word for. For example, she started saying, "bye eat" to request the Kong toy we filled with peanut butter every time we go to work. She did not only say this once or twice. She said it nearly every day when we were preparing to leave, or if it took us longer to leave than usual.

"Bye eat?" I asked. "You want to leave and eat somewhere else? Or we are going to leave then you will eat when we come back?" I stared at Stella, trying to figure out what she meant.

Stella licked her lips. I grabbed my bag, lunch box, and water bottle, tossed Stella's Kong into her kennel for her, and rushed out the door. Ten minutes into my drive, the answer popped into my head. *Duh*, I thought. *She was trying to tell me she wanted me to leave so she could have her peanut butter.*

This was yet another important lesson to not dismiss communication if we do not understand it right away. Just because the adult may not connect the dots immediately, it does not mean the communication was random or unmeaningful. This happens all the time with toddlers. The last time I was with my one-year-old niece, Clara, I watched this exact same scenario unfold. Clara sat in her high chair, waiting for her food.

"Paper towel," she said.

"Here you go." I set a paper towel down on her tray.

"Oh, she wants a clementine," Kate, my older sister, said.

"What?" I asked.

"Every time Clara eats a clementine, she likes putting the peel on a paper towel."

Kate was very aware of Clara's routines, which allowed her to understand this communication without skipping a beat. Clara knew how to say "paper towel" but did not know how to say "clementine" yet. She said what she could to communicate her desire. If I had been alone with Clara, there was no way I would have jumped to the understanding that she wanted a clementine. Just because I did not understand did not mean it was unmeaningful. Sure enough, when Kate opened the fridge and pulled out a clementine, Clara started clapping.

"Beach play," Stella said. I was in the middle of making dinner. Stella kept asking for the beach, but I knew the three of us were going to visit the beach later that night after dinner.

"Beach play later, Stella," I said.

Stella barked at me. I walked over to her board.

"You sound mad, girl." I said. "Stella mad. Beach later," I modeled.

Stella stood next to the door whining. I returned to the kitchen, but I could still hear her in the living room. I stirred the soup on the stove and thought back to my speech therapy sessions with toddlers. If a child asked for something we could not play with at the time or asked to go somewhere, I would not only say "no" or "later" and leave it at that. I would have offered the child something else to do instead. Giving the child options for activities we could do in the moment helped him feel in control and showed him that there were other fun toys we could use. Maybe Stella needed a little more direction. Maybe she would benefit from having options too.

I walked back into the living room. "Beach later Stella," I said. "Want play toy now?" I modeled "want play now" while pointing to Stella's toy bin. "Or want bed?" I modeled "want bed" and pulled her bed out to the kitchen so she could lie and watch me cook if she wanted. Stella became quiet. She looked around the room and back at me. She picked up a toy, squeaked it, then dropped it. Stella walked over to her bed. She plopped right down and watched me finish making dinner. "Good Stella," I said. "Good Stella on bed now."

With so many frequent communication advancements, I created Hunger for Words Facebook and Instagram accounts. I had continued writing blog posts and updating a couple of new featured videos on the homepage of my website every couple of weeks. My audience was mostly friends, family members, and friends of friends. But every so often, I would notice some strangers stumbling upon my blog and following along to see Stella updates.

I was hesitant to return to the world of social media. I had created the space I needed in my life to be able to progress this far with Stella and focus on what was important to me without mental clutter standing in the way. But I also had so many videos of Stella talking that I wanted others to see. It was fine for people to read about her communication stories through my blog posts, but it was always more striking actually seeing her in action. I hoped these videos would help people start thinking about communication potential in both humans and animals in a new way. I started sharing videos of Stella talking, and writing captions to explain the skills she was demonstrating and what I was noticing.

In July, only four months after launching my website, and six months after I moved all Stella's buttons to her first board, I received an email from a writer at the alumni magazine at my graduate school, Northern Illinois University. She had heard about my work with Stella and asked to write a piece on me.

"My first interview!" I shouted to Jake.

"The first of many, I'm sure," he said.

I could not wait for the chance to talk about speech therapy, AAC, and Stella's success in a way that could potentially reach a large audience. The writer sent me the list of questions she was planning to ask. I mulled them over for multiple days, practiced responses, and wrote down talking points. I wanted to represent my work in the best way I could.

After the piece came out, I gained more followers on my social media pages and email subscribers. I received a few thoughtful emails from fellow alumni, sending well wishes and excitement about my work. Now a few hundred people were following us along on our journey. I wanted this story to spread because of the messages it represented. Everyone deserves a voice. And dogs say and think about so much more than we ever thought they could.

At the end of the summer in 2019, we moved to a new apartment near the dog beach. It was heaven for Stella. There was a giant park across the street from us on the right, and the path to the dog beach on the left. We drove to this area all the time after work and on the weekends anyway, so we figured we might as well live where we spent the majority of our free time. I wondered how Stella would react to moving again. I knew it would not be nearly as traumatic as moving across the country, but I was worried she would panic seeing our home emptied out. I wondered if she would use her words at all during this transition. Last year when we moved, she needed some adjustment time to become comfortable in her new space before she said much. But now, Stella was older, had significantly stronger communication skills, and a board that kept her words in the same locations. I was eager to see how she would do.

On the first evening in our new apartment, we emptied out half our boxes. Stella sniffed everything we unpacked and carefully watched us set up our new space. Her gaze tracked our every movements. This apartment was still a one-bedroom unit, but it was slightly larger than our last one. The twelve-foot-tall ceilings and large windows in the living room made it feel much more spacious. We placed Stella's board a few feet away from the door, at the edge of our living room.

"I want to show her where we can walk to now," I said. "Let's take her to the beach!" Stella came running over to me. She must have heard her favorite word. "Yes, beach. Let's go to the beach, Stella."

As soon as we reached the elevated bike path that led to the dog beach, Stella smiled and bolted for the shore. She and I ran together, both equally excited about our new neighborhood. When we returned from our sunset playtime, Stella walked straight to her board.

"Beach play love you," she said.

"She is going to be so happy living here," Jake said.

The next Saturday morning, Jake and I woke up early to resume unpacking and rearranging our furniture. We were debating on the location of our couch and had moved it back and forth across the living room three or four times by now. Each time we lifted the couch, Stella jumped back as far away from us as she could go while still keeping an eye on us.

"You're right, I think it's better over there," I said. "Let's move it back. Final decision."

Jake and I took our positions. We squatted down to lift it. Jake started counting. "1, 2, . . ."

Stella barked and ran to her board. We paused.

"All done walk happy walk happy want," she said.

"I know you want us to be all done now. Hang on, Stella, walk later," I said. We moved the couch across the room and continued unpacking for a few more minutes. Stella walked back to her board.

"Stella bye love you," she said. She sat in front of the door, leaning against it. She was absolutely ready to leave the chaos.

The location of our new apartment brought even more understanding of the meaning behind Stella's words. Across the street, there was a clear fork in the road where the beach was to the left, and the park was to the right. If Stella said, "park," but I really wanted to go to the beach and tried walking her that way, she would lie down in the middle of the sidewalk until I turned the right way. Even though she did not have her board out on walks with her, she found a clear way to tell me that she meant what she said. I learned that the beach and the park were not equal experiences for her. I do not know exactly what made her more in the mood for the park instead of the beach some days, and vice versa, but she clearly had a reason and a preference, like we all do. Maybe some days she wanted to see the squirrels at the park, and on others she wanted to chase birds down the shore. Maybe some days she felt like rolling around in the grass, but on others she wanted to dig in the sand. I wondered if she had more vocabulary available if she would be able to tell us exactly what she wanted to do during her playtime.

Stella's commitment to her own wants and needs inspired me. She did not back down from her own desires when I tried taking her where I wanted to go. This was further proof to me that Stella's sole purpose in life was not to do what we say. She had her own mind and ideas. Everyone has the right to their own opinion and their own wants. Now that I saw first-hand that Stella had a specific vision for her playtime, and did not appreciate me trying to change it, I tried finding a balance between what Stella wanted and what Jake or I wanted and talking about it first. Before we left, I would model "Christina want beach," or "Christina want walk." Then I would ask, "What Stella want?" We always took Stella's wants into consideration like we would with another human. Some days we all had the same wants, other days we picked where Stella wanted to go, and sometimes we chose where Jake or I wanted. When we told Stella beforehand where we were going, she would not lie down in protest. She just needed us to tell her what was happening so she could understand.

I opened another new box of Recordable Answer Buzzers. Now that Stella used all her words consistently, it was time to add more buttons for her. Stella's behavior around her board always showed me when she really needed an expanded vocabulary. After she had learned all her words and used them all independently, sometimes she walked through the rows and whined or stood on her board whining. This made me wonder if she was trying to tell me something that she did not have a word for. Stella watched me remove the buttons. Her tail wagged and she licked the box.

"Happy want," Stella said. She walked back to me and licked the box of buttons again.

This time, I added fringe words for Stella: *ball, toy, couch, inside*. Since Stella was communicating with such ease and at such high frequencies, I figured it was time for some more specific vocabulary to help her make her messages even clearer. I modeled phrases like "Stella play ball," "play ball inside," "want ball," every time we played with a ball. I said, "Stella play toy," "play toy inside," or "help toy couch" when her toy slid under the couch.

One weeknight at the beach, Stella found a ratty scrap of some other dog's toy buried in the sand. It was disgusting. But Stella would not let it go. She carried it the whole way home. When we reached the sidewalk outside of our apartment, we told Stella to "leave it," and ran inside before she could pick it up again. When we walked inside, Stella stood by the front door with her nose pressed against it. She kept sniffing and pawing at the door. A few minutes later, Stella walked over to her board.

"Toy inside," she said.

"You want to bring the toy inside?"

Stella wagged her tail and ran back to the door.

"Let's play toy outside, Stella. Come on, girl." I clipped Stella's leash on again and took her back outside. Stella pounced on the toy. She clenched it in her mouth and shook it back and forth. I still did not want to bring it inside, so I let her play for a few more minutes outside before being all done for the night.

While Stella's vocabulary was growing, the situations she talked about were also becoming more and more complex. New and unusual circumstances led to greater revelations about Stella's cognition. One morning, Stella accidentally bumped the reset tab on her "beach" button. It made a loud sound, then erased the word.

"Mad," Stella said.

"I know, Stella, let me fix it. Christina help." Stella tracked my every move. She always watched closely when I intervened with her device. I picked the button off her board and tried recording "beach" again. But it didn't work. The button had broken after so much use.

"Sorry, girl," I said. We didn't have any spare buttons.

About five minutes later, Stella approached her board. She put her paw on the empty space where "beach" was supposed to be, then sniffed it. Stella paused on her device, looking around to her other buttons.

"Help water outside," she said.

"Oh my gosh . . ." I said.

Stella had the understanding and the problem-solving skills to figure out a way to talk about her broken "beach" button. This was the first time we had a malfunction with her "beach" buzzer. We had never practiced anything like this or talked about this situation. Stella was using words in unique ways during brand-new circumstances.

A couple of days later, we ran out of Stella's typical food. I took it upon myself to make her a special dinner instead of running out to buy more food right away. I plopped the rice, chicken, and vegetable medley into her bowl. "Here you go, Stella."

Stella sniffed her food then took a couple of small bites. She looked up to me.

"Stella eat," I said.

Stella sniffed her food again, then walked to her board. "Eat no," she said. Stella hopped on the couch and curled into a ball. I assumed she would have enjoyed a different (and home-cooked) meal. But she didn't go near it the rest of the night.

The next day, after we bought more of her normal food, Stella scarfed down her bowl then walked to her board.

"Happy eat," she said.

I was glad Stella had a way to express even simple opinions about what we fed her every day. I really didn't know she enjoyed her specific food so much until she said "happy eat."

A couple of weeks later, Jake, Stella, and I spent a weekend visiting several of Jake's friends. When we arrived to a living room full of people, Stella ran to greet each person. I set her board down against the wall while Stella enjoyed all the attention. Everyone formed a circle around her, taking turns petting her and giving Stella lots of love.

I stepped into the circle. "Stella, come here," I called. I wanted to pet her too.

Stella glanced over to me, then walked to her board.

"Christina later," she said.

My jaw dropped. Jake burst out laughing. Our dog just told me she wanted to hang out with her new friends instead of me right now.

It felt like we hit a sweet spot with the now twenty-nine words on Stella's device. We had a great combination of core words and fringe words for her to be able to talk about most of her daily activities. The number of words is not everything. Having a solid group of vocabulary options available for Stella to talk about several different situations is far more important than having tons of words that do not really impact how she communicates. But remember, we all know thousands of words, yet the same three hundred to four hundred words make up 80 percent of our everyday speech.[41] I still wanted to add more words to the empty space on Stella's board, but I was so happy with the balance of words we had achieved so far.

I experimented with some words along the way that I did not end up keeping on her device because they did not serve a unique purpose for Stella. I tried *get, go, kennel, then.* I thought *get* might be a useful addition when I realized how often I say "get your toy," or "get your ball." But Stella ended up using *want* in all the scenarios where *get* would also be appropriate. *Go* is a great word, which I would normally always recommend adding, but Stella had learned to say the specific places she wanted to go to already. Also, she had started using *bye* like *go.* If I were starting over again, I probably would have incorporated *go* earlier on. Stella used *bed* to talk about her kennel since her bed was in there. And *later* was more functional for us than *then.* We could use *later* on its own, like "beach later," or in combination with what we were doing now—"Eat now beach later." But we could not use *then* on its own, only in combination with what was happening now. It would not make sense to just say "then beach."

Little differences in vocabulary uses like these can go a long way in picking which words are on a communication device. In a perfect world, we could have all the words available for Stella as we do on human communication devices, but we are not at that point yet. So for now, selecting the words that gave Stella the most bang for her buck worked out well.

TAKEAWAYS FOR TEACHING *YOUR* DOG

- **Introduce time concepts to help your dog differentiate between something that already happened, is happening now, or will occur later.** Model "now" in combination with what you are currently doing and "later" if you plan on doing a specific activity later in the day. If your dog says "now," try as best you can to react quickly!

- **Give your dog a way to say "all done."** Having words like "finished" or "stop" or a phrase such as "all done" gives your dog the power to say when she wants something to be done. Model "all done" at the conclusion of your dog's activities to help her learn its meaning.

- **Talk to your dog about what's happening.** I learned with Stella that if I told her what we were doing beforehand, she was less startled, and reacted more calmly to changes in her routine, or an activity that was different from what she requested. We are all more understanding when we know what's going on.

CHAPTER 17

Hello, World

————

At sunrise on October 30, 2019, I opened my journal and wrote on the top of the page, "Wouldn't it be amazing if . . . ?" This is one of my favorite early-morning activities, letting my imagination run wild before the rest of the world wakes up. "Wouldn't it be amazing if my Stella posts attracted hundreds and thousands of new fans bursting with enthusiasm? Wouldn't it be amazing if someday I got to speak to large groups of people about my work with Stella? Wouldn't it be amazing if someday I was doing interviews on TV about Stella and AAC?" I sat with those ideas, completely crazy to me at the time, and let myself feel how wonderful it would be to experience all that.

The next day, I parked my car in front of a beachside apartment building with a few minutes to kill before my next speech therapy session started. I checked my email to see one new message with the subject line "People Magazine Calling!" I opened the email, expecting it to be some sort of spam. My eyes widened when I saw that it was not spam at all. It was a legitimate email from a *People* magazine writer, Hilary Shenfeld, who happened to see my videos of Stella on social media. She wanted to write about Stella and me.

I freaked out. Barely anyone knew about my work with Stella. A lot of my friends did not even know what I was doing. But suddenly, one of the few hundred people in my social media audience happened to be a writer for *People*? What are the chances? I took a screenshot of the email and sent it to Jake, along with a row of exclamation points.

Three days later, on the eve of the scheduled interview, I opened a text from one of my SLP friends: You didn't tell me you were going to be in the Leader this month!! it read. The *ASHA Leader* is the professional magazine for speech-language pathologists and audiologists.

What?? I didn't know I was going to be! I haven't gotten my copy yet, what is it? I texted back.

She sent a picture of one of the first pages of the magazine, a column written by Dr. Shari Robertson, the president of the American Speech and Hearing Association at the time. I loved her work. I ripped out her previous columns and saved them to read whenever I needed a dose of inspiration. And now, she knew of me. The column was titled "Celebrating the Bold Thinking of ASHA Imaginologists." My eyes were glued to the screen:

I cannot think of a better use for my last column as ASHA's president than to highlight the stories of some of our colleagues who have dared to push their personal boundaries beyond the safe and familiar. While each is unique, each began with the seed of an idea, that fertilized with equal measures of passion, vision, and hard work, eventually blossomed into reality. I hope the four stories I have chosen to share here will delight, inspire, and challenge you to imagine more and imagine better.[42]

In the next paragraph, entitled "A hunger for words," Dr. Robertson wrote about the work I had done with Stella. I truly could not believe it. I had completely forgotten that a few months ago I submitted a blurb about Stella's communication journey to ASHA for a chance to be featured on their social media accounts. I never dreamed the president would see it and end up writing about it.

This news could not have come at a more perfect time. I was excited for my phone interview with *People* the next day, but ever since I created my website, I was a little nervous about what ASHA would think. I was proud of my career and my profession. All I wanted was to represent the field of speech-language pathology as best as I could. Now, seeing such enthusiastic support from the president of ASHA, I was fueled to keep going and to keep sharing. It felt like a permission slip to continue my pursuit.

November 4, 2019, started out like any other Monday. I listened to an inspiring podcast while I drank a cup of coffee, had three speech therapy sessions, and stopped home for lunch. But, instead of eating lunch and taking Stella for a quick walk, I had a phone interview with Hilary from *People* magazine. Unlike my interview with the NIU alumni magazine writer, I had no idea what the questions would be.

"Are you sure you're ready for this?" she asked. "Millions of people will see it. And I just want to warn you, there are some really mean people who will find something negative to say about even the most positive stories."

I took a deep breath. "I'm ready," I said. "This is too important not to share, regardless of what anybody else thinks."

Hilary told me she didn't know when the article would run. "Sometimes it's a couple of days, and sometimes it's a couple of weeks. I'll send you the link when it's up though."

Forty-five minutes later, I was off the phone and on the road again to my next client. I received a last-minute text from the parent of my 3:00 session saying they had to cancel. So this was my last session of the day.

I could not stop running everything I said back through my head. Except I could not even remember what I said. It was such a blur. I hope I represented what I was doing well enough. I hope I explained the concept in a way that everyone would understand. Thankfully, my job is not one where I can keep ruminating on something in my head while continuing to work. Toddlers require full attention and truly keep you in the moment. Their stream of energy, curiosity, and wonder about everything around them, and desire to play is magnetic. There was nothing else for me to do now except to play, laugh, have fun, and, my favorite thing of all, teach more words.

At the end of the session we sang the cleanup song and I pulled my phone out of my bag to write my session note. My screen was filled with notifications from Gmail and Instagram, and a text from Hilary. *She probably has a follow-up question*, I thought.

But I unlocked my phone to see the words It's up! with a link to an article headlined "Dog Learning to Talk By Using a Custom Soundboard." I quickly scrolled down to see pictures of Stella with her AAC device, and the two of us together. I had not mentally prepared at all for this. I had no idea it would be posted so quickly. I was so focused on getting through the interview that I did not even think about what might happen when it was online. My heart pounded. I so badly wanted to read it. But I was sitting on the floor of a client's living room, needing to write my session note so his mom could sign it.

As soon as I shut the front door behind me, I clicked on the article link again. I sat in my driver's seat not believing that there were pictures of Stella and me in a *People* article. Immediately, I texted it to Jake, my family, and friends. I opened Instagram to see that I already had a couple thousand new followers in the hour since it was posted. Jake picked up champagne on his way home. We toasted to a growing community of fans and my work officially being "out there."

Before we poured a single glass of champagne, my in-box was rapidly filling up with questions, pictures of dogs from passionate new followers, usage permissions for my videos from random news outlets, and all kinds of media requests. I had no idea that other news outlets would want to write about this story once they saw it in *People*, and I had no idea this would all happen so quickly.

Inside Edition wanted to come film a segment at our apartment. They said they needed an answer right then because they move on to new stories pretty quickly. I didn't want to miss an opportunity, so I said yes. I refreshed my in-box to see that *Popular Mechanics* asked to interview me the next day, and CNN wanted to conduct a Skype interview the day after that. I couldn't even drink a glass of champagne. I had to figure out what to do. I still had a job. I had a full week of kids to see. Was I supposed to give these people permission to use my videos? I had absolutely no idea. How many interviews should I do? Would these requests be the only ones I would ever be asked to do, or would they still be interested in the future? Nobody I knew had been through anything like this.

For the rest of the night, Jake and I grew dizzy as we watched my number of followers keep jumping, new spin-off articles being posted rapidly, and the story bouncing through Twitter and Reddit.

You're trending on Apple News! my sister texted our family group chat. We all took guesses on how many followers I would reach by the end of the night, and my dad kept sending screen-shots of heartwarming comments on my Instagram videos. I figured this was going to be the peak, that in the next day or two it would all slow back down again, and these would be a fun couple of nights to remember. When we went to bed, I was at about ten thousand followers. I never imagined I would go from six hundred to ten thousand in one single day.

The next morning, I woke up to thirty thousand followers. People were now commenting in different languages. A text from my cousin Rachel read: I had the news on this morning and all of a sudden they were talking about you!! She attached a video clip of *CBS This Morning*. Gayle King was talking about Stella and me. A picture of Stella's face took up the entire backdrop behind the anchors, and one of my Instagram videos of Stella talking played. Random acquaintances from middle school through college were coming out of the woodwork, messaging me screenshots of people they knew posting articles about me. This was completely wild. "I can't believe I have a session with a two-year-old in an hour," I said. "How in the world am I supposed to focus?"

In between therapy sessions, I pulled into a gas station parking lot and had a phone interview with *Popular Mechanics*. Then, I scheduled *NBC Nightly News*'s visit to our apartment.

Parents of the children I worked with were seeing articles about me. When I showed up at the front door of a client's house ready for therapy, the mom opened the door. "There's the face I've been seeing all over the news," she said. "Someone showed me a Spanish news clip about a talking dog, and I screamed when I saw it was you!"

I often pictured how my work with Stella would become known to the public. I thought I'd gain a slow but steady following. I thought it would catch the attention of someone in the dog world and that person would pass it around to other people in the dog field. That's what had started to happen with the speech therapy community. I pictured myself teaching several different dogs before it really gained the attention of the public. But I truly believed this would not stay hidden forever. Stella's progress was all too incredible. I did not know exactly what would happen, or when, but I felt somewhere deep in my core that this would all come out in some way, shape, or form.

All the threads that came together at the right time in the right way astounded me. Sending my website to my former professors led to the NIU Alumni Association reaching out for an interview. The article in the university magazine attracted a lot of people in the area, especially speech-language pathologists. One speech therapist who saw that article shared one of my videos of Stella on Facebook. Her cousin, a writer for *People*, saw the video and reached out to me. Every single small step I took in moving my project forward was necessary for it to be shared with the world.

Thursday morning an *Inside Edition* camera crew from L.A. parked on the street outside of our apartment. Two men in their late thirties stepped out of the van. Stella immediately ran up to the interviewer with her typical body wiggle and smile. He stood near the curb with his arms crossed, looking down to her. "I didn't think she would be energetic," he said.

"Oh, yeah. She's only one . . . she's just excited," I said. "She loves people." He patted her head once, then did not interact with her again.

Jake and I exchanged glances that said, *I sure hope this was a good idea.*

I was incredibly nervous. I had no idea how Stella would react to cameras or if she would talk with complete strangers and her space overtaken by video equipment. I tried keeping Stella entertained and comfortable while they set up their equipment in our living room. The cameraman squatted down to Stella's level while carrying a three-foot-long, bulky camera on his shoulder. He trailed behind her, following her every move. Stella looked back at the camera and trotted over to her board.

"All done," she said. Stella ran into the bedroom and hid behind the bed.

"Let's do your interview first," he said. "We'll give her some time to get used to us."

Over the two hours that they stayed at our apartment, Stella said several different words. She said when she wanted to go to the park, play with her ball, she was mad that we could not go outside again, and said "bye" when they started packing up. I was so relieved that Stella adjusted well and that they could capture footage of her talking. I could not wait to see what they would use when they ran the segment.

Two hours later, I signed onto Skype for an interview with *CNN International.* I had no idea who was interviewing me, or what they looked like. I had to stare at a black screen while the two anchors talked between themselves and asked me questions. It was strange being unable to see what was happening, and knowing that they, along with all the viewers, could see me.

"I don't think I can ever watch that," I said to Jake. "I don't even want to know what I looked like or said."

When the *NBC* crew arrived from New York and Los Angeles that Friday, I felt a little less nervous now that I knew Stella would probably react well. I already had two interviews under my belt and knew what types of questions to expect. The *CNN* segment had aired and made its way around. They put together an excellent compilation of videos of Stella talking, the interview, and pictures. It turned out much better than I expected it would.

Instead of only two people, the *NBC* crew consisted of five. They brought in more equipment than I thought could fit in our entire apartment. We rearranged some of our living room furniture to make it all fit. Lighting umbrellas surrounded Stella's board; cameras were set up at every possible angle. We could all barely squeeze into our small space. Once they finished preparing the setup, everyone sat in a row on our chaise lounger, dining stools, and living room chairs staring at Stella. Stella looked at everyone and walked over to her board.

"Hi," she said. She wagged her tail and walked over to greet them again. Stella must have been so confused. Suddenly there were so many new people coming over and putting all kinds of strange objects around her board.

Inside Edition had asked me several questions about language, AAC, and Stella's progress. I was disappointed when they aired the segment, though. They did not include any of my responses. The quotes they chose from me were, "Yeah, it's crazy" and me answering the question about what her least favorite words were. It was worse with *NBC*. They spent over five hours at our apartment. I took the day off from working with my kids. We even all went to the dog beach together. After all that, they did not end up airing the segment. It was due to the news cycle. I had no idea it was not a guarantee. Still, the potential of the breakthroughs I had made with Stella was clearer than ever. The writer from *People* left a voice mail saying that article was one of the most well-received stories they had ever published. Thousands of kind people emailed me asking to learn more, or to share stories about what their dogs understood.

Two weeks after the *People* article came out, I had over five hundred thousand followers on Instagram. My posts were flooded with comments and questions. My parents put together a little booklet of some touching comments for me to look at when I needed to remember the bigger picture of what I was doing. It was such an outpouring of support, excitement, enthusiasm, and joy. I felt like the world was ready for my work. It was time for me to figure out how to share even more of it, and how we reached this point.

Even though it was thrilling to see the great interest, I quickly came to see that it would not matter to me what anyone else thought about what I was doing. Stella's accomplishments were all that mattered to me.

This quote from Deepak Chopra struck me during this time of extremely heightened visibility: "Happiness for a reason is just another form of misery because the reason can be taken away from us at any time."

I did not want my feelings toward my work to be contingent on anyone else's perceptions of it. I did not want to start the habit of saying, "There are so many positive comments on this video, I'm so happy," then seeing a negative comment and being upset by it. I wanted to feel good about the work, and free myself from the approval or disapproval of an internet stranger. I started the habit of checking in with myself to ask myself if I was happy with what I was doing and with Stella's progress. Or I would ask myself, *If I didn't have a bunch of people watching me, what would I do?* Then I would proceed to do that.

The media requests and emails still poured in. Somehow, Jake and I were both receiving phone calls from international radio stations asking to speak with me. A French station repeatedly called and texted Jake. Radio stations called my parents' home in Illinois. I still have no idea how anyone found our numbers. A Canadian news station called the speech therapy company I worked for, looking to talk to me. Local news anchors sent me friend requests to try making contact. It was all complete chaos.

At one point, I turned off the lights in my bedroom and pulled the sheets over my head. Jake rubbed my back. "It feels like hundreds of thousands of people are tugging on my shirt all at once, asking me for things," I said. I still had kids to see and a job to do. I desperately wanted to teach people, but I could not explain speech therapy and a year and a half full of observations in Instagram comments or in thousands of email replies. If I tried responding to everything, I would not have time to do anything else in the day. I needed to figure out what I wanted. "How am I supposed to manage all this?" I asked. If I had had any idea this was going to be so big, I would have tried to prepare myself first.

I soon realized that the depth of this story could not be reflected in the quick news cycles. I would not be able to communicate my patterns of thinking as a speech therapist and the past year and a half of progress and observations in minute-long video clips. It was not even up to me to choose which of my lines were used or not. I wanted to be able to tell our story and help people all over the world see dog communication and potential through the lens of a speech-language pathologist. And I did not want to leave it up to anyone else to share my work, this exciting new idea, for the first time.

I had offers to do absolutely everything I could think of: speaking engagements, TV show ideas, interviews, documentaries, product creations, course creations, and one subject line of an email that caught my attention the most: "Write a book?"

CHAPTER 18

This Is the Beginning

_____

After the media craziness died down, I filled up the rest of Stella's board and continued teaching her new words. With the three new additions, *blanket*, *like*, *where*, we reached thirty-two buttons. The first time Stella used "like" was when we found one of her favorite balls that had been lost under the couch for months. When we rolled it out, Stella picked up her ball, said "ball like," and continued playing with it for hours.

I added "where" to see if Stella would be able to ask us questions. "Where" is one of the first question words that toddlers start using. "Where Mom?" "Where Dad?" "Where ball?" are all common phrases for toddlers. I modeled "where" every time I asked Stella where she wanted to go, or where one of her toys was. After only a few days of modeling, when Jake and I would put our shoes on, she asked "where?" When we would return from the store, she sniffed the bags and asked "where?" When I was talking to Jake on speakerphone, Stella asked "where?" and looked out the window. When her toys or blanket were out of sight, she would ask, "blanket where?" or "where toy?" When I came home from work one day, I asked, "Want to go for a walk?"

Stella paused for a few moments. "Where?" she asked. She looked back up to me.

"Walk on beach," I said.

Stella wagged her tail and said, "Walk outside."

She cared about where we were going and what we were doing. I wondered how long she had been wanting to ask us "where," after we had asked her "Where do you want to go?" for months. What else was Stella wondering? What else was she waiting to be able to say? I guess I would need more space and more buttons to find out.

So what happened when I used speech therapy techniques to teach words to my puppy? When Stella was eight weeks old, I introduced just one button that said "outside." My initial plans were to give Stella a way to say a few different words so we would know what she wanted. I recognized all the other ways she was communicating with gestures and vocalizations, how she was understanding words, then continued to add more and more vocabulary as we progressed together. My vision became clearer with each step forward I took. As Martin Luther King Jr. said, "Faith is taking the first step even when you don't see the whole staircase."

Now, Stella uses nouns, verbs, names, adjectives, and question words to tell me what she wants to do, where she wants to go, when she is thinking about me, what we are doing, what she likes, when she is mad, when she is happy, when she needs alone time, when we are being good, to answer questions, to ask questions, to participate in short conversations, and to make her own unique phrases every single day. My process of teaching Stella language certainly was not perfect. It took several months before I even had the idea to put all her words together on one cohesive board for her. I hope dogs of the future will continue reaching new milestones that even Stella has not achieved yet. This is just the start. It is the door opening to show what is possible, and all that we as a society have to explore and learn.

The question I am asked the most is "How did you come up with this idea?" The easiest explanation is that I worked with lots of children who use communication devices to talk. I recognized prelinguistic skills in Stella's communication that toddlers demonstrate before they start saying words. So I wondered if Stella could say words if she had a communication device.

But the real reason is so much deeper than my experience as a speech-language pathologist. I had no preconceived notions of what could or could not be achieved. I had never spent time reading about why dogs cannot talk, or why animals will never use human words. I was completely dedicated to my field of speech therapy and saw a fun opportunity to try it out in a new way. I saw all the reasons why it could be possible. I looked for the possibilities rather than the potential problems. I put faith into my own professional experiences rather than looking at others' expertise as the gold standard. I put weight into my own ideas instead of what the world thought was possible. I did not have any limiting beliefs stopping me from discovering more.

What would have happened if Thomas Edison gave up on his experiments because someone else did not share his vision?

What would have happened if the Wright Brothers allowed other people's ideas of what was possible to stop them from trying something new? All great ideas and discoveries come not from focusing on "what is," but from imagining what "could be." After all, as Albert Einstein said, "Logic will take you from A to B. Imagination will take you everywhere." I choose to live in a world where visions of what "could be" are celebrated and prioritized.

Language is often viewed as the last barrier we have from the human to the animal world. What happens when that barrier dissolves? We realize that we are all connected in more ways than we can even begin to comprehend. We are not as separate from animals as many think we are. We all think, we all feel, we all have opinions, we all communicate, and we all want to connect.

I am a firm believer that our beliefs about the world shape our own individual experiences. I challenge you to think in terms of possibilities instead of problems. Ask yourself, *What if it does work? What if the results are even better than I thought?* I challenge you to look at the world through the lens of un-tapped potential everywhere you turn. I challenge you to follow your curiosities, no matter how wild or unlikely they may seem at first. I challenge you to let go of all the excuses you can think of for why something couldn't work and hold on to the reasons why it could. At the start of any pursuit, you have no idea what it could become.

Starting from the first days I spent with little Stella, I watched her progress through stages of language development in ways extremely similar to human children. When I gave Stella the opportunity to use words, she continually pushed the envelope and acquired new skills beyond my expectations. She always found ways to use words in unique situations, make longer phrases, and communicate about new experiences. On average, Stella said between twenty-five and forty different utterances each day. Sometimes, she even said between fifty and sixty different words or phrases on a given day. She had so much to say and so badly wanted to communicate with us about the world we were all living in together.

I thought bringing home a puppy would change my life in all the predictable ways. I expected to play with Stella, and to cuddle with her. I expected to go for more walks, to watch her grow, to care for her, and to learn about her personality. I expected to have a companion who would stay by Jake's and my side as we began our life together.

But Stella gave me so much more than this. She completely changed my life. I can never go back to the way I looked at the world before Stella learned to talk. Stella opened my eyes to the glaring similarities between dog and human communication skills. She made me spend my spare time contemplating humans' relationships with the animal world. She made me never question a single child's communication potential ever again. She made me work my hardest to get AAC devices for children. She taught me to make the most out of every window of opportunity. She taught me how powerful believing in potential can be. She taught me that everyone deserves a chance to use their voice and that everyone has something important to say. She made me realize how desperately I wanted to open the world's eyes to the power of communication. She introduced me to my life's purpose.

Stella's and my journey represents the beginning of a field bursting at the seams with possibility. We have so much to experiment with, so many questions to ask, and so many ideas to test out. What other words can dogs learn? What is the range of normal for dogs' language skills? Is there a critical period for language learning? How long would it take older dogs to learn to use words in comparison to puppies? Do dog breeds differ in language capabilities? What are dogs' collective syntax patterns? How do device setups impact language use? Will service dogs be able to help their owners more if they can communicate with words? How can we adapt devices for dogs with special needs? How does having access to words change a dog's awareness and perception of their environment? Will we stop assuming that we know everything our pets are thinking? Will we stop talking for our animals and instead let them speak up for themselves?

Will this open new doors for interspecies communication research? What animals could be next? How will our new communication with dogs change how we treat them? How will this change our pets' lives? How will this change ours?

It is time for us to start searching for the answers to these questions and many more. It is time to unite the human and animal worlds through language. It is time for a communication revolution. And I cannot wait to see what we all discover together.

Helping Your Dog Learn to Talk

———

Talk to your dog!

All dogs, regardless of their age, are bursting with communication potential. Narrate your dog's actions and activities in short, simple phrases. If you are not sure what to say, ask yourself, *What is happening right now?* Examples of narration include "Stella eat," "Play toy," "Stella Christina walk," "Water!"

Observe your dog's nonverbal and verbal communication

How does your dog currently communicate? Does she paw at objects? Does she whine when trying to grab your attention? Does her tail wag when she is happy? Does she bark at you when she needs something? Notice all the ways your dog communicates and start responding. We want to respond to all communication, not only to words. The more we acknowledge all forms of communication, the more likely your dog will be to communicate with words.

Try modeling words when your dog is communicating verbally or nonverbally. When you see your dog pawing at the door, say "outside." If your dog whines near her leash, say "walk." If your dog looks at a toy that is stuck under the couch, say "help." Pairing words with gestures or vocalizations that your dog already uses helps her learn the meanings of the words.

Pay attention to words your dog is understanding

Which words cause your dog to become excited, turn her head back and forth, or run in from the other room? Are there any words you have to spell out, so your dog does not hear what you are planning? Keep track of these words. Dogs will likely learn to say words that they already know the fastest.

Select words to teach

Ask yourself the following questions: Which words is my dog already understanding? What is my dog already communicating to me with gestures and vocalizations? Which words are frequently occurring? Which words would help her communicate about a variety of experiences? Which words would be most beneficial for all of us if she could say them? What does my dog love to do? Use the answers to these questions to guide your decisions. Start with words that your dog will want to say and will have plenty of opportunities to say.

Set your dog's device up in a convenient location
that is easy to access for you and your dog

Find a space in your home where your dog naturally spends time already. Try picking a spot that has room to support potential growth and that will stay clear of clutter covering or hiding the buttons.

Keep talking to your dog, but push the corresponding buttons when you talk

Keep narrating your dog's actions but use your dog's buttons to talk as well! This is called *aided language input.* The more we use communication devices as we are talking, the more AAC users learn how to use their device to say words. Before you take your dog outside, say "outside" verbally and with her button. For even more learning, set a goal for yourself to repeat a single word between five and ten times before moving on. Refer to Chapter 5 for an example of how to incorporate this into your routines.

Pay attention for signs that your dog is observing your modeling

It might take time for your dog to notice the buttons or device, or to really pay attention to you modeling words. Even if it does not look like your dog is watching, keep on modeling. She is still hearing the words you are saying. Look for signs that your dog might be becoming aware of the device. Does your dog look at your foot, or up to you? Does your dog glance down at the button while walking past? These are all signs that your dog is headed in the direction of exploring the words.

When your dog is becoming more aware of your modeling, create communication opportunities within your routines

When you see your dog noticing your modeling or noticing the buttons, turn your routine interactions into language-facilitating opportunities. The greatest cue we can provide is a long, silent pause to give the AAC user a chance to process what is happening and try exploring her words. When you see your dog communicate through a gesture or vocalization, stay quiet for at least ten to fifteen seconds. At the end of fifteen seconds, if your dog looks like she might be walking toward her buttons or is looking at them, continue staying quiet. If you have not seen an indication that she might try saying a word, add the next level of naturalistic cueing.

Add naturalistic cues if necessary

After you have already tried staying silent, you can try standing next to your dog's buttons or pointing at them. Dogs respond to human gestural social cues as early as six weeks old! If pointing or standing near the buttons does not work, you can try tapping it with your finger or foot, not pushing it to activate it. You can also try adding an open-ended verbal prompt such as, "What do you want?" Avoid telling your dog exactly what to say or forcing your dog to push a button with their paw. This can cause prompt dependency and keep your dog from learning how to use words independently.

If none of these prompts encourage your dog to try saying a word, simply model it again verbally and with the button, and carry on with the appropriate action.

Continue responding to all forms of communication

Do not withhold food, water, trips outside, playtime, or anything from your dog until she says a word. Respond to all forms of communication, and allow for a minute or two of opportunity for your dog to try using a word.

Provide positive praise when your dog tries to use their device

If your dog approaches the device, sniffs it, paws at it, licks it, stares at it, be excited! Show your dog that you are proud that she is exploring and testing out the new object in her space. If your dog successfully pushes a button, respond to it! Even if you think it was accidental or she was just pushing it to explore, respond! Your dog will learn the meaning of the words by observing your reactions whenever she uses it.

Respond to words

Especially while your dog is in the beginning stages of learning, respond to your dog's words as frequently and as best you can. Again, even if you do not yet know if they are intentional words, keep responding as if they are. Providing the appropriate response will help your dog learn how to use each word intentionally. If your dog says a word, but you think she really meant to say something else, still respond to the word your dog said. This provides a great opportunity for your dog to distinguish between words. After you respond to the original word, you can model the word you thought your dog was wanting to say.

Keep modeling

When your dog starts using words, do not stop modeling! The more you use your dog's device, the more she will continue to learn and use it on her own. Try to model words in a variety of contexts. This will help your dog generalize the meaning of words to multiple situations and show her the many different ways she can use it.

Keep adding vocabulary that will allow your dog to talk about a variety of experiences

When in doubt, try adding more words! You might be surprised by how much your dog learns to say or what she prefers to talk about. Think again about the words you use often when talking to your dog, her daily activities, and different functions of communication. Does your dog have words that she could use for communication functions other than requesting? Does she have a way to tell you "no" or "all done"? Can she call you over, or let you know when she is happy or mad?

Model two-word phrases when your dog starts using single words
As your dog reaches new milestones, keep modeling the next level up. Model short phrases such as "play outside," "walk outside," "come play." If you are finding that the vocabulary you have makes it challenging to combine words, try adding more verbs instead of nouns. If it is difficult for you to combine words with your dog's vocabulary, it will be even more challenging for your dog.

Have fun!
Teaching your dog words, learning more about her thoughts and personality, and connecting on a deeper level is incredibly rewarding. Enjoy the process and be proud of any progress that you and your dog make together.

Troubleshooting

What to do if . . .

You are wondering how to teach a specific word
Think about your own communication. In which contexts do *you* naturally use this word? These are the situations in which you should model it. For example, "How do I use the word *want*?" I use *want* when I am requesting an object or activity.

So every time I see Stella requesting an object or activity, I will model *want* to go along with her words or gestures.

Your dog says a word that you were not expecting to hear or that seems "random"

Respond to it! Your dog may be exploring new vocabulary. The only way she will learn the meaning of each word is by seeing your response to it. If after you respond, your dog seems to not have received what she expected, model the word you think she meant to say, then follow through with that natural response.

Your dog is scared of the buttons or device

Don't force your dog to try using the buttons or be near them. Keep the buttons out for a few days before you try using them again. Spend time sitting or standing by the buttons so your dog sees that they are not harmful. If possible, call your dog over to pet her while near the buttons. When your dog is calm, try modeling a word again and providing the appropriate response. The calmer you are, the calmer your dog will feel.

Your dog only says words on your command, not spontaneously

Stop using the verbal prompts you are giving immediately. Your dog has learned the pattern of waiting for you to give a cue, then saying a word rather than using the buttons on her own. Instead of asking "Do you want to go outside?" or saying, "Tell me outside," simply say "outside" verbally and with the button before taking your dog out. When you notice your dog gesturing or vocalizing to go outside, provide subtle, naturalistic cues. Start with silently standing near the button or looking at it. Increase to pointing at it or tapping it if necessary.

Remember to wait at least ten to fifteen seconds before adding a cue. Sometimes a long pause is all that is needed.

Your dog continuously requests the same object or activity

If your dog has a solid understanding of the word for the object or activity, incorporate an "all done," "finished," "stop," or "later" button. You can respond by saying "all done walk" or "walk later" both verbally and with the buttons. Provide a suggestion for what your dog could do now instead: "all done walk, play now!" then start playing. Or "all done walk, bed now" and pat your dog's bed.

Also, consider the amount of vocabulary you have available for your dog. If your dog only has a few words, think about if your dog might be using one word to communicate several different wants or needs. Providing access to more words helps your dog differentiate their different meanings.

Your dog is not using the buttons after you have been modeling them for a few weeks

Look for subtle changes in your dog's progress. Is your dog stopping to look at the buttons? Is she walking slower past them? Is she watching you model? Is she standing by the buttons? All these are steps in the right direction. Strive for these stages before striving to hear your dog's first words. Progress can take time, and steps forward can be subtle.

You can also try adding and modeling new words. Your dog might be more excited to say a different word than you thought she would be!

You need to switch your dog's setup

Understand that changing devices will take time for your dog to relearn the locations of her words. If possible, keep the old device out and available for at least the first couple of days, and model words on the new device. This can be less traumatic than completely removing a familiar setup. Help your dog through this transition by providing high-frequency models on the new device, being aware of all your dog's forms of communication, and providing lots of positive praise and encouragement when your dog explores the new device.

If You're Not Seeing the Progress You Expected, Ask Yourself:

Are your dog's basic needs being met?

Is she feeling safe and secure in her environment? Is she well rested? Is she getting enough playtime? How your dog is feeling impacts her ability to learn. If she is stressed, tired, sick, scared, or overwhelmed, it will be more difficult for her to learn new information.

Is the environment chaotic when you're modeling?

It might be difficult for your dog to concentrate if there are a lot of other noises or activities happening. Try modeling words and working with your dog when the environment is calmer.

Is everyone in the household modeling?

The more people who use your dog's communication device to talk, the better your dog will learn. Consistency is important!

Are you providing a long pause before you give another cue?

Before jumping in to use one of your dog's buttons, wait at least ten to fifteen seconds. AAC users and emerging communicators benefit from time to think and process what is happening.

Are the words motivating for your dog?
Make sure the first words you select are words that you think your dog would want to say! Think about what your dog already communicates via gestures and vocalizations, and which words she is excited to hear you say.

Do you have too few words available?
Having more vocabulary available to model and incorporate into your routines can help your dog learn faster. Greater exposure leads to greater learning.

Are you directing your dog to talk on command?
Telling your dog what to say and when can hinder their ability to use words independently. They learn to say what you tell them instead of what they want to say. The ultimate goal is spontaneous communication with words, not talking on command. Instead of giving your dog a command to say a specific word, model each word in the appropriate contexts.

Is your device in an easy-to-access location for your dog?
Make sure to keep your dog's buttons or device in a room where she naturally spends a lot of time.

Are you keeping your buttons in the same location?
Moving word locations around can be confusing for your dog. This would be the equivalent of switching the location of the keys on the keyboard every time you typed. Keeping the words in the same spots will lead to the fastest learning.

Resources and Recommended Reading

———

To learn more about augmentative and alternative communication, language development, or speech therapy, visit:

Hunger for Words: www.hungerforwords.com
Hunger for Words was created by Christina Hunger to share her communication journey with Stella, educate readers about speech therapy and AAC, and inspire others to teach their pets to talk. You can find videos of Stella talking, answers to frequently asked questions, and resources to help you on your journey with your dog.

The American Speech and Hearing Association (ASHA): www.asha.org
The American Speech-Language-Hearing Association (ASHA) is the national professional, scientific, and credentialing association

for audiologists and speech-language pathologists. ASHA provides information about the speech therapy scope of practice, research materials, and evidence-based interventions.

AssistiveWare: www.assistiveware.com

AssistiveWare is an assistive technology company whose website includes a multitude of easy-to-read articles about important AAC topics. Their "Learn AAC" section is an excellent place to start if you are looking to read about presuming competence, modeling, different functions of communication, and how to be a good communication partner.

Language Acquisition through Motor Planning (LAMP): www.aacandautism.com/lamp

LAMP is a therapy approach developed by a speech-language pathologist and an occupational therapist. Based on the principles of motor learning and natural language development, the LAMP approach is highly effective in teaching words and improving functional communication. The LAMP website shares information about the power of learning words through motor planning and important AAC device features.

PrAACtical AAC: www.praacticalaac.org

PrAACtical AAC is a blog created by AAC researcher and professor Carole Zangari. PrAACtical AAC has a wealth of therapy tips and strategies for helping AAC users become effective communicators.

AAC Language Lab: www.aaclanguagelab.com/language-stages

Created by one of the leading AAC device manufacturers, PRC, the AAC Language Lab provides support materials for speech-language pathologists, teachers, and parents of AAC users. Their "Language Stages" gives excellent descriptions of each phase of language development, and objectives to target during each one.

The Hanen Centre: www.hanen.org
The Hanen Centre, a nonprofit founded by a speech-language pathologist, trains parents on how to help their young children develop language and communication skills. They offer courses, guidebooks, workshops, and several free articles about effective language facilitation strategies.

Recommended Reading

Thirty Million Words: Building a Child's Brain by Dana L. Suskind

Chasing Doctor Dolittle: Learning the Language of Animals by Con Slobodchikoff

Chaser: Unlocking the Genius of the Dog Who Knows a Thousand Words by John Pilley and Hilary Hinzmann

The Inner Life of Animals by Peter Wohllben

The Education of Koko by Francine Patterson

The Genius of Dogs by Brian Hare and Vanessa Woods

The Soul of an Octopus: A Surprising Exploration into the Wonder of Consciousness by Sy Montgomery

Acknowledgments

———

To my parents, Laura and Brian Hunger, thank you for raising me to be the person that I am today. You taught me from
such a young age that my voice and opinions matter, and to
speak up for what I believe in. Thank you for encouraging me
to think differently from the crowd and for your constant love
and support.

To my big sisters, Sarah Hunger and Kate Elliott, thank you
for being such incredible role models for me while growing up.
You both trailblazed your own paths and inspired me to create
my own as well. You have no idea how much I wanted to grow
up to be like you two.

To my great friend, Grace Stevens, I truly believe that our
meeting and working together was written in the stars. Thank
you for always giving such sound advice about both speech
therapy and life, brainstorming ideas about Stella's AAC with
me, reading drafts of my book, and being a fantastic friend.

To my wonderful friend Sarah Reece, thank you for coming up with the name Hunger for Words and for all of our AAC-inspired discussions. You are quite possibly the only person I know who would remind me to bring my iPad whenever we hung out so we could talk to each other using AAC. All of your students are so lucky to have you as their speech therapist.

To the entire Northern Illinois University Speech-Language Pathology department, thank you for equipping me with an excellent education and for introducing me to the fascinating world of augmentative communication. And thank you to Michelle O'Loughlin, my first clinical supervisor, mentor, and now great friend. You taught me the importance of listening to myself and thinking outside of the box.

To my literary agents, Christopher Hermelin and Ryan Fischer-Harbage, I am so grateful for all of your ideas, encouragement, and enthusiasm throughout my entire book-writing process. Christopher, you have been such a wonderful literary agent, sounding board, and friend to me. Thank you for living in the land of possibilities with me and for helping me share my voice with the world. Ryan, thank you so much for your devotion to my book. No matter what was going on, I could always count on you to give such excellent advice. Thank you both for introducing me to this next phase of my life.

To my editor, Mauro DiPreta, thank you for believing in my potential to write this book. I have learned so much from working with you and am incredibly grateful for all of your comments, suggestions, and editorial visions. You helped me turn my ideas for *How Stella Learned to Talk* into a wonderful reality.

To the entire William Morrow team, thank you so much for all of your hard work in bringing my book to life and sharing it with the world. Tavia, Jamie, Vedika, and Kelly, it has been so fun getting to know you and working with you all. I could not have asked for a better group of people to guide me through this process and work on this book.

To my Hunger for Words community and to all of my readers, thank you so much for being a part of this journey. I can't believe how far this movement is spreading, and that is all thanks to you. I am so unbelievably proud seeing how many of you are using AAC with your own dogs (and other pets!). You are all an important part of this new era of interspecies communication, and are showing the world that everyone has a voice.

To my husband, Jake, to whom this book is dedicated, words cannot begin to describe how thankful I am for your unconditional love and support. You have believed in me every single day through every single pursuit, and it has truly meant the world to me. Thank you for teaching Stella with me, reading each draft of my book multiple times, and for being the biggest supporter of all my dreams. I can't wait to see what we do together next.

And finally, thank you to Stella. I knew from the moment we met that we were in for a special journey together, but this is wilder than I could have ever imagined. Thank you, sweet girl, for your kisses, body wiggles, smiles, and love. You are my inspiration. I love you so much.

Notes

---

1. "Catahoula Leopard Dog," DogTime, accessed September 9, 2020. https://dogtime.com/dog-breeds/catahoula-leopard-dog.

2. "Australian Cattle Dog Breed Information, Pictures, Characteristics & Facts," DogTime, accessed September 9, 2020. https://dogtime .com/dog-breeds/australian-cattle-dog.

3. Jana M. Iverson and Susan Goldin-Meadow, "Gesture Paves the Way for Language Development," *Psychological Science* 16, no. 5 (May 1, 2005): 367–71. https://doi.org/10.1111/j.0956-7976.2005.01542.x.

4. Louis Michael Rossetti, *The Rossetti Infant Toddler Language Scale: A Measure of Communication and Interaction* (Austin, TX: PRO-ED, Inc., 2005).

5. Rossetti, *The Rossetti Infant Toddler Language Scale.*

6. Janet R. Lanza and Lynn K. Flahive, *Guide to Communication Milestones* (East Moline, IL: LinguiSystems, 2008).

7. Gregg Vanderheiden, "A Journey Through Early Augmentative Communication and Computer Access," *Journal of Rehabilitation Research and Development* 39, no. 6 (2002): 39–53.

8. John W. Pilley and Alliston K. Reid, "Border Collie Comprehends Object Names as Verbal Referents," *Behavioural Processes* 86, no. 2 (2011): 184–95. https://doi.org/10.1016/j.beproc.2010.11.007.

9. John W. Pilley, "Border Collie Comprehends Sentences Containing a Prepositional Object, Verb, and Direct Object," *Learning and Motivation* 44, no. 4 (November 1, 2013): 229–40. https://doi.org/10.1016/j.lmot.2013.02.003.

10. Attila Andics, Anna Gábor, Márta Gácsi, Tamás Faragó, Dora Szabo, and Adam Miklosi, "Neural Mechanisms for Lexical Processing in Dogs," *Science* 353, no. 6303 (September 2, 2016): 1030–32. https://doi.org/10.1126/science.aan3276.

11. Nell Greenfieldboyce, "Their Masters' Voices: Dogs Understand Tone and Meaning of Words," NPR, August 30, 2016, www.npr.org/sections/health-shots/2016/08/30/491935800/their-masters-voices-dogs-understand-tone-and-meaning-of-words.

12. Tara O'Neill, Janice Light, and Lauramarie Pope, "Effects of Interventions That Include Aided Augmentative and Alternative Communication Input on the Communication of Individuals with Complex Communication Needs: A Meta-Analysis," *Journal of Speech, Language, and Hearing Research* 61, no. 7 (July 13, 2018): 1743–65. https://doi.org/10.1044/2018_jslhr-l-17-0132.

13. Luigi Girolametto, Patsy Steig Pearce, and Elaine Weitzman, "Interactive Focused Stimulation for Toddlers with Expressive Vocabulary Delays," *Journal of Speech and Hearing Research* 39, no. 6 (December 1, 1996): 1274–83. https://doi.org/10.1044/jshr.3906.1274.

14. Shakila Dada and Erna Alant, "The Effect of Aided Language Stimulation on Vocabulary Acquisition in Children with Little or No Functional Speech," *American Journal of Speech–Language Pathology* 18, no. 1 (February 1, 2009): 50–64. https://doi.org/10.1044/1058-0360(2008/07-0018).

15. Napolean Hill, *Think and Grow Rich* (New York: Jeremy P. Tarcher/Penguin, 2005).

16. Hill, *Think and Grow Rich*.

17. Erinn H. Finke, Jennifer M. Davis, Morgan Benedict, Lauren Goga, Jennifer Kelly, Lauren Palumbo, Tanika Peart, and Samantha Waters, "Effects of a Least-to-Most Prompting Procedure on Multisymbol Message Production in Children with Autism Spectrum Disorder Who Use Augmentative and Alternative Communication," *American Journal of Speech–Language Pathology* 26, no. 1 (2017): 81–98. https://doi.org/10.1044/2016_ajslp-14-0187.

18. Hilary Mathis, "The Effect of Pause Time Upon the Communicative Interactions of Young People Who Use Augmentative and Al-

ternative Communication," *International Journal of Speech–Language Pathology* 13, no. 5 (2011): 411–21. https://doi.org/10.3109/17549507.2011.524709.

19. "Dogs' Intelligence on Par with Two-Year-Old Human, Canine Researcher Says," American Psychological Association, August 10, 2009. https://www.apa.org/news/press/releases/2009/08/dogs-think.

20. Gregg Vanderheiden and David Kelso, "Comparative Analysis of Fixed-Vocabulary Communication Acceleration Techniques," *Augmentative and Alternative Communication* 3, no. 4 (1987): 196–206. https://doi.org/10.1080/07434618712331274519.

21. John Halloran and Cindy Halloran, *LAMP: Language Acquisition through Motor Planning* (Wooster, OH: The Center for AAC and Autism, 2006).

22. Halloran and Halloran, *LAMP*.

23. Halloran and Halloran, *LAMP*.

24. Jennifer J. Thistle, Stephanie A. Holmes, Madeline M. Horn, and Alyson M. Reum, "Consistent Symbol Location Affects Motor Learning in Preschoolers Without Disabilities: Implications for Designing Augmentative and Alternative Communication Displays," *American Journal of Speech-Language Pathology* 27, no. 3 (2018): 1010–17. https://doi.org/10.1044/2018_ajslp-17-0129.

25. Juliann Woods, Shubha Kashinath, and Howard Goldstein, "Effects of Embedding Caregiver-Implemented Teaching Strategies in Daily Routines on Children's Communication Outcomes," *Journal of Early Intervention* 26, no. 3 (April 1, 2004): 175–93. https://doi.org/10.1177/105381510402600302.

26. Joshua Becker, "Display What You Value Most," Becoming Minimalist, October 2, 2019. https://www.becomingminimalist.com/benefit-display-what-you-value-most/.

27. Saul Mcleod, "Maslow's Hierarchy of Needs," Simply Psychology, March 20, 2020. https://www.simplypsychology.org/maslow.html.

28. Jennifer Kent-Walsh, Kimberly A. Murza, Melissa D. Malani, and Cathy Binger, "Effects of Communication Partner Instruction on the Communication of Individuals Using AAC: A Meta-Analysis." *Augmentative and Alternative Communication* 31, no. 4 (2015): 271–84. https://doi.org/10.3109/07434618.2015.1052153.

29. Rossetti, *The Rossetti Infant Toddler Language Scale.*

30. Halloran and Halloran, *LAMP*.

31.   "Augmentative and Alternative Communication Decisions," American Speech-Language-Hearing Association (ASHA), accessed September 9, 2020. https://www.asha.org/public/speech/disorders /CommunicationDecisions/.

32.   Daniel H. Pink, *Drive: The Surprising Truth About What Motivates Us* (Edinburgh, UK: Canongate Books Ltd., 2018).

33.   Pink, *Drive*.

34.   Pink, *Drive*.

35.   David Crystal, "Roger Brown, A First Language: The Early Stages. Cambridge, MA: Harvard University Press, 1973. Pp. Xi 437," *Journal of Child Language* 1, no. 2 (1974): 289–307. https://doi.org/10.1017 /s030500090000074x.

36.   Nancy J. Scherer and Lesley B. Olswang, "Role of Mothers' Expansions in Stimulating Children's Language Production," *Journal of Speech, Language, and Hearing Research* 27, no. 3 (1984): 387–96. https://doi.org/10.1044/jshr.2703.387.

37.   Rossetti, *The Rossetti Infant Toddler Language Scale*.

38.   Halloran and Halloran, *LAMP*.

39.   Erika Hoff, *Language Development* (Belmont, CA: Wadsworth/ Thomson Learning, 2005).

40.   Julia Riedel, Katrin Schumann, Juliane Kaminski, Josep Call, and Michael Tomasello, "The Early Ontogeny of Human–Dog Communication," *Animal Behaviour* 75, no. 3 (2008): 1003–14. https://doi .org/10.1016/j.anbehav.2007.08.010.

41.   Vanderheiden and Kelso, "Comparative Analysis."

42.   Shari Robertson, "Celebrating the Bold Thinking of ASHA Imaginologists," *The ASHA Leader* 24, no. 11 (2019): 8–10. https://doi .org/10.1044/leader.ftp.24112019.8.